# A GEOGRAPHY
# OF EUROPE

**FOURTH
EDITION**

# A GEOGRAPHY
# OF EUROPE

## JEAN GOTTMANN
### University of Oxford

**HOLT, RINEHART AND WINSTON**
New York · Chicago · San Francisco · Atlanta
Dallas · Montreal · Toronto · London · Sydney

Front end papers: *Nova Europae Descriptio,* a map of Europe in the seventeenth century, first drawn by I. Hondius and revised in 1644 by N. Picart in Paris. (Reproduced by permission from the original in the collection of the Bibliothèque Nationale, Paris)

The map testifies to the somewhat inadequate knowledge of the contours and topography of Europe at the time. The North Atlantic was believed to be rather narrow, as the position of Greenland in the northwest corner of the map implies. Above the map are drawings of the major European cities: London, Paris, and Rome of course, but also Venice, Toledo, and Lisbon. Along the sides are portrayals of various peoples of Europe during the first half of the seventeenth century: on the left, the English, French, Belgians, Castillians, and Venetians; on the right, the Germans, Hungarians, Bohemians, Poles, and Greeks. It is interesting to compare the general outline of this map with the map of Europe in 1960 on the back endpapers.

# PREFACE

The first edition of *A Geography of Europe*, published in 1950, dealt with a shattered continent endeavoring to heal the many scars left upon it by World War II. Reconstruction was then the predominant problem of Europe. A second edition of this book (1954), then a third (1962) recorded the stages of the reconstruction, which was practically completed by 1960, and of the economic and political reorganization that went on, rejuvenating this old continent, while the material destruction of wartime was being repaired. As the fourth edition goes to press, Europe looks very different not only from what it was twenty years ago—when it was an impoverished and war-ravaged part of the world—but also from what it was earlier in this century. The old political and social partitioning of European space and society has acquired a fluidity that requires new molds. The search for the new forms goes on actively. We are looking now at a continent in flux in terms of its internal structures as well as in terms of its part in the modern world.

Geography is dedicated to the description and analysis of constantly changing facts and situations. It looks for the relationships governing the change, for the elements of stability and the factors of diversity. Old Europe is now having an exciting time as it is once more experiencing rapid expansion and internal reform. This is a time of crisis but also of progress. To record the momentum of recent years, many changes have had to be made while revising this book for the present edition. A great many of the changes have brought up to date a large number of factual details concerning the locational and statistical characteristics of the countries and places described. But a wider revision has been necessary which has affected the general outline of the book. In the former editions, after a first part devoted to the general characteristics of the whole of Europe, we studied successively Western Europe, Central Europe, then Mediterranean Europe, and completed the regional chapters with a section on the European parts of the Soviet Union. It has seemed now preferable to take into account the rapid evolution of the Mediterranean countries and their increasing links with the West European countries, so the chapters on Mediterranean Europe now follow those on Western Europe. The section on Central Europe comes afterward, bringing the reader gradually through the eastern countries of Central Europe to the borders of the Soviet Union. True, this outline leaves in Central Europe the study of Germany, which finds itself separated by all the Mediterranean chapters from the study of Western Europe with which the Federal Republic of Germany has been increasingly coalescing politically and economically. Still this is a better order to adopt, as it makes the reader clearly aware of the many links West Germany keeps with the areas to the east of its present border and of the essential problem left now on the political map of this old continent: the slow-thawing "iron curtain" across Central Europe, an area over the whole of which extends the shadow of the Soviet Union. The division of Germany and the future evolution of Central Europe will long remain decisive elements in the continent's fate.

*A Geography of Europe* was written mainly for American students by a European who has had the privilege of teaching and working in the United States and Canada as well as in several European countries. With this transatlantic experience, the author sought to present *A Geography of Europe* with the insight of a native and some of the objectivity of an outsider. European studies are important to people the world over because Europe in past centuries discovered the rest of the world, because this small continent's culture swept the other, vaster continents with little resistance, and because even today it continues to play a part in the world quite disproportionate with its size or even its population. The momentum of history is constantly present in European geography, and it has been recorded there better than in any other part of the world. It is, therefore, particularly important to stress the inheritance of the past, the historical evolution that has brought about the present forms and functions of the various parts of Europe.

This edition has kept the emphasis on the historical and cultural factors in the geography of the European countries, which the former editions of this book brought to the fore. This geography emphasizes people, their ways of life, their divisions, and their endeavors to solve their problems and to adapt the regional environmental conditions to their ways and means. Previous editions of this book have been widely used in American universities as well as in universities and research institutes around the world. Translations have been published in Spanish and Singhalese. The author has felt that while revising the volume for the present edition he ought to remain within the tradition that the former editions had established over almost twenty years. Besides updating the details and modifying somewhat the regional layout, he has had to rewrite entirely many sections of the book, particularly those having to do with the use of resources in Europe as a whole and in most of the different countries. One more country, Malta, which recently achieved independence, has been added in the section on Mediterranean Europe. Some new photographs and maps have been included.

In the preparation of this volume, I have benefited for many years from the help and advice of friends and colleagues both in America and in Europe. With every edition, the list of acknowledgments would greatly lengthen. Making here such a full list would considerably increase the size of the book. It will be possible to mention only the few institutions and persons whose help has been generously given throughout the twenty years of the author's work on this geography of Europe. Such special gratitude is owed to the American Geographical Society of New York, the Institute for Advanced Study in Princeton, the Institut d'Études Politiques of the University of Paris, and to many of my colleagues in the universities where I taught, visited, or did research in an area extending from the Pacific coast of North America to the shores of the Aegean Sea and the banks of the Vistula River. I wish to mention with special gratefulness Professors H. G. J. Daysh, of the University of Newcastle; William Mead, of the University of London; J. O. M. Broek, of the University of Minnesota; A. A. Michel and Peter Nash, of the University of Rhode Island; Gunnar Myrdal, of the University of Stockholm; A. C. de Vooys and C. Van Paassen, of the University of Utrecht; Dr. Edvard Hambro and Mr. Carl Hambro, of Oslo.

Most of all, this book is indebted to the students to whom I have repeatedly taught the elements of European geography or of some parts of Europe, and to the students who, having used the book with other teachers, have written me remarks about it.

Milwaukee, Wisconsin                                                    J. G.
April 1969

# CONTENTS

# PART II   WESTERN EUROPE

# PART III   MEDITERRANEAN EUROPE

## PART VI CONCLUSION

# Introduction

On a map of the world there are two large land masses: the Old World and the New World. The former has the greater land area and the bulkier shape of the two. However, in its northwestern section the lands of the Old World do not look bulky at all. Between the heavy land masses of Asia and Africa, there is a sort of puzzle of mingling lands and seas called Europe. Between the Arctic Ocean, the North Atlantic, the Mediterranean Sea, and the widening forests and shrublands of Soviet Asia, the European lands consist of peninsular and isthmian areas, plus a scattering of islands all around. It scarcely deserves to be called a continent. However, it is and has always been an exceedingly important part of the globe.

For centuries Europe was at the root of every important world trend: modern civilization stemmed from it; science, art, trade, and migrations fanned out of it and imposed European supremacy on the other parts of the world; standards were set according to European normality. Thus, so long as Europe was the center of the world, it did not matter whether it was a continent or an agglomeration of peninsulas, islands, and isthmuses.

Today, in the middle of the twentieth century, the position of Europe has changed substantially. Its size, shape, and climate are the same, but these stable physical features no longer carry the same meaning. The political and economic structure which puts them to use has changed so much as to call for a general re-evaluation. Europe is a problem for Europeans as well as for the world outside. Although the two major powers of the present world stemmed from Europe, they are no longer actually European. One of them, the Soviet Union, is physically attached to Europe; a large portion of its territory, the more populated and better

1

organized portion, is in Europe, but as a result of Russian colonization, it has spread widely over Asia. The other, the United States, is separated from Europe by the width of the Atlantic Ocean. Although related to Europe by links of blood and culture, America is another part of the world. Both of these superpowers have their own civilizations, which differ in many respects from the classical one born and developed in the Western and Mediterranean parts of Europe.

Europe still finds itself in the midst of the turmoil of history, but this time it is unable to direct world trends. Its geographical position makes of it a buffer between the two new leaders; moreover, one half of its area is part of the Soviet Union. Europe has always been an area deeply divided within, and every part of it has tried to be linked with the outside. Its traditions of lively internal division and active outside relations make Europe's geography rather complicated, but also more important and interesting. Nature endowed this small part of the world with a diversified and chiseled physical pattern; out of it, through thousands of years, men worked a delicate mosaic of countries, provinces, cantons, and other divisions, each of which is proud of its personality and of its historical past. The past of Europe is a long story. It cannot be told, with all its regional aspects, in a geographical study, but the geographer must keep the past in mind if he wants to understand the "whys" behind the present problems and the present landscapes.

Geography aims at an accurate picture of some part of a moving world. When the motion is accelerated to the extent that it is at present, a still picture is bound to be fuzzy. In an endeavor to give a clear representation of Europe and its varied parts, projection in time and in space will often be necessary in order to make the picture clearer. As an eminent geographer once remarked, mankind is so passionately interested in its own past because it provides the only materials for imagining the future. To take time into account is imperative, for, while the expansion of Europe over the other continents has interrupted the development of local life to frame it in a new setting, the flow of history in Europe proper has not been interrupted by a major break for at least two thousand years. This continuity of development has contributed to the originality of Europe; it has enabled men and nature, through a slow and steady process, to cooperate in elaborating delicate skills, strong regionalisms, and a great diversity of ways of life.

It takes much human labor to master and reshape the natural conditions of an area. Europe seems to have been densely populated for a long time. On eight percent of the world's land area, it concentrates at present about one fifth of the world's population. Heavy population pressure raises problems that present a challenge which spurs people in the search for a solution. One attempt at solution consists in putting the mass of the people to work under a severe discipline to provide the bare necessities of life for everyone and greater benefits to a small group in which authority is vested. This method has often been applied under various labels in European countries as elsewhere, but it was challenged earlier and more consistently in this part of the world than in others. The moral laws of the Bible found in Europe a fertile ground which was altogether lacking in more massive lands. Armed with the logic of the Greeks, who coined the term *democracy*, generation after generation of Europeans battled for more freedom, greater social justice, and fuller liberation of the individual.

The long and uninterrupted history of Europe is full of wars, revolutions, and all kinds of bloodshed that created division, hatred, and prejudice; but out of these conflicts came progress. It was the most creative development that history has recorded, although—and perhaps because—it was the most tumultuous. The endless struggle still goes on. Its greatest successes have been achieved outside the area: looking for new riches or new roads, European adventurers and merchants discovered new, far-off lands, and trickles of refugees—unconquered, though defeated in the European fight for more freedom and a better life—went soon to the newly opened spaces. Europeans escaped in all directions—America, Australia, South Africa, Siberia, Palestine. In a few cases, among which the United States is most notable, they succeeded in establishing an actual political democracy, a government "of the people, by the people, for the people," and a higher standard of living—all things of which Europe has been dreaming for ages, probably more passionately than other sections of mankind.

The distinctive features of Europe belong to the pattern of culture rather than to the natural environment. Inside the area we shall review a great number of regions differentiated by their landscapes and by the way in which the natural conditions are managed. To what extent are these regional patterns the effect of the physical environment? The question has been asked over a long period of time. It has been explored with the aid of constantly improved scientific methods and a growing mass of observations, but nothing warrants the hypothesis of appreciable change of climatic conditions during the historical period. Local changes in the topography have had some influence on local details, but never on general trends. On the other hand, Europeans away from home have shown a remarkable and indisputable ability to manage under conditions quite different from those existing in their country of origin. If the concept of environment is limited to stable physical factors, it does not seem to determine human behavior. Social factors build up much more effective pressure on men. Certainly the social environment puts its imprint on people's ways of living and acting, particularly on their understanding of the physical milieu. All modern studies in medicine, sociology, and economic history concur in the conclusion that variations in the social environment often determine changes in human behavior much more effectively than do variations in physical conditions.

But the stable, permanent features of the physical environment are the raw material out of which men model the finished product, the work of art that appears to the stranger as a "local landscape." It has taken long centuries of continued effort to produce most of the regions of Europe. The same material has had different values at different periods, depending on the techniques and the tools used by the craftsmen, on the varying tastes and the varying ideas about the kind of life desired. Any raw material has its limitations, but it may also offer the advantages of plasticity. The geographer never leaves out of account the material provided by nature, nor does he neglect the qualities and abilities of the craftsman. The space of Europe is not very wide, but it presents some marvels of organization and a whole gamut of the different possible styles of management.

In the second half of the twentieth century a study of the general features of Europe and of its regional aspects and problems presents many difficulties. Not only is the world changing, but we are looking at a continent in flux, and it clarifies nothing to say that Europe is at the crossroads—many of the possible roads of the future are dim and uncertain. Europe is an old continent; it is undergoing a mutation that may bring about a rejuvenation. Now that the wartime wounds are healed, a new spirit rises: Europeans are concerned about their own welfare; they want to catch up with the higher American standard of living. Consumption and production are expanding. This economic revival owes much to a rejuvenated demography, and to a novel understanding of Europe's resources and of the contribution the continent can make to our time. On both sides of the "iron curtain" which still divides Europe into two separate realms, new endeavors call for reassessment of the system of external relations under which the European peoples have been living. Europe is the largest group of well-developed nations in the world, and it is gathering strength and self-assurance as it seeks a new role and new spirit.

# Part I

## The General Features of Europe

A lake in the Highlands of Scotland, one of the oldest, most deeply eroded lands in the world. Clouds cling to the higher crests. In ancient times, Strabo, circumnavigating Britain, reported it to be a land so damp that it was hard to separate land, sea, and sky. (*British Information Services*)

# 1

## The Physical Pattern

A continent is generally a bulky mass, and Europe is no exception. On the map, the whole of Europe appears to be a big peninsula attached to Asia by a wide base in the east, jutting westward toward the Atlantic Ocean, and steadily narrowing down until it looks like a chain of isthmuses between the Mediterranean Sea and the ocean.

### THE SIZE AND SHAPE OF EUROPE

Among the vast pieces of land called continents, Europe is the smallest and the most irregularly shaped. Covering 3.9 million square miles, less than one half of North America and less than one fourth of Asia, it has a queer, scalloped outline, for here the sea penetrates deeply into the land, dividing it into narrow compartments stretching lengthwise as peninsulas.

Like the limbs of a tree, smaller peninsulas extend in all directions from the main body, the jettylike aspect of which is reinforced by the generally east-west axis of the main mountain ranges that build up the spine of the continent. Groups of islands and smaller peninsulas encircle the bordering seas, divide them into basins, and extend interrupted links, like blown-up bridges, across the water spaces. Europe is indeed the part of the world where land and sea interpenetrate most deeply and most intricately. One has to look carefully for a point on the continent that is beyond a thousand miles of some shoreline. The only such area—and it is not wide—is the middle of Russia; there the continent

7

widens eastward where it is strongly welded to the big body of Asia.

There have been many discussions as to the actual eastern limit of Europe. Europe has been described as one of the peninsulas or even as a cape of the Asiatic continent. Some geographers, on the other hand, wish to define Europe as extending deep into Siberia. God made the earth, the land, and the sea, but He left it to men to give them names. Adam was not enough of a geographer to coin once and forever the terms to describe the world and its different parts, and today geographical terms do not always carry absolutely defined meanings — some interpretation is necessary on the fringes. The situation may be simpler on the other continents because their European discoverers wrote their contours and names on the maps. Being in the midst of the then-known world, Europe took less interest in defining itself — especially as the boundaries of its countries were constantly being changed. There is little use in changing the meaning of a geographical name, and there is no imperative reason to reconsider now the limits of the space traditionally called Europe. These usual limits are clear except to the east: the Arctic Ocean to the north, the wide open spaces of the Atlantic to the west (Iceland still being considered as part of Europe), the Mediterranean and Black seas with the Straits linking them to the regions south and southeast. The eastern limit follows traditionally the "line of the Urals" — that is, the crest of the Ural Mountain range from the Arctic shores southward, then the course of the Ural River which empties into the Caspian Sea; the limit crosses the Caspian southward and swings back to the Black Sea westward along the crest of the Caucasus range.

Within this frame Europe, though varied, has a certain unity: a unity of shape through the interpenetration of land and sea; a unity of climate which does not become too extreme at any point in any way; a unity of structure on the whole; and, last but not least, the historical unity of populations that have lived together maintaining uninterrupted contact for a few thousand years. Whether these limits follow political boundaries does not matter greatly. French "metropolitan territory," for instance, has spanned the Atlantic since the French West Indies were put under the same administrative regime as the environs of Paris. But such considerations could not induce us to include a part of the Caribbean islands in our concept of Europe. The same reasoning applies to Greenland, administratively an integral part of the kingdom of Denmark. The Soviet Union stretches across the Urals to the Pacific Ocean; Britain, a group of islands off the coast of the European mainland, is part of a commonwealth whose lands are scattered the world over — political relationships are only one of the many aspects of geographical reality. Distribution of land and sea is a much more decisive, because a more permanent, factor. European peoples have lived of necessity within a given environment, and escape from it for large groups became possible only recently. We shall respect the old mold from which history has been so long cast.

## THE SEAS AROUND AND INSIDE EUROPE

The seas framing Europe have an outstanding influence on the conditions of life on the continent as well as on its division into natural regions. Penetrating deeply and in an irregular way into the continent, the seas have isolated some parts of it from others. They have made outside communication difficult for peoples who ignored the art of navigation; they have, on the other hand, opened wide and almost boundless horizons to those skilled in the technique of sailing. The maritime factor has made itself felt far inland, through its influence on drainage and climate. Three features of the sea contribute to the importance of the maritime influence. First, the water spaces evaporate into the air as humidity which, carried away by the wind, is redistributed over the land in the condensed form of rain, snow, dew, etc. Second, water has the physical property of warming up and cooling off more slowly than solid ground, so that the sea acts as an enormous reservoir of warmth or coolness according to the season, moderating in both cases the climate of the continental area. And third, since all the maritime masses are fluid and communicate with one another (with the exception of big lakes like the Caspian Sea), a general sea level exists all around the globe, remains relatively stable, and receives most of the continental drainage flow.

These three properties make the proximity of the sea a valuable asset. In the case of Europe, the maritime influence is particularly beneficial to the climate and, through it, to hydrography, soils, vegetation, and even communication, owing to the fact that the surrounding seas are warm. The maritime factor would indeed lose much of its significance if the sea froze, as it does for prolonged periods in certain areas. Very few of the European coasts are ice-bound in winter: parts of the Baltic Sea and the Caspian and White seas, all of them inland water spaces, freeze regularly, but the outer ring of seas and bays never freezes. During the winter the sea continues to act as a reservoir of both humidity and heat. This is a considerable help to navigation and fishing; it is even more important for the climatic consequences it determines.

On the eastern seaboard of North America facing Europe, winter freezing and cold are much more severe. Southward as far as Baltimore, large ports have to maintain icebreakers to be sure of remaining open to traffic through the winter. Baltimore, south of the 40th Parallel, is about the latitude of Lisbon, one of the southernmost corners of Europe.

Lisbon has never dreamt of icebreakers, and the Norwegian port of Narvik, above the 68th Parallel, stays ice-free all the year round. At similar latitudes in North America, one finds the icecap of Greenland or the seldom-navigated northern coast of Canada. This maritime influence on Europe, with its climatic and other effects, decreases gradually toward the east as the continent increases in width and massiveness. It is still felt, to some extent, up to the Urals. There is almost no desert, whether created by cold or by aridity, in Europe; and this would not be so without the deep penetration inland of warm seas.

The warmth of the water masses off the European shores cannot be explained by local conditions. For a sea such as the Mediterranean to the south of Europe, consisting of a string of deep basins, at middle latitude, and in a sunny climate, these conditions are decisive; the water mass of the Mediterranean can store during the warm season enough heat to remain warm through the winter, which is seldom severe or long. Such considerations, however, would not account for the quality of the waters encountered along the western shores of Europe up to the threshold of the Arctic Ocean. These are "tropical" water masses, easy to identify through the combination of their temperature (usually above 52°F.) and their high salinity (35.5 to 36.7 per 1000). Polar water masses flowing from the high latitudes, and largely originating from melting ice, are cold and of lower salinity. While temperature, at least on the surface, may vary with local conditions, salinity does not. It is also well known that water masses of different salinity and temperature do not combine when they meet in large volumes: no compromise mixture is formed.

The waters that warm up European shores have to come from the tropics. The traditional explanation of this phenomenon, as given in the eighteenth century by Benjamin Franklin, remains famous under the name of Gulf Stream. Franklin saw a powerful current leaving the Gulf of Mexico through the Florida Strait, rolling northward along the American coast to the vicinity of Newfoundland, then swinging eastward to cross the Atlantic and spread its tropical waters around the European shores to the Danish straits, to the North Cape, and even to the Russian Arctic port of Murmansk. Today the heating function of the Gulf Stream is seriously questioned — it would be a long trip for warm waters from Florida to Norway; and the volume of the original current that was supposed to irrigate and heat up most of the North Atlantic would have to be enormous. There is no doubt that a hot current follows the American coast from Florida to Newfoundland where it meets, in the area known to hydrographers as the Cold Wall, the polar water masses of the Labrador Current. From there on, the heating power of the Gulf Stream diminishes rapidly. True, the predominant eastward winds or *Westerlies* of the middle latitudes push toward Europe a steady surface

Temperatures in Europe. As these are actual temperatures, that is, not reduced to sea level, the main anomalies indicate the main features of the topography.

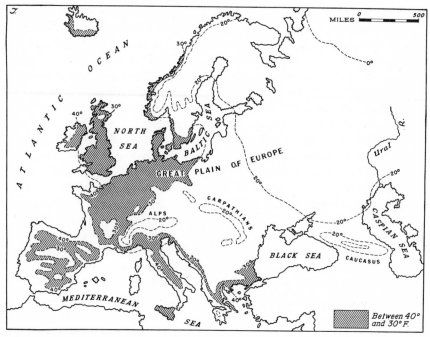

Isotherms in Europe in January.

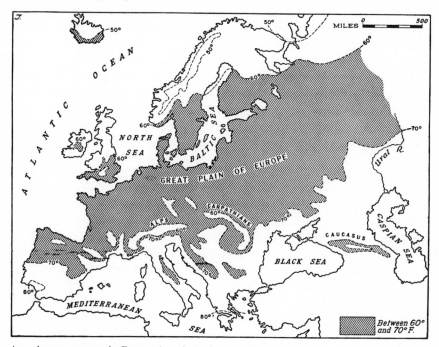

Actual temperatures in Europe in July in degrees Fahrenheit.

current called the North Atlantic Drift, and ships going to America feel its resistance slowing them down. But oceanographers admit now that this drift of the waters toward Europe has no particular thermic function. Some of them are led to believe that an expansion of tropical waters takes place every year in the vast mass of the central, tropical Atlantic Ocean. The drift of these waters northward is deflected to its right—that is, to the northeast, where Europe lies—through the impulse of the earth's rotation. The waters can flow easily in this direction because of the general outline of the submarine topography and also because the icy waters flowing southward from the Arctic get oriented by a similar deflection toward the west—that is, the American shores. Thus, the thermic dissymmetry between the ocean's banks—which holds in the Pacific as well as in the Atlantic—can be explained without the necessity of postulating a current all across the ocean. A bigger and closer source than the Gulf of Mexico is found for the warm waters that bathe Europe. The heat accumulated by solar radiation in the tropics in the huge mass of the ocean is thus redistributed to less sunny areas in a way benefiting chiefly the northeastern shores of the immense basin.

This influx of tropical waters is not equally distributed every year and everywhere around Europe, and the force of the expansion and its volume vary from year to year. The mechanism governing this kind of tide is not yet fully understood, but details of the distribution in the European seas are somewhat better known: it varies not only in time but also in space, according to the submarine topography and other local conditions. Little of these waters enters the Mediterranean through the Strait of Gibraltar, but that southern sea has its own supply of heat through solar radiation, and its stores of saline waters in the depths of its closed and isolated basins, which were probably filled long ago in the geological past. The Mediterranean is actually a *continental sea,* although it communicates with the ocean. Its influence is felt in the lands around it in a special way, and will be examined in its own regional frame.

Another continental sea is the Baltic, which penetrates deeply into northern Europe. It is a shallow sea, with depths averaging 300 feet and seldom going below 600, and the Straits of Denmark, connecting it with the more open North Sea, are narrow, winding, and shallow. Numerous rivers of the surrounding lands feed into the Baltic the sweet waters of their wide basins. The salinity of the Baltic waters is thus low and their temperature rather cool. The parts of the Baltic reaching farthest into the continent, such as the Gulfs of Finland and Bothnia, freeze every winter. Most of the sea is ice-bound for a few weeks each year. The maritime influence this sea can exert is thus substantially reduced, but it is almost an exception in Europe. The only case at all similar is the White Sea, a deep bay of the Arctic Ocean penetrating into north Russia,

but much smaller than the Baltic and situated entirely to the north of
the 64th Parallel. These two cases contrast sharply with the general
features of the border seas to the west.

The maritime space to the west of Europe is divided into basins by the
contours of the coastline and by the submarine relief. The wide, open
oceanic spaces come directly up to the western shores of Portugal, Spain,
Brittany, Ireland, and Norway. The broad, open gulf situated between
the western coast of France and the northern coast of Spain is called the
Bay of Biscay: it is a stormy area, since it faces the northwest, where
storms often originate; most of it is deep and naturally partakes of
oceanic circulation.

Between Brittany and Norway extend several shallow seas, screened
from the ocean by the British Isles. These seas cover a wide westward extension of the continental shelf, a submarine platform which borders the
continent and over which the sea never reaches a depth of more than
100 fathoms. There are three border seas in this area: the Irish Sea,
between the isles of Ireland and Britain; the English Channel (in French,
*La Manche*), between the southern coast of England and the northwestern shore of France, leading to the Strait of Dover, which opens on
the North Sea; and the North Sea itself, the widest and in all respects
the most important of the border seas of Europe. It stretches between
Great Britain and the northwestern part of the continent, communicates
with the Baltic and the Channel, and opens widely northward on the
Atlantic. For several centuries it has been the richest fishing area and the
main trade hub of the world. All these warm seas have their periods of
stormy weather in winter. Navigation is not always easy there. When the
air is still, dense fog often rises during the cold season over the warm
waters. But the water mass regulates the thermal regime all over western
Europe.

The whole of the continent looks indeed like a peninsula or a bridge
thrown across a maritime realm from Asia to northwest Africa. In the
west, France could almost be described as an isthmus between the
Atlantic and the Mediterranean; in the east, the western section of the
Soviet Union is just another isthmus between the Baltic and Black seas;
Finland is again an isthmus between the Baltic and the White Sea. Such
a scalloped design means a complicated geological structure.

## THE ARCHITECTURE OF THE CONTINENT

The coastline is not the only feature of Europe to present such an
intricate outline. The topography of the continent is broken into small
sections, and is so varied from section to section, that to group all these
aspects in a few main physiographic regions is not the fairly simple

proposition that it is for larger and more massive continents such as the Americas, Asia, or Africa. An *irregular checkerboard* seems to be the best that can be offered in the way of a definition.

The earth's crust is endowed with some plasticity. Under the pressure of internal forces, some compartments of it are raised, others sunken; certain sections are folded through tangential pressure; others remain rigid, like resistant shields, amid the greater fluidity of their surroundings. Thus the surface of our whole globe has been molded, shaped, and reshaped through the geological periods; oceans and continents have changed places and reorganized their contours. But the major hypotheses elaborated to explain the geological history of the globe do not concern this present study of one region of the world aside from their effect on our understanding of the present architecture of Europe. The complicated and chiseled nature of this architecture is due to the tectonic strains affecting the crust's structure, which have piled up there with greater density and variety than in any other region. A frequent alternation of depressed and raised compartments has resulted in a deeper interpenetration of land and sea. Europe has no mountain ranges comparable in height or size to the Andes or the Himalayas; the seas around it do not reach such abysmal depths as are encountered along certain American or Asiatic shores. It seems that the tectonic forces have not reached their greatest intensity in the European region, but that almost all their major moves have met in the European hub, leaving their successive imprints on its topography. The scale is somewhat reduced—although contrasts are sharp enough—but diversity and complexity make up for size.

Generalization is dangerous in the face of such a structure, but a rapid outline can be attempted, if one keeps in mind the variability of the details that will appear in the regional study. The main lines of Europe's architecture can be compared to a triangle with an acute angle pointed southwestward—toward Gibraltar. The three sides of the triangle consist mostly of lofty highlands, the lowlands being inside. These three sides are not, of course, continuous but are interrupted by wide gaps. To the east is the Ural range; to the south the involved mass of highlands bordering the Mediterranean from the Spanish Sierras to the Caucasus range, with the Alps as the main link in the middle; to the west and northwest are the many ranges which, through Portugal and Spain, Ireland, Scotland, and Norway, fringe the Atlantic. The two main systems of the European highlands could thus be classified as an Atlantic system to the northwest, with a general southwest-northeast orientation, and a Mediterranean or, better, Alpine system to the south, with a general west-east axis. Within the V formed by these two orientations develops the system of European plains with the hills and small ranges that stud them. The southern system of mountains has more continuity, diversity, and ramifications, and a higher altitude than the Atlantic one. Both of them were erected along big troughs in the earth's crust: this proximity of raised compartments to sunken ones strikes some kind of balance in the tectonic pressures. The instability is greater along the Mediterranean area, where active volcanism is widespread and earthquakes are frequent; the Atlantic shores seem to be more settled, although legends still abound along them of kingdoms which have disappeared under the waves. Few changes of importance seem to have been brought about by the play of tectonic forces during historical time, which in Europe goes back several thousand years. The geological past was more eventful, and the age of the existing structures has to be kept in mind to understand their morphology.

There are old and young structures amid the mountains and plateaus of Europe. The oldest ones are the system of the Atlantic ranges to the northwest. They were folded and erected first among the very old Huronian ranges (in what geology calls the Proterozoic period); then they belonged to the Caledonian system of foldings (Paleozoic era); erosion brought their altitude lower and flattened them gradually to a *peneplain*. After many vicissitudes, masses of these old rocks were raised again at the time when the Atlantic trough was formed (Tertiary era). The present coast of Norway follows the line of contact between the major raised compartment (now called Scandinavia) and the sunken one. The strain which developed along this fracture of the earth's crust caused many faults and some flow of volcanic material, remnants of which are still being found. Most of Scandinavia and Finland are thus made of one big mass of very old, hard, resistant rock. This area is called the *Fenno-Scandian Shield*, as it has a slightly ventricose or domelike shape, and as it has been the main buttress around which recent trends in the upbuilding of northern Europe have molded their effects. The hearts of these areas are rugged highlands of medium altitude; the highlands of Scotland, Wales, and Ireland belong to the same system, which should be referred to as the *old Atlantic mountainous system* of Europe. Its predominant orientation is southwest-northeast.

Dating back also to the Primary era, but more recent than the Atlantic ranges, is another system of folds called Hercynian. This covered for a while a large part of Western and Central Europe, then was peneplaned, subsided, and was covered by seas which, during the ages, deposited successive layers of sediments upon the old, resistant Hercynian strata. With the reshaping of all this section of the earth's crust in the Tertiary era, and with the erection through the south of Europe of new lofty ranges, the Hercynian system was "given the works." It was broken into blocks, some of which were uplifted, some sunk deeper, and

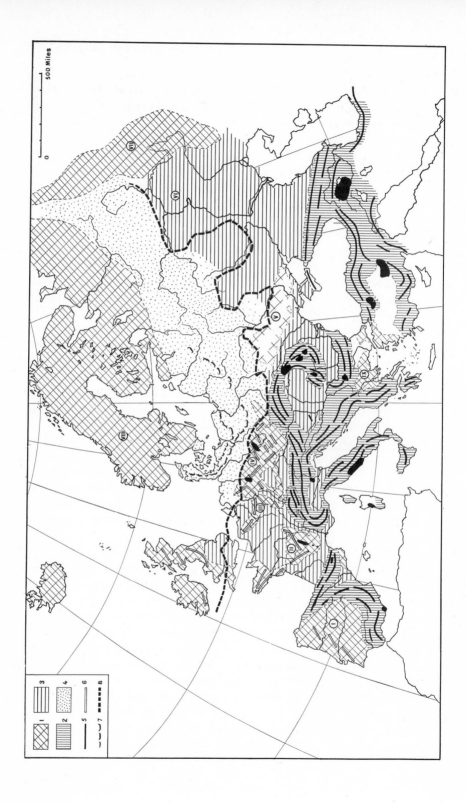

some split into several pieces or faulted after having been raised. The result is one of the most intricate elements of the European checkerboard. In the middle of Europe are found high tablelands or hilly massives of irregular shapes and sizes disposed without any order, sometimes bearing pieces of the sedimentary layers that once covered them and were largely carried away by erosion after the uplifting. Some of these massives display forms very close to those of the Appalachian Mountains in the United States; others bear testimony to recent and powerful volcanic activity. The central plateau of France, the isolated massives of western Germany, the ranges forming the "Bohemian square" in Czechoslovakia, are among the main pieces of the disorderly Hercynian system, in the middle of which numerous depressions remain filled with recent sedimentary layers. According to German terminology, a raised block of resistant material is called *horst* and the sunken section or trough is called *graben*. These terms have become classical in physical geography. Vast sections of the old Hercynian system were involved in the turmoil of the erection of younger ranges through the southern parts of Europe. Some of them, raised very high, constituted the nuclei of the main knobs of these new ranges; others, large horsts, remained as faulted tablelands encircled by the folds, which were then endowed with greater plasticity.

The youngest and most spectacular system of mountainous ranges is thus in the south of Europe, along the Mediterranean. Some of its powerful limbs circle deep into the middle of the continent. These ranges come under the general name of the *Alpine system,* taken from the range of the Alps, the highest of them and the best studied. These Alpine mountains are higher, because, being younger, the forces of erosion have had much less time to flatten them; but erosion is working

---

(*Opposite*) The structure of Europe. Explanation of legend (at upper left):

   1. Ancient crystalline masses (I, Spanish Meseta; II, central plateau of France; III, Ardennes-Palatinate area; IV, Bohemian square and small Hercynian massives of Germany; V, the Don-Donetz dome of the Ukraine; VI, the central Russian shield; VII, the Ural range; VIII, the Fenno-Scandian Shield; IX, the Balkan ranges. The group of ancient highlands of Ireland, Scotland, and Wales has not been given a numeral.)

   2. Alpine ranges and folds.

   3. Sedimentary areas, not much affected by foldings.

   4. The great plain of Europe, largely glaciated.

   5. General directions of alpine folds.

   6. General orientation of ancient folds (mainly Hercynian).

   7. Main groupings of morainic hills.

   8. Limit of the maximum extension of the great northern icecap.

Volcanic areas are indicated by plain black patches.

Domes of ancient foldings reduced to peneplains in Eastern Europe are in large part masked by a superficial cover of more recent formations, which explains the shades around figures V and VI other than shade 1.

in full swing on the steep slopes and gives them sharp and bold aspects of great beauty. The chief ranges of the Alpine system are, from west to east, the Pyrenees, the Alps, the Tatras, the Carpathians, and the Caucasus. The first and last of these are almost continuous, one-block barriers, extending along a straight line on a predominantly west-east axis. The other ranges, including the Alps, are more manifold and curved, divided into sections by deep valleys connected by wide passes. The curved outline is frequent and is explained by the irregular pre-Alpine structure of compartments of older, more resistant materials in the earth's crust that were squeezed inside the vice of the strains developed by the Alpine uplifting. These compartments went up or down, while the strata (made plastic through terrific internal pressure) infiltrated, overflowed, folded themselves, and curved along the lines of least resistance. When a compartment was uplifted, it constituted a plateau or tableland inside the system, of which the Spanish *Meseta* is typical; when it went down the ranges curved around a depression filled in either by a sea (such as the Adriatic or the western Mediterranean basin) or by recent sediment (such as the Pannonian depression of Hungary).

Thus the architecture of Europe could, in spite of all our warnings, be compared even to that of North America: there are old rugged mountains of moderate elevation in the north and northwest of Europe, like the Appalachians and the Canadian shield in the eastern and northeastern parts of North America; there is a lower and flatter area of plains and plateaus, widening eastward in the center of Europe, like the Great Plains in the heart of North America; and in the south of Europe there is an area of complicated topography, made up of lofty and young ranges with tablelands or basins in the middle of them, as there is in western North America. The American features have more continuity and develop on a larger scale than the European architecture. Both continents could be divided into three main natural regions. To be more precise, however, one should further divide into two belts the inner lower lands of Europe: the Great European Plain extends from the shores of the North Sea to the Urals, but it is separated from the Alpine belt to the south by the mosaic of uplifted blocks and depressions making up the Hercynian belt that stretches from the Channel to the Black Sea. Another and much more important difference between the continents on the two sides of the northern Atlantic is that, while the main axis of the North American architecture is oriented north-south, the European one is chiefly east-west. Altogether, Europe is a continent of shades rather than contrasts; but a certain number of contrasts were created by the tectonic forces, particularly in the vertical movements of the surface, enabling deep or shallow seas to penetrate into the very heart of the continent to a much greater extent than in America. The penetration of the Mediterranean and Black Sea inland has a total length equal to the greatest width of the American continent.

Such is the architecture of Europe, erected by the tectonic forces. It has been still further diversified and ornamented through the constant sculpturing by the forces of erosion.

## EROSION AND ACCUMULATION

Through the geological ages erosion flattened many a part of Europe, bringing what had been originally lofty mountainous ranges to the state of low-lying peneplains. The materials thus carried away from the heights were deposited around the raised area, on the continent or on the bottoms of seas and lakes. Erosion goes on daily through the action of rain, wind, snow, run-off waters that gather into streams, and glaciers. There have been periods in the recent geological past, during what have been called *quaternary* times, when the action of *normal* erosion—which in Europe is predominantly erosion by flowing water—was superseded by more powerful action—glaciers and winds. Glaciers are still the most important agent of erosion in cold areas that are humid enough to provide for a development of ice masses on a large scale; winds are a major factor in the morphology of dry, desertic areas (*eolian* erosion). According to the climatic conditions of past periods glaciers or winds took the leading role in the sculpture of the relief and in the transportation and accumulation of the debris. The work of the glaciers during the so-called *great quaternary glaciations* was particularly appalling, and the results are still evident in Europe.

Several times and for prolonged periods these glaciations spread over the world. They left their imprint over many continents; but it is in Europe and North America that their effects have been the better studied. As a result of climatic changes, whose nature and duration are still under dispute, tremendous icecaps arose and covered large sections of the continents. They were similar to the present icecap of Greenland or, when on a smaller scale, to the mass of glaciers now covering the better part of the St. Elias range in Alaska.

Two main centers of glaciation existed in Europe: one in the north, on the Fenno-Scandian Shield, the other in the center, on the higher section of the Alps. An icecap that at least twice reached tremendous dimensions covered all of northern Europe, including Fenno-Scandia, the Baltic and the plains south and east of that sea, as well as the northwestern section of Russia. Another icecap of lesser size submerged the Alps and overflowed on all the neighborhood. Smaller centers of glaciation were scattered over the mountains of Europe: the Pyrenees, the Carpathians, certain Balkan ranges, even some of the Spanish and Portuguese highlands.

extensive, but its marks are the clearest. In between the glaciations, drier and perhaps warmer periods occurred. The aridity of interglacial times seems to have been the decisive factor preventing the formation of glaciers. At those times desertlike climates probably existed all over Europe or at least over large portions of it. As always in arid climates, wind erosion developed; the sculpture it probably imprinted on the topography was rubbed off by the ensuing glacial or normal erosion, but quaternary soils retain the mark of such periods. After the retreat of the glaciers, winds were able to raise immense clouds of particles ground small by the ice tongues and sheets. They were transported varying distances and formed vast deposits south of the glaciated areas. To such an eolian origin are ascribed the large patches of rich soil, known as *loess*, that are found through the plains of Europe. Although this explanation of the loess deposits has recently been disputed, there is no doubt that in the interglacial periods wind erosion and accumulation were important.

The distribution of the main centers of glaciation in Europe is rather curious, and it seems to be linked to the present distribution of humidity rather than of temperature — most of the centers are in the western half of Europe, which enjoys a damper climate. Ice being made out of water, one should not be too surprised by this observation; similar trends were recorded in the distribution of glaciers over North America, where the drier west had much less of them. This leads to the conclusion that the general pattern of the climatic map of Europe has changed little since the Ice Age, in so far as distribution of humidity is concerned. It also makes it appear that glacial and wind erosion, even in the details of their action, depend mainly on climate. This is true as well of normal erosion, which is influenced, of course, by the nature of the soil and subsoil and by the slope which gives force to the water current, but essentially by the climate which determines the amount of moisture and its distribution over the year.

## MODERATION OF CLIMATE AND INSTABILITY OF WEATHER

The climate of Europe is above all a remarkably moderate one. The extremes there are closer to the average figures than on the other continents. It is also a varied climate, with many gradations throughout the year and a rather regular division of the year into four quarters, the usual four distinct seasons. These features are due to the geographical position of Europe and its design: the moderation of the climate is due largely to the interpenetration of the lands with warm seas. Since the first long records of meteorological data and the first classical works on climatology were made in Western and Central

The flattened, flooded, wooded, almost amphibious landscape of the lower land of the Fenno-Scandian Shield. *(Swedish Information Service)*

A "loch" in the Highlands of Scotland—glacial erosion of an old, flattened, crystalline range. *(British Information Services)*

Europe, the climate described and analyzed there has been put forth as the *normal* one. In world terms such a climate is actually no more normal than the European interpenetration of land and sea; both would be better called *exceptional*. Even the moderate climate, with its four regular seasons, is restricted to the northwest and a part of the center of the continent. Other types of climate have developed elsewhere. True, each type of climate found in Europe is a rather mild example of its category, but such a general proximity to averages cannot be designated as normalcy. Climate is largely a matter of contrasts and weather of instability: even in the moderate, maritime Europe such contrasts and such instability are frequent.

The distribution of temperature and humidity over Europe, as well as their variations in time, reflect the struggle between the opposed influences of the ocean to the west and the massive continent of Asia to the east. In conjunction with the usual differences between north and south, this struggle between east and west overlays the checkered topography of Europe with a climatic map that looks like a mosaic. To understand the mechanism and its caprices, the general trends of atmospheric circulation must be taken into account.

The distribution of atmospheric pressure, ruling the direction and intensity of air currents, depends on the latitude and on the distribution of temperature. Determinant causes of geographical phenomena are never purely *local;* they are often regional—that is, affected by the situation of a given area with respect to other regions surrounding it. The geographical *environment* is a notion in space: it is influenced more by conditions surrounding an area studied than by the area's internal conditions. Europe is situated between the Arctic and the subtropical belt. Throughout the year the latter is crossed by a string of *anticyclones* or high-pressure areas, from which air masses diverge in various directions: chiefly toward *cyclonic areas*—that is, areas of low pressure. Most of the European continent is within the middle latitudes, a domain of somewhat unstable air currents directed chiefly eastward. The important current in this system is the procession of centers of low pressure or cyclones from west to east (which may mean northeastward or southeastward).

The eastward flow of air masses and of cyclones is directed by the land-sea contrast in longitude: to the east, Europe becomes increasingly massive as it nears Asia, the largest of all the continents. The continental mass constitutes a source of thermic changes within the year: in the winter it is very cold; in the summer it is heated up much more than the surrounding areas on the globe. In winter, Siberia and central Asia are covered by a powerful anticyclone, for cold air is heavy and the pressure is high; in summer the same area is very hot, the heated air masses rise,

The Alps—peaks of the Sella range in Switzerland. *(Official Information Bureau of Switzerland)*

A valley near Mont Pelvoux in France, in sharp contrast with the much older ranges flattened during previous geological periods (see pp. 20–23). Glaciation here created sharp forms. Note the huge alluvial fans of pebbles accumulating in the valley at the bottom of the slopes. *(French Cultural Services)*

and the pressure is low. Thus, to the east of Europe, the Asiatic continent is a source of heavy polar air masses in the cold season and of low pressures attracting winds and cyclones in the warm season. Therefore Europe, particularly its eastern parts, feels more the impact of the continent, cold and dry, in wintertime, while the maritime influences, bringing moderate temperatures and moisture, penetrate far eastward during the summer. The contrast between the seasons is greatest in Russia and is minimized on the articulated Atlantic shores.

An action from the south will introduce another regional aspect in the picture. The subtropical anticyclone, extending over the Atlantic Ocean as well as western Africa, is responsible for maintaining in the Sahara the greatest desert in the world. This high-pressure area bears the name "anticyclone of the Azores," as it is considered to be centered over this small archipelago in the Atlantic. But since it owes its existence to its position in latitude—that is, to some relationship to the distribution of solar radiation over the earth's surface—it moves up and down in latitude according to the movement of the sun between the Tropics. At the time of the winter solstice, when the rays of sun are vertical near the Southern Tropic, this anticyclone extends southward and frees the Mediterranean and southern Europe from its influence; in the summer, following the movement of the sun, its high-pressure area extends northward, covering the Mediterranean and the part of the Atlantic bordering the southwestern coast of Europe.

As a result of this oscillation of the high-pressure zone, southern Europe belongs to the Mediterranean climatic zone. It is opened to western—that is, oceanic—influences, which bring in moisture and storms in winter or the intermediate seasons, but stays dry and hot in the summer, though largely occupied by a sea. The isolation of the Mediterranean basin from the rest of the continent is increased by the lofty Alpine ranges to the north, screening the moderating and rainy influences from the oceanic northwest. East, south, and northwest are thus the three poles of the atmospheric mechanism of Europe.

The effect of the European mingling of land and sea is modified by several factors: high pressures over the Mediterranean restrict its maritime value to summer climates; and the partial freezing of the Baltic, with its shallow and little salted hydrography, reduces its climatic moderating and moistening influence during the winter. *"Les Pyrénées sont hautes"* (high are the Pyrenees) is an old French saying that is all the more true when the extension of the Azores anticyclone reaches them in summer. The climate of Western Europe is bounded on the south by the high ranges of the Pyrenees and Alps. Mountains form a dividing line, not only for atmospheric currents but for all kinds of traffic: what happens to be true in climatology applies also to other fields—even to politics, the sphere in which that dictum about the Pyrenees originated.

High altitude does not only influence the climate because of its two opposing slopes: it also means lower temperatures all the year round, sharper temperature differences due to exposure, stronger winds, a tendency to stop the onward march of cyclones and to attract eventually an expansion of high pressures from a neighboring anticyclone. The spine of highlands, mostly Alpine ranges, which stretches across Europe helps to establish at times "a barometric spine," or narrow belt of higher pressures, linking the Russian anticyclone with the Azorian in winter and subjecting most of Europe to the predominance of polar air flowing from Siberia.

The weather over Europe is determined therefore by factors acting in Asia, in Africa, over the Atlantic, and above the Alps. The procession of low-pressure centers, main agents of movement and instability, has its roots around Iceland and Newfoundland, or in the middle of the Atlantic—wherever air masses of polar and tropical origin can meet to generate a whirlwind strong enough to survive and move eastward. Europe, the hub where all these and other influences meet, could not have stable weather conditions, particularly as any combination of air masses is bound to be reshaped when it passes over from sea to land or vice versa. And such situations occur frequently within the region. Weather forecasts are generally less precise and accurate in Europe than in the eastern United States, both because the changing conditions on the seas around Europe are more difficult to survey adequately, and because of the greater instability of the general situation.

The resultant of an equation including all the factors that make up Europe's weather is still a moderate one. In January, monthly average temperatures vary between 17° Fahrenheit in the northeast and over the high central ranges and 45° to 50° on the shores of the Mediterranean and the Bay of Biscay. In July these averages rise to between 60° around the North Sea and about 80° in the southern sections of Mediterranean peninsulas. The extremes over the continent are closer together in summer, when the maritime influence penetrates deeper. The range within the year increases eastward. It is not a very impressive range, even in Russia, until the very threshold of Asia is reached. (See maps, p. 11.)

A similar moderation is demonstrated by annual precipitation figures: most of Europe gets 20 to 40 inches. This average tops 80 on a few slopes exposed to the northwest in Scotland, southern Norway, or the Alps; it is under 15 inches in the Arctic lands, and falls below 10 inches—a desertic regime—only on the northern shores of the Caspian Sea at the gate of the arid belt of central Asia. The seasonal distribution of this moisture is most regular on the western shores of Ireland (over 210

Pine forest in southwestern France where some of the trees have been tapped for rosin. This is a dense forest in sandy soil along the Atlantic shore (see regional description, p. 349). *(French Cultural Services)*

The European summer rainfall. The average July rainfall is more important than the January average because of the ripening crops. The unity of Europe is evident here, with the extremes of the high ranges and the Mediterranean area most obvious.

Key: 1, more than 4 inches; 2, 2 to 4 inches; 3, 1 to 2 inches; 4, less than 1 inch. (Compare with maps of temperatures in July and January p. 11.)

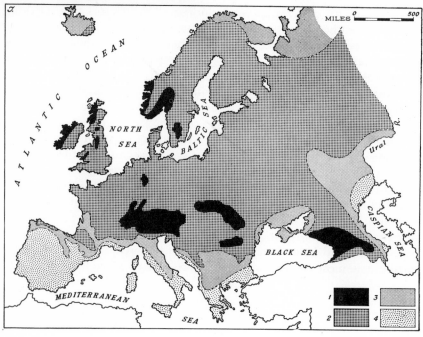

rainy days per year) and France (about 180 rainy days, the maxima occurring at intermediate seasons). The frequency as well as the total amount of precipitation decreases toward the east and south, with a concentration during the summer for Russia and during the autumn for most of the Mediterranean.

Strong winds are common only in some corners of Europe, notably on the Atlantic margins and along the Mediterranean shores, especially during the winter. Such winds are determined by considerable contrasts in pressure within small areas. Those conditions occur during the cold season in regions where highlands come close to the seashore: these highlands are much colder, and often covered with snow and ice while the sea is still warm in the same vicinity. Thus strong winds develop along the shores of Norway and in the parts of the Pyrenees that are close to the shore. The same is true of most of the Balkan peninsula. The central part of the Atlantic façade, though it consists of lower ground, is not free from such strong winds in winter, as the British Isles and the North Sea form an area attracting cyclonic depressions. These low-pressure centers may cause strong whirls to develop, particularly when high-pressure conditions are established on neighboring continental areas. Freak weather conditions are rare on the whole in Europe except on the Arctic and Asiatic fringes, where the influence of warm seas is less effective. European weather generally is capricious, but reasonably so. The vegetation suffers from excessive cold only in high altitudes or high latitudes; elsewhere, long droughts are the only serious threat.

## SOILS, PLANTS, AND WILD LIFE

The influences of geology, topography, past and present forces of erosion, and climate combine to vary the soil map of Europe. The top layer of the soil is thus affected by many factors. A general classification of soils was proposed at the end of the nineteenth century by the Russian Imperial Bureau of Soils, which outlined long stretches through Europe and Asia oriented along the parallels and differentiated by physical and chemical properties. This differentiation was explained by differences in climate and was said to be reflected by the color of the soils. Thus the Mediterranean climate, which is very special indeed, was considered responsible for the red coloring of most of the soils around that sea. In the subarctic areas the soils are grayish white, of an ashlike shade; for this reason they were termed *podzols* (ash being *zola* in Russian). Southward the color turns brown, chestnut, and even black in the case of deep soils rich in humus, such as those of the Ukrainian steppe.

While such a classification may be acceptable for the vast, flat Russian spaces, where the climate changes gradually with the latitude and where the belts of vegetation follow on the whole the same regular east-west axis, the listing was far too simple for the rest of Europe. The soils contribute to the complicated variety of European nature. In Scandinavia and the north of Russia, podzols actually predominate. Southward, glacial influences have been most important: the boulder clay alternates with light sandy soils, partly of eolian origin. Farther south, around the Hercynian massives, wide patches of loess appear, as well as rich loams that cover the limestone plateaus or recent alluvial deposits which fill in the main valleys. The weathering of granite and other crystalline rock on the old peneplains produces rather heavy, clayish, nonpermeable soil. Another stratification, in altitude this time, clothes the slopes of the high Alpine ranges, with deep alluvials in the bottom of the valleys and podzols on those parts of the high summits that are not scraped down to barren rock. Finally, around the Mediterranean, the predominance of *terra rossa* does not preclude other types and shades of soil. The "red earth" seems to result from the weathering of limestone and may be due more to the parent rock than to the local climate.

The quality of a soil depends more on the degree to which it is leached than on its original constitution. More recent soils have a greater fertility on the average than older soils of the same kind — alluvial deposits are an obvious example. Other soils — the podzol type, for instance — when leached develop at a certain depth a solid crust which restricts the percolation of water and the push of roots downward. Such deterioration can be combated in different ways, through a proper system of tilling or through the planting of certain plants. The development of scientific agricultural techniques has greatly improved or helped to maintain the fertility of European soils. Involved crop-rotation cycles, careful planning of reforestation, and the large-scale use of chemical fertilizers have considerably modified the natural aspect of the soils over large stretches of Europe. In some cases, nature has anticipated man; volcanic ashes irregularly fertilize the lands around some active volcanoes such as Vesuvius and Etna in Italy; manure from large herds of animals fertilizes grazing areas. Peasants all over the continent have long been aware of such fertilization: everyone in Europe knows how much a flock of sheep improves the land on which it grazes for an appreciable period of time; volcanic soils, even less recent than those of southern Italy, have always attracted populations and yielded rich harvests. And natural action is particularly helpful in the form of a regular and moderate moistening of the land all the year round; the abundant fog and dew, the long drizzling rains every month in the year are certainly one of the main reasons why the soils in northwestern Europe are not so much leached as elsewhere.

New York City authorities have struggled for years to protect the Egyptian obelisk erected in Central Park against rapid deterioration; but a similar, larger obelisk has stood for a century and a half in the center of the Place de la Concorde in Paris without causing headaches. This contrast, familiar to many tourists who have visited both cities, illustrates the difference between the two areas in the leaching of soils and weathering of rocks. In most of the countries of Europe, long organized by men, land-conservation practices have been developed, which also helped to retard leaching. Classifications of soils based, like the Russian one, on purely natural factors are only of relative accuracy and value on this old continent; human action, which has varied from country to country and province to province, has further elaborated the mosaic on the soil map.

What is true of the soil holds for the vegetation. There is little left of the natural primary cover in Europe, originally forested land with a general zoning in latitude like the general classification of the soils. In the Arctic, cold reduces the annual vegetation period to very little: mosses with a low, sparse brush, covering a poor soil, frozen several months a year and marshy in the summer, form the landscape of the *tundra* found in the north of Russia and of Scandinavia. To the south, trees, growing gradually denser, form a forest which is rather thin in the coldest areas. Coniferous trees — that is, trees with needles instead of leaves — predominate in the northern forests: firs, pines, spruces, mixed with birch trees in varying quantities. The birch predominates in wide areas of the Russian forests where the peasants use its wood as raw material for their handicrafts; even the silvery bark of the birch served as footwear in the past.

In warmer regions the coniferous trees are less frequent; they may constitute dense woods of a homogeneous type in certain conditions — pines on drier, sandy soils or firs on certain mountain slopes. The broad-leaved forests of temperate countries, which used to be typical of Central and Western European landscapes, have been reduced by the clearing of the land to patches, some of which are still impressive. The oak tree used to play a predominant part in these areas; today the forests are very mixed, many of the species having been imported from remote countries. But a few virgin forests can still be found in the far northern sections of Europe or on the vast marshes of the eastern countries (particularly in the area of the Pinsk marshes in White Russia). Vast stretches of forest remain on the main mountain ranges, especially on the slopes looking northward or westward; since these receive more rain and less sunshine, the natives cleared them less than the better-exposed slopes. Grass and tundralike formations prevail on the highest summits because of the cold and the force of the wind. Trees sometimes have difficulty

Bent by the seashore winds, such trees, especially pines, are quite common along the rocky coasts of Europe. The scene is typical of the Mediterranean area: a rocky limestone coast, deeply eroded by the waves; a cliff top with a patch of low, dense brush quite characteristic of the *garrigue* (see p. 33, and regional Mediterranean descriptions, pp. 410–424). *(French Government Tourist Office)*

in developing in the too-windy coastlands of Western Europe: woods may then be replaced by a lower brush.

Toward the south and southeast, increased aridity restricts forest development. A high grassland landscape, with rare scattered clusters of trees, predominates in the areas known as *steppes* (a Russian word describing a type of vegetation very similar to the American prairie). The steppe is a transition to the desert, which in extreme form is never reached in Europe. The main extension of the steppe is in the southern part of the Soviet Union, across the Ukraine and the lands of the Lower Volga River. A smaller steppic area covers the Hungarian depression, and another the center of Spain. The origin of the steppe in such areas as Spain or the Ukraine has been discussed many times. Is it the result of natural, mainly climatic forces? Or did it develop as a result of the inability of the forest to reconstitute itself under a marginal climate after active deforestation by man? Deforestation by fire may have been easy in dry periods, for these lands have been set afire many times in the past, either in wars or to clear the way for grazing herds.

The influence of depleted forest has for ages been decisive in shaping the Mediterranean vegetation. Most of the hills along the southern shores of Europe were forested in ancient times, but few remain wooded —the flocks of sheep needed open grazing ground, and the shepherd set fire repeatedly to the land. Out went the trees, and low brush, rich in thorny and odorous species, predominated, its aspect varying with the kind of soil. The crystalline areas grow the *maquis,* while limestone is usually covered with the *garrigue* (both French terms). The Mediterranean trees are of a somewhat different type than those to the north. The brevity and infrequency of the periods of frost in winter have favored the plants staying green or the trees keeping their leaves all the year round. Examples are the famous olive, the cork oak, and the holm oak (holly). Many coniferous species are originally Mediterranean, such as the Lebanon cedar or the much more common Aleppo pine (*Pinus Aleppensis*). Various kinds of pines spreading an umbrella of needles characterize the Mediterranean landscape. The olive and cork trees are cultivated, and the Aleppo pine is found in plantations far beyond the Mediterranean area, for instance, as far up as the western coast of Brittany. To define the exact extent of vegetation zones in Europe is a difficult task today. Many classifications have been attempted and revised, but they become rapidly out-dated on so old and civilized a continent. The traveler who comes to some parts of the Atlantic façade marked on vegetation maps as being the domain of maritime pine, may well find hay pastures enclosed with hedges planted with willows. The vast plains around Paris, intensively cultivated at present, used to be covered with deep forests which most specialists think con-

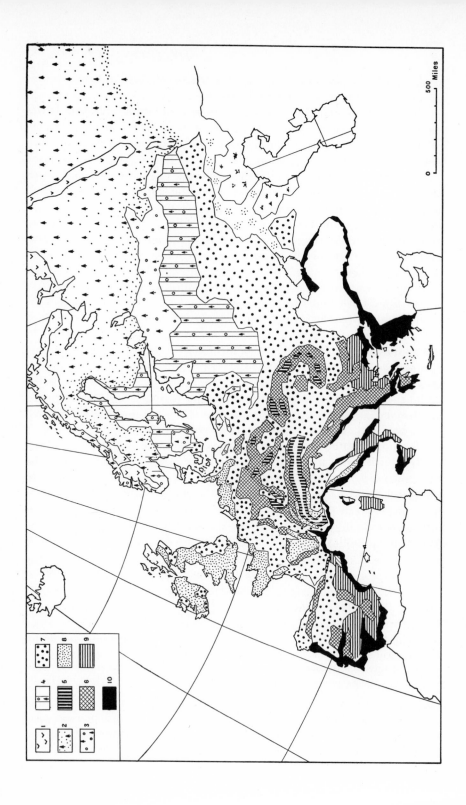

500 Miles

0

sisted chiefly of oak trees, although some experts believe beech groves predominated at first. Man has been so active for so long a time in Europe that one must think nowadays in terms of land utilization rather than of natural vegetation. The natural conditions affected considerably of course the general distribution of crops and modes of land use (see map, p. 34).

The biological elements in the landscape seem to be the most easily affected by human action. The fauna, even more than the flora, has been transformed by men, and wild life is restricted to a very few areas. Practically all the large animals that may have lived here have been wiped out or domesticated. A few bison remain in one Eastern European forest and are referred to in textbooks as "a vestige." Wolves, wild boars, and stags have taken refuge in the forests. Successfully hunted, restricted more and more in their wanderings by the impact of widening civilization, they have had to be specially protected for conservation purposes. Wild animals are more abundant in the eastern than in the western half of Europe. Every year boars migrate westward from the center of the continent to the French forests, replenishing the stock. Small animals, particularly of the rodent family, are of course abundant; they seem to thrive as parasites around human agglomerations. Birds and fishes have had to be preserved by complicated legislation; as a result selected species are practically raised, and it may be said that wild life is becoming artificial or "controlled" in Europe.

The domesticated species of animals are numerous, varied, and generally similar, with a few exceptions, to the American ones: there has been so much intercourse between the United States and Europe that most of the useful species have been exchanged. The European peoples have shown a remarkable ability for the domestication of animals, much more so than most of the extra-European peoples: cattle, sheep and goats, pigs, poultry — all abound throughout Europe. The climate im-

---

(*Opposite*) Vegetation and land use in Europe. In most of Europe, man has reshaped the natural landscape so thoroughly that vegetation cannot be studied aside from land use. This map shows in a schematic way the predominant types of land use in Europe through the dominant features of the vegetation as it appears in the present landscape. Explanation of legend (at upper left): 1, tundra and poorer northern windswept moors; 2, northern forest (predominantly conifers with some birch trees); 3, mixed forest (coniferous and deciduous); 4, zone of cleared forests where tilled areas alternate with woodlands; 5, forest and meadows of alpine mountains (higher zone of poor pastures and glaciers is left in blank); 6, zone of mixed Hercynian woodlands with clearings; 7, zone of intensive cultivation, with predominance of grains; 8, zone of intense cultivation oriented toward a cattle economy; 9, zone of Mediterranean agriculture affected by altitude or backwardness; 10, zone of intense Mediterranean polyculture, oriented toward vines, orchards, truck farming, and the like.

poses few limitations. The Arctic lands have, of course, their own fauna and specialize in the raising of reindeer and the hunting of fur animals. Drier areas have difficulty in supplying enough grassland for cattle and therefore prefer sheep herding. The only limitation is the absence of hot climate: plants and animals from hot or tropical countries cannot live freely in Europe. Otherwise an almost complete range of cold and temperate land animals can be obtained.

Laws of conservation developed differently in Europe — and through a longer process than in the Americas — at times when science was neither advanced nor popular. The areas that might have played the part of the national parks were simply those to which access was very difficult: the highest parts of the main mountainous ranges, certain Arctic areas, and wide marshes such as the Pripyat marshes or the Rhone River delta on the Mediterranean coast of France. Even these marshes are little by little being conquered by that process of reorganization by man known as civilization.

Natural conditions have been so mismanaged by people armed with modern techniques that new situations have developed in which agricultural populations as well as city dwellers looking for truly rural landscapes have become worried about the growing artificiality of the land. Now many groups are seeking the protection of nature, not only because certain economic ends might be thus better served, but also because the belief is spreading that the physical pattern should not be disturbed too deeply if and when this can be avoided. Europeans often saw reservoirs, built in mountain areas behind dams to produce power, ensilted with unexpected rapidity; deforestation and overgrazing on the steep slopes caused increased erosion, and alluvials accumulated in the bottom of the valleys behind the dams; in other cases they increased the strength of river floods. The more civilized nations are, the more intensely they now survey their local physical conditions, in order to establish a better balance between the network of natural forces and the action of men, striving to organize them for their own purposes. These purposes change, however, with time and social evolution. For instance, in days of yore, European farmers welcomed the spread of rabbits, which supplied some meat and cheap fur, and kept down certain weeds. In recent years, with greater affluence and more scientific methods of tilling, they grew less tolerant of the multiplying rabbit population and were happy in the late 1940s and early 1950s to see the new virus of *myxomatosis* considerably reduce the number of these animals.

As rabbits became scarce in the western European forests, the species of trees found in some of them began to appear modified. While they were very numerous, the rabbits apparently kept down the species of young plants which they ate; their elimination modified the ecological balance of the woodlands. Many such stories could be told, showing how the successive changes in the flora and fauna of Europe responded to various stages of the social and political history of the various nations.

The greater need for outdoor recreation of large crowds of urban dwellers, who enjoy more leisure and longer vacations, require a new management of the land outside metropolitan areas. Public authority must now provide for the hunting, fishing, camping, swimming, and other outdoor recreational activities of millions of people. Special legislation has been approved; new species of plants, animals, and fish are being introduced; others are strictly protected. National or regional parks are being created; wildlife or wilderness areas are being established. The conservationists must keep up a daily struggle for the preservation of various natural features of the changing environment. The European landscapes are undergoing a thorough reorganization in our time.

# 2

## Man's Organization of Space

It takes time for man to reorganize the natural setting of the place he lives in. In Europe people have had plenty of time to do this, and plenty of changing, ever-improving techniques. Men had of course to keep in mind the physical features of their land and seas. This physical environment impressed its influence on human ways and means on a very broad scale; the main climatic belts are an example: the Mediterranean lands could not be managed the same way the cold subarctic spaces were in northern Scandinavia or Russia. The physical environment was also a determining factor on a small local scale: a peasant necessarily differentiated between the bottom of the valley, the sunny slope, and the shadowy

The château and town of Luynes, France. The small town of Luynes symbolizes the involved past of the organization of European space, a past still very much alive and weighing heavily on the present. The massive medieval castle on the hilltop dominates the small town, with its congested, narrow streets and small buildings, nestling in the shadow of the local authority that once granted security and provided jobs and trade. In the foreground is the cemetery, with an older pentagonal section to the right and a more recent extension to the left, added as the town grew older. In the background, beyond the grounds of the castle, are a chapel and broken fields, fitted to a diversified agriculture: regular rows of vines, then small rectangles of ploughed land; in the upper right corner, fruit trees are scattered in a hedge-enclosed pasture. Between the fields there are several roads lined with hedges or rows of trees. This landscape has not changed a great deal in several centuries; however, the town is still prosperous in its own way. *(French Government Tourist Office)*

39

Èze, an old fortified town atop a hill on the Mediterranean coast, a location protected from pirates in the Middle Ages. Olive groves and terraces cover the hillside. This place is now a famed tourist attraction on the French Riviera. *(French Government Tourist Office)*

An Irish farm. These two different types of rural life suggest the regional variety of modes of life in Europe. *(Irish Tourist Bureau)*

one; he would generally have some pastures in the damp bottom, while he would till fields on the sunny slope and let woods grow on the shadowy side. Most regional differentiation that is important in present-day geography does not belong, however, to either of these two scales: the very broad areas and small local management. On the scale that chiefly concerns us, physical factors had incidental importance; their meaning was constantly interpreted and reinterpreted by the inhabitants. These physical features have not changed much in historical times; the occupying populations changed, and even more frequently their techniques and practical purposes changed. More change than ever is developing at present.

## FACTORS OF REGIONAL DIFFERENTIATION

The physical features of Europe could be classified, on the whole, by grouping them into a small number of main regions, but a similar task would not be worth while with respect to peoples — their actual diversity is too great. The complexity of its topographical checkerboard has been cited as the main reason for Europe's numerous political and administrative divisions. Such a relationship may have had an influence on certain political forms at certain periods, but a detailed examination of the political structures, past and present, reveals few cases of lasting coincidence between natural divides, such as mountain crests or rivers, and political boundaries. These boundaries between nations or within a national unit have been subject to rapid shifts throughout history, while all available data confirm the stability of natural conditions, topographic as well as climatic; only vegetation changed appreciably.

Many classifications of the present regions and landscapes of Europe are possible, each based on one specific feature. There are well-known classifications, established by linguists, of the Germanic, Slavonic, and Romance language families. Other systems follow "racial" lines, chiefly the predominance of one or another shape of skull, but these are so vague that they have generally had to be related to linguistic divisions to become understandable. Distinction between maritime and continental peoples does not lead very far either. Some island peoples, such as the Irish or the Sardinians, have been little interested in seafaring for the last thousand years, while the Russians, the most continental of all European nations, show a considerable interest in the sea, and the Swiss, though deeply landlocked, have at times maintained ships on the high seas. In any case, a classification based on a single feature would be of little practical use, for human nature and activities are so manifold and the "personality" of every nation is so complicated a mode of behavior. What the geographer is interested in is the combination of elements that makes any given region inhabited by a given people so different from any other. This differentiation occurs with a greater frequency and per-haps a greater intensity in Europe than on any other continent. Among the causes of this differentiation, the physical pattern is certainly impor-tant in minor matters, but in no way is it immediately and directly determining. We should beware of easy and oversimplified explanations of human behavior in terms of instincts dictated by natural influences. The longer physicians and biologists study man, the stronger grows their conviction of the predominance of social motives and impulses over instinctive ones. Civilization consists largely of series of conventions im-posed by society upon individuals — and most of these conventions order the suppression or control of the instinctive impulses. This is true not only of relations among men but also of relations between men and their natural environment, between men and resources.

The *patterns of culture* are recognized by anthropologists as a deter-mining factor in the behavior of primitive peoples. It would be ridicu-lous to suppose that the way of life of Englishmen, Frenchmen, or Russians is influenced more by natural conditions than is the way of life of natives of the Fiji or Solomon islands in the Pacific. European patterns of culture are more complicated because they are older and more ad-vanced and are based on a more involved stratification of past contri-butions. Actually they are more than "patterns"; they are "cultures" in-deed, and even civilizations. For a clearer understanding of the present map of Europe in all its variety, it is necessary to make a rapid survey of the past ages during which the organization of European space by its inhabitants was brought about.

## THE CONTINUITY OF EUROPEAN SETTLEMENT

Man has lived in Europe for several thousand years. Rich remnants of early human settlement have been found in various parts of the conti-nent, and their antiquity has been determined by the kind of tools used and the features of the skulls found in graves and caves. Man encountered in Europe climatic and biological conditions quite different from those he had known in former periods elsewhere. It is certain that he witnessed the last phase of the glacial periods, the last extension of the icesheets. At that time his habitat was, of course, limited to the ice-free areas, mainly in the south. Though mountainous, the Mediterranean region served as a refuge for the men and animals who could not thrive on the frozen lands. After the glaciers retreated, settlers moved toward the newly opened areas from the south and the southeast.

Even in these early times links existed between the European shores of the Mediterranean and the African and Asiatic lands around that in-land sea. It is probable that more land bridges existed then than do today, for the Turkish Straits and the Strait of Gibraltar are of recent origin. According to certain interpretations, the big shock that caused the tidal wave described in the Bible as the Deluge occurred at the time of the active faulting that opened these straits. Whether by land or by sea, active exchanges of population between the continents took place within the Mediterranean area. During the Paleolithic period the races of Italy and southern France were rather long headed (dolichocephalic) and of short stature, probably similar to the Berbers of present-day North Africa. A little later some populations with Negroid features inhabited these same parts. Then, from the beginning of the Neolithic period, other races of a round-headed (or brachycephalic) type appeared throughout Southern Europe. (Both round-headed and long-headed skeletons have been found in the same graves.) Mingling of different races, some probably African and others Asiatic in origin, began early in Europe.

After the melting of the glaciers and the drying up of the land, the vast European area opened to settlement attracted new people. A steady flow of population came from the east – that is, from Asia. All linguistic theories concur on this point, for the different languages of Europe are all related to those of Asia. The linguistic argument has not convinced all the biologists, however. It has often happened that entire nations adopted the language of a conquering foreigner, while the actual mixing of blood between conqueror and conquered would generally occur on a rather restricted scale. True, communications with the wide continent of Asia to the east have been for long periods easier and more active than with other parts of the world. The migration from the east is known to have been in progress in Neolithic times, and it continued through the pre-historic era and a good part of the ancient periods for which we have historical records.

Such records are not precise enough to inform us on the numerical importance of the migrations. It may well be, as specialists of prehistoric epochs are inclined to think, that numerically important elements came also from other directions, and that the natural increase of already sta-bilized European populations should not be underestimated. There was a great deal of activity, trade, and displacement of persons all along the Atlantic margins of Europe in remote times. A Western European group of peoples probably did exist early in prehistory, a group which mixed with elements immigrating from various parts; and the conquerors from the east never erased racially or even culturally these old foundations. What we know of the Celts and their expansion and culture, as well as of the early roads followed by the Norse expansion in the Middle Ages, all points toward a strongly organized basis in the west as far back as one can go.

Stabilization came with the rise of civilization, beginning in the Mediterranean area. Sedentary life requires more advanced techniques than nomadism. A longer experiencing of local conditions, the fight for survival in areas drying up in the south while the ice melted in the north, continuous ties with other countries, and the increase of population — all probably contributed to the advancement of the Mediterranean peoples. Once mature, the great civilizations of the Greek and Italian peninsulas expanded in different directions: the Greek colonization spread around the Mediterranean and Black seas; the Roman Empire reached the North Sea and crossed the Danube River. But such expansion was a phenomenon more of colonization than of settlement, and the numbers of natives from the peninsulas who settled in these distant lands were rather small. Mass migrations, however, continued from the northeast toward both the Atlantic and the Mediterranean.

In Europe, as in almost all other parts of the world, the coastal areas exerted a curious power of attraction on the populations of the interior of the continent. The maritime areas developed more rapidly because they were more populated and longer occupied, and economic motives strengthened this attraction. A contrast developed between the south and west on the one hand and the interior and east on the other. For a few centuries in the beginning of the Christian Era, it was the contrast between the civilized Roman Empire and the barbaric lands of the interior. The age of settlement, with its implications of stabilization and advancement of peoples, began to divide Europe into cultural areas.

The general features of European topography are oriented according to an east-west axis, and this disposition made early communications easier in these directions. The main source of settlers was in the east; to the west the wide Atlantic Ocean imposed until recently an impassable barrier to migration. Inevitably, populations becoming crowded in the west put up a growing resistance to the newcomers from the east. In the early Middle Ages, groups of easterners, generally in small numbers, broke through to the western shores. The Visigoths for a while conquered a large part of the Iberian peninsula; the Ostrogoths broke into Italy; the Vandals, after setting France afire, went to northwest Africa; the Franks endowed France with its modern name; and Mongol hordes rushed through Europe, leaving a memory of terror that centuries did not erase. A great many other tribes or groups, whose feats were less spectacular, infiltrated into the center, west, and south of the continent. These migrations do not seem ever to have wiped out the inhabitants of the territories they invaded or conquered. Sometimes, however, the names, language, and customs of the conquerors predominated; the path of these conquests can be traced on the map by geographic names and patronymics. Racially they caused only an increased mingling — Europe has been a melting pot for thousands of years. Most of the settlers who came to the continent belonged to the white race. Some were Mongols, very few were Negroes or had Negroid features; and these elements of the yellow and black races were assimilated in the white mass. Practically all the population of Europe is white, and it is from Europe that the white race has spread throughout the world.

Strong resistance to the westward migration began in the Middle Ages. Germanic peoples, feeling crowded in Central Europe and unable to proceed in the traditional direction, turned back eastward, though other populations, the Slavs, were still pressing from the east. As a result there developed a sharp conflict between Slavs and Germans that thereafter underlay most of the troubled history of Central and Eastern Europe; it added greatly to the confusion of the ethnic and political map of these lands and erected forever a partition between east and west. Eastward drives were attempted many times. The famous German *Drang nach Osten* brought some momentary political results and settled small nuclei of people in the East. But these never succeeded in outnumbering the Slavs or Eastern peoples on any significant territory. The only actual expansion of Europeans eastward was the Russian settlement that marched on across Siberia to the Pacific, but that was again an extra-European achievement. In Europe itself, the successive waves of migration and settlement along the east-west axis created antagonisms; boundaries began to be defined from north to south, and these political divisions cut across the natural regions that, because of topography as well as climate, varied more in latitude than longitude.

Opposition developed between the two axes: an east-west axis of structure and migration, a north-south axis of political organization. Nuclei of organization, or centers of trouble, arose at their many intersections, and the European map changed rapidly as a result. Had some invasion and conquest submerged these shaky and numerous structures, they might have been of far less importance; coming from the outside, such an invasion might have erased the existing divisions and shaped a new map on a continental scale. But nothing of that kind happened in Europe, and a slow but continuous settlement went on, creating a disordered but continuous history. Every province, almost every town, has for many centuries had its own network of relations, its own memories of long-standing friendships and hatreds, of slowly and patiently elaborated traditions and skills—hence the great force of regionalism and nationalism. They are strongly rooted, and they bear testimony to a proud and highly competitive spirit, a state of mind that was instrumental in developing such an advanced civilization as the Western one. Europeans have shown an extraordinary capacity of resistance to unfavorable odds posed either by men or by nature. They have proved able to insure their continuity against all the difficulties accumulated by time. This heavy heritage rendered extremely important and, at the same time, very fragile the whole system of transportation inside and around the continent.

## ROUTES, TRAFFIC, AND CROSSROADS

Europe is well organized for traffic. Nature paved the way, and man took full advantage of her paving. The facility of communication and transportation was a trump card that greatly helped the cultural advances and the spread of techniques, preparing for the mastery of European man over nature and for his expansion over continents with peoples less trained to dominate and organize space. The natural advantages that Europe offers to traffic are threefold: the discontinuous and chiseled quality of the mountain ranges; the density and regularity of the river network; the deep penetration of the seas inland. All three, however, presented enough local challenges to induce a desire for improved techniques and for a reorganization by man. The job that was done in response to these challenges has brought the whole system close to perfection in many areas.

In spite of its intricate topography, Europe still unrolls long stretches of lowland. The Great Plain of Europe from the North Sea to the Urals is the easiest section for land travel. With the exception of its spinal range, the Fenno-Scandian Shield has been flattened enough to offer no serious barrier to traffic—its topography gets massive and rugged mainly in the north, where the severe climate increases the difficulties—but actually the Shield constitutes only a small corner of Europe. The Hercynian belt is so broken down into mountainous or hilly ranges, plateaus, and depressions, that, even if some detours are necessary, traffic is not seriously impeded; it is simply more strictly channeled in places along depressed corridors. The lowlands widen eastward, establishing an easy and flat area for communication from the shores of the Baltic and White seas on the one hand to those of the Black and Caspian seas on the other. The topography rises and serious difficulties begin with the Alpine belt. Still, there are not very many long stretches of continuously high crests; convenient depressions open up between the ranges, such as the French Languedoc between the Alps and the Pyrenees, the Danube valley between the Alps and the Carpathians, and the depression followed by the valleys of the Morava and Vardar rivers amid the Balkan ranges. The longest ranges, the Alps and the Carpathians, have been sculpted deeply within by glaciers and other forces of erosion, so that valleys penetrate between their main blocks to the very heart of the mountain system, and passes connect the main

A Viking ship in which Norsemen crossed the northern Atlantic to Iceland, Greenland, and perhaps beyond (as exhibited in the museum at Oslo). *(Norwegian Information Service)*

The difficulty of European communications is demonstrated by the problem of building railroads through the Swiss Alps. This railroad winds across a valley by means of tunnels and bridges. Halfway down the steep slope a road follows the river. See the map of trans-Alpine traffic, page 388. *(Official Information Bureau of Switzerland)*

valleys between them. Only the Pyrenees and the Caucasus are powerful and continuous barriers, with sidewalks along the seashore on their extremities and few and high passes in their midst. These two ranges are situated respectively in the southwest and southeast corners of the continent and are not major obstacles to over-all traffic. The most difficult topography is still that of the Mediterranean peninsulas, which are quite mountainous and are partitioned in most cases into small ranges, basins, and narrow valleys, or with massive interior tablelands like those in central Spain. Indeed, the difficulty of land transportation in these regions may well have been an incentive for an early development of the skills of navigation.

Water has a considerable advantage over land for transportation purposes: it carries the vessel, provided the craft has either been made of light enough material or been given a proper shape. A river provides a track. To be navigable, it has to have a regular *regime* — that is, enough depth the year round and a gentle slope without falls or rapids. Nature has organized the European hydrography very well: large basins have developed through the Great Plain and the Hercynian belt, and many streams have their headwaters in one of the Alpine ranges. The variety of sources of supply can balance itself to insure an abundant and regular flow. Such is the case of two of the main rivers of Europe: the Rhine and the Danube; their gradients are gentle enough to open the longer sections of their courses to navigation. On the Great Plain, several vast basins enjoying a well-watered climate feed into navigable streams flowing to the North, Baltic, Black, and Caspian seas: in Germany, the Weser, Elbe, and Oder rivers; in Poland, the Vistula; in Russia, the two Dvinas, the Dnieper, the Don, and the Volga. The last of these, the Volga, is the longest and most powerful river in Europe. It drains more than half of European Russia and links the Moscow area with the Caspian; its two defects are that it empties into a closed sea and that it freezes for a prolonged period in winter. Freezing affects several of these rivers and their tributaries, many of which are navigable for a section of their course, but the freezing happens in different ways according to the place and to the year. The Russian rivers are the only ones affected as long as several months a year; in the west, freezing is exceptional.

The central section of the Alps and the hub of central Europe, where in Czechoslovakia the Alpine and Hercynian belts mingle, constitute the water tower of Europe (Russia excluded). Rivers radiate from this area in a fanlike design in all directions. Their lower, most navigable sections have been connected first by portages and later by canals, so that man was able to put the whole of the network to the best possible use. Several transcontinental waterways cross Europe, linking together all its bordering seas. Some of the routes followed by such rivers (or their valleys, when the rivers were not regularly navigable) have played a considerable part in history: thus the Rhine-Saône-Rhone itinerary, linking the North Sea to the western Mediterranean, the Rhine-Main-Danube diagonal route from the North to the Black Sea, the Morava-Vardar route from the Danubian basin to the eastern Mediterranean, and the Western Dvina-Dnieper connection from the Baltic to the Black Sea. At times empires were erected on these waterways systems — generally they proved fragile, for often rivers acted as boundaries. The dilemma of whether a river divides or unites remains to be solved. In any case, most of the rivers in Europe carry heavy trade; some of them which have steeper slopes, smaller basins, and less regular rainfall (mainly in the Mediterranean area), are not navigable; their valleys served as roads of penetration.

Topography and climate combine to make land transportation difficult in the Mediterranean area. The length of the indented peninsulas, the abundance of islands, and the frequency of luminous, calm weather — all favored an early development of navigation on this sea. Even more important were the serious population pressures on some of these peninsulas and the rise around the eastern basin of the Mediterranean of the major civilizations of antiquity — Egypt, Phoenicia, Palestine, the Hittites, Mesopotamia, and the Greek and Cretan cultures. Communications and trade by sea were bound to develop among them, and the expansions of the Greeks and Phoenicians proceeded chiefly by sea. The Mediterraneans enjoyed a tideless sea, with steady currents and a system of winds that they quickly learned to use; coastwise navigation was easy, as the proximity of mountains to the water's edge made orientation simpler. Early the Greeks went into the Black Sea and all around it; then they followed the Phoenicians' lead westward and, after creating a Greater Greece in Sicily, sailed past the Strait of Gibraltar along the Atlantic coast of Europe.

Navigating skills developed also, but with a slightly different technique, along the Atlantic and Baltic shores. The strong tides and frequent fogs and storms did not prevent the northern countries from navigating, and long before the Christian Era close contacts existed between the British Isles and the continent, particularly with Brittany. These peoples, however, left fewer records of their activities, and we know less about their past. It seems probable that the Mediterranean skills and organization developed better and earlier in antiquity than the rest of Europe's because the social and political order was more advanced in these Eastern civilizations; but we should not assume that the Mediterraneans brought their techniques to the Atlantic peoples. Navigation, like any other technique, may well have been developed in several places at about the same period — the Mediterranean and Atlantic sails and boats were of somewhat different shapes. Evolution followed different paths, and the Vikings sailed across the Atlantic and settled in Greenland several centuries before Columbus discovered the West Indies and the New World.

Whatever the detailed history of navigation, the seas around Europe early carried men and cargoes. Competition between land and sea transportation started in ancient times, one or the other taking the lead according to the advances of technology. On land Europeans became great specialists in the domestication of animals, and horses, donkeys, and oxen carried packs until the discovery of the wheel and the use of the harness led to the traction of vehicles. The horse-drawn car, used three thousand years ago by the Egyptians for military purposes, remained the chief means of transportation on land routes until the railroad came in the nineteenth century and the motor car in the twentieth. The economy of traction has been an involved and respected science for a long time; until very recently, harnessmakers were one of the most important guilds in European towns. Horse raising was a noble profession, and certain races of horses brought international fame to their places of origin.

The limited power of traction of a horse or of a team of horses restricted the cargo that could be loaded on a cart, and the transportation of heavy cargoes necessitated such long caravans of carts that they were seldom economical. These limitations did not apply to the sea or even the rivers. Techniques improved rapidly, enabling men to build navies of appreciable proportions. Using the currents and winds saved a great deal of traction power—even going upstream on rivers, it is possible to pull a cargo many times heavier if it floats on water than if it rolls on solid ground. Until the middle of the nineteenth century the development of resources that involved the transport of bulky materials was practically restricted to the vicinity of waterways—seashores or navigable streams. Maritime areas acquired a marked advantage over continental regions; this favored Europe as against more massive continents, and it had a definite impact on the pattern of settlement inside Europe. The better organized nations on the continent engaged in the construction of canals to supplement artificially the natural network of waterways, or they endeavored to regularize existing rivers and make them more navigable. France started large-scale canal building in the seventeenth century, Germany in the nineteenth, Russia in the twentieth. With the steady increase in the size of ships and cargoes, waterways had to be gradually improved, enlarged, and deepened; some of them that were not capable of such improvement declined or were abandoned.

Navigation developments explain much about the location and functions of European cities and towns. Thus cities along the Loire River in France used to be thriving centers when the stream was navigable, but silting and lack of depth reduced the traffic to small rafts in the eighteenth century, and now the Loire flows along sleepy local market towns that still display monuments of bygone splendor. Cities in Flanders were built on rivers at the points reached by the tidal currents, which provided easy access to and from the sea. Competition between ports created many conflicts — the struggle of Venice and Genoa for the control of Mediterranean sea lanes and trade routes across the Alps was an important factor in medieval politics. More recently Rotterdam and Antwerp fought bitterly for the privileged position of main seaport at the mouth of the Rhine and Meuse rivers.

Cooperation between land, river, and sea traffic was at least as important as competition. Points where these different means of transportation met, or where several roads and rivers came together, became hubs of trade where goods and ideas were exchanged. Meetings of merchants from different countries were instrumental in the growth of important cities and even capitals. Merchants preferred to meet in safe places, and the best guarantee of security was the presence of some local authority powerful enough to keep any threat away. During the disturbed thousand years known as the Middle Ages, such an authority was either feudal (a powerful lord) or spiritual (a respected bishop). Trade centers thus arose in the shadows of castles or cathedrals, preferably at a hub of natural routes. The name of Copenhagen, the Danish capital, means "the merchants' harbor," and the city did start as such, on the strait at the entrance of the Baltic Sea, under a bishop's auspices. Paris is a natural hub around which radiate the valleys of the navigable Seine, Oise, Marne, and Yonne rivers as well as land routes over flat plateaus. Certain cities, enriched by trade and boasting a population that was impressive for the period, established by themselves strong, democratic authorities with a secure grasp on the reins of power. Such were the Greek and Italian cities of antiquity; thus rose Athens and Republican Rome. Later a similar pattern was followed in the merchant republic of Venice and by the burghers of Flemish cities such as Ghent and Bruges.

Trade crossroads thus account for the scattering of urban developments in Europe. Trade centers attracted merchants and craftsmen and later industries; together, they agglomerated population. Very important in the geography of settlement and power in Europe were the regular annual market gatherings called *fairs*, and the location of these old commanding centers of the caravan trade is important to an understanding of the modern network of intra-European trade. Cities such as Lyon in France, Milan in Italy, Frankfurt-am-Main and Leipzig in Germany, Gorki (then Nizhny-Novgorod) in Russia, and Kharkov in the Ukraine grew up largely owing to the success of their fairs.

Transportation is so important a factor in geography because it establishes connections and unites or opposes different areas. It has to be organized according to economic and political considerations, and often the political ones have been dominant. The Roman Empire would never have had such an impact on European history after its decline, if it had not left behind a road network that took centuries to build. The Roman highway, or *via*, was strongly paved; well-cemented bridges spanned rivers; and its route was carefully planned. Built to facilitate the march of the Imperial legions, the *via* became a favored route for peaceful traffic as well. The Imperial network of highways across the Mediterranean and western countries of Europe established durable links on which a whole structure of economic and cultural relations grew with time.

"All roads lead to Rome"—this ancient dictum existing in all European languages was almost literally true. What Rome achieved, at the expense of tremendous capital investment, with the technical means of antiquity, modern powers have also endeavored to achieve, each within its national or imperial framework. The centralization of the French networks of highways, railroads, and waterways toward Paris, and the similar pattern centering on Moscow, worked out on a wider scale by the Soviet government, are typical examples. A durable political organization needs an adequate infrastructure of means of transportation. The Roman Empire could have been distinguished from the "barbarian" countries around as the "land with roads," and its heritage left a rift between the two parts of Europe. In the centuries following the Dark Ages, strenuous efforts were made by the western countries to develop public works, mainly ports, canals, fortifications, and highways, so that by 1900 statesmen could again speak of the existence of two Europes: the Europe that had roads and the Europe that did not have them. At that time this applied mainly to railroads, but with the rise of motor transportation in the twentieth century the highways regained importance. Hitler in Germany and Mussolini in Italy were proud of their roadbuilding achievements, for those countries had not theretofore been so well equipped as the countries of the Atlantic seaboard. However, the density of transportation facilities still varies greatly between east and west.

Transportation facilities are not proportional to the density of the population, but they are an essential measure of the accessibility of resources and of the mastery won by society over space and nature in general.

In the middle of the twentieth century, techniques of transportation are so numerous and involved that a full survey would require several volumes. Europe's network is well integrated, but Europe can no longer claim its former superiority in the whole field. During their transconti-

In Italy, many roads still follow the straight line along which a Roman road was built some two thousand years ago. The heavy inheritance of history is obvious in the landscape, as the road passes picturesque ruins testifying to past grandeur and much antiquated equipment still travels on it. Seen from America, Europe is divided into two parts, one of which is burdened with aged, useless equipment, and the other almost undeveloped. Even so, Europe is still ahead of many other parts of the world. *(Italian National Tourist Office)*

nental march westward, the American people developed techniques of transportation to a degree that was unknown in most of Europe. If Europe can compare with the United States in the field of railroads, canals, and seaports, it lags definitely behind in the development of air transportation, motor traffic, and pipeline construction.

The higher density of population in Europe has less to do with transportation facilities than is sometimes believed. China and India, with a much higher density, have much less traffic. It must be remembered that the European economy was organized within a vast oceanic framework for the countries of the Atlantic seaboard, and within a strictly regional frame for most of the inland territories. Difficulties of land transportation forced the inhabitants of the interior to live on local resources; very few could afford the high prices of goods transported from any distance. Imported merchandise was a luxury until a century ago.

The price of transportation was always high, even along the main streams or on the banks of the narrow seas. At every strait, ford, narrow gorge, or bridge, on the frontier of every state or county, local authorities stationed guards and levied fees on traffic going through. Danish princes taxed ships passing through their straits; German noblemen erected strings of proud castles along those great waterways, the Rhine and the Danube; almost every king had covered his realm with a tight network of gates at which tolls had to be paid. With the exception of a few places on the seashore, imported goods were expensive everywhere. One of the great achievements of the French Revolution — and one that made it so popular throughout Europe — was the breaking down of all this elaborate system of barriers in France and in some of the surrounding countries. The German *Zollverein*, or customs union, was the next step. Little by little Europe liberated itself from obstacles to trade inside the continent, making possible a more efficient and rational utilization of resources.

This process goes on. National tariff barriers are remnants of the old oppressive system, and a notable trend toward lowering them has developed since World War II, partly under American pressure and partly out of sheer logic. While commissions and conferences discuss the application of free trade on the international scale, agreements are being written for some regions of Europe: new entities appear, such as the Common Market and other groupings. Under the weight of so long a history, the emergence of such wider regional frames can result only from painful negotiations — Europeans are passionately attached to the local frame in which they were brought up. This is not simply conservative spirit; it is much more an emotional tie to something which for so many generations cost so much blood, sweat, and tears.

## OCEAN AND CONTINENT IN ECONOMICS

Until the development of the railroads, continental influences in economics worked toward a restriction of transportation facilities and, consequently, more investment in the development of local resources. Thus soil conservation practices were devised early, and mineral resources were surveyed and mined even under difficult conditions. In many cases Europeans utilized successfully what in other areas would be considered desperately poor soils or unproductive ores. At the price of hard toil for prolonged periods, Europeans turned into assets what would have been neglected elsewhere. To achieve this a vast expenditure of human labor along lines directed by highly developed techniques has been indispensable. The abundance of skilled manpower resulting from this economic system was both a strength and a weakness: a strength because it made easier the fuller use of resources and because the thirst of better educated people for improvement was in all fields a factor of progress; a weakness because, where and when certain skills had been applied with success for some time, drastic changes were difficult and unpopular. It was also a weakness because wide markets were needed for a large-scale production of manufactured goods, while standardization was difficult among such regional and national diversity. In a long economic evolution, assets and liabilities mingle in some way to raise problems and contradictions. In the course of better fitting herself for self-sufficiency, Europe, as a whole or in parts, experienced a constant need for expanding markets.

The simplest way of expanding markets is trade between different regions: the greater the differences in environmental conditions and techniques, the better the prospects for exchange. Transcontinental trade relations across Europe existed in prehistoric periods, demonstrated by the distribution of tools — for one example, the polished stone axes discovered in areas far from those where that stone is found. At first it was only expensive, finished goods that could stand the cost of transportation; but precious raw materials early began to be carried along special routes, such as the amber road from Northern Europe and the silk route which reached the eastern gates of Europe after crossing all of Asia. The variety of the regional settings in the European checkerboard, the frequent contrasts, both natural and human, stimulated an active commercial circulation. Local specialization appeared early and lasted long, owing to the persistence of skilled manpower: in an area that has mined silver and raised cattle for many centuries, in Italy, Florence is still famous today for silverwork and leatherware.

The most active traffic routes are still linked to waterways, and the most important are those crossing the continent from coast to coast, particularly in the north-south direction. This was the axis of more rapid change in natural conditions, as demonstrated by the boundaries in the Treaty of Verdun (see map p. 70). Continental trade was linked very early with maritime navigation. Fishing was one of the very first skills man developed, and the sea therefore brought to coastal areas an important addition to man's diet. However, it was the commercial possibilities of the sea that rapidly became essential.

The hub of the world trade in antiquity was in the Mediterranean. In its midst, Rome erected a vast urban center, with a crowded population that needed the foodstuffs and raw materials of other countries. The Empire was mainly circum-Mediterranean but stretched also along the Atlantic shores to the northwest. Navigation brought quantities of products: wheat from Egypt and Tunisia, cotton and silk from the eastern shores of the Mediterranean, lead and tin (so important for making bronze) from Brittany and Cornwall. Slaves and mercenaries arrived from overseas, as well as merchants coming to buy the manufactured products of the Roman industries. In the Middle Ages the decay of the Empire, insecurity on the sea, and, above all, the Moslem conquest westward after the sixth century, disorganized maritime connections. The Mediterranean was thus eventually cut into two irreconcilable parts: Christians in great numbers no longer lived in Moslem countries and Moslems were expelled from most of Europe. A few individuals, mostly Jews, were admitted to both sides of that religious and political front—an early "iron curtain"—and very few were able to maintain even restricted commercial relations. The prosperity and the whole economic organization of the Southern European areas slowly disintegrated. The Middle Ages marked a return from a maritime and intercontinental to an intracontinental, regional economic system.

Still navigation skills were not lost, and maritime interests developed among peoples of the north of Europe. The Baltic Sea served as an important link there; the Swedes became, in a way, the Greeks, if not the Romans, of the Baltic and brought trade and maritime life to many areas, among them Russia. *Russ* was the name given first to Swedes who, coming chiefly from a place north of Stockholm, established themselves on the eastern reaches of the Baltic among Slavonic tribes which soon also adopted that name for themselves. From the Baltic, associations of seafaring merchants colonized the North Sea. The famous Hansa awakened the oceanic vocation on many points of the Atlantic coasts— for instance, in London, which became an active port when the Hansa traders, coming up the Thames River, founded an establishment on the Strand.

From Norway, daring mariners had already set out westward. Today it appears that the Vikings had regular connections with North America, via Iceland and Greenland; they even settled in Greenland in the twelfth and thirteenth centuries, long before Columbus sailed westward. Earlier, Norsemen had invaded from the sea several countries of the Atlantic seaboard. From the French shores, the duke of Normandy conquered England. Regular ties were established across the sea between the British Isles and the French and Flemish coasts — wines imported from the Anjou and Bordeaux areas chased the vines from Britain, where once they supplied a poor quality beverage. The main beneficiary of this North Sea development at first appeared to be the coastal area of the Low Countries. The excellent waterways of the Rhine, Meuse, and Schelde rivers, with their tributaries and easy land-route connections with the rest of the continent, made them the central crossroads of maritime and continental lanes. A magnificent commercial civilization blossomed with rich growing cities gathering money and skills, erecting monuments, spreading industries into the surrounding rural areas, and investing capital heavily in the improvement of the soil and the equipment of farms. Improvement in relations with the Byzantine and Moslem powers brought some revival of Mediterranean sea trade. From the tenth century onward, Italian cities such as Venice, Genoa, and Pisa developed splendid commercial enterprises at the Mediterranean extremity of a much-traveled transcontinental route, connecting Italy with the Low Countries through the Alps, France, Switzerland, and southwestern Germany over land and to some extent with Byzantium over the sea.

But there were still too many hindrances to the developing trade of the European cities with the Far East across the Moslem Near East. Navigators from Southern Europe looked for an all-sea route to the countries producing spices, silk, cotton, gems, and ivory. The Venetian Marco Polo made his famous trip to China; Portuguese seamen began to seek a route to the east around Africa, avoiding the Moslem Near East; Columbus sailed westward to find India, and his discovery of America may be said to have stemmed from the spirit of protest that developed in European merchants against the narrow regional frame of their continent and the barrier erected by religious antagonism in the Moslem countries.

The great discoveries of the fifteenth and sixteenth centuries made the Atlantic Ocean the chief field of European expansion, and the Atlantic-façade countries rose to the highest level of prosperity, culture, and power. The commerical West, with better utilized local resources and vast investments abroad, came to be characterized by dense population, urbanization, industrialization, comparatively democratic political regimes, and world-wide connections. The contrast with the more continental East was striking, for that area was more agricultural, less developed, more thinly populated, living on a much more "localized" self-sufficiency. Eastern Europe also expanded, but it expanded on the continent of Asia, where Russia built up an impressive empire. The standards of living in east and west remained for almost a millennium in sharp contrast. This contrast was not without relation to the importance of foreign trade: Europe had dominated world trade and for four centuries had concentrated all its control in the hands of people living between Gibraltar and the Danish straits; Russia had only a small share in the whole network and traffic.

Today the history of trade in relation to the continental and maritime positions of the various countries still plays an essential part in the economic problems and systems of Europe, in the present division between east and west, and in the continental orientation of the landlocked Eastern powers and the Atlantic orientation of the Western ones. Recent technical transformations of the means of transportation have affected little the general economic pattern inherited from a longcontinued history, but they herald substantial changes for the future. Large-scale development of resources is no longer restricted to the seashores, and the advantages from overseas, acquired in old times by the Western powers through their capital investments abroad and the political control of imperial territories, may vanish or be transformed.

The importance of the advantages that come to European countries from their relations with overseas countries can hardly be assessed. The necessary statistics do not exist for most countries, and it would be futile to attempt an evaluation. After World War II, what had been a gradual evolution was brought to a sharp turn. New trends have started. The decisive problem now is to know how to better manage the continent's environment.

## MAN-MADE LANDSCAPES

Sweat has flowed freely to bring European landscapes to their present shape. The climate and topography of the continent did not determine its present aspect. Once dense forests covered areas in France, Germany, and Russia that are now almost treeless and completely under the plow. Where brush once predominated, pine woods grow. Where played the waves of the sea, rich harvests of wheat sway in the wind. Where desert marshes stretched, now great cities stand. These results were a long time in the making. While the most spectacular changes were achieved recently with the help of modern techniques and machines, immense areas were reshaped earlier, before this help was available, and slowly, by the tenacious efforts of generations bent over a soil that was often barren to begin with. Most impressive of all is the centuries-old struggle of the Dutch and Flemish populations to wrest from the sea new land for cultivation, and their constantly vigilant struggle to keep these lands dry, against the attempts of the sea to reconquer the territory. Elsewhere the work of men is less spectacular.

The clearing of the European forests was a Herculean job. It was done slowly, according to the amount of open space needed. Little remains of the predominantly oak forest that probably covered most of the northern half of France two thousand years ago. Central Russia is still largely wooded, but the cities of today, including Moscow itself, were started in small clearings less than a thousand years ago. Once wood cutting progressed far, erosion developed with a new and threatening force, particularly on sloping ground. Reforestation was started and wide official programs drawn beginning in the middle of the nineteenth century in Western and Central Europe. In some parts of the Alps, modern engineers found it necessary to rebuild eroded slopes, a procedure that was by no means original with modern science.

Whoever has traveled in the Mediterranean area has noticed the many terraces that clothe the hilly slopes. With varying regularity and more or less careful maintenance, the slope is shaped into a flight of large stairs protected by a stone edging. Thus the good soil is prevented from slipping down the slope, and the erosive force of the water flowing downward is much reduced. On the steepest slopes of the Alps, the Swiss peasant has maintained the top layer of his soil by tireless care, fetching back from the bottom of the valley what a violent storm may have swept away, carrying the earth up in big baskets on his back to retrieve his land. On the chalky, convex slopes of Picardy in northern France, the peasants broke the slope with little terraces, each planted with a line of trees that are called *rideaux* (screens). Curtains of trees were also used to screen farms and crops against certain winds, a frequent sight on the plains and hills of maritime regions. The seaboard was not only windy but also damp, and the humid climate favored the growth of grass. Hence, as animal husbandry, particularly cattle raising, took an increased part in the European economy, open fields were enclosed so that behind stony walls or thick hedges the animals could be left to graze unattended, saving manpower. Thus the *enclosures* developed in England, France, and many other countries, changing the landscape of open fields into a quite different, almost wooded, aspect.

Both the dampness of the soil in marshy areas and the dryness of the climate, suggesting the need for irrigation, induced a reorganization of the drainage system, and most of Europe at some period underwent some work for water control. Vast areas of meadows are thus irrigated with trickles of water from neighboring streams—in Limousin (central

The man-made soil of southern France. Terraces, gardening, aqueducts, and tunnels are necessary to organize the land. *(French Cultural Services)*

France), in Lombardy (northern Italy), and in southwestern Germany. Other areas were marshy or too damp and had to be drained constantly by an intricate system of canals and pipes. Berlin and Leningrad (then St. Petersburg) were built in the eighteenth century amid drained marshes. The wide Po valley and a number of smaller areas had to be drained in Italy where good flatland is rather restricted; the drainage of the Pontine marshes south of Rome was completed in the 1930s. Similar jobs had been performed in France in the Vendée and Breton marshes, and in the draining and planting of vast pine woods on the sandy moors of the Landes. Dutchmen gained a well-deserved world-wide reputation as experts in water control after the great work they accomplished in conquering *polders* on the submerged or tidal lands. Their province of Zeeland has been defined as "a masterpiece of masonry," but the greatest job in this line that they have tackled is now in progress, the conversion into polders of the larger part of the Zuider Zee, a bay of the North Sea. Along the banks of the North Sea many polders, reclaimed from under the sea, exist on the coasts of Flanders, eastern England, Denmark, and Germany.

Marshy areas were the safest shelters for wild life in Europe, but the extent of such areas has been severely reduced. However, some wide stretches remain in Russia, where lack of space is not yet a problem. The hydrographic network throughout the continent is still being reshaped by human action, aimed at the improvement of navigability, the control of torrential erosion, particularly in the mountains, and the production of hydroelectric power.

Clearing and reforestation, drainage and irrigation, correction of streams and control of erosion have led Europeans to alter their land-scape greatly in order to maintain their activities on the land. The famous Swiss anthropologist Professor Eugene Pittard used to caution against too much pride in being a European, since Europe received from other continents the early skills and inventions on which its own tech-niques and ways of life were founded. Much was achieved, however, in the adaptation and improvement of these crafts. Although the cultiva-tion of plants appears to have originated on other continents, scientific agriculture was highly developed by Europeans. Fertilization of the soils often changed completely their productivity. Actually the soil of Europe is to a large extent the production of man rather than of nature, particularly in the west of the continent. The vineyards producing the famous French wines of Champagne and Burgundy, for instance, grow on ground that has been specially treated for centuries. There the vine-grower knows the special features of every parcel of his farm, for he has a secret family recipe dictating what earth taken from nearby quar-ries or fields should be added and at what intervals to keep the soil producing a certain quality of grape. Thus the earth of his vineyard for several yards in depth consists of that special blend and has little relation to what it would have been if left to natural evolution.

Although such completely man-made soils are exceptional, the human factor has been significant everywhere in pedology. Specialists in Mediterranean argriculture doubt very much that the Russian classification of *terra rossa* types would apply in these old countries, where the action of men has interfered so much with weathering processes. Some of them have suggested the use of a special term such as *grounds* instead of *soils* to emphasize the artificial character of this surface layer. The main method used to maintain, restore, or improve the fertility of the land consisted in the addition of fertilizer. The oldest form is manure produced by animals and spread over the fields. The European farmer has generally endeavored to combine the cultivation of crops with stock raising. Sheep grazing on stubble fields after the harvest applied direct fertilization to the land, but manure mixed with straw was carefully prepared on every farm having stables. It was accumulated at a chosen point in the farmyard or even on the sidewalk of the village street, a custom that many tourists probably have found distasteful or unhygienic. They should remember that the peasant has had to maintain the productivity of a soil on which the pressure of demand by a growing population was continually increasing; there were no more free lands, and products from other regions could not be used widely because transportation was too expensive and difficult. Manure helped local self-sufficiency, and it was abundantly applied, especially in the more populated parts of the continent. Since the middle of the nineteenth century the railroad has made land transportation much cheaper, and the progress of chemistry has led to the widespread use of chemical fertilizer. Phosphates from Poland, Russia, and North Africa, nitrates from Chile, potash from Germany and France and, more recently, synthetic ammonia—all have been used on a large scale; they complemented manure without replacing it. As a result many poor soils have been much improved chemically and fitted for crops that could not be grown on them previously. With the rise in the standard of living of urban populations, the refuse of the cities and towns grew in volume and variety to enrich the vast stretches of poor soil in which it was buried. Some areas formerly reputed barren began thus to bear harvests.

The size and versatility of European production grew steadily as agriculture became more scientific. Agricultural techniques have changed more within the last hundred years than in ten preceding centuries. Still mechanization is just beginning, and the modern plough is a newcomer to some parts of Southern and Eastern Europe. Particularly important also has been the system of crop rotation; in this field Europe can certainly claim leadership. The European peasant discovered early how easy it was to exhaust even the richest soil by growing the same crop on it year after year, and he began to allow his ground rest periods. Traditionally Europe was divided into two zones with respect to crop rotation: the zone of the biennial rotation (one year under cultivation, one year fallow) and the zone of the triennial or three-course rotation (one year grains, one year roots, and one year fallow). An elaboration of the three-course system replaced the fallow period with hay or fodder crops. Then more intricate rotations were developed, creating cycles extending over four to eight years. Fallow periods were replaced by an adequate combination that did not exhaust the land too much, and fertility was maintained by abundant organic and chemical fertilization. This system is used of course only in areas of intensive, scientific cultivation, mostly in the northwestern part of the continent. Mediterranean lands had the old system of biennial rotation with a year of fallow, the ancestor of what was called *dry farming* in the arid American West. Three-course rotation originated in the northwest, where the combination of animal and grain raising was also worked out and where the best races of cattle originated. Holstein, Charolais, and Jersey are place names of northwestern Europe, as well as Lincoln and Rambouillet, both famous for the races of sheep they produce. Crop rotation and mechanization are gaining rapidly in the eastern part of the continent. But the problem of crop rotation carries many more complications than one would expect: it affects the whole agrarian system, the distribution of farms throughout the countryside, and land ownership. Public opinion inclines to look on the landscapes of urban and industrial regions as definitely artificial and man-made, but it looks for "natural" scenery in the rural country. Such is not the lesson of European geography.

## RURAL HABITAT AND AGRARIAN PROBLEMS

The distribution of habitat, the material and shape of the buildings, the kind of enclosures, the design and size of fields — all play an important part in shaping scenery, giving it a special coloring and flavor. These features have greatly interested geographers who mapped them and endeavored to explain them by the physical environment. Local conditions greatly influence the organization of habitat in countries where self-sufficiency within narrow regional frames has been the rule for long centuries. Still, nature conditioned few of the actually important aspects. Climate restricted the range of crops that could be produced; it suggested to men certain efforts for protection against the possible extremes. The soil or subsoil supplied the material for building: brick on clayish lowlands, stone on limestone plateaus or hills, timber in wooded lands.

But a choice could often be made, for instance between timber and stone in many hilly areas; the decision was dictated by budgetary reasons and by tradition, rather than by climatic considerations. As a matter of fact, modern architects think many of the patterns of farm-building in olden times were unhealthy and wrong and that local materials could have been used much more rationally. Peasants were looking less for comfort than for security and for the social standing that the external appearance of the buildings suggested.

More important than the building materials is the plan and general layout of the farm. According to the classification outlined for Europe by the French geographer Albert Demangeon, farmsteads fall into two main types: those built in one block and those with a yard or court. The block farm could be built horizontally, on the ground, with only one floor above the ground floor, the different sections placed side by side; or it could be built vertically with several stories, the stables being on the ground floor, living quarters above it, and the barn on top. Such "houses in height" seem to be frequent in sloping areas, particularly in the Alpine and Mediterranean belts. Sometimes, owing to the slope, the barn at the top would be level with the ground at the back of the building. The court farm consisted of several buildings, separated or built at right angles surrounding a yard or scattered through an enclosed court. The courts seem to be always associated with an emphasis on livestock-raising in the local economy. Some of these court farms take very picturesque and original shapes, and some of them, such as the farms of the Pays de Caux in Normandy, seem quite unrelated to those of neighboring regions enjoying a similar climate and type of agriculture. There are many cultural influences mingled in every type of farm, and there are so many farms in the old lands of Europe. Each bears the imprints of the successive economic periods of its past. The farm buildings constitute the farmer's main tool; they express his technical background and the tastes of his fathers. With the development of quick and cheap transportation and the breaking down of regional isolation, some standardization is taking place, but in spite of wars and destruction, most European farms have very old buildings, and even the new ones bear some resemblance to the local type — the peasant feels more comfortable in familiar surroundings. Social discipline has a strong impact on rural areas, and the whole past enforces it.

The strength of social traditions appears in the distribution of habitat: farms can be agglomerated in large villages, grouped in small hamlets, or scattered throughout the countryside. The distribution of buildings gives a distinctive character to the scenery, apparent at first glance. Certain geographers early advanced an explanation based on water resources: men clustered around the main springs in areas where water

Mountain habitat. *(Above)* A tall farmhouse in the Swiss Alps near St. Gallen *(Official Information Bureau of Switzerland)*. *(Below)* The agglomerated village of Utelle in the French Alps near the Mediterranean coast *(French Cultural Services)*.

was scarce and scattered in areas where water was running abundantly on the surface. However, comparison with the geological map does not bear out this relationship. Germany, for instance, seemed to be predominantly an area of concentrated habitat, but Germany, as well as most of Northwestern Europe, is a humid area; in the areas farther south scattering was more frequent. In fact the concentration of habitat in older times depended on a number of conditions; security was an important one, and the defense of a compact community was easier. Thus concentration was a rule in the Middle Ages — on Mediterranean shores open to incursions by Saracens or other pirates, and on the open flat plains of Central or Northwestern Europe through which armies often marched. The system of landownership and crop rotation was another factor: where some of the land was owned, grazed, or tilled in common (possibly owned by a distant authority and tilled according to regulations worked out in common), it was wise for men to group together in a convenient spot, preferably in the middle of the grounds to be attended. The three-course crop rotation required some collective discipline, and traffic through the fields during tillage or harvest was much easier if the fields were open with no separations between them and if everyone conformed to the discipline. That system favored large villages situated in the center of their lands without any scattered habitation; every farmer had a plot in each of three divisions or *fields* (called *soles* in France). Collective ownership of a meadow was very helpful for poorer peasants who had not enough land of their own to raise animals. Similar collective arrangements helped people when a new house had to be built, or in any other crucial period.

If the collective provisions of this agrarian common law had not been of great force and importance in the country from which the Pilgrims came, Bostonians perhaps would not have located their grassy Common in the middle of the city, and New Englanders perhaps would not have insisted on the town-meeting tradition. In fact, the whole settlement of the eastern United States might have been quite different. In the seventeenth and eighteenth centuries, the rural structure of England underwent broad reforms. The enclosures led to a predominance of large private holdings, restricting the application of the old collective customs from which the poorer elements were the main beneficiaries. Refugees in New England intended to preserve these customs. Britain was not the only country where such common-law measures were deeply rooted: there were the countries around the North Sea and along the Great Plain of Europe down to Russia, where the villages used to be organized in associations for tilling, called *mir*. Some German scholars have ascribed these customs to the "racial" features of the peoples speaking Germanic languages, thus claiming for Germany all the areas of concentrated habitat and traditional three-course rotation. Actually the impulse toward collective organization in the northern half of Europe may be linked to the tribal organization that for a long time ruled the countries little affected by the Roman Empire. Common law in Europe used to be the opposite of Roman law. The Germanic tribes, since they were mostly outside the Roman Empire, needed more collective protection. But Portugal has a triennial rotation in contrast to Spain, where the biennial was the rule, and this could not be explained by German racial or even cultural influences. Many parts of the destroyed Roman Empire turned to concentrated habitat for security reasons during the troubled period of the early Middle Ages. Finally areas cleared and settled or resettled in recent times, belonging to strongly organized states, show a trend toward the scattering of habitat; such is the case even of parts of the Hercynian hills in and around Germany. Large valleys in the Pyrenees have superimposed two levels of settlement: old large villages on the valley floor and scattered farms climbing the recently cleared slopes. Since olden times, the scattering of habitat seems to have been associated with the predominance of livestock raising and with a more advanced civilization, insuring greater social security to individuals.

Still, how could individualism rise in a predominantly rural economy without access to landownership for the common man? For a very long time, landownership in Europe was concentrated in the hands of a very few. The Middle Ages were a decisive period when feudal lords, the powerful aristocracy, gathered land titles into their hands, reducing almost all the peasant masses to serfdom. This trend varied in intensity and duration with the countries. In Eastern Europe, a small but ranking group of landlords controlled the rural revenues of most of the countries as late as the beginning of the twentieth century. In the west, the early growth of the middle class led to greater equality in the distribution of land and of the income from it. From the seventeenth century on, the Lowlands and France showed trends toward small holdings; the revolutionary period at the end of the eighteenth century removed most of the servitudes remaining from feudal times. In Southern and Eastern Europe large estates, or *latifundia,* as they were called in Roman law, were until recently the rule; the Soviet Revolution of 1917 broke down the system in Russia and replaced it by collectivization and state ownership. Since 1920, agrarian reforms have been taking place under varying influences in Eastern and Southern Europe, dividing the estates and bringing the peasants closer to owning—collectively if not individually—the land they till. In the West heavier taxation is bringing about the break-up of most of the large estates. Mechanization helps to expand the area that can be cared for by one family, so that the trend would appear to be in favor

Old house of a Norman peasant.
*(French Government Tourist Office)*

Mont St. Michel, famous fortified
medieval abbey on a rocky island
off the French Channel coast. *(French
Government Tourist Office)*

of medium-sized farms, neither too large nor too small, with the optimum size varying, of course, from region to region. Western individualism and Eastern collectivism seem to be again contrasted today. The opposition has certainly no ethnic foundation, but it does have some explanation in the historical past—for instance, few peasants in the East have ever possessed their land freely—and in different cultural ties.

## CULTURAL REGIONS AND THE SPIRITUAL FACTOR

The rural scenery of Europe has been deeply imprinted, through the crop systems and the agrarian laws, with the mark of the culture or cultures predominant in a given area. Economics is most important, of course, but every people has its own way of assessing values and planning its budget. Differences of appreciation of conditions and resources lie generally in the cultural variations. These are frequent and considerable in Europe. That small continent has been divided into many national units within which generally there are subdivisions; "historical" provinces deserve attention, particularly when they are occupied by "national minorities." Historical provinces cannot be suppressed or reshaped by an edict; their roots are too deep, buried in the landscape and the way of life as well as in politics. National minorities are groups claiming to be different from the majority of the surrounding national groups by their cultures, by their past history, and by their political aspirations. The basis of all such claims, whether they concern a group of people or a region, is cultural: the people thus estranging themselves somehow differ from their neighbors in civilization; it may be in language, religion, some tradition of which the minority is proud, memories from the past; often it is all of these put together.

An easy method of classification has been to divide the European peoples in three main families according to linguistic differences: these are the Germanic, Slavonic, and Latin peoples. Recently it has been the fashion to call these divisions "races," as they seem to correspond to the three main stages of the settlement. The Latin strata, occupying the Southwest (Portugal, Spain, France, Italy, part of Belgium, and part of Switzerland), would be the oldest, linked to the Roman Empire; the Germanic strata came later and ruled during the early Middle Ages, keeping the Northwest and Central Europe as its realm (Britain, Scandinavia, the Lowlands, Germany, Austria, part of Switzerland, and scattered areas in the east); the most recent strata, the last civilized and the last arrived from Asia, would be the Slavonic (Czechoslovakia, Poland, Yugoslavia, Bulgaria, Russia, and the Ukraine). The picture is complicated by the existence amid these groups of other, miscellaneous peoples speaking different languages. Rumanian is closest to the Latin

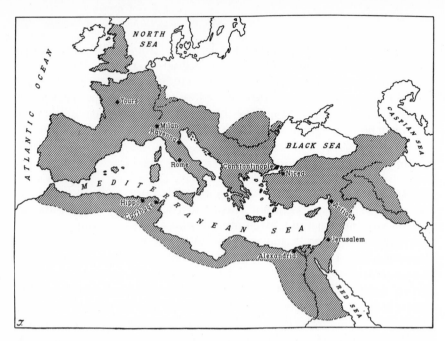

The Roman Empire, A.D. 180. (After Charles G. Haines and Warren B. Walsh, *The Development of Western Civilization*)

The division of Charlemagne's empire according to the Treaty of Verdun, 843. (After Charles G. Haines and Warren B. Walsh, *The Development of Western Civilization*)

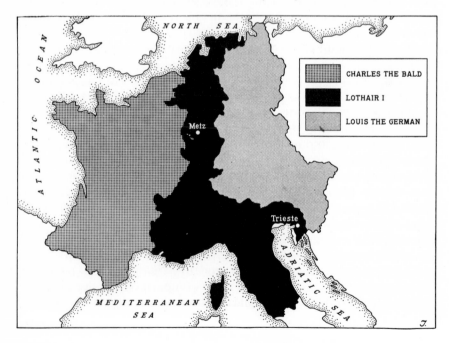

family; Hungarian, Finnish, and Estonian are of a fourth group, closer to the Mongol family of languages. The Gaelic language of Ireland is something else again, surviving from a very old Celtic cultural area that stretched over the Atlantic seaboard of Europe. Albania has a language made of many different elements taken from the Latin, Slavonic, Turkish, and Greek languages. Finally Greece has its own language and a special position, for it erected the first great civilization in Europe, which taught logic and government to the rest of the continent.

The three main linguistic areas do not correspond clearly to different races, for many of the people speaking any of the European languages descend in large part from local stock that belonged to other cultures and spoke another language before the spread of the present one. They also correspond — and this is very important — to the three great political constellations of European history: the Roman Empire, the official language of which was Latin; the Germanic empire (which called itself at first the Holy Roman Empire, to stress its inheritance of authority with the conquest of the city of Rome), the main language of which eventually became German; and the Eastern empire, at first Greek, then Byzantine after the Roman Emperor Constantine moved his capital in A.D. 330 to Constantinople (Byzantium) on the straits at the entrance of the Black Sea. After the fifteenth century, the Turks having conquered Byzantium, the sultans claimed to be the Eastern rulers and for centuries kept a large section of southeastern Europe within their empire. But Moscow, capital of the Russians, claimed to be the heir of the Eastern Orthodox Christian imperium of Greco-Roman origin and the "third Rome."

As we attempt to stride rapidly through European history, we may catch a view of a sort of oscillation of the main center of power in Europe from east to west and back again. The oscillation is not a regular one, and the pendulum does not always stop at the same spot, but there is an alternation between west and east. In ancient times, the laurels pass from Greece to Rome and switch back to Constantinople, in the Greek area; about A.D. 800 they shift westward again, with Charlemagne proclaimed Emperor of the Occident with an unstable capital wandering between Aachen and Rome; later, with the Hapsburgs, the Germanic Holy Roman Empire settles in Vienna, on the Danube, then moves to Madrid in Spain; from there the main center of European power moves northward to Paris in the seventeenth and eighteenth centuries, culminating with the Napoleonic period. The fall of the French emperor leaves the Russian emperor Alexander I the supreme arbiter on the continent; a rivalry shapes between St. Petersburg, predominating on the continent, and London, ruling the seas. Berlin emerges at the end of the nineteenth century for a brief and troubled period, which ends with Hitler and the emergence of Moscow as the headquarters of the continental superpower, while the weakened West looks for support toward an extra-European, transatlantic capital in Washington.

All these oscillations seem to be an inheritance of the old cultural rivalry between east and west, between Rome and Byzantium, between an Oriental power, linked to Asia, and an Occidental power committed to expansion overseas and Atlantic relations. Thus more partitions were created between east and west than between north and south. When Charlemagne's Occidental empire had to be divided up between the three brothers who were his heirs, the most important settlement was made in 843 by the Treaty of Verdun: a long conference was held in Metz, gathering over one hundred experts and wizards who, after careful study and deliberation, traced the limits of the respective realms assigned to Charlemagne's grandsons. The youngest, Charles the Bald, was given the west, what is now France without its eastern parts; Louis, called the German, was given the east, an area east of the Rhine and north of the main Alpine watershed, touching the Mediterranean near the present location of Trieste; the eldest brother, Lothair, was given Italy, with the imperial title and a corridor running through to the North Sea and including parts of what are now eastern France, Switzerland, western Germany, Belgium, and the Netherlands. The three entities thus born became France, Germany, and Lotharingia. The latter, situated in the middle, remains to this day the field of Franco-German rivalry; several local entities developed from Lotharingia; other parts were divided up between the two more powerful neighbors. When tracing the frontiers, the experts of the day gave considerable attention to the variety of resources needed by each of the three princes, and a division into territories stretching from north to south—and thus cutting across natural zones of climate and vegetation—was considered fairest and most workable. Long discussions at Metz hinged upon the proper amount of area of rich meadows, vines, and orchards producing different wines and fruits, to be given to each prince. The economic factor thus worked in favor of an east-west differentiation, through north-south boundaries.

The Treaty of Verdun, however, would not have had such lasting influence had it not divided Europe into clear-cut cultural areas, a division that endured. Lotharingia, the most involved of the three and the most ingenious as an economic setup, did not work; it disintegrated because, instead of being based on a cultural unit, it was astride a cultural boundary. The economic factor has often yielded to the cultural in the organization of space; this remains true among countries as well as among villages.

All the wars and conquests, the empires and partitions, left cultural influences spreading in their wake. Every new authority, if it were alien to the culture existing in the acquired territory, endeavored to change its new possessions and assimilate them to its own culture, for experience showed that only such cultural ties were lasting and could outlive political shifts and economic reforms. In most of the countries of Europe a great number of different cultural strata were thus deposited. Every individual and every community had to choose one of them or work out something special for local use in order to maintain a personality. So many allegiances, so many different faiths were offered them, that the European was forced to choose something and stick to it in order to keep his soul. Thus arose a tradition of the preservation of old beliefs, biases, and customs, a tradition of resisting change — because too many changes were occurring. Man needs some strong psychological foundation on which to base his life and thinking. Through the turmoil of European history and the continuous, rapidly rising stratification of cultural influence, every region worked out its personality. In the most disputed areas, such as the central tidal land of contact between Germans and Slavs, numerous areas became internally divided, some sections of the population having chosen one side, others another; the growing rift discouraged intermarriage, and each group quickly claimed racial difference and national minority status. In places where stabilization and fusion of the diverse elements occurred, large and united nations formed.

France is usually credited with being the "oldest nation" of Europe. It was constituted a separate political unit in 843 and under the feudal system developed a strong administrative structure during the twelfth to fifteenth centuries. Her boundaries underwent many minor alterations, but these were peripheral and local only. This country has been a pole of stability in the west. In the east the Russian people spread over vast areas and arrived at a strongly organized uniformity in the central area around Moscow in the fifteenth to sixteenth centuries; thence the state expanded in all directions and remained a permanent element of dynamism in the east. In the north the Swedish people were well organized and strongly united in the Middle Ages; they expanded all around the Baltic and went deep into the continent, only to retreat back into their peninsula — primarily as a result of the Russian push westward — to become the northern pillar of the European political structure.

The rest of Europe has been deeply divided in all respects. Partitions were almost a common event in some areas, such as the Balkans, the Danubian lands, and Poland; even Italy and Germany had been divided in different ways many times before they achieved national unity around 1870. For certain nations their very positions as crossroads and hubs of influence constituted an incentive to group themselves and to gain distinct personalities in order to stand against all the surrounding divided world. Such entities which achieved unity and national status out of instability and variety were usually small in size, and most of them are situated along that cultural melting pot that formed on the borders of Roman domination. Most typical of these, and the first to obtain independence, was the Swiss nation, born in 1291 out of a mountaineer's association in the heart of the Alps. A little later the Netherlands were constituted as a unit, from which Belgium separated itself in 1830. These small but rich nations, parts of the Lotharingia of the ninth century, were erected at major crossroads of the European system. The mosaic appears much better stabilized in the west than in the east, the stabilization resulting from long practice in good neighborliness and in general freedom of creed and language. There are two official languages in Belgium and four in Switzerland; nevertheless, few nations are more distinct from their neighbors than these two small groups of peoples.

Common life has long been difficult — almost impossible — for people of different creeds in Europe. At first, it was the division between those who believed in the gods and Caesars of Rome and those, the Barbarians, who did not. Then the Roman Empire became gradually Christianized; and when the Emperor Constantine was baptized in 337, he moved his capital to Constantinople in the Greek area. An opposition that grew in metaphysical differentiation developed between the Bishop of Rome — the Pope, heir of Saint Peter and head of the Roman Catholic Church — and the Basileus, a Christian Caesar, reigning in Byzantium and favoring his Greek Orthodox Church. Later the Russian tsars claimed to have inherited the latter's functions and directed the Orthodox Church in the east, while Catholicism was spreading in the west and the center of Europe. During the Middle Ages another rift developed between Christian and Moslem Europe, the latter headed first by Arab caliphs and then by Turkish sultans in Constantinople. Inside the Catholic West schisms developed early and finally led to the great Reformation, engendering the religious wars, some of the toughest and bloodiest struggles Europe has known. They terminated on the international scene with the Treaties of Westphalia (1648), which committed the signatories to the principle of giving to a state the religion of its sovereign (*Cujus regio ejus religio*). Thus national boundaries became spiritual and cultural barriers.

A slow and gradually developing process broke down a social and political structure based on intolerance. The spiritual factor has been decisive throughout European history in shaping local oppositions and regional differences. The Roman Catholic faith remains predominant in Central and Southern Europe, while the Reformed Churches predominate mainly in the northwest. The Orthodox Church

In a U-shaped glacial valley of Wales are a church, a graveyard, small farms amid enclosed fields, and pastures and woods on the slopes. *(British Information Services)*

An old bridge guarded by towers at Mostar in the south of Yugoslavia. Beyond it is a typical Mediterranean landscape, with a mosque and minaret as reminders of Islamic influences. *(Yugoslav Information Center)*

is still predominant in the East, but it has fallen into the shadow in the Soviet Union and at times has had to go underground, while, since 1917, communism has spread not only as a political doctrine but as a new faith, opposing other religions.

The fact that, at the end of long and intense struggle, the formula *Cujus regio ejus religio* emerged as the most acceptable to Europeans illustrates well the decisive part that the spiritual factor has long played in the shaping of European regionalisms. To be distinct from its surroundings, a region needs much more than a mountain or a valley, a given language or certain skills; it needs essentially a strong belief based on some religious creed, some social viewpoint, or some pattern of political memories, and often a combination of all three. Thus regionalism has what might be called an *iconography* as its foundation: each community has found for itself or was given an icon, a symbol slightly different from those cherished by its neighbors. For centuries the icon was cared for, adorned with whatever riches and jewels the community could supply. In many cases such an amount of labor and capital was invested that what started as a belief, or as the cult of or even the memory of a military feat, grew into a considerable economic investment around which the interests of an economic region united.

European archeology shows that early travelers throughout the continent felt the need of protection at every crossroad. The modern motorist gets such protection from the red and green lights at major intersections and from the many signs and regulations controlling traffic. But a long time elapsed before such a traffic system was devised, and it is still somewhat primitive in parts of Europe. Almost everywhere, however, monuments were placed at the crossroads. In the Middle Ages, the Church found it necessary to erect crosses, small chapels, or icons at the crossroads in order to exorcize them and give the passer-by a feeling of security by reminding everyone of the supreme authority of God. Feudal lords established bands of armed men to police the roads at selected points, where travelers usually had to pay tolls; those who benefited by the security thus provided paid to enjoy it. Thus religious, political and economic authorities together developed in early times a pattern of regional security which was not entirely lost for later political divisions.

It is hard to overstate the part played by the network of means of transportation and communication in shaping the present pattern of the organization of European space. Traffic all along this network and its many ramifications makes for exchange of people, goods, techniques, and ideas. In brief, it makes for change and for unification. But the smooth flow of all these forms of traffic requires a set of controls policing the network to insure security of movement. These controls were particularly indispensable in days of yore: all kinds of authorities, including the spiritual ones, participated in securing the best possible conditions — for that time — for movement across land and along the waterways. To maintain easier control, and more profit from it, local authorities rooted the main operations of exchange and trade, and the policing thereof, at certain points. A system meant to insure free movement had to have a stabilizing influence over the network of flow and a dividing-up influence over the organization of space. It made for partitioning of space.

The more historians study the economic organization of the past, the better they perceive the growth of the complicated network of toll-houses and monopoly regulations that formed the backbone of the political organization of continental space. Thus, from the white or black stones laid out by prehistoric men at their crossroads, and later the crosses or icons erected by the churches, to the highway policemen in white gloves directing traffic at intersections, we find an unbroken thread, woven through the history of every European region, showing how the factor of movement, which meant progress, and the local iconography, which meant resistance to change, combined to support the establishment of political authority over a certain area.

Techniques often change while beliefs stay. The partitioning of European space is complicated, because, through the continuity of a very long history in which a great many different influences have met, rigid partitions have been erected in people's minds. One should never forget this factor in reviewing European countries and problems; it is what makes geography so involved and so delicate a science. Some opposition between East and West appears to be a permanent European problem: this is the result neither of differences of climate nor of racial divisions; it is rather the mark of two different zones of civilization. The physical pattern, of course, has some bearing, for the two civilizations are contrasted in one decisive respect: the western zone is maritime and the eastern continental. Man is, after all, a land animal: the empty, endless horizons of the ocean affect him differently than the broad open spaces of the land.

Modern means of transportation, especially by air, tend to obliterate such old historical differences. All the countries of Europe seem bent today on a great endeavor toward industrialization and urbanization, which reshape land use and modes of life. These contemporary trends work for more uniformity, at least in terms of their imprint on the landscape. In every region, however, the utilization of resources remains largely determined by a cultural heritage rooted in a distant past.

The new Harbor Building in Amsterdam was the first high office tower in a city where building in height seemed precluded. Notice the port's cranes in the background and the line of tourists waiting for a ship ride on the canals in the foreground. *(The Netherlands National Tourist Office)*

# 3

## The Utilization of Resources

Now Europe finds itself in the midst of complete reorganization. Before World War II, some parts of the continent were developing satisfactorily, but most countries suffered from economic stagnation. Immediately after the war, which badly destroyed most of Europe, its resources seemed diminished and no longer adequate to carry on the economic and social leadership it had assumed for so long a period in the past. Other parts of the world, growing faster, appeared on the way to achieve better living conditions; constant comparison with the United States made European countries *feel* poorer and weaker than before. Europe began to consider itself a "have not" or dissatisfied area. Dissatisfaction, however, often stimulates change and brings about progress. Since the 1950s, the recovery of the European economy has been spectacular. Never has Europe produced so much of all kinds of goods as it does now; nor has it ever consumed so much; the rate of growth, on the whole, is steep and steady. Some dissatisfaction, nevertheless, lingers on; and it is particularly interesting to look at the continent's resources at a moment when they are still undergoing active reappraisal.

The relation of man to space in Europe is an unusual one. About 600 million people live on that continent, and 8 percent of the world's land area accounts for close to 20 percent of the world's population. Similar and even higher densities are found in parts of the Far East, in India, China, Japan; but in those countries the crowding has its counterpart in a very low standard of living. This is not true of Europe. Until the middle of the twentieth century, Europeans on the average managed to enjoy more comfort than the inhabitants of any other part of the world, with the sole exception, recently emerged, of the United States.

Some authorities have explained this prosperity as resulting from the importance of Europe's "natural resources"; others have ascribed it to Europe's domination of almost all the other continents. According to this second view, Europeans had all other peoples working for them; if cut off from the sources of riches overseas, European prosperity could not endure. Between these two divergent explanations some balance must be found. Europe developed both the fields open to her activities — inside and outside the continent — far beyond what was achieved by other continents. She put, as we have stressed, much of her blood, sweat, and tears into her soil; she also put much of them into lands overseas and into the organization of the high seas. The originality of her economy lies probably in the balance she achieved between continental and overseas endeavors.

The European market expanded with the number of consumers and their rate of consumption. The market of European goods expanded also on other continents with the colonization of certain areas and the settlement of others. Not all of Europe played the same part as yet: the West, more populated and more advanced in arts and skills, became the manufacturing and trading center of the world; for the past fifty years it has had to share this function with North America. Eastern Europe until recently had an economy aimed at complementing Western Europe, a so-called "young" economy, exporting surpluses of foodstuffs and raw materials and importing manufactured goods. A remarkable contrast developed between the standards of living and the scales of wages in West and East. Since the Soviet Revolution of 1917, Russia, then the whole of Eastern Europe, has taken a different course, aimed at rivalry rather than cooperation with the West. The East has never had a numerous *bourgeoisie* or middle class; it decided to jump over such stratification to take another course. For several centuries, in fact, there have been two Europes in social structure just as there have been two Europes as developed by the transportation networks: in the West a Europe with roads and a *bourgeoisie;* in the East, another Europe with neither. The distinction has been determined largely by history and the distribution of land and sea, and only very little by soil, climate, and natural resources. The actual riches of Europe lay in the abundance and quality of manpower. Material resources may be limited, but a European people will save them and work hard, spending human labor liberally, to maintain and even to develop an adequate economic basis.

POPULATION PRESSURE AND RESOURCES

The late French geographer André Siegfried once formulated the main difference between the European and the North American civilizations in this way: "Europe saves materials and wastes men; America wastes materials and saves men." People have been abundant in Europe for quite some time, and one could afford to waste them. The present average density of the population on that small continent reaches 166 inhabitants per square mile. This figure is twice that of Asia, six times that of Africa; the average density for the whole of the Americas is one sixth that of Europe, and the United States has just one third of Europe's density.

The steady rise of this population was interrupted several times during the Middle Ages, the last of these setbacks, and a major one, being the Black Plague of the fourteenth century. The religious wars again decimated certain areas in the sixteenth and seventeenth centuries. But since 1700 growth has been stupendous: in 250 years the number of Europeans has increased almost five times, despite wars and epidemics. It was estimated at 187 million in 1800, 400 million in 1900, and 625 in 1965. This growth occurred at a period when a continuous and increasing flow of emigration was carrying Europeans toward the Americas, the British Dominions overseas, and the Russian territories in Asia. For a period the rate of this overflow reached more than one million emigrants a year. Meanwhile no appreciable immigration entered Europe, where the natural increase of population by surplus of births over deaths has been substantial and sustained for 200 years.

Population density and rate of increase are not equally distributed all over Europe. Any map of population density would show scattered patches of great crowding (more than 800 persons per square mile) to the west of the line of 20° of longitude east of Greenwich. On the average the density thins out eastward, but a belt of high density (over 250 per square mile) stretches in an east-west direction, from a wide base on the North Sea shores toward a narrowing eastern tip in the Ukraine. This belt follows the contact of the Hercynian zone with the Great Plain of Europe; it is associated with some of the richest soils and a heavily mineralized area grouping the most important coalfields. Another heavily populated area is Italy, with 450 inhabitants to the square mile; this figure is surpassed only by the densities of the Netherlands and Belgium (900 per square mile), the United Kingdom (585), and Germany. Lowest densities are found in the north and east of the continent: even a Western country such as Norway has only 28 persons per square mile, and about one half of European Russia has less than Norway. But in the first half of the century the rate of increase was much higher in the East than in the West; World War II changed these trends and precipitated an increase almost everywhere. During the period 1958–1965 it was particularly rapid in Albania (annual population increase of 3.1 percent), Switzerland (1.9 percent), the Netherlands (1.4 percent), France, West Germany, and Poland (all three, 1.3 percent).

These rates of population increase seem relatively low compared to

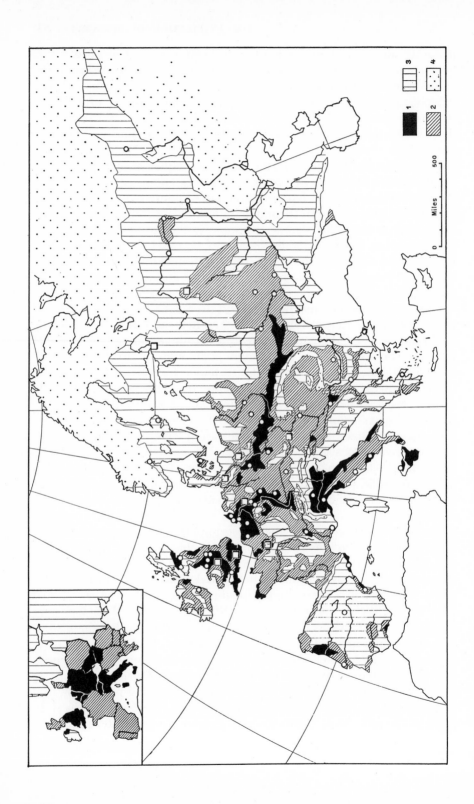

1   2   3   4

0        500
    Miles

those of the underdeveloped countries, where annual rates above 2 percent and 3 percent are common. The rapid natural increase in Albania may be explained by the fact that it was certainly the least developed and in many ways the least "European" country of Europe. But among the more advanced countries, those of Europe fare relatively well when they are compared with the United States (where the annual rate of increase reached 1.5 percent in the same period), Canada (2 percent), Australia (2.1 percent), Japan (1.0 percent). Still, as a whole, the number of Europeans is not increasing as fast as the rest of mankind, though the emigration from Europe has decreased considerably. In most of the European nations in 1958–1965, the rate of increase was below 1 percent annually, reflecting a steady and substantial decrease of the birth rates. The crude birth rate in 1965 stood at 19.9 in the Netherlands instead of 25.3 in 1948, at 19.2 instead of 21.9 in Italy, at 15.9 instead of 18.4 in Sweden, at 13.1 instead of 21 in Hungary. The mortality rates had decreased too, but proportionately less because they were already rather low in most of Europe.

The annual rate of population change reflects not only the balance of mortality and natality but also the *net balance* of migration, and the latter is largely responsible for the present variations in these trends: in 1958–1965, East Germany was still losing about 0.2 percent of its population annually, and Ireland and Malta appeared to be almost stabilized mainly owing to emigration. On the contrary, the favorable performance of Switzerland, France, and West Germany was due largely to immigration during those years. The steady economic expansion of Western Europe since the 1950s created a demand in the more industrialized countries for cheaper manpower, which was supplied to a large extent by migration from southern Europe, which still has a "surplus" of poor and inadequately employed people.

---

(*Opposite*) Distribution of population densities in Europe. Population is rather unequally distributed throughout Europe, as this map demonstrates. Generally density of population is indicated by the four shades, the darker indicating the greater concentration. Shade 1 (see legend lower right) represents densities of more than 250 inhabitants per square mile; shade 2 shows densities of 125 to 250; shade 3 shows densities between 25 and 125; shade 4 (in Scandinavia and Russia) shows densities of less than 25 inhabitants per square mile. To complement this general picture of the total population, the main agglomerations in conurbations are stressed by these symbols: a small circle, representing a conurbation of 500,000 to 2,000,000 inhabitants; a square, meaning urban agglomeration of more than 2 million people (there are only 9 such centers in Europe). The inset map (upper left) shows the distribution of population using the same scale of shades by countries, as of 1950. Note that the dark shade stresses the "Rome-Berlin Axis" of 1937–1940. The larger map shows the actual situation with its regional variety and problems. The patches of shade 1 could be related to the location of the coal basins on which modern industries have been built, but also to the best-developed soils and the great crossroads of European trade. (Compare with map p. 105.)

It is estimated that during the last twenty years more than 10 million people migrated from the Mediterranean countries of Europe northwestward. To this main current were added the trickling of East German refugees toward West Germany and the brief but massive migration (close to 1 million) of inhabitants of European stock from Algeria toward France in 1962–1963. The two latter movements had political as well as economic causes, but the steady flow of Mediterranean labor northward is to be explained by the economic prosperity and expansion of the West European countries. They even began attracting manpower from overseas, as West Indians flowed to Britain, North Africans to France. Essentially, the migratory currents remain intra-European; some of them displace people temporarily; some lead to permanent resettlement. As economic conditions evolve, these flows may be altered. The gradual coming on the labor market of the more numerous generation born during the post-World War II "baby boom" and the growing automation of many stages of production have begun, since 1965, to decrease the demand for the little-skilled personnel supplied by these migrations.

Still, according to the forecasts of demographic trends until 1980 published by the Organization for Economic Cooperation and Development net immigration is expected to continue for West Germany, Switzerland, Sweden, France, and even for Great Britain and the Netherlands, and net emigration is expected for Ireland, Norway, Spain, Portugal, Italy, and Greece. These migrations help to equalize the effects of the existing differences in natural demographic trends among the European countries. On the whole, it appears that the pre-World War II contrast between the rapid natural increase in the Eastern countries and the rather steady demography of the West has been greatly smoothed out. Beyond the "iron curtain," natality has substantially decreased. Economic expansion in the West and the improvement of birth rates in several nations have made the West an area of substantial population growth. For the period of 1965–1970, a total natural increase of between 2 percent and 5 percent, disregarding migration, is expected for most European countries. For the whole period, 1965–1980, an average increase of about 11 percent seems likely, but with variations according to countries (thus, Germany and Austria are expected to be below the average, while Ireland, Portugal, the Netherlands, Poland, and Albania are expected to experience increases much above the average).

Once again, migration within Europe will certainly redistribute part of the natural increases, bringing about less variation between nations than would have developed had the boundaries been closed. The general trend is toward more fluidity and more interpenetration between the various countries, especially in the two main sections of Europe divided by the "iron curtain." But the redistribution of people between countries may be of lesser portent to the general economic and social life of the continent than the general and rapid migration toward the cities inside every nation.

## THE BALANCE BETWEEN CITY AND COUNTRY

Draining marshes, keeping the tides away from the polders, and fertilizing sterile grounds helped to expand the agricultural wealth of Europe. Still the carrying and feeding capacity of the rural areas could not alone have supported, in the past, both material progress and population increase. Urbanization, an exodus from the rural areas toward the cities, accounts for the higher densities. Since the eighteenth century the trend has been general in Europe; its intensity varied in time and space. Urbanization has been closely associated with the industrialization. Large industrial plants, their personnel crowding near by, appeared and spread with the use of steam for power generation. Energy thus produced could not be transported any notable distance from the generating plant: industries had to be operated in large units, and small villages swelled to become large towns.

Coal was the principal and cheapest source of power, and it had to be mined in scattered deposits all over the continent. Most of these deposits were situated in the carboniferous strata of old rocks and were found close to the surface all around the old mountainous massives, particularly of the Hercynian belt. On every coalfield industries congregated. Others established themselves along the good waterways, bringing coal cheaply from a not-too-distant mining center. If there were no natural waterways, canals or railroads were provided. The combination of means of transportation and sources of power was the necessary and sufficient condition for industrial sites. Since the beginning of the nineteenth century, new sources of power have been devised: waterfalls, mineral oil, lignite or brown coal, natural gas. Transportation of power in the form of high-tension electric current was introduced; importation by sea of huge quantities of either coal and oil or raw materials for manufacturing invited the industries to the seaports. Industrial centers scattered, yet big industrial "basins" were constituted in which a convenient pool of power, transportation, and manpower resources was achieved. Industries attracted industries by the mere proximity of existing facilities, and the large basins, most of which were established on coal, could not be decentralized. The Ruhr in Germany, Upper Silesia in Poland, the

The black-country landscape. Europe wants more power, steel, and industry. It is also struggling against pollution and the heavy inheritance of the old equipment. *(Val Doone, British Information Services)*

Franco-Belgian coalfields area, the Scottish Lowlands, Lancashire and the Midlands in England, the Donetz Basin in the Ukraine are the main examples.

Industries also located at important crossroads and old fair sites, where trade had created easy access to raw materials, markets, and manpower; such were the Gate of Burgundy, or the Basel-Mulhouse-Belfort area, Lyon and its surroundings in France, Milan in Italy, Frankfurt-am-Main and Leipzig in Germany; and many seaports like Rotterdam and Antwerp, Marseille and Genoa, Copenhagen and Göteborg, Hamburg and Bremen, Bordeaux and Le Havre belong to the same category. Sometimes a crossroads happened to be also a large city, an important political capital, and therefore a large center of consumption and redistribution. Such a center was bound to attract industries, and such were the cases of Paris, London, Berlin, Vienna, Moscow, and Madrid. Finally in certain areas of rich rural activity, crafts had been developed and for a long time had been scattered throughout farms and villages. This happened both in many mountain ranges and in lowlands; the presence of skilled personnel, still closely associated with the local rural life, often kept the industries on the spot, though some differentiation was worked out between the agricultural and industrial occupations. The distribution of power through the countryside with the extension of the grid system of electrification greatly helped these areas to keep their dual system of activities, especially in the Western European countries.

Some balance had to be struck between the rural and urban populations and between the industrial and agricultural activities. Countries with an "old economy" were urbanized, industrialized, and dependent on their foreign trade for supplies of foodstuffs and raw materials and for the marketing of a large part of their production. "Younger" countries were on the contrary mostly rural and agricultural. Falling between these two types were "mature" economies, the least dependent on foreign trade for the maintenance of their standard of living. Europe ran the whole gamut of the scale. Three countries can be used to illustrate these three economic categories: Britain as the "old economy"—an extreme example of it, in fact—so attached to overseas patrons or dependencies that it appears almost extra-European; France as a "mature economy," probably the best-balanced in Europe; Rumania as the "young economy," almost a "colonial" dependency of Western Europe until the 1930s. By 1961 these regional differences still remained, although the acceleration in a general trend toward urbanization caused the more advanced economies to look rejuvenated or "younger," while the backward and more rural countries looked "older."

Modern technology has made it possible for adequately equipped farms to produce increasing quantities of most agricultural products on

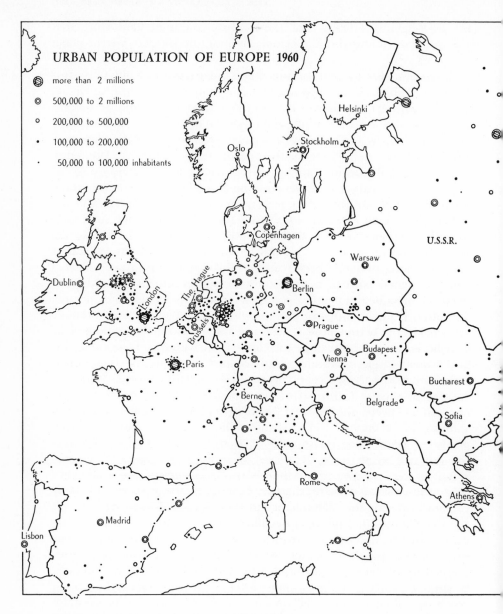

Distribution of cities of more than 50,000 inhabitants.

*less* land with *less labor.* The migration of rural population toward urbanized areas has thus been accelerated; in Europe this movement still affects large numbers of people. The cities meanwhile are growing faster and breaking out of old bounds. The urban uses of the land are no longer confined to rather small, densely built-up areas; the suburban sprawl redistributes residences and industrial and commercial establishments over a wide radius around the major cities. New towns are springing up, often in the orbit of a large metropolis. Entire regions are becoming urbanized and suburbanized, so that new *urban regions* arise, each of them constituting a constellation of cities and towns, without necessarily covering the whole area with buildings. Such metropolitan areas or urban regions are shaping on a larger scale than the "conurbations," or areas of continuous urbanization, first defined in Britain.

Indeed, Europe is becoming urbanized on a huge scale. Britain was the first country in which the proportion of farm population in the total dropped to 6 percent as early as 1911. In most European countries today, a majority of the population live in urban or suburban centers. Many of the residents of areas classified as rural are working in cities or towns. The percentage of agricultural employment in the labor force is steadily decreasing all over the continent. In the West, it is becoming a small minority: 16 percent in France, 10 percent in West Germany, still about 20 percent in Italy; these percentages were much higher by 1950 (respectively 28 percent, 25 percent, and 44 percent). They are higher, of course, to the southeast, but even in Greece and Rumania they are below 40 percent, and in Czechoslovakia and Poland below 10 percent.

The nonfarm majority do not all live in cities; there are still many in villages and small towns. But their basic incomes come from sources other than agriculture, forestry, and fisheries, and this means an urban way of life founded on resources associated with an urbanized and industrialized economy. The cities have, therefore, recently grown very fast, and they will keep on growing. The old concept of a numerical balance between urban and rural population has been abandoned. The city is increasingly dominating the economy of Europe. It is spreading to regions that in the past were considered remote and unfit for dense settlement, such as high mountain slopes or long stretches of rocky seashore; greater affluence and longer leisure time are fostering an enormous development of tourism and vacationing at various seasons of the year. Tens of millions of Europeans are thus on the move at vacation time, particularly in the summer, and specialized towns and cities are being built or enlarged to house and entertain these seasonal migrations.

Every nation endeavors, nevertheless, to preserve agricultural regions, interspersed with the urbanizing areas, within its borders. National and regional parks are also being organized to provide for the recreation and education of urbanites, whose lives are too often divorced from regular contact with unspoiled nature; in addition, wildlife and wilderness areas are being established for the conservation of a flora and fauna rapidly modified by man's action. Thus, a new balance between city and country determines a reshuffling of land use and of the geographical distribution of resources.

## UNDERDEVELOPED AND OVERDEVELOPED COUNTRIES

The maps of consumption describing the variations of the standard of living also stress the fact that economic and social progress cannot use the same recipes in different parts of Europe. Some countries, especially in the southeast, appear frankly backward, or according to the terminology presently in vogue, *underdeveloped.* Such is certainly the case of countries where the annual consumption of all forms of energy per capita stayed in 1965 below the equivalent of 1.5 tons of coal: such was the case of Portugal, Spain, Greece, Yugoslavia, Albania, and Malta. In a similar way, no country is "normally" developed, in mid-twentieth century terms, that has more than eighty inhabitants for every car in use, and such was still the case, in 1965, of Poland, Hungary, Rumania, and the whole of the Balkan peninsula. Although we do not get much statistical information concerning the European area of the Soviet Union, we know enough about its standard of living to assume safely that most of it belongs as well to the underdeveloped category. For all these countries, the main problem is to build up their own resources and achieve better development, which means more investment, more equipment of all kinds, more production, and more transportation.

Quite different is the problem of those Western countries where the standard of living used to be the highest known and is still fairly high. The main worry here is that of maintenance, of avoiding loss of ground with respect to the general upward trend of standards. The economic systems of these countries were established on a foundation of international trade on a large scale, on the easy supply of cheap raw materials and wide markets for their exports of manufactured goods. In foreign markets, inside as well as outside Europe, all these countries at present encounter much greater difficulty in buying their supplies and in selling their products. These difficulties are due to several causes, but in particular to two main factors: European industrialized countries find the United States, Japan, and sometimes also Canada and others as competitors in international markets; they encounter also the competition of national industries, as every important country in the world attempts industrialization.

A British expert once commented that "Great Britain is as great an antithesis to the underdeveloped areas of Mr. Truman's 'Fourth Point' as could ever be imagined. The industrialization of the nineteenth century led at one time and the same time to a vast increase in population and to the exhaustion of most of our natural resources, which were never very considerable. Great Britain is an example of a country which is almost ready for another kind of programme: a programme for the restitution of overpopulated and overdeveloped areas" (Dr. S. Zuckerman, in *Journal of the Science of Food and Agriculture,* 1950, No. 9, pp. 255–263). To a large extent, Germany, the Netherlands, Belgium, and Switzerland belong in the category thus defined for Great Britain. Even Denmark, Sweden, and France could be included in that category, although their local resources are proportionately greater. This is a group of countries that built up their past prosperity on a system of international trade that was organized in the nineteenth century but could not be restored after World War II. Since then they have been constantly striving to readapt themselves.

The "iron curtain" that divides Europe into two main political halves follows approximately the line of partition between the overdeveloped and the underdeveloped countries, with the exception that it leaves with the Western section the three underdeveloped Mediterranean peninsulas and includes with the Eastern section well-developed areas such as the Bohemian region of Czechoslovakia and Eastern Germany. To make things clearer we are justified in dividing Europe into four main parts: the overdeveloped, densely populated area of Western Europe, looking outside Europe and striving at a new organization of its economy; the complicated mixture of Central Europe, where highly developed Germany borders on the more backward lands of Poland and the Danubian basin, the whole area being divided between two political constellations; the underdeveloped and overpopulated Mediterranean peninsulas; and last but not least the areas now encompassed in the territory of the Soviet Union and being developed according to a specially conceived and strictly planned economy.

These four major divisions are so different one from another, because of their natural setting, their past background, and their present organization, that few problems can be mentioned that concern all four of them in a similar manner. The important problems must and will be considered on a regional scale, in their proper frame. A few general trends only should be mentioned at present.

To begin with, all European nations feel that they are today somewhat behind the time, and all of them look toward the United States, some with cordiality and some with hostility, but all with a common aim to catch up as fast as possible. The result of this attitude is a general endeavor to increase the national production. Since 1950, the aim has no

Logging down a Swedish river. *(Swedish Information Service)*

Industrial development in Yugoslavia. *(Yugoslav Information Center)*

longer been only to restore prewar levels of production, but to increase output further and at a faster rate than it had been done in the first half of the century. Within the area of Soviet supremacy, rapid industrialization is pushed ahead while agricultural production is being mechanized and, wherever possible, increased. Within the more advanced area of free Europe, industrialization is also progressing either in the form of modernizing methods of production or of increasing the quantities and the variety of the industrial output. This is why figures of production are steadily growing on the whole and why never before has Europe produced and consumed as much as it does at present, even per capita.

While industrialization in Europe is forging ahead, consumption has also been increasing, both because of claims for higher living standards and because of demographic growth. Representative figures can be found in the statistics of international sea-borne trade, as established by the Statistical Office of the United Nations, for each continent in the world: while the total of the goods unloaded in the seaports of the world (in international trade) grew from 470 million metric tons in 1929 to 1640 in 1965, Europe accounted for 264 in 1929 and 799 in 1965, showing a smaller increase than the world total. In the same period, Europe saw the goods loaded in its ports increasing in tonnage, from 223 in 1929 to only 255 in 1965. In North America, the evolution has been quite different between 1929 and 1965: the goods loaded went up from 104 to 314 and the goods unloaded from 83 to 362. On the whole, however, Europe's trade is still the most important in the world, and it is now expanding again. In 1953, already the imports of Europe west of the "iron curtain" amounted to 42.7 percent in value of the free world imports, and its exports to 38.3 percent of the free world exports. The continent as a whole imported, then, more than the rest of the world and exported just a little less than the rest of the world; in 1965, Europe took 51 percent of the world imports and supplied 52 percent of all exports. Indeed, Europe was regaining the role of the central hub of world trade that World War II had temporarily displaced. But this was a new system of relations, announcing still more shifts for the immediate future.

The most stubborn trend is the emphasis on more exchange within the continent. In the Soviet orbit, the European satellites trade mainly with the USSR; several of them however have endeavored to develop their commercial relations with the underdeveloped countries, and also with their European neighbors to the west. The trend toward economic integration in the western half of the small continent has produced spectacular results. Still, the trade relations of Europe with the other parts of the world keep producing a deficit that is covered chiefly by the services the European countries can supply to the outsiders, but the European balance of payments was greatly helped by a steady flow of American capital to Europe. Such are the volume and the variety of the European trade that practically every category of goods can be found regularly imported and exported, though not always by the same country. The deficit of the trade, however, is caused by the steady need for three major categories of imports: foodstuffs, fuels, and textile raw materials.

The high density and standards of living of Europe explain the dependence on imports of foodstuffs, especially of grain, meat, and "exotic" food that grows in sunnier climates. Similarly Europe is a heavy importer of cotton, wool, and silk. While agricultural production can still be expanded, though at a cost, there is little likelihood that textile fibers could be produced on a large enough scale on the small continent, unless they are manmade fibers. The major element in this picture of the European dependency on outside supplies is the supply of coal and oil. Europe used to be the main exporter of coal in the world, chiefly from Great Britain and Western Germany. Nowadays Europe imports rather than exports coal—a few dozen million tons a year in periods of great industrial activity; most of these imports come from the United States. Frantic efforts have been made by many countries to increase their own output of coal, and some have succeeded in this trend, mainly the Soviet Union, Poland, and, to a smaller extent, France. More was achieved by the development of water-power resources, which is being pushed in many countries, and of natural gas, enormous finds of which have brightened the prospects of Western Europe and European Russia.

The chief addition to the old supply in sources of energy came from oil. The need for oil products grows with the increase in motor transportation, with the mechanization of agriculture, and with the development of new chemical industries. Europe produces very little oil outside the Soviet Union. It imports from other continents, chiefly the Middle East and South America, most of what it consumes, which is over 500 million metric tons of crude oil. These imports weigh heavily on this continent's balance of payments, especially for the more mechanized Western section. This was made especially obvious during the Suez crisis in 1956 and in 1967, the aftermath of which cost large sums in dollar currency to the Western countries, particularly to Britain. In recent years, the Soviet Union has launched a drive to export crude petroleum to various countries of the free world, with little success as yet in Europe west of the "iron curtain."

More coal and more oil. More tools and more food. More industries and more large cities. All around, Europe asks for more. To achieve some of its aims, it feels the need of deep changes in its structure.

The Eagle Dam on the Dordogne River, harnessing the waterpower of the central plateau of France. *(French Cultural Services)*

Trains loaded with bauxite leaving the mines in southern France. *(French Cultural Services)*

## THE STANDARD OF LIVING IN EUROPE

The standard of living and financial prosperity of a nation used to be proportional to its industrialization and urbanization; Europeans used to estimate the actual power of a country by the volume of its foreign trade, preferably figured per head of population as well as in total size. Those were, in fact, specifically the standards of nineteenth-century Europe. The happiness and prosperity of a nation actually consists of an involved combination that must be in harmony with the national aspirations of the moment. It cannot be worked out on a purely statistical basis.

Many questions are being asked anew about the economic organization that would be "logical" for Europe after the continent got back on its feet after the tough ordeal of World War II in which it was the main battlefield. The war has not only destroyed many material assets, it has not only induced the spending of most of the overseas investments, it has also caused a reorganization of the world economy which is now centered on the United States and the American dollar. Last but not least, the aftermath of the war has virtually cut Europe into two parts and greatly strained relations between them. The overpopulated continent appeared to many experts inside and out to be seriously threatened. Will it still be able to feed its population? How can the standard of living be kept up at adequate levels? Would birth control, increased exports, or emigration help bring about a solution? All these questions and many others are interesting and worth consideration; generally they transcend the field of geography by projecting too many factors into a dim future. The 1960s brought great prosperity, economic expansion, and social progress. Still one basic aspect of the European problem must be taken into account each time the whole of Europe or a part of it is reviewed with reference to its present potential. To use the available resources, what is the driving motive?

For over twenty centuries, Europe rode the crest of the wave of history and was quite conscious of it, but early in the twentieth century some doubt and even some pessimism set in. The small and scalloped continent was no longer sure of leading the world and directing its destiny. This consciousness found expression in several important books about the decline of Europe, published just before and after World War I. The chief and most permanent factor in reducing Europe's domination over the rest of the world had been the settlement of Europeans in large numbers on other continents and the growth there of nations that could well compare in their material development with European countries. North America has been the most spectacular and decisive case. Other areas with few European settlers learned from European contacts skills that brought them closer to competing with the former monopolist. Having generously undertaken to teach the world, Europe, succeeding in many respects, discovered that not all her pupils accepted the ideas and spirit of their teacher, although they were taking good advantage of her techniques and skills. Two World Wars and the depression of the 1930s created, within the first half of this century, three periods when international trade was disrupted and when economic regionalism developed, making Europe's economy less important to the rest of the world.

Having destroyed many assets, Europe badly needed a period of prosperity with wide-open horizons and free channels of supply and marketing. Instead, she found more barriers erected — barriers to foreign trade (for extra-European countries wanted to protect their own young industries and leaned toward a general orientation of their commerce about the richer American market and the stronger dollar currency) and barriers also inside Europe (for the USSR isolated itself behind a "Chinese Great Wall" after 1917 and then lowered another "curtain" between its satellites and the West after 1945). Overpopulated urban and industrial Western Europe saw the trade relations so essential to its prosperity being jeopardized inside and outside of the continent. In the late 1950s, however, international relations improved, and trade barriers were lowered within Europe as well as in overseas commerce. Despite a considerable effort at self-sufficiency, the two blocks of "Western" and "Socialist" countries in Europe continue to need supplies from the outside on a large scale; to pay for them, each country fosters the expansion of its capacity to export goods and services.

The recent changes have not greatly affected the fertility of European soils, nor did they deplete the mineral resources. Statistically, it looked as though local production could feed the Europeans and supply a good part of their textile needs, at least in years of reasonably good harvests. But one should not overlook the fact that percentages in quantities produced and in numbers of inhabitants do not provide an accurate key to actual consumption requirements. The average standard of living in Europe, though below that of the United States, was far above the world mean. Thus Europe needed to import about 10 million tons of wheat annually before World War II, and at that time a large part of the European population, particularly in the Soviet Union, did not have plenty of wheat. And European requirements are much greater, comparatively, for textiles, iron, and chemicals than for wheat. Still, whatever may be the expansion of its production, this continent must remain a great importer.

The standard of living remains, however, a vague measure when estimated for entire continents. Within Europe itself, the standard of

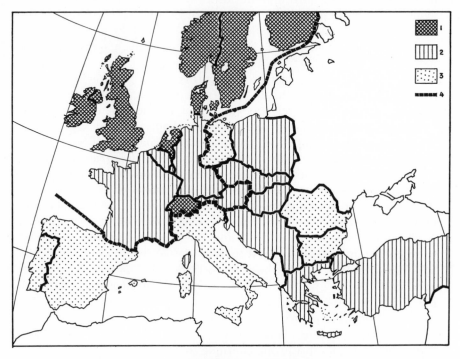

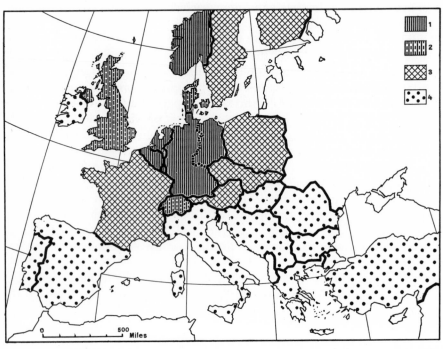

living varies greatly; we have attempted to show the picture of its distribution on four maps presenting the consumption of food, energy, fertilizers, and automobiles in the different countries of Europe. The general picture offered by these four maps shows a decline in the amount of consumption, and therefore in the standard of living, from north to south and particularly from the northwest to the southeast. The four maps point out, however, that some countries have emphasized certain aspects of consumption at the expense of others; thus France ranks high in the density of automobiles (7 inhabitants per car in use) while its consumption of fertilizers is relatively low (40 kilograms per year and per hectare of agricultural land) and its total consumption of power, of which the gasoline for the cars is part, shows only as average (2.36 units, equivalent to a ton of coal per year per capita). The maps (see pages 98 and 100) present the situation as of 1958; they make use of official statistics, which do not always accurately reflect reality: thus France appears less well fed than the United Kingdom, and Denmark a little less well fed than Norway, while anyone who has recently traveled through those countries cannot help being convinced of the contrary. The fact is that food consumption is much better assessed in countries where most of the food is imported and therefore checked by customs, which is the case in both Britain and Norway, while the figures of agricultural production in rich agricultural countries such as France and Denmark may easily

---

(*Opposite*) Standards of living in Europe. The "standard of living" is a much more elusive notion than it may appear to be, and economic statistics for Europe are not adequate for a simple index to be illustrative and true for the various countries. Maps I to IV attempt a graphic description.

Map I (*above*) gives an idea of the level of food consumption in terms of calories consumed per inhabitant and per day in 1958, according to official statistics. Explanation of legend: 1, Countries with an average of more than 3000 calories. 2, Countries with an average of 2700 to 3000 calories. 3, Countries with an average of less than 2700 calories. 4, Line limiting the countries where more than 25 percent of the calories consumed come from animal proteins; these countries are to the northwest of the line; countries to its south and east have less than 25 percent of animal proteins in their diet. The total calorie intake is not adequate as data unless corrected by some indication of the proportion of elements of animal origin. The general contrast between northwestern Europe and the southeast is striking. There is no comparable data available on food consumption in the Soviet Union.

Map II (*below*) shows the consumption of chemical fertilizers, a measure of the intensity of agricultural production on the lands tilled. It gives the amount used in 1958 in kilograms per hectare (1 hectare equals 2.5 acres) of agricultural land: shade 1, over 100 kilograms per hectare; shade 2, between 50 and 100 kilograms; shade 3, between 30 and 49; shade 4, less than 30 kilograms. The great endeavor to produce food at home with modern methods is thus striking in Germany and the Benelux countries, as well as in Norway, where agricultural land accounts, however, for only a small part of the total area. More fertilization could substantially increase yields in Mediterranean Europe, in the East, and even in France.

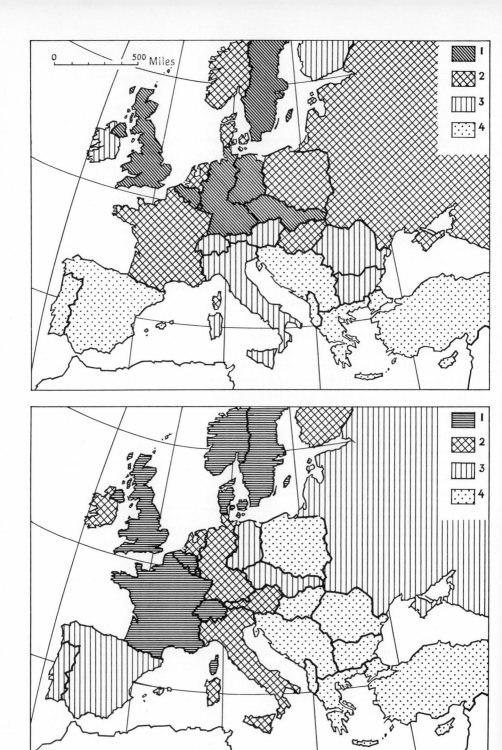

be underestimated, for peasants do not always state fully the real quantities produced; in France the underestimation, largely due to reasons of fiscal evasion, is traditional.

Taken for whatever they are worth, the statistics of consumption still express the general trends of distribution of standard of living in European space. On all scores European figures, even for the best served countries, are definitely below the average corresponding figures for the United States. European nations thus have lost their old feeling of economic and social leadership in the world, being constantly reminded of better living conditions in North America. This comparison is enough to create a certain amount of frustration and demand for improvement. The highest standard of living cannot be defined in quantities: it corresponds for a given community to the highest level this community knows about. The bare fact that so many European nations are dissatisfied with their present standard of living does not mean that they have not regained a level equivalent to the prewar level, nor does it mean resignation to a second-rank level. Indeed, the generalization of such dissatisfaction is becoming a factor of general progress.

It would be wishful thinking, however, to pretend that Europe can easily improve its present level of consumption. The scars of World War II were on the whole healed by 1956, but the changed position this continent now occupies in the world economy required deep transformations in the economic geography of many countries, a number of reforms that are not easy to bring about. Still, much improvement has been achieved from 1956 to 1968, partly as a result of reconstruction, and partly through straightforward economic development. In some respects, the progress already attained has sharpened some regional differences, for instance in the levels of prosperity of Spain or Greece on the one hand and Benelux or Switzerland on the other. But the "revolution of rising expectations" did proceed faster in Europe than in the less developed

---

Map III *(above)* shows the distribution of consumption of energy per inhabitant and per year as of 1958; it takes into account all commercial sources of power and expresses the total in units equivalent to the calorific power of one metric ton of coal. The legend shows four shades: 1, over 3 such units per inhabitant; 2, between 2 and 3; 3, between 1 and 2; 4, less than 1.

Map IV *(below)* shows the density of motor vehicles in use in 1958, by country, in relation to the population. The density is expressed in terms of the number of inhabitants per motor car (including trucks). The legend shows four shades: 1, 5 to 25 inhabitants per car (7 is the lowest figure in Europe, achieved in 1958 in both France and Sweden); 2, 26 to 50 inhabitants per car; 3, 51 to 100; 4, over 100 (for example, 170 for Poland and 286 for Yugoslavia). As a matter of comparison we may mention that in the same year there were less than 13 inhabitants per car in use in the United States and about 870 per car in use in India.

parts of the world. Many European countries have recently shown unusual optimism in this connection: official statements have promised to the Russians and to the French a standard of living equivalent to that of the American people sometime in the 1970s.

There has been an acceleration of the process by means of which the European standard of living has been rising steadily during the last three centuries. The religious wars that accompanied and followed the Reformation had important economic consequences. It is noteworthy that the Reformation condemned the too-great prosperity and economic role of the Roman Catholic Church and that its strongest support came from trading countries rather than from purely agricultural areas. Protestants succeeded better on the whole in urbanization and trade development than did the more Catholic agricultural sections of Europe. The map of industrialization during the eighteenth and nineteenth centuries coincides curiously with the map of Protestantism. The only notable exception in Europe is the area of Belgium and northern France, which remained strongly Catholic: but this region has had a powerful *bourgeoisie* since the Middle Ages, and it was from here that John Calvin, born in Picardy, went on to lead the Reformation in Geneva.

The struggle for the freedom of religion has been associated with the struggle for the freedom from want. In both cases it was a struggle for social justice. King Henry IV of France, originally a Protestant, is credited with the policy that "every French home should have a chicken in the pot every Sunday." Around 1600 any kind of meat was an unusual luxury in the European diet. Three centuries later chicken was still rather expensive, but steak had become a popular and fairly ordinary dish. Both World War periods, however, made rationing necessary. Rationing was maintained in Russia after the Revolution of 1917 and in Germany under the Nazi regime of total preparedness for war. After World War II, all countries in Europe rationed at least some foods and consumer goods. Will the trend tôward increased consumption now resumed be carried forward? Europe is again divided into two camps: this is not only a political and economic fight; it is today a spiritual conflict, which recalls many features of the religious wars of the sixteenth and seventeenth centuries, or even of the time when the Mediterranean world was split between the Crescent and the Cross. Perhaps the opposition that has arisen between Western democracy and Eastern communism may be interpreted as the new shape of the everlasting struggle for more social justice that appears to be a specialty of Europe.

Realizing somewhat late the importance of the American methods in developing average individual consumption as a factor of economic expansion and, in the long run, of industrial and political might, the Western nations of Europe set out in the 1950s to end the stagnation that had been plaguing too many of them in periods of peace. In his celebrated volume on the *Wealth of Nations*, Adam Smith said: "Consumption is the sole end and purpose of production; and the interest of the producer ought to be attended to, only so far as it may be necessary for promoting that of the consumer." By a constant emphasis on exports of their produce the more industrialized countries of Europe had often neglected their domestic market, that is, the mass of the consumers in their own nation. Some correction has been introduced and we have seen the standard of living rise. Still, to fulfill the promise of a level of consumption equivalent to that of America, the production of Europe must be greatly expanded. The recognition by the economic leadership of major European countries that the American experiment was a model to be studied and followed in order to achieve economic expansion and "catch up" with the times has led to an extensive "Americanization" of European ways of living and working. Still, the similarities are to be found chiefly in the cities of Western Europe.

Europeans remain attached to many special features of their own environments and modes of life as they shaped them. Many more local differences remain and will be preserved in the various parts of Europe than can be observed in North America. An improved economic system means to the Europeans more social security benefits, longer annual vacations with full pay, greater stability of employment, better free public education (with easier access to the universities), and better housing. This is all being achieved gradually. Progress in housing is notable, though the supply of new lower-income housing is still far from being equal to the demand. The construction industry is becoming one of the most important in Europe, and it is concentrating on high-rise apartment buildings rather than on more expensive one-family detached houses. The forest of cranes rising above the urban landscape has been, in recent years, characteristic of economic growth from Lisbon to Moscow.

It is in the production of cement that the European Common Market first achieved world leadership. All the varied industries supplying urban equipment should follow this trend. But Europeans are still far from achieving American levels of per capita consumption for capital goods, hardware and software alike. Perhaps it is not necessary to be so wasteful of material goods as the more advanced groups of industrial society have been. The rhythm of obsolescence is slower in Europe. And the average consumer is asking for more services and benefits in the form of public or collective facilities.

## PROBLEMS OF LAGGING REGIONS

The benefits of modernization, urbanization, and economic expansion are distributed very unequally over the map of Europe. The larger urban regions attract most of the massive addition of jobs and people.

Some other areas that used to have only secondary agglomerations are growing very fast because of locations there of special natural or cultural amenities. But many regions lag behind the general progress, which is, in fact, quite concentrated on a few fractions of every nation's land.

Thus, the rate and mode of urbanization greatly vary from area to area. The largest metropolitan regions in Europe are London (about 15 million people densely agglomerated in and around the British capital), Paris (nearly 10 million in the metropolitan region), and Moscow — at least among conurbations formed around a single central city. Looser urbanized groupings are found in many other places on the Continent and in Britain. Most of England proper (without Wales and perhaps also excluding Cornwall) is already highly urbanized and suburbanized to a large extent, as some observers had foreseen long ago. Dense urbanization is gaining in most of Benelux, melting in places with the adjacent German Rhineland, encompassing the Ruhr industrial district. Projecting this growth into the future, one can visualize a huge area of urbanization taking shape across the continent from the North Sea to the Mediterranean in Italy (see map, p. 88), along the medieval trade routes from Venice and Genoa to Amsterdam and Bruges. The Alps are no longer a barrier, as their valleys and slopes are being invaded by industries attracted by the availability of hydroelectric power, the abundance of skilled labor, the vicinity of well-entrenched centers of trade and culture, and last but not least, the proximity to skiing and tourist resorts. Seasonal towns in former rural areas may occasionally grow into substantial cities and even industrial centers (Nice and Annecy being two cases in point).

This evolution reflects a far-reaching mutation, involving displacement of many activities and obvious migratory flows toward the new poles of growth. This change is developing at the expense of less rapidly growing or declining regions. There is more territory that is being thinned out or emptied than is blossoming and gathering new strength. In every nation, a process of geographical concentration of population and economic activity threatens the old distribution, the extant structures.

Most of the regions which feel disadvantaged in this present reshuffling are not actually declining, but they are *lagging* behind the general national and international trend of progress. They are found all over the Continent: in western and central France, in southern and eastern Belgium, in central parts of West Germany, in southern Italy, northern Greece, southeastern Poland, etc. Every country has such lagging regions. One of two types of regional economy is usually at the root of the matter: either it is a rural region with a densely settled farm popu-

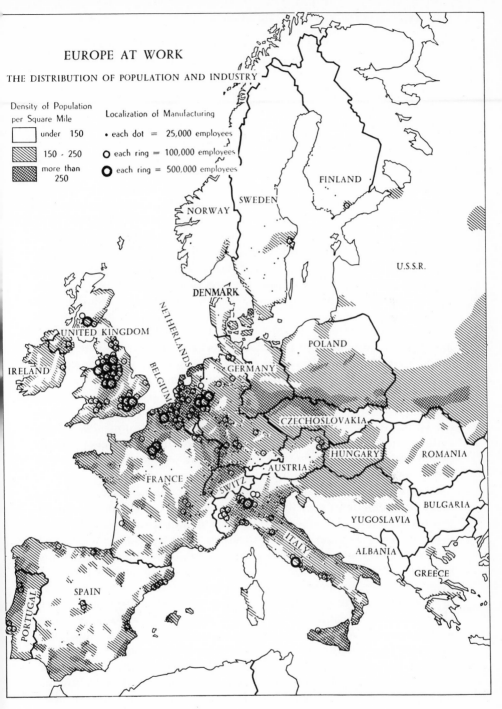

EUROPE AT WORK

THE DISTRIBUTION OF POPULATION AND INDUSTRY

Density of Population
per Square Mile

under 150

150 - 250

more than
250

Localization of Manufacturing

• each dot = 25,000 employees

○ each ring = 100,000 employees

◎ each ring = 500,000 employees

NORWAY

SWEDEN

FINLAND

DENMARK

U.S.S.R.

UNITED KINGDOM

IRELAND

NETHERLANDS

BELGIUM

GERMANY

POLAND

CZECHOSLOVAKIA

HUNGARY

ROMANIA

FRANCE

AUSTRIA

SWITZ

BULGARIA

YUGOSLAVIA

ITALY

ALBANIA

GREECE

PORTUGAL

SPAIN

Data on manufacturing employment was available for Europe only west of the "iron curtain."

lation whose small farms are not suited to modern large-scale methods of production (Brittany in France, Galicia in Spain, Slovakia, and eastern Poland are four cases among many) or it is an old industrial region, burdened with outdated equipment and a larger labor force than automating industries can use (the textile areas of Lancashire, the mining and metallurgical sections of Belgian Wallonia, and coal-mining districts in various countries are in this category).

The planning policy in almost all European countries is aimed at stemming the rapid growth of the more successful regions in order to bring relief and greater development to these that are lagging. It is thought that the political and economic domestic problems would be attenuated if people could be provided with satisfactory means of livelihood where they are, if migrations crowding the more rapidly growing areas could be slowed down. Techniques of spurring on growth in lagging regions vary from country to country: in the Western nations, they include supports for small family farms and for coal miners; in almost every European country, legislation fosters decentralization of industry and of many government agencies. "Decentralization" means restricting any addition to the existing activities and institutions in the large flourishing centers; thus, new growth has to go to other regions which have been lagging behind. It was first and most generally applied as a policy of location or relocation of manufacturing plants. In many countries, it has been applied more recently also to the location of government agencies and large offices. Although this kind of regulation remains on the books, decentralization has not succeeded in arresting the growth of the major regions where economic activities had a tendency to conglomerate. It may have helped somewhat to reduce the gap between these more successful areas and the lagging ones.

Causes for the lag are many: In some cases, it is the decline in employment and sometimes even in production of certain old industries, of which coal-mining is the most important in Europe; in other cases, it is the growing automation of agriculture, industry, warehousing, and even transportation; and in almost every case, the out-migration of the farm population toward the cities continues to be a major factor. Such migration does not develop equally toward all cities; it is not simply proportional to the size of the receiving cities or metropolitan areas. Other variables are at play: The younger generation is looking for better living conditions, particularly for places to live where they may expect more amenities, both physical (a better climate, sea, and ski, etc.) and cultural (for their education as well as their recreation). And a basic amenity is the hope for more economic opportunity and social fluidity. As a general rule, the young girls leave the lagging regions first; after a while, the boys follow. A top-heavy age pyramid is usually characteristic of the lagging regions, particularly of those more difficult to help. Realizing the complexity of the problem, national and local authorities are trying to develop amenities and cultural centers to prevent the out-migration from these regions. However, that process has been only slowed down. The concentration of many economic activities in large metropolitan nuclei is largely determined by the greater efficiency of work. The scattering works often at cross-purposes with both the incentives of technical planning and the desire of a large part of the personnel. The lagging regions constitute, of course, a political headache as their people and politicians complain about the too-rapid growth of the other regions.

This inequality in the geographical distribution of the rate of growth and the benefits of expansion as they may be demonstrated by the national statistics have been one of the major concerns of economic planning in almost every European country. It has been one more reason to develop and enforce planning, and it has often worked against the sheer logic of an expansionist policy.

ATTEMPTS AT REORGANIZATION

World War II seems to have taught at least one definite lesson to the European public opinion. It has felt the weakness inherent in the small scale of its national territories. As it looks at the economic development achieved in the United States or in the Soviet Union, it feels too small and begins to understand the advantages of being big, as a nation and as a market; the nations on the continent think more in terms of internal European reorganization. The importance of the size of the American domestic market in promoting the economic development and power of the United States is being increasingly recognized. Several attempts at economic or tariff unions were considered by the Scandinavian countries, by France and Italy, and by the "Benelux" group of Belgium, the Netherlands, and Luxembourg in the late 1940s. Benelux finally came of age, but at a time when broader communities had already been formed, superseding it.

First to improve the conditions of working together was the Organization for European Economic Cooperation. Formed in 1948 by all the European nations participating in the Marshall Plan, it was later widened by the admission of West Germany and Spain and by the association of the United States and Canada with it. The OEEC accomplished considerable work in coordinating among its members the distribution of the benefits of American aid during the postwar reconstruction period; it then fostered cooperation among them in their endeavors toward economic progress and development. In recent years it has dealt with

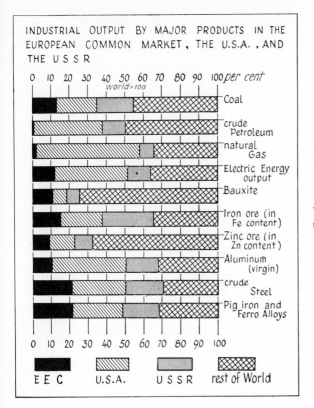

INDUSTRIAL OUTPUT BY MAJOR PRODUCTS IN THE EUROPEAN COMMON MARKET, THE U.S.A., AND THE USSR

0 10 20 30 40 50 60 70 80 90 100 *per cent*
*world=100*

Coal
crude Petroleum
natural Gas
Electric Energy output
Bauxite
Iron ore (in Fe content)
Zinc ore (in Zn content)
Aluminum (virgin)
crude Steel
Pig iron and Ferro Alloys

0 10 20 30 40 50 60 70 80 90 100

EEC    U.S.A.    USSR    rest of World

The graph shows industrial output of the Common Market compared to that of the United States, the USSR, and the rest of the world. In 1961 Greece was accepted as an associate member of the EEC (the Six), while Finland was asking to become an associate of the EFTA (the Seven). Britain also began to consider entering the EEC, an action that could unite the Western countries of Europe in the Community and the Association.

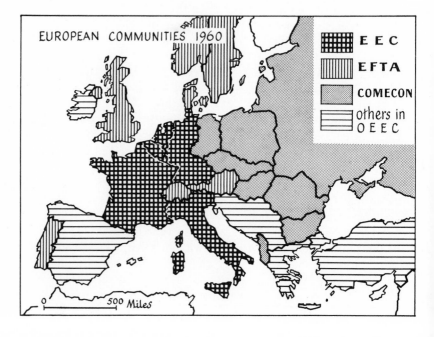

EUROPEAN COMMUNITIES 1960

EEC
EFTA
COMECON
others in OEEC

0    500 Miles

monetary matters, the liberalization of trade and the movement of capital, with the joint construction of nuclear energy plants, pooling scientific and technical personnel, and with productivity. The successful work of the OEEC seems to have spurred on the Soviet Union and its European satellites to the establishment, after 1949, of a Council for Mutual Economic Aid, or COMECON, which, under the authoritarian supervision of the USSR, has become a tool to control economic planning and cooperation in Europe east of the "iron curtain." From 1947 on, the United Nations also maintained an Economic Commission for Europe—with headquarters in Geneva—which helped further cooperation among the European powers in economic matters and even promoted some development of East-West trade through the "iron curtain."

Neither the U.N. Commission nor the OEEC, which changed its name to Organization for Economic Cooperation and Development, or OECD, had any power to enforce decisions on the member states, or to infringe in any way upon their national sovereignty. A growing desire for more economic integration accordingly brought about the creation of new international institutions endowed with a degree of supranational authority. The new groupings are often referred to as the "European Communities." By 1960 there were three of them, consisting of the same six powers: France, West Germany, Belgium, Luxembourg, the Netherlands, and Italy. This grouping was sometimes called the "Inner Six" or "Little Europe." More voluntary economic integration has been gradually achieved by this group than any other in the free world. A first stage was reached when, pursuant to the Schuman Plan, the Six adopted the Paris treaty of 1951 organizing a European Coal and Steel Community, usually known as the "coal and steel pool." In practice a common market for coal, iron ore, scrap and pig iron, and steel was gradually established by 1958. In that year two other common efforts of the Six came into operation, as outlined in the Rome treaties of 1957: a European Atomic Energy Community, or "Euratom," and a European Economic Community (EEC), popularly referred to as "the Common Market." Euratom introduced a common market for nuclear products, set up common nuclear research centers, and signed agreements with the United States and Canada providing for joint work programs. It also conducts projects jointly with the Nuclear Energy Agency of the OECD. The greatest success of all has been the EEC, which in its first three years brought considerable economic development and prosperity to the six partners, to the envy of many other countries. The coal and steel pool had done much to prepare the way for the smooth operation of the Common Market of the Six; the contiguity of the area involved also helped. Many old neighborly links could at last blossom and bear fruit in an impressive way.

The Six planned a twelve-year period of transition to bring about by 1970 a genuine common market providing for the free exchange within the whole area of goods, capital, labor, and services. As a tariff union it would surround itself with a common tariff wall toward the outside world. In 1960, there was already some discussion about the possibility of a political confederation of the Six. The early success of the scheme led the participants to lower tariffs between the member countries faster than had been planned. By 1961, the tariffs for industrial goods had been cut by 50 percent, though progress with respect to agricultural goods and the liberalization of labor migration was by no means as great. What was achieved in three years came, however, as a surprise to most Europeans who had been generally skeptical about the possibility of such integration. Optimism set in, and the pace accelerated: in 1962, the Six agreed on extending the Common Market to agricultural goods. The first steps in this area began August 1, 1962, when, as a Swiss editorialist commented: "Several independent nations accepted to pool for the first time in history the resources of which their very flesh and blood were made." Negotiations developed between the governments of the Six to integrate their labor markets and unify their social security systems. In 1967, an Italian worker could enjoy, in West Germany, the same rights and benefits as a German worker, and he could move to Belgium without losing the benefits earned on his German social security account. Co-ordination was established between the major airlines of the Six, and discussion of financial integration was started. All tariffs on industrial goods among the Six were to be erased by July 1968, two years ahead of the original schedule. And already in 1967, the three original Communities (the Coal and Steel Pool, the EEC, and Euratom) were merged into a single central authority located at Brussels. The Common Market's output and capability could be compared to those of the two superpowers of our time (see graphs, pp. 108–113). The rate of growth of the EEC was strong until 1965; then a slight recession set in, but in some parts of the whole area, and particularly in Italy, growth continued buoyant.

The successful organization of the EEC induced the seven Western countries of Europe, which had declined to participate in the Communities, to form, in 1959, a European Free Trade Association, or EFTA, often called the "Outer Seven" because its members (the United Kingdom, Norway, Sweden, Denmark, Switzerland, Austria, and Portugal) are distributed around the block of the "Inner Six." The EFTA proposed to eliminate gradually quantitative restrictions, customs duties, and assimilable charges on industrial goods traded between its members. Its constitution, as formulated in the Stockholm Treaty of 1959, was less comprehensive than that of the EEC but proposed to follow closely the latter's schedule of tariff reduction. All import duties between the Seven were also planned to be eliminated by 1970. No supranational authorities were set up by them, however, as had been done for the Six. The EFTA did not experience either comparable expansion or a pace of integration similar to that of the EEC.

In 1961, the senior partner of the Seven, the United Kingdom, moved first to join the Common Market, a move which would have greatly strengthened that economic organization and would have considerably increased its global industrial and financial weight. Difficult negotiations ensued, and in 1963 the French government vetoed British entry. Another round of negotiations took place in 1967 without much success. In the interval, a period of economic difficulties led the British government to establish temporarily a 25 percent tariff surtax on the importation of manufactured goods, and in 1967 the pound sterling was devalued. All these events weakened the progress of the EFTA. It seemed that despite present economic and political difficulties, all the thirteen nations concerned were moving toward closer association and most probably toward the formation, in a not too distant future, of a larger Common Market with which several other European countries would be associated. Greece and Turkey are already associates of the EEC. Austria and even Yugoslavia are negotiating to the same aim. As it stands in 1968, the EEC is the largest world unit in terms of foreign trade. It is also the largest cement producer. Once the Common Market is extended to most of the continent west of the "iron curtain," it would constitute a very powerful economic unit.

There has been talk of political integration following the economic one. It will certainly take longer but for the first time in history such a prospect can be reasonably considered. An important factor is the freer movement of labor across all national borders, establishing new and durable links, despite some temporary tensions. The rapid growth of international tourist travel has also been an integrating factor, as every year it mixes millions of Europeans coming to spend vacations in other European countries. Both the labor market and tourism contribute to mixing along a north-south axis, bringing somewhat closer together the poorer and richer nations in the Western half of Europe.

Another axis of relations between distinct parts of Europe and which has been historically of essential significance to Europeans is, of course, the East-West axis. After World War II, the high barrier dividing the Western countries of Free Europe associated with the United States and the Eastern countries bound to Russia by military alliance and by the predominance of the Communist party in their governments was aptly described by Winston Churchill as an iron curtain. After Stalin's death in 1953 and the thaw that gradually set in in the external relations of the Soviet Union, more contact developed between the Eastern and Western parts of Europe. Trade relations were the first to improve. In 1955, the Eastern countries of Europe imported in all goods for a value of $4,750 million, of which $1,790 million were imports of the smaller countries from the USSR; in 1965, these same figures stood at $12,460 million in total, and $4,550 million from the USSR; Western Europe supplied to the East $1,100 million in 1955, $3,320 million in 1965, and $3,570 million in 1967. The USSR has given to Fiat, the largest Italian automobile firm, a contract to build and help operate a large plant which will be making Fiat motor cars in Russia for the Soviet market. People are traveling more freely across the "iron curtain" either for business or tourism. Groups of Soviet tourists may be seen around the major landmarks of Paris, London, or Athens. Increasing numbers of Europeans enjoy vacations hunting or skiing in Poland, bathing on the Black Sea shores in Rumania or Bulgaria, or visiting the sights of Moscow and Prague.

Still, these relations are just a trickle compared to the massive currents developing among the Western countries of Europe. One country, ruled by a Communist regime, has served, to some extent, as a hinge between the two blocks: Yugoslavia has been associated with both sides of the curtain in different ways; it is a member of the OECD. The improvement in East-West relations is important to Europeans in general. It reflects better relations between the United States and the Soviet Union and some warming up of the "cold war." Westerners are looking for more markets that they hope to develop in the Eastern countries where consumption is still low and somewhat rationed. Easterners are expecting technical and economic help from the West to improve their lagging condition, and they are thirsty for the information, travel, culture, and excitement that more contacts with the West can offer after the long period of seclusion of the Stalin era.

Despite these signs of progress, Europe remains divided into two blocks. Various incidents and the partition of Berlin by an actual wall remind the Europeans of this division. The Eastern countries are organized in a tight trade association (COMECON, or CEMA) under Soviet leadership and in a military alliance formulated in the Warsaw Pact. The Western countries have their own regional community, of which EEC is by far the most integrated and successful, and in a military alliance with the United States and Canada, the North Atlantic Treaty Organization, or NATO, with headquarters now at Brussels. A few West European countries have kept out of or withdrawn from NATO (notably Switzerland, Sweden, and since 1967 France). But all are economically closely associated with the United States, and their foreign policies are founded on the assumption that they are assured of the protection of American nuclear power in case of crisis.

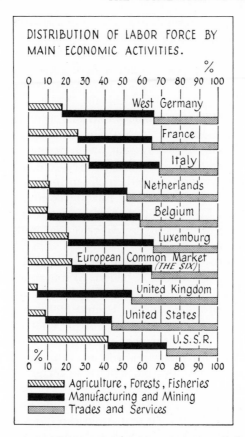

DISTRIBUTION OF LABOR FORCE BY MAIN ECONOMIC ACTIVITIES.

Agriculture, Forests, Fisheries
Manufacturing and Mining
Trades and Services

In the management of its internal and external policies, Europe gives a very special importance to the complex network of its relationship with the United States. The Atlantic partnership has worked well for more than twenty years and has provided the Western parts of Europe with a period of peace, reconstruction, and economic expansion which has been greatly appreciated. However, this very successful association, which binds together across the Atlantic the two richer and more prosperous parts of the world, does not work without inner tensions and lively debates. In the late 1940s, the Western European countries, ravaged and impoverished by the war, were happy to be helped, supported, and protected by the United States. But these proud nations were not resigned to the status of poor relations. They worked hard at improving their own conditions and reorganizing their political and economic systems to gain greater strength for the future. Their endeavors of reorganization and integration were aimed at a European community that might become comparable to the United States not only in standard of living per capita but also in global strength. Such a goal appears quite remote for the present, but the economic role of Europe, which still remains a rather divided plurality, is increasing.

Twenty years ago, Europe's finances were plagued with a lack of dollars or hard currency at a time when most European countries suffered from deficits in their balance of payments. This was the period of the "dollar gap"; after 1958, the financial currents across the North Atlantic were considerably modified. Many of the Western European nations, with a favorable balance of payments, accumulated large holdings in dollars, part of which they converted into gold. The deficit of the United States balance of payments worked chiefly in favor of Western Europe. The dollar gap was replaced by what Europeans considered to be a dollar surplus situation. Much of this surplus appeared to have accumulated as a result of large investments by American corporations in Western European enterprises. At the beginning of 1951, American direct private investment in Europe amounted to about $1.7 billion. In the beginning of 1966, it stood at $14 billion. At that time, European direct investments in the United States amounted to $6 billion. If the total assets owned by Europeans in the United States were valued at $34 billion, the total United States assets in Europe stood at $30 billion only. But as a by-product of this financial interplay, American corporations, many of them giant organizations, held a very powerful position in European industry and business, particularly in oil, automotive, mechanical, chemical, and electronic industries; on the other hand, European financial participation in the American economy was a minor factor. Several European countries felt that American interests were acquiring an overwhelming position of direction in their economic life. The United States may have felt similarly about British and French investments in the American economy in the latter part of the nineteenth century, but this European position had been erased as a consequence of two World Wars and also of the stupendous American economic expansion.

Still, owing to the recent American plant investment in Europe, European holdings of dollars amounted in 1967 to more than $20 billion; that is, much more than the gold reserve of the U.S. Treasury. This imbalance of international monetary relations has caused a reconsideration of the whole basis of the world monetary system founded on a certain price of gold labeled in dollars. New devices have been introduced in recent years on the credit markets in the form of "Eurodollars" and "Eurobonds." More important is the agreement achieved in 1967 in Geneva to liberalize the conditions of trade between Europe and America (the so-called "Kennedy Round Agreements") and also to create under the aegis of the International Monetary Fund in Washington special drawing rights to be used by the governments of the various countries to settle the accounts between them arising from imbalance in payments. These agreements and innovations were brought about essentially because of difficulties in the economic relations between the United States and the Western European countries, but they will modify in the long run the working of the world economy.

These new devices and agreements should facilitate economic relations across the Atlantic in the future; many causes for concern in the general Atlantic relationship will remain. American economic superiority is becoming more obvious to Europeans as they strive to catch up with the United States. It is no longer the dollar gap, a transitory situation, that worries them but a technological, managerial, and financial gap. Europeans complain about the "brain drain," that is, the steady emigration to the United States of large numbers of the best-trained elements of the European youth. It is estimated that from 1962 through 1966 more than 60,000 professional and technical workers came from Europe to the United States, where better incentives and working conditions were offered. A wide gap remains in the actual levels of opportunity and organizational skill, and Europe suffers from it. Political speeches and best-selling books have brought this debate into the limelight, and it is bound to affect trans-Atlantic relations.

The evolution of Europe is a dynamic one and, as in the past, it is interwoven with the trends of other parts of the world. The role of Europe and its use of resources, domestic and external, have been greatly modified in the last twenty years. The present attempts at reform and reorganization herald more change for the immediate future. Basically, however, Europe remains a deeply divided continent, and its different parts are moving in different rhythms.

# Part II

## Western Europe

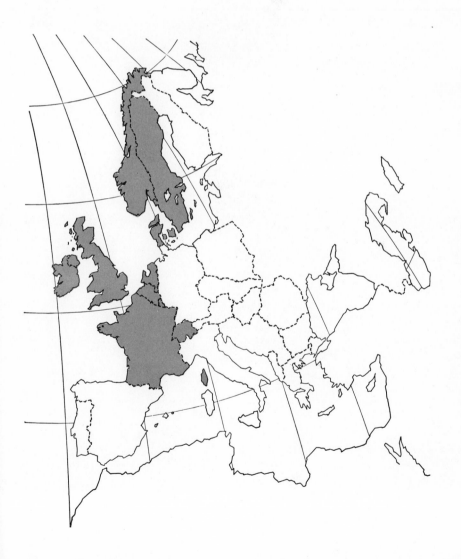

A corner of the postwar port of London. *(Combine Photos)*

# 4

## The Personality of Western Europe

The Atlantic façade of Europe has a distinct personality. East and West have been so often and for so long opposed on this continent that a quite different Western section was bound to form. Its personality is particularly obvious from overseas, for the countries of the Western section were generally what people meant when they used the term *Europe*. Even inside the continent the leadership of these Western countries has been recognized for some 300 years. They were the preponderant powers in the economic and cultural fields, if not always in the military. They built vast colonial empires abroad and developed the network of world trade on the basis of their capital investments. Thus what we call *Western* turns out to be the quintessence of the notion of Europe, and should be given a precise definition.

Western Europe has a diversified topography and a temperate oceanic climate, a four-seasonal division without sharp contrasts in the year. It is an area of old culture that has known many civilizations, has participated in the Celtic development, has absorbed strong Roman influences, and has always been open to continental inflows from the east. Politically it is the most stable part of Europe where, during the last century and a half, changes have happened in a moderate way, and where the force of public opinion has imposed democratic forms of government with strongly maintained freedoms and a wide participation by the people in the administration of public affairs. It is also the best-educated part of Europe, and its civilization has radiated all over the world to the point where it is commonly called "Western civilization." By active navigation on the high seas, the maritime nations of the West established a wheel of world relations of which they remained the hub for three centuries. An involved economic system, based on relations with faraway lands, scientific utilization of local resources, a unique commercial knowhow, and huge amounts of savings, maintained dense populations at a high standard of living. Almost every one of these countries has had an empire in Europe and abroad and has sent settlers to other continents. Such are the most apparent features that individualize Western Europe and make it different from neighboring lands.

## THE LIMITS OF WESTERN EUROPE

For the purpose of this study, Western Europe is limited to the following group of countries: Britain, Ireland, Iceland, Norway, Sweden, Denmark, the Netherlands, Belgium, Luxembourg, France, and Switzerland. As any other, this classification can be challenged: the Scandinavian countries are usually put aside, in a northern section of Europe, and Switzerland is ordinarily included in Central Europe. We shall include these two areas in the Western realm to which they belong because of some physical and many economic and social features. Western Europe thus defined constitutes a zone of civilization as opposed to the countries southward and eastward.

The wide-open oceanic spaces of the Atlantic are the boundary to the west. Iceland, though at a substantial distance from the mainland, has to be included, since for about a thousand years it was closely linked to the Scandinavian countries, particularly to Denmark. To the south, the limit is set by the main divide of the high ranges, the Pyrenees and the Alps; on the other side of these ranges one enters a peninsular world with a drier climate, a different history, and an economy that from the eighteenth century until recently has participated little in the social evolution of Western Europe. To the east, the Rhine is a boundary, for the lands across that river felt little Latin influence and have remained a tidal land where political stabilization has been difficult. From the point where the Rhine divides itself in many arms and mingles in its delta with the Meuse, the northeastern boundary of our region stretches across the base of the Jutland peninsula and through the Baltic and its Gulf of Bothnia to the Arctic. Most of the Swiss territory is inside the elbow outlined by the crest of the Alps to the St. Gotthard Massif and the Rhine valley that starts from there. Most of Germany is to the east of the line we draw, and we shall leave the whole of it out, for Prussia, the nucleus around which modern Germany was assembled and from which it had been directed, never belonged in Western Europe, and because the present partition has put East Germany in the realm of Soviet control.

The line of division thus followed by the Pyrenees, the Alps, the Rhine, and the Baltic carries some meaning in physical geography too. The topography of this region is remarkable for its irregularity—a typically European characteristic. No vast stretch of continuous land-scape exists, no real massivity in the general outline. The loftiest ranges, such as the Alps, are deeply indented and chiseled inside; the most massive unit, the Scandinavian peninsula with its spinal range, is an old shield, planed by erosion, polished and sculpted by the glaciers, indented with fjords, and strewn with lakes, and has no high crests of considerable altitude. On the mainland, the checkered topography of plateaus, small ranges, plains, and basins does not permit any ensemble to develop. The Great Plain of Europe may begin on the North Sea shores, but in the Low Countries and in France it is so narrow, so broken up by dams, river branches, or bays, that one does not get the feeling of continuity or of the broad open spaces that begin east of the Rhine.

Most of the highlands inside Western Europe belong to the old Primary era foldings of the Caledonian or Hercynian systems. They are strongly mineralized. Depressions between or around them often bear coal deposits. In other points ore deposits of high metallic content were found, such as the famous Swedish iron ores, the tin ores of south-western England, zinc and lead in Belgium, and some wolfram in Brittany. In the more recent strata, other minerals are found: chiefly, the iron ores of Lorraine and of the English Midlands, the bauxite of southern France, the natural gas of Groningen, and the potash of Alsace. The topographic diversity has something to do with the variety of mineral resources; it also determined much more directly an abundance of waterfalls, either in the glaciated area of the north or in the Alpine ranges to the south. Here hydroelectric power could be easily developed and coupled with power produced from coal. The whole area seems to be deficient in mineral oil, although rich deposits of natural gas have recently been located in the North Sea, in the Netherlands, and southwestern France.

The varied topography determines, of course, many local nuances in the climate, which is bound to change over an area that stretches from 42° to 72° North latitude, and which reaches in altitude over 10,000 feet on several crests. Vegetation zones translate the gradual change in latitude or altitude, but the transitions are generally slow. The surrounding warm seas are felt all around. Their moderating action keeps the average temperature of the coldest month in Tromsö (Norway, lat. 69°39′ N.) around 25° Fahrenheit, and that of the warmest month in Toulouse (France, 43°37′) at 70°. Precipitation is abundant everywhere.

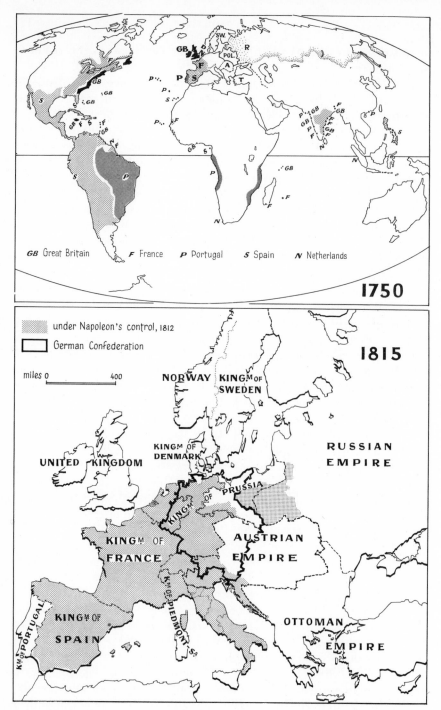

**1750**

under Napoleon's control, 1812

German Confederation

**1815**

miles 0      400

NORWAY KINGᴹOF SWEDEN

KINGᴹ OF DENMARK

RUSSIAN EMPIRE

UNITED KINGDOM

KINGᴹ OF PRUSSIA

KINGᴹ OF FRANCE

AUSTRIAN EMPIRE

Kᴹᴳ OF PORTUGAL

KINGᴹ OF SPAIN

Kᴹ OF PIEDMONT

OTTOMAN EMPIRE

The evolution of the political geography of Western Europe, I.

Only the highlands, Switzerland and Scandinavia, are covered with snow in winter. The number of rainy days is above 150 for most of the area. The thin, drizzling rain, the abundant dew, and the frequent mists keep the soil continuously moist, and in a few places only, too damp. Violent storms and torrential rains as well as prolonged droughts are rare occurrences, so that vegetation or crops are assured a regular supply of water. Soils are slowly weathered, seldom washed out. Thick heavy loams can form under such conditions on flat terrain. Seasonal changes happen slowly, gradually: there are indeed four seasons, corresponding almost exactly to the quarters of the year. Contrasts in the seasons are felt more at higher latitudes and altitudes, but over the major part of the region nature seems organized for distributing heat, sunshine, and humidity in small, regular doses. Such a combination of climate, topography, and vegetation has been a great favor, of course, bestowed on the area from the moment man started working hard to use its soil.

It would be difficult to agree with the theory of certain geographers, particularly the late Ellsworth Huntington of Yale University, that the climate of Northwestern Europe fitted the people living in it for higher cultural development and intensive activities. Italy and the Middle West of the United States, in quite different climatic conditions, have also shown ability for high civilization and prosperity during certain periods. It would be difficult to contend that the dampness of the Lowlands was only an asset and the fogs of London an incentive for the development of one of the chief seaports in the world. As in every climate there are good and bad aspects of the weather conditions of Western Europe. The local populations were able to turn most of these conditions to their advantage, and the moderation and regularity of the climate could be interpreted as an element of stability for agriculture. We are far, however, from being able thus to explain the involved civilization of the Western region.

The mixing of the populations along the Atlantic façade, which was for long a dead end for westward European migrations, suggests also the mingling of cultural influences: the Latin order and organization, the adventurous spirit of Atlantic navigation, the Barbarians' thirst for freedom and equality—these three currents at least and probably many others less well known contributed to the Western spirit that later spread with such force in all directions. The old and permanent axis around which the Western unity revolved was the great transcontinental route linking the northern seas with the Mediterranean. This route of the Rhine and Meuse toward the Rhone and the Alpine passes was perhaps nature's greatest gift to the area. It led the Roman legions northward, the Barbarians southward, and trade, from ancient to modern times, to and fro. Along this axis was designed medieval Lot-

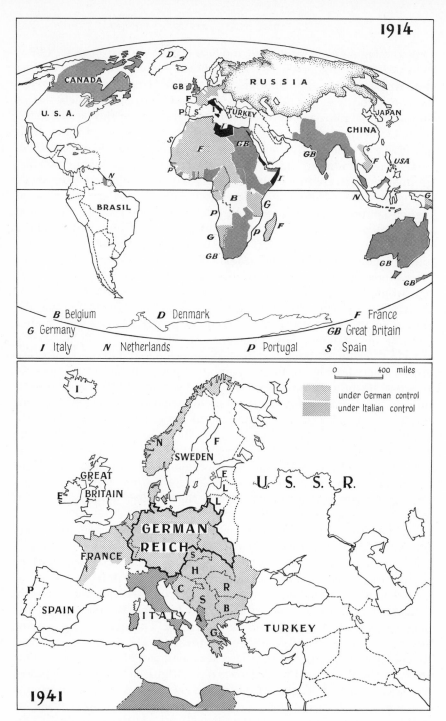

The evolution of the political geography of Western Europe, II.

haringia, which soon broke into parts. When the Lowlands proclaimed their independence from Spain, they gained it under the dynasty of the House of Orange, which still reigns in the Netherlands: Orange, a town on the lower Rhone, and Holland are at the two extremities of the famous route.

Many landmarks stake out the north-south line, demonstrating the ties between various sections of this region and the unity of its culture. There is an air of close relationship between the great cities along the Rhine and those of Holland and Flanders: Strasbourg makes one think at times of Amsterdam or Bruges; Basel reminds one of Ghent. Geneva has much in common with Nice, and Bern with The Hague. Even Lyon on the Rhone has something of Rotterdam and perhaps of Copenhagen. Every one of these cities has a clearcut, distinct individuality, and yet all belong to one great family. The north-south axis was extended by the sea to Scandinavia: the Norse came to Normandy and Paris, even to the western Mediterranean. French influence was strong in the north through the seventeenth to nineteenth centuries. Uppsala was rebuilt in its present shape by French architects, and the House of Bernadotte, reigning in Sweden, came from France.

Similar ties, perhaps even more spectacular, could be listed as existing between the Western countries and others in Europe. But still they did not bring about a general unity in the development and structure of the nations such as exists throughout the Western region.

## THE MARITIME VOCATION

The foundation of the Western community rests on the sea. Landlocked Switzerland is present in Rotterdam and Antwerp by the numerous Rhine river boats flying the Swiss flag, and the passes through the Alps give the Swiss a decisive position in communications between the seas. Curiously enough, insular Ireland, after having had a network of maritime relations in the Middle Ages, stepped aside from the great Atlantic sea trade—or perhaps was kept out of it by the powerful shadow of her British neighbor and master. From the eighteenth century to World War II, Britian ruled the high seas. Her whole national life was linked to the oceans and to the Royal Navy. The domination of the seas was maintained through the control of strategic position on the straits and in the midst of narrow or wide seas the world over, as well as by the supremacy of naval and merchant tonnage. When some important position on a sea lane was not under British aegis, it was held generally by the Dutch, the French, the Danes, or several of them. On the whole, Western Europe had the mastery of the seas for two centuries at least.

In 1939, on the eve of World War II, seven Western European nations accounted for a merchant marine of 32 million tons out of a world total of 68.5 million. The end of the war found the European share seriously diminished, mainly replaced by the growth of American tonnage. But reconstruction of merchant marines was one of the first postwar achievements, and in 1966, the figures of 1939 were surpassed, as the ten powers registered together 57 million tons out of a world total of 171 million. They owned more that flew flags of convenience, and they launched, in 1966, 1 million tons of new ships or 28 percent of the world's new tonnage.

Before the great oceanic trade ever developed, seafaring became an important resource because of fishing, and the seas off the north European coasts are among the richest fishing grounds in the world. In olden times fish was essential in the European diet: meat was scarce and expensive and its preservation difficult. There was plenty of fish in the sea, and prehistoric people knew the techniques for catching fish in the lakes; they were simple, and the equipment could be manufactured out of local materials anywhere. Fish could be salted, marinated, or smoked at small expense, then shipped far inland. Herring thus became a staple on the menu of Europeans, even of the poorest people in the East who had access to markets visited by merchants from the West. Over the centuries Dutchmen and Danes sold to the continent inestimable loads of herring and other preserved fish. In the Russian language herring is still called by its Danish name, *sild*, and Amsterdam claims to have been built "on carcasses of herrings," for this trade brought great fortunes to the Western ports. Today in the small French Channel port of Fécamp, one can still visit the plants where herring is smoked before being put on the French and African markets. With refrigeration and manufacture of ice, transportation of fresh fish became simple, and ever-increasing quantities were caught by the Western fleets.

The fish catch was estimated in 1965 at nearly 7.2 million tons, or 14 percent of the world total and 45 percent of the European total; Britain, Iceland, and Norway supplied more than one million tons each. Part of this catch came from distant fishing grounds: the sea around Newfoundland or off the western coast of Africa. For centuries European powers, particularly France and Britain, have disputed the rights to the Newfoundland fisheries where cod was caught; British and Norwegians knew a period of rivalry in whaling in the southern Atlantic. But the main bulk of the fish catch came always from the bordering shallow seas, particularly the North Sea.

Every country of Western Europe (with the exception of Switzerland and Ireland) has at least a narrow coastal area on the North Sea.

In recent centuries it has been the most navigated sea in the world and has yielded a greater seafood catch than any other. A shallow body of water, it is less than 300 feet in depth over most of its area. In the center, on the Dogger Bank, a famous meeting place for fishing boats — there are more than 30,000 — the depth of the water is less than 130 feet. The bottom of the sea slopes gently northward where a trough follows the Norwegian coast, and great, oceanic depths of more than 500 fathoms begin north of Scotland. Navigation is far from easy: visibility is rarely good owing to the damp, foggy climate; sandbanks on the shallow bottom are frequent and strangely shaped. Many of these banks are erected as a result of the meeting of tides and tidal currents. The range of the tides in such a funnel-shaped basin is great — it reaches 25 feet 11 inches at Boulogne at the entrance of the Channel on the French coast. Spring tides rise 20 feet at London Bridge, and in stormy weather certain tidal waves have scoured the British shores at a speed of over 90 miles an hour. Torrential currents may develop in narrow straits, reshaping the sandbanks; big liners may be checked and stranded by heavy seas. In some places dangerous swirls develop and have frightened mariners over the centuries.

The North Sea is remarkable for the variety of waters that mingle without quite mixing within its basin. The large rivers that empty into it, particularly the Rhine and Meuse, carry great volumes of fresh water; through the Strait of Dover and through the wider opening in the north, masses of warmer and saline Atlantic waters flow; the Baltic supplies through the Danish straits some colder and less saline water. Most of the North Sea waters have a uniform salinity around 34.5 per 1000; this is higher as a rule near the north and south openings of the sea than in the middle, and it is usually higher along the British shores than along those of the continent, from which the fresh and colder water flows in. That diversity of qualities of water is very important for the development of animal life in the sea. It has been said that fish like to have "hot and cold running water," but in any case the changes of temperature and salinity in the North Sea according to the seasonal variations of the inflow of Atlantic waters, and the mingling of waters from such different origins in large quantities, has helped many species of fish to come and swarm in large shoals in the midst of this sea. The constant circulation of the water masses renews the fertile elements and particularly the food or *plankton* on which the fish thrive. The bottom of the marginal seas of Europe has been likened to luxuriant pastures on which the fish swarm and leave a tremendous harvest. (The herring lays on the average only 31,000 eggs, but the turbot achieves the figure of 8.6 million!) The tremendous size of the annual catch should not be surprising.

Rhine barges crowded together in the port of Rotterdam, at present the largest seaport in the world in terms of amount of goods handled in international trade.

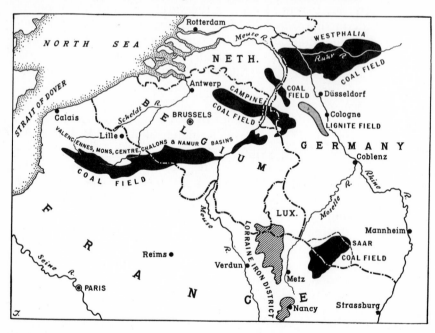

The coalfields of France, Belgium, the Netherlands, the Lower Rhine, and the Saar. France, Belgium, and Germany share one coalfield, located close to the sea and the navigable Rhine, with the Lorraine ore district completing the basis for great industrial power. The presence of resources of coal and iron ore in the same area with a dense population and an excellent system of waterways centered on the Rhine made this corner of Western Europe a great hub of trade. (*U.S. Geological Survey*)

The variety of the fish is considerable: cod, herring, mackerel, plaice, sole, turbot, and flounder are the main species caught. The Dogger Bank—*Dogger* means cod in Dutch—has a role comparable to that of the Grand Bank of Newfoundland off the American shores. There the British, Dutch, and Scandinavian ships are plying and fishing the year round. In the war period of 1940–1944 little fishing could be done because of military operations and the abundance of floating mines. In 1945 the depleted fleets again began to put to sea, sometimes against the Admiralties' instructions. But they brought home a miraculous catch, and mountains of silvery mackerels were landed in April–May 1945 in the main fishing ports of France. The variety of the catch is not less important than its size. Swarms of different species arrive with the kind of water they prefer. With the annual ebb and flow of the Atlantic and continental waters, seasons of fishing succeed one another, and trawlers bring successively to the market and to the processing plant the different kinds of seafood.

To assess the whole importance of this fishing economy on these shores, one must remember that for centuries, from Hammerfest in the north to Bayonne in the south, fishermen sailed to faraway banks in order to add the catch of the remote Atlantic to the local one. And it is from North Sea and Channel ports that the ships leave to fish off the coasts of Iceland, West Africa, and even Newfoundland (where they meet the American fishermen) and here is based also the largest part of the world fleet of whalers. On the continental side, the Western European ports supplied a large part of Europe and some parts of Africa and Asia with preserved fish.

Fishing was the origin of the fortune of several great ports, and today it is one of the main functions of towns on the shore, such as Boulogne, Dieppe, Fécamp, Concarneau, and Douarnenez in France, Aberdeen, Grimsby, Yarmouth, Padstow, and Falmouth in Britain, Ijmuiden in Holland, Stavanger, Trondheim, Bergen, Tromsö, and many others in Norway. In olden times every port of appreciable size engaged in some fishing, but other vessels put out to sea: merchantmen, privateers, men-of-war. A specialization of the seaports was slowly worked out. Naval bases, great commercial ports, industrial centers, fishing or passenger ports are many along the Western European coasts. These ports form a chain of crossroads connecting by joints the continental and oceanic economies. On them was based the mastery of the seas that the Western European powers, particularly Britain, held from the seventeenth century to the middle of the twentieth. Nowhere else did sea traffic develop with comparable intensity. London, Antwerp, Rotterdam, and Hamburg are in the twentieth century four of the greatest seaports in the world, by tonnage as well as by number of calling ships. The North Atlantic route from the Channel ports to New York remains by far the

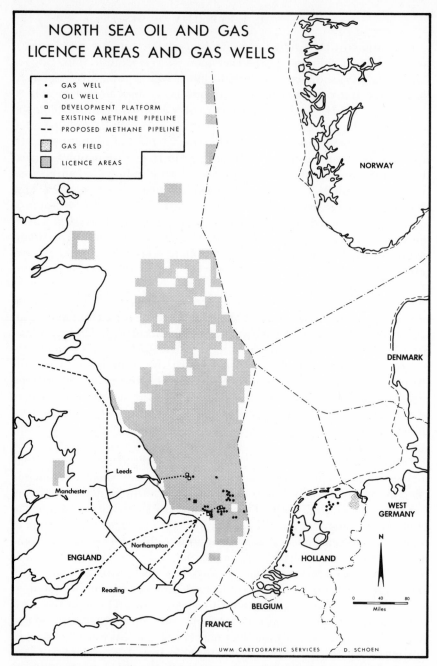

North Sea oil and gas. The map shows the sections of the North Sea apportioned to the various Riparian Powers. Notice the license areas and operating wells (as of February 1968) in the British sector and the importance of the gas fields in the Netherlands, which triggered the exploration of the Sea. *(Based on map and data supplied by the Northern Gas Board, Newcastle-upon-Tyne)*

most traveled by passenger liners. The largest and most luxurious ships in history were built for this run.

In the 1960s, the North Sea has become a source of useful minerals. During the last twenty years, several new strikes were made of oil and natural gas on the lands bordering the sea, particularly in the Netherlands and West Germany. The most spectacular of these finds was the discovery of one of the largest world deposits of natural gas in the Dutch province of Groningen. As a result, exploration started offshore and proceeded apace in the bottom of this shallow sea. Many wells, producing large quantities of natural gas and some oil, are rising out of the waves in several sectors of the North Sea. The most important production as yet is that of natural gas off the eastern shore of England, and it promises to supply a large part of the British requirement of gas. Exploitation of the sea bottom has led to a significant evolution in the international law of the sea. Not only did the Riparian Powers extend the width of the territorial seas they claim from three miles to six or nine, but a new international convention has been adopted under United Nations auspices which extends the control of the Riparian Power, and for all practical purposes, its sovereignty, over the whole Continental Shelf adjacent to its shores. In the case of the North Sea, the whole sea has the Continental Shelf for bottom, with the exception of a narrow deep trough which follows part of the Norwegian coast. The international convention divides such shallow seas with various independent states on several sides according to a median line between the shores. The median lines cut up the bottom of the North Sea into sectors like sections of an apple pie; each sector is attributed to the nation on the adjacent land; Great Britain, Norway, Denmark, Sweden, West Germany, Belgium, and even France, in a southern corner, share in this way the ownership of the bottom of the sea. This new way of appropriating the Continental Shelf under the high seas does not affect the international traditional freedom of navigation and fishing on the high seas, that is, beyond the limit of the territorial seas as claimed by the Riparian Powers.

The North Sea is now serving as a basic laboratory for the new legislation and regulation of the sea in terms of use of the mineral resources that can be extracted from its bottom. At present only the Continental Shelf has come under such regulation, because it is the only part of the seas' bottoms that is easily accessible. However, in the particular case of the North Sea and to avoid discrimination against Norway, the Riparian Powers have agreed to waive enforcement of the rule of the continuity of the shelf, and the sector of the sea appropriated by Norway has been drawn up without consideration of the interruption by a narrow deep trough. Similar agreements may be expected to be drawn up, as the need

The drilling rig "Orion" used in the British sector of the North Sea by the Gas Council/ Amoco Group. *(Northern Gas Board, Newcastle-upon-Tyne; photo, Maurice Broomfield, London)*

arises, to divide among the Riparian Powers the right to use the resources of the adjacent maritime spaces beyond the old limits of territorial seas. In the case of Western Europe, several border seas or gulfs may be expected to be so allocated: the Channel, the Irish Sea, the Baltic, the Bay of Biscay, possibly even the Mediterranean, although it is a much deeper sea.

Fishing remains open to any nation on any high sea. The West European nations are beginning, however, to be concerned about the increasing activity of trawlers fishing in large numbers in their border seas and flying the flags of distant nations; the increased presence of Soviet fishing fleets in the border seas of Western Europe is a case in point. However, Western Europe has for centuries claimed and defended the freedom of navigation and fishing over all the high seas of the world. More than any other part of the world it has reaped the benefits of the freedom of the high seas. As the greatest crossroads of maritime trade, it still needs to maintain this freedom, and it is not likely that it will now adopt principles of local control over large sea spaces. Still, its share in the practical use of the high seas and its share of the maritime equipment plying the seas have been considerably decreased in recent years by the great expansion of newcomers, as the merchant marines, the fishing and the shipbuilding of Japan, the Soviet Union, some east and south European nations expanded steadily. The maritime vocation of the peoples around the North Sea and the Channel has laid the foundation of a magnificent economic and cultural development.

## A GLOBAL ECONOMY

Recently the economic system of Western Europe has been shattered by two great wars with a serious depression between them. It still shows extraordinary abilities for recovery; its large network of world connections is a very considerable advantage in peacetime and provided greater mobility and transportation capacity in wartime. But it has also worked out an involved economy with a variety of resources in every country, so that the local basis enables some degree of isolation if necessary.

The total population of Western Europe, as we define it, numbers about 156 million inhabitants, with the highest densities in the Netherlands, Belgium, and the industrial areas of Britain and France; the lowest are in the north of Scandinavia. The total is still impressive, and the average density is almost four times that of the United States. The average standard of living is rather high, though lower than that of the United States. Such a population has been maintained by a constant expansion of its material basis through use of a diversity of combined resources.

In the field of agriculture, crops were combined early with livestock raising. Animals were fed first on empty space, then, when very little unoccupied area remained, on fodder crops, irrigated meadows, and high mountain pastures. For centuries an annual migration, famous in France under the name of *transhumance*, has taken the livestock from stables or lowland winter pastures to the high summer grassy prairies, called *alpages*, on the lofty Alps. Cattle as well as sheep circulate in this way. By the Middle Ages the shepherds of southern France had already developed special routes and even specially built graveled roads called *drailles.* The movements of the flocks on the *draille du Languedoc,* for instance, are still today an impressive sight, although now there are far fewer sheep in Europe. With the increasing number of cattle and the improved strains, the feeding became better organized and called for feed imported from other parts of the world. Thus large quantites of wheat, corn, and even barley are imported. During the lean years of war, the farmers often fed all kinds of grain to their animals, reducing substantially the quantities of meat supply put at the disposal of the population. But a steady trend increases the role of livestock in the farming economy of Western Europe, and even the isolation of the years 1940–1945 did not interrupt this seriously.

As crop rotations became more and more complicated, agricultural practices were gradually mechanized, and increased amounts of fertilizer were needed. The average yields are high, but the total harvest is on the whole insufficient to feed the population adequately. With the rise of the standard of living, many exotic foods became necessities, particularly products of tropical climates, such as coffee, tea, cocoa, many fruits, and oils. European history shows a constant but accelerated development in the variety of foodstuffs considered "necessary." In 1700, the first *café* or coffeehouse, a luxury for a select public, appeared on the boulevards in Paris. Since then coffee has become a first-rate basic food, and the same is true of chocolate, citrus fruits, bananas, and peanut oil. The quantities consumed rose with the variety. Today social and economic progress means for Western Europe greater interdependence with other countries.

This is even more true of the industrial picture. Agglomerations in urban centers require a great many jobs, and the problem of marketing is not so easy. Here comparison with the United States in its pre-1950 situation is striking: Western Europe, slightly less populated, needed many more outside markets to maintain, with a lower standard of living and lower wages, a smaller number of working people; the domestic market in the United States, by its tremendous consumption and its unity, made things much simpler. Western European countries exchanged among themselves about 38 percent of their total exports in

1938 and 55 percent in 1966. Close to one half of the foreign trade of Western Europe is transacted outside the regional frame. It is an economy geared to the global scale. It must be stressed that the regional market is extraordinarily important: proximity and unity of civilization are powerful factors in trade. The total foreign trade of Western European powers represents one fourth of the world trade in value; about one eighth of all the international transactions on the globe are performed within this small area of Western Europe. The internal traffic of every country is still more active than its external relations; Switzerland alone may be an exception. Still, the intensity of traffic cannot compare with that of the United States: for instance the railways freight traffic, figured out in ton-kilometers, shows for 1965 65 billion in France and 25 billion in the United Kingdom, where coastwise navigation is more important, but rises to 1029 in the United States. Such comparisons suggest the idea, many times advanced, that a lowering of national tariff barriers and a great increasing of consumption in a unified Western European market would bring a considerable increase in activity, as demonstrated by the first years of the EEC.

Local resources are still much smaller in Western Europe than in the United States in so far as area of fertile soil and known mineral deposits are concerned. These resources are put to use with more costly methods: the maintenance of the fertility of the soil involves more investment and, particularly, much more labor. The same is true for the mines, which are scattered, smaller in size, and produce usually poorer grade raw materials. Most of the iron ores mined in France and Britain, for instance, belong in categories that are considered not worth being used on a large scale in North America. Western Europe compensates by consuming large quantities of human labor, particularly of skilled, high-quality manpower. Its system of trade consists in importing foodstuffs and industrial materials and exporting mainly finished, manufactured goods. Ships come to its ports heavily filled with bulky cargoes; they leave high above the water. These countries import much more than they export, in tonnage and in value. This deficit in volume of the foreign-trade balance had little importance; it was compensated by adequate freight rates. But the deficit in value had a much greater significance: purchases abroad had to be paid for with foreign money, especially when they came from foreign lands and not from colonial dependencies. Even the intraimperial trade of such colonial powers as Britain, France, or the Netherlands had to be balanced in some way.

Western Europe developed an intricate but essential chapter in its income through what has been called *services*. This region was able to provide others with a certain number of services in different fields against payment. Transportation on the high seas was one of these

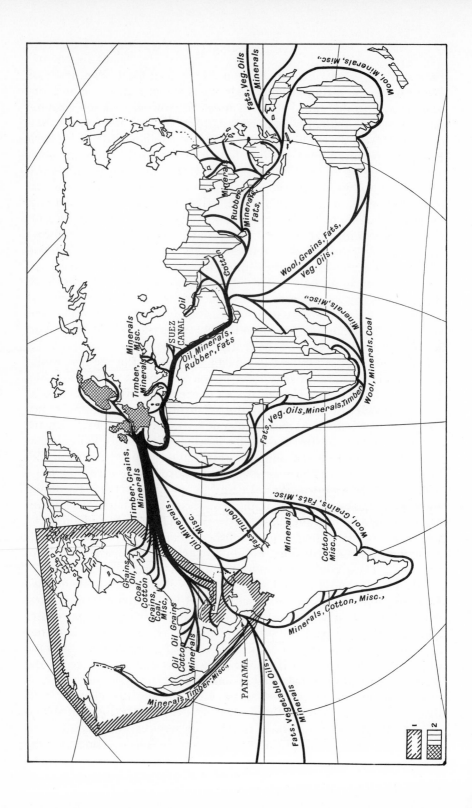

Wool, Veg. Oils
Minerals
Wool, Minerals, Misc.,
Rubber
Minerals
Fats
Wool, Grains, Fats,
Veg. Oils,
Minerals
Rubber,
Minerals,
Fats,
Cotton
Minerals, Misc.
Wool, Minerals, Coal
Minerals
Oil
SUEZ
CANAL
Timber,
Minerals
Misc.
Oil, Minerals,
Rubber, Fats
Fats, Veg. Oils, Minerals, Timber
Wool, Grains, Fats, Misc.
Timber, Grains,
Minerals
Oil, Minerals
Misc.
Fats, Timber
Minerals
Cotton,
Misc.
Grains,
Oil,
Coal,
Cotton
Grains,
Coal,
Misc.
Oil  Oil Grains
Cotton
Minerals
Minerals, Cotton, Misc.,
PANAMA
Minerals, Timber, Misc.
Fats, Vegetable Oils,
Minerals

1
2

services, for instance, the carrying of bulky materials from Asia to America in British or Dutch bottoms, or Venezuelan oils to other American countries in Norwegian tankers, or Chilean iron ore to Baltimore in Swedish ore ships. Lending money was another important service: interest paid on these loans was an important source of revenue, particularly for Britain, France, Belgium, and Switzerland. Insuring and re-insuring people all over the world brought a third chapter of income. The famous London institution of Lloyd's has been for almost two centuries the world center of insurance, particularly against transportation risks, and Switzerland is another hub of insurance, trading on a world-wide scale. Warehousing and redistribution of goods were again services extended to the whole world; at the center of world trade, exchange and warehousing facilities were available to such an extent that a buyer was always sure to find on that market any quality and any quantity of the kind of material he may need. Thus London was for a long time the world store for a number of tropical goods such as tea, coffee, and rubber, none of which was produced in Britain. It had a similar re-distributing function for other raw materials, such as gold, wool, and tobacco. Amsterdam had similar functions on a smaller scale for some time.

Western Europe was capable of extending such services to the international economy because it had large amounts of capital saved and available for investment. The commercial activities and the saving tradition of Western European populations, particularly of the *bourgeoisie*, have paved the ground for financial expansion. While some investments were made in insurance, merchant marine, and foreign loans, others went into buying land, building plants, developing other lands in all kinds of ways. Investments abroad yielded a steady and increased flow of capital back toward the financing countries, until economic nationalism, exchange difficulties, and controls complicated the circuit and reduced the inflow of profits from overseas investments. To organize and direct the development of the enterprises thus started, Western Europe supplied generally the top-ranking personnel: engineers, managers, and the like. There was a constant export of skilled personnel and even of skills under the form of patents and licences. The most advanced

---

(*Opposite*) The world-wide system of supply in Western Europe. This map summarizes the intricate system of imports to Western Europe, the foodstuffs and industrial raw materials it must buy in other parts of the world. Shaded areas: 1, line surrounding the dollar area; 2, shading indicating the limits of Western Europe as defined in this book (darker shade) and the main overseas areas economically dependent on Western European powers (such as the British Commonwealth and the French Union) as of July 1953 (lighter shading). Note the paramount importance of the traffic crossing the North Atlantic from the dollar area toward Western Europe; note also the importance of the Suez Canal for imports from nondollar areas.

civilization had the best developed techniques. All these were exports of "brains."

The deficit of the trade balance was filled in or the favorable trade balance largely improved by such *invisible* items as services, investments, or "brains exports." Altogether the balance of payments between Western Europe and the rest of the world was largely to this region's benefit until recently. The network of this economy was indeed global, in space as well as in structure, and was devised to maintain the region's domination of the rest of the world in the economic and even in the cultural fields. It must be remembered that most of the important technical advances in the eighteenth and nineteenth centuries were made by Western Europeans: the steam and Diesel engines, the utilization of electric power, the blast furnace and ovens used in the iron and steel industries, mechanical spinning and weaving of textiles—the list could be a long one.

The rapid industrialization and urban concentration brought about by the Industrial Revolution accelerated social trends in Europe. The important reforms leading to a better distribution of income and giving greater freedom of association to labor for the defense of its rights started in Europe in the West. Here the first large organizations of co-operatives and trade unions were founded and permitted to share in the administration of public affairs. This evolution had been prepared for by the respected role played in these countries by professional guilds since olden times, and also by the existence of a middle class or *bourgeoisie* participating in government. The concentration of economic and political power in the hands of a small aristocracy and of the Roman Catholic Church had been softened up by a gradual and slow process. Social pressure was very strong as a result of the economic evolution, but it affected a flexible and diversified structure; with the exception of the French Revolution of 1789–1799, it did not bring to the Western countries any grave internal conflicts after the religious wars of the seventeenth century. Before World War II all the Western countries were quite advanced in their democratic evolution, in the freedom given and attention paid to the voice of the laboring masses. The social security system was sometimes involved, but it was applied generally and equitably.

It was easier to manage such a gradual transition, with labor and management both showing some generosity, when the country was rich and the future prospects were good. In fact, for about three centuries Western Europe managed the world economy and built an admirable civilization at home, founded on a prosperity that required the consent, given freely or not, of other parts of the world. In the twentieth century, however, the relative dominance of this region was decreased.

## THE TWENTIETH-CENTURY CRISIS

World War II precipitated a trend begun several decades earlier with what has been called "the revolt of massive continents." It was a revolt against the economic and political domination of Western Europe. The decisive element in this revolt was the emergence of the United States as a world power. This rise occurred gradually and in close cooperation with Western European powers. Until World War I, Europeans were not quite aware of what was happening across the Atlantic. When in the 1940s Western Europe had to be liberated from Nazi domination by an Allied effort, which was mainly American insofar as high command, personnel, equipment, and financing were concerned, it became obvious that leadership had moved across the ocean.

This change in the geographical location of the headquarters of the world was strengthened as a result of the destruction undergone by the Western European countries and the quick spending of their assets abroad for war and reconstruction needs. The capital available in Western Europe had been greatly diminished, and the whole manifold and involved structure of the region's economy appeared shattered. With less revenue from "invisible" and "brains" exports and fewer investments abroad, it was hard to compensate for the deficit in the balance of payments. The plight of Western Europe did not appear to open long-range opportunities to the United States. The national American economy was geared much more to the domestic market than to international world trade. Other parts of the world had not been provided with ways and means to obtain dollars, as they had been previously for the pound sterling or the French and Swiss francs. The structure of the world economy, which was of the greatest concern to the United States, had been centered around the North Sea, and reorganizing it was a long and intricate process. The isolation of Russia after 1917 was extended after 1945 to another section of the continent of Europe. Horizons of the international commercial system, based on sea trade, were narrowing.

The solidarity of the Western civilization, stemming from the great maritime discoveries of the Renaissance, was splendidly confirmed through the considerable help that the United States gave in different ways to the Western European nations. Relief and rehabilitation help, government loans, and establishment of the European Recovery Program were the main steps of a general policy aimed at helping Europe to get back on its feet.

This help has been substantial and will serve to tighten the links that the Western countries have had with North America, but transition from the former status of supremacy to a new and as yet undefined one will take time. The main directions which Western Europe has set for its

A corner of the large Renault motor works at Flins near Paris demonstrates advanced automation in the automotive industry. *(French Cultural Services)*

Western Europe has succeeded in preserving old landscapes and even some old equipment while evolving fast: windmills in the Netherlands still stand along canals draining polders and testifying to ancient ways of harnessing the natural environment to man's purposes. *(Netherland Information Service)*

reconstruction work may be summed up, however, as follows: to maintain and develop its maritime functions; to increase the production of exportable products, with rationing (when necessary) of the scarce commodities; to make a careful survey of foreign assets and drastic restrictions on dollar expenditure; to raise the rate of capital formation at home; to develop further local resources.

Such trends imposed on the governments and other public authorities heavy responsibilities. To face them, these authorities claimed more power, and there arose a tendency for more centralized government control of all stages of the peacetime economy of each nation, with a great deal of planning. Even in Britain and France, these citadels of economic liberalism, the government "nationalized" the main banks and the ownership of large transportation systems. Labor organizations gained an increased part in government responsibilities. The ordeal of the war and the misery of the period that followed caused a serious upheaval of social pressure and an outcry for a better distribution of the available resources. The problem was made all the more serious as many governments faced the necessity of restoring or maintaining at prewar levels the general standard of living while the foundations of the old structure were badly damaged.

The question of the standard of living is dominant in the minds of the European peoples. In the East the claim is for higher standards—indeed they were low in most cases. In the West it was at first a claim for the restoration of the previous prosperity; then, with the contagious example of the Eastern countries and after a prolonged period of privations, it became also a claim for increased and improved conditions, eventually beyond the pre-1940 situation, which of course had not been ideal. A better realization of the higher level existing in the United States was one more incentive. Thus, social pressures increased as a result of the meeting, at the tip of the massive Eurasian continent, of influences coming from land and sea.

The improvement of social conditions requires a widening of the economic basis. It could be made by trade expansion abroad, by a better technique in the utilization of existing resources on the spot, and by the increase of local resources when new ones could be discovered. Every country and even every region finds itself in a special case, because densities of population and extent of development of resources vary greatly from place to place. Undergoing a wave of pessimism, many local authorities feel that the material basis of Western Europe is too narrow, that the large urban crowds of the industrial centers cannot exist without very wide systems of supply and marketing, involving international trade on a large scale. Before World War II Europeans thought they could specialize in the higher stages of manufacturing, exporting skill and brains;

today they have to share largely with the United States even in this field. The higher stages of manufacturing have been mechanized to a considerable extent; during World War II, most of the technical advances — and they were many — occurred or were developed in America. The rift created by the unequal strength and stability of the currencies is hard to span. A lag remains in the technological and financial sectors, where Europeans used to dominate. More than ever Western Europe feels the necessity of being closely associated with the United States, although it intends to remain European, as geography made it, and to keep its own culture and ways of life, as history shaped them.

The conflict between East and West — more exactly, between the oceanic and continental attractions — is acute in Western Europe. It may be softened by the working out of a better balance between the population pressure, the social urge, the exploitation of resources, and the distribution of income. The heaviest densities of population are found there; still one does not experience there the feeling of *surplus* mankind that overwhelms a Western visitor in some parts of Mediterranean and Central Europe. Through a long history Western European nations succeeded in establishing at home a harmony of long standing which they strive hard nowadays to preserve.

## TODAY'S BASIC PROBLEMS

The problem of reconstruction is not merely one of rebuilding the physical facilities destroyed during World War II. Most of that task was completed by 1960. Actual destruction has not been quantitatively so important as it may have seemed in the immediate postwar period. In 1946 the industrial capacity of Western Europe was rather greater than in 1938. In France, which was one of the countries most hurt by the Nazi war effort, and where destruction by military operations was impressive, gross damage to the industrial equipment has been shown to amount only to 8.5 percent of the total. Motive power installed in industry was greater in 1946 than in 1938 by 16 percent in Norway, 23 in the Netherlands, 35 in Denmark, 38 in Sweden, and about 50 in Switzerland. Agriculture had suffered chiefly through heavy losses of livestock, resulting from a shortage of feed which lasted till 1948. The heaviest destruction was in the field of transportation, and this caused temporary paralysis of many other activities: not only had merchant shipping been depleted, but railway rolling stock was totally inadequate, as was the barge fleet, which was reduced to about one fourth of the prewar tonnage. The only seaport of importance that had not been too much affected by physical destruction was Antwerp. Four fifths of the capacity of the French ports and most of the Rotterdam harbor were out of commission. Reconstruction proceeded apace, restricted, however, by shortages in the materials needed until about 1952, and in some of the means of payment in the years following.

Reconstruction was no more a basic problem after 1957 in Western Europe. The only serious shortages still left by that time appeared due to the rapid increase in the demands of the average consumer. In many ways the period of reconstruction produced an awakening of the demand for and expectation of social progress, useful impulses in a part of the world that had been very satisfied with itself for some time. Reconstruction injected new money, new ideas, and new desires into the hearts of the people. A large city and seaport like Bordeaux complained in 1960 that it had not enjoyed any of the advantages that came in the wake of wartime destruction to such damaged cities like Le Havre, Marseille, or Boulogne. In the whole of Western Europe the pace of economic activity quickened in the 1950s. The coming of age in the 1960s of the more numerous, and probably more demanding, postwar generation still bolstered this momentum further.

One of the fields where the demand still runs ahead of the supply in most of Western Europe is housing. This is partly the result of accumulated backlog, and partly the result of urbanization, for construction has been proceeding apace. France is still the least well housed of the nations in the area (see graphs on the maps, p. 146), while Britain is better off but asks for more. In the period between the two World Wars better large-scale housing and town planning were found in Switzerland, the Netherlands, and Sweden; and as one compares housing standards of the Western European countries to what is available to their east and south (see maps, p. 146), this remains on the whole the best-housed part of the continent and of the Old World. Such general considerations cannot however erase the persistence of slums, the rapid aging of pre-1920 buildings, the insufficient provision made for the forthcoming growth. To maintain its lead, Western Europe requires vision, and to provide adequately for a future that may still be great, it needs at least self-confidence, which recently has seemed lacking.

Housing is only one item, although a basic one, in the general tableau of the needs, now openly exposed, of these nations which do not feel they belong to the "haves" any more. They realize, of course, their advantages over the "underdeveloped" parts of the world, but they prefer to compare their status to conditions in the United States. They worry about the relative slowness of Europe in mechanizing and industrializing, and about their own loss of influence and power in the world. Many people in Western Europe erroneously imagine their conditions of living inferior to those of the Russians, and they envy the rise of prestige and power of the Soviet Union since the war. Not only have Britain and France realized they have been surpassed by the two superpowers in industrial magnitude, but they also see Japan and Western Germany

A rural road in County Waterford, Ireland—a beautiful landscape with an antiquated look. *(Irish Tourist Bureau)*

forging ahead of them on this score, while Canada is nearing an equivalent rank. The Suez crisis of 1956 vividly demonstrated the inability of France and Britain, even when united, to protect by themselves their vital interests abroad. Most of the nations of Western Europe also feel diminished as their former colonial dependencies achieve independence and break away from a political system previously organized and headed by Britain, France, the Netherlands, or Belgium. By 1962 all these former colonial empires were liquidated or in process of liquidation, and what was left of them looked more like a burden than an asset for the Europeans (see maps, pp. 122, 124).

The former empires have left, however, a heritage of economic and cultural links that remain important factors in the political and commercial geography of the present world. In some ways this inheritance compels the former colonial powers to shoulder continued expenditure in the form of financial help to their former colonies; it is not only money that is at stake but also the need to provide the new nations with expert and academic staffs, and to help the marketing of some of their products that otherwise may have difficulties finding buyers. The Commonwealth is thus a costly asset to Britain, while the French Communauté and the maintenance of good relations with Algeria, Morocco, Cambodia, and Malagasy are even costlier to France. The two superpowers are now sharing with the former colonial powers the financial burden of keeping running, and where possible stimulating, the independent but underdeveloped countries of Africa and southern Asia. A new form of association is developing between Europe and America in expediting this task. For all practical purposes the *triangular trade* between Western Europe, North America, and the tropical areas around the Atlantic Ocean which flourished during the eighteenth century is reappearing again under a new guise: in the 1950s, while still keeping a trade deficit with North America, Western Europe found it easier to export on a wide scale to "third markets," that is, to Latin America, Africa, and the Asiatic countries which were then better supplied with dollar credits, and from which the United States was importing. Such a triangular exchange helped to overcome the dollar shortage. Since 1958, the aims of such triangular exchanges have shifted, and during the temporary outflow of gold from the dollar area toward the Western European central banks, new proposals have been offered.

For some of the Western European powers, and particularly for the United Kingdom, the solution of the pending economic problems could hardly be provided by less than a vast Atlantic economic community, associating the United States with Western Europe. Such a group would represent nowadays an overwhelming economic superiority and attract easily in its orbit all the nations that have not yet been politically vas-

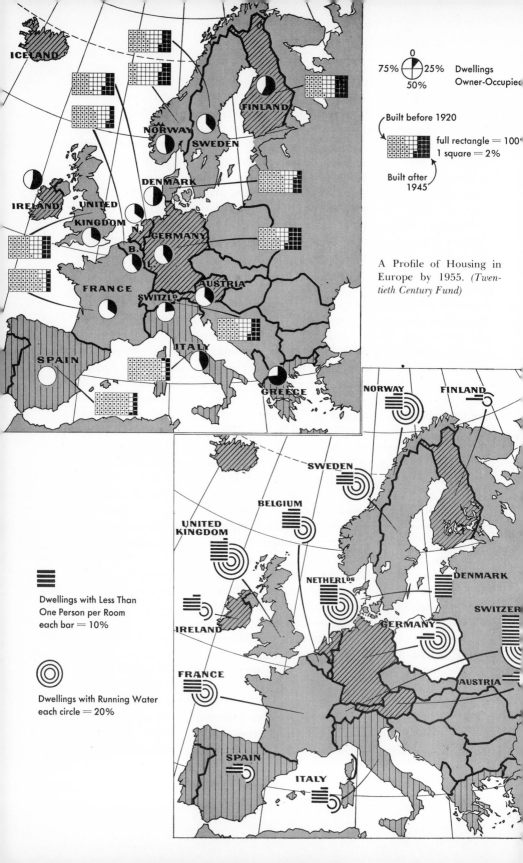

ICELAND

NORWAY

SWEDEN

FINLAND

DENMARK

IRELAND

UNITED KINGDOM

N.B.

GERMANY

AUSTRIA

FRANCE

SWITZLD

ITALY

SPAIN

GREECE

0
75% ⊕ 25%  Dwellings
50%           Owner-Occupied

Built before 1920

full rectangle = 100
1 square = 2%

Built after 1945

A Profile of Housing in Europe by 1955. *(Twentieth Century Fund)*

NORWAY

FINLAND

SWEDEN

BELGIUM

UNITED KINGDOM

NETHERLDS

DENMARK

SWITZER

GERMANY

IRELAND

AUSTRIA

FRANCE

SPAIN

ITALY

Dwellings with Less Than One Person per Room each bar = 10%

Dwellings with Running Water each circle = 20%

salized by the Communists. On the other hand, France and Belgium, more strongly rooted in the continent of Europe despite their great network of international relations, have been thinking in more narrow terms of the "European Communities," and particularly since 1958 in terms of the Common Market. The Six have progressed much faster than the Seven in the period 1958–1961, and Britain has even applied to join the Common Market. The Inner Six have let France delay the entry of Britain, which probably would be accompanied by Denmark, Norway, and Switzerland.

Despite the present political and economic difficulties between the Western European nations, their economies are gradually growing closer together and becoming more and more interwoven. Not only is there more trade between them and more movement of people either for business or pleasure, but there is also integration of transportation networks and power distributing systems. A special cable under the Channel connects the power grids of Britain and France, taking the surplus capacity of electricity produced in one country to the other in one direction at certain hours of the day and in the opposite direction at other hours, for the peak hours do not coincide. The market for oil products and natural gas is being slowly integrated under the aegis of the major international companies producing or distributing oil products throughout Western Europe. At the same time that the French government once more was blocking Britain's entry in the EEC, Franco-British talks were progressing in 1967 toward the ultimate contracts that will lay the foundation for the railroad tunnel under the Straits of Dover. Work on the tunnel is scheduled to start only in 1970, but it may be expected that during the 1970s some of the last elements of isolation and insularity left among the West European countries will fade away.

Such integration does not mean uniformization over the whole area. Each country, and many of the countries' distinctive provinces, intends to maintain its own traditions in the way of life; a few queer systems of differentiation from neighbors may be removed (thus motor traffic in Sweden shifted to the right side of the road in 1967 to conform to the general usage in Europe, and Britain is preparing to adopt a decimal monetary system for the pound sterling); more standardization of consumer goods will develop; but essential differences will remain in the ways of behaving and in the general arrangement of the local environment. More political integration on the international level may very well mean more regional differentiation based on old cultural and historical traditions. A Scottish nationalist party has suddenly appeared, claiming more autonomy; Belgium is more divided than ever on cultural and religious grounds; even in France there is talk of more regional autonomy.

An aerial view of the new center of Rotterdam, evidence of the new vitality demonstrated by postwar Europe. The city was hard-hit during World War II, but once again office buildings, factories, and apartment houses line its central arteries. Compare with the wider view of this area of Rotterdam, page 308.

While it evolves toward greater unity as a general economic and political system, Western Europe also stresses its links with the outside parts of the world with which it was traditionally associated. France and the Benelux countries have been more closely associated than ever with Italy and West Germany in the new frame of the EEC. All the countries around the North Sea have established new links or reinforced old ones with the countries of Mediterranean Europe because they imported labor from the latter area and sent to it more tourists than ever. Trade is developing with the Eastern European bloc. But basic to the present and future of Western Europe is its relationship to North America. Britain and the Netherlands have particularly close relations, economic and social, with the United States; Britain and France with Canada. The main cleavage delaying Western European integration is a certain disagreement between Britain and France as to the basic idea of the new Europe to be built: The British see it as rooted in the North Atlantic tradition and supported by a tight partnership with the United States and Canada; the French see the new Europe as a future third superpower that could be the rival of either of the present Big Two. However, everyone realizes that it is owing to the umbrella of American power protecting it, and to the relatively peaceful relations between the United States and the Soviet Union, that Western Europe has been able to achieve twenty years of internal peace and a great deal of economic expansion and social progress.

Despite the forces that seem to push and pull the countries in this area in different directions, the personality of Western Europe as a whole remains certain. Although their ways of life have been very much influenced in recent years by the American way of life, these nations feel less envy than others of the United States and they hesitate more to adopt more fully the American pattern. Their hesitation is due to a mixture of pride in their own ways, of respect for their own traditions, and of doubts as to the final value of unlimited mechanization and standardization. While they too progress on the technological paths of our time, they still preserve old ways and means, a certain stability of society, old landscapes and buildings, with a stubbornness that stems from the hope of elaborating soon their own version of this century and maintaining some continuity with their past. Western Europe has been going through a grave psychological crisis; twenty years ago it seemed to have lost confidence in itself. Then some of this confidence has been regained in the process of reconstruction, reform, and internal expansion. Since 1968, doubts and unrest have revived the crisis, especially among the young.

Stockholm, with Lake Mälar and the town hall in the background. Some almost rural aspects remain within this city. *(Swedish Information Service)*

# 5

## The Scandinavian Countries

Scandinavia begins at 54° N. latitude and extends as far as 71°. This is the latitude of Alaska, Greenland, and some of the vast barren solitudes of Siberia. But outside Europe no important economic centers have developed at such high latitudes, and in Europe the Scandinavian countries are much more populated and advanced than is the north of Russia. Although it borders on the warm Atlantic, Scandinavia is definitely not a mild or easy country in so far as climate and topography are concerned. Men have made it what it is: an important and extremely lively area of Western Europe, a great center of industry, trade, and democratic tradition. In no other part of Europe does the impact of human endeavor appear with such force. There are four countries grouped under the general label of *Scandinavia*. Their unity is one of civilization, and they have a strong personality that makes them different from their neighbors. To have succeeded as they did in their rough environment, the Scandinavian people performed a genuine miracle.

### THE SHIELD AND ITS ENVIRONMENT

A very old land, Scandinavia is part of the vast block of crystalline, Primary rocks called the *Fenno-Scandian Shield*, which extends over most of the Scandinavian peninsula (Sweden and Norway), Finland, and the Kola peninsula in the northwest of Russia. It is a nucleus of resistance in the general structure of the earth's crust, hence it has been called a "shield." To resist such pressures, the materials out of which the north-

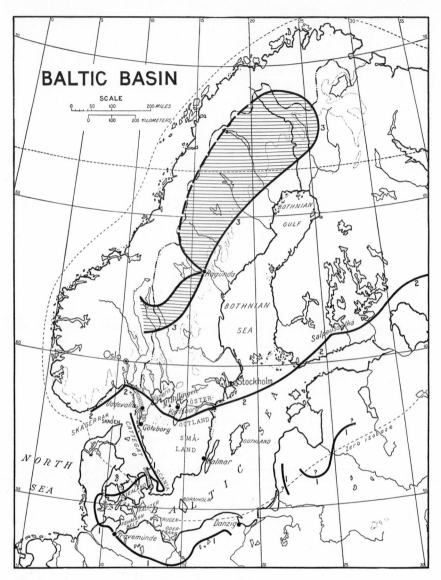

Map illustrating the late glacial and postglacial history of the Baltic Basin. The numbered lines indicate the position of the ice edge at the beginning of the (1) Gotiglacial, (2) Finiglacial, and (3) postglacial time respectively. Ice remnants in Sweden at the beginning of the postglacial epoch are shown by shading; the light broken line is the zero isobase. *(The Geographical Review)*

ern peninsula is made have to be very hard. They are surrounded with more recent and softer strata. The area we generally call Scandinavia consists of Sweden and Norway, two countries sharing the large peninsula to the north; then Denmark, made of a smaller peninsula and a group of islands, entirely in the bordering area of softer materials; and finally Iceland, an outlying large island in the ocean, reminding one of the structural connections existing between the northern lands of Eurasia and American underneath the Atlantic.

The large peninsula in the north is made of gneiss, with injections of nuclei of granitic or porphyric rocks. The porphyry often contains high-grade iron ores and also quartzite layers. Since the Primary era a number of events have occurred that added variety to the geological map; when the sea recovered all or part of the shield, layers of sedimentary rock were deposited: limestones, schists, and quartzites. During the Primary period they were taken into a powerful folding. This folding affected the western or Norwegian slope of the shield much more than the eastern or Swedish one. In Sweden, the structure is rather tabular, gently sloping eastward and southward; in Norway tectonic pressures were much greater, as the main push was westward; from the Hardanger Fjord to Lapland in the north, a range extends, in places showing badly crushed, almost vertical strata. This range provides the Scandinavian peninsula with a spine.

Since these happenings in the Primary era, the shield has remained erect, generally above the surrounding seas. Recent sedimentary deposits were laid only along its border in a few places such as Scania at the southernmost tip of the peninsula. The highlands were planed by erosion, and several cycles of erosion gave to the Scandinavian landforms the massive, tabular aspect of today. The heights erected by the Caledonian foldings, being made of softer materials on the whole than the surrounding old rocks, were the first to be erased. Today the remnants are found in depressions amid the overlooking harder mass of crystalline rock. During the tectonic movements of the Tertiary era, when the Alpine ranges were erected, the Fenno-Scandian Shield remained stable, but it was affected several times, reacting by deep faults and some tilting. The general layout of the relief and the main valleys inside the shield were already well shaped at the beginning of the Quaternary era, when the ice times set in.

The Scandinavian highlands became the main center of accumulation and outflow of the great icecap of northern Europe. Three successive glaciations have been diagnosed on the Danish peninsula, and the Scandinavian peninsula probably underwent four of them, of which the third was the most extensive. Of the last two glaciations in Scandinavia, the former has been compared to the present icecap re-covering the

Antarctic continent and the latter to the present icecap of Greenland. The third glaciation was so powerful that it erased almost all signs of the previous ones. It did most of the work still apparent in the details of the Scandinavian landscape, excavating the deep fjords and the U-shaped valleys later invaded by the sea or filled with water from the thaw of the glaciers. Innumerable depressions, rounded heights, scalloped forms of the coastline, even the relief of the bottom of the sea along the Norwegian coasts, were sculpted by the glacier. The last episode of the glaciations—the thaw—is best known through the accumulated morainic deposits that it left.

Practically all the soils of Scandinavia are of glacial or postglacial origin. Geologists and geographers have studied in all its detail the topography left by the retreating ice sheets. Famous scientists such as Gerard de Geer, H. Munthe, and Hans W:son Ahlmann analyzed the effects of glaciers and retraced their history. According to the estimates of de Geer, the melting of the icecap began in Sweden some 16,500 years ago. A first period of slow, gradual retreat, called the *Gotiglacial period*, lasted 7000 years; then the thaw stopped for some 250 years during which high morainic ramparts of an arched form were accumulated along the stabilized tip of the tongues. After this stoppage, the retreat was resumed at a quicker rate; this was the *Finiglacial period*, when the ice disappeared leaving only small-size accumulations in the wake of its speedy thaw; it lasted 1000 years. The postglacial times have now lasted some 8500 years—a brief period on the geological scale, and its brevity explains why so few changes have been made by the normal forces of erosion in the tremendous work accomplished by the glaciers.

Of that work two lines of morainic hills marking two stages in the retreat of the last glaciation are of utmost importance; according to de Geer, they mark the extent of the ice sheet at the beginning and at the end of the Gotiglacial period. The biggest and oldest line circles around the Baltic, along the eastern and southern shores of this sea. It has certainly influenced the shape of the sea and constitutes the main line of heights through the flat Great Plain of Europe. The second, more recent line of morainic heights encloses to the south the largest lakes of Sweden: the Vätter and Vänern. While the icecap was retreating, seas or lakes of varied shapes and levels formed on the liberated areas. The thaw of the immense mass of ice sent to the seas such quantities of water that the average sea level rose, covering a large section of the Fenno-Scandian Shield; then the whole mass of the Scandinavian peninsula began to rise through the film of water covering it. This steady uplifting of the land mass has been explained as a normal balancing move of a section in the earth's crust relieved from the enormous weight of the icecap that had been pressing it down. This uplifting still goes on, and in the last centuries the advances of shoreline into the sea have caused the displacement of several ports on the coast of Sweden.

Local accidents deepened certain valleys or raised depressed parts, reshaping some details of the topography left by the icecap. The land continuity between Sweden and the Danish peninsula of Jutland was broken, and the Danish straits linked the Baltic and North Seas, leading each year a tongue of warmer saline waters from the Atlantic into the continental sea. During the whole period of advance and retreat of the ice, the climate was changing—the glaciations could not be accounted for otherwise. The last noticeable change seems to have occurred around 500 B.C. when the present climate, humid and rather rough, set in. Although the uplifting of the land goes on slowly, there is a rise in the average level of the lakes; more springs flow with abundance; marshes show trends to expand. Archeologists noted that the Iron Age (500 B.C. to A.D. 100) left fewer and poorer traces than the preceding Bronze Age (1800 to 500 B.C.). This last change in climate may have caused a migration southward of the local Germanic tribes in the beginning of the Christian Era. It has not, however, prevented the Scandinavian peoples from doing nicely in climatic conditions that may be less pleasant than those of the Bronze Age.

The glaciers left a striking contrast in Scandinavia between the interior, thoroughly planed and converted to rugged tabular highlands generally called *fjeld*, and the coastal areas, with deep and wide valleys between steep slopes, the *fjord*. The work was much more thorough and the digging deeper on the Norwegian side than on the Swedish side, with steeper slopes than in Preglacial times. The landscape on the Swedish peneplain is a rather confused one: an irregular network of ups and downs, some small U-shaped valleys filled with water, called *fjaerdar*, and a few isolated hills, flattened at their top, remnants of older high platforms, often highly mineralized. Amid the lower lands the moraines have left an irregular network of lines of sand and gravel accumulation, called *ösar*, which look like natural dikes in damp areas. They provided the first settlers with natural lanes or bridges and fixed the sites of many towns or roads. Postglacial lakes or bays of the sea deposited beaches of sandy-clayish soils which are among the most fertile in central Sweden. To the south, on more recent strata, the soils are better and the climate warmer.

Scandinavia is a damp country. Water flows everywhere or rests in limpid lakes. Two thousand square miles, a larger area than on the Alps, are still occupied by glaciers the majority of which are on the Norwegian highlands. The hydrography of running waters still bears the imprint of the Ice Age. The drainage is undecided; divides between the river basins are often unprecise; rivers divide themselves in several

The deserted, icy yet scenic landscape of Svalbard, a Norwegian archipelago in the Arctic.

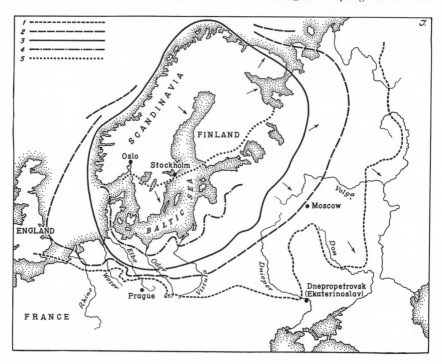

The extent of the Scandinavian ice sheet. Key: 1, end moraine; 2 and 3, recessional phases; 4, Baltic phase; 5, Finiglacial phase. (After Raoul Blanchard and Raymond E. Crist, *A Geography of Europe*)

arms; interconnections through lakes are common, and it is sometimes difficult to guess whether a water area is a section of a river's course or just a lake. The total area of the lakes is estimated at 15,000 square miles in Sweden and about 5000 in Norway. The fjords give an impressive appearance to the lower course of short streams, and waterfalls and rapids are frequent. This topography is similar to that of eastern Canada, where the Laurentian Shield also was once covered with a great ice sheet.

The largest rivers in Scandinavia are in the northern half of the peninsula on the Swedish side. Their flow is determined by the spring thaw of the snow, floods coming after May, in late spring and summer, winter being the season of low waters. South of 59° N. latitude, rivers are smaller in size and less abundantly fed; their high waters come in winter and early spring, the summer heat increasing the evaporation of land and plants and diminishing the run-off. The streams play a most important part in the Scandinavian economy. Though cut by rapids, most of them are navigable and served as the normal network of transportation before the railroads began to wind along the valleys. Today timber is still floated downstream to the industrial plants of seaports. The energy of the waterfalls helped the spread of industries. The water is limpid, having been filtered by several lakes, and carries little silt as the rocks are usually hard and crystalline. The blue mirrors of the lakes and the white splendor of the waterfalls add a beautiful touch to the delicate scenery endowed with some grandiose sites that are the results of sculpturing by the glaciers.

Visitors always admire the quality of light in Scandinavia, where the latitude creates very special conditions. On June 21 along the 60°, which is the latitude of Uppsala, Oslo, and Bergen, daytime lasts 18 hours and 49 minutes, but on December 22, only 5 hours and 42 minutes. In the north of the peninsula and in Iceland the sun does not set for a period of days during June, and darkness prevails without interruption in December. All of Scandinavia knows some dark days in the winter and some "white nights" in summertime, and in June cruises are organized along the Norwegian coast to admire the fjords under the "midnight sun." The Scandinavians have a deep love of sunlight and utterly dislike the dark days of early winter. The urban planning of a city such as Bergen takes into careful consideration the duration of the sunlight in every section of the city's area. The most restless labor organizations of Sweden are those in the Far North, beyond the Arctic circle, which stress, among other claims, their obligation to work in the dark for weeks in wintertime.

The climate on the whole is exceedingly warm for the latitude; Scandinavia shows the greatest positive anomaly in the distribution of temperatures on our globe. Proximity to the pole reduces the length of the intermediate seasons: in Stockholm, winter lasts 121 days, spring 57,

(Above) Herring is a staple food of Scandinavia, and herring fishing is one of the oldest industries. *(Swedish Information Service) (Below)* The codfishing fleet off the Lofoten Islands of northern Norway. *(Norwegian Information Service)*

summer 124, and autumn 63; in Lapland, winter lasts more than 200 days, in Copenhagen, no more than 75. The lengthy and severe cold season is a major problem in Scandinavia—for agriculture, for transportation, and for the general morale of the people. The cold season, however, varies greatly from year to year, as the country is situated almost directly in between the two determining centers of influence: the moderating warm Atlantic and the extreme continental mass of Eurasia.

The maritime influence predominates all over Scandinavia, making it indeed part of Western Europe. It reigns over Iceland, Norway, and Denmark almost all the year round, and is strongly felt everywhere in Sweden, although the latter looks eastward toward the Baltic Sea and a continent frozen in winter. The weather in the cold season is determined by the struggle between the cold polar air masses diverging from the Siberian anticyclone and the warm maritime air of the Atlantic flowing in behind cyclonic depressions that progress eastward. The Baltic Sea, though shallow and small, plays an important part in delaying the winter colds, prolonging the fall and attracting the cyclones. There still is a clearcut contrast between the east and west coasts of each of the two peninsulas, particularly between Sweden and Norway. In the north of Sweden, on the Baltic coast, Haparanda has an average yearly temperature of 32.5°, with 10.6° in February, the coldest month. Copenhagen, in a maritime position in the south, records 45.9° as yearly average, 31.8° for February and 61.9° in July. All of Scandinavia is well watered, especially for an area where the period of active evaporation is short. The mountainous Atlantic coastland of Norway gets the maximum rainfall, over 80 inches per year, while in most of Denmark and Sweden average is around 25 inches. Only in northern Sweden is the film of rain below 16 inches—it drops to 12 inches at Abisko in Swedish Lapland—but most of the winter precipitations fall in the form of snow which is preserved until the summer, therefore insuring a decent supply of humidity to vegetation during the period of growth.

The Scandinavian countries were destined by nature to be wooded, with the exception perhaps of Iceland. Deep forests occupied the two peninsulas, and men had a big job to clear them. Forests are still typical of the Swedish and Norwegian landscapes, with a predominance of coniferous species, particularly the spruce. There is, of course, a zoning with the latitude which is repeated in altitude. The Far North has vast barren areas, with a meager brush of tundralike character; farther south trees appear and assemble: first the birch, then the spruce and the pine. In the south of Sweden and in Denmark broad-leaved trees appear, mingling with the conifers, particularly the oak, maple, linden, and hazel. In recent centuries the spruce, particularly the picea kind (*Picea obovata*), seems to have pushed triumphantly southward, replacing the pine and the oak. The pine largely replaced the oak and maple in the south, while the birch was mingling with the spruce in the Norrland. These migrations of the species southward have been linked to a greater dampness and perhaps a warming up in the climate. All over the Arctic, recent observations point to a warming up of climatic conditions and to a new retreat of the existing glaciers until about 1950; in most recent years, a new offensive of the cold seems to have set in. Such changes may seriously influence natural conditions. Human influence may have had its part in bringing about changes in the vegetation—for instance, the oak occupied the best soils in southern Sweden, but those were the most thoroughly cleared and cultivated. The Scandinavians feel that they live on a fringe, on a frontier of nature; they see their soil rising, their glaciers receding, their trees migrating, and, quite understandably, they tend to explain much of what happens to them by relating it to shifts in natural conditions. They have behind them, however, a history somewhat shorter, but no less brilliant, than that of other parts of Europe.

## THE SCANDINAVIAN "MIRACLE"

Historians of antiquity used to tell about the Greek "miracle," how a handful of men on a rugged peninsula in the midst of the Mediterranean developed suddenly a civilization that taught a great deal to the whole of mankind and in some respects has never been surpassed. Geographers could well speak in a similar way of the Scandinavian "miracle," how small numbers of men have established under difficult physical conditions one of the zones of more advanced civilization.

The history of Scandinavia begins late, much more recently than that of the Mediterranean countries. About 8000 B.C. some dense populations had already occupied the eastern fjords of Denmark; their main occupations were fishing and some hunting. Around 3000 B.C. settlement had spread to the whole periphery of the Scandinavian peninsula, and agriculture had started; the Danish Neolithic period was an active one. To the south of the Limfjord, an important center of worship, meeting of peoples, and marketing, there existed a hub of trade in the vicinity of the present town of Viborg. Great development occurred in the interior of Denmark and in Scania during the Bronze Age; forests were cleared, and animal husbandry was conducted parallel with the extension of agriculture to heavy, clayish soils. The push inland in Denmark may have resulted from the development of Norse piracy on the sea. In Sweden a strong agricultural belt developed northward along the coastal areas up to the Dal älv valley. Wheat, barley, and millet were grown on the plain, which was expanded with the rise of the land and the retreat of the water's edge; cattle and sheep were raised, and the horse had been introduced; copper was utilized, and the Bronze Age was one of expansion. With the Iron Age it seems that harder climatic conditions stopped the progress inland, and the peoples of Scandinavia began to look for better lands overseas. The maritime vocation became an early urge, and ties began to link the countries bordering on the Baltic and North seas. In the second century of the Christian Era the island of Gotland assumed the role of a great center of trade and communication in the middle of the Baltic.

In the first centuries of this era Tacitus and Ptolemaeus mentioned the peoples of the Goths and of the Sveas. In that period the Scandinavian countries were populated by a mixture of races among which the long-headed, tall, blond type predominated. All spoke one language, yet out of that ethnic unity came three nations with slightly different languages, the differentiation occurring during the Middle Ages. The Danes, more advanced, had the first great political expansion and attempted to unite under their authority all the Scandinavian peoples. But they did not succeed for long. A move toward national unity in Norway had sent a number of Norse tribes on an emigration by sea. Paris still keeps a memory of horror of the attacks by Norsemen who ransacked the city in the ninth century and established themselves on the lower course of the Seine—the French province of Normandy. While the Danes too were on the move, the Swedes were united under the kings of the Sveas in the fifth century; soon afterward they colonized the eastern shores of the Baltic, and Swedish settlers, known as *Russ*, founded the town of Novgorod and began to trade across the continent with the Black Sea. Later, in the seventeenth century, the Swedish empire encircled the whole of the Baltic but thereafter retreated steadily under the pressure of Russian expansion. Still, the reigning dynasty of Russia was descended from Rurik, a Swede.

Only in recent times have the Scandinavian countries given up imperial dreams and engaged in peaceful pursuits, in which their contribution has been surprisingly great and varied for so small a group of people (14.2 million in the four countries). In the cultural field they may claim one of the richest literatures of Western civilization in the last century: the works of Hans Christian Andersen, Henrik Ibsen, Soren Kierkegaard, Georg Brandes, Selma Lagerlöf, Sigrid Undset, and August Strindberg have become international classics. Andersen's fairy tales about the little mermaid and others have left their imprint on the youthful imagination of generations of children in Europe and elsewhere; Ibsen may have been one of the greatest playwrights of all times. In the field of science the Swede Linne (or Linnaeus) classified the known plants and laid the foundation of modern botanical studies; more recently Niels Bohr of Denmark made one of the greatest contributions

The Kramfors sawmill on the Angerman älv. Timber has been collected and worked here at the meeting of river and maritime navigation since 1740. *(Swedish Information Service)*

Harnessing waterpower in Norway. *(Norwegian Information Service)*

of the twentieth century to theoretical physics with his quantum theory, and Vilhelm Bjerknes of Norway brought about significant changes in our understanding of climatology. The early exploration of polar regions could be written mostly in terms of such Scandinavian names as Otto Nordenskjold, Fritjof Nansen, and Roald Amundsen, who first reached the South Pole. Gerard de Geer founded modern glacial geology, and the chronology of prehistoric periods is based on his calculations. Sven Hedin explored the Central Asiatic highlands. Many scientific treatises and textbooks that are known the world over were written by Scandinavians.

The contribution was not less in the field of technical invention and industrial development: the marine Diesel engine came from Denmark; safety matches, dynamite, ball bearings, kerosene stoves, refrigerators, and steam turbines were first developed in Sweden. These inventions, and the knowledge they indicate, generated exports: "brains" brought a great deal of money when exported in the form of patents and licences and helped the establishment of industrial enterprises throughout the world which bear the names of SKF, Delaval, Ericsson, or "Swedish matches." It is natural that Sweden, with some cooperation from Norway, awards the famous Nobel prizes, considered the highest existing distinction for scientific achievements, literature, and service to peace. In the cultural work performed in Scandinavia one is struck by the efforts to apply all new discoveries to practical pursuits. This is apparent in their talent for industrial organization and even more in the rapidity with which social progress advanced in these countries, making their social studies and their social security system, as well as the organization of their labor unions, models for the Western world. Scandinavians in the twentieth century played a part in world affairs all out of proportion to the number of the population, the size of the land, and the wealth of their economy. Indeed a Scandinavian "miracle" is more apparent today than in older times when Norsemen invaded France or Swedish armies ruled Germany.

A remarkable feature of Scandinavian culture has been its ability to develop in a rather narrow frame, in not-too-comfortable physical conditions, and to profit by contacts with the outside, assimilating foreign ideas and methods but applying them in their own special way. Roman influence was felt, but rather late, and left no clear imprint or problem. The region was Christianized late, too. Scandinavia was converted to Catholicism from the tenth to twelfth centuries, but accepted the tenets of the Reformation unanimously and more readily than any other part of Europe. The Reformed Lutheran Church is the state church in all four countries. There is a unified Scandinavian culture, but it has been differentiated by history, and the differences were aided by geography:

Iceland is an island; Denmark is a group of insular and peninsular lands at the gate of the Baltic; Sweden and Norway are the two opposed slopes of a peninsula screening the Baltic from the Atlantic.

The maritime influence is thus predominant over the Scandinavian world. Since the time of the old civilization of fishermen near the fjords of Denmark, the sea has always played a part in the regional life, a determining part perhaps, as the originality of every country may be traced to a certain relationship with one of the surrounding seas. Three nations (Iceland being a very small one) have important merchant marines, with a total tonnage of 23.7 million afloat in 1966, but each nation gives a different emphasis to maritime activities in its national life.

By its geology and structure, by the ethnic unity of the population, by its remarkable growth on the fringe of the Arctic, Scandinavia is an area of its own, but by its present economy, social structure, and culture it is part of Western Europe.

## SWEDEN

Sweden is the largest Scandinavian power—in area, in population, and in economic development. It is also the most continental or at least the most Baltic. Although it borders on the Danish straits and on the Skagerrak, a bay of the North Sea, Sweden has been generally oriented by its topography toward its wide façade on the Baltic. For long centuries it endeavored to follow this natural inclination. The Swedish nation seems to have been born out of the union, achieved by military force about A.D. 400, of the Goths and the Sveas under the authoritarian rule of the king of the Sveas, whose capital was Uppsala in the Uppland. The Goths lived in the south of the peninsula, and in the regional life of the country a division and some rivalry are still very much alive between the southern and the central areas. But this union laid the foundation for an expansion eastward. Finland was colonized in the ninth to the fourteenth centuries. At the end of this period, Stockholm was the great capital of the Gulf of Bothnia, and it was called a "Northern Venice," not only because ships passed through the very heart of the city built on several islands, but also because it was a great center of trade. In the 1520s King Gustaf Vasa defeated the Danes who had tried to bring all of Scandinavia under their supremacy. In the seventeenth century came the period of greatness, the *Storhetstid*, when the Swedes controlled all the areas at the mouths of the main streams emptying into the Baltic and when the foundation of the port and city of Göteborg on the Skagerrak shore marked a drive toward the Atlantic.

Then began a retreat on the continent, a retreat chiefly before the advances of Russia but also an evacuation of Germany because of the rise of

Prussia. In 1809 Finland, the oldest overseas dependency, was lost to Russia; in the nineteenth century also the center of Swedish interest migrated toward the southwest, following the developing participation in the maritime international economy. Still Sweden could not forget its continental ties. But instead of Baltic horizons, the Swedes turned toward fuller development of their national territory, and an actual rush was started northward that still is in progress. In the Norrland, Sweden has what may be considered the last frontier and pioneer fringe in the west of the old continent of Europe, and this newly settled area begins less than 100 miles from Uppsala. Such a proximity of old and young areas in Sweden adds to the regional contrasts and to the general dynamism of the country.

Stretched on thirteen degrees of latitude (from 55° N. lat. to 68°), Sweden should be divided in regions from north to south: there is the vast Norrland; then central Sweden, the country of the great lakes; and finally southern Sweden, of which Scania in the very tip is the main section.

The *Norrland* covers some 100,000 square miles, more than one half of the total area of Sweden. The lower valley of the Dal älv is considered its southern limit. As a Swedish saying puts it: "Above it there are no more oaks, crayfish, or nobles." Most of it is covered with an immense forest where pine and spruce mix with birch. It is a splendid country to cross in the early autumn, when the sun is still bright in a clear sky above a colorful combination of the deep green of spruce dotted with the golden leaves and silvery stems of birch trees, while a brown carpet of dead needles and leaves covers the soil. The silent solitude of the woods is often interrupted by the murmur of wide blue streams and lakes. The Norrland has several large rivers or *älv*, and the Angerman, the Lule älv, the Indals älv, and the Dal älv carry abundant waters through stairways of rapids from the mountains along the Norwegian border to the Gulf of Bothnia. Timber is floated down the streams, and hydroelectric plants harness the power developed in the falls. The Norrland is credited with 80 percent of the total potential waterpower of Sweden, much of which is still to be utilized. But towns have been established at the mouth of every important river, and the valleys serve as roads of penetration inland.

Settlement of the coastal plain was well advanced by the fourteenth century, and a number of towns were built around 1600. The string of ports at the mouth of the rivers begins with Haparanda on the Finnish border; then southward come Lulea, Pitea, Skellefte, Umea, Hernösand, Sundsvall, and Söderhamn. The uplifting of the land has carried the old cities inland, and new seaports have had to be built several miles farther downstream. The old road crossed the peninsula from Sundsvall into

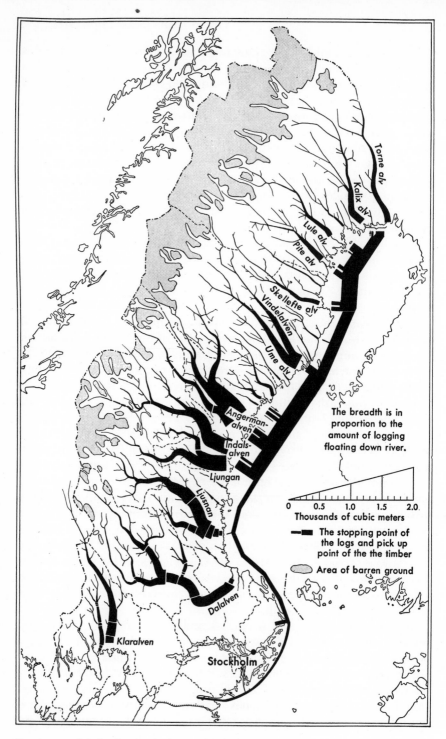

The breadth is in proportion to the amount of logging floating down river.

0   0.5   1.0   1.5   2.0
Thousands of cubic meters

■━■ The stopping point of the logs and pick up point of the the timber

Area of barren ground

Torne alv
Kalix alv
Lule alv
Pite alv
Skellefte alv
Vindelalven
Ume alv
Angerman-alven
Indals-alven
Ljungan
Ljusnan
Dalalven
Klaralven
Stockholm

Sketch map of timber logging in the Norrland, showing the floating of logs down the rivers and along the coast. (After O. Hedblom and I. Winberg, 1935)

Norway, across the high fjeld of the central range, because of the early development around Öestersund, in a piedmont position in the interior of the Jemtland. This region was favored by a wide outcropping of schist, sandstone, and limestone, providing better soils and drier bottoms in a place where a lowering of the Norwegian crests opened more to Atlantic air masses. The Jemtland, a favored oasis with beautiful, calm lakes and active agriculture in the midst of damp woods and barren, frozen fjeld, also helped some penetration inside the Norrland. But with this exception and the coastal plain settlements, the Norrland remained asleep and empty until the 1850s. Then it was "discovered" as the great reserve of Sweden, and people talked about its "unlimited possibilities" almost as Americans did about their West.

At first the frontier penetrated inland and northward to obtain more timber, and large industries were built to use wood for timber, pulp, and charcoal. Sundsvall became a center of important chemical industries, while lumbering populated the Norrland and went farther. The harnessing of the waterfalls, by the dam at Porjus and many others, provided the area with cheap and abundant energy. A railroad began to wind northward and in 1887 reached Gällivare and Lulea, opening the way for the development of the iron ores of the Norrbotten, the Swedish Lapland.

The Norrbotten is subarctic land; a large part of it is high fjeld with little vegetation, only tundra and clusters of stunted birch trees. Here a scanty population of Lapps raise reindeers on poor pastures. But several hills, rising over the gently sloping plain, bear rich deposits of high-grade iron ore (60 to 70 percent). Their use, however, was held up by their phosphorus content until about 1880, when adequate techniques were developed. Then the rail linked Galliväre with the port of Lulea on the Baltic, proceeded to the richer deposit of Kiruna, and linked both of them, over the mountains, to the Norwegian port of Narvik on the Atlantic, icefree all the year round. The strategic importance of these ores for European industries was illustrated by the Allied expedition against Narvik in 1940, which attempted to cut off access to the iron for the Germans (who then occupied most of Norway) during the winter months, when Lulea was icebound. Now several million tons of these ores are exported yearly to European and American furnaces, and Sweden has built iron and steel works at Lulea under government management. Industrialization in these parts spurred on some agricultural production, and today strawberries, potatoes, and other vegetables are produced during the brief summer, when daytime is long and growth therefore accelerated.

In the heart of the Norrbotten is Kiruna, the main iron-ore town. It is an unusual place for Europe, for it is a center of pioneering and a boom

Norra Fjällnäs, a village in southern Swedish Lapland. *(Swedish Information Service)*

Open-pit iron-ore mining at Kiruna. *(Swedish Information Service)*

town, yet when the twentieth century began, only Lapp tents and herds of reindeer were to be found. Today a brand new town climbs a slope facing two oddly shaped hills, Kiirunavaara and Luossavaara, heights that look like artificial mounds so flattened are their tops and so gigantic the staircases of regular terraces which replace the slopes on the sides. Through the middle of each of these two hills has been dug an enormous trench, which, starting from top, is steadily deepening as dynamite blows up and heavily mechanized equipment excavates out the rich iron ore deposited in a thick, almost vertical layer. And the work goes on day and night, everything being floodlighted at night and during the dark winter period. From the beginning of October until April, the cold is severe and sharp winds often blow, but the cars filled with ore keep rolling out of the bottom of the two hills and, in long trains, proceed to the seashore — to Narvik on the Atlantic or to Lulea on the Baltic. Gällivare, with its older iron hill of Malmberget, is on that same railway, as is the town of Boden, a military center and the headquarters of the defense of the Swedish northern frontiers.

Around Kiruna (30,000 people) the Lapps retain their seminomadism. In the streets and shops of the modern town, where money is abundant one sees daily a few Lapps in their traditional, picturesque clothes, doing errands and shopping. The church of Kiruna has been built to resemble a grandiose Lapp's tent, so that the natives, recently Christianized, will feel more at home. The contact of the two civilizations, one rather primitive and the other ultramodern, apparently has worked well; the country gives a definite impression of prosperity. This situation may well continue, because the iron resources are considerable, and at the present rate extraction can continue until about 1970 before the bottom of the hills is reached and the digging of pits underground is necessitated. The total reserves of iron ore of the Norrbotten are estimated at about 2 billion tons.

The Norrland has other ores than iron: copper has been mined near Gällivare, and south of the Lapland is a diversified and major mining development (copper, arsenic, gold, and silver) in the field along the Skellefte älv, the main center of which is Boliden. The abundance of waterfalls opens wide possibilities for the erection of electrometallurgical and electrochemical industries. Ore mining and lumbering are now the two great local resources of the newly developed Norrland. There still is little agriculture, although the farms are always well equipped and maintained. The Norrland imports its food and ships out many millions of tons of bulky materials annually. Lulea, the Norrbotten's capital, has a steel mill and strives to increase its population of 35,000 and the size of its harbor. The whole province accounts for 260,000; important urban and industrial centers are farther south: Sundsvall, one of the capitals of timber and pulp, was the first city of more than 25,000 (60,000 in 1966).

One has to reach the mouth of the Dal älv to encounter an old urban center of some importance. Such is Gävle (60,000) at the point of contact between the Norrland and *central Sweden*. By its age, its size, and the variety of its industries, Gävle belongs to central Sweden. Southward the landscape changes slowly: a gradual transition brings in a greater diversity of trees, more clearings in the forest cover, and wider areas under active cultivation. The main contrast is still in the intensity and variety of human activities and in the established aspect of the towns. Lakes and fast-flowing rivers with rapids are many. The soils are somewhat different; the subsoil is more varied, a number of tectonic depressions (with a few *horsts* between them) and lines of morainic accumulations helping to increase the variety. Woods have been better preserved on poor rocky or sandy soils; the areas with better soils (clays and loams) are well tilled, and the warmer climate permits some wheat to be grown with other grain and fodder crops. Cattle is one of the basic resources—a few centuries ago parts of this region used to be taxed in heads of cattle.

Much more special to central Sweden than the type of rural economy is the thick network of industrial towns that covers it, for here some association between tillage, livestock raising, and manufacturing pursuits is very ancient. Today it is the urban and industrial aspects that predominate. The old traditions have led toward a production of high-quality goods, involving a great deal of skill and labor—it is largely to the products of this area that the Swedish industries owe their prestige on the world markets for high-grade finished articles.

Again timber and iron are at the foundation of these industries, and they have been used for a long time. These areas are the heart of the land of the Svea. Uppsala, their old capital, built anew after a fire in the beginning of the eighteenth century, had a remarkable network of roads radiating from it in all directions as early as the fifth century. Today it is a center of university studies and research, with a few industries (milling, bicycles), a regional market, and 95,000 inhabitants. In the middle of this zone of contact between the old lands and the Norrland is situated the keystone of Swedish industrial tradition, the region known as the *bergslagen*. This name was coined in the Middle Ages to describe a kind of miners' organization chartered by the king, endowed with some autonomy and privileges, and owning the mines together with some forests and lands. Each *bergslag* constituted an almost self-sufficient economic group, with peasants farming the land and supplying the food, while miners and craftsmen worked the iron and maintained a system of transportation inside their territory. In the seventeenth century there were fifteen *bergslagen*, most of them directly north of Uppsala. Later this form of

economy developed and moved westward, and now the whole area of
scattered industrial centers north of the great lakes is commonly called
by the name of the organization that started the development and gave
its special physiognomy to the region.

The old but varied rocks of the subsoil provide a diversity of high-
grade ores: iron and manganese, copper, zinc and lead, some gold and
silver. Waterfalls and a deep forest of pines and spruces provide power.
In and around the bergslagen, towns like Falun, Sala, Grangesberg,
Sadviken, Domnarvet, and many others have built up a string of plants
working metals or wood. Metallurgy is predominant in the central and
eastern sections, and Sandviken is famous all over the world for some of
the best steels ever made. Part of the iron is still smelted with charcoal;
some of the ores extracted at Grangesberg reach 80 percent of iron content. Westward, wood and pulp gain and the metallic industries weaken.
One must reach the banks of the great Swedish lakes in the south of the
bergslagen area to find larger towns with a variety of industries (mostly
finishing), most of which have long been related to the woods and metals
of the area to the north. One should not underestimate the importance
of the bergslagen organizations as a training in social solidarity and as a
preparation for the democratic system that Sweden has so rapidly and
peacefully applied to its government.

This interesting region reaches to the northern banks of the three
great lakes of Sweden. Lake Mälar is a long fjord oriented eastwest,
with a ramified contour, communicating with the Baltic through a narrow
bottleneck, on which Stockholm is established; Lake Vätter, farther
south, is an elongated fracture oriented north-south; Lake Vänern, to
the west, is practically a small inland sea. These three lakes have a total
area of about 3500 square miles. Their limit is clearly indicated in the
south by the alignment of morainic heights accumulated by the icecap
at the beginning of the Finiglacial period. North of this limit the relatively
flat, only gently rolling plains of central Sweden are partitioned by the
morainic dams of the *ösars*. Along these natural dikes highways wind and
strings of towns are laid out. Many rivers or water channels link the lakes;
a famous internal route of navigation called the Göta Canal winds across
central Sweden from Göteborg on the west coast to Norrköping on the
east shore. The same checkerboard of fields on good soils and woods on
poorer ones continues, but here better soils cover more land in the areas
where marine deposits have been preserved. Here too the growth of
industries has eclipsed rural pursuits. Some towns that were important
in a less industrial era are now small and sleepy, such as Strangnas, just
a local rural center. Others following manufacturing pursuits have had
a rapid rise.

Around Lake Mälar, Köping has mechanical plants. Västeras (110,000

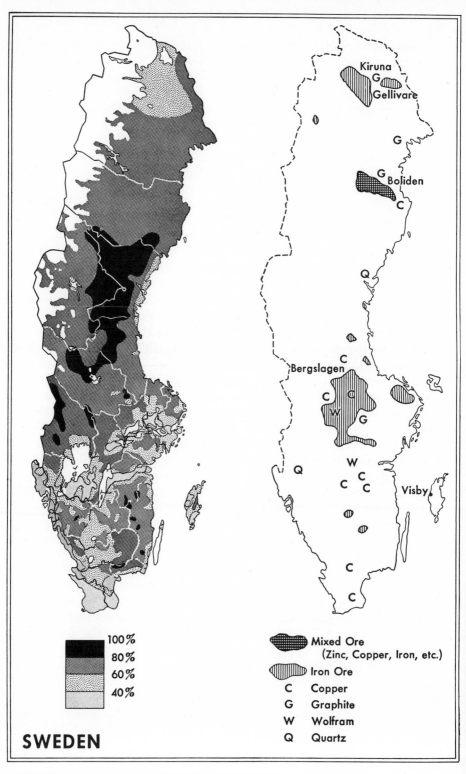

| | |
|---|---|
| 100% | |
| 80% | |
| 60% | |
| 40% | |

**SWEDEN**

| | |
|---|---|
| Mixed Ore (Zinc, Copper, Iron, etc.) | |
| Iron Ore | |
| C | Copper |
| G | Graphite |
| W | Wolfram |
| Q | Quartz |

Kiruna
G
Gellivare
G
G
Boliden
C
G
Q
C
Bergslagen
C
G
G
C
W
G
W
C
C
Q
C
Visby

Forested area (in percentage of the total area) and main mineral deposits. (*Sverige Industri*, 1948) inhabitants) leads the field of electrical engineering, with the ASEA corporation (Allmänna Svensha Electriska AB.) making turbines, engines, locomotives, tramways, transformers, and many articles of nonferrous materials. And in Eskilstuna (60,000), the arsenal of Sweden since 1654, the iron work has been concentrated, disputing Sheffield and Solingen for supremacy in high-grade cutlery on the international market. Actually the modern arsenal today is the small town of Bofors, situated farther inland in the midst of a large patch of woods, where a large corporation manufactures precision guns and ammunition, mainly for antiaircraft and antitank use. Bofors guns of world-wide fame played an important part in World War II, and several other countries manufacture them under licences from the Bofors Corporation. Near the small town of Bofors, development begun around 1911 has led to the creation of the new urban center of Karlskoga (38,000). Houses and cottages spread out over a vast area from a central square, on which stand the town hall and the hotel, some of the most modern structures of Scandinavia and a monument of gratitude to the Bofors Corporation.

More ancient and no less thriving are the cities among which Karlskoga rises. At the western extremity of Lake Hjelmar, on a large *ösar*, stands Örebro (82,000), one of the centers of paper making, with large shoe factories also and the main repair shops of the Swedish railroads. Then to the west, on the northern shore of Lake Vänern, Kristinehamn (22,000) builds turbines, and Karlstad (52,000) makes the equipment for pulp and paper plants and works the wood floated down to its port on the lake. Another east-wing string of cities crosses the great lakes area farther south. Some of them like Linköping (77,000) and Vadstena were important religious centers before the Reformation; others like Motala on Lake Vätter kept some importance as ports on the Göta Canal system. The only city in this area, Norrköping (94,000) is located on a deep fjord of the Baltic; it is the chief textile town of Sweden, producing woolens, cotton, and linen; it also has paper mills.

Although they increased their population by 25 to 50 percent in the period of 1930–1945, these cities are slowed down in their development because all of central Sweden is now overshadowed by *Stockholm*. The capital of Sweden rose at the entrance of Lake Mälar in 1272 as a fortress protecting the interior from attacks by the Baltic pirates. The old city with its royal palace was built on the island of Staden, in the midst of the Norrstrom, a channel of communication between the Baltic and Lake Mälar. The flow of the Norrström is irregular, for it depends on the water supply pouring into the lake from the surrounding lands. During the spring thaw high waters flowing toward the sea can sometimes flood the center of the city; after a drought, the level of the lake sinks, and the Norrström may reverse its course to fill up with Baltic waters.

The long shadows of autumn across a typical rural scene in central Sweden. *(Swedish In-formation Service)*

Norrköping, the main textile center of Sweden. *(Swedish Information Service)*

Icebreakers now keep the port open all year round, but with the decrease in importance of the Baltic trade, Stockholm is not the active seaport that it was. The population of the city has risen rapidly from 16,000 in 1635, to 93,000 in 1850, to 300,000 in 1900, and to 808,000 in 1960. Recently large suburbs have spread out, some with numerous high, modern buildings, others with scattered, comfortable cottages with small gardens. It is an elegant city, with beautiful monuments reminding one of its great history and the stages of its development. An intense traffic roars down the too-narrow streets of the business section. Few European capitals give the same feeling of concentrated and relentless effort, of prosperity and efficiency, in a frame of natural and manmade beauty.

Until 1850 Stockholm was the great export center of Sweden. The kings favored it by granting to it the privilege of concentrating most of the trade coming from the bergslagen and the Norrland. And Stockholm merited the name of "Venice of the North" not only because of the deep penetration of water channels and sea navigation inside the built-up area, but equally because of the role it played in the Baltic area as the commercial metropolis. Although the main port functions have moved to Göteborg, Stockholm remains a thriving city, concentrating the political and financial direction of the country, increasing its cultural and academic function, developing a suburban industrial belt where a number of factories produce finished complicated goods (telephone equipment, moving pictures, kerosene stoves, electrical machinery and appliances, cream separators). The trend in the administration of public affairs in Sweden is rather toward centralization, and the capital takes full advantage of it. Now, since the close of World War II, it gives an impression of "booming" development; its destiny will be a symbol of that of the whole country. The metropolitan region of Stockholm encompassed at least 1,300,000 by 1966; the capital was surrounded with a constellation of satellite cities such as Djursholm, Lidingö, Nacka, Solna, Sundbyberg, and Vaxholm, entirely dependent on the central city for all their economic activities, but completely separate administrative units for government purposes. Some recently built suburbs, such as Vällingby, have been carefully planned with a garden-city idea in mind, although they include large blocks of high-rise apartment buildings. An electric railway system links the suburbs to the city, which is being largely redeveloped, to make it soon the most modern of the old capitals of Europe. Besides these densely occupied towns, a "summer Stockholm" subsists of small summer cottages scattered along many lakes within commuting distance from the city. Two thirds of the Swedish population live now in cities and suburban zones; metropolitan Stockholm alone makes up one sixth of the nation.

Vällingby, a carefully planned residential suburb of Stockholm, is designed for commuters. It alternates wooden-frame high-rise towers with smaller apartment buildings. Residents commute by rail, either walking to the station or driving and using the parking lot provided there. *(Swedish Information Service)*

The large steel mill and new town of Mo-i-Rana was developed in the 1950s in the Norwegian Nordland. *(Norwegian Information Service)*

Because Stockholm dominates the whole of central Sweden, other important urban centers are situated at some distance, in the *southern* section of the country. South of the great lakes, the climate is warmer as the maritime influences of the North Sea penetrate deeper. In this section are the two richest agricultural provinces of Sweden: Vestergötland in the northwest and Scania in the south. Between them the larger Smaland looks empty. The northern region is mainly a block of gneiss surrounded by the lakes and the Danish straits, but the glacial and postglacial accumulation provided it with richer soils. This was one of the first densely populated parts of the country, and Skara, a small town, was the first bishopric of Sweden. The rural country specializes in livestock economy: oats, beets, potatoes, and turnips are the chief crops; and cattle are more numerous than in any other province. Scattered farms produce milk and cheese for the whole country. The towns are small and rather rural: Skara, Falköping, Lidköping, and Skövde are just large villages, and Tidaholm alone has large plants (matches and motor cars). The population decreases, moving toward the periphery, with poorer soils but more industries. Closer to the sea, Boras (70,000) makes textiles. At the junction of the Göta Canal with Lake Vänern, Trollhättan (40,000) is a Swedish Niagara; its dams produce 250,000 h.p.; its plants make locomotives, fertilizers, cyanamid, paper and pulp, shoes and leatherware, plastics and matches; and a whole constellation of specialized industrial towns surrounds it and uses its power. To the southeast Jönköping (53,000) was born of its site at the southern extremity of Lake Vätter, at an important crossroads; it has immense match factories and a variety of metallic articles (hardware, bicycles) in its suburbs. This is the threshold of Smaland.

The province of Smaland in the center of southern Sweden is known for its poverty. It has no good soils, a colder and cloudy atmosphere; even the forest is meager, often replaced by heath and moors. Briarwood and honey were the only local resources until a factory for glass was established in the eighteenth century. Since then the Smaland has acquired an industry, for now it manufactures most of the ordinary and artistic Swedish glassware, exporting handsome articles made out of its sterile sands. The glass industry spread eastward to the Baltic coast, where the soils are better and some beet sugar is produced. Kalmar is the local town trading with the islands offshore, and farther south Karlskrona, on a splendid well-protected roadstead, remains the great naval base. The two islands of Gotland and Öland rise from the sea with steep cliffs, fragments of a limestone plateau. The former has better soils, raises cattle, and has truck farming; the latter specializes in sheep herding. Gotland has a great history: its port of Visby used to be one of the main headquarters of the Hansa, a merchants' metropolis, and vast treasures of silver were found here, but now it is a sleepy rural and tourist center, proud of its medieval walls and Gothic churches.

All the commercial activity of southern Sweden has migrated westward to the coast of the Skagerrak and Kattegat, straits between the North Sea and the Baltic. This indented coast was conquered from the Danes in 1645. Its maritime vocation is ancient, and today a number of small ports are actively engaged in fishing, participating in the normal life of the North Sea. But the land is poor, with few forests and some heath, and supports only flocks of sheep. In the midst of this coast, on the mouth of the Göta älv leading into Lake Vänern, King Gustav-Adolf established in 1618 the port of Göteborg (or Gothenburg), which is now the chief seaport of Sweden, accounting for almost one half of the foreign trade of the country. Most of central Sweden trades through this port. Göteborg has several important shipping concerns, such as the Brostrom Line, the Johnson Line, and the Swedish-American Line, and it sends liners and tramps all over the Atlantic. It is also a large center of shipbuilding, and the modern yards of the Göta Works are the pride of the Swedish industry, the largest shipbuilding firm in the world outside of Japan. In the second ranking city in Sweden, Göteborg's 450,000 inhabitants do not all live off the sea trades. Large factories produce electric and textile machinery or weave cotton and flax, and here is the home of the famed SKF ball bearings. Long lines of industrial towns radiate from Göteborg along the valleys leading inland, with food, textile, and chemical industries scattered throughout. Indeed Göteborg looks like a regional capital; with its satellites it aggregates half a million people, yet its central section is modest and fresh. No other important town or port in the vicinity could withstand its competition. Only Halmstad (41,000) to the south has recently developed some metallurgical plants and a market for agricultural products; it stands almost at the entrance of Scania.

Sweden terminates its territory in the south with a small peninsula at the tip of the big one. This land of some 4500 square miles has a very special importance: it accounts for a population of close to 1 million, one eighth of the nation. It extends southward like a bridge toward Denmark and therefore the main bulk of the European continent. Only the *Sund*, a few miles wide, separates it from the Danish islands; it is also a geological bridge, establishing the transition from the old crystalline rocks of the Fenno-Scandian Shield to the sedimentary strata of the great European Plain. It has therefore better soils; its latitude and maritime position warrant a warmer climate with an average winter temperature close to the freezing point. Here even the section uplifted in postglacial times ends—Scania has been sinking slightly. These natural conditions made of Scania the granary of Sweden, with a rich, intensive agriculture closely related to the Danish rural life. The district of Malmö tills 75 percent of its total area. A systematic rotation of wheat, sugar beet, and fodder crops has been followed, maintaining the soil's fertility but requiring intensive fertilization. These crops are associated with an economy of cattle, dairy production, and poultry farming. There are about 20,000 farms in Scania, and many of them are over 50 acres. The southwestern part, overlooking the Sund is the richer, by the quality of the soils as well as by its commercial and industrial activities. Malmö is the third city of Sweden: a great city in the sixteenth century, ruined and reduced to only 1236 inhabitants in 1720, it rose to 250,000. Farther north, Hälsingborg (80,000) has followed in its footsteps. Both ports have ferry connection with Copenhagen and many industries, including sugar, flour, fertilizers, and agricultural implements. Malmö is truly the capital of Scania. On the main railroad from Stockholm to the continent, it takes advantage of the proximity of a small coalfield; it is known for its cement, edible oil, soap, beer, and machinery; it builds ships, and some of its suburbs engage in fishing. Nowhere else in Sweden, with the sole exception of the capital region, is there such a density of population and such a widespread activity as on the southern extremity of the peninsula. Close to Malmö, the town of Lund (46,000) with its bishopric and university retains the directing influence in the cultural activities of southern Sweden.

Such are the regional aspects of Sweden. It is indeed the heart of the "Scandinavian miracle": a population of 8 million people, spread over a total area of 170,000 square miles, has built up on the fringes of the Arctic one of the greatest centers of world industry and culture. The recent period has been mostly one of industrialization and urbanization, and that process is still going on, but it still can claim a large margin of underdeveloped resources throughout its territory. The Swedish people have a real passion for their country, the nature, the sunshine, the vegetation. Green plants are everywhere, and everyone goes out of town as often as possible to enjoy the countryside. In 1947, almost one third of the population still lived in towns of not more than 20,000 inhabitants; by 1965, 54 percent of the population was urban, and farming employed only 9 percent of the labor force.

Agriculture became a third-rank resource only recently. The land produces more than ever owing to better management and mechanization. In 1961 there were 232,900 active farms with more than 5 acres of arable land each; of these only 37,800 had over 50 acres. The number of the farms was decreasing as many small-size family farms were going out of business. The area under cultivation was remaining almost stable, around 9 million acres, while the natural meadows were shrinking (1.3 million acres compared to 2.4 in 1944) and the forested area was slowly expanding; the forests covered 56.3 million acres, about 55 percent of the total land area and 800,000 acres more than in 1944. Oats,wheat, barley, rye, potatoes, and hay were the main crops. There were in 1965, 2.3 million head of cattle, 2 million hogs, 170,000 farm tractors in use, and still some 110,000 horses. This agriculture could not feed the population adequately and foodstuffs made up about 15 percent of the country's total imports. Farming was of course subsidized in Sweden, and the dairy economy enjoyed a high margin of protection.

Forestry is still the country's main category of land use and natural resource. The overcutting that prevailed earlier in this century has been replaced by careful methods of long-range forest management. Although there are some 200,000 small woodlot owners, these own less than half of the total forested area. The rest is owned, and scientifically managed, either by public authorities or large industrial concerns; some of the latter have domains of over a million acres of woods. About 86 percent of the Swedish stands consists of conifers, that is, pine and spruce, which are favored by the developing and powerfully organized pulp and paper industry. The forests produce annually about 50 million cubic meters of roundwood, of which about one third is destined to the needs of the domestic market and two thirds are intended for export purposes, but mainly in the form of pulp or manufactured goods. Rather than overcutting again, Sweden prefers nowadays to import more roundwood (from Norway and Finland) than it exports.

The industrial potential of Sweden is based on a few raw materials available on the spot, such as timber, iron, and some other ores, but even more it is based on the quality of the Swedish manpower and technique. Traditionally an exporter of raw or semifinished materials (iron ore, timber, wood, and pulp), Sweden now is endeavoring to transform much of it at home and sell the finished product. It already has, of course, a great tradition in the field—the reputation of Swedish glassware and furniture, of Sweden's Eskilstuna cutlery, Primus stoves, ball bearings, matches, electric and telephone equipment, even of its ships, does not need to be improved. But the competition in all these specialties is increasing. Swedish industry is handicapped by its lack of coal and petroleum; the Scanian coalfields supply only some 60,000 tons of coal, and several million tons have to be imported annually; the emphasis put on hydroelectric development and the use of charcoal cannot balance this deficit. The scale of wages is rather high and requires adequate prices to accommodate it. Sweden must keep open to its products the markets of rich and prosperous countries.

Since the war, every year has brought a rise in the industrial activity of Sweden, although there was no destruction to repair. Total consumption of energy expressed in units equivalent to a million metric tons of coal rose from 15.7 in 1937 to 19.6 in 1949 and 34.8 in 1965. In 1966, when many records of production were broken throughout the world,

Sweden produced 2,500,000 tons of pig iron and ferroalloys (804,000 in 1948), 4,800,000 tons of crude steel (1,257,000 in 1948), and 7,400,000 tons of wood pulp, thus making her the largest European producer of pulp, and second only to the United States and Canada elsewhere. While the weaving of rayon fabrics developed greatly during the war, other textile industries did not show comparable progress. Sweden prefers to specialize in certain aspects of industrial activity for which it is better endowed: forest products, machinery, instruments, and ships. The foreign trade balance normally shows a small deficit, which is compensated for by net income from shipping (5.9 million gross tons registered in 1966) and from patents and other services. The main shortage in Sweden's economy is coal and oil; but the country's resources in water power are estimated at 80 billion kwhr per year: 8.1 were produced in 1940 and 50 in 1966.

Sweden has had the great privilege of escaping the two world wars; it has known no armed conflict since 1815. The Swedes are deeply impressed with the conviction that international peace through mutual understanding can be brought about. But their main worries are domestic problems. They are today the most isolationist people of Europe, refusing to participate in the North Atlantic military alliance and affirming their intention to remain neutral and to maintain good relations with both sides. This attitude toward the East is curious. By their culture, their social, and economic structure, the Swedes are Westerners; their former empire has been ruined and taken over by Russia. Yet they occupy a slope that goes down to the Baltic, and they feel, underneath all their historical grievances, some responsibility to the East, which they helped civilize, especially a responsibility toward Finland, which was part of Sweden for several centuries. The Swedes have the highest per capita ratio of motor cars in Europe; but their "insularity" made them drive on the left side of the road until 1967, when they shifted to the right side.

External problems are being dealt with behind a strong defensive organization. Sweden has kept a vigilant guard on its northern boundary. It also has established a policy of strong economic protection, particularly after the weakening of its financial position in the dollar area. Still the balance of payments has been difficult to maintain with a high and rising standard of living in the rapidly increasing urban populations. Heavy taxation and generous government expenditure to improve the comfort of the people has helped to bring about a truly democratic situation, and the middle class is largely predominant in Sweden. Having achieved "social democracy," the Swedes are striving now for "economic democracy." They have the highest gross national product per capita after the United States.

In recent years, Sweden presented the interesting and paradoxical picture of the most Americanlike country outside North America and also of the last European country on the continent—in the sense of the good old traditional Europe of the 1900s. It seems to achieve a synthesis of many of the good qualities and few of the evils of the two sides of the Atlantic, a fortunate situation, but one difficult to maintain.

## NORWAY

Norway is all mountain and sea. The contrast between the two slopes of the Scandinavian peninsula is sharp, the Atlantic slope being warmer, damper, and much steeper. The steepness gave greater force to erosion, whether glacial or normal. Widening and deepening the valleys, the glaciers pushed far into the sea (as some of those on the Alaskan coast now do) and sculpted the land far below sea level, creating deep fjords that penetrate inland. In the north, where Norway narrows to less than fifty miles in many places, the fjords or the valleys cut the land to pieces, making almost a string of islands. Southward, where the land is wider, there is still little unity, for the southwestern lobe of the peninsula, entirely Norwegian, is occupied by the most elevated and massive of all Scandinavian highlands with many summits rising about 6000 feet.

Settlement is concentrated on the periphery—that is, on the coast or in the valleys cutting inland from the coast. The great German geographer Friedrich Ratzel noted that the distribution of the population in Norway made a clear outline of the hydrography: it is the result of the steepness of the slope and of the massiveness of the highlands where they can develop. Norway is a country without plains; fjords and high fjelds is all that it has. The fjords are so effectively isolated one from another that each of them seems almost an independent cell. Until A.D. 872, there was little unity between the many tribes and clans scattered along the western coast; at that date Harald Haarfager, coming from the east, achieved political unification, but only with considerable losses. Many of the Vikings revolted, preferring emigration overseas to obedience at home, and while some ransacked the coasts of Western Europe, others settled in Iceland, Greenland, and perhaps even on the North American mainland. America was first discovered by Norwegian individualism, or regionalism, as a gesture of resistance to oppression.

Centered either in Trondheim or in Bergen, the kingdom of Norway flourished on its maritime expansion from the tenth to the fourteenth centuries. Then it was ravaged by the Black Plague of 1349, conquered by the Danes, and after 1814 controlled by the Swedes; it regained full independence only in 1905 and is a "young" nation on the European scale. Although its national capital has been located in the east since the seventeenth century—Oslo (Christiania) was closer to Denmark and Sweden and better situated for the export of the timber from the southern forests to the Netherlands—Norway never took a genuine interest in Baltic affairs. It resented domination either by the Danes or by the Swedes, and its love of freedom for the individual was a strongly rooted way of resisting "foreign controls." Norwegian interests are indeed on the vast open spaces of the ocean.

Over its area of 125,000 square miles, distances are long, not only as a result of the stretch in latitude, but also because the road from Oslo to Finnmark has to be measured on the sea. The airplane has improved the situation, but north of Bergen the Norwegian airlines use seaplanes because there is insufficient flat space in the vicinity of towns for landing strips. Frequent fogs make flying schedules somewhat irregular. The total population of 3,800,000 in 1968 is therefore unequally distributed: the greatest densities are in the southeastern section (100 to 200 per square mile); elsewhere the density is below 50, and the average of 29 per square mile is one of the lowest in Europe. The two main cities together account for one sixth of the total population. Distribution by profession shows that about 15 percent depend on agriculture and forestry, another 35 percent on industry, and some 38 percent on trade, services, and fishing. Thus it can be said that a substantial portion of the Norwegian population lives on the high seas. Many Norwegian authorities claim that over one half the people have moved overseas, close to 4 million Americans and Canadians being of Norwegian extraction or descent. The natural increase of population reaches 30,000 to 40,000 annually.

Although the sea creates some unity and, with the help of topography, opposes the coast to the interior, some differentiation was natural in thirteen degrees of latitude, the more so as the inland structure varies from north to south. Northern Norway (above 65°N. lat.) is only a scalloped, narrow, steep slope. It has been rather neglected; the settlement is thin—4 per square mile in the Finnmark and 17 in the Nordland—and concentrated in fishing ports. The extreme north, where Finnmark borders on Finland (and since 1945 on Soviet Russia) on the Arctic coast, is exceptional country even for Norway: very cold in winter, a rugged plateau covered with a meager tundra, inhabited by Lapps, who raise reindeers and combine inland nomadism with periods of fishing on the sea—a combination which is rather unique.

Then begins the string of fishing ports, free of ice, visited by the "midnight-sun cruises." The interior is made of hard, barren rock with little vegetation, but the sea is rich indeed: Hammerfest, Tromsö Harstad, and Narvik are the chief fishing centers with many scattered small places between them. Tromsö (34,000) is the regional capital, while Narvik lives mainly as the Atlantic outlet of the Swedish Norrland. A vast railroad yard and an impressive pier serve the ore traffic (about 16 million tons of iron ore annually) Narvik seems almost a Swedish appendix in Norwegian territory, and the house of the Swedish consul proudly overlooks the town. Narvik is built on a beautiful fjord, and its houses climb the steep cliff rising from it. Violently disputed during the campaign of 1940, the town was almost completely destroyed by the Allied attack. Today it has two distinct parts: the older one untouched by the war and the newly rebuilt, quite modern, larger section. Off this coast the two groups of islands called the Lofoten and the Vesteraalen are active centers of fishing, catching cod and herring in the winter in prodigious quantities. The unedible remains of the fish serve as feed for the cattle raised on the island or as fertilizer for the tilled plots. Farther south Bodö (14,000) is the only appreciable town until the fjord of Trondheim is reached. A railroad is being built through the Nordland and now reaches Bodö; towns are connected by boats, seaplanes, and buses that use ferries to cross the fjords. There is a rejuvenation going on in the north, and it began largely with the reconstruction of the severe material damage suffered in World War II.

The *North Norway Plan* adopted in Oslo after detailed economic surveys of Finnmark, Troms, and Nordland set forth a carefully elaborated program of development of the area's resources. As it is gradually carried out a new frontier is developing in the northern third of the country, which holds only one fifth of its woodlands, less than one tenth of its potential water power, and one eighth of its population. A new authority was established in 1951 for the northern fishing industry, to increase the catch and expand the shipping of refrigerated fresh fish to consuming markets, while also elaborating by-products. Two large processing plants were established at Batsfjord and Honningsvag. To help also the old farm fishing association, in which the seasonally employed fishermen lived on small subsistence farms, drainage work has been started to provide more arable land, and dairying and pig-raising have been supported to give greater self-sufficiency to the region's food supply. Finally large-scale industrialization has been launched with the largest Norwegian iron and steel plant built, the state-owned Norsk Jernverk at Mo-i-Rana, situated on a fjord near the Syd-Varanger iron mines and on a good water-power site, with a specially developed oven that requires a great deal of power in order to save on imported coke in the making of steel. The iron ore, shipped by the mines in concentrated briquettes (at 66 percent of metal content), is also exported to Britain and West Germany in this form. The north is thus being developed, its highway network expanded, and a full electrification program enforced. It expects to play an increasing part in the expanding Norwegian economy.

The port of Bergen, with the picturesque buildings of the old Hanseatic town. *(Norwegian Information Service)*

Cattle going to the higher summer pastures in the Norwegian säter system. *(Norwegian Information Service)*

At the latitude of Trondheim the central or, better, the *western section* of Norway begins. It is not very different from the north in the climate of its coast: in February, the coldest month, the temperature averages 25° at Tromsö, 26.8° at Trondheim, and 33.6° at Bergen, while the averages for July are 51.8°, 57.2°, and 57.9° respectively. The yearly rainfall is abundant and depends on the screening from the sea: 31 inches annually at Trondheim, but 81 inches at more exposed Bergen. The uniqueness of this coast is its topography: it is more massive; the fjords penetrate more deeply; high mountainous scenery rises straight from the ocean's edge. The calm blue mirror of the water, almost unaffected by tides or storms, reflects Alpine landscapes with bold peaks and snow-capped heights. Such is the Romsdal Fjord in the vicinity of Trondheim and, farther south, many other fjords of which the Hardanger is perhaps the most impressive. The grandeur of this landscape has a well-deserved reputation among tourists, but it does not make for an amiable nature. Trondheim (115,000) has been favored by a lowering of the mountains in its hinterland, with easy passes to the Swedish Jemtland or to Oslo, and two railways follow these routes. Moreover, relatively wide and arable spaces lie at low altitudes, aiding rural activities. It seems quite natural that Trondheim was the first capital and holy city of Norway. It is now the metropolis of the developing north, and a booming city which doubled its population from 1950 to 1965. Its largest employer is the Norwegian Technological Institute. Southward the bulk of the mountains rises, the land widens, and the barren fjeld reigns. At altitudes of about 3000 feet it is hard to imagine a ruder solitude: plateaus like the Hardangervidda are practically arctic, almost uninhabited. A few generations ago men from the fjords went there to hunt the reindeer on the fjeld; now only small herds remain. Little grows on the hard crystalline surface polished by the ice. There is little wood, but once a few pastures were used on the slopes. As in the Alps, but for much shorter distances, the Norwegians had a summer migration of herds upward to the *säters* (mountain outfarms of the herders who were farmers from the seashore). This combination of modes of life still exists, but today men are farmers or fishermen according to the season. In such an environment people have had to try all possible ways to make a living.

The only source of plenty was the sea, and urban life is concentrated in a few ports. Kristiansund and Aalesund, established on small islands off the mainshore, specialize in cod and herring. Aalesund also commissions some whalers; Sundalsöra makes aluminum. They are linked with the rest of the country by the railway of the Romsdal Fjord. On a deep fjord screened by a group of islands stands Bergen, now the capital of the western coast and the second city of Norway (118,000). For a long time this port had no hinterland: behind it the Hardangervidda was a dead end; but it did have a "foreland" on the fjords and the islands, and herring fishing has been a chief activity there for a long time. In the Middle Ages the Hansa merchants came to Bergen and chose it as their main center for the trade in dried fish. Next to the old royal castle the Hansa built its own walled city within the city, enjoying special privileges and holding the monopoly of trade. They ruled the place until 1750, and Bergen is still proud of its well-preserved Hanseatic section. Although the Norwegians took over the trade when they took over the city, Bergen, which in 1600 had been the largest northern city with 15,000 people, had to bow to Oslo. It still is Norway's largest center of fish trading and fish processing and the first port for imports. Over one million tons of shipping are registered there, ships that ply on faraway seas or link Bergen to other ports on the Atlantic, especially Newcastle and New York. Its suburbs have shipyards and flour and textile mills. Its university makes Bergen the cultural capital of Norway's western seaboard. In 1909 the railroad crossed the Hardangervidda to establish a good connection with Oslo.

Along the fjords farmers raise some wheat, rye, and potatoes, while herders take the livestock up and down the hills to the *säters*. With progress in harnessing the immense waterfalls flowing from the highlands, various industries were built, mainly textile, aluminum, and chemical plants, and especially along Sogne Fjord. Farther south more fishing centers attract people: Haugesund (27,000) specializes in herring and Stavanger (78,000) in anchovies and fishmeal; and the latter also has large canning factories. The warmer climate of the southern tip of the peninsula stimulates the growth of grass, and dairy cattle are important there. Kristiansand (50,000) is a local market and ships some timber, because, with the coast veering northward, a dense forest of pines and broad-leaved trees has spread on the hills. Electrochemical and metallurgical plants scatter around these towns.

*Eastern Norway* is very different from the Atlantic coast. With the exception of Oslo Bay, the fjords have been replaced by wide flat-bottomed valleys, opening the way to agriculture and meadows, while a rich, dense forest clothes the valley slopes. Fields and woods replace the ocean as basic resources. Curiously the climate is tougher — colder in winter, warmer and drier in the summer. Oslo is the hottest town of Scandinavia in July (63.1°), and the meadows at the bottom of the large valley often require irrigation. Still, these conditions are much more favorable to vegetation and rural pursuits, and the use of the land has attracted men and deterred emigration. In 1891 the Atlantic slope accounted for 1,025,000 inhabitants and eastern Norway for 795,000; in 1966 the figures were 1,850,000 and 1,920,000, revealing the advance

A fjord advances deep in the Norwegian hills. *(Norwegian Information Service)*

Oslo: a new town, rapidly spreading upward, with an impressive front on the port in the foreground and high wooded crests in the background. *(Norwegian Information Service)*

made by Oslo and the rural east. Lumbering provides the basis of several large industries such as electrochemical plants, pulp, and paper. The annual natural increase of the Norwegian forests is estimated at 13.5 million cubic meters; about 9 million are cut yearly and account for one sixth of the country's exports, largely in the form of pulp and paper.

Approaching Oslo one finds a special type of rural civilization, with a rich folklore and beautiful wood carvings on buildings and farmhouses, particularly in the valleys of Telemark. But the conservative rural population often clashes with the urban population recently crowded into a great number of small industrial towns and now won over to socialist ideas. Here industry and agriculture seem to have concentrated and united in a recent growth, and even fishing and connected manufacturing are present. Tönsberg and Sandefjord are the homes of the world's largest fleet of whalers, which go hunting in the Antarctic; they also manufacture the equipment for this fleet, while Frederikstad refines the whale oil. The largest town, Drammen (47,000), produces pulp, paper, and cellulose, but it looks almost like a distant suburb of Oslo.

The Norwegian capital stands at the end of a wide, scenic fjord surrounded by steep hills. It is a dynamic city of some 500,000 people, with an atmosphere of simplicity and cordiality. Actually its growth began around 1850, and its national function is still recent, but, though impressive monuments are few, it nonetheless administers the country with efficiency and understanding. Oslo is the first port of Norway and its main hub of railroads for internal as well as external communication. Industries are rapidly developing: metallurgy, oil refineries, cotton mills, and a great variety of finished consumer goods. Truly Norwegian, the site has little flat space, so that the residential sections climb the slopes and the plants scatter along the valleys and the routes of the railroads. The conurbation has added over 100,000 people in the last ten years. It is only strange that Oslo has no part in the fishing activities; its rise marks a somewhat new orientation of the national economy.

Since its independence Norway has built up a great merchant marine. In 1939 it had a gross tonnage of close to 5 millions, and though the losses in World War II amounted to about one half of this total, the 1966 figure was 16.4 million. This merchant fleet, second only to the American and British merchant marines, played an important part in the war — one out of every ten ships in the Channel on D-Day flew the Norwegian colors. The importance of the oil tankers in this fleet is worth noting: in 1966, 8.8 out of 16.4 million gross tons were tankers. Norwegian ships carry oil all over the world under long-term contract with the great American and British oil companies. Since the war, however, Norway has encountered in this field of activity acute competition from other flags specializing in oil transportation, particularly those of the Republics of Panama and Liberia, where the burden of taxation and social benefits is lighter. The income from such activities greatly helps the Norwegian balance of payments. Fishing and whaling also add to the riches yielded by the sea: fresh-fish landings reached 2,280,000 tons in 1965, a figure second to none in Europe and second only to those of Peru, Japan and the United States elsewhere; in whaling, Norway — formerly undisputed world leader — rivals Japan and the USSR since 1958, catching 4,751 whales in the 1965-1966 season.

There is still a limit to what can be done in the maritime field by this small race of great seamen, and that limit seems almost to have been reached. The narrow ribbons of arable land, about 3 percent of the total area, restrict further agricultural development. In order to provide sustenance for its expanding population, Norway has engaged daringly in industrialization, basing its hopes on two resources: timber in the east and waterpower around the periphery of its highlands. The steepness of the slope and the humidity of the climate combine to make the country extremely rich in hydroelectric potential. But harnessing this potential requires heavy investments, and Norway does not possess large capital assets. Power could be exported to Sweden and Denmark; once available at cheap rates and in large quantities, it alone would help to build up large industries. The whole world learned of this trend in the specialization of Norwegian industry in 1943, when the Allies had to bomb out the plants making the heavy water needed for atomic research. The total potential of the Norwegian waterfalls is estimated at 131 billion kilowatt-hours per year; about 10 were produced in 1938-1939 and 50 in 1967. Most of the electricity produced is consumed in the production of nitrogen, carbide, ferrosilicium, aluminum, zinc, steel, and paper and pulp. Norway also endeavors to develop whatever mineral resources have been found — mostly pyrites, some iron, copper, and zinc ores — and her molybdenum and nickel deposits are being worked.

But the lack of coal and oil is a major hindrance. Electricity could fill this need, but Norwegian authorities hesitate because of the heavy capital investment — for instance, in the case of the railroads. Sweden once offered to help finance the harnessing of the waterfalls in return for a share in the power produced — because of the greater slope, electricity would be much cheaper in Norway — but Norway refused in a gesture to preserve its economy from foreign interference. Norway is a young country, passionately attached to every shade of its independence. Parts of it were hard hit during the war; its economy was shattered; food rationing in the 1940s was severe; fish alone was abundant, for the financial situation did not permit large imports of much-needed foodstuffs. The last rationing, of automobiles, was abolished only in 1960. With an admirable tenacity the Norwegians carry on alone the upbuilding of their national destiny, in the creases of their land as well as on the sea.

## DENMARK

The contrast is sharp indeed when, crossing the Skagerrak, one passes from Norway to Denmark. Here is a low, flat country, densely populated, predominantly agricultural, though very much interested in the sea from a commercial standpoint. Denmark is a small country and knows it: its area of 16,576 square miles supports a population of 4,900,000. With their habitual joviality, the Danes talk about the impossibility of now defending their territory—the whole of it could be taken within eight hours in case of aggression by a major power. Denmark is comprised of Jutland, a peninsula jutting northward from the Great Plain of Europe, and a group of islands filling in the bottleneck at the entrance to the Baltic. The country looks like a dike (with a few fissures) enclosing the Baltic, or like a shattered bridge linking the continental mainland to the Scandinavian peninsula. In any case, it is a place of transit, and therefore of trade.

Nature seems to have endowed Denmark much better than the countries to the north. The geological structure is simple and consists of sediments deposited by seas bordering the crystalline shield to the south during the Secondary and Tertiary periods. Most of it is limestone, interstratified with some clays and sands and with chalk at its base. Only on the isolated island of Bornholm is there an outcropping of Primary rock. The whole territory has been glaciated, and all the topography and soils of Denmark are the work of glacial or postglacial actions. Moraines are responsible for the scattered hills, the complexity of the drainage, and the top layers of the stratigraphy. No point in Denmark rises above 600 feet. The shoreline is, of course, very long: regular low coast on the North Sea, with sand dunes and vast beaches making navigation difficult; easy access on the Baltic side, with lines of cliffs and numerous little bays (pretentiously called fjords). In their northerly retreat the glaciers left Denmark much earlier than even the south of Sweden. The land therefore has dried up better, and the soil formations have been better weathered during a longer postglacial period. The climate is also milder and cannot help being maritime everywhere. The temperature, fairly uniform throughout the country, averages 32° in winter and 62° in summer. Sometimes an expansion of eastern continental influences creates a

Harvesting in Denmark. *(Swedish Information Service)*

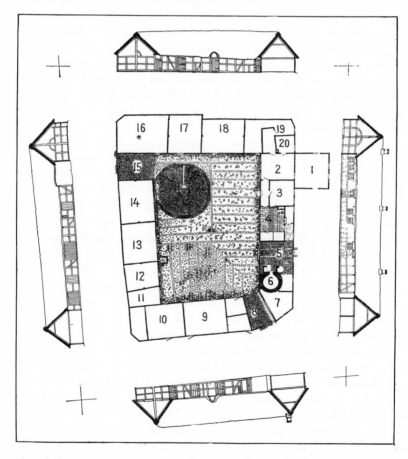

Plan of a Danish quadrangular farm, Lundager, County of Odense, Fünen: 1 and 2, main rooms; 3, small room; 4, kitchen; 5, brew house; 6, bakery; 7, peat store; 8, gate; 9, stable; 10, cattle shed; 11, cart shed; 12, byre; 13 and 17, threshing floors; 14, rye granary; 15, main entrance; 16, barley granary; 18, granary; 19, chamber; 20, guestroom. *(After the original in the Danish Folk Museum, Copenhagen; The Geographical Review)*

heat or a cold wave according to the season, but ordinarily mildness is the rule — dampness, too, with the relative humidity oscillating from 75 to 92 percent.

Originally Denmark belonged to the great forest belt of Middle Europe; now oak and, principally, beech are common, and plantations of coniferous trees were made only recently. Vast areas were under heath; moors and marshes were frequent; and a belt of wide and dangerous marshes crossed Jutland from coast to coast in its south, making the peninsula almost inaccessible by land in old times, so that Denmark at first developed like an archipelago. Man occupied the land rather early; in the fifth millenium b.c. the interior was colonized. Agriculture was well developed during the Bronze Age, when the climate was perhaps warmer, and the tradition was maintained. Settlement proceeded by large villages with few scattered farms, the woods being cleared in the Middle Ages. In the eleventh century the Danes also settled the coastline and looked toward the sea, erecting rings of castles around the islands to protect them against piracy. Copenhagen was founded then, as were Aarhus, Aalborg, and other towns. The maritime and military expansion had already started, and for a while the Danish empire included a part of Britain. Then it conquered some of the Baltic lands and held Norway from 1397 until 1814. But a long conflict with the German cities of the Hansa followed by rivalry with Sweden caused the gradual ruin of the empire in the Baltic and even in Norway. The strain imposed on a small people by this brilliant history weakened Denmark around the sixteenth century and brought retreat before the Swedish expansion. The Virgin Islands were sold to the United States in 1917; even Iceland was lost in 1918; Greenland and a few distant isles are all that remain of a vast empire.

Since the end of the eighteenth century Denmark has definitely directed its main endeavors toward its internal domestic problems. In this field it succeeded in a splendid way and became one of the most prosperous nations in Europe. While its population rose from 797,000 in 1769 to 4,767,000 in 1965, the number of the people living in the cities rose from 159,000 to almost 2,500,000. This growth of cities was due to a commercial development based both on maritime relations and on the production of the land. Agricultural progress started after 1780, when the peasants were freed and the lands reassembled in individual holdings. Most of large villages were broken up, the ties of communal discipline dissolved, and isolated farms scattered through the countryside. This evolution also determined a trend emphasizing animal husbandry and requiring fewer men on the land. An exodus toward the cities started, favoring especially the capital.

There still are miniature pioneer fringes open to settlement in Jutland.

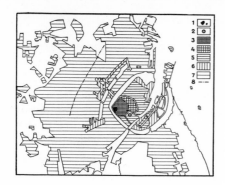 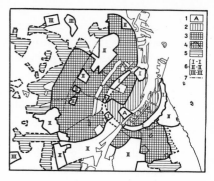

*(Left)* The evolution of Copenhagen proper: 1, approximate site of first village and harbor; 2, Bishop Absalon's castle (1167); 3, the first town, probably as in Bishop Absalon's time; 4, urban area within the fortifications at the close of the thirteenth century; 5, urban area about 1700, within Christian IV's fortifications in the seventeenth century; 6, urban area about 1854; 7, urban area about 1921; 8, boundary line in the year 1660. *(Right)* Map of Copenhagen proper: 1, Slottsholmen ("The Castle Island"), population density 1100 per square kilometer; 2, "city" area, density 24,900 per square kilometer, with the naval and commercial harbors on the east; 3, area of close settlement, density 40,000–82,000 per square kilometer; 4, part of Frederiksberg, within 3, that has a density of only 25,000 per square kilometer; 5, area that was being built up in 1928, density varying about 25,000 per square kilometer; 6, three open belts of parks, hospitals, cemeteries, station yards, airdrome, and the like. *(The Geographical Review)*

Copenhagen. By means of canals, the port penetrates the old city, and the smokestacks of modern industries tower above it. *(Swedish Information Service)*

Nature has not been easy on the peninsula, and its use is incomplete. This land, a barrier between two seas, seems largely aloof to the traffic going on around it; it is isolated and deeply rural. Dunes, marshes, and heathland have had to be conquered, and in 1965 the average density on Jutland was only 189 per square mile, far below the Danish average of 288. The north of the peninsula, very windy, is mostly pastoral, and Skagen, at the tip of the land, is a fishing port. Maritime activity penetrates deeply into the land along the Limfjord, on which stands the old and picturesque town of Aalborg (100,000). Here diversified plants have centered (beer, fertilizer, cement), and near by the Lilla Vildmose is the largest peat bog in Denmark. A diversified topography, with better lands intensively tilled and with patches of wood, occupies the eastern section of Jutland. Here wheat and barley, sugar beets, and oats are grown, cattle and poultry are raised, and industrial towns have arisen. Aarhus (187,000), the second city in Denmark, is a regional capital with mechanical and clothing industries; Randers (42,000) makes gloves and builds railroad cars; Horsens (37,000) has textile mills. The contrast is great between the active eastern coast and the sandy western coast covered with heath and pine woods. But recent colonization has advanced in the latter area, marls being dug out and mixed with the sand, damp soils being drained, and some polders being created, as the Danes followed the example of the Dutch. Cattle were put on the reclaimed territory, and more polders are being planned. The entirely artificial port of Esbjerg was built on the inhospitable coast to send butter, milk, and bacon to England; it became a town of 56,000 people and a thriving local market. In the south of Jutland, Schleswig, annexed by Germany from 1864 to 1920, has been returned to Denmark: it has benefited less from the Danish agricultural progress and is slightly Germanized.

About one half of the Jutland area consists of islands, richer, more thickly populated, and seemingly utilized to the limit of their possibilities. This habitat seems also to have reached an optimum status, and its general layout has changed little in recent times. The two largest islands are Funen to the west and Zealand to the east, a number of smaller ones completing the archipelago. Funen has numerous small farms of less than 20 acres and produces sugar beets, flowers, and fruits; its capital, Odense (133,000), is an important rail hub and has long been famous for its fairs. The southern islands, with many small towns scattered on them, also have a combination of the sugar beet and fodder economies. Zealand is by far the largest and richest island; its excellent soils, maintained with great care, support an intensive culture of grains, beets, and fodder crops. Here the predominant type of farm ranges between 50 and 150 acres. The landscape is flat, open, almost monotonous, and the farms are often surrounded with a screen of trees. The whole island is under the direct impact of its capital city, *Copenhagen,* the largest urban center in Scandinavia.

The Danish capital is a thriving conurbation of more than 1.3 million people, suburbs included, and thus concentrates more than one fourth of the whole Danish nation. The merchants' harbor (*Köpmanna Havn*), built by the archbishop in the twelfth century, has been considerably developed. At the gate of the Baltic, even without an empire, Copenhagen is a great center of shipping, international trade, and manufacturing for the world market. The port penetrates deep inside a city, in which are beautiful palaces and other monuments to remind one continually of the great historical past. And Copenhagen is a great cultural center, whose influence is still felt throughout Northern and Western Europe, its university and museums well deserving their fame. In the busy, winding streets of the central section, too narrow for its present traffic, one feels the tradition of old culture and the open-mindedness and eagerness of a people who always have sailed broad seas and mingled with foreigners. Copenhagen is indeed a worldly city, with great charm, a quick rhythm, a stubborn cheerfulness despite the odds of the time. In the midst of the port, off an elegant boardwalk, a statue of the Little Mermaid rises from the water, recalling Andersen's fairy tale and the attraction of the sea.

In the last two hundred years Copenhagen has developed chiefly in concentric circles: the port is its heart, but the industrial boom created rings of expansion. The city is practically the only heavy-industry center of Denmark, with shipyards, vast textile mills, food industries, electrical engineering plants, breweries, and all kinds of mechanical equipment — diesel engines are a Danish specialty. Copenhagen also makes the Danish porcelain, fine china, and silverware that have such great repute. This is indeed a powerful industrial capital for a small agricultural country. But Danish agriculture is as thoroughly organized — almost industrialized — and as dependent on marketing abroad as the capital that befits the national economy.

Denmark is largely man-made, and more and more this is true as Copenhagen's industries expand and Jutland's reclamation of sands, heaths, and polders proceeds. Seventy-six percent of its land area is cultivated, and with most scientific methods, so that average yields of most crops grown in Denmark are superior to those in almost any other country of Europe or the world with the exception of the Netherlands. In some respects the Danes have learned from the Dutch how to manage an intensive agriculture with limited, damp land and few people (18 percent of the labor force work on farms). They went further than any other country in the efficient management of the production and the standardization of the high-grade dairy products—poultry, eggs, ham, and bacon—which they export on a large scale. Danish standards are considered "tops" in this field in Europe. The spread of cooperative organizations for production, processing, and marketing organized, helped, and controlled the rural production, offering the small farms most of the advantages of large-scale enterprise.

Danish economy is thus geared to a wide-open international economy. Its exports include dairy and meat products, sugar, beer, cattle, ships, machinery, and chinaware, but it must import large quantities of foodstuffs (especially grains), fuels, coal, metal, textile fibers, and fertilizer. Denmark has no mineral riches. It has a very active fishing fleet and a merchant marine of about 2.9 million tons, and Copenhagen sees through its port an important transit traffic. All this, however, does not quite balance foreign payments, unless good prices are paid for the exported goods. More than any Scandinavian country, Denmark depends on foreign marketing. Formerly its best markets were in Western and Central Europe, particularly in overindustrialized Britain and Germany. Politically as well as economically, Denmark balanced between them. Since 1945, Denmark has felt closer to Britain, but the trade with Germany was expanding again.

Of its former empire, Denmark keeps a few islands. In the Baltic, Bornholm, rocky, crystalline, important as a source of clays and kaolin for chinaware, engages actively in fishing and cattle raising. In the Atlantic, halfway between Scotland and Iceland, the Faroe islands (34,000 inhabitants on 540 square miles) are a small archipelago of old basaltic lava blocks, glaciated, barren and peaty, though with a mild climate and regular rainfall. The population grows potatoes and raises sheep, but the main resource is fishing, the catch of cod, halibut, and herring being largely salted; the principal port and town is Thorshavn. These islands are considered part of Denmark proper. The only large possession left therefore is Greenland—a vast icecap with a few Eskimos on the fringes—and the defense of Greenland is undertaken by the United States according to an agreement signed in 1951 as it is Danish territory in North America.

## ICELAND

In the Atlantic Ocean just south of the Arctic Circle is Iceland, a large island of 40,000 square miles, the westernmost land of Europe, populated by Scandinavian settlers since the ninth century. Formed of a big mass of old basalt, it has gone through a whole cycle of erosion, including glaciation. Many faults and still-active volcanism have added their action to that of glaciers to shape a diversified topography. The island is mountainous, and a main range crosses it from east to west, with many heights above 5000 feet and vast areas still covered by glaciers, perhaps the remnants of an old and much larger ice sheet. Proximity to Greenland is felt. The climate is a temperate one, with the monthly average temperature between 30° and 51° except in the vicinity of the large glaciers such as the Vatnajökull. Rough winds and the abundance of very recent, not-yet-weathered deposits of active volcanoes reduce the tree growth; on the heights a dull tundra reigns. Iceland is still warmed from beneath by the volcanism that built it. Earthquakes and eruptions are frequent — the eruptions of volcanoes capped with ice and snow often produce curious effects. And the violence of some volcanoes still affects the history of the island — the Laki's eruption in 1783 killed one fifth of the population and one half of the livestock. Hot springs are numerous, and their waters have long been used to heat the homes and irrigate some lands. These natural advantages do not compensate for the the fact that glaciers cover 12 percent of the whole land area and another 65 percent is devoid of vegetation.

Irish monks apparently came to Iceland about A.D. 800, but the bulk of the settlement came after 874 when the Norse fled from the new centralizing rule in Norway. It is believed that the population reached 25,000 around 900, and a republican and democratic constitution was voted by the people in 930 — Iceland claims to have the oldest parliament and constitution of Europe. In 1263 an act of union was signed with Norway, and in 1381 Iceland fell under Danish rule; it regained its independence slowly, becoming a sovereign state in 1918 and severing all ties with the Crown of Denmark to become a republic again in 1944. After a period of decay from the fourteenth to the nineteenth centuries, the island is regaining strength quickly. In 1967 its population reached 200,000; its inland agriculture grows grains, potatoes, and turnips; sheep are raised, and horses are numerous; irrigation with warm water helps truck farming. The towns on the periphery still account for most of the people: fishing and its processing (dried cod, cod-liver oil, etc.) is the main resource and supplies 95 percent of the exports. Improved methods of fishing brought about a "herring boom" for a few years; the fish catches rose to 1.3 million tons in 1966. The capital and main port of Reykjavik (80,000) has an airport that was a relay station on the North Atlantic air lane during World War II, and the United States still has an air base there. The frequency of heavy fogs and cyclonic depressions, however, do not favor much through air traffic. The United States armed forces stationed on the island as the "Iceland Defence Force," under the North Atlantic Treaty, are the only military element in the country; and they have become the main pillar of its present prosperity.

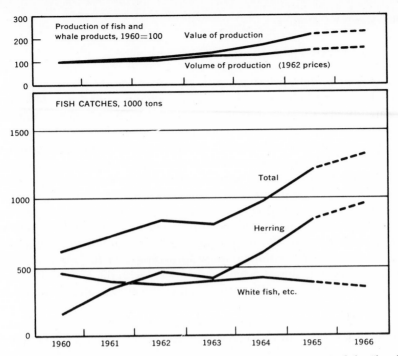

Icelandic fish catches and fish processing during the years 1960–1965 of the "herring boom." *(OECD Economic Surveys, 1967)*

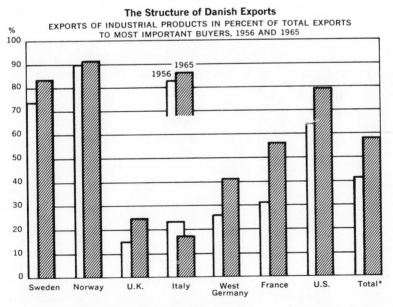

**The Structure of Danish Exports**

Notice the rapid growth of the share of the United States, France, and West Germany. After 1966 the agricultural integration of the Common Market made the German share in agricultural products decrease substantially. *(OECD Economic Surveys, 1967)*

## THE PROBLEMS OF SCANDINAVIA

Few regions in the world have such an actual unity in many respects as
have the four Scandinavian countries. All enjoy a moderate, cool, humid
climate; all are situated in high latitude and have been deeply affected
by the Quaternary glaciations. Their people belong approximately to the
same stock and have been living and dealing together for thousands of
years. Their languages are so similar that at Scandinavian conferences
each speaks his own tongue and is understood by the others without an
interpreter. As a result there is a deep cultural unity, worked out with
great similarities in legislation and procedure, with regular meetings
gathering the associations of lawyers, bankers, physicians, engineers,
traders, and artists of all four peoples. Still never in history was there an
effective political or economic unity spreading over the whole of Scandinavia. Denmark almost achieved it in 1397 with the Union of Kalmar
but could not bring in Sweden. Sweden never was able to dominate
Denmark.

   Today, in the middle of the twentieth century there are many practical
reasons for a close working together of the four countries. They occupy

Recent suburban housing development at Etterstad on the fringes of Oslo. Compare with
the view of the residential suburb of Stockholm (p. 176). The new suburban sprawl around
European capitals has increasingly taken on the pattern of large multistoried apartment
buildings with some open space preserved between and around them.

a strategic positon directly in between the Soviet area and the area of the Anglo-Saxon powers in the high latitudes where the distances are the shortest; in a way they almost span the North Atlantic. Divided, each is a small military power; united, they would form a substantial force. In economics, each looks for a widening of its commercial horizons, for larger markets and easier sources of supply. During the period 1947 – 1950 conferences met and committees worked on the possible establishment of a Scandinavian "bloc," or at least of a tariff union. A great deal could be achieved in the economic field: Denmark needs the timber, pulp, and paper of Sweden and Norway, both of which need the meat and dairy products of Denmark; Sweden and Denmark need the electric power that Norway could supply cheaply, and Norway and Iceland need the ships and machinery built by those countries.

Everyone is aware of the possibilities but also of the difficulties. Sweden, the greatest power of the four, is worried about Danish competition with her own agriculture and livestock, less well organized and often sustaining higher costs. Norway, just developing her "young" industry, is afraid that she would be strangled by the competition of the much more powerful and richer Swedish manufacturing. In fact each country is to some extent suspicious of the other three. The emotional reaction aroused by memories of the past is decisive. Iceland fears being dominated anew by Denmark so shortly after its full political emancipation; Norway has a similar attitude toward Sweden and wonders whether even economic coordination would not restore some of the authority from which it was emancipated less than fifty years ago. All of them enjoy working together – but in a larger frame, when many other powers take part and democracy has full play. At general international conferences it is customary for one spokesman to expound the views of all four Scandinavian powers; all of them have participated in the Economic Commission for Europe of the United Nations and in the OEEC. Sweden, Norway, and Denmark joined the Seven of the EFTA, but they feel just as linked by trade to the Six of the Common Market. When the question of the North Atlantic Pact was raised in 1949, Denmark and Norway joined, but Sweden stepped aside. There is still an opposition of the two slopes, the Atlantic and the Baltic, and Sweden remains somewhat insular. The routes of the Vikings and the Varangians are different.

The role now played by Scandinavian statesmen in international organizations is nevertheless outstanding: the two first Secretaries General of the United Nations have been Scandinavians, as well as the first postwar executive Secretary of ECE in Geneva and registrar of the International Court of Justice at The Hague. In part this role might be explained by the geographical position of the Scandinavian area in high latitude in between the two big land masses of North America and the Soviet Union; in part it can be explained also by the systematic coordination that seems to exist between the foreign policies of the Scandinavian powers and that of Great Britain. Most of this international prestige is still due to the quality of the men.

The "Scandinavian miracle" vividly illustrates the European skill in utilizing and reforming the physical environment and the strength of European regionalism rooted in a long history. It required tremendous stubbornness to achieve under difficult conditions what the Scandinavians did in material and social organization; that same stubbornness is bound to make hard the solution of regional problems. Now the Scandinavian countries are facing the problem of European integration. Old ties and the EFTA bind them to Britain, but if the latter were to join the Common Market, the Scandinavian countries would certainly follow and their entry would not cause the same difficulties as have arisen in the negotiations with the British. Denmark is the most interested in joining the EEC: West Germany has been the major purchaser of its agricultural exports; in recent years, this rich and expanding market has been slowly shifting its purchases to its partners in the EEC, particularly to The Netherlands and France. Norway would also like to join, though with hesitation: the Lutheran Church of Norway has been wary of a situation in which the small Protestant nations would be absorbed into a large, predominantly Roman Catholic system. Swedish reluctance would be more influenced by political factors and the trend of the Common Market to establish supranational authorities.

Geographically located in an outlying position, in a peripheral corner of the densely inhabited world, in higher latitude, the Scandinavian nations have shown great interest in the rest of the world. Their economy and culture rests more by tradition on their network of outside linkages than on their local resources. First they went out on the high seas to distant shores, exploring, ransacking, and conquering. Then, in recent times, they became peaceful traders and developed a deep missionary concern for the welfare of mankind. To the ancient maritime vocation they have added active air navigation: the SAS group of airlines is one of the most successful among the international air traffic networks, and it is quite out of proportion with the purely Scandinavian needs in this area. Even more remarkable has been the scientific production, the share of the Scandinavians in modern technological innovation. This world role is reflected in the transactional activity of their major cities, which have developed a metropolitan function also out of proportion to their size. All this has been particularly characteristic of the Swedes in the first half of this century; the Danes and the Norwegians have been catching up fast recently in several respects.

Each country reacts in its own way, according to its own emotions rooted in cultural and historical grounds. Still it seems that economic integration would benefit greatly all of Scandinavia if it came on a large scale, encompassing most of the western half of Europe. Scandinavians feel, however, very Atlantic, too: millions of cousins live in North America. The tradition of association with Britain is also strong, and Scandinavia today faces a difficult situation in Europe. So many forces seem to be at work toward the gradual economic integration of Western Europe that the trend could hardly be reversed.

# 6

---

# The
# British Isles

The geography of the United Kingdom is an extraordinary phenomenon. The British nation erected on its small island a huge structure and developed powerful economic machinery which dominated the seas and, beyond them, many distant lands. Such an involved structure needed constant maintenance and readaptation to a changing world. Never was British power made up of sheer strength. This is especially obvious to the geographer, since the national territory was rather small and never produced a single pound of many of the materials which were traded and processed to produce national prosperity. The management of the British economic and political power always required much shrewd steadiness, a leading characteristic of this nation. In many ways the United Kingdom could be likened to a great ship anchored to the ground, but with her antennas alive with radio waves going to and coming from all parts of the globe. No country has been more deeply involved in the present crisis of Western Europe. None is endeavoring more to overcome the difficulties of the time.

## POSITION AND DESTINY

The United Kingdom of Great Britain and Northern Ireland and the Republic of Ireland occupy a group of islands to the northwest of the mainland of Europe, between the open Atlantic and the North Sea. By its structure the British archipelago belongs to Europe, from which it is separated only by shallow seas—the Channel and the North Sea. Its highlands belong either to the Caledonian or to the Hercynian system; many of its structural lines have prolongations that have been traced on the continent. Insular position has always been a decisive factor, giving a special personality to British history.

The British Isles participated in the early stages of European history, but only as a passive, almost marginal land. Parts of them were included at different times in the Celtic zone of civilization, the Roman Empire, the westward Germanic migrations, the Danish realm, and the trading area of the Hansa. All these influences left their mark, yet none was overwhelming. The greatest outside influence was probably the French Norman that followed in the wake of William the Conqueror, who took over the English crown after his victory at Hastings in 1066. As a result, it seemed for a while that some unity might develop between the French and English kingdoms, but after the Hundred Years' War the English were ejected from the continent and the Norman element was assimilated within the insular frame. What happened in Britain at that time was not of great importance to the continent, for the country lived unto itself, rather isolated. A considerable change occurred, however, in the sixteenth century when the great maritime discoveries and Europe's expansion on the oceans made a springboard of the western Atlantic façade. The British Isles were exactly in the middle of this façade and more maritime than any other country. The British do not seem to have had much early nautical experience, but most of the influences reaching them by sea brought in people who were among the best seamen on the continent: Danes, Norse, French. In an insular but deeply rural country, the most remarkable of all modern seafaring civilizations flourished suddenly, beginning in the reign of Queen Elizabeth I.

In the eighteenth century Britain, having united all of the archipelago under one rule, gained the mastery of the seas throughout the world and established a broad empire scattered on all the continents. In the nineteenth century, reinforcing its position, Britain rose to virtual supremacy as the first world power. In the twentieth century her position has been weakened by the growth of new nations out of the reach of naval power, and by the "economic revolt" of the massive lands. Her participation in the two World Wars accelerated the crisis by absorbing much of her labor for long periods and much of her assets overseas. Still, in the 1920s it could be said, as a demonstration of her strength, that the British Empire produced over one half of the essential raw materials in the world. The awakening of remote lands with wider spaces and greater resources, lands that were settled or developed by people of British stock or associated culture, profited Britain for only a century or two. The newly developed areas demanded more self-government as their strength rose—they did not want to remain a dependency of the land from which the whole process had begun, now weakened by the world wars. This breakup of empire is the basis of the crisis of Europe in the twentieth century; it has been the destiny of all overseas empires beginning with the Greeks and Phoenicians. But in the case of the British Isles the consequences have reached further than for most of the countries on the continent.

Until the 1920s none of the large countries of Europe was richer than Britain, and none had established a more involved economy based on overseas connections. Britain had more ships afloat, more capital investments abroad, and a larger share in the international trade and insurance network than any other country in the world. Owing to this unique position, she had also a greater density of population with a higher standard of living than any other major power. And the population has continued to increase: in 1961 the total for the British Isles reached 55.5 million, of which 52.7 lived in the United Kingdom. This was a small fraction of the total population of the Commonwealth or of the English-speaking world, but it meant that on the 121,630 square miles of the archipelago the average density was 455 (almost 560 for the United Kingdom). This was greater than the densities of Germany or Italy, two overpopulated countries which have long complained. In the bitter disputes between the "have-not" and "have" powers in the 1930s, the fact that Britain was able to live well with so dense a population was ascribed generally to the advantages she obtained from her empire. In fact, the structure of British prosperity was much more complicated and manifold: it was built on the sea and on far-off shores, but it was also built largely in lands over which Britain had no direct control. As Albert Demangeon put it: "In an overpopulated Europe the British Isles form the most striking instance of a country in which the accumulated toil of past generations enables the present inhabitants to earn a livelihood." Still, the results of that toil had been largely invested outside the island shores: it was a maritime system, of truly global conception. It had brought about a situation in which any change not initiated by the British was a threat to their well-being. For some time Britain had been able to show that on the scales of political and economic power the small could outweigh the large; the twentieth century was beginning to put it the other way around.

Now, more than ever, the people of the British Isles look at their national territory with the hope of rebuilding the base of their existence so that it can again support the lofty and involved national structure that previous generations had erected. The actual significance of a given geographical position changes as world history rolls on: there is no longer a European springboard on the Atlantic on which Britain has a central and advanced position. She still is on the great North Atlantic

Wales. At the foot of the Snowdon range, in a glacial-eroded valley between barren slopes, are both industries and small woods. *(British Information Services)*

A typical English countryside in the center of the London basin. Hedges enclose the fields, and grazing sheep testify to the old-farm predominance of livestock raising. *(British Information Services)*

way between Europe and America, but the world is being decentralized, and air transportation spans land and sea with equal ease. What the islands' position is worth at present is being questioned and their relationship to the European continent is being reconsidered.

## NATURAL AND HUMAN REGIONS

The seas that isolate the British Isles have shaped scalloped shore lines. Great Britain is deeply penetrated by tidal waters on all its sides; Ireland has a more rounded contour but still has profound indentations on its periphery. No point in either island is situated at more than 100 miles from tidal water. The sea thus provided easy transportation around the islands and even to some extent inland. The tide is felt on many rivers upstream, and the traffic of small craft in the port of London still takes advantage of the tidal currents to move up or down the Thames River. Many of the leading ports are established at some point upstream on these more-or-less wide rivers or channels, such being the case of London, Southampton, Bristol, Hull, Newcastle-upon-Tyne, and Glasgow.

The maritime influence brought also some unity in the climatic conditions. Britain and Ireland are moderate in temperature and damp all year around: the actual annual temperature stays between 40° and 50° over the whole country; bathed in the warm Atlantic waters, they have a small range of temperatures within the year and abundant rainfall equally distributed among the four seasons. The topography varies the degree of penetration of the maritime influences. Situated definitely in the zone of the Westerlies—that is, of winds from the west, blowing chiefly behind the cyclonic depressions, the eastward procession of which goes on the year round—the islands will show some contrasts between their east and west coasts, all the more so as the North Sea, being smaller and shallow, permits some continental influences to cross over from the east occasionally, while only oceanic influences come in from the west. Thus the east is colder in winter and drier all the year round, but particularly in winter; the south and southeast are hotter in summer. These contrasts are sharper in Britain than in Ireland, as the former is larger, more extended in latitude, closer to the continent, and endowed with a more accentuated relief. On the southwestern coast of Ireland, the meteorological station of Valentia is commonly cited in Europe as the perfect example of the maritime climate: its yearly average temperature is 50.8° and its rainfall 55.6 inches. The range of temperatures between the coldest and warmest months averages 14.6°; the absolute minimum and maximum recorded are 20° and 81°. The rainfall is equally distributed over the year, no month having less than 5 or more than 12 percent of the annual total. The winter half-year gets 58 percent of this total. There are close to 300 rainy or foggy days every year; between certain heavy fogs and the steady drizzle of rain, it is sometimes difficult to draw a line; generally the sky is overcast; and there are only 1442 hours of sunshine, or 31 percent of the total number of daytime hours.

It must be remembered that Valentia is situated at 52° N. latitude, that of southern Labrador or of Calgary, Alberta. This gives a fair idea of what the climate is in the British Isles, although to the southeast, seasonal contrasts increase, the sun shines a little more, and rains are less abundant and more concentrated in time. Scotland and Ireland are thus substantially different from warmer and drier England. When in antiquity navigators from the Mediterranean reached the shores of Scotland, they brought back the tale of a region where one could not quite differentiate between sky, land, and sea—indeed the end of the continental world!

The structure of the British Isles sharpens the contrast between east and west and accentuates the impression of a land's-end area. The highlands are to the north and northwest, remnants of old Primary era foldings of the Caledonian and Hercynian systems; the general axis of the folding was northeast-southwest, with sometimes a perpendicular direction superimposed on it. The more recent Alpine movements have found some echo in these old resistant blocks, causing cracks, faulting, and volcanism in some spots. They have also slightly undulated the sedimentary strata to the southeast, for, in between the periods of tectonic surrection, seas occupied the lower parts of the present islands and deposited thick layers of sandstones, limestones, chalk, sands, and clays. Only narrow belts of such deposits are to be found in the northern and western sections of the islands; almost all the subsoil of Ireland is of ancient (Primary or Paleozoic) rock. It is only in southern and eastern England that the sedimentary layers, disposed in gently sloping basins, cover a wide expanse. These areas are structurally connected with the plains of the continent across the Channel or the North Sea. Scotland, on the contrary, is linked by its structure to the Scandinavian range.

Such an architecture seems logical. The old resistant sections of it are disposed to the northwest, closer to the edge of the continental shelf, bordering on the great Atlantic troughs; they may have acted as shields for some pressures coming from the west in the earth's crust; they also act as climatic screens to sharpen the contrast between northwestern and southeastern sections of the isles.

The differences in geological structure and in climate have obvious consequences in the distribution of soils, plants, and agricultural activities. These regional differences have been accentuated again by the glaciations. In the Ice Age glaciers covered all the isles southward to a line following approximately the present valley of the Thames River; the area south of a London-Oxford-Bristol line remained unglaciated— a new motive for contrast. The action of the glaciers was, of course, varied. The ice was much thicker and its action had much greater effect on the topography and soils in the colder and damper areas to the north and west: the morainic accumulation left a strong imprint on Ireland, where long lines of dikelike embankments similar to the Swedish *ösar* are called *eskers;* Scotland has fjords that may compare, though on a smaller scale, with those of Norway; the mountains of Wales offer types of glacial *cirque* formation as perfect as some of the Alpine lofty ranges. The plains of the islands have sometimes benefited by morainic soils; the boulder-clay formation covers vast areas and is supposed to come from the bottom moraine laid underneath the ice tongues. The drainage was also affected, valleys were deepened and widened, and the penetration of the sea inland was favored thereby.

Natural action throughout the ages thus prepared a division into natural regions and human influences coming from the outside, and acted parallel with environmental conditions to shape the regional map. The outside influences came from the continent, and on the whole they were bound to reinforce the local differences or contrasts resulting from the geological structure and the maritime influences. The Danes came mainly to the east of Britain and so did the Anglo-Saxon Germanic tribes; the Roman colonization occupied England but did not reach the north; the Norman conquest again came from the southeast. Norsemen had been visiting Scotland, and the narrowness of the North Channel between the Atlantic and the Irish Sea brought about closer ties between the settlement of northern Ireland and Scotland than between southern Ireland and England; still another transitional unit developed in Wales.

In its details, regionalism in England was influenced by a historical evolution similar to that of the rest of Western Europe, with the formation of feudal estates and of historical provinces followed by a stronger central authority shaped at the royal courts and in Parliament. After many centuries of opposition and war, the two kingdoms of Scotland and England were drawn together in their insular frame and united in 1707. Wales had been joined to England in the Middle Ages, and through a long series of wars waged between the thirteenth and seventeenth centuries the British achieved the conquest of Ireland. Thus in the eighteenth and nineteenth centuries the British Isles were united in one political structure, with one king who wore more than one crown. A number of local autonomies were preserved, and certain shades of culture continued to differentiate England and Scotland. Under a special regime, colonial in some ways, Ireland was restive and longed

The glaciated landscape of County Donegal, showing one of the poorer and more barren sections of Ireland. *(Irish Tourist Bureau)*

Cahersiveen Cohr, County Kerry. In the background, rounded hilltops demonstrate the same aspects of Irish terrain as the mountains of Donegal *(above)*, but in the valley nestles an attractive little town with a large church to the left, a castle at the bridge, and a checkering of rectangular fields beyond the river. *(Irish Tourist Bureau)*

for greater independence; after a gradual evolution, the Irish Free State was born in 1921, covering most of the western island, while six counties to the northeast, under the name of Northern Ireland, remained part of the United Kingdom. Southern Ireland or Eire continued to drift away from the British framework, and a fully independent Republic of Ireland was proclaimed in 1949.

The two main islands are thus politically distinct. They have followed also different economic evolutions. Under a regime of large estates owned by a small number of absentee landlords, Ireland has remained mainly a rural country; with the exception of a few towns on its northeastern coast, closely associated with Britain, the country did not take an active part in the maritime and industrial expansion of Britain. The larger island accomplished alone almost all the immense, world-wide development on which its greatness was founded. Commercial and industrial power drew the population toward the main port areas and toward the lowlands. In the eighteenth and nineteenth centuries the population concentrated in the areas of the coalfields. Great Britain owed to its geographical structure the existence of deep and continuous layers of coal in many parts of its territory, on the periphery of the old Primary massives, and therefore on the coasts rather than inland. With the advent of the steam engine and turbine, coal became the essential source of power for manufacturing and transportation, and the British built their power on the rich coalfields close to the sea. Industrialization and urbanization proceeded chiefly on coal until World War I (see map, p. 234). London, the national and imperial capital and the first seaport, was the only very large agglomeration of population independent of coal. This stressed again the opposition between high and low-lying areas, between the different slopes and the different orientations of the coasts. It helped stabilize the growing population of Great Britain, while Ireland, though less thickly populated, underwent greater economic pressures and had to relieve them through mass emigration. Therefore although the physical environment is relatively uniform, the British Isles contain striking contrasts, on which strong regionalisms have grown up, to be reinforced in a few cases by recent trends.

## IRELAND

The general topography of Ireland can be described as an old, low, and glaciated plateau. The subsoil of the main bulk, the central section of the island, is formed by a mass of limestone of the carboniferous period, with outcroppings of coal-measures strata on the fringe. Most of this central part of the island is below 500 feet of elevation. Its topography and topsoil are the result of glacial action. To the north and south of

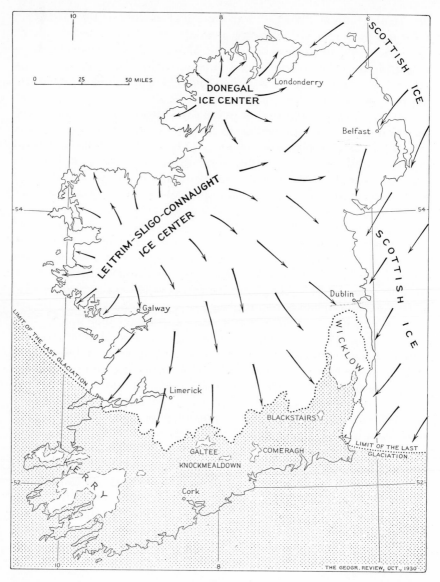

Glaciation of Ireland during the regime of the last ice sheet. Dotted line shows the limitation of the icecap glaciation at this epoch imposed by Scottish ice and by ice from two Irish
centers (arrows show approximate directions of ice movement). Broken lines show the
limits of local glaciation by valley glaciers in the highlands south of the main ice mass
(each local center is named). *(The Geographical Review)*

the island the altitude rises, and the topography is more diversified. In both cases a general northeast-southwest orientation prevails. In the northern section, a continuation of the structure of Scotland is found; there are three elements from west to east: the old rocky mass of crystalline materials making the mountains of Donegal; the large basaltic plateau of Antrim with a large lake, the Lough Neagh, in its midst, and picturesque sea-erosion of the basalt mass shaping landscapes such as the Giants' Causeway on the coast; and finally the granitic intrusion of the Mourne Mountains to the east. The heights have been sculpted by the ice which gave sharp contours to the land forms; a few summits rise above 2000 feet. To the south of the central plain, small hilly ranges align themselves along the outcroppings of old red sandstone anticlines, which alternate with limestone valleys. This string of massives begins immediately to the south of Dublin with the Wicklow Mountains, rising to 3039 feet, due to the intrusion of another mass of igneous rock. But the highest summit of Ireland is situated at its southwestern corner in the mountains of Kerry, where Carrantuohill reaches 3414. On the whole, Ireland is made of a central plain, which opens more widely eastward on the Irish Sea and is higher and more rugged on the periphery, particularly to the north and to the southwest.

Drainage is always difficult in a basin-shaped area. Glaciers have disorganized it and left a humid land on which the moraines have accumulated irregular barriers to the flow of water. The persisting uncertainty of the drainage is obvious on the hydrographic map, with the great number of strangely shaped lakes and a great number of streams flowing in all directions. The River Shannon, actually a long string of lakes, drains most of central Ireland, but its basin is interconnected by many channels with those of other rivers flowing in different directions. The humidity of the climate and this uncertainty of the surface drainage have favored the formation of marshes and peat bogs, which are common throughout the central and western sections of Ireland. Climate and topography combine to make a better drainage along the western and southern coasts. The great acidity and dampness of the soils was never favorable to forest growth. Moreover, Ireland was thickly populated from an early period, and a great deal of the existing woods was cleared.

Such an environment is not always easy to manage. It might have been developed, like some of the damp and naturally poor areas of the Netherlands or Denmark, if enough capital and labor had been put into it over long centuries. Instead, political history imposed other trends. Different traditions seem to have differentiated the evolutions of Ireland and England. The smaller island to the west belonged to the area of the old Celtic civilization, in which Scotland, Wales, Cornwall, and

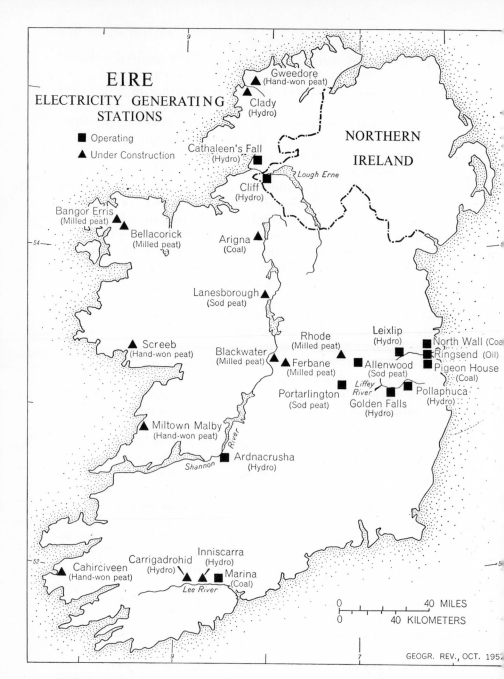

# EIRE
## ELECTRICITY GENERATING
## STATIONS

■ Operating

▲ Under Construction

Gweedore
(Hand-won peat)

Clady
(Hydro)

Cathaleen's Fall
(Hydro)

NORTHERN

IRELAND

Cliff
(Hydro)

Lough Erne

Bangor Erris
(Milled peat)

Bellacorick
(Milled peat)

Arigna
(Coal)

Lanesborough
(Sod peat)

Rhode
(Milled peat)

Leixlip
(Hydro)

North Wall (Coal)

Screeb
(Hand-won peat)

Blackwater
(Milled peat)

Ferbane
(Milled peat)

Allenwood
(Sod peat)

Ringsend (Oil)

Pigeon House
(Coal)

Portarlington
(Sod peat)

Liffey
River

Golden Falls
(Hydro)

Pollaphuca
(Hydro)

Miltown Malby
(Hand-won peat)

River

Ardnacrusha
(Hydro)

Shannon

Inniscarra
(Hydro)

Carrigadrohid
(Hydro)

Marina
(Coal)

Cahirciveen
(Hand-won peat)

Lee River

0   40 MILES

0   40 KILOMETERS

GEOGR. REV., OCT. 1957

Stations marked as under construction were completed by 1961. Notice the continuing importance of both hydroelectricity and peat in the production of power. Both these sources of energy have been inherited from the glacial and damp past of the island. (*The Geographical Review*)

Brittany participated. It was not much affected by the Germanic invasions which swept England and was the seat in the fifth to the ninth centuries of an extraordinarily brilliant cultural development led by the Roman Catholic Church. Irish monasteries were at that time the great meeting places and seats of learning for scholars in Western Europe. They had many ties with France and Spain and went overseas, settling even in Iceland. From Scotland a steady flow of population came to Ireland, and from the twelfth century on the kings of England and Wales began taking an interest in the island.

During long centuries the British dominated Ireland — and the Irish fought back stubbornly. The rural landscape was organized not so much for the purpose of supplying the local needs as to complement the British economy. The soil and climate of Ireland were well fitted for a rapid growth of grass, and the specialty of Ireland became livestock husbandry on large estates owned generally by the British. (In 1903 some 750 landlords owned more than half the island.) This was a green island indeed, and the green of grass has remained the national color. According to a well-known rule, true all around the world, a rural population takes little care of the land if it is not admitted to a large share in the production. Such was the case for centuries in Ireland, and the economy remained rather backward. The peasants lived on small plots of land or cultivated the large estates. They produced potatoes for food, flax and some wool for textiles. When the potato crop was bad, famine threatened the whole population. Such was the case in 1846, when the disease of the potato started the great Irish migration overseas: in the second half of the nineteenth century about 4 million people left the island, most of them for North America. Western Ireland particularly, the damper and poorer part, lost a considerable percentage of its population. The parallel political struggle continued, bringing the British government to grant Home Rule and finally independence to the larger section of Ireland. Since 1922 the economic trends have been so different in Eire, now the Republic of Ireland, and Northern Ireland that they must be studied separately.

THE REPUBLIC OF IRELAND

In 1966 the Republic of Ireland's land area of 17 million acres was inhabited by about 2.9 million people. The population had slowly decreased, although the flow of emigration to the United States had been checked by the latter's restrictions on immigration and by the endeavors of the Irish government to develop the national economy. Great reforms have been undertaken and carried out since the establishment of an autonomous Irish Free State in 1921. The first measures concerned the breaking up of the large estates and the distribution of the lands in small or medium-sized farms. The trend, begun in the 1870s under Home Rule, was accelerated, and today Eire is a country of small farmers, most of whom own their lands. Next, the Irish economy, geared toward export of dairy and meat products to Britain, was directed more toward self-sufficiency. In 1958 two crops that were negligible before 1920 occupied substantial areas—wheat (418,000 acres) and sugar beets (84,600) but they declined again in the 1960s (to 182,000 and 65,500 acres, respectively, in 1965), while the traditional culture of oats (284,000 acres), potatoes (174,000), turnips (105,000), barley (464,000), and hay (1,953,000) was continued. The main crop changes have occurred in the south of the central plain in the famous Golden Vale of Limerick and Tipperary and in the east with its better soils and warmer climate, wheat and sugar beets being given the best soils and the latter prospering particularly in the Barrow Valley. There were also 5.4 million head of cattle, 5 million sheep, and numerous horses and pigs. Animal husbandry still predominated, but tilled agriculture had increased its part. Still, the cultivated area in the mid-1960s was smaller than it had been in the mid-1940s, during the period of great shortages of food in the wake of the war. Irish agriculture has not been as prosperous and profitable in times of abundance; it has even become the problem area of the Irish economy, which used to be essentially agricultural. The bad harvests of the cold and rainy summers too frequently repeated in the 1954–1965 period made things worse. The exodus away from the farms increased and was responsible for the emigration that made the Irish republic the only country in the free world with a decreasing population during the 1950s, stabilizing in the 1960s.

Finally Eire has started to industrialize and urbanize itself. Dublin, its capital, is also the main port and the principal industrial center, and in 1966 it was an agglomeration of 750,000 people, about one fourth of the total population of Eire. Its traditional industries were founded on the agricultural production of the hinterland, such as dairy products, beer, and alcohol made from potatoes. Now it has sugar refineries, glass, cement, textiles, clothing, and boot and shoe factories as well as a printing and publishing industry. Some metallurgy has also started, and a large plant assembles motor vehicles. The port equipment has been improved, and about one half of the foreign trade of Eire now goes through it. The other thriving urban centers are worth mentioning: on the southern coast, Cork (122,000 people, but 150,000 with the suburbs), with its roadstead of Cobh at which large liners call, and on the western coast, at the bottom of the shallow and wide mouth of the Shannon River, Limerick (57,000), a peaceful, prosperous, and handsome town in the midst of one of the richest and greenest sections of the island. Both these towns are becoming industrialized, although their main function still is to service the rural areas of southern Ireland. Cork has fertilizer plants and a rubber industry; Limerick has electronic plants and, in its vicinity, Shannon Airport, one of the main relays of transatlantic flights, although losing in importance as the range of airplanes increases.

For large-scale industrialization Eire lacks raw materials, capital, and markets. Coal has been mined (186,000 tons in 1943, 230,000 in 1959, but 178,000 only in 1965), but the extraction is small and the coal is second-rate; waterpower is harnessed on the Shannon, Lee, and a few other rivers. An extensive electrification program has multiplied the generating stations, many of which use peat. From 1948 to 1966 the output of electricity has risen from 709 to 3,750 million kwhr, one third of which is now supplied by water power. Industries have expanded using this power or imported coal and oil. The abundant and inexpensive labor available in Ireland is being gradually put to work in more profitable fashion than would be possible on a small farm, owing to an inflow of foreign capital; during the 1950s, American, Dutch, German, and Japanese investments have spurred the growth of manufacturing, producing goods for export. In the 1960s, most of the influx of capital came from Britain.

Traditionally, Irish exports reflected the rural character of the country: live animals usually constituted half of the domestic exports in value, the rest being butter, bacon, ham, beer, some linen and leather goods. Now, manufactured goods, including textiles, machinery, and some electronic apparatus, have come to form a notable part of the domestic exports: in 1957, they made up one fifth of these exports; in 1961, one third (equaling for the first time the value of the live animals exported); and in 1966, again one fourth. The cattle economy remains the basic pillar of the Irish rural economy and still supplies the major and most stable component of its exports. In 1967, in the fright of contamination coming from Britain, where an epidemic of hoof-and-mouth disease decimated the cattle, Ireland forbade Irish residents in England to return home for Christmas. This meant a substantial loss in terms of receipts from tourism. Foreign visitors in Ireland numbered more than 15 million annually in recent years; their expenditures help the Irish balance of payments. Most of them come from the United Kingdom, which is also the main customer for Irish exports: Britain and Northern Ireland used to take more than 90 percent of all Irish exports; this proportion came down to about 80 percent in 1960, and 70 percent in 1966; the United Kingdom also supplies at least one half of all Irish imports. An Anglo-Irish free trade agreement was signed in 1965, promising to remove gradually all duty between the two countries by July 1975. Economics still integrate the Republic of Ireland with the

Peat cutting in Eire. Peat is still an important fuel for domestic use in Ireland. *(Irish Tourist Bureau)*

Map of a part of the central lowland, showing some of the eskers left by the glaciers *(The Geographical Review)*

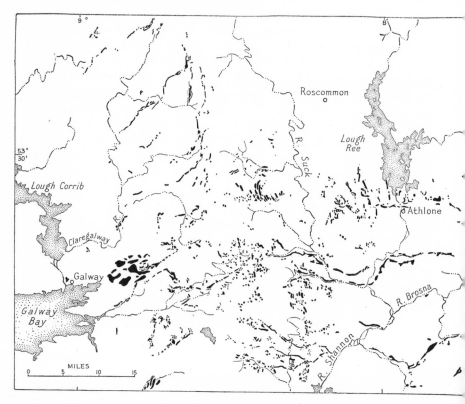

The port of Dublin. *(Irish Tourist Bureau)*

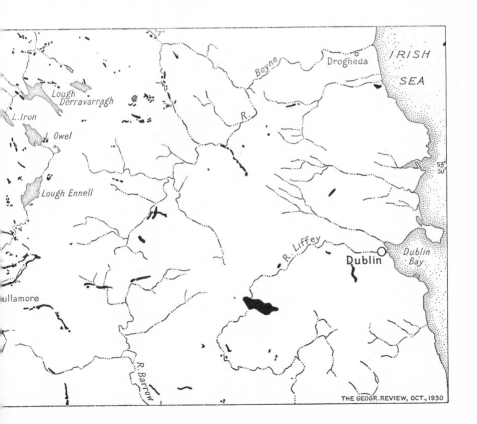

British Isles, although the recent decade has widened the horizon and the commercial relations with the Common Market countries and the United States.

Politically, Dublin's relations with London have improved greatly. It is still to England that most of the Irish emigrate in search of work, and it is mainly British capital that helps build Irish industry. In the 1960s urbanization and industrialization reached a point which reduced to about 20,000 the annual outflow of emigrants, so that the population balance of the country was righted for the first time in a century, and the total population of Ireland did not decrease. Occasional strain with Britain flares up at times, not only because of recently acquired independence but more often because of partition of the island; the Northern counties remained part of the United Kingdom and voted again in favor of this status in 1949, but they are *terra irredenta* for the Dublin government. The deep feeling of national integrity within the frame of the shoreline is naturally and deeply rooted in the Irish heart. There are many relationships between the two states on the same island, but there is a great deal of opposition, too, arising partly from economic structures, but even more from spiritual differences: Eire is predominantly and devoutly Roman Catholic, while Northern Ireland is, in the majority, Protestant. Barriers of the spirit are the most difficult to overcome.

## NORTHERN IRELAND

Ulster or Northern Ireland has a total area of 5,460 sq. miles supporting a population of 1.5 million inhabitants. More than one third of these are concentrated in the two main cities, indicating a fairly advanced stage of urbanization. The agricultural economy follows the traditional pattern of Ireland, without the recent changes introduced by Eire since its independence; hay, oats, potatoes, barley, and flax are the important crops, indicating a clear specialization in cattle raising; sheep, pigs, and poultry are important, too, with a greater emphasis on hogs than in the south. There are about 72,000 holdings in the area, most of them small, and the farmers are in process of completing the purchase of their lands. Under the Land Purchase Act, an agrarian reform similar to that of Eire, though more gradual, is being performed in Northern Ireland.

Ulster may claim a diversified economy as a result of the existence of two large-scale industries in its two main towns. The oldest local industry is manufacturing linen from the flax grown in the island, and Londonderry (54,000 inhabitants in 1961) is the main linen center. The other industry, centered at Belfast, is shipbuilding. Both industries were started there by Scottish interests but now have deep local roots. Belfast is a thriving city of nearly 500,000 people, and its shipyards have a capacity of over 200,000 tons per year. But the steel and coal must be brought from Britain, and indeed this industry looks like a subsidiary of the great shipyard zone of the Clyde on the Scottish shores facing those of Antrim. The textile industry, which is important in Belfast, too, was expanded since World War II by the addition of manmade fibers woven on machinery which previously served for linen only. Most of the linen production is exported overseas and has won a high reputation in the international market. Recently aircraft manufacture, textile, machinery, and electronics have become major industries, especially in the Belfast area. Still, serious civil trouble erupted in 1969.

Northern Ireland has a small parliament of its own, which sits in Belfast and makes decisions concerning local affairs. It continues to participate normally in the political life of the United Kingdom and sends members to the House of Commons in London. The local government is assisted in several respects, particularly in so far as finances are concerned, by the British Treasury, and the population now benefits from its association with the greater neighbor to the east.

## SCOTLAND

Scotland is one of the most remarkable and picturesque countries of Europe; it is also an example of successful achievement by man in an unfavorable physical environment. Most of the country resembles western Norway with its fjelds and fjords, but in the lower areas an industrial and commercial activity has developed without parallel in Scandinavia. The topography divides Scotland clearly into three sections that are in strong opposition: the highlands in the north, the Midland valley in the center, and the southern uplands in the south. In all these regions, which stretch from coast to coast across the island, there are important differences between east and west.

The *highlands* are a glaciated crystalline plateau sloping down to the southeast. Mature, heavy landforms predominate on the high level, above 1000 feet. The moorland, a landscape with few trees, stretches over vast areas on which the density of population often does not exceed 1 per square mile. A few bold summits rise above the general level, Ben Nevis in the west reaching 4406 feet. Deep valleys break up the continuity of the plateau and divide it into so many ridges and hills that in many parts the highlands take on the aspect of mountains. Most of the wide and deep valleys, though sculpted by the glaciers, have a structural orientation northeast-southwest and are called *glens;* elongated lakes often occupy part of their bottoms and are called *lochs;* at their extremities they widen in funnel-shaped bays, which increase rapidly in depth and are called *firths* or sounds. The most impressive of these valleys is

Glen More, cutting across the island from the Moray Firth in the northeast to the Firth of Lorne in the southwest and separating the northwest highlands from the Grampian Mountains, which are more massive and stretch more widely from west to east.

Some glens and lochs were dug so deeply by the glaciers that they became sea channels, cutting off islands from the main island: such is the case of the Inner Hebrides along the west coast and the Outer Hebrides across the Minch. Off the northern coast, the highlands send an arm to the northeast marked by the Orkneys and the Shetland Islands. There is a picturesque grandeur in these solitudes created by the highlands and their contact with the sea, particularly to the west. The Inner Hebrides are formed in part of lava plateaus dominating the sea by vertical cliffs. In the basalt, the waves have eroded high walls (such as on the Isle of Skye) or gigantic columns and grottoes (such as on the island of Mull, famous for its Fingal's Cave, into which the high tide rushes with a terrifying roar).

The highlands cover six tenths of Scotland but support little of its population. Lakes, peat bogs, and barren rocks are the main element of the landscape and offer little resources. Large estates are still common here, with wide areas reserved for hunting grounds or deer forests. Sheep pasture on the meager grass. To the north of Scotland, the Shetland Islands are well known for their breed of sheep. But the highlands' main resource is fishing; the sea has attracted to the periphery most of the population and its activities. Narrow coastal plains are harbored on the eastern fringe of the highlands, with fields of oats, potatoes, and turnips.

Larger areas are under hay. Some cattle is raised, particularly of the Aberdeen-Angus and Shorthorn breeds, on the low-lying meadows in the east. On the whole, the highlands are the poorest agricultural region of Great Britain. The only important development, growing up around the specialization in cattle, centers in Aberdeen (185,000 inhabitants), one of the chief fishing ports of the North Sea and the only large town in the highlands. Inverness has only 30,000 people and Thurso, in the far north, once the hub of Scottish relations with Scandinavia, had been reduced to very little until it started growing again in the 1950s.

Although their total number is small, Highlanders are famous for their clans, their long-lived feuds, the traditions to which they cling stubbornly, and particularly for their kilts and tartans. The rough environment of the highlands provides good training in tenacity. The medieval castles overlooking the lochs, the monotonous music of the pipers, the old traditions of the populations—all add greatly to the charm of the country. The Highlanders have remained so isolated that in the northwestern section there is still a majority of people who speak

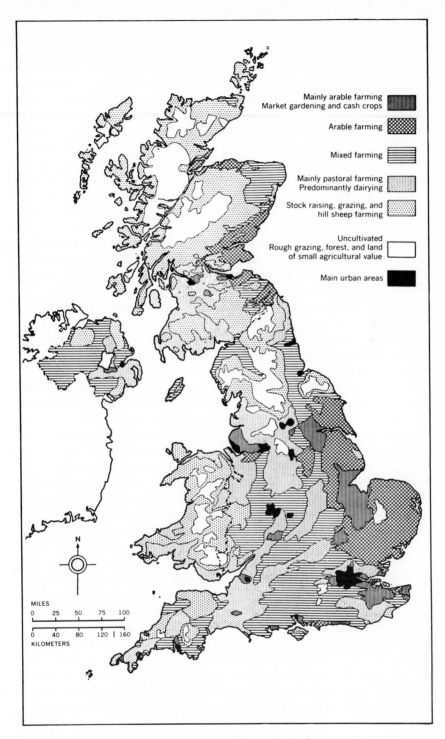

Agriculture in Great Britain in the 1960s. *(Ministry of Agriculture)*

the Gaelic language of ancient times. Thousands of years pass without seeming to make much effect on the local way of life; in fact, however, afforestation, modern methods of sheep raising, and efficient trawlers at sea have been introduced since the nineteenth century. More recently, some industry has come to the highlands to utilize some of its water-power resources, most of which are still unharnessed. Indeed, in many respects this region recalls western Norway; it even has some plants making aluminum with hydro-electric power. But so ancient are the rocks and so immovable the traditions that tales have spread of animals of remote geological periods still living in the highlands—thus the re-current rumor about the monster of the Loch Ness that rests at the bot-tom of the Glen More.

The highlands are the stronghold of Scotland, and they continue to influence the rest of the country, even Britain, as they send a contin-uous stream of the surplus population southward, especially to the Midland valley.

The *Midland valley* is a large trough deeply penetrated by firths and strewn with small groups of hills; a little more excavation might have converted it into a sea channel and the highlands into a separate island. It is the heart of Scotland, concentrating over two thirds of its popu-lation and almost nine tenths of its resources. Here stretch, mainly on the eastern side, the best agricultural lands of Scotland, on the sediment-ary layers preserved at the bottom of the trench. Eruptive rocks caused the hills that are scattered through the depression and often crowned with beautiful castles. Rich alluvial soils have filled the valleys, particu-larly that of the Forth. "Better a link of Forth than the province of Moray," runs an old saying. Man has worked hard on the narrow bot-tomlands that held out enough promise: swamps were drained, scienti-fically calculated crop rotations applied, and much fertilizer added. Wheat, oats, barley, potatoes, turnips, clover, and alfalfa are grown with care and produce some of the highest yields in Great Britain. The recent trend has been toward more intensive cattle raising and toward orch-ards; nurseries of trees and flower gardens are important too. In the farms, which are generally 150 to 200 acres in size, landowners have invested large capital to create this advanced, almost scientific, agri-culture. But the main resource is still not the land. Since olden times it has been the sea, then the coalfields and a variety of productions among which Scotch whisky is not the least.

A few towns that were important in old times as local centers, cross-roads, and seats of feudal authority are scattered through the Midland valley. Stirling and Perth (41,200) are among them; the latter is on an estuary and has some textile factories. Linen and jute mills are spread all along the Firth of Tay. Dundee is by far the main center of these industries. In the nineteenth century it had almost a monopoly of large-scale manufacturing of goods from jute, which was imported from India. Since then, jute mills have been built in many other places, particularly in Calcutta, close to the producing area; linen made with flax from the Baltic countries also has lost in importance. With its 183,000 inhabitants, Dundee is still a notable regional center, and a number of factories can the fruits of the valley's orchards, make watches, electrical machinery, hats, and clothing, but the large-scale industries and main agglomerations are to be found farther south, along the Firth of Forth and the Clyde River, where coal is also abundant.

The Clyde River basin is one of the important industrial areas of Britain. The river is rather narrow and reaches the firth through a sharp bend; neither the foggy and windy climate nor the topography seemed to favor seaport activities or agriculture around the town of Glasgow, which numbered only 14,000 inhabitants in 1661. It was in the eighteenth century that Glasgow and the Clyde started to develop; in the beginning of that century, the union of Scotland with England opened the possibility of trade with the colonies in America and, looking westward, the Clyde sent ships to Maryland and Virginia ports. Glasgow specialized in the tobacco trade and around 1775 is supposed to have imported half of the tobacco coming into Europe, immense warehouses being built there. Sugar, rum, and other tropical goods were added to tobacco, and the capital amassed in this trade served to build up the harbor facilities, and to build ships and manufacturing plants. Dredging opened Glasgow to the largest ships afloat, and a string of satellite towns, mostly industrial suburbs, expanded downstream. At the end of the eighteenth century large deposits of coal with shallow seams were found in the neighborhood, sometimes interstratified with iron ores. This gave rise to a large iron and steel industry—James Watt made some of his main experiments with the steam engine in Glasgow. Engineering then became the chief activity, putting trade in a secondary position. Large engineering plants, building a vast gamut of machinery from pipes to locomotives, motorcars, sewing machines, cranes, and pumps, grew up on the Clyde on a large scale; but the main industry is still shipbuilding and associated manufacturing. The Clyde yards have built a large percentage of the British naval and merchant tonnage: 50 percent in the 1870s and about 25 percent in the 1930s, including the famous *Queen Mary* and *Queen Elizabeth*, which were for many years the largest luxury liners afloat until their retirement in 1968.

Industrial development attracts still more industry: a great variety of plants grew up and goods were manufactured along the Clyde and in smaller towns scattered about the western part of the Midland valley; textiles and chemicals assumed an important size. Thus a "black-country"

Edinburgh, the heart of the Scottish capital. The railroad (lower left) passes through the loch, which has been drained, leaving a narrow valley between the medieval castle on the hill (background, left) and Princes Street (right), with its heavy traffic, modern shops, and monument to Sir Walter Scott *(British Information Services)*

Crofters cutting hay in the fields above Loch Inchard. *(British Information Services)*

belt developed around Glasgow, and the port's main function became the servicing of these industries. The exports have decreased, as almost no coal is now being shipped overseas, and instead huge quantities of petroleum are brought in and refined. The collieries around Glasgow have decreased their output more rapidly than the British average, for their seams are shallow but thin and the quality is not always excellent. Still they supply the local consumption, and it is huge. The metallurgical zone around Glasgow produces about 14 percent of British pig iron and steel, and the chemical industries require increasing quantities of coal. The local iron ores are almost exhausted and most of the ores have to be imported. The prosperity of the area is again largely based on the ports of the Clyde. During World War II they functioned as one of the main debarkation points for American troops in Britain, as the two *Queens* shuttled between New York and Greenock, their birthplace, well protected by the fogs and its distance from German-controlled shores. These two advantages were obvious also in the few cases of bombing of Scottish industries by enemy planes and resulted in greater efficiency of wartime production. With 1,055,000 inhabitants, Glasgow rivals Birmingham for second place among Britain's cities. The Clyde-side conurbation amounted to 1,800,000 people in 1961. It is the in-dustrial keystone of Scotland, but the heart of the Scottish national life is to be found eastward—on the Forth.

Edinburgh, the old and beautiful capital of Scotland, cannot compare with the banks of the Clyde for industrial or commercial activity. It is, however, a thriving city of 468,000 with an active port in its suburb of Leith, and greater independence from England than Clyde has achieved in its development. With its towering Castle Rock, its cathedral, abbey, the houses of Parliament, its castles, many museums and monuments, Edinburgh looks like a real capital. Its university is an old and renowned center of learning and research; the Royal Scottish Geographical Society carries on a well-established tradition in its own field, and many great scientists have worked and taught at Edinburgh. The city has a special part in the history of economics, for its banks laid the foundations of modern banking methods. And through the importance of its banks and insurance companies, Edinburgh is still the financial capital of Scotland, as well as its cultural and national metropolis. The industrial function is not entirely absent from the city: there is coal mining in its vicinity, and the Midlothian field has recently increased its importance; a small oil field is also situated near by. But heavy manufacturing was attracted westward, and Edinburgh specialized in lighter crafts, in electronics, in paper making, printing, and publishing—again recalling the "brains" function of this city—and is perhaps the least industrialized and the handsomest of large British towns.

South of the Midland valley, the topography rises again, but the *southern uplands* do not have the massivity or the altitude of the high-lands. The highest summits range between 2500 and 2800 feet, and most of the area is below 1500 feet. Silurian schists have been more easily sculpted by erosion than the old crystalline plateaus of the north; the predominance of the Caledonian structural axis is less apparent; and wide valleys go in all directions from the central group of higher crests. Outcroppings of granite give more relief and mass to the western section of the uplands; grass, heathland, and moors still predominate on the hills. Eastward the topography is more broken, and one main stream, the Tweed, drains most of the region, including part of the Cheviot Hills, along which winds the boundary between Scotland and England. Cheviot and Tweed are famous names in the terminology of woolen goods. The uplands are indeed fitted for sheep raising, and this has long been their chief resource. The abundance of high-grade wool gave birth to the industry, concentrated mainly in the long valley of the Tweed at places such as Peebles, Galashiels, and Selkirk. Today most of the raw wool is imported from overseas, but the local clip of the Cheviots remains substantial and of good quality. In the low-lying areas rural life is active, with emphasis on grain crops in the sunnier east and on the fattening of cattle in the damper west. The uplands are a picturesque area with many historical sites and castles scattered throughout the hills, for this borderland was devastated by border warfare between Scotland and England for some 700 years; Berwick, Dunbar, Peebles, and Selkirk were primarily fortresses in medieval times. The four border counties of Berwick, Peebles, Roxburgh, and Selkirk look like "old country"; they have had rather low fertility rates in recent decades, and, with some emigration, their population has decreased.

The total population of Scotland, however, has been increasing. Between 1951 and 1961, it gained 82,075 and reached at the 1961 census the figure of 5,178,490, the highest on record. It had been reduced by about 254,700 as a result of migration over the ten years. Within Scotland itself, the concentration of the people in the Midland valley went on, for besides the border counties, the seven crofting counties also lost about 2.8 percent of their population in 1951-1961, despite a high birth rate. In the Midland valley, the city of Glasgow counted a slight loss in population, a rather normal trend nowadays for central cities of more than a million in Western countries. Edinburgh and Dundee had slight increases; but the main gathering went on in the valley around and in between the major cities. Several new towns, founded in the late 1940s, developed well through the 1950s, thus East Kilbride (28,000) and Cumbernauld near Glasgow and Glenrothes near Kirkcaldy. The Falkirk-Grangemouth area seemed to be growing at the more substantial rate, indicating a trend of the metropolitan regions of Edinburgh and Glasgow to extend toward one another. To the west the Ayr-Prestwick area also showed some progress. Similar trends prevailed in the 1960s; the total population of Scotland reached 5,200,000 in 1968. The new industries expanding in the valley are mainly engineering and chemicals (including petrochemistry, dyes, and pharmaceuticals). Increasingly, the bulk of the people and resources of Scotland are concentrated in the small area of the Midland valley, but the higher lands framing it have contributed greatly to shape the nation, giving it its originality and special temperament. Scots are famous for their tenacity, their efficiency, and their skill at saving and investing money. They also are noted for imagination and venturesome disposition. The difficult environment for a rapidly increasing people may be responsible for some of these traits. Lack of resources at home favored emigration; centuries ago large numbers emigrated to Northern Ireland and then farther overseas. The Act of Union opened the English colonies to them, and during the eighteenth and nineteenth centuries Scots formed strong settlements throughout the Americas, in Australia, and elsewhere. Often they succeeded better than the English in the new countries, gaining fortune and influence, particularly in the Americas, where their role has been outstanding from Montreal to Punta-Arenas. A steady flow of emigration took Scots to England proper as well. A British reporter noted the following definition given in the 1920s at the League of Nations in Geneva: "One Scot — a savings bank; two Scots — a game of golf; three Scots — the British Government."

## ENGLAND AND WALES

South of the Scottish border the structure of Great Britain assumes new forms. After a narrow section, the island widens; the lower areas increase, particularly in the east; the structural northeast-southwest axis is replaced by a dominant north-south orientation, with some interference in an east-west direction. The human picture changes also. The urban and industrial agglomerations are more frequent; the densities are higher; the agriculture expands in a milder climate, but it is an intensively mechanized kind of agriculture with emphasis on cattle; although most of the forest cover has been cleared, the frequent hedges planted with trees give a wooded aspect to the landscape. As in Western Europe, the present scenery is far removed from the original natural one and has changed several times. An ancient rural civilization, tilling the land with the hoe, covered parts of the plains with open, square fields, still visible in an aerial photograph under the present checkerboard of elongated parcels. The introduction of the wheeled plough from the continental shores of the North Sea made horse-drawn tillage more efficient and lengthy fields more convenient, and in the eleventh century Norman armies marched through open fields where now hedges and trees enclose most of the parcels of land. The change was accomplished from the thirteenth to the eighteenth centuries through an agrarian evolution, leading to enclosures around fields and meadows and an increased emphasis on grass and livestock—cattle on the better lands, sheep on the meager pastures. Considerable effort went into the production of the foodstuffs for which the climate, the soil, and the system of tenure fitted England. Still there was little improvement and development of land to an extent that could compare with that achieved in Denmark or the Low Countries; since she became a great power, the main resources of England have been in commerce, shipping, and manufacturing.

The structure and climate of England have increased the regional differences owing to the contrasts between east and west coasts and owing also to the existence of a wide plain in the south. We shall review the whole area by dividing it into five regions: north, south, and east England, the central plain in the midst, and Wales in the west.

Northern England is a vast region stretching as far southward as the Wash on the eastern coast and Wales on the western. It is formed by a hilly spinal area, the Pennine chain, stretching north-south between two fairly different coastal plains, both widening toward the south but the eastern plain being much wider and richer on the whole. The Pennines are formed by a large anticline. The vault of its arch changes in nature along the chain: in the north, crystalline rocks are still frequent, and the Hercynian folds appear in places; southward the altitude decreases, more recent strata cover the old materials, the range of hills narrows and plunges suddenly under the sedimentary plain of the Midlands along 53° latitude. Several rivers cut through the range in deep gaps, with the Tyne and Airdale gaps opening the way to transversal communications and railroads. Most of the hills are covered with heath and moor, flocks of sheep alternating between the higher summer pastures and the lower winter ones. Grass, hay, and cattle appear in the valleys.

In the area south of the Scottish border, the Pennines stretch across the entire width of the island; they are still massive and the high peaks reach about 3000 feet. The Tyne gap and the wider, north-south-oriented Eden valley break the hills into sections and canalize the through traffic. The westernmost section of the chain, the Cumbrian Mountains, is dissected by radiating glaciated valleys with elongated lakes between forested slopes. This lake district of England offers charming scenery quite different from that of Scotland. North of these ridges a flat area develops along the Solway Firth; this Solway plain, many times disputed between Scotland and England, is now a quiet rural district: the town of Carlisle (71,000) has little industry, and that chiefly engineering and cloth printing. The industrial section of Cumberland is on the narrow coastal plain to the west, on a coalfield, and it was the proximity of this coal to deposits of high-grade iron ore that favored the development of iron and steel industries. Both minerals, however, were soon found to be available in inadequate quantities: Cumberland's iron and steel has only a secondary importance in England, and the blast furnaces and steel works of Barrow-in-Furness and Workington receive their raw materials by sea. Shipyards are the main industry of Barrow, and most of its metallurgy belongs to the renowned firm of Vickers. The first large British nuclear power plant, Calder Hall, is located in Cumberland.

A road crossing sheep pastures and following approximately a line of Roman fortifications against the Scots leads eastward over the hills from Cumberland into the valley of the Tyne in Northumberland. Quiet rural life still predominates in these valleys, which are cut in carboniferous limestone and largely devoted to a prosperous mixed farming. Fox hunting remains a lively traditional pastime in this green country. It contrasts strikingly with the lower land along the seashore from Blyth southward and along the tidal estuary of the Tyne.

The Tyneside early became one of the leading industrial areas of Britain. It benefited by the proximity of the rich Northumberland and Durham collieries on both sides of the river, and by the presence of iron ore at a small distance inland. The nearby seams of coal are relatively thin and the pits shallow, but the coal is of high quality, particularly for coke making. These seams plunge eastward under the sea, and some mining galleries have gone under the water. As the coal of the upper layers was exhausted, mining went deeper, and some pits presently go more than 3000 feet down. As often happens in coal-mining areas, many galleries went under built-up districts, causing the soil to subside under the buildings. Not infrequently in these northeastern coal-basin regions one sees houses specially propped up to prevent collapse. Coal extraction started early and helped develop both industrial activities and the sea trade of the ports on the deep estuaries of the rivers Tyne, Wear, and Tees.

Newcastle-upon-Tyne (270,000) is the regional capital and main port of the English northeast. As early as the fourteenth century it shipped coal to London, and by the nineteenth, to the whole world. "Carrying coal to Newcastle" became a proverbial expression of redundant effort. The fact is, however, that before the war Newcastle received anthracite from Wales, and in certain years recently it has even imported

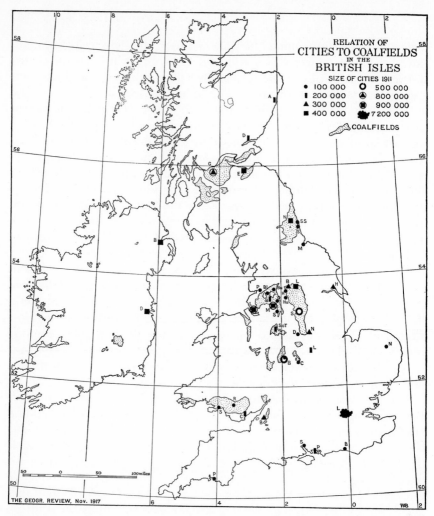

RELATION OF
**CITIES TO COALFIELDS**
IN THE
**BRITISH ISLES**
SIZE OF CITIES 1911
●  100 000   ○  500 000
▮  200 000   ◉  800 000
▲  300 000   ⬢  900 000
■  400 000   ✸ 7 200 000

COALFIELDS

This map is chiefly of historical interest, as it shows the close relationship existing until 1920 between urban growth and the distribution of the coalfields. Though the determining influence of coal is declining in British trade and industry, large cities cannot be easily moved, and their present distribution must be adapted to new conditions. Compare this map with the current map, opposite. The principal cities are indicated by their initials. Population figures are according to the 1911 census. *(The Geographical Review)*

Cities and industries in the United Kingdom, 1951. Key: 1, iron; 2, steel; 3, cotton; 4, wool; 5, linen; 6, silk; 7, chemicals; 8, commercial ports; 9, fishing ports; 10, shipyards; 11, tin; 12, lead; 13, principal railroads. The size of population is indicated by the type of lettering for the names of cities: block capitals mean over 1,000,000 inhabitants; slanted capitals, 500,000 to 1,000,000; block letters, 100,000 to 500,000. Compare this map with that for coalfields and growth of cities, opposite. The important mechanical and food industries could not be shown on this map because they are so widespread.

The monotony of the industrial might of England: workers' residences in Newcastle-upon-Tyne.*(British Information Services)*

Thirty-five miles in length, the Manchester Ship Canal has twelve miles of wharves, facilities for annually docking 500 vessels up to 15,000 tons, and oil refineries and many other plants along its banks. *(British Information Services)*

some ordinary coal. The supply of the local mines is no longer overabundant, as it used to be. Some exports still go out, chiefly to the North Sea and occasionally to the Mediterranean areas. A solid line of industrial towns along the Tyneside, from Newcastle to Tynemouth, produces a great variety of metals and machinery, builds and repairs many ships (the Tyne disputes the Clyde for first rank among shipbuilding centers of Great Britain), and manufactures chemical products. To the south of Newcastle, an important group of varied industries has developed recently in the Team Valley. Newcastle itself is an impressive and lively city, carrying on proudly long traditions that have left their imprint on the architecture of many streets. The whole conurbation accounts for 850,000 people. It forms the main urban center of the northeastern region of England, which has been one of the regions most affected by the twentieth-century crisis, where unemployment was extremely high between 1920 and 1940 and where a stubborn fight is now being put up against the factors of decline.

Durham, the historical capital of that county, is still a small town with an old university. Built by the prince-bishops who held the land against the Scots, Durham occupies a fortified position on a peninsula surrounded by a river meander and dominated by the massive cathedral that looks much like a fortress. Farther south, at the mouth of the Wear, is Sunderland, which builds more ships and used to export coal, but which went through a serious crisis in the 1930s, when the Durham mines, inadequately equipped, experienced a difficult period.

On the Tees estuary, the northeast coalfield nears the Cleveland iron-ore beds. Middlesbrough (now 161,000 inhabitants), on the mouth of the Tees, became the main center of blast furnaces and pig-iron production of Great Britain around 1900. The local ore, however, was of high phosphoric content and could be used only after the invention of the Thomas process; after 1920 the use of this ore decreased and with it Middlesbrough's leading part in iron making. Great quantities of imported, higher grade ores had to be used, and in 1965, the whole northeastern coast was making only 20 percent of the pig iron and 18 percent of the steel produced in the United Kingdom. Upstream along the Tees, machine works and big metallurgical constructions are carried on at Stockton, Darlington, and elsewhere. In 1968 a new county borough of Teesside was created around Middlesbrough, bringing under one governmental authority this thriving conurbation.

From 1945 to 1960, the northeast was considered a "development area," in which economic growth was helped by the government. The various measures taken under this policy greatly benefited the region; a good deal of prosperity was restored to it, although the general progress lagged somewhat behind national averages. The major pillars of the regional economy remained steel, chemicals, and heavy engineering (especially shipbuilding and repairing). But many lighter industries were introduced and flourished, particularly in the framework of the "trading estates," or industrial parks, which first developed here under government auspices. There are several large trading estates in the northeast, as in Team Valley at Gateshead-on-Tyne; by 1958 North Eastern Trading Estates, Ltd. had provided 36 sites or estates in Northumberland, Durham, and North Yorkshire, where about 55,000 people were employed in over 12 million square feet of factory space. Industrial expansion and diversification came also as large firms established new plants in the region, such as one of the largest knitting-wool factories in the world recently built at Darlington. However, the region's rate of population growth has remained somewhat inferior to the national average; in 1960 coal mining still was the largest single industry here, employing 14 percent of the insured population. The northeast was the second iron- and steel-producing region of Britain after South Wales. But it was trying to develop, on a large scale, new industries, particularly chemical, and to take advantage of its proximity to the natural gas fields of the North Sea. Newcastle had adopted a bold new plan of urban renewal centered around its expanding young university and an impressive Civic Center. A new town to count 100,000 inhabitants is being laid out south of the Tyneside, at a place named Washington, bringing the most modern kind of urban design to the northeast coast.

South of the Tees, the eastern plain widens rapidly; a few plateau areas maintain stretches of moorland close to the coast, but rich agricultural areas develop inland with a string of teaming industrial centers following the foot of the Pennines. This is the county of Yorkshire — "the biggest and the best of England," say the local people. The county extends broadly westward across the Pennines almost to the western coastal plain. Here the chain is more broken and pierced through by a network of gaps, and in early days east-west traffic used this zone of easier passage. It was one of the routes of westward penetration taken by the Anglo-Saxon tribes who arrived by sea on the eastern shores. York has played a special part in the formation of the English nation and culture, and its archbishop ranks second in the hierarchy of the Church of England. As its destiny varied, it was a Roman, a Danish, and a Norman stronghold, a port on the North Sea, and a regional capital. Today it is a principal railway town, has a lively university, and is the hub of a rich rural country in the central part of the fertile valley of York, where high yields are obtained from grain crops and some of the best cattle and hog breeds are raised. The maritime activities of Yorkshire are concentrated on the coast along the deep estuary of the Humber: Grimsby (95,000) is the largest British fishing port on the North Sea, from which London and the Midlands are supplied with sea food; nearby Hull (303,000) remains one of the largest ports of Britain, importing foodstuffs, pitprops, and oil seed, exporting steel, textile goods, machinery, and some coal and rivaling Grimsby as a fishing port.

The most striking development of Yorkshire has taken place in its coalfields, along the foot of the Pennines, with factories spreading along the valleys that penetrate the range. The larger area—known as the West Riding district—is devoted to textiles, especially woolens and worsteds. Leeds (510,000) and Bradford (296,000) are the two chief centers of wool combing and worsted making and do much of the woolen weaving of Britain. They are among the few large cities in Britain with still increasing population. A number of smaller places—such as Halifax, Huddersfield, Keighley, and Wakefield—work the wool and rayon. Doncaster is the main center of coal mining. Some oil and potash have been found in that region. There has been since the beginning of the century an increased concentration of the woolen industry in west Yorkshire, and, rather better than the cotton industry, this branch of manufacturing has withstood the difficulties of the period. The West Yorkshire conurbation counted 1.7 million people in 1961. South of the woolen region, iron and steel rises in importance again, with the famous steel center of Sheffield (530,000) producing about 12 percent of the United Kingdom's steel output. Iron has been worked at Sheffield for centuries, as some ore was extracted in the vicinity and smelted with charcoal from the Pennine forests. Piedmont waterfalls supplied the power that helped run the forges and shops, as Sheffield's cutlery became rapidly known for its quality, and demand for export overseas grew. In 1853 Bessemer invented and first applied in Sheffield the open-hearth process for the large-scale production of steel. Steel rapidly became the specialty of the place, and from Middlesbrough and elsewhere pig iron was brought in for final processing and turning into finished steel goods. Guns and armor plate, looms, axles, and wheels are produced here, as well as the older specialties such as knives, scissors, and files. Sheffield exemplifies in a striking way how manufacturing may cling to a site devoid of all advantages except the presence of coal and of skilled manpower.

In Sheffield's orbit, several medium-size towns work steel. Eastward, the fertile county of Lincoln rolls to the sea, continuing the grain and livestock economy of Yorkshire. Southward, the collieries stretch through an area dotted with mining and manufacturing towns to the threshold of the Midland plain; this eastern industrial fringe of the Pennines ends with Derby (132,000), which was a market for lead extracted in nearby mountains, then became a center for delicate textiles, silks, hosiery, ceramics, the building of Rolls Royce cars and of railroad rolling stock.

There, on the river Trent, stands Nottingham (312,000), commanding the gate of the Midlands. A town of considerable strategic importance in local wars, it developed a commercial function that led to industry: cotton hosiery, tulles, and laces are its specialty; it builds machinery and bicycles, and manufactures chemicals. Several of its rivals on the continent — Calais in France, Plauen in Germany — have long been dependent on Nottingham for their tooling. But cotton manufacturing seems somewhat lost in the east of England; one must cross the Pennines to find its stronghold on the western plain and valleys, in Lancashire.

The damp climate of the Cheshire plain, looking toward the northwest across the Irish Sea, favors the growth of grass, hay, and oats, while cattle and pigs feed on the farms that supply the dense urban centers. This same dampness used to be given as the reason for the rise in Lancashire of the main cotton-spinning and weaving district of Britain and, for a long time, of the world. But there are a great many other damp areas in Western Europe and several industrial districts working cotton that are not so damp. Actually the industry came to Lancashire through the trade with colonial areas developed successfully by the port of Liverpool at the mouth of the Mersey River. This port started as a British springboard of penetration into Ireland. In the seventeenth century the trade with the West Indies began; in the eighteenth century Liverpool engaged in the slave trade and specialized more successfully than any other European port in the "triangular trade" across the Atlantic. This meant taking some weapons, ammunition, and manufactured goods to the west coast of Africa, exchanging this cargo for "black ivory," and carrying the slaves across the ocean to sell them on the plantations of the West Indies and the southern United States, from which loads of tropical goods, especially cotton, were brought back to the home port. Great fortunes were built on this trade; and at Liverpool vast warehouses were erected, the port enlarged and equipped, and tropical goods redistributed to England and the continent. Even at present Liverpool re-exports a part of its imports. Transatlantic relations remained the main current of trade — Liverpool is the home of the Cunard Line and was one of the main ports of debarkation during World War II even when it was hard hit by German bombings. The population of this second port of the United Kingdom rose from 25,000 in 1760 to 165,000 in 1831, 855,000 in 1931 and 747,000 in 1961. Though the city proper declined, the conurbation is still growing, reaching 1,386,000 in 1961, with suburbs crowding the Merseyside which were cities in their own rights — Birkenhead with 142,000, Wallasey with 103,000, and Bootle with 83,000 people. The new town of Kirkby, with its thriving industrial estate, rose from 3,145 in 1951 to 52,200 in 1961. Much trade was bound to develop many industries, and the Merseyside is today a teaming avenue of factories: at present chemical and food industries predominate. Cotton from all parts of the world has long had here its chief market, before being reshipped elsewhere, mostly to Manchester, where in the eighteenth century some woolen manufacturing had been displaced by cotton mills started under the impulse and partly with the capital of Liverpool.

Manchester had been famous for its linen and woolen cloth beginning in the fourteenth century. Then it turned to cotton, and its craftsmen developed most of the automatic machinery used for cotton processing. In the late eighteenth century steam entered the picture, and a large coal deposit was discovered and mined north of the Manchester-Liverpool line. Large-scale industrialization started. It was in Lancashire that early labor troubles occurred, and the jobless workers set out to smash the machinery they blamed for their plight. And it was the Manchester school of economists who, headed by Cobden, started the fight to repeal the Corn Laws and made England turn to free trade to become the world's mill, supplied from overseas with most of its food and raw materials. South Lancashire became the typical heavily industrialized and specialized industrial district, supplying the whole world with certain qualities of cotton goods. Every valley or town specialized in some fabric, each working for a given country. Manchester became the "cottonopolis," setting the pace for the international trade of the raw material as well as the finished cloth. Manufacturing was spread through the neighborhood; merchandising centralized in the city; a ship canal was built from the Mersey to let Manchester import cotton directly without transshipment in Liverpool. The city reached 766,000 inhabitants in 1931, 661,000 in 1961. The conurbation centered on it goes on expanding in area but its population remains close to 2.4 million.

With the beginning of the twentieth century signs of rising competition appeared throughout the world: on the continent of Europe, in North America, and then in Japan. With Japanese industrialization, a powerful rival arose using much cheaper labor. The foundation of Manchester's prosperity was shattered along with the free-trade system and the general commercial supremacy of Britain; the rapid industrialization of the United States and Gandhi's campaign of passive resistance and boycott of British goods were decisive. Long before 1940 Lancashire experienced a grave and permanent crisis, and though the total population stayed close to 5 million during 1911–1951, its textile industries showed many signs of decline. World War II brought more difficulties because of the blitz and the general commercial situation. The textile industry today needs re-equipping; it needs also more markets abroad and cheaper raw materials. In 1946 the Labor Government closed down the cotton exchange in Liverpool—in Britain the era of free trade and textile-

But the reconstruction proceeds apace, and the city in 1961 numbered about 305,000 people, an increase of 135 percent over 1921 and 332,000 in 1966. The industrial Midlands form the south part of a U-shaped industrialized area that frames the Pennine chain. Within this region the geographical distribution shows a migration of the more prosperous industries toward the southeast, which touches the outskirts of East Anglia, the drier and richest agricultural region of Britain. The metropolitan periphery around Birmingham has boomed in the 1960s with renewed vitality and has become the second pole of attraction in Britain.

Between the Wash and the mouth of the Thames, the flat East Anglian plain, bulging eastward, has been traditionally the granary of England. More sunshine over heavy alluvials and loams, or over the Fens where marshes were drained and the fertility of these carefully embanked polders maintained by addition of fertilizers, tells the story of this part of Britain; nature granted some privileges, and men did the rest. Here is concentrated the bulk of the wheat and sugar-beet production of the United Kingdom; yields are quite comparable to those of the best-tilled rich loams of the continent. Since 1940 careful planning has improved the land as mechanization modernized the equipment, and both cattle and pigs are fattened in the stables. A few towns with some manufacturing functions are scattered through the plain, the more important being Cambridge with its famed and old university. Norwich is a regional capital and the seat of the new University of East Anglia. The ports of Great Yarmouth and Lowestoft on the coast are engaged in large-scale fishing.

The plain, animated by a few escarpments and lines of small hills, stretches farther to the south and west. The basin of the Thames River occupies the central part of the area, with a predominance of rural scenery, grass and cattle economy, and small local market towns, contrasting sharply with the "black country" on the one hand and on the other with the tremendous agglomeration of London, a world in itself that must be studied outside the local framework. Most of the towns around the plain are beginning to be defined chiefly by their relation to London, though Oxford, the old center of learning in the upper Thames valley, enjoys a special status. Recently industry has invaded the quiet town; automotive and other mechanical works have given it a new rhythm, and huge laboratories add to the modernization of the place (106,000). The two communities within the city, the academic and the industrial, have little in common other than proximity. The industrial community, one of the larger automotive construction centers in Europe, has contributed a new research College, Nuffield College, to the University; still, it is largely ignored in the academic area. For eight centuries, Oxford has stood as one of the greatest centers of learning, a capital of the humanities and the arts, where a large part of the English-speaking world's leadership was trained, as it is still today. Less than an hour and a quarter from London, Oxford was never a remote academic community; in the shadow of the famous towers and cupolas, the colleges carry on their traditions of meditation as well as of active participation in the social and political life of the country and beyond.

North of the lower Thames, in the region where East Anglia meets the metropolitan growth of London eastward, the counties of Essex and Hertford have experienced the fastest population growth of the 1950s. To a prosperous agriculture, which profits by its proximity to the Greater London markets, have been added new towns, bringing new industries and trade. Thus in Essex, the towns of Basildon and Harlow, founded in 1949 and 1947, had become cities of more than 50,000 each by 1961. On the north bank of the Thames' estuary, Southend (165,000) had grown to be the largest British seaside resort. This area, with that immediately south of Greater London, has experienced the most impressive recent growth and expansion in Britain.

South of the Thames, on unglaciated territory, extends an irregular checkering of vales and higher grounds called "downs," generally occupied by low-grade pastures suitable for sheep. Directly to the south of London, the Weald, a formerly forested area, presents a quaint topography owing to its origin as a low anticline or dome, excavated by erosion and cut through by the Strait of Dover. The chalky hillocks of the downs end along the water's edge in long lines of white cliffs facing the nearby continent are classified in Europe as the typical first view one gets of England. The white color of the chalk gave birth to the name *Albion* often applied to Britain. Here and there the lines of cliffs break into wide-open chasms, in which are ports linking England to France and the Lowlands: Dover, Folkestone, and Newhaven serve annually hundreds of thousands of passengers. On the deep bay screened from the sea by the Isle of Wight, two large ports have grown up: the naval base of Portsmouth and the deep-sea port of Southampton, the oceanic gateway to London and the port of call of the great liners of all nationalities plying through the Channel. A large oil-refining center has been in operation near Southampton since 1952.

Seaside resorts are mushrooming along the southern seaboard. Brighton (163,000), Bournemouth, Eastbourne, and, to the east, Margate and Ramsgate are important cities even measured by their permanent, out of season, population. Urbanization progresses as various forms of tourism and leisure bring more people and income to this southeastern corner of England; as one moves closer to Greater London, one encounters more rapidly growing districts, and several large new towns, especially Crawley. In a lovely and still rural landscape, east of the North Downs, the historic town of Canterbury—seat of the Archbishop and primate of the Church of England and dominated by its magnificent medieval cathedral—has also sprawled beyond the old ramparts. The new University of Kent is located at Canterbury, and that of Sussex at Brighton.

The rest of southern England seems to be the summer park of London and the industrial Midlands, for the coast is strewn with beaches and sea resorts. One has to reach the banks of the Severn to find again the rich agricultural scenery of the plain of Somerset. Here too is the important industrial and commercial center of Bristol, a large port and the sixteenth- and seventeenth-century base for colonial expansion. Terribly destroyed by the blitz, it is once again a thriving city of 436,000 that works hard at its reconstruction while carrying on its historical role of regional capital in the southwest. For several centuries the second largest city in England, Bristol held the sixth rank in 1801, and the seventh in 1961. Its conurbation has about half a million people. Engineering provides its main industry, and from railway rolling-stock manufacturing, Bristol went into building bicycles, cars, and finally aircraft. It is now the largest center of aircraft manufacturing in Britain.

Farther south and west Great Britain ends in the narrowing and rocky peninsula of Cornwall. Here again some granite and older rocks outcrop, with higher grounds and wider stretches of moorland, but a more animated and varied landscape—Londoners go to summer homes in Devon and Cornwall as though going into the wilderness. Cornwall is one of Europe's land's ends, and the small group of the Scilly Islands or Cape Lizard are often the first land one sees on an eastbound voyage across the Atlantic. The two coasts of Cornwall are rocky and indented; the climatic contrast is sharp between the northern, humid, windy, and colder shore and the screened, warmer, and sunnier southern coast, reputed to be the warmest spot of Britain. Plymouth is a large naval base and fishing port. The higher sections inland are called moors (Exmoor, Dartmoor, Bodmin moors), and a poor type of rural economy reigns. Cornwall is a rugged country, now losing population, and it anticipates Wales in a modest way; it mines some tin, slate, and china clay.

The only important group of mountains south of Scotland cover almost the whole of Wales, the massive peninsula west of England. The higher altitude and rugged topography have helped to isolate the country and therefore to preserve the originality of the Welsh. Like the Scots they have often emigrated toward England and played a notable part in national life. The importance of Wales cannot, however, be compared to that of Scotland, either in size or in nature. This country

The Welsh border, a restful rural landscape. In the foreground, sheep and the enclosures between fields; in the background, the steep barren slope shaped by erosion. *(British Information Services)*

The Welsh black country: Rhondda coalfield in south Wales *(British Information Services)*

# WALES
# COAL AND SLATE MINES

□    Anthracite collieries
+    Steam and bituminous collieries
━    Generalized limit of coal field
○    Active slate quarries
●    Active slate mines
///   Areas in which cleavage is well developed
     The lines follow the general trend of
     cleavage planes (after F. J. North)

SCOTLAND

ENGLAND

WALES

100 MILES
100 KM.

—54°

—52° 30′

2°

Liverpool

Llandudno

ANGLESEY

Port Penrhyn
Bangor
Bethesda
Port Dinorwic
Penrhyn Quarries
Caernarvon
Llanberis
Dinorwic
Nantlle
Llanrwst

FLINTSHIRE

DENBIGHSHIRE

Corwen
Llangollen FLINT SHIRE

CAERNARVONSHIRE

Ffestiniog

Portmadoc
Tremadoc
Bala

MERIONETHSHIRE

Llangynog

Barmouth
Dolgelley

CARDIGAN

Corris

Towyn
MONTGOMERYSHIRE
Machynlleth

BAY

RADNORSHIRE

CARDIGANSHIRE

BRECKNOCKSHIRE

PEMBROKESHIRE
CARMARTHENSHIRE

St. Brides
Bay

Ammanford
Merthyr Tydfil
Tredegar
Ebbw Vale
Blaenavon
Pontypool

Burry Port
Llanelly
Rhondda

Carmarthen
Bay

G
L
A
Glyncorrwg
Swansea
Pontypridd
MONMOUTHSHIRE
Port Talbot
Maesteg
Caerphilly
Newport

Bridgend
Llanharan
R
G
A
N
Cardiff
Mouth of the Severn

BRISTOL CHANNEL

30 MILES
30 KILOMETERS

is all mountains: old folds, planed by erosion, then made to look young again with sharp crests, bold peaks, and deep cirques, owing to the rejuvenating action of the glaciers. Few countries can display as beautiful specimens of glacial topography as Wales. But these highlands are poor; sheep graze up and down the slopes, some of which are well forested, and the mountain folk live a simple and isolated kind of life. Many of them, however, continue to leave Wales and move to England. The peninsula is fringed with coastal plains covered with deep, rich glacial drift. A few wide valleys do penetrate into hills, and in these lower lands agriculture has developed, geared to cattle production, particularly the Welsh Black breed. These plains have always fed the mountaineers, and their conquest by the English in the thirteenth century brought about the submission of all of Wales. Most of the population is crowded on the periphery—in rural communities in the north (except for a small coalfield on the northeast coast), but mainly in the southern industrial district along the shore of the Bristol Channel.

South Wales is a major coalfield of Britain. It is larger and better endowed with thicker seams than are the Scottish or northeastern fields. Still the output per manshift at the face remains at 2.18 tons as against 2.30 in 1938 and 3.17 for the whole of Great Britain in 1951; the equipment is somewhat outdated; production is costly, though the quality of coals is generally high. Most of the coal used to be exported, but foreign shipments had fallen from 61 percent of the output in 1913 to 49 percent in 1938. Here an important industrial district has been erected on the coal and on the older traditions of metal smelting and working, because iron ore was also found interstratified with coal, and tin-ore deposits of the nearby Cornwall have been famous since the Bronze Age. In the present Iron Age, south Wales has specialized in tin-plate, but today it works with imported iron and tin, using the local fuel and labor. Tin-plate, sheet-tin, and galvanizing works are spread through the coalfield and east of it, in many small towns with Celtic names such as Pontypool, Pontnewynydd, Aberdulais, Ystalyfera, Llantrisant, Cwmavon. (Some people in Wales speak the Brythonic dialect, rather close to the Gaelic Breton dialect of France.) Other nonferrous metal works (copper, zinc, and nickel) have been attracted there. The main port and center of the metal industry is Swansea (166,000), surrounded by a whole constellation of hardworking cities, all making a truly "black country" scenery that has eliminated most of the vegetation even from surrounding slopes.

The chief port and city of south Wales is still farther east on the river Taff—Cardiff (256,000)—disputing Newcastle for first rank among coal-shipping ports in days of yore. For years Cardiff prices of coal were followed by all of Europe and many lands abroad with great attention, for

Cardiff shipped bunker coal as well as anthracite. After the decay of the coal export trade the city remained the commercial center of south Wales, building large food and chemical industries. An inland "black-country" belt links Swansea to Cardiff; the main industrial towns inland are Rhondda (100,000) and Merthyr-Tydfil (59,000). But the population and activity of the area have been decreasing since the 1920s, and south Wales was classified between the two World Wars as one of the "depressed areas" of Britain. Government policy favors building of new industries in this area to absorb available labor. Large steel mills were established there as Britain recently expanded its steel capacity. In 1965, south Wales produced 10 percent of the British output of coal, 27 percent of the pig iron, and 25 percent of the steel.

A few islands around Great Britain must be mentioned. In the Irish Sea is the large Isle of Man, a structural westward prolongation of Cumberland; its rural life is similar to that of northwestern England; a large-scale fishing activity has developed, and the beautiful landscape attracts crowds of summer tourists. Even more picturesque perhaps are the Anglo-Norman islands in the Channel. Jersey, Guernsey, and Alderney are closer to the French than the English coast; they are the remnants of the lands that Norman kings of England claimed on the continent; the population, still speaking French, has concentrated on cattle raising. The Norman breed is known under the name of Jersey throughout the English-speaking world. Tourism is enhanced by the absence on the islands of many of the excise taxes levied in Britain or France.

LONDON

In the rural southeast of Great Britain, away from coal and ore mines, has been erected the largest conurbation of Britain and Europe—London—only recently outstripped by New York and Tokyo as the greatest city in the world. At the head of the Thames tidal estuary, London was also on the old Roman road crossing the river at the Westminster Ford. Tacitus spoke of the town as being active in commerce, but the maritime vocation arose when the merchants of the Hanseatic League established there a port trading with the continent; in the sixteenth century local merchants began going abroad. Until then London's fortune had been based on the export of wool of the English sheep—the Lord Chancellor in the House of Lords sits on the woolsack, thus symbolizing the foundation of English wealth and power. But with the maritime discoveries and expansion, London began trading with remote lands and importing all kinds of tropical products that were resold in Britain or re-exported to the continent. In the eighteenth century London achieved the part of the greatest emporium of colonial goods in the

The Thames and Westminster in the heart of London, with Whitehall and the Houses of Parliament in the foreground. This aerial view was taken before the Blitz. See also the photograph on page 118 of the docks of the port of London. *(British Information Services)*

The port of Southampton, with a light carrier in the foreground and the *Queen Mary* in the background. *(British Information Services)*

world, becoming the hub of world trade. Most of the European transactions in coffee, tea, rice, cotton, wool, silk, indigo, furs, sugar, hardwood, and gold passed through London. In the nineteenth century the
Industrial Revolution boosted the volume of international trade to such
an extent that no one port could handle it; the rise of nationalism in
Europe also led to direct transportation from producing to consuming
areas.

Still London continued to grow. Its population reached 670,000 in
1682, passed the million mark soon after 1800, rose to 2,800,000 in
1861, and Greater London counted 8.3 million people in 1951 but
only 7.9 in 1967. Its port still is one of the largest in the world, its docks
stretching along the banks of the Thames for over 25 miles. Merchandise from all over the world was gathered here, but less often for redistribution to consuming markets than to feed the population and factories
of London itself and a part of England. Something of the *entrepôt* trade
and redistribution function survives, especially for wool, tea, and rubber.
In the midst of World War II, a manufacturer in New York could get
a shipload of Australian wool more easily from London than from
Melbourne.

Such a tremendous accumulation of stockpiled materials meant a permanent long-range investment of huge sums of money. From its commerce and trade London had a capitalization that its brokers and banks
used with great art, making of the City the clearinghouse of the world's
financial accounts. The Bank of England for money and Lloyd's for
insurance were until the beginning of the twentieth century the apex
of the pyramid of international financing. Anything could be bought,
sold, insured, or rented through London, and the offices in the City
took a commission on every one of the innumerable businesses they
helped to transact directly or indirectly; goods and ships did not need
to clear through the docks or warehouses of London or even Britain
to bring some income to the Londoners. In the human and economic
structure of Britain, London is indeed a region by itself, a special and
essential one.

The meteoric rise of the town and its power would not have been
possible without the practical help granted by the crown and the government. The capital of the United Kingdom and of the Empire added to
its trading and financial functions a political and administrative one of
considerable import for the successful management of business. In the
sixteenth to the eighteenth centuries the growing centralization of the
British Isles under a single political authority sitting in London was
important. And beyond the Isles was all the breadth and width of the
Empire. London carries its historical function proudly; this is obvious
from its size and the intense rhythm of its manifold activities as well as

the variety and beauty of its monuments. The city itself, which was granted so many privileges and rose to such pre-eminence, has an area of only 675 acres and very few residents; it is exclusively an office and business district around which London stretches widely. Residential sections have gone to the "outer ring," particularly during the period of the bombings in 1940–1945, but this was a natural trend. The best residential quarters and even the elegant shopping section (from Knightsbridge to Regent street) are situated to the west: the West End means high social standing. The port, with its docks, large plants, and teeming labor, expanded eastward and downstream as the increase in the size of ships and the volume of trade required more space closer to the sea. The East End is the poorest, most overpopulated part of the conurbation and the hardest hit by the blitz. The central section along Oxford and Fleet Streets also suffered; around St. Paul's Cathedral, which remained untouched, a wide area was practically razed by explosions and fire, and beautifully rebuilt after 1950.

Despite its fogs and drizzling rain, its widely stretching sections of standardized rows of brick houses, London has considerable beauty and charm. It is not all due to the wealth of historical memories and of noteworthy institutions lined up from Westminster Abbey to the Bank, nor is it due solely to the select clubs, the smart hotels and residences, and wideopen parks of the West End—the charm comes mostly from the human climate of this hard-laboring but prosperous people, satisfied with their endeavor, carrying on some of the best traditions of Western democracy and culture. It is to be hoped that the ordeal of the war and the hardships of the peace will not affect too deeply the character that lies at the basis of English greatness and strength. For Londoners have to struggle hard to readapt their involved and fragile structure to the changing economic conditions of the day. The great city has lost much of its financial and commercial importance; it fights to keep and to develop both its function as a cultural capital and its industries. It is still the second money and credit market in the world, after New York. London is the largest British center of finishing industries, particularly in engineering, clothing, and chemical manufacturing; moreover vast foodstuff industries and power and gas plants have grown out of the importance of the local market. There is an established law for the survival of large urban centers after their zone of economic and political influence has shrunk. A large city generates some *raison d'être* for itself, but it is at the price of a profound reorganization and often of a substantial reduction of its standard of living. The case of London is that of the whole British economy; but this versatile conurbation has shown greater adaptability than many a large industrial district in Britain.

Already in the 1680s Sir William Petty, projecting the growth of London he then observed into the future, could forecast that this growth would stop of itself before 1800, as London would have gathered all the population of England, and perhaps covered all the realm's area by that time. In fact, the conurbation of London is still growing, and attracting a constantly increasing proportion of Britain's people and economic activities. The *City* itself stopped growing in the 1850s; but even in Petty's time it was obvious that London had expanded far beyond the City of London limits. In 1961 the census showed that even the County of London and Greater London were losing population as the migration of residence out toward the periphery of the conurbation went on. The County of London saw its population drop from 3.35 million in 1951 to 3.2 million in 1961; similarly, Greater London decreased from 8.35 to 8.17 million; in 1951 the number of jobs in the conurbation was already 4 percent above the figure of the employed population resident within its limits, which meant that there was steady commuting from beyond the territory defined as the conurbation. And, as could have been expected, the 1961 census showed that of all the counties of Britain the greatest increases in population during the last ten years had occurred in the counties surrounding Greater London, that is, Hertfordshire, Essex, West Sussex, Buckinghamshire, Berkshire, and Bedfordshire. A whole constellation of recent new towns is happily developing all around Greater London, with such substantial young cities as Basildon, Harlow, Crawley, Bracknell, Hemel Hempstead, Hatfield, Welwyn Garden City, and Stevenage; and more are planned.

Not all the people who live in this outer ring, much of which still looks rather rural, work in Greater London; but there is little doubt that the proximity to the great capital was the determinant factor in the establishment and growth there of all these urban and suburban communities. In 1947, when London needed a great deal of reconstruction and could be somewhat replanned, a remarkable new plan was drawn. It bore the imprint of the thinking of the nineteenth-century "Utopists" who had been struggling for the concept of the garden-city, especially Ebenezer Howard. The new London planned at mid-twentieth century favored small one-family houses with small gardens when feasible, organized in not too-large new towns; belts of green space were to be provided around the dense residential areas, and between them and the industrial sectors. Whether or not London will be able to direct its development along the lines and principles of the postwar plan, the philosophy of it has already put its imprint on land use and the landscape, and it has helped the conurbation to break out of old bounds and sprawl over the surrounding land.

It becomes increasingly difficult to define the limits of the London urban area. The "continuously built-up area" can hardly be a working concept at a time when the need for green belts and open space for recreation within the conurbation is officially recognized. The geographer T. W. Freeman remarked that "never in history has there been a civilization so thoroughly of the town as that of modern Britain." But he stressed that "a town is a dynamic entity . . . the main social problem for the future will lie not in the town centres of the present, nor in many of the older and better residential areas, but in the suburbs built since 1919." This is especially true in Greater London and all around it, for this still is at present the most dynamic region in Britain. As it sprawls northwards and southwards, this vast advance of urbanization may well meet soon with other such sprawls extending from the Midlands or the southern shore cities toward London. An interesting symbiosis of urban and rural is thus developing (see map of commuting on p. 368). On the whole the London urbanized region encompasses some 15 million people and it continues to grow. The number commuting toward its central core, which used to be considered London in the beginning of this century, increases every year. Decentralization of much of the growth toward the periphery and beyond does not prevent more concentration of offices and transactional business activities in the central section.

Like most of the great cities of today, London becomes essentially a center for management of public and private affairs, national as well as international; and a vast organization of the markets of mass media, money, ideas, and talent, closely associated with management, has developed. The University of London is growing rapidly and claiming new means for expansion in all directions. Central sectors of the enormous city, strewn along an axis that parallels the Thames River, acquire new functions and a new appearance, distinguishing it from the old *City*, the financial district, which rebuilds in height without modifying its quiet and aristocratic way of expediting business, and from the bohemian section of Chelsea. A few tall towers are beginning to form a skyline of modernistic style, which in the next years will probably become more pronounced.

London has long resisted the concentration of the "office industry" and architectural skyscraping, but leading planning authorities now recognize the necessity of letting this growth develop in the heart of Britain: it is as indispensable to the functioning of modern economy and society as the agglomeration of large industrial plants making up the "black country" landscape was needed in the time of the Industrial Revolution. The present expansion has given London a cultural and scientific role which it used to ignore: now Oxford and Cambridge rely for their futures on their relative proximity to the great capital. The London airport is the busiest crossroads of air traffic in Europe. In the central core of the city, traffic has become incredibly dense and has had to be strictly regulated. To keep it moving on the streets, rules were laid down against parking and standing which have made many people abandon the idea of using individual cars to come into these sections. An efficient network of buses and underground and suburban rail lines keeps the city functioning and permits it to grow and face its daily problems with relatively little changes in the general design and cityscape.

Still, the life of London changes constantly. As more residences move outward, more offices, stores, and other services take their place; a great general impression of affluence permeates much of the city; new styles and fashions are launched here. In the eighteenth century, Dr. Johnson remarked that "the best prospect a Scotsman ever saw was the high road to London." This prospect has opened up, with the increase in the mobility of people, for other, more distant populations. In the 1940s London became the central focus of Polish exiles, and about 40,000 Poles settled there; in the 1950s, West Indians began coming in large numbers; and in the 1960s, British subjects of Indian and Pakistani origin joined the flow of newcomers. Ethnic problems have now arisen on the streets of London, and in 1968 legislation was passed restricting this immigration. Hardly anything shakes any part of the globe without causing an echo and some change in this enormous and lively international crossroad.

As the distinguished planner, Lord Holford, noted: "Despite all the necessary restrictions on industrial and office growth, despite improved standards of density and more space for education and amenities, despite transport costs and traffic congestion—despite all this, social, administrative and commercial activities contrive to grow; and the night population of the County of London and its immediate suburban ring continues to diminish." There is little doubt that modern society needs such enormous urban agglomerations, and the continued expansion of London appears as one of the best illustrations of the country's dynamism.

## THE CHANGING ECONOMIC STRUCTURE OF BRITAIN

A gradual evolution, accelerated by World War II, is slowly reshaping the structure on which British prosperity was based. The economic system founded on the past supremacy in manufacturing and shipping and on the world's reliance on the pound sterling underwent many crises in the twentieth century. The densely populated island with a rather high standard of living saw the pillars of the old structures shattered by two long and costly wars and by the economic depression of the early 1930s. The latter caused the British Government to renounce its century-old free trade tradition and adopt protectionist and imperial preference policies. A steady trend toward self-sufficiency developed which has at times led to increase domestic production even in fields requiring costly support; and at times of acute crisis measures were taken to decrease internal consumption. The rationing of the British consumer was drastic during World War II and had to be retained for several years afterward under the label of the "austerity program." After the general conditions of the international economy recovered from the wartime destruction and shortages, the rationing of consumer goods was terminated, but some austerity policies recurred in periods of financial stress, restricting government expenditures, tightening credit, and limiting the outflow of money abroad.

Land use and agricultural policies reflect rather well the oscillations of Britain between the inward and outward approaches to its use of resources. Between the two world wars, British agriculture suffered a long depression. A careful survey of land utilization, county by county, was prepared as a preliminary to planning for an efficient and scientific use of the soil. Still, agricultural activity declined through the 1930s. Much land once tilled was then under permanent grass. In wartime the government was endowed with authority to plan and direct agricultural production in detail: 7 million acres of the permanent grass were plowed; the area under potatoes and barley doubled, that under wheat increased by one third; cattle increased slightly while the rest of the live-stock figures declined. Scarce wartime manpower accelerated the trend toward mechanization, which kept on after 1945. In 1948, the number of tractor-drawn plows surpassed that of the horse-drawn; the British farms had three times as many tractors as in 1939 and six times as many combined harvester-threshers. As the emergency shortages due to the war receded around the world, it seemed at first that war-time progress of tilled area and grain production was stopped and even reversed. As the nation's consumption of food, kept down by rationing and other governmental measures until the early 1950s, expanded again in the prosperity of the late 1950s, it seemed that Britain could scarcely hope to produce at home a large part of the food it needed. Feeding the British nation is a gigantic problem and not an easy one. The United Kingdom's imports of food and animal feedstuffs made up, in the 1930s, about one tenth in value of all the world trade and about two fifths of the total trade in food. If this proportion has decreased, it has been due more to an expansion of world trade than to a decrease in British food needs. Still, domestic agriculture produced, in the 1960s, a much higher percentage of the country's food supplies than was the case before World War II: According to official statistics of the Ministry of Agriculture, home production provided, in 1963, 41 percent of the total supplies of wheat and flour (as against 23 percent in an average prewar year); for

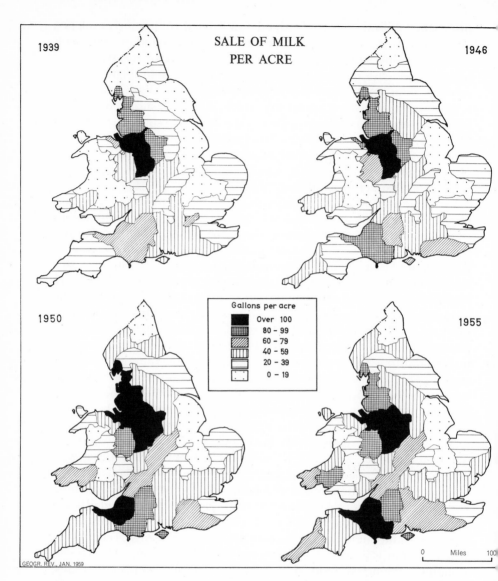

SALE OF MILK
PER ACRE

1939

1946

1950

1955

Gallons per acre

- Over 100
- 80 – 99
- 60 – 79
- 40 – 59
- 20 – 39
- 0 – 19

0    Miles    100

The expansion of dairy farming, particularly for the production of milk, has been impressive in the years since 1939. Notice the progress of milk produced per acre in the west and south of England, that is, in the rural areas close to the major conurbations of London, the Midlands, and Lancashire. This trend of associating milk production to the suburban economy is found in several other industrialized countries. *(The Geographical Review)* refined sugar home supplies made up 23 percent of the total instead of 17 percent prewar; carcass meat stood at 69 percent instead of 51 percent; bacon and ham at 38 percent instead of 32 percent; cheese at 43 percent instead of 24 percent; shell eggs at 98 percent instead of 71 percent; condensed milk at 95 percent instead of 70 percent.

Since 1955, the livestock economy was considerably expanded, not only for cattle but even more for pigs and poultry. At the same time it was found possible, owing to improved technology of wheat and barley growing, to considerably expand grain production. Crop yields of 2 tons of wheat per acre are no longer unusual, and in 1965, the harvest of wheat surpassed 4 million tons, breaking all records. Still, the most important farm product of Britain, and the only one supplying domestic consumption fully, is fluid milk (see map, page 258). This substantial expansion of farm production was achieved through mechanization, rationalization of technology, and the concentration of production on larger, more compact, and better-equipped farms. The trend of abandoning marginal lands, particularly in the highlands of Scotland and Wales, will certainly continue. From 1939 to 1963, the volume of agricultural production increased by some 60 percent while about 4 percent of the total agricultural area was withdrawn from farm use. Modern agriculture, when properly equipped and financed, requires less hands and less acres to produce more. Land abandoned by agriculture is partly built up as a result of urban and suburban sprawl, but most of it returns to natural vegetation growth. Since 1919, the United Kingdom has had a Forestry Commission to promote forestry and establish state forests. However the Forestry Commission has done most of its work since 1947. Of the present 4.2 million acres under wood, one half has been planted since 1919, and more than one third in the last twenty years. There are still several million acres of poor land in Britain, suitable for afforestation on purely physical grounds; not all of it is available for planting, but some will be converted to woodland as present trends develop.

Grain production may be expanded somewhat further. But climate and soil endow Britain particularly well for grass growth and specialization in animal husbandry; the latter has long been also a specialty of its expert farmers. In 1965–1966, livestock and livestock products represented two thirds of the gross output of British agriculture (the total amount of which rose to 1,849 million pounds sterling). There were about 12 million head of cattle in the United Kingdom, 30 million sheep and lamb, 8 million pigs, and about 118 million poultry. In 1967–1968, an unfortunate epidemic of hoof-and-mouth disease worked terrible havoc in Britain and greatly reduced these figures.

Agriculture has managed to maintain in the United Kingdom a role which can hardly be understood on other grounds than the urge for some self-sufficiency in foodstuffs in time of crisis that might cause isolation. The rapid progress of urbanization reduced agricultural employment to less than 4 percent of the nation's labor force; as the conurbations sprawled in all directions even the arable lands necessary to the farms were besieged and threatened, all the more so as the population migration toward the southeast continued. But the farming areas, which usually vote conservative, could upset the balance of power in Parliament if such a mood developed among farmers. The stronger positions and expansionist trends farming assumed during the period of food shortage in wartime and during the war's aftermath can thus be maintained for good reasons of domestic politics. By 1960 the protection of Britain's agriculture was a serious international problem; it was one of the obstacles in the way of the economic integration of Britain with the countries facing it across the sea on the continent of Europe, countries which were threatened with increasing domestic surpluses of key agricultural products.

The British economy needs much more than food in terms of supplies from abroad. Around 1925 it seemed that British power was based on cotton, petroleum, wool, tobacco, tea, rubber, gold, and diamonds, goods that, except for wool, the British had never produced, but in which they dominated international trade. Coal was still plentiful at that time but on a downward trend in production as well as in exports; and the relative importance of coal was already receding, with more coalfields being developed all around the globe and more waterpower and petroleum being produced and consumed in most countries.

Trade alone does not explain all the economic power and prosperity of Great Britain in the nineteenth and the early twentieth centuries. The main island was the workshop of the world. For almost two centuries now agriculture has been of second-rate importance. Industry was paramount, and even more so since the decay of the redistributing trade. The industrial power at home was founded on three assets: vast coal resources, abundant skilled manpower and good conditions of supply resulting from the trade organization. Coal had proved to be handy in many ways: to propel machines, to combine with iron in the form of coke in blast furnaces, to supply steamships, and to fill the bottoms of ships going out from British ports to all the other parts of the world to bring back a variety of raw materials and foods. In 1913, the United Kingdom produced 292 million tons of coal and exported 96 million; in 1937, 240 million tons were produced and 52 exported; in 1947, 197 were produced and 5.5 exported; in 1965, 187 were produced and about 4 exported. Available stocks of coal are kept so low that in periods of sudden increase in industrial consumption, such as the second half of 1950 for instance, Great Britain must import coal from abroad. The domestic consumption, being close to 180 million tons annually, almost equals the present output and declines steadily.

After 1900, coal shipments from Britain found tough competition from German, American, Polish, Australian, and other sources; at the same time many countries reduced their imports through development of local resources. The shrinking foreign market and the decline of the consumption in certain branches even on the domestic market (as against waterpower and use of petroleum products) created a situation that deprived the collieries of incentive to improve their equipment, dig new pits, or modernize their tooling. There were also growing difficulties in recruiting personnel for the deeper mines; coal mining was no longer popular, either among labor or among owners. During the 1937–1947 period, output decreased in all coalfields, with the exception of those of Derbyshire and Nottinghamshire. Decline was particularly felt in southern Wales and northeastern England. This time, however, it was not for lack of a market: from 1945 till 1953, the continent of Europe was desperately short of coal; most of the continent's coal deficit was met by shipments from the United States, but cargoes of Australian or South African coal have occasionally landed in Scandinavian ports! Great Britain was unable to restore its production: only in 1952 did it reach again the level of 1935–1938, after many efforts and some modernization. Net output per underground worker per year now reaches close to 490 tons; decrease of colliery manpower has been achieved to some extent although with difficulty. Public management of the collieries improved the problem of investment and equipment. The fact remains that Great Britain seems to be mining its coal as fast as the established resources permit. Meanwhile, the total consumption of energy increases: measured in units equivalent to tons of coal per capita it went from 4.28 in 1937 to 4.30 in 1949 and 5.15 in 1965. Thus one understands that the consumption of coal stood at 190 million tons in 1937 and again in 1962; the increase in consumption is provided to a large extent by imported oil and to a smaller extent by nuclear and waterpower developments. The arrival of the North Sea natural gas on the market will lessen still more the dependence on coal.

Frantic efforts have been made to find more mineral resources within the insular kingdom. Two tiny oilfields have been worked that supply yearly about 100,000 tons of crude oil (less than 0.2 percent of the needs). The output of iron ore, of poor quality, having slightly declined immediately after the war, remains in 1955–1965 close to an annual average of 4.4 million tons (in iron content), less than one third of the needs of a powerful iron and steel industry. That industry has always been one of Great Britain's most active. During the war and after 1945, steel-making capacity was expanded and new modern mills put into operation. The annual output of pig iron and ferroalloys rose from the vicinity of 8 million tons in 1936–1940 to more than 13 million since 1960 (16 in 1966). The increase in the crude steel output was even more notable: from 13.2 million in 1937 and again in 1942–1943, it rose to more than 18 million every year since 1954 and 27.4 in 1966. Further expansion of the steel output depends on the prospects of the international market and also on the cost of supply of high-grade iron ore, usually imported from such areas as Sweden, Norway, Canada, and various African territories. British interests are participating in the development of new sources of ore, especially in Africa.

Great Britain is nearly self-sufficient in terms of iron and steel scrap but must import almost all her needs of additive metals for steel making, such as manganese, chromium, nickel, and tungsten. Nonferrous metals are imported, too; the British consumption of all these metals is an important one, usually second only to that of the United States and possibly the Soviet Union. In recent years Great Britain consumed annually about 500,000 tons of manganese, 640,000 tons of copper, 300,000 tons of zinc and lead, 24,000 tons of tin, and 500,000 tons of aluminum. A large part of the imports of all these metals or ores comes from the Commonwealth. However some of the imports originate in the dollar area, chiefly in the United States and Canada, and another part has to come from other foreign countries.

To pay for all these imports, Britain used to export large quantities of manufactured metallurgical goods. Since the 1930s, and even more after World War II, British industries turned increasingly towards finished products in all fields, towards complicated engineering requiring a great deal of skilled labor. The quality and work of British manpower, the efficiency of industrial and commercial organization made it possible to supply the nation with always-improved goods and to pay for the raw materials imported with exports of these products of British industrial plants. The total number of people employed in "metals, engineering, vehicles, shipbuilding, and electrical goods" rose from 2,590,000 in 1938 to 4,659,000 in 1943 owing to the war effort, decreased to 3,289,000 in 1946 then rose again steadily up to 4 million in 1951–1965, that is, 18.2 percent of the total civil employment in 1951 and 15 percent in 1965. The number of workers in mining and quarrying decreased in total numbers from 850,000 to 625,000 and in percentage of civil employment from 5 in 1938 to 2.5 in 1965.

The distribution of the labor force shows also a steady growth of chemical and allied industries and the decline of textile and leather industries. Thus it is not surprising to find that while the British output of cars and trucks rose from 445,000 in 1938 to 2,100,000 in 1966, the output of radio and television sets from 1,918,000 in 1937 to 2,900,000 in 1965, the output of sulfuric acid from 1,068,000 tons in 1937 to 3,168,000 in 1966, the output of rayon yarn and staple fibre from 67,000 tons in 1937 to 400,000 in 1966, other productions declined, among them the older kinds of textiles, such as cotton and wool, which used to be great British specialities. Wool yarn production stood at 256,600 tons in 1937 and 247,300 in 1966; however the industrial consumption of wool in terms of weight seems to have been slightly superior in a few years to the prewar period. Cotton declined in a more obvious way: the industrial consumption of the United Kingdom fell from 583,000 tons of ginned cotton in 1938–1939 to 463,000 in 1950–1951 and only 226,000 in 1965. The decline in the consumption of silk was even sharper, but partly to be explained by the rise of rayon, nylon, and dacron. The textile industries of Britain used to be the largest and best equipped in the world. This situation has been considerably altered: a great deal of the British textile equipment now looks old; other countries have developed great textile industries: not only last-century competitors such as France and Germany, but also newcomers in the field of international trade in fabrics. Gandhi's spinning-wheel is displayed on the flag of the Republic of India, and that country's industrial consumption of cotton averages at present 1,100,000 tons annually, almost five times the British consumption. The greatest exporter of cotton fabrics today is again Japan, and the Japanese consumption of cotton surpassed the British in 1951–1952 to reach triple its weight in 1965. It is understandable therefore that great centers of mechanical and engineering works have become more important in the British economy than the older centers of textiles and heavy metallurgy: thus the Midlands, London, and the Southeast gain in comparison with Lancashire, Durham, and south Wales. This displacement in the geographical center of gravity of the country is difficult to counteract: it has already shown its impact on the evolution of domestic politics in Britain during the twentieth century.

## THE STRUGGLE FOR ECONOMIC RECOVERY

During the depression of the early 1930s, Great Britain became aware of the relative decline of its position in the world and started a long and stubborn struggle for recovering a strong position within the international economic system. After World War II, which impoverished Britain further and brought about in a spectacular fashion the general leadership of the American economy in the world, the British no longer expect to regain the predominance they held before 1914. The first years that followed the war were a difficult period for the British economy, and the statistics for the years 1946–1948 demonstrate it plainly.

Since 1949 a steady and substantial trend of recovery has brightened future perspectives.

Britain remains as dependent as before—perhaps more so—on the outside supply of food and raw materials. The prices of these goods on the international market determine a great deal about Britain's final balance of payments and her solvency. Such an economy benefits from terms of trade resulting from a fall in the prices of raw materials and foods if prices of manufactured products do not follow the same trend. Thus Britain's terms of trade were rather favorable during the period between the World Wars. Since 1939, however, prices of raw materials have gone up much more rapidly than prices of industrial finished goods. To pay for 10 tons of wheat, the United Kingdom would have had to export 26 bicycles in 1938, but 38 in 1952; to pay for one ton of copper 16 sewing machines were needed in 1938 and 21 in 1952. An official source estimated that the deterioration in Britain's terms of trade between 1938 and 1952 was responsible for an increase of about 2.7 billion dollars in the country's spending in 1952. To a large extent terms of trade in the international markets depend on what happens on the domestic market of the United States. A bumper crop of grain in North America may affect to a major degree world prices of food. Stockpiling purchases of raw materials by the United States sends world prices skyrocketing.

Britain strongly organized the whole economy of the Commonwealth in order to protect as much as possible the balance of payments between the dollar area—to which Canada belongs, one of the principal producers of raw materials and foodstuffs in the world—and the sterling area, including most of the Commonwealth countries. As the sterling area is on the whole a great producer of a number of raw materials needed in the dollar area, it could benefit to some extent from a rise in prices and from increased purchases by the United States; although the British economy in the islands could suffer as a result of such trends, the whole of the sterling area economy could benefit by such a situation. Among the materials for which the sterling area regularly has surpluses to be sold to the dollar area, as well as to other foreign countries, the more important are wool, rubber, tin, copper, bauxite, and manganese. The trade in raw materials on the whole, in average years, does not favor the sterling area: exports of manufactured goods and various services have to make up for the deficit.

The total exports of goods and services remained for a number of postwar years below the total imports of goods and services. For the year 1952, however, the balance of payments of the United Kingdom showed a surplus of 170 million pounds sterling even excluding defence aid. The previous year had shown a heavy deficit. The better balance for 1952 reflected many events and factors at play throughout the world:

the temporary closing of the oilfields and refinery in Iran and the decreased receipts from the Malayan exports of rubber and tin had been unfavorable factors, as also was the rather low level of revenue from foreign assets (only 61 million pounds in 1952); but lower prices of imported raw materials, a steady expansion of exports, the good performance of shipping were the main factors redressing the balance. The British economy is extremely sensitive to almost everything that happens anywhere in the world. This is the ransom for the nation's prosperity and power established on a world-wide network of commercial relations. The unhappy outcome of the Suez expedition of 1956 shattered once more the financial stability of the pound, but was followed by speedy recovery in 1957–1958. The closing of the Suez Canal in June 1967 again adversely affected the British economy; but this time a lag in industrial expansion, several prolonged strikes, and other factors delayed recovery.

Normally the cost of Britain's imports has been higher than the receipts from exports insofar as goods alone are considered. This annual deficit is compensated for by earnings from investments abroad and from the export of services, such as shipping, banking, insurance, patents, and brokerage on a variety of international transactions. Such services were exported more easily than goods at a time of economic nationalism and high protective tariffs around the globe, as it had been the case during the interwar period (1920–1940). The postwar emergence of the United States as the senior partner of the international system somewhat restricted the market for the exportation of the kinds of services from which Britain drew much of its "invisible" foreign earnings. While the volume and variety of international commerce expanded rapidly through the 1950s, Britain could not keep up with the pace of the rest of the world.

In 1938, the total international trade of the free world in goods (excluding the USSR and its present satellites) amounted in U. S. dollars to 48.8 billion, and the United Kingdom's foreign trade to 10.7 billion, or 22 percent of the world's total. In 1950, the free world's trade had risen to 115.3 billion U. S. dollars and in 1959 to 211.7 billion, while the British trade came up to 13.1 and 20.1 respectively, its share dropping to 11.3 percent in 1950 and 9.5 percent in 1959. Taking into account the Communist countries, the decrease in relative importance of the United Kingdom's trade would have appeared even steeper. True, almost half of the expanded world trade was still being transacted in sterling currency and this helped British exports of services, but even these did not seem to grow fast enough. The British merchant marine, a traditional earner of "invisible exports," counted 17.7 million gross tons registered in 1938 (about 26 percent of the world's merchant shipping)

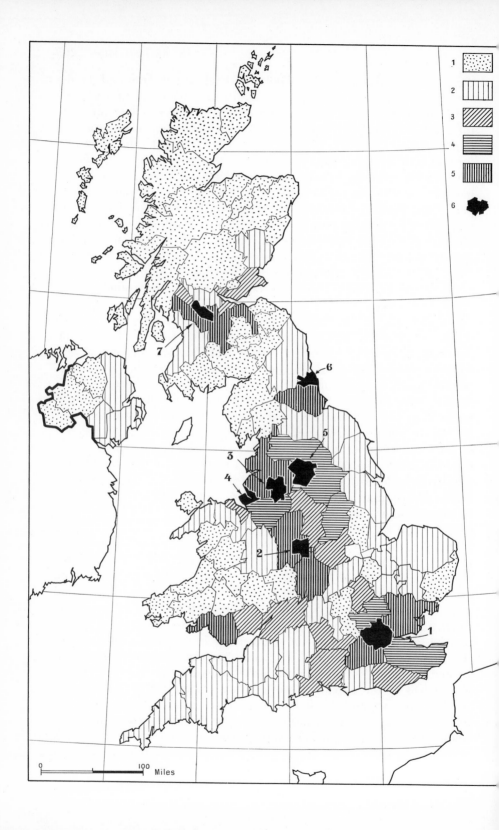

and 21.5 million tons in 1966 (only 13 percent of the world total). Among seagoing merchant fleets it was once more the world's largest, having regained, in 1965, a slim lead over the United States flag. But the total British tonnage seemed stabilized while several rivals were fast catching up with it: Liberia, a flag of convenience, and, more importantly, the Soviet Union, Norway, Greece, and Japan.

Increasing concentration on financial and technological services to be provided to foreign countries or to the Commonwealth was a constant endeavor, and partly responsible for the growth of the office industry and metropolitan ring of London; but it did not appear adequate to swing favorably the balance of payments. In 1958, a rather good year, exports of goods and services topped the imports, bringing a net income of 269 million pounds. The following years however were less favorable: a serious deficit developed in the 1960s. After 1964, following a general trend in Western Europe, industrial production grew slowly and in some critical sectors, slightly declined. Exports of manufactured goods, this main pillar of British prosperity, increased more rapidly in value and less in quantity than in most other advanced and competing nations. The average international index of unit value based on 1958 = 100 for manufactured-goods exports rose to 108 by 1966 but reached 117 for the United Kingdom (as against 109 for the United States, 112 for West Germany, 106 for France, and 90 for Japan); in the same period, the United Nations quantum index of the same exports reached an average of 196 but registered only 136 for the United Kingdom. This lag, due to higher costs, announced the need for a devaluation of the pound, which came at the end of 1967. Growth ratios of the British economy looked slow compared to the Common Market countries and some other industrialized nations. The British government was faced with the need for an agonizing reappraisal of its foreign economic relations, and for a new period of austerity at home.

The more the British crisis was analyzed the more problems seemed to boil down to the following dilemma: the "overdevelopment" of the

---

(*Opposite*) Population in the United Kingdom, 1951. Key: 1, less than 200 inhabitants per square mile; 2, 201 to 500; 3, 501 to 875; 4, 876 to 1250; 5, over 1250; 6, conurbations as defined in 1951 census. The conurbations are numbered: 1 is Greater London (8.3 million inhabitants); 2 is west Midlands (2.2); 3 is southeast Lancashire (2.4); 4 is Merseyside (1.4); 5 is west Yorkshire (1.7); 6 is Tyneside (0.83); and 7 is Clydeside (1.8). The densities are shown by counties and conurbations. The two major masses of population appear well localized: one around London, the second in central England all around the Pennine range. There are few counties showing a density below 200 inhabitants per square mile in England proper, and few counties showing densities above 200 per square mile in Scotland, Wales, and northern Ireland. This general distribution of population densities changed little by 1961, but to understand the trend, see map p. 235.

British economy was founded on a world-wide system of active commercial relations centered on London; now that the world economy has been reorganized and is centered elsewhere (that is, for the free world mainly in New York City and Washington, D.C.), the old British structure, even if rehauled, cannot satisfactorily develop if based on a domestic market of about 56 million consumers. The final accounting of the British economy rests on the balance between the value of what is produced and what is consumed by the nation. In the postwar years the British accepted an austerity policy which was well managed and helped bring about speedy reconstruction and bettered conditions of public welfare. Despite the country's effort in the field of services and white-collar activities, the proportion of the civil employment occupied in distributive trades decreased from 16.5 in 1938 to 11.8 percent in 1951. Manpower had been steered to the more productive professions, while an inverse process accompanied the period of restrictions and reconstruction in several other Western European countries. In the mid-1950s, the British, reaping the rewards of their steadfast endeavors, which had won the admiration of the world began to enjoy a genuine prosperity in a freer economy with a rapidly rising standard of living. But the evolution of the balance of payments cast a shadow over this bright picture. As the domestic market was better supplied and consumed more, imports swelled faster than exports, and the trade deficit widened. Were Britons living beyond their means? Their standard of living did not seem on the whole much higher than that of the Benelux countries or Switzerland, much smaller nations and hardly better endowed by nature at home. It seemed strange that the British could not afford as much while working as hard. The more this problem was studied, the more it appeared that in recent years, while the other European nations had succeeded in broadening the scope of their commercial horizons, the British economic opportunity had been increasingly fenced in in several parts of the world.

## BRITAIN, THE COMMONWEALTH, AND EUROPE

The foreign economic policies of Britain are closely linked with her general political position. Physically the British Isles are part and parcel of Europe, but humanly they are different. Until the sixteenth century Britain was on the fringe of the continent, a marginal land; after that period, history, economics, cultural and blood ties linked her more with other parts of the world. To consider her therefore as participating in Europe's life like any power on the continent would be a mistake. The British geographers L. Dudley Stamp and S. H. Beaver wrote in 1933 in *The British Isles:* "It is still not too much to say that the British Isles do not really belong to Europe. If the Utopian idea of a United States of Europe be achieved, Britain will scarcely form one of those states. A glance at the foreign news page of one of our important daily papers stresses the orientation of the British viewpoint toward America and the overseas dominions, rather than toward the continent of Europe." Several countries of Western Europe feel the same way, without having always had the same ties as England with the New World; this is a result of the maritime vocation and a heritage of the world-wide economy organized by Western Europe, on which its prosperity was founded. America may be, however, the region where, in this century, British commerce comes up against the strongest competition. The United States has inherited much of British and other European skills and has perfected them on a larger scale, with wider natural and human resources. But between Britain and the United States, as well as several of the Dominions, there is a contrast in the age of the civilization and in the proportion of economic structure to its geographical basis. By all measurements, Britain is European, and her aim is to conserve the heritage of tradition and history: her orientation toward the new worlds creates within herself a fundamental conflict.

Europe may not seem essential to Britain; the fact was demonstrated in 1940–1941, when she fought alone against the continent. She found herself in a similar position for a longer time in the Napoleonic period, but still the British people would not care to have such ordeals repeated more than once a century. The great master of British geography Sir Halford Mackinder may have suggested in 1943 that instead of a European community there was an Atlantic community, centered in North America, of which Britain was a "moated airdrome" facing Europe; but where is the independent greatness and prosperity of such a stronghold? Britain has a considerable part to play in world trade, which she, more than any other nation, instrumented. In fact she could not carry on her domestic economy without such a part. And Europe still plays a decisive part in this trade — nowhere else are there as many potential consumers for goods that Britain wishes to export; nowhere else could there be more "complementary" markets. In 1938, 31 percent of the imports of the United Kingdom came from the present sterling area, 24 percent from nonsterling OEEC countries and their possessions, 8 percent from European countries east of the present "iron curtain," and 23.3 percent from the dollar area; in 1951 the four percentages were 36, 26, 5, and 20. Thus the share of both the dollar area and the Soviet zone had decreased in the total British imports. The share of the United States stood at 12.9 in 1938, 9.7 in 1951, and 9.3 in 1959. The concentration of purchases in soft-currency areas is evident. In the export trade the picture is somewhat different: in 1938 the shares of the same four groups of countries were set at 45, 25, 6, and 11 percent; in 1951 these percentages were 50.3, 23.6, 2.3, and 12.5. Exports have been thus flowing increasingly towards the sterling and dollar areas: it was easier to keep the markets in the former; strenuous efforts were made to conquer markets in the latter. The share of the United States in these exports remained stabilized, 5.4 percent in 1938, 5.2 in 1951, then rose to 10.9 in 1959.

The 1960s brought to British foreign trade new problems and opportunities. The constitution in 1958–1959, of the two rival European economic groupings, the EEC and the EFTA, provided a new framework for commercial relations with Europe. At the same time, the economic relationship across the Atlantic between the United States and Western Europe was being modified: the "dollar gap" which has obsessed European economics since World War II was fading away. After 1958, the United States balance of payments ran, rather consistently, a large deficit, chiefly in favor of the European countries, the members of the EEC and a few others, such as Switzerland, Norway, and Sweden. Gold holdings of the countries on the Continent rose steadily. The dollar and sterling holdings of the continental countries also increased, and they usually preferred dollar to sterling, particularly in a period of slow economic growth in Britain. The larger holders of foreign currencies, such as West Germany and France, began buying gold to ensure themselves against a threatening depreciation in the purchasing power of the reserve currencies. These policies on the Continent made the financial position of Britain more difficult. At the same time, its exports to the EEC countries were held up in terms of their possible expansion as the members of the Common Market lowered tariffs and other trade barriers among themselves at the expense of the outsiders. EFTA did not succeed as well as EEC. Moreover, Britain was the only large member of EFTA, while EEC grouped three large and growing economies. In 1961, Britain, followed by some of its associates in EFTA, began negotiating for admission into the EEC. It seemed that it was taking the road of European unification. The negotiations were blocked by a French veto in January 1963. They were resumed in 1967 and again postponed by French objections. It was becoming obvious that Britain felt more European than previously despite its will to maintain the Commonwealth and keep close relations with countries outside the European continent, particularly the United States.

For a country as dependent as Britain on overseas trade, the distribution of imports and exports remains very significant. In 1966, out of a total value of 5,954 million pounds, the British imports came from the EFTA countries for 14 percent, from Ireland for 3.1 percent, from the EEC for 18.4 percent, from the United States for 12 percent,

## The Gas Council Natural Gas Transmission System

——————— Existing Natural Gas Pipeline
— — — — Proposed Natural Gas Pipeline
—··—··— Natural Gas Pipeline Under Construction
············ Sub-Marine Pipeline

EDINBURGH
GLASGOW
Ayr
Scottish Gas Bd.
Dumfries
CARLISLE
Northern Gas Bd.
NEWCASTLE
MIDDLESBROUGH

0  10  20  30  40  50
**Scale of miles**

North Eastern Gas Bd.
LEEDS
HULL
WEST SOLE FIELD
British Petroleum
Killingholme
EASINGTON
North Western Gas Bd.
SCUNTHORPE
MANCHESTER
SHEFFIELD
LIVERPOOL
LEMAN BANK FIELD
Shell/Esso &
Gas Council/Amoco
East Midlands Gas Bd.
NOTTINGHAM
SHREWSBURY
BACTON
LEICESTER
West Midlands Gas Bd.
Coleshill
Lowestoft
Wales Gas Bd.
BIRMINGHAM
COVENTRY
RUGBY
NORTHAMPTON
Eastern
Gas Bd.
Cambridge
IPSWICH
Hitchin
GLOUCESTER
Dunstable
Chelmsford
SWANSEA
CARDIFF
Avonmouth
SWINDON
READING
North
Thames
Bromley
Canvey Terminal
BRISTOL
Bath
Slough
Gas Bd.
E. Greenwich
Southern
Gas Bd.
Maidstone
Guildford
South Eastern Gas Bd.
Salisbury
South West Gas Bd.
SOUTHAMPTON
Exeter
PLYMOUTH

The Gas Council, Nov. 1967

The Natural Gas Transmission system is designed to bring North Sea gas to all of Great Britain from three main reservoirs now established at Canvey, Bacton, and Easington. This map shows the planning as of November 1967. *(Northern Gas Board, Newcastle-upon-Tyne)* and from the Commonwealth countries for 27.4 percent. The Commonwealth was still the leading category among the groups of countries supplying Britain; its share, however, was lower than that of the European countries surrounding Britain; if the percentages of the EEC, EFTA, and the Irish Republic were added up, they amounted to a total of 35.5 percent of all the imports. Exports of British products were distributed, in 1966, in rather similar fashion: EEC took 19 percent, EFTA 15 percent, Ireland 3.6 percent, the United States 12.4 percent, and the Commonwealth 26 percent. Europe's share as a buyer of British goods appeared higher than in the sales to Britain. EFTA, EEC, and the Irish Republic accounted for 37.7 percent of British exports. As the British exports aim at developing the high-quality, more expensive manufactured goods, the potential market would be obviously in Europe, including Eastern Europe, rather than in the Commonwealth countries.

Britain, in the 1960s, seems to be in the grip of a Shakespearean dilemma. It stands on the threshold of a new period in its history. The great world-wide network of economic relations, on which its greatness and prosperity had been founded for the last three centuries and that had permitted it to disassociate itself from Europe on many occasions, no longer provides the expected results. In fact, some of this inheritance weakens rather than supports the British economy in the present process of its reorganization. But the dilemma is not simply a choice between Commonwealth preference and European integration. Britain feels also that the latter choice would weaken its association with North America. Memories of the common struggle during World War II and recognition of the new position of dominance acquired by the United States on the world scene both contribute to make Britain feel the special importance to it of British-American ties. The United States and Canada are also essential markets for exports and the region in the world where foodstuffs and some of the other raw materials Britain needs can now be purchased at the lowest price. British and American interests are closely interwoven throughout the world. Not only is there much British capital invested in the United States and much more American investment in Britain (more than in any country outside the Western Hemisphere), but British and American capital and management have long been associated in large international corporations dealing in oil, chemicals, soap, and fats, divers mechanical manufacturing, banking, and mining. Intricate association among British and United States firms is found not only in those countries themselves, in Canada and Australia, but throughout Europe west of the "iron curtain," and in Africa. Seen from the United States, Britain is a close relative, a natural ally, and a good customer for many American exports. The United States has generously helped the reconstruction of Britain and the maintenance of the pound sterling as one of the two international reserve currencies. American corporations have made considerable investments in Britain and by now own or participate in ownership of wide sectors of British industry. This complex intertwining of British and American economic and cultural interests does not preclude a great deal of rivalry and competition in various fields.

The lively economic, political, and cultural ties still binding Britain to the Commonwealth countries cannot prevent the latter from expanding their relations with the United States, with other European countries, and even with the Soviet Union or Communist China. Britain's share in world exports of manufactured goods has been steadily decreasing, while the shares of some of its competitors, particularly West Germany and Japan, have been rising. Britain has also found that the maintenance of substantial military forces in various parts of the world no longer corresponds to its actual means and needs. In 1967, the decision was taken to restrict considerably British military involvement east of Suez. In the long run, the new policy could save a good deal of expenditure abroad and help the British balance of payments. It may also limit the possibility of local conflicts with former dependencies throughout the world. The recent evolution of British policy seems to indicate a slow shift back toward integration in a European framework. The British attempt at isolation in the 1950s seems to have brought about a stronger impact of the regional environment that welds it to Europe. There are many factors at play in the international arena that influence the evolution of the British position: the discovery of great local resources of energy in the form of natural gas in the North Sea basin may be one of these factors; the indisputable economic success of the integration of six very different powers in the EEC is another factor; the shifting away of the less developed countries, including many of the Commonwealth members, toward closer association with the superpowers of the day; the recovery of prosperity and political liveliness on the continent of Europe; all these and many other factors are now instrumental in the British decision to link itself closely to Western Europe; perhaps nothing could help Europe so much to regain some of its past role as Britain's integration with the Western countries, which could not fail to unite the Six of the EEC with the Seven of the EFTA, making up altogether a very substantial new political unit. And every country in Western Europe shares in some way the British need and tradition of a dynamic system of wide overseas relations.

The great dike of Holland, cutting off the Zuider Zee from the North Sea — a *chef d'oeuvre* of man's mastery over nature. *(The Netherlands Information Bureau)*

# 7

---

# The
# Benelux Countries

Although it is a recently coined term, *Benelux* is already widely used to designate three countries of Northwestern Europe—Belgium, the Netherlands, and Luxembourg—among the smallest European powers in area but among the most important in the economic and cultural fields. Benelux, as a whole, covers only 25,600 square miles but supports a population of 22,700,000 inhabitants. The average density of 890 people to the square mile, a steadily increasing one, is higher than that of other European nations. It is also the highest density for an area with such a high standard of living, for the people of Benelux before the war were among the most prosperous in Europe and their national income seemed well distributed. Today, economic unity is being brought about through the organization of the Common Market in an area politically divided into three sovereign states. Belgium and the Netherlands have had great histories. The Netherlands was one of the leading Western powers from the sixteenth to the eighteenth centuries, with a vast colonial empire, and it still has some dependent territories overseas. Belgium has had a shorter history as an independent country but has already commanded a large empire in Central Africa. Both are great centers of trade and industry. The smaller Luxembourg also has industrial significance. All three countries belong to the coastal area of the North Sea and have participated actively in the maritime activities characteristic of Western Europe.

Situated on one of the northwestern shores of the continent, the Benelux countries were reached by two major expansions of the past: the Roman Empire and the Germanic migrations. In mixing, the two influences have created special regional features that are at the same time different from and related to both the zones of civilization stretching to the south (France and the Latin area) and the east (Germany). Here is the northern section of the Lotharingia of the Verdun partition, stubbornly disputed by those who claimed the imperial heritage in the Occident and even more stubbornly defended by the local populations against outside control. But the hardships that helped to shape the personality of these countries did not all come from human and historical causes: the physical environment has been the cause of many difficulties; the extreme dampness and flatness of the coastal area has several times led the sea to invade portions of it. The fight against the sea and the struggle to improve the local conditions to enable them to support such a dense population have become models for the whole Western world. Before *Benelux* was coined, this area was called the Low Countries, and no other area in Europe is more man-made.

## THE CHALLENGE OF THE LOWLANDS

The structure and topography of the Benelux area are simple: it is the beginning of the Great Plain of Europe, a flat plain fringed to the southeast by low plateaus, the fringe of the Hercynian zone. The contrast between the plain and the peneplain is sharp. The low sedimentary plain is flat, and the courses of the streams have not dug much below the general level, while in the old rock of the peneplain, called here the Ardennes plateau, deep valleys have cut through. The maritime climate of the plain is in opposition to the stronger variations of the peneplain's altitude; the rich alluvial soil of the plain contrasts with the poorer heath and moorland of the plateau. But the plain covers practically all of the Netherlands and most of Belgium—the plateau in the southeast never reaches above 2200 feet and in general not more than 1300. Closer to the shore, an almost sea-level altitude prevails; indeed certain parts are below sea level. This whole area has been affected by some fractures that oriented details of the topography, and it slopes gently from the southeast to the northwest—in the latter section the province of Holland means "hollow land." Along this slope there are four levels: the crystalline plateau, the Belgian sedimentary plain, the delta of the Lowlands, and the hollow parts along the shore.

A large part of the northern lowlands was glaciated, and therefore it was flattened even more by the ice sheet and endowed with some morainic topography, some hillocks of gravel, depressed basins, and a confused drainage. After the glacier's retreat, large streams draining wide basins inland came to empty through the Low Countries into the North Sea. That is how the northern half of the area became a delta: alluvials were deposited and spread, and the coastline was somewhat regularized and fringed with a line of sand dunes and beaches. But the waters from the interior had great difficulty in reaching the sea; their gradient was very low, and there was practically no slope in their lower course. Consequently floods covered the surrounding lands, and the rivers meandered across the territory through numerous and unstable channels. At times of high tides, the sea broke through the line of dunes and rushed inland, flooding some of the land again. Soils of clay and peat are not permeable (water stays on it), and the climate is damp, very similar to that of the British Isles, with rains and fogs throughout the whole year. Here indeed was a territory where it was hard to differentiate land from sea, but, as a Dutch author put it, "God having created the land and the sea, the Dutch took care of the coasts."

Through the ages, the Dutch population has worked out an effective control of the water flow and mastered all threats, whether they came from the inland drainage or from the marine tidal waves. But all danger has not been averted once and for all, and permanent vigilance is required in the lower lands close to the sea. In January 1916, a high tide flooded some 40,000 acres near Amsterdam with saline water; infiltration continues elsewhere, and continuous pumping is necessary to evacuate waters in places. On February 1, 1953, heavy seas again broke through the dams in Zeeland along the lower Rhine, wreaking terrible havoc. The Dutch needed the help of Allied forces in Europe to stem the flood and rescue people in the devastated areas. The challenge has led to a magnificent riposte: the sea was conquered along the shore and on the wide oceans; instead of a threat, the rivers brought trade and riches. Such was particularly the story of the Netherlands, and of the province of Flanders in coastal Belgium. For centuries men dug into the peat bogs for fuel, and lakes spread, filling the excavated parts. Dikes were built around the lakes that were pumped dry and reclaimed, becoming *droogmakerijen*. The flood of 1953 led to the *Delta* project.

A piece of land is defended or conquered from the water through the erection of a protective dam — any parcel of territory so enclosed by dikes is called a *polder*. A polder cannot exist independently of the environment, and owners of the land have to work together for successful defense. Such combined operations appeared early: in Flanders there are associations of polderland holders, dating back to the twelfth century and still carrying on under the name of *wateringen*. This was a wonderful school for self-government and democracy; these associations — the Dutch would call them *waterschap* or *heemraadschap* — had their own finances, officers, and rules; they were the vigilantes of the water. The Polderland developed parallelly along the seashore and along the main rivers of the Rhine and Meuse. In the fifteenth century, several major

Polders and hothouses: two solutions that give the Lowlanders control over their hostile environment. *(The Netherlands Information Bureau)*

breakthroughs of the sea inland from the sand dunes of the shore made necessary an organized attack, and public authorities came to its aid. In the seventeenth century the techniques of damming, pumping out the waters (chiefly with the power of windmills), and channeling them through a series of locks to river or sea were well advanced. The Dutch even started a national organization for water control under a special government department; they began draining swamps and lakes inland, then conquering the tidal lands along the seashore, uniting islands to the mainland, and maintaining the river floods between high embankments. The first great artificial polder was drained in the years 1608–1612 in northern Holland—the Beemstermeer polder maintained with the help of forty windmills had an area of 18,000 acres. The former landscape of Holland, dotted with lakes, disappeared and was replaced by a regular chessboard of narrow canals. The great work of the nineteenth century was the draining of the inland lake of the Haarlemmermeer. The twentieth century, with increased technical means, went further, and work was begun to convert into a lake and drain the Zuider Zee, the large bay penetrating into the northern coast of the Netherlands. Now the former Zuider Zee is being made into polders, with the lake of Ijssel in the middle, behind an enormous dam that is one of the great public works of our age. Flooded during World War II, the new polderland was reclaimed in 1945–1946, and settlement is again progressing. To satisfy the demand for land of an increasing population, the Netherlands creates more land; nearly 40 percent of its land area is polderland.

The Dutch have exported their technology of water control: they taught poldermaking to other European nations, such as the French, the British, and the Danes, and there are few great hydraulic enterprises in the world in which the Dutch have not participated in some way. But they did not restrict their contacts with water to chasing it away: they went out on the high seas and played an outstanding part in Europe's mastery of the seas. The legend of the flying Dutchman haunted more than the Atlantic. The Low Countries became the main façade of the continent on the North Sea, a façade that was greatly aided by the design of the hydrographic network of Western Europe.

The Low Countries are indeed a delta, and a delta of several rivers: the Rhine, the Meuse, and the Schelde join their courses and waters in this flat area in such a puzzle that it is difficult to determine which river is where. They empty through channels that cross Holland in all directions and are mostly old or modern arms of the Rhine; then they mix their waters in a deep inlet of the sea, a common mouth for the three streams, half filled with the islands of Zeeland. All three rivers are navigable, the Schelde and the Meuse draining basins through northern

France and Belgium that have the regular rainfall and dampness of the Atlantic climate. But the Rhine is a large stream with a more involved feeding. It comes down from the Swiss Alps and has an abundant flow of water, with heavy floods in spring and summer from the thaw of snow and ice in that lofty range. It crosses lakes that act like reservoirs and moderate the regime; then it receives many tributaries from France and Germany, some of them important rivers in their own right, such as the Neckar, the Main, and the Moselle, which bring more water from the plain and low Hercynian ranges in fall and winter than in the warm season when evaporation is strongest. The combination of its upper regime with its middle-course tributaries feeds the Lower Rhine with an abundant and regular gauge all the year round. It is the ideal waterway of Europe and carries large barges upstream to Basel. Through the tributaries and canals that link them with other streams, especially in Germany and France, the ports at the mouth of the Rhine-Meuse-Schelde system serve as transshipment points for a large part of Western and Central Europe.

Since antiquity these rivers have been carrying traffic to and from the North Sea shores. Until the Germanic invasions westward these shores were a marginal area; then the North Sea became a Germanic sea, and the Viking tribes, from Denmark and Norway, came to rule parts of Italy and Spain. In the beginning of the ninth century, Charlemagne restored the empire in the west and carried Western and Christian rule eastward to the Elbe River. Instead of being a frontier, the Rhine became the main street of this Occidental empire, and the countries at its point of contact with the North Sea became great hubs of trade and traffic. For a thousand years they remained one of the essential crossroads of international trade. And once again it is commerce—this time with a slightly different aspect, that of a hinge linking together the continental and the maritime economies and civilizations—that helped develop in the Low Countries a rich, dense, cultivated population and a balanced economy—an economy of cities that have still made the most out of a rather difficult rural environment.

The challenge of the natural environment was turned into an asset. Although dependent on commerce, the stubborn and efficient populations of the Lowlands are deeply rooted and passionately attached to their soil, and the regional frame gave rise to local patriotism leading to the political division of a naturally unified region.

## THE NETHERLANDS

The Netherlands occupies principally the delta of the Rhine and Meuse, and its boundaries do not follow any natural limits. As a political unit and as a geographical area it is indeed man-made, linked to the solidarity of interests of a people who, established on a flooded gate, united to fight against the waters and foreign interference. The historical kernel is the county of Holland to the west. Isolated by the extension of the sea inland in the thirteenth century, Holland had only fisheries and the meadows on its sandy soils for resources, plus a fee from every ship passing on the arm of the Rhine before the Dutch stronghold at Dordrecht. But slowly the Dutch built up their state against the richer Flanders. They devised the preserving of salted herring in barrels and exported herring to the continent without submitting to the Hansa monopoly of this trade; in the sixteenth century their fleets defeated the Hansa and established free access to North Sea and Baltic ports, Amsterdam then becoming an emporium of trade between the northern and southern countries of Europe. At the time of the Reformation, the Low Countries were divided. Holland and other provinces in the north joined the Protestants; the southern counties, including Flanders and Brabant, remained Catholic. The rule of the Most Catholic King of Spain started in 1568 a religious war that divided the Netherlands from Belgium ten years later when the United Protestant Provinces declared their independence. When in 1648 the Netherlands was recognized by other European powers as independent, it already ranked as a great power; its naval and merchant marine, its agricultural and commercial skill, and its advanced system of education were already admired throughout the world.

After a brief period of reunion with the Belgian provinces during the years 1815–1830, the Netherlands received its present boundaries, with a piece of territory stretching upstream along the Meuse to the town of Maastricht. An area of 12,868 square miles, it has a population of 12.7 million inhabitants. This rapidly increasing population (only 6.8 million in 1920) is no longer purely Protestant; Roman Catholics accounted for about 42 percent in 1960, chiefly in the southern provinces and the principal cities. The national tradition is founded on a rich historical background, on the Dutch language and Dutch culture. Here is a highly individualized country, quite different from all its neighbors on the continent or the sea. The Netherlands — or Holland, as the whole country is often called — is a homogeneous nation, whose contribution to Western civilization has been considerable. One could also speak of a "Dutch miracle."

The Netherlands has the most artificial land of any European state. There are three main soil regions: the ribbon of sand dunes of the western coast, chiefly occupied by a string of towns; the polderland, which occupies the western part of the country, and finally, the sandy and peaty lands of the east. The polders are the most intensively cultivated section of the whole: a large part is in meadows, but there are also rich crops produced on the drained land. Wheat and beets are grown on the Wieringermeer which until 1930 was under the North Sea; fields of tulips cover part of the sand dunes near Haarlem every spring; north of Amsterdam the permanent grassland dominates, and the green of the polder, checkered with the deeper green of the water canals, is dotted with the black and white patches of the Dutch cows (a breed closely related to the Holstein). A similar landscape fringes the northern coast where polders have advanced on tidal lands.

The interior in the east and center of the country used to be a heath-land of sand with many lakes and peat bogs throughout. This was the result of the morainic action to which the delta has added more recent sands and humidity. The average altitude is above sea level, and the roads, instead of following the ditches above the fields and meadows, are distinctly on or below the general level. A few clusters of wood and heath remain on the worst sands, but the Dutch could not afford to lose so much land. Sandy soils were reclaimed with marls and fertilizer, but the best job was performed on the large and numerous peat bogs. There the peat was extracted, the sand at its bottom was enriched with marls and clays carried from a distance, and all kinds of necessary ferti-lizers added until the new mixture became good, rich soil. These re-claimed peat bogs were called *veenkolonien;* they started on a large scale in the Middle Ages not far from the town of Groningen in the northeast and have since spread through the country and to Germany and Den-mark, In the center and southeast, afforestation is replacing heath with woods. The stubborn labor and "know-how" of the small Dutch farmer turned the sandy *Geest* into fields and pastures. Polders predominate again in the lower valley of the Rhine and Meuse and achieve perfection in the insular or coastal Zeeland at the mouth of the streams. But ever since the tenth century the population has had to maintain a relentless guard against possible incursions of the waves—the case of the West-kapelle Dam on the isle of Walcheren is famous. Many of these islands were actually built out of many smaller ones that were united and ce-mented together. The province of Zeeland with its motto of *"Luctor et emergo"* has been rightly described as "a masterpiece of masonry."

The soil created by such stubborn toil was fitted for an intensive use. A total area of 5.6 million acres are cultivated, permanent grass account-ing for about 3.3 million. On the rest the most extensive crops are pota-toes (either directly for food or for potato flour), rye, oats, wheat, barley, sugar and fodder beets, colza, carrots, peas, and flax. An important crop is flowers, especially the flower bulbs that are exported all over the world, and 32,000 acres are given up to bulb production; nurseries are quite important too (8,600 acres). This agricultural production is far from sufficient to feed the population adequately, and a large part of

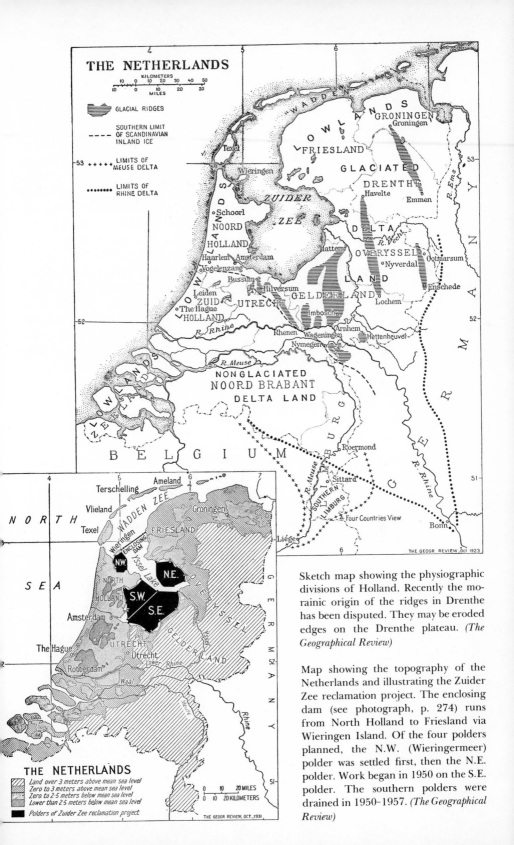

# THE NETHERLANDS

KILOMETERS
10  0  10  20  30  40  50
10  0  10  20  30
MILES

- GLACIAL RIDGES
- SOUTHERN LIMIT OF SCANDINAVIAN INLAND ICE
- 53 +++++ LIMITS OF MEUSE DELTA
- •••••• LIMITS OF RHINE DELTA

WADDEN
LOWLANDS
GRONINGEN
Groningen
FRIESLAND
GLACIATED
Texel
DRENTHE
Wieringen
Havelte
ZUIDER
Emmen
ZEE
R. Ems
Schoorl
NOORD
DELTA
HOLLAND
R. Vecht
OVERYSSEL
Haarlem
Amsterdam
Hattem
Nyverdal
Oothmarsum
Vogelenzang
LAND
Bussum
Enschede
Leiden
Hilversum
GELDERLAND
Lochem
ZUID
UTRECHT
The Hague
HOLLAND
Imbosch
R. Rhine
Rhenen
Wageningen
Arnhem
Hettenheuvel
Nymegen
R. Meuse
NONGLACIATED
NOORD BRABANT
DELTA LAND
BELGIUM
LIMBURG
Roermond
R. Meuse
SOUTHERN
Sittard
LIMBURG
R. Rhine
Four Countries View
Bonn

THE GEOGR. REVIEW, OCT 1923

53
53
52
52
51

N O R T H
S E A

THE NETHERLANDS

Terschelling
Ameland
Vlieland
WADDEN ZEE
Groningen
Texel
Wieringen
FRIESLAND
ENCLOSING DAM
N.W.
NORTH
HOLLAND
Yssel Lake
N.E.
S.W.
S.E.
OVERYSSEL
Amsterdam
GELDERLAND
The Hague
UTRECHT
Utrecht
Lower Rhine
Rotterdam
Waal
Meuse
Rhine
GERMANY

Land over 3 meters above mean sea level
Zero to 3 meters above mean sea level
Zero to 2·5 meters below mean sea level
Lower than 2·5 meters below mean sea level
Polders of Zuider Zee reclamation project

0   10        20 MILES
0   10   20 KILOMETERS
THE GEOGR. REVIEW, OCT.,1931

Sketch map showing the physiographic divisions of Holland. Recently the morainic origin of the ridges in Drenthe has been disputed. They may be eroded edges on the Drenthe plateau. (*The Geographical Review*)

Map showing the topography of the Netherlands and illustrating the Zuider Zee reclamation project. The enclosing dam (see photograph, p. 274) runs from North Holland to Friesland via Wieringen Island. Of the four polders planned, the N.W. (Wieringermeer) polder was settled first, then the N.E. polder. Work began in 1950 on the S.E. polder. The southern polders were drained in 1950–1957. (*The Geographical Review*)

Rich cropland with modern scattered farms has emerged from under the former Zuider Zee. The bridge to the right, over one of the channels left to drain water toward the North Sea, connects the new dyke on which runs a highway to older land which has a different pattern of land use. (*Netherlands Information Service*)

Dutch shipping going through one of the many sluices necessitated by the variety of water tables in a flat country. (*The Netherlands Information Bureau*)

Holland's food, especially grain, has to be imported. The rural activities are mainly geared to livestock raising, and there Holland can rival Denmark for first rank in modern methods and quality of production. The livestock, somewhat depleted by the war, is now much above the prewar level with 4 million head of cattle and 4.3 million pigs. Holland cheese, eggs, and butter are well known and are exported in large quantities; yet on the morrow of the war it was the flowers and bulbs that were the most valuable export of the products of the land. Small farms are generally well equipped, grouped in cooperatives, and specialized. As the soil is artificial, agriculture is almost completely industrialized. In the general economy it is now less important than industry or commercial activities but still supplies one third of the total exports.

Commercial and industrial pursuits early created an active urban life. In 1966 there were fifteen cities of more than 100,000 inhabitants, totaling 40 percent of the population. The main group of cities lies along the meeting of the western coastal sandy belt with the polders, from Amsterdam to Rotterdam, the two main cities and ports. Amsterdam is the old capital city of Holland. It is built on the former Zuider Zee and forms, with its suburbs, a conurbation of more than a million people. It began to rise in the fourteenth century as a trading post on the route from Hamburg to Flanders; then it entered the great maritime trade and appeared in the middle of the seventeenth century as the foremost emporium of the Western world, before being displaced by London. The Dutch dominated the trade with the East Indies and the route around Africa. Their shipbuilding was reputed the best, and Peter the Great, when Tsar of Russia, came to learn shipbuilding, working as an ordinary Dutchman in the yards. Famous writers, such as Locke, Descartes, and Voltaire, published books in Amsterdam, a citadel of freedom and culture. The city expanded, being built not exactly as has been said "on carcasses of herrings" but on millions of timberlogs driven into the swampy ground to help support its heavy structures. The redistribution trade passed to London in the eighteenth century, but a new commercial development took place in the nineteenth; and since 1876 a ship canal has linked Amsterdam directly with the North Sea at Ijmuiden, where huge locks were built able to receive the largest of ships. A new and wide canal links the port of Amsterdam to the Rhine, now that trade with independent Indonesia is no longer so active. From its old links with South Africa a diamond-cutting industry and large diamond market arose. But the main current of traffic is based on the trade with tropical countries such as the West Indies or Indonesia. Tin, sugar, and rubber from Java; tea, coffee, spices, copra, and tobacco—all are stored in vast warehouses. With the capital accumulated from centuries of trade, large industries have been erected: foods and chemicals, shipyards,

Amsterdam, with its royal castle designed in 1648. A whole forest of timber logs was sunk in the marshy ground to strengthen the foundations of such buildings. Now tons of sand and cement are used. *(The Netherlands Information Bureau)*

The Dutch milch cows, with their black and white pattern, originate in polders below sea level as illustrated here. An ocean-going ship follows a waterway kept by levees above the level of the land it crosses. *(Netherlands Information Service)*

engineering, and timber works are the main activities in the city itself and in a wide belt of busy and expanding suburbs.

Built of brick, Amsterdam is an extremely active city with its busy crowds flowing up and down streets too narrow for their present traffic, many of them paralleled by canals. In the midst of the business section barges are loaded from warehouses of original Renaissance style. To the south and west stretch new residential sections with large modern apartment houses and an abundance of flowers on the streets and balconies. The University of Amsterdam carries on a great tradition, and Rembrandt's house stands, piously preserved, on the old Jewish street. The population has begun to migrate to the periphery, to independent suburbs such as Hilversum (103,000) and Zaandam (56,000). Fishing boats and foreign liners use the port of Ijmuiden, where a large steel mill and a cement plant are in operation. Although in recent years Rotterdam has been growing more rapidly than Amsterdam both as a seaport and as an industrial center, Amsterdam has retained the functions of the financial capital as the main center of banking and industrial management, as well as remaining the leading cultural center of the Netherlands. Along some of the quiet, romantic *grachten* (canals) in the heart of the historic city, seventeenth-century mansions are being refitted behind their preserved façades and occupied by rapidly spreading offices; and near the central railroad station, overlooking the port, has risen the first skyscraper of Holland, grouping the offices of maritime interests. Amsterdam proudly carries on as the capital of the Netherlands, though it is not the seat of the government; in many ways it is now the northern extremity of a vast urbanized region which still preserves some farmland in its midst and is thus referred to as the *Randstadt* (or circular city) of Holland, agglomerating about 4 million people.

The great road southward from Amsterdam to the mouth of the Rhine and Meuse is a continuous line of large and prosperous cities. Haarlem (170,000) is the capital of the flower and bulb trade and has many food industries, textile plants, mechanical works, and shipyards. Leyden (100,000) used to be a great Rhine port and is still the seat of a university of repute; it too has some textile and mechanical plants. The Hague (745,000) with suburbs is a small Washington, with the government's offices and the Queen's residence, the Parliament, the International Court of Justice (which sits in the Peace Palace built with Andrew Carnegie's endowment), and many officials, active and retired—a city of dignity and serenity. This traditional picture was somewhat disturbed when oil was struck under the northern section of the city, near the elegant seaside suburb of Scheveningen. A few derricks now rise and trains of tank cars run amidst a respectable garden-city landscape. A few hundred yards south of the oilfield the headquarters of the Royal Dutch

Company has long been managing petroleum interests all around the globe. The Hague has also attracted the offices of other large international concerns, such as the Iranian Oil Consortium, and European headquarters of several American corporations. One barely has left the suburbs of The Hague when one enters the old city of Delft (78,000), which has long been famous for its chinaware and which now houses a variety of food industries, large distilleries, and a large Institute of Technology with atomic laboratories. To the south one then comes to Schiedam (82,000), an industrial suburb of Rotterdam.

Rotterdam (730,000) is the second city of Holland and now its chief port on the Rhine. It is the port function that defines the city, which stands on the Nieuw Maas, where the Meuse and Rhine waters mix to form an impressive waterway. Hundreds of riverboats come alongside ocean-going ships, and all the flags of the world fly on their masts, including that of the Swiss. Through Rotterdam the basin of the Rhine is fed with cargoes from overseas. Before 1939 the total tonnage of the traffic made Rotterdam one of the great seaports of the world, but it suffered greatly through bombings during World War II and the great fire of 1940, from being cut off from the sea thereafter by Allied blockade, and finally after 1945 from the reduced activity in the German Rhineland. This is an international and Atlantic port, largely dependent on transit trade, but from trade much industry has been born here: chemical and mechanical manufacturing, flour and cotton mills, oil and sugar refineries, glass and soap factories, and the like. The factories push downstream along the new waterway that ends in the sea, located between two big jetties advancing far out from the shoreline.

Since 1947 Rotterdam's recovery has been spectacular, and it now ranks as the first seaport on the continent of Europe, with 130 million tons of goods loaded and unloaded by seagoing ships in 1966. This figure was much above that of 1938, when the traffic of the port reached 42.4 million tons. During this period the characteristics of the port's traffic have changed: petroleum products have greatly increased their share and volume, rising from 3 million tons in 1938 to 68 in 1965; the share of the Dutch exports and imports has also increased, now making up about half of the huge port's traffic, a figure which shows clearly the pace of postwar industrialization in the Netherlands. Rotterdam, by 1966, had an international traffic far above that of London and could claim to be the world's largest in international movement of goods, and altogether the second largest port in the world, after New York. The city has built large industries; its three new oil refineries have a combined capacity of 35 million metric tons a year. An ambitious scheme was started in 1958, an advanced extension of the port on the Nieuwe Waterweg, opposite the Hook of Holland, that will be able to receive the

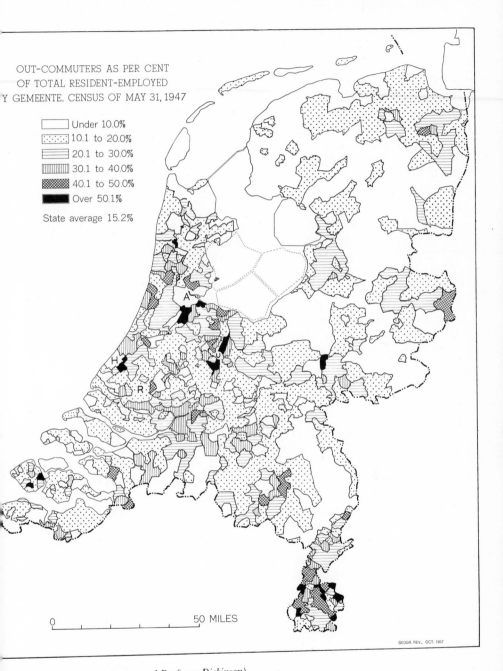

OUT-COMMUTERS AS PER CENT
OF TOTAL RESIDENT-EMPLOYED
Y GEMEENTE. CENSUS OF MAY 31, 1947

Under 10.0%
10.1 to 20.0%
20.1 to 30.0%
30.1 to 40.0%
40.1 to 50.0%
Over 50.1%

State average 15.2%

0                    50 MILES

GEOGR. REV., OCT. 1957

*(The Geographical Review and Professor Dickinson)*

largest ships (up to 100,000 tons deadweight) and provide 4000 acres of docks and industrial establishments. Rotterdam nowadays sees its future on a grand scale. The new project of the *Europoort* assumes that the city is becoming the major maritime gate to the Common Market and perhaps an even wider European community. The central business district of Rotterdam has been rebuilt with similar daring vision. Its new shopping area, the Lijnbaan, has been cited by planners as a model. As the navigation on the Upper Rhine is being improved, and the Moselle canalized, the waterways in the hinterland of the port will be extending to an ever larger section of eastern France and Switzerland. But for all this trade, Rotterdam still competes with Amsterdam (which keeps a respectable traffic of 21.8 million tons by maritime vessels plus 10.4 by fluvial navigation), Antwerp, and even Bremen, Hamburg, and Dunkirk.

Industrial centers abound inland all along the old and new branches of the Meuse and Rhine. Thus Utrecht (430,000 with suburbs), which used to be a great regional capital, still has a large university, railroad yards and shops, sugar and fertilizer factories. Gouda (46,000) specializes in cheese, as does Alkmaar farther north. The textile and leather industries are spread among the cities of southern Netherlands: Tilburg, Nijmegen, Arnhem, Eindhoven (the capital of electronics) and Breda each have over 100,000. Cotton is important at Enschede (135,000) and Hengelo. Groningen is the capital of the northeast, close to the German border; it used to be isolated from Germany by a wide stretch of impassable swamps, but these have been transformed into *veenkolonien*. An enormous deposit of natural gas was found and is being developed near Groningen which now becomes a great node of pipelines. To the southeast the isolated province of Limburg is dominated by the old stronghold of Maastricht (95,000), which took on a new importance with the development between the two World Wars of the only coalfield in Holland; it supplies all the needs of the domestic market (14 million tons in 1937 but only 10.3 million in 1966). A small oilfield is also worked here.

The Netherlands has succeeded in the flattest and most monotonous country in Europe in creating a diversified and attractive scenery: it is made up of canals and flower fields, of clean, old little towns and teeming cities that still retain some Renaissance flavor, of the now disappearing windmills and a scattering of black and white cows, and of a mild atmosphere with subtle shades of light. The whole country gives a general impression of comfort and efficiency. Its prosperity, however, was shattered deeply by World War II and the postwar economic crisis.

Holland was one of the bankers of the world, and it cannot afford to carry on. One of the chief foundations of Dutch prosperity was the well-developed colonial empire in the East Indies; now Indonesia has emancipated itself and the other islands no longer produce the same output

The destruction of Rotterdam. Only the railroad station was left standing in an area that before May 1940 was a busy central section of the city. Reconstruction was begun in 1947. Compare the view in 1960 (p. 308); the crossroads in the foreground correspond to the plaza in the lower left corner of the view of the rebuilt area. *(Royal Dutch Airlines)*

or the same income. The Dutch are very active on the seas—in tonnage, ships adding up to about 5 million tons fly their flag—and Dutch directors sit on the boards of Unilever and the Royal Dutch-Shell Company—the Dutch island of Curaçao, off the coast of Venezuela, is one of the great oil refining centers in the world. But all this still did not seem enough to maintain for the hard-working but increasing population of the Netherlands the high standard of living it was accustomed to. The Dutch government has needed to engage in systematic planning, of which the most impressive item is the drainage of the Zuider Zee. On the monument in the midst of the huge dam cutting the bay from the sea there has been inscribed: "A wise people provides for its future." And the Dutch certainly do their best at home: this project added 550,-000 acres of fertile land to the rural country. Then a more ambitious plan considers the possibility of building a dam along the arch of the Frisian Islands and draining the Wadden Zee—beyond that the land area cannot be extended. Holland is close to achieving its agricultural maximum. The future requires more trade and manufacturing and an economic system of a new kind to replace the structure of past centuries shattered by external developments and the loss of the East Indies. The Dutch problem has been extremely well managed. Through Benelux at first, then the EEC, the markets were expanded and the new industrial and commercial structure fortified. At the same time the economic recovery of West Germany greatly helped Rotterdam and the Rhine traffic. Dutch interests remain closely associated with British and American interests in various international concerns. The Netherlands thus remain a senior partner of the free world's economic system. And they also remain most conscious of their need to develop to the limit their domestic resources.

Recently some oil has been found in the Netherlands (2.4 million tons produced in 1966) and a great deal of natural gas. But the fundamental difficulties are more basic: to preserve the agricultural land built up at such cost, the Dutch must carefully ration its use and the urban sprawl that could devour too much space. Vast areas are covered with glass, and truck farming goes on all year round in the hot houses, especially in southern Holland. Another shortage looms on the horizon as urbanization and industrialization progress: that of fresh water as the demand rises for domestic and industrial uses. Thus was launched the *Delta* plan, which consists in damming up the large inlets of the sea between the islands of southern Holland and Zeeland, with the double aim of keeping the highest tides out (to avoid repetition of such disastrous floods as occurred in 1953), and of creating behind these dams vast reservoirs of the fresh water brought by the Rhine and the Meuse. Immense works have begun, to be completed in 1977, erecting these dams. At the same time the Dutch insist on measures against the pollution of the international streams, the water they will ultimately drink. No other nation in Europe has been forced by its very environment to plan and provide for its future to the same extent.

## BELGIUM

Smaller in area (11,755 square miles) and less populated (9.7 million inhabitants) than Holland, Belgium is much younger as an independent nation. It received its present status in 1839 when the union with the Netherlands, attempted after 1815, proved an unhappy one. Since the Middle Ages the Belgians have been ruled successively by many outside authorities: they belonged to Charlemagne's empire, then to Lotharingia, then to the duke of Burgundy, a powerful French prince; they passed under Spanish, then Austrian, rule with the Hapsburgs; they were conquered by the French at the time of the Revolution and the Napoleonic empire; and they were united with the Dutch by the Congress of Vienna. Against all these interferences they fought with tenacity—and also with some philosophy, for they felt much smaller than the empires surrounding them. Always they tried to work out a balance of power between whatever country governed them and England, who was deeply interested in the control of the continental coast that faced her. There was an old economic unity of interests with England, for English wool sold on the continent was manufactured into cloth in Flanders, and Bruges, Ghent, and Antwerp redistributed British products inland. After its independence was achieved, Belgium wished to work in peace and to stay neutral in politics. She was not able to remain so after the German armies invaded her in 1914 and again in 1940.

Belgium is definitely situated south of the Meuse and Rhine delta, but through the lower course of the Schelde, on which Antwerp is built, it participates in the North Sea and Rhine trades. Few countries have been as long disputed among continental powers and between influences of the Latin and of the Germanic zones of civilization. To avoid being definitely torn to pieces and to take advantage of their intermediate position, the Belgians strengthened their regionalism and built a small but patriotic national unit; but there still remains at its very foundation an element of instability.

The present Belgian state results from the merger of three important units of the feudal Middle Ages, the counties of Flanders, Brabant, and Hainaut. All three were rich and powerful units of olden times; all of them were transitional lands; spiritually all were united by the Roman Catholic faith, but culturally they were different. There are still two official languages in Belgium: Flemish, a Germanic tongue, quite close to Dutch, and French. About one fifth of the population is truly bilingual, but the proportion of the Flemish element is estimated at 55 percent and that of the Walloon or French-speaking element at 33 percent. The linguistic boundary follows an east-west line that passes immediately south of Brussels — although the capital city itself speaks predominantly French. This duality of language and culture has caused in such a small area considerable diversity and some tensions, but no sharp contrasts.

The physical frame is simple: a gentle slope from the Hercynian plateau of the Ardennes in the southeast to the low North Sea coast in the northwest. Three belts of topography and different landscapes have developed: the plateau, the plain in the middle, and the coastal lowland. These must be classified as three regions, at once historical and economic: the Ardennes, the central plain, and Flanders.

The plateau of Ardennes is rugged and of a continental shade. The northeast-southeast axis of the old folds is still apparent in the topography. The highest summits seldom reach more than 2000 feet; a level around 1200 predominates in the southeast, while the tableland slopes gently under the sedimentary strata to the northwest. The landforms are generally old, mature, and thoroughly planed. On the highland the climate may become rugged — there are 145 days of frost a year in Bastogne, 98 in Spa. Woods of spruce and beech cover the plateau; moorland extends onto some parts and is called *fagnes*. It is a region of difficult passage, once considered as a "mountain" and a dead end. Twice during World War II, looking for weaker parts of the Allied front, German armies attempted to break through precisely across this plateau; they succeeded in May 1940, but they were checked in December 1944 at the Battle of the Bulge. The country is not thickly populated, but neither is it poor; since the end of the nineteenth century a farming development has taken place, improving the soil, turning it into good pastures and meadows. Cattle and hogs are the main resource, and there is a good local breed of horses. The towns are just large villages, with urban activities concentrated in the main valleys. The Meuse River crosses the Ardennes, at first cutting from south to north across hard schist and sandstone; its classical meanderings with interlocking spurs have been often studied and attract tourists. The Meuse used to be a major road guarded by the town of Dinant, which was affiliated with the Hansa but now is rather sleepy, though with some textile mills. All the intense life of the plateau has been drained toward the Meuse downstream of Namur and the Sambre valley upstream of that town. The Sambre-Meuse depression for a length of 100 miles follows the contact of the plateau with the plain, marked by outcroppings of carboniferous limestone and rich coal layers in depth.

This is a "black country," established on coal and built up along an

The Meuse at Dinant. This impressive fortified church stands near a bridge over the river that cuts through the Ardennes plateau from the French border to Namur. Two highways, a railroad, and a canal follow the narrow valley between the cliffs. This valley is lined with towns, suburbs, and industrial plants, proclaiming the much larger concentration of people and industries of the Sambre-Meuse coal basin. *(Belgian Government Information Center)*

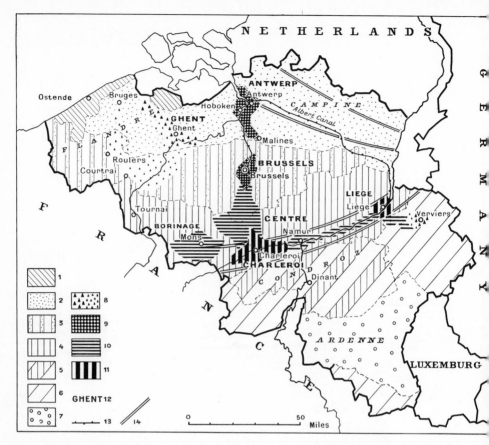

Economic map of Belgium. Key: 1, polder areas (mainly agricultural with predominance of grains, hay, and potatoes); 2, region of sandy soils, heavily fertilized (with a cattle economy predominating); 3, region of loamy soils with sandy patches (wheat and dairy economy); 4, region of heavy-loam soils and most intensive farming (grains and sugar beet with some flax); 5, predominance of meadows with some grain; 6, predominance of a grass economy, hay and pastures; 7, forests and pastures of the Ardennes plateau; 8, textile industries (size of triangular dot indicating average size of factories); 9, zones of heavy concentration of varied industries; 10, areas of scattered manufactures; 11, areas of heavy industrial concentration; 12, names of major concentrations of manufactures; 13, main ship canals; 14, schematic limits of the coal-mining areas (the older collieries of the Sambre and Meuse valleys and the new development of the Campine basin).

This map does not show the most recent and very important trend of residential areas and large industrial plants scattered along the general axis of the Albert Canal between Antwerp and Liège, since including these would result in an overcrowded map. These two conurbations are advancing along the canal and will shortly meet, so a new manufacturing area will be formed on the double asset of Campine coal and canal navigation. Thus a new industrial axis from Antwerp to Liège will be added to the two older manufacturing belts that cross Belgian territory: one based on currents of trade from Antwerp to Mons; the other based on both waterways and coal from Mons to Liège. The triangle thus outlined constantly attracts new population and industries at the expense of the southern and western sections of Belgium.

old waterway of Western European traffic. Today it links the industrial basin of northern France with the industrial German Rhineland, and smoke from the factories showers coal dust everywhere, while conic hills of slag characterize the landscape. In fact industry has put its imprint of homogeneity over many different physiographic regions. A string of industrial cities have for a long time worked some local iron ores with the charcoal from the Ardennes forest; the modern development started in the 1820s when, with the help of English technicians, the first blast furnace on the continent and the first large-scale metallurgy with steam were started here, the French and the Germans learning from the Belgian experiment. Coal mining swelled from 8 million tons annually in the 1850s to 24 million in the 1920s; since then it has risen only to decline again. But iron and steel industries thrived on the coal; though the local ores were soon exhausted, foreign ores were imported on a large scale, and soon the Sambre-Meuse area specialized in finished steel products and in engineering.

The main collieries were at first in the south around Mons; then they shifted toward Courtrai and Liège. The Borinage region of Mons (27,000) lost population, and large-scale iron and steel production in all its aspects begins with the group of towns around Charleroi (25,000 in the city, but 450,000 in the conurbation), where electronics and electrical engineering are rapidly developing. Here, too, are such associated chemical industries as soda ash, sulfuric acid, and glassware. Mechanical industries predominate around Namur (34,000), and so one reaches the wide and deep valley of the Meuse, between steep limestone cliffs in the vicinity of Liège. This city with 156,000 inhabitants is truly the regional capital of eastern Belgium: as early as the eighth century it was a powerful bishopric, a hub of trade, and a center of iron works. It specializes now in fine metallurgy, and its cutlery and weapons are renowned — Liège used to export guns and pistols all over the world. Out of nearby mines of zinc and silver ore, nonferrous metallurgy sprang up; here was formed in 1837 the *Société de la Vieille Montagne*, one of the leading world companies in zinc trade and manufacturing. Liège imports ore and re-exports metal throughout Western Europe; copper, brass, and lead industries have developed, as well as rubber, soap, electrical equipment, piano factories, and paper mills. Liège has a beautiful location, and its activities and even the lack of planning show the old traditions of its rich burghers. Its industries have spread into the surrounding valleys and the metropolitan region counts some 600,000 people. In one such valley a very remarkable specialization in high quality woolen weaving developed around the town of Verviers (37,000), and the cloth of Verviers is famous in Europe.

West of this string of old industrial towns one enters the flat plain of central Belgium. It has a monotonous and level topography, with gentle slopes. The chalk, sand, or clay that forms the subsoil is covered by a uniform carpet of thick, heavy loam. Sand outcroppings south of Brussels or northward in the Campine area are marked by woods of beech or pine. The rest of the area has been cleared of an original oak forest, and now lines of trees just screen a few villages. An intensive scientific agriculture grows high yields of wheat, oats, sugar beets, and fodder crops on the loamy soils. Large agglomerated villages, built of bricks, are scattered throughout with such density that the traveler wonders whether he is in a rural or suburban area. Some large farms are isolated and look like old strongholds. And so they were, for they served in such capacity in many a war—the battle of Waterloo was fought in the midst of this monotonous plain.

In the middle of the rich plain, about halfway between the cities of Flanders and the industrious valley of the Meuse, stands the mushrooming Belgian capital. Brussels, with a conurbation of 1.5 million inhabitants, has developed because of its administrative function and also out of the prosperity of the surrounding plain. Like most of the centers born amid rural wealth, Brussels has a definite liking for arts and smart, comfortable living. It is a very beautiful city, animated, elegant, with famous theaters and an important university, and it is closer in its aspect and way of life to Paris than to the cities of the North Sea–Rhine commercial region. The importance of the conurbation attracted industries to the suburbs—textiles and clothing, finishing work on leather and metals, foodstuffs, paper, printing—but the heavier Belgian industry concentrated along the valley of the Senne River downstream toward Antwerp. Such an important city could not remain cut off from the sea, and since 1922 a ship canal brings ocean-going ships to Brussels and links it to the Schelde River, the principal waterway of central Belgium.

With the Schelde valley the loamy plain establishes contact with the maritime plain. This last western section of Belgium has a poorer soil made of sandy materials first, then of heavy clays along the coast. The sandy, or interior, Flanders was the domain of heathland and meager woods until the modern reclamation fertilized the soils, checkered them with live hedges, and planted trees to give the landscape a wooded aspect. This is a rural scenery now frequently encountered in Western Europe and is known by its French name of *bocage*. Farther down the soil becomes clayey, humid, and nonpermeable; drainage by a regular design of the trenches turned it into polders. Thus we come to the country of green meadows and dairy cattle.

All of Flanders is a beautiful garden, artificial but fertile. The main resources, however, are of a different nature. Since the Middle Ages the cities of Flanders have been to the west of Europe what the Greek cities

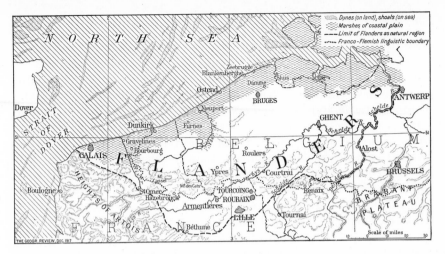

Sketch map of Flanders and its limits as a natural region. *(After R. Blanchard; The Geographical Review)*

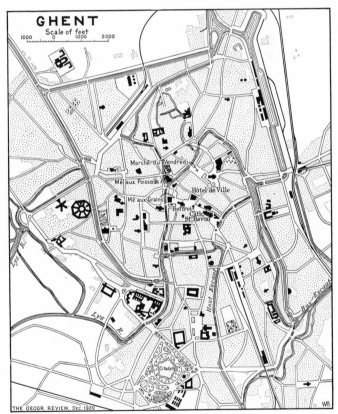

Town map of Ghent. The commercial interests of Ghent are evidenced by the various markets and the guild halls. *(The Geographical Review)*

were to the ancient Mediterranean: to resist too much interference by foreign or local authorities, the people found that the city, *intra muros*, was the best basis for resistance and security. Thus since the twelfth century these cities have been rich commercial intermediaries in the European trade and large centers of textile manufacturing. A genuine symbiosis has been established between the urban center and the surrounding rural areas, which turned chiefly to cattle raising and truck farming to produce dairy products, meat, and vegetables for the town market. On the farms the women became textile workers, looms were spread throughout the countryside, and the trade and finishing of textiles (chiefly linen and woolen) was centered in the cities.

Bruges and Ghent were the main ports and urban centers of Flanders. Both are inland ports, from which the sea trade retreated with the silting of the coast and with the increase in the size of the ships. A ship canal still brings maritime navigation to Ghent. Bruges, now a sleepy local market with 52,000 people, was in the thirteenth to the fifteenth centuries a metropolis of trade and industry, ruling the international market of wool. Only memories and an extraordinary array of grandiose monuments remain, attracting crowds of tourists, though there has been a slight revival recently with the construction of a larger canal to the advanced port of Zeebrugge on the shore. Quite different is Ghent, now the third city of Belgium with 158,000 inhabitants, and its central monumental section shows how the capital of Flanders was a proud rival of Bruges and, later, of Amsterdam. In the sixteenth century it became a center of linen manufacturing, importing the flax fiber from Russia; in the nineteenth, it turned to cotton, and a new ring of suburbs circled the old city, tripling its population from 1800 to 1900, when the present figure was already reached. To its benefit Ghent has concentrated the industrial work carried on earlier in the rural country, but it has ceased to grow—once a Belgian Manchester, it now attempts to adapt itself by developing mechanical industries in satellite towns of a conurbation aggregating about 450,000 people.

In the north the Belgian plain is poorer than in the center: the sands emerge from under the loam; heathland predominates. Maritime life did not penetrate east of the Schelde, and so this Campine region was kept out of the early development of Flanders; reclamation came only at the end of the eighteenth and in the nineteenth centuries, applying here the methods worked out in Flanders and Holland. Capital investments from Antwerp helped the transformation; pinewoods spread; the cattle economy was strongly organized; and a belt of intensive truck farming extended from Antwerp's suburbs to Malines, the old town of lace making and the seat of the archbishop who heads the Belgian Church. The greatest transformation began with the discovery of the coal basin of

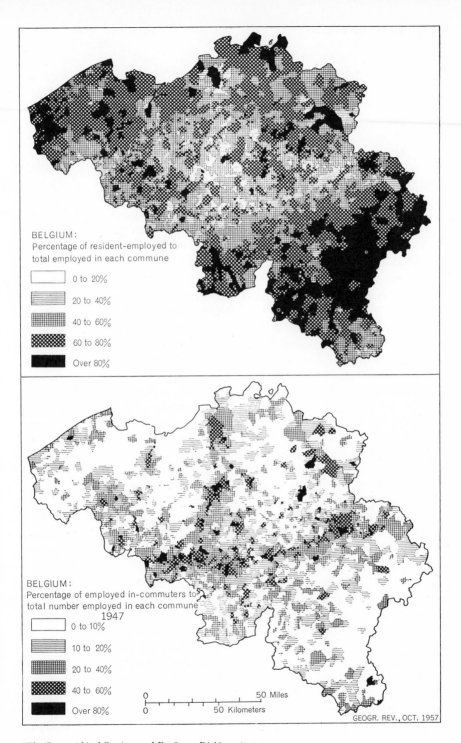

BELGIUM:
Percentage of resident-employed to
total employed in each commune

| | 0 to 20% |
| | 20 to 40% |
| | 40 to 60% |
| | 60 to 80% |
| | Over 80% |

BELGIUM:
Percentage of employed in-commuters to
total number employed in each commune
1947

| | 0 to 10% |
| | 10 to 20% |
| | 20 to 40% |
| | 40 to 60% |
| | Over 80% |

0        50 Miles
0        50 Kilometers

GEOGR. REV., OCT. 1957

*(The Geographical Review and Professor Dickinson)*

Limburg, rich in depth—the Campine boasts more reserves of better coal than the Meuse—and since 1924 output has increased steadily. Coal mining stimulated urban life and attracted industries. A wide waterway, the Albert Canal, now links the Meuse to Antwerp through the Campine, along the Dutch border; it did not have all the strategic efficiency the military had expected, but it did bring easy communications with the outside to what had been the most isolated and marginal province of Belgium. The population of the province of Limburg rose from 367,000 in 1930 to about 615,000 in 1965. This northern section has the advantage of forming the immediate hinterland of Antwerp.

The second city, the great port of Antwerp, has always been an essential part of the Belgian nation and economy. At the mouth of the Schelde, it offers the modern version of the Flemish tradition of oceanic trade and participation in the Rhine River traffic. Antwerp had great fairs, visited by French, German, and Italian traders, as long ago as the fourteenth century. It allied itself with London to sell English cloth on the continent in competition with Bruges and Ghent; in the sixteenth century it replaced Bruges as the Flemish emporium of North Sea and Baltic trade; it supplied naval stores to the Spanish and Portuguese fleets at the time of the great maritime discoveries and drew in payment most of the Portuguese trade in spices, replacing Venice in this market function, and of the gold and silver brought by Spanish galleons from the New World. Antwerp rivaled Amsterdam for control of Baltic supplies. The independence of the Netherlands brought to a head the competition between these two great ports, and Amsterdam decided to close the waters of Zeeland to Schelde traffic, cutting off Antwerp from the sea and the Rhine. Not until 1793, after two centuries of paralysis, was the principle of free international use of the major streams imposed by the French Revolution. But Rotterdam persuaded the Dutch authorities to levy a heavy fee on ships entering Antwerp, and free competition was not restored until 1839. It may be said that the rivalry of the ports was instrumental in bringing about the independence of Belgium. Within a century, Antwerp became one of the great seaports of the world. It does over 80 percent of Belgium's maritime traffic; it is a great center of commerce, handling the capital hoarded in Belgium over centuries for transactions in the merchandise going through the port; it is also a great hub of transit and transshipment on an international scale. Perhaps no other port on the continent has such a wide and varied network of maritime connections: the excellent, man-made facilities of the port, the facility of warehousing, the rapidity of railroad connection, and the dynamism of local capital and banks gave Antwerp a privileged position. In the 1950s close to 270 regular shipping lines linked Antwerp with all the seaports of the world. Germany, northern France, and Switzerland sometimes used this port rather than their own for cargoes requiring speed. The city is quite impressive, consisting of an ancient nucleus of Renaissance style and a new ring built since 1840. Its population of 260,000 lives essentially from the port. Heavy industries do exist but have a secondary importance, and, owing to an immigration of Jewish refugees in the twentieth century, Antwerp also developed a diamond-cutting and polishing industry which outranks Amsterdam. The only large port left in good shape by World War II on the west European shores, Antwerp picked up rapidly after 1945. Industrialization continues to gain in its suburbs—Deurne with 75,000 people, Hoboken 31,000, Merksem 33,000, Wilryck 32,000. The whole conurbation aggregates over half a million people. But Antwerp still needs more free trade across Europe and its competition with Rotterdam is an exciting bout to watch.

Relations with the countries of the Rhine basin are not quite so important for the prosperity of Antwerp as they are for that of Rotterdam. During World War I, when Antwerp fought on the side of the Allies, most of the German commercial interests that had been centered there moved to Rotterdam which was a neutral port. Rotterdam is better situated with respect to the Rhine navigation, and all the measures by which Antwerp endeavors to keep a larger portion of the transit trade towards Germany and Switzerland cannot balance the natural advantages of the Dutch harbor. But Antwerp has other resources: of all the large European ports it has the best balanced traffic. In 1964, out of a total international sea traffic of 53 million tons of goods in this port, 68 percent were unloaded and 32 loaded. Such balance is a record in Europe where the main seaports import a great deal of bulky goods and export usually much lighter cargoes. Antwerp has been able to obtain preferential rates on the Belgian railroads for goods transiting through its port and going to or coming from foreign countries. It has an excellent system of canals linking it with northern France. It has powerful port equipment, handling merchandise of all kinds carefully and quickly. Almost any kind of shipment of manufactured goods from Western Europe has a better chance here of rapidly finding a ship for whatever destination overseas is desired than at any other port. Thus Antwerp attracts more general cargo from neighboring countries than any other European port. Out of the 35 million tons handled in 1958, about 4 million were in transit to or from France: this amounted to about one tenth of the total French maritime foreign trade if crude oil shipments (which do not pass through Antwerp) are excluded. Seaports of northwestern France such as Dunkirk and Le Havre complain bitterly about the competition of Antwerp.

Owing to the importance of Belgian textile industries and the raw

Antwerp: A section of the monumental waterfront of the great port. *(Belgian Government Information Center)*

Barges on a canal in a small Belgian town. *(Belgian Government Information Center)*

material production of the then Belgian Congo, Antwerp built up a relatively important exchange in commodities, particularly wool and copper. This market works in close touch with British interests. However, the stronger international position of the Belgian currency has led to an increased activity on the markets of Antwerp.

With the growth of Antwerp and the industrialization of the Campine, all the territory of Belgium (with the exception of the highlands of the Ardennes) is covered with a dual landscape of intensive "gardening" agriculture and scattered industrial towns. There is less emphasis on agriculture and livestock and much more on manufacturing than in the Netherlands; the commercial development of Antwerp could not have happened with such speed and scope without the networks of trade relations established by Bruges, Ghent, Brussels, and Liège centuries ago and maintained for the trade of their textile and metal works. A great amount of capital was accumulated by the hardworking farmers and workers and invested at home as well as abroad. Small Belgium was one of the bankers of the world. Curiously enough, a specialty of Belgian investors was transportation, particularly the streetcar companies that Belgian capital created in many cities from Turkey to Argentina, from China to Poland.

Manufacturing has a predominant part in the Belgian economy. For its small size, Belgium is surprisingly important for a wide range of industries. The local base is restricted chiefly to coal (30 million tons mined in 1955, 17.5 in 1966), roofing slates, some building materials, and rather negligible quantities of ores. As in Britain, most of the raw materials are imported. Belgium produced in 1966 8.3 million tons of pig iron and ferroalloys, and 9 million tons of crude steel (an all time high). About 37 percent of this steel production was consumed within the country. The textile industries consumed recently about 80,000 tons of cotton and 45,000 tons of wool per annum, definitely more than in prewar years. If the rayon and linen industries are taken into consideration, it appears that in the field of textiles, Belgium holds the fifth rank in Europe, after Britain, France, Germany, and Italy (the Soviet Union being excluded). Chemical industries are very important, too, and engineering is becoming more and more an important specialty. American firms have joined with Belgian interests to establish new industries, mainly mechanical and chemical, in various cities (near Antwerp and also in Louvain and Malines). Brussels has fought valiantly to become an international metropolis. In recent years a great deal of urban renewal and redevelopment has been carried out in the Belgian capital, for the International Fair of 1958 and afterwards. High modern office towers have risen and new throughways crisscross the city. Brussels thus won the headquarters of the Common Market, and has been developing a

European function. In 1967, the Supreme Headquarters of the North Atlantic Treaty Organization moved from Paris to Brussels, broadening the international role. Its metropolitan region, centrally located in Belgium and on the great Amsterdam-Paris axis, has recently been attracting more Belgian immigrants than any other part of the country. Basically a French-speaking city, it is now surrounded with a complex checkerboard of Walloon and Flemish communities.

For a long time it seemed that the duality of language and culture reflected in the division of the Belgian nation between Flemish and Walloons was strengthening rather than weakening the national unity. The tension between the two, however, has recently grown threatening owing to a steady decline of importance of the Walloons. The Flemish element has been increasing faster, due to a higher birth rate; it inhabited the parts of Belgium which have been developing and industrializing faster since the 1920s. The Flemish people are devout Roman Catholics and vote for the Christian Social party, while the Walloons are much less church-goers and vote predominantly for the Belgian Socialist party. Since they saw their regional economy remain rather stagnant while the Flemish-speaking areas were developing fast, the Walloons felt that in the 1950s the predominantly Christian Social governments had favored their Flemish supporters at the expense of the French-speaking areas. Mounting resentment erupted in the form of a strike and violence, especially in the region of Liège, during the winter of 1960–1961, soon after the loss of the Belgian Congo in Africa. In 1966–1968, more trouble developed as the two linguistic groups clashed at Louvain, in the older and larger Belgian university, causing a government crisis.

In the nineteenth century, King Leopold built up for himself quite a sizable property in Central Africa, but in 1908 he gave his vast Congo domain to the Belgian people. The Belgian Congo covered some 900,000 square miles, and its riches have contributed much to strengthening Belgium's international position. Mining of ores yielding important quantities of copper, gold, silver, lead, tin, and cobalt has been developed. Through its mines of Haut-Katanga the Congo became the main world source of cobalt and radium and, after 1940, the first world exporter of uranium, chiefly to the United States. In 1960, after some trouble had arisen in the principal cities, Belgium abruptly granted independence to the Congo, where a period of anarchy and political struggle ensued.

Having lost its African empire, where some economic interests are retained, and despite some serious tension at home, Belgium remains an important economic unit of Western Europe. Because it had been less destroyed in World War II and had a better dollar balance right after liberation, Belgium may have appeared in the postwar period to have been in better position than her neighbors. In the long run, her problems were not very much different, and like the other members of the EEC, Belgium has substantially benefited by the widening of economic opportunity resulting from reorganization and the trend toward integration of Europe.

## LUXEMBOURG

The third country of Benelux is the Grand Duchy of Luxembourg; by its size (999 square miles) and population (350,000), this is the smallest fully independent country of Europe. In the heart of the Ardennes plateau, it remains the survivor of a much larger feudal state and a buffer between Germany on the one hand and France and Belgium on the other. Disputed by both, Luxembourg is deeply influenced by both Latin and Germanic cultures; yet its border position fostered local patriotism, and since 1867 it has been an independent and neutral state.

Traditionally Luxembourg was a country of woods and small farms growing oats (40,000 tons on 42,000 acres in 1958), wheat (53,000 tons on 58,000 acres), potatoes, and hay and raising cattle and pigs. The abundance of cattle and oak trees helped the development of leather tanning, and the forest also supplied the charcoal for the iron works using local ores. The south of the duchy, where limestone outcrops and the soils are the best, was always called the *Gutland* (good land): there after 1874 large-scale iron and steel industries were built up on an abundant local supply of iron ores. Beyond the French border this same metallurgy is continued in Lorraine: the same kind of ore is smelted with imported coal. The Luxembourg output was greatly reduced by coal shortage in wartime but is picking up, being dependent on the availability of coke from the Ruhr. The 1966 production of 4 million tons of pig iron and 4.4 million tons of steel showed that prewar levels had been surpassed. This heavy industry gives Luxembourg a notable weight in Europe as an economic power. Since 1922 economic union with Belgium opened to the iron and steel products and the leather and clothing industries of Luxembourg the wider Belgian market and the maritime gate of Antwerp. Through its metallurgy, close ties have been added to the historic friendship with France. Such a wide network of relationships resulting from its disturbed history has helped this small state to erect an appreciable industrial might.

The headquarters of the European Coal and Steel Community was set up at Luxembourg, a city of about 80,000 which stands on the rim of the Ardennes plateau, close to the Gutland. Few countries in the world can boast of as perfect land utilization throughout their territory. Out of their small land, the people of Luxembourg have certainly made a

# Rotterdam

The reconstructed center of Rotterdam next to the railroad station occupies the area devastated by the bombings and fire of 1940 (see photo p. 291). Notice the modern design of the new shopping center of the Lijnbaan, admired by city planners all over the world, and the new port installations on the Maas in the background. This area is one of the best achievements of European reconstruction and, in terms of economic activity, a huge success. *(The Netherlands National Tourist Office)* maximum use. The soils of the Ardennes are here much better tilled and more productive than in either Belgium or France. Every corner of picturesque landscape has been developed for tourism, on weekends attracting crowds from other parts of Benelux. This small country gives the impression that every parcel of land is used to the utmost and that a fair prosperity has been achieved for its people, much more than in the neighboring regions of either France or Germany.

## THE PLACE OF BENELUX IN EUROPE

In the twentieth century, with the emergence of great countries with vast domestic markets and rapid industrialization, it appears more and more imperative that the economy of an industrial country be based on an important market from which no tariff barrier can eliminate its products. The small countries of the Lowlands face this situation with considerable anxiety. They feel that their costs of production rise above those of larger economic units, and they strive for a widening of their own markets: self-sufficiency is impossible for them; hence the domestic market cannot provide the solution. An idea developed to bring about a general improvement through a tariff and economic union of Belgium and the Netherlands, in which Luxembourg (already united to Belgium) would also participate. The present political relations of the three countries are cordial; no major conflict divides them and such economic coordination looks promising to all.

Belgium has a considerable surplus of manufactured goods, which are imported generally by the Netherlands; Holland on the other hand has a surplus of dairy products and certain meats that are badly needed in Belgium. There were other elements of complementarity. Thus each country doubles its domestic market by a tariff union. The Benelux Customs Union came into being in 1948; several transitional years were necessary to bring it into full force. By that time its three participants were also members of the European Coal and Steel Community, and in 1957 they entered also into the Common Market and Euratom. All three seem to have profited from these greatly widened commercial horizons; the benefits may be more striking in the case of the Netherlands, whose economy seemed more shaky until the mid-1950s but displayed great strength in the 1960s. That all the countries of Benelux would profit greatly from such measures directed toward a European economic integration of which they are part cannot be doubted. They have in common the highest population pressure in the Western world and the narrowest areal base to support it. However advantageous their location on the North Sea and in the delta of the Rhine and Meuse, they can put this geographical asset to use only if commercial relations with the outside are opened up on a large scale.

History, sometimes painfully, has taught the peoples of the Low Countries how to be good neighbors in a crowded world. Their experience may be of great value to them and their neighbors in the present European experiment. Although they have achieved full employment by 1960 to a surprising extent and despite their high density of population, the Netherlands and Belgium remain potentially countries of emigration. The Dutch government has since the war officially encouraged and sponsored Dutch emigration overseas (reduced however to about 25,000 persons annually in recent years, while the annual population increase reached about 150,000). Belgians have often migrated to work in France. These nations would greatly be relieved concerning their future needs of space and employment if European integration also resulted in a widening of the labor market. The Dutch and the Belgians especially could supply the quality labor so much in demand.

The Netherlands and Belgium are certainly the most heavily urbanized corner of the European continent. A great deal of their urbanization has proceeded piecemeal and, until recently, unplanned. They do not have any one enormous city such as London or Paris, or even Berlin; but they have a continuous network of large medium-sized cities and towns covering most of their countryside with a dense urban mosaic. Only a few areas, such as the Belgian Ardennes or the northeastern provinces of the Netherlands, still have wide-open rural spaces. The population of Belgium increased particularly fast between the two world wars, when it was the most densely settled country in Europe. Since 1945, its rate of population growth declined while that of the Netherlands accelerated, and the Dutch gained the crown of density. Present conservative forecasts indicate, for 1980, a population of 15.2 million in the Netherlands, that is, an increase of 25 percent over 1965.

To provide for the future of its rapidly thickening population and to avoid a large emigration, Dutch authorities have ironed out bold plans for economic expansion, coupled with a strict control of their environment. On one hand, the remarkable economic growth of Rotterdam as a city and as a port, after the ordeal of the war, illustrates the quality of this dynamic planning. The growth of manufactures and employment has been carefully decentralized and spread around the country as much as possible without disturbing the imperatives of efficiency. The Dutch deeply feel the need of widening their horizons and building networks of outside relations to keep their own economy and their cultural life active and growing.

The Institute of Social Studies at The Hague started a study of the vast urban triangle in northwestern Europe that already extends in a somewhat continuous fashion from Amsterdam to Cologne and the Ruhr in Germany, and to Lille in France, encompassing most of Belgium within its frame. Such plans illustrate the concept slowly developed in the Benelux countries of establishing there, at the mouth of the great rivers of Western Europe, along the chain of old seaports and centers of trade and industry, a European megalopolis, to become the capital region of the gradually integrating Western half of Europe.

The Belgians, despite their traditional distrust of Dutch policies, are working along similar lines. They have obtained for Brussels the head-quarters of both EEC and NATO. Their capital, struggling to face the pressures of this rapid growth, is becoming increasingly the seat of the governing institution of the new Europe. It is, however, a sad paradox that both these two very European and internationalistic countries are deeply divided within, each by cultural tensions. Between their dynam-ism and prosperity they experience recurrent political crises due to religious or linguistic divisions. The Dutch are divided between Pro-testants and Catholics, the latter being predominant in the southern provinces. The struggle between the two religions affects planning even in terms of industrial location and even in terms of the religion of the settlers assigned to the new villages of the newly developed polders in the north. Belgium is divided between the Flemish and the French-speaking elements in its population; this struggle has come to threaten the integrity of the country.

The Netherlands and Belgium are both rather small nations, well knit by their past traditions, and homogeneous in the sense that they count a minimum of exotic elements in their midst. Still, cultural dif-ferences create deep variations and inner conflicts, all the more so as they are rooted in different geographical regions of each country. Despite the high population density in both countries, there is a striking contrast between the careful planning of land use and urban growth in the Netherlands and the rather chaotic lack of such planning in Belgium. These characteristics and inner conflicts illustrate how the partitioning of Europe into small units survives amid the process of gradual integra-tion and apparent lowering of old national boundaries.

Paris. "The French capital has a greater concentration of the reins of government than any other capital of a major power." *(French Government Tourist Office)*

# 8

---

# France

France is the oldest nation in Europe, with frontiers that for several centuries have changed only in details. In the center of the western façade of Europe, she occupies a geographical crossroad, extending over 212,000 square miles, with a population of 50 million. Her history, with that of Britain, used to sum up all the history of the Western world for the last thousand years; while Britain has been more active on the oceans, France has been more closely linked to the life of the continent she has oriented for so long. No other country has had in the past a more radiant culture: for ages French has been the language of the cultivated people of Europe and, during the eighteenth century, of most of the world; French literature was perhaps more classical than any other from the seventeenth to the nineteenth centuries; decimal notation and the metric system of measurement are originally French. Three times France built large empires overseas: in the Mediterranean at the time of the Crusades, in America and India in the eighteenth century, in Africa and Indochina after 1830. She probably has been more often invaded than any other of the leading countries. Such a destiny has meant many hardships and many sacrifices for the population; but it has also enabled the country to mature earlier, to evolve more quickly a better balanced economic system and a more stable way of life.

## THE WESTERN HUB OF EUROPE

French destiny has had some of its roots in the position of France on the continent of Europe. Her territory lies at the southwestern tip of the mainland, just before Europe breaks up into peninsulas. It has a general hexagonal shape, and its boundaries often follow the seashore of the crestline of lofty mountainous ranges, giving them a more "natural" aspect. Position has given France the considerable advantage of being relatively well screened from the continent, which made military defense somewhat easier, and of having a direct coastline opening on several seas: the North Sea, the English Channel, the Atlantic Ocean, and the Mediterranean. Thus France has participated actively in the life of both the Mediterranean and the North Sea, the two main poles of traffic and culture in Europe. Since the Atlantic Ocean ceased to be a dead end, France has had a wide-open window on it.

Though the continental frontiers are marked by highlands, they are not a continuous barrier, and many low and wide passes or deep valleys make overland relations with other parts of Europe easy. In the north, France opens broadly on the Belgian plain between the plateau of Ardennes and the North Sea. In fact France has a share in each of the major physical divisions we outlined on the continent, with the sole exception of the northern Fenno-Scandian Shield. Along the Belgian frontier in the north, the Great Plain of Europe penetrates deep into France: the loamy plains stretch without interruption from Brussels to Paris and to the River Loire; on the coast of the North Sea is the French, that is, the western, extremity of Flanders with some Flemish-speaking population, polders, and wateringen. The plains of the northern half of France are fringed with a semicircular frame of Hercynian higher lands, low plateaus (like the Armorican massif of Brittany), or small mountainous ranges (like the Vosges). A bulky central plateau occupies the middle of the southern half of France, giving a large extension to the Hercynian structure in the country. To the south and southeast the lofty ranges of the Pyrenees and Alps erect a belt of folded high mountains of the Alpine type. This Alpine zone is interrupted in the southeast by a depression in which the Mediterranean Sea drives the Gulf of Lyon inside the continent. Mediterranean influences were thus allowed to penetrate deeply and easily in the country; the southeastern coast is definitely part of the Mediterranean area, and the island of Corsica adds to the French participation in Mediterranean Europe. Great Plain, Hercynian zone, Alpine ranges, and Mediterranean world—all are present in France; in her natural regions she almost could sum up the physical geography of most of Europe. This variety helped regional differentiation and the division of the country into provinces, but it also allowed France to participate actively in all the historic processes agitating the various parts of Europe.

The great geographer Vidal de la Blache explained the personality of the French nation as having been born out of the constant mingling within its territory of two elements: the Mediterranean element, reaching her through the southeastern shores and the passes of the Alps and Pyrenees, and the continental element coming in through the Great

Plain, the depressions of the Hercynian zone, and even the North Sea. The Mediterranean influences were not only Roman and Latin: at times they were Arabic, Moorish, Turkish, Greek, Lombard, Venetian, and Florentine. The continental influences have been Germanic and also, at times, Slavic, Dutch, Flemish, Swiss, and others. It may be wise to add today a third element to those stressed by Vidal de la Blache: the Atlantic element, for one cannot call "continental" the influences that came by sea—Norse, Irish, Scottish, and, for the past two centuries, American—to land on the beaches of Normandy or on the estuary of the Gironde. The Mediterranean alone does not suffice to describe the maritime interests and activities of France. The Roman domination Latinized the country of Gaul and linked it once and forever with its southern neighbors. These ties might not have survived with such strength had a constant pressure, bringing trouble and bloodshed, been exercised from the Mediterranean. But that kind of pressure came to France mostly from the continental east, with the westward flow of the Germanic tribes and and the later expansions of the Holy Roman Empire. The main barriers had to be erected against the continent, along artificial lines crossing a flat or low and confused topography. Thus came the idea, inherited from Rome, of the natural frontier of the Rhine and Alps.

The mingling of so many different structural and historical influences made of French territory the western hub of Europe and brought to it a greater unity. It is not a paradox to maintain that, in proper conditions, physical diversity helps human unity. Varied resources put together from contrasted natural regions form a better balanced, more self-sufficient economy; contacts with many different worlds generally will reinforce regionalism and strengthen local patriotism. To obtain such results from natural variety, a strong common cultural background is necessary; otherwise narrow regional frames will tend to form small national units, as happened in Belgium or Switzerland on France's borders. But in France the cultural heritage was very strong and made of several layers.

The oldest layer we can speak of is probably the Celtic civilization that covered most of Gaul: although divided into tribes and clans, warring among themselves, the Gauls that the Romans found formed a distinct unit; they had no difficulties in gathering at Lyon, at a major crossroads, assemblies to which all cities sent delegates. Bringing peace, law, and order, the Roman domination worked powerfully for homogeneity. Out of Latin came the French language that became the cementing factor—the kings reigning in Paris claimed all French-speaking lands. The continuity of the royal dynasty which labored toward unification and steady territorial expansion should not be overlooked either. All these historical factors could not have been applied with such success if the people of the territory that became France had not desired for a long time to live in common. There existed an old spiritual unity which the Church of France helped to maintain, a strongly Catholic Church, which fought the Reformation bitterly, chasing most of the Huguenots out of the country, but a Catholic Church which boasted of privileges of autonomy in a trend called *gallicanism* against too strict obedience to Rome. The patron saint of France, Joan of Arc, was a peasant girl from Lorraine who came to Bourges, in the center of the country, to lead under divine instructions the royal armies against those of a king who held Paris, who was Norman and who spoke French, but whose base was London. Sainte Geneviève, the patron saint of Paris, comforted the city at the time of the Norman invasions and saved it from pillage. Among the French people there was a feeling of long standing that their nationality was holy—other Europeans felt this too and almost resented it.

French history is stormy. The western hub of Europe has seen constant hordes and armies marching through it, partly because of its strategic position, partly because it was famous throughout the ages for its wealth. As an isthmus between the North Sea and the Mediterranean, France played a considerable part in European traffic: there is no easier penetration from Mediterranean shores to the heart of the continent than the deep north-south corridor of the Rhone and Saône valleys. From the upper Saône one can pass through the low and wide Gate of Burgundy to reach the Rhine, where it becomes navigable, and go down along it to western Germany, the Lowlands, and the Great Plain; from the Saône valley, another route leads through the flat plateaus and plains of Burgundy and Champagne either to Flanders or to Paris, Normandy, and the Channel. The economic history of much of Europe could be written in terms of the great fairs of Lyon, Burgundy, Champagne, Paris, Flanders, and the Rhine valley. Even when Lotharingia was founded, France had a large access to this transcontinental road, for the boundary followed the Rhone-Saône depression. Merchants followed the north-south road, while armies generally preferred the east-west passages.

Commenting on all these doors opening out and through which external influences entered, Vidal de la Blache observed that "a civilization is like a clock"—it needs frequently external interference to keep it running, to wind it up. An isolated civilization, living in a closed frame, stops progressing and cannot remain up to date. The geographical position, the general outline of its topography, and the troubled history kept the French clock running on time for two thousand years at least. A symbiosis of a unique strength has been established between the people and the land: it favored the development of a way of life famous for its charm, delicacy, and artistic beauty and to which the French people are profoundly attached. Through the centuries of organizing their space, the French have translated this way of life into the architecture of their monuments and farms, into the planning of their cities and their rural scenery.

## PARK AND MUSEUM PATTERNS

The beauty of the French landscapes enjoys a wide reputation, generally attributed to the quality of the soil and to the favorable climate. As usual in Western Europe, most of the landscape is man-made. Forests have been displaced; the oak woods around Paris are cleared, but a dense pine forest still covers the swamps and heaths of the southwestern coastland. Drainage of swamps and polders was in some cases recent, in others very old, possibly prehistoric, as Camille Jullian, the great historian of Gaul, thinks was the case with the Limagne depression in the central plateau. In the south, French agriculture applied biennial rotation and in the north, three-course rotation, before the present more involved systems were introduced. The Romans brought in the cultivation of the olive tree and of the grapevine for wine. They also taught the Gauls how to build well-paved roads and gave to the country all this "stone culture," as Jullian put it, which led to an architecture of stone for houses, monuments, temples, bridges and aqueducts—a truly Mediterranean contribution to a forested country. It gave a more monumental aspect to French buildings and endowed the landscape with some stability—one does not move a stone structure with ease.

The handling of stone and the development of masonry skills, maintained by an immigration of Italian specialists, led to a rapid blossoming of architectural art, and in the Middle Ages the Church covered France with that "mantle of cathedrals," the density and majesty of which has not been repeated. One is amazed at the total amount of labor and capital invested in this array of gigantic structures; it bears witness to the cultural advancement and economic prosperity of the country in the Middle Ages. Then came the period of castles surrounded with parks that dotted the countryside during the sixteenth to the eighteenth centuries. The architects who planned them drew their inspiration from the surrounding landscape as well as from the teachings of Italian masters—the many cupolas and turrets of the Château of Chambord reproduced accurately a village of the Loire country rebuilt in stone on the terrace roof; the *parterre* of the French gardens is an artistic interpretation of the layout of open fields in the country; alleys in the park of Versailles are roads through the forest. From the eighteenth century on the art of gardening and park planning backfired on the rural scene from which their original inspiration had been drawn; civil engineers—trained specially for the public works administration or the management of large estates—endeavoring to create a beautiful landscape, wanted the national highways to look like alleys of a royal park, and the vault of foliage over many roads in France is still being maintained (see photographs, pp. 319 and 321).

Town planning early followed definite patterns, and the French system of radiating avenues around a circle, so beautifully applied in Paris, was used in many other places, including Washington, D. C. But the regular checkerboard of perpendicular streets with a central block converted into a market place, is more familiar, especially in the southern section and among cities built anew or created in the thirteenth and fourteenth centuries. Attention was paid quite early to the conservation of monuments and of entire sections of towns characterized by a definite style. Many French cities thus became, at least in sections, living museums; new developments within the city limits were usually carried out with an eye for the style and general effect. It took the recent mushrooming of industrial and suburban districts to give a more impersonal aspect to a number of cities.

The "park and museum" patterns of the French scenery have greatly added to the attractive views encountered in areas of rather monotonous topography; in other parts the natural frame plays, of course, a decisive part. There are many possible ways of dealing with the details of the difficult environment of high valleys, but French mountaineers seem to have achieved some balance of efficiency with systematic, almost geometrical layout. No other European country has molded its scenery with such art and skill over vast areas. The labor invested, however, has made the French reluctant to make frequent change—a museum curator's state of mind has to be conservative by definition. Moreover, when the general appearance of a whole region has to be looked after, a few slight changes may involve considerable expenditure. Reforms of certain features in the French organization of space are difficult problems because of both the conservative tradition and the cost. Inevitable traditionalism in a "masterpiece" country has helped preserve the regional aspects and some quaint, picturesque landscapes. The Frenchman usually has a great attachment for his original province; he likes to talk about it and wants it to keep its folklore and special character.

Still, unification has proceeded apace through the whole territory. The kings brought some of it in their fight against local feudal authority; the Revolution advanced it by leveling all economic and administrative barriers that might have restricted the freedom of movement of men and goods; the Revolutionary period and, subsequently, Napoleon centralized more power and organization in Paris than the kings had been able to do for centuries. It was then that the Republic was proclaimed

The Castle of Villandry in the Loire country. The garden in the foreground seems to reproduce in miniature the landscape in the background, which is bocage country. *(French Government Tourist Office)*

"one and indivisible." In the nineteenth and twentieth centuries the appearance of easy and cheap transportation of bulky materials by canal and rail furthered standardization. Brick and some qualities of stone became cheaper than local materials for building; barbed wire replaced many rows of hedges; mechanization of tillage and transportation made scattered trees a liability; and rows of stereotyped houses spread through new residential districts. Still the French do attempt some stylization and decoration as soon as things are stabilized—if they can afford it.

In the regional pattern, the historical "provinces" are almost more important than purely economic factors. This may be explained by the variety of the resources and the age of the economic development: every province has practically its own wealth, and every province has to some extent remained attached to the system of resource utilization that it developed long ago. The industrial and agricultural maps of France are complicated because of so many survivals, but some generalization can be attempted. The regional pattern would follow geological, historical, and economic lines simultaneously if we divided France broadly into two halves, northern and southern, along a line following approximately the 47th parallel and passing along the northern edge of the central plateau. Paris is the heart of northern France, but the city has achieved such national and international importance that, like London, it deserves separate consideration.

## NORTHERN FRANCE

The northern half of France is predominantly a lowland with altitudes below 1500 feet; only on its eastern periphery do some crests rise above this level. The general structure of the area is shaped like a circular basin centered on Paris: what the geologists call the *Paris Basin* has been notched in to the northwest by the eastward penetration of the Channel. Gentle slopes rise all around Paris toward the periphery of the basin, which is framed with an irregular half-circle of Hercynian old crystalline blocks raised in recent geological periods. The uplifting of this Hercynian compartment has been greater to the east and southeast—that is, in the direction more directly affected by the push of the erection of the Alps. A section of the Ardennes plateau to the northeast, the Vosges Mountains to the east, the Jura Range to the southeast, the central plateau to the south, and the Armorican massif to the west are the Hercynian horsts or more recent foldings (this is the case for the Jura, which is not a Hercynian chain) encircling the basin. To the northwest, the basin opens on the Channel across which the English lowland outlines another basinlike structure around London. Northward in Belgium the basin melts into the beginning of the Great European Plain, in an easy transi-

Along a road in France (see map, p. 322). *(French Government Tourist Office)*

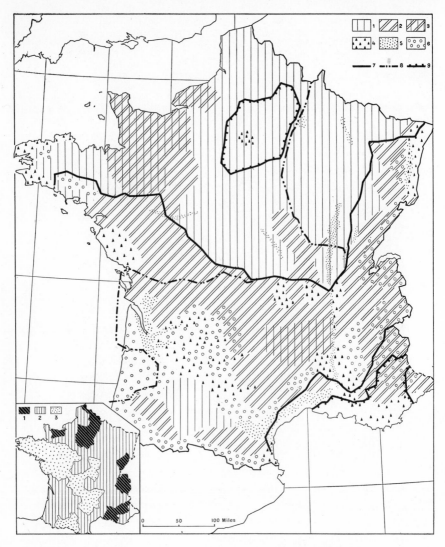

Agriculture in France. The six different shades show the distribution of the principal kinds of land use according to the predominant kind of crop; the three lines drawn on the map show the limits of certain phenomena that are basic to the present agricultural organization of the country; the inset map gives the distribution of tractors in January 1952.

Key to the main map: 1, predominance of grains, in rotation with beets; 2, predominance of forage crops and meadows; 3, areas of mixed agriculture: grains and meadows; 4, areas of mixed agriculture with predominance of truck farming, orchards, or specialized crops; 5, areas with predominance of vineyards; 6, areas predominantly under forest; 7, in the area between these lines farmers still use oxen widely for traction (chiefly southeastern part of France); 8, in the area south and east of this line the majority of farmers own their land; 9, limits of the areas where farms of more than 250 acres predominate (region of Paris and part of the southeast).

Key to inset map (density of tractors): 1, acres with one farm tractor for every 200 acres at the most; 2, areas with one farm tractor per 200 to 450 acres; 3, areas with one farm tractor per more than 450 acres.

This map gives the distribution of the main crops. Of necessity it presents land use in tion marked simply by a Hercynian outcropping in the scooped-out dome of Boulonnais, the northern extremity of which shapes the Weald in southern England.

Within that Hercynian frame, many geological seas have deposited sedimentary layers with an alternation of limestone, sand, and clay strata. The most recent layers are found at the bottom of the basin — that is, in the midst of it around Paris — and are hard limestone horizontal layers, cut through by the river valleys, and generally covered with a carpet of thick rich loam comparable to that of central Belgium. Traveling from Paris to some point on the periphery of the basin, one crosses outcroppings of layers of more and more ancient deposits until the old crystalline rocks appear. The circular disposition of outcroppings is particularly regular eastward; the outcroppings also form narrower ribbons, as the slope increases from the uplifted mountains to the bottom of the basin. Erosion by the rivers has shaped the present features of the topography in a way that affected the economic and political development.

Paris stands in the midst of a striking convergence of rivers: the Oise, Marne, upper Seine, Yonne, Loing, and Eure converge toward the central and lower part of the basin, from which the lower Seine channel carries their waters to the sea. This convergence of drainage puts Paris in an extremely favorable position, at a node of traffic lanes following the valleys or using the rivers as waterways, for most of them were navigable owing to the gentle slope and to the abundant, regular rainfall. The erosion exerted by these rivers and their many tributaries had another effect — it worked differently across the successive outcropping layers according to their hardness; softer materials were eroded more quickly and depressions dug out along their outcroppings, while harder layers were cut only into pieces of plain divided by deep valleys. Owing to steeper slope of the basin structure east of Paris, this northeastern section of France offers a classical case of *cuesta* topography, with struc-

---

terms of the predominant element in complicated crop rotations. No areas besides those occupied by vines or forests specialize in one crop only; there are always rotations and often a mixture of pastures and fields on each farm, even very small ones. The three lines drawn over the shaded map help to explain the underlying factors: small landownership by farmers (involving farming units of too small a size) extends chiefly over the southern half of France, employing old techniques (such as traction by oxen) and inadequate equipment (lack of tractors). However, the predominance of free tenure does not have the same regrettable consequences over most of the northeastern area. The inset map underlines the more progressive areas, with a greater density of tractors on the land, chiefly situated outside the area in which, for the most part, small farmers own their lands. Thus a contrast has developed between northern agriculture and that carried on by peasants with backward and less commercialized methods; there is, however, a more advanced agricultural section in the Mediterranean southeast. By 1966 there were many more tractors at work, but the general distribution of relatively mechanized regions remained the same.

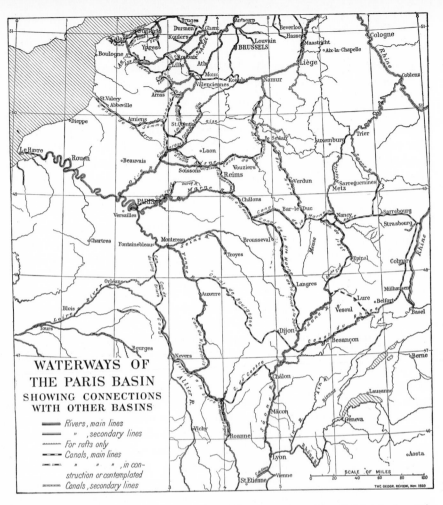

## WATERWAYS OF
## THE PARIS BASIN
### SHOWING CONNECTIONS
### WITH OTHER BASINS

| | |
|---|---|
| ▬▬▬ | Rivers, main lines |
| ——— | " , secondary lines |
| ┼┼┼┼┼ | For rafts only |
| ▭▭▭ | Canals, main lines |
| ▬ ▭ ▬ | " " " , in construction or contemplated |
| ▨▨▨▨ | Canals, secondary lines |

SCALE OF MILES
0    20    40    60    80    100

THE GEOGR. REVIEW, Nov. 1920

*(Above)* The waterways of the Paris basin and its connection with adjoining basins. *(The Geographical Review) (Below)* A section of the port of Dunkirk as it was being rebuilt after having been razed in the battle of 1940. By 1966 the port was already handling 16 million tons of goods. *(French Government Tourist Office)*

tural limestone platforms alternating with clayey depressions and over-looking these depressions with steep cliffs turned toward the east. There are at least three such concentric arches of escarpments between Paris and the Vosges or Ardennes heights. Each is a natural rampart, easy to fortify against an enemy coming in from the east. Paris is well defended on this side, and it is from the north that most of the modern invasions reached deep into France. The Belgian Plain has been the weak link in the continental defenses of France, for there no major topographic line, with the exception of the wide and flat-bottomed valley of the Somme River, could serve as a natural defense.

The western half of the basin is less regularly shaped, and the slope of the layers toward the middle is gentler. Still, although the distribution in a regular half-circle is broken on this side by the drainage of several rivers directly to the sea, hard limestone provided flat structural plat-forms, while lower lying depressions correspond to outcroppings of sand or clay. Throughout the Parisian basin this alternation of drier (because of the permeability of the subsoil) and flatter *campagnes* with damper and more dug-in depressions in materials with less resistance to erosion has given some variety to the landscape and to the land utilization of these plains. The climate varies mainly from west to east: the range in temperature and the inequality of seasonal rainfall distribution increase with the great continentality eastward; the decrease of maritime in-fluence cuts down the total annual amount of precipitation to make the winters much colder and somewhat drier. Lorraine is thus definitely more continental than Brittany: Paris is still very temperate, maritime, and rather rainy. Yet the climate of Paris is quite different from that of London, for it is sunnier, with more rain falling in brief showers during the summer, with less fog, but with occasional periods of frost in winter.

Though connections with the south are easy, through structural de-pressions, Mediterranean influences have been on the whole over-shadowed by those of continental and Atlantic origin. In older times France used to be divided into two linguistic areas: *langue d'oc* in the south and *langue d'oïl* in the north, where *oïl* (the northern pronunciation of the word *yes*) was the ancestor of the modern *oui*. And the boundary between the two areas had for centuries a practical significance in the modes of transportation, tillage, and in law; the *langue d'oc* country had been more under Roman influences and also had received an Oriental, Moorish contribution. Then, too, the northern half of the country had many advantages over the southern; wider stretches of lowlands, better soils (particularly the thick loam), more regular rainfall, easier com-munications, a more centralized network of navigable rivers. In recent centuries, the proximity of the North Sea and Channel, these hubs of world navigation, and the discovery of large coal and iron deposits helped considerably the economic development of the north, which groups the main industrial areas, the richest agricultural districts, and the largest concentrations of population.

Curiously enough the largest industrial district of France coincided with the section of most intensive agriculture, in the northernmost corner of the country. The old provinces of Flanders and Artois owe to their proximity to the North Sea and to the Strait of Dover their traditions of intensive land use (with polderland and involved crop rotations) and of commercial activities (with fishing on the sea, international trade, and many crafts spread throughout the farms). This is the French section of the Low Countries, finally annexed to the French kingdom in the seventeenth century. Presently the two departments of Nord and Pas-de-Calais account for a total of 3.6 million people and half of the French coal output. Coal mining attracted iron, steel, and chemical industries there in the nineteenth century; and steam concentrated in large mills the textile work formerly spread over the farms. A "black-country" landscape developed, continuing westward the long string of industrial districts strewn across Belgium and western Germany. From the Ruhr to the Pas-de-Calais an overindustrialized and overcrowded zone has been erected on a double foundation of old commercial traditions and coal.

The northern French coalfield suffers from many handicaps: seams are generally thin; thickness allowing the miner to work standing upright in a gallery is exceptional; and the continuity of the seams is often interrupted by faulting. While bituminous coal for gas is abundant, the usable qualities for the production of metallurgical coke are scarce. Mechanization was slow at the beginning of this century, but following the destructions of the two World Wars, reconstruction progressed rapidly after 1946, and the basin has produced since 1948 more coal than it did in 1938. The collieries, started around the town of Valenciennes, have progressed westward, and the bulk of the production is now extracted around Béthune. Some 60,000 miners are employed in the mines, and their standardized residential towns, with monotonous brick houses, alternate with large industrial plants. The collieries have been nationalized and since 1945 under government-controlled management.

Abundance of power, manpower, and easy transportation on the rivers, canals, and railways of the lowlands favored industrialization. Iron and steel industries came to a region that had been weaving cloth for centuries. All over the coalfields heavy metallurgy operates at full blast: the iron ore from abroad or pig iron from Lorraine is turned into finished steel; nonferrous ores are smelted; and large engineering plants have developed, making all kinds of heavy machinery, rolling stock, bridges, and the like. Founded on the same coal are also the chemical, textile, glass, and pottery industries.

Lille is the main city and regional capital of this industrial area; born in a swampy environment, on the River Deule, it is the farthest point reached by upstream river navigation coming from the Schelde and Lys; long ago it made cloth which it sold through Antwerp and also traded with the fairs of Champagne. With coal Lille became a great industrial center of steel finishing industries, engineering, and linen and cotton mills. The city counted 195,000 people in 1962; some decentralization has developed, and two periods of occupation have weakened its regional independence. As a banking center it has become a satellite of Paris, three hours away by train. But a whole constellation of smaller industrial towns surrounds Lille; Fives builds locomotives; Armentières spins and weaves linen; further on Roubaix and Tourcoing are two sizable towns already united in their suburbs and centralizing most of the French trade in wool and woolen manufacturing. The Lille-Roubaix-Tourcoing metropolitan area has an over-all population of about a million people. In between its urban developments the plain has some of the richest fields in France, producing the best yields in the country of wheat, oats, sugar beets, potatoes, clover, and turnips. A large foodstuffs industry has developed there, producing flour, sugar, beer, and large quantities of alcohol for industrial use. Following the Flemish tradition, dairy cattle are numerous in the stables and on the polders.

Three ports are important on the seashore, all three rebuilt after thorough wartime destruction. Dunkirk, famous for its evacuation in 1940, was built in the seventeenth century as a naval base on the North Sea by Marshal Vauban, the great engineer who fortified Lille and other frontier towns of the French northern border. It is an artificial port with locks, the regional seagate of the industrial basin near by; it imports foodstuffs, ores, wool, timber and pulp, jute, and oil. Dunkirk (143,000) has now completed reconstruction, with a large new steel mill, shipyards, and more plants having come to its suburbs. Still the city is purely a regional port, dependent on its hinterland, financially a vassal of Lille and Paris, besides suffering from the competition of Antwerp for the export of products of the northern industries. On the protuberance called the Nose of Calais, within some twenty miles of the English shores, Calais rivals Boulogne in serving the passenger trade to the British islands. (Heavy goods go through Dunkirk, which also has regular ferry service across the Strait to Dover.) Calais is also an industrial center, manufacturing rayon and some cloth, specializing also in delicate laces. Boulogne is the first fishing port of France, sending trawlers all over the North Sea and supplying the north down to Paris with fresh fish. It also makes steel, cement, and office supplies, and in the surrounding country was raised the famous breed of heavy horses called Boulonnais.

In many ways this area is under the direct impact of Paris, and commuting to the great city is easy by road or rail. Still the north has its own aristocracy of intellectuals and big businessmen, although it has lost most of its financial independence. A steady decentralization of industries in France and an improvement in the intensive cultivation of some other areas have somewhat diminished the impact of the Flanders coal-basin area on the French economy. South of it, toward Paris, stretches a gently rolling plain, part of the rich agricultural belt that feeds the country. Small towns are scattered through it, every one with some industries and often with a beautiful cathedral recalling its importance of old. The underlying rocks are formed of chalky layers—in Picardy these layers make a regularly rolling landscape, with convex slopes on which the farmers have built terraces, screens of trees being planted at the edge to retain the soil. The soil is a heavy clay with flints on which grains and beets are grown. The chief towns are in the flat-bottomed valley of the Somme: Amiens (136,000), an industrial center surrounded with a truck-farming area on damp bottom lands; Saint-Quentin, with famous old velvet factories. Southward the chalk is replaced by Tertiary limestone covered with loam, and here the cattle economy increases in importance, while the sugar beet reigns as a cash crop. A string of large plants, many of which are sugar refineries, follows the valley of the canalized River Oise, the main waterway from the northern district toward Paris. Outcroppings of sand, before reaching the Parisian conurbation, keep their forest cover. Here the small town of Liancourt makes agricultural machinery; Beauvais is famous for its ancient tapestry manufacture and serves as a market town.

Today all around Paris the limestone plains covered with loam offer the sight of purely rural areas with an intensive and highly mechanized kind of agriculture of an almost American type. The circle of plain is divided in sectors by the wide valleys of the Seine and its tributaries. The three main sectors are, to the east, the Brie between the Marne and the Seine, to the south of the Seine, the Beauce, and, to the west, the Vexin between Seine and Oise. This whole agricultural area belongs to the old province of Île de France, the historical heart of the nation, and its granary. The aristocracy, and later the businessmen, of Paris invested large sums of money in the estates that they owned in these plains—but the regional rural economy is not quite of the traditional French kind, for the holdings are managed by the tenants rather than by the owners (among whom are many banks or industrial corporations). Large farms are scattered through the countryside, each with large barns, abundant machinery, a repair shop, silos, and often a distillery; they look much like a factory and apply involved crop rotations in which wheat, sugar beet, and fodder crops play the major part. The plain around is flat, dry, covered with fields, and almost treeless; such is the case throughout most of the Beauce. The same scenery extends westward north of the Seine to the seaboard; to the traveler on the railroad between Rouen and Le Havre, the plain of the Pays de Caux may appear as a well-cultivated desert: he sees fields with small clusters of trees, but no habitations. The farms of this original section of the plain, hidden behind screens of trees, are often of a very picturesque Norman style, with low, thatched buildings scattered across a grassy yard.

In this western direction, Normandy begins not far from Paris. This prosperous country consists of alternating *campagnes* of loam over limestone and depressions where, on clayey soil, the land is checkered with live hedges planted with trees; this latter landscape is called *bocage* and covers large stretches in the west of the country. The green scenery of the bocage looks from afar like woodland, and one must enter inside to understand its organization with the fields and meadows it encloses. The trees and bushes supply some wood, charcoal, and stable litter. They occupy considerable space and make circulation difficult, but their main use is to enclose the area in which the cattle is left alone to graze, thus saving manpower and keeping the cattle from wandering on the neighbor's land. The hedges are therefore linked to an economy centered on cattle raising and grasslands with rather little mechanization. In their advance through Normandy after the landings in 1944, American forces found progress complicated by the hedges; once in a while even tanks had difficulties in overcoming the barriers devised to stop a bull.

Bocage and campagne alternate in Normandy according to the nature of the subsoil. Westward, the bocage gains as marls extend and the sedimentary strata finally is replaced by crystalline rocks in the Armorican massif, to which belong the peninsulas of Britanny and Normandy (or Cotentin). The main cities of Normandy are not in the bocage: the two largest are on the lower course of the Seine River, this avenue leading from Paris to the sea and lined by large factories making such products as cement, paper, sugar, and chemicals. This lower Seine is the site of the main group of oil refineries in France, and motor tank-barges carry the fuel to Paris. Rouen (121,000, but 370,000 with the suburbs) was the historic capital of Normandy and possessed a marvellous array of monuments, many of which were destroyed or damaged during the fighting. In its suburb of Grand Couronne, iron and steel is produced with imported coal and ores from the Norman and North African mines. Rouen's main industry is cotton, which replaced linen in the eighteenth century; it spins and weaves, dyes the cloth, and even tailors it into finished articles. Once spread over the surrounding farms, the industry now is concentrated in mills in the town itself or smaller centers in the

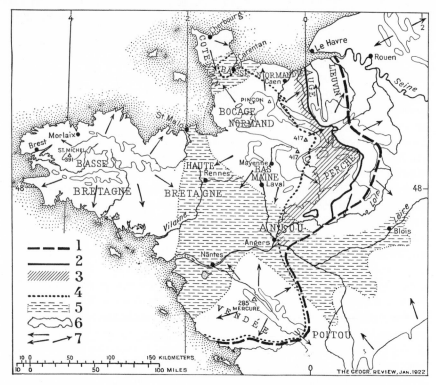

The west of France. Key: 1, eastern limit of the bocage and the "west"; 2, western limit of the clay-with-flints plateau; 3, depressed zone at the foot of 2; 4, eastern limit of the ancient terrains of the Armorican massif; 5, area invaded by the *faluns* sea of Miocene times; 6, land above 200 meters altitude; 7, direction of slope of the peneplain surfaces. *(The Geographical Review)*

The bocage country of Brittany (Finistère). *(French Government Tourist Office)*

surrounding valleys; but the women in rural districts still make most of the French production of cotton shirts. The city has also shipyards, oil refining, and chemical and engineering plants. Access to Rouen, an advanced seagate to Paris, has been kept open to ocean-going ships by dredging and the port receives timber and pulp from the Baltic, ores and wine from North Africa, coal from America, and many other materials for its own area or for the conurbation of Paris. On the estuary of the Seine stands Le Havre, the main oceanic gate of France; its port handled 30.5 million tons of foreign trade in 1966 (while Rouen handled 12.4). Since the sixteenth century when it was built, many Norman navigators and traders have set out from Le Havre; it is the home of the French Line, and its chief relations are with America; coffee, cotton, hardwood, and oil are imported. Terribly destroyed by the Allied bombings, perhaps more than any other city in France, Le Havre, because of the depth and width of its harbor, rapidly became after 1945 one of the main ports of the transatlantic trade, receiving most of the shipments of coal from America and oil from Kuwait or Iraq. The city has been rebuilt in monumental style and has many industries, and its population (247,000) has grown. Still, Le Havre seems one of the liveliest places around Paris, of which it is naturally the ocean pier. It can receive at any time the largest ships afloat.

Few other towns have developed on either side of the Seine estuary. On the coast of Pays de Caux, Fécamp and Dieppe, instead of the privateers of the seventeenth and eighteenth centuries, send trawlers to sea, and Dieppe has a shuttle service for passengers to the English port of Newhaven. West of the Seine, several beaches, such as Deauville and Trouville, have become fashionable sea resorts. A few miles inland, but linked by a canal to the sea, stands Caen (152,000), another historic center rebuilt since the war, with an old university and some modern metallurgy. Around Caen stretches a flat campagne made of a hard limestone that the Norman kings found useful to build St. Paul's Cathedral in London. Iron-ore deposits, of a higher grade than in Lorraine but with smaller reserves, brought mining to the rural country and blast furnaces to Caen. Some ore was exported to England and Germany. Around the campagne of Caen, bocage landscape predominates and widens to the west. The cattle country begins here, and milestones at the crossroads spell a geography of cheese: Camembert, Livarot, Pont l'Evêque, and Port-Salut are small Norman towns. Other towns like Falaise (where, in the medieval castle, William the Conqueror was born), Saint-Lô, and Avranches have since 1944 had their place in the history of the United States, as have the nearby Omaha and Utah beaches. At the tip of the crystalline peninsula of Cotentin, Cherbourg is mainly a port of call, visited by transatlantic liners.

The same economy of bocage and cattle raising extends westward and southward in the old provinces of Brittany, Anjou, and Maine. The small farm does not pay nowadays, and this region is a hotbed of agrarian unrest. Granite, schist, and crystalline sandstone form the rock bases of a gently rolling peneplain. Small, scattered farms predominate, and the housing is often rather primitive, especially in the interior of Brittany peninsula. This land, jutting westward toward the ocean, is one of the principal land's ends of Europe. It is beautiful and picturesque. The poor, wooded interior is partly heathland, with a small range of hills whose crest has such grandiose views made up of fogs, winds, and moors that it reminds one of Northern Ireland and Scotland. The maritime periphery, on the other hand, is progressive, teeming with a variety of activities.

Everywhere the coast of Brittany is rocky, scalloped, and fringed with islands. Navigation has always been difficult along it in the ocean's mists or storms. So many wrecks have occurred off the Breton shores that the inhabitants have even been credited with instigating some in order to plunder the wreckage. As the saying goes: "He who sees Ushant sees his own blood." But Bretons sailed well and they sailed far; at the border of Normandy the port of Saint-Malo was the main French base for cod-fishing off Newfoundland; at the western tip of the peninsula, on a deep and wide bay or *ria,* Brest is the chief French naval base on the Atlantic. The southern shore is somewhat warmer and the more active: Lorient, Douarnenez, and Concarneau are the great fishing ports and centers of fish and vegetable canning; the best soils of the coastal plains are devoted to intensive truck farming, producing especially peas, carrots, and potatoes. The southern and western coasts have kept their archaic traditions of dress, and the lace headgear of the women varies in every township. All this seaboard is lined with summer resorts and tourist attractions, the most famous of which is the medieval abbey of Mont St. Michel, off the northeastern shore.

In the interior, cattle and horse raising with a much poorer agriculture spreads over poorer soils in a cooler climate. The capital of Brittany is in the interior but toward the west, at the point of contact with the richer and grassy bocage: Rennes (200,000) is quite a regional capital with large automotive industries, breweries, and some metallurgy. In the vicinity the old rocks of the peneplain contain some deposits of high-grade ores of wolfram, tin, and iron, which as yet have not been much developed. The economic capital of Brittany is still farther south, at the mouth of the Loire River; Nantes (400,000 inhabitants) used to be the great colonial port, trading with the West Indies and West Africa in the seventeenth and eighteenth centuries, when the Loire Valley was a prosperous, major thoroughfare. In the nineteenth century with less navigation, the silting on the Loire, and the rise of Le Havre and Bordeaux, the port of Nantes dried up, and the city became an industrial center rather than a hub of trade. Nantes now builds ships, cans meats and vegetables, makes tin-plate, refines oil and sugar, and manufactures fertilizers, soap, paper, and glass. With the increase in the size of ships, an advanced port was built at the entrance of the estuary: Saint-Nazaire (badly hit in 1943) developed the largest shipyards of France and has built all the main French liners, big tankers, and men-of-war. A whole metallurgical industry servicing the shipyards sprang up on the Loire estuary, a small French Clyde.

Normans and Bretons have for long played an outstanding part on the French national stage; not only did they supply most of the personnel for the expansion overseas, they also greatly influenced the domestic evolution. Both peoples have a taste for adventure—and stubbornness. The Norman is smarter, noncommittal, efficient, tenacious; the Breton is more extreme, also more generous and openhearted. Breton life has an imprint of traditionalism and austerity; it is quite different from that of the populations of the Loire upstream from the estuary.

The story of the Loire has been often told: now famous among tourists for its châteaux and wines, it was until the eighteenth century a major economic area with a string of prosperous cities. In old times Orléans rivaled Paris as a site for the capital. These cities are rather sleepy though handsome places, living off local trade and on industries based on the regional agricultural production with some electronics, printing, shoemaking, and railroad yards. Navigation no longer counts, for the Loire and the road to Spain have lost much in importance. The climate is mild and warm: a few centuries ago this was the Riviera of France, and it is dotted with beautiful castles and châteaux that kings and barons built along the river and its tributaries. Vines clothe the southern or eastern slopes. Angers, Tours, Blois, and Orléans are the main towns, and each of these names carries with it abundant historical memories. The 1960s brought them a revival, with new universities at Tours and Orléans and manufacturing plants (electronics at Angers, machinery at Tours). Described by many writers, it is a charming country with one of the most simple, free, and comfortable ways of life in France.

This rural district extends southward, with the same charm and the same type of châteaux, almost to the edge of the central plateau. Only to the southwest does Brittany extend some of its extreme and austere character into the province of Vendée, a land of heaths and polders, much of which has been reclaimed since the Revolution when it was the citadel of Royalist resistance. But in the interior the mildness of the Loire reigns over its southern tributaries. Inside the big bend of the

A corner of Rouen, the capital of Normandy and a museum city before the destruction of 1944. *(French Government Tourist Office)*

New urban developments often include such monumental apartment houses as this one, a "Cité Radieuse" in Nantes, designed by the architect Le Corbusier. *(French Cultural Services)*

river a wide outcropping of sands creates a forested and swampy landscape. With large estates that are used in part for hunting grounds, deer forests, bee cultivation, and poor potato growing, this wide stretch of territory in the northern half of France was badly in need of reclamation. Now a special authority has been formed to reclaim the Sologne marshy area, and work is progressing slowly. Farther south limestone plains rise again, more fertile in their western sections, more barren but still cultivated and used for sheep-growing in the eastern province of Berry. The plain is so flat in parts, and the habitat is so concentrated, that one sees from afar like a towering hill the huge structure of the cathedral of Bourges, the historic capital of Berry and the capital of France for a while during the retreat period of the Hundred Years' War. It was at Bourges that Joan of Arc came to fetch the King and to start the French reconquest. Bourges (60,000) was a great center of trade, with important fairs, banking activities, and woolen manufacturing in the Middle Ages—the size of its cathedral and the prosperous mansions still standing in its old section bear testimony to this. Then traffic avoided it, preferring other routes to the northeast along the Loire or through the land of Burgundy. South of the campagne a new depression appears in the marls, at the foot of the central plateau, with bocage, cattle, and quiet rural life. Something throughout this section of the Loire basin, the geographical center of French territory, gives the impression of a dead end.

The permanent transcontinental route, the main artery of traffic, passes east of the central plateau. Other activity appears along the middle valley of the Loire: vineyards and truck farming following the river and livestock near by. The small towns have benefited by a system of canals linking this section of the Loire to the Seine and to the Saône; Gien, Briare, Cosne, La Charité, Nevers—all have some small industries and trade, but the rural activities still predominate. East of the Loire one enters Burgundy, the southeastern section of the Paris Basin. Burgundy was a powerful country in the Middle Ages. Its dukes threatened the king in Paris, and Charles the Bold of Burgundy held Louis XI in custody. The duchy is established on a major crossroads: the Saône depression directs the north-south traffic, and many arteries diverge from it across the plateaus to the west or northeast through the Gate of Burgundy to the Rhine. Here is the handle of the fan of roads across eastern France. But there is a difference between the "two Burgundies" separated by the Saône: to the west is the duchy, part of the kingdom of France, and to the east the free county (or Franche-Comté) which became French later and until then was a part of the Hapsburg Empire.

The heart of Burgundy is the depression of the Saône. Here the river flows slowly through the flat bottom of a tectonic trough that has been

A bituminous coal mine in Burgundy near Autun, to the northeast of the central plateau. *(French Cultural Services)*

Sketch map showing the means of access by water to the river port of Strasbourg, which handled 7.2 million tons of goods in 1966. *(The Geographical Review)*

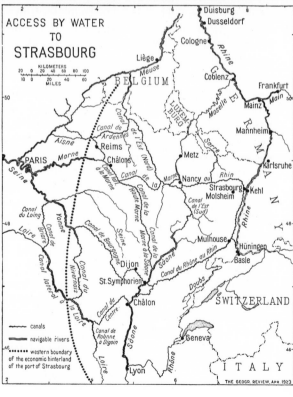

ACCESS BY WATER
TO
STRASBOURG

KILOMETERS
20 0 20 40 60 80 100
10 0 20 40 60
MILES

— canals
— navigable rivers
•••••• western boundary of the economic hinterland of the port of Strasbourg

THE GEOGR. REVIEW, APR. 1923

filled up by recent alluvials of considerable thickness. Along the stream the lands are marshy, covered by some meadows and rich truck farms; rich and even more intensive agriculture prevails on slightly higher and drier soil. A steep cliff overlooks the low-lying valley to the west, the sharp edge of the limestone plateau of Burgundy. At its foot, on a gentler slope and on alluvials mixed with much else that the farmers have brought in, are soils of a special kind, warmed by the sun's rays from the east. This narrow belt along the foot of the cliff is the vineyard that produces Burgundy wines, and the names of its towns have thus become famous: Mâcon, Beaune, Nuits-St. George, Meursault. The vineyard ends to the north near Dijon, the capital of Burgundy, a city of old monuments, a university, famous foodstuffs industries (particularly mustard, gingerbread, liquors) and engineering factories, and one of the main rail hubs of eastern France. Dijon (184,000) has taken full advantage of the fact that the valleys lead westward by relatively easy passes across the limestone plateau toward Paris.

West of the cliff the higher lands of Burgundy are of a complicated structure. A small Hercynian block of hills has pushed north here amid the limestone strata: it is the Morvan, with wooded heights and verdant, grassy depressions, a good land for fattening beef cattle. A great culture developed in the Middle Ages around Morvan, where some of the most famous abbeys in France such as Cluny, Citeaux, Vezelay, and Paray-le-Monial are found. To the north and east the campagne landscape reappears, but more often without much loam or good topsoil; it is rather the campagne landscape of barren limestone, with woods and heathland, a poor agriculture on sandy reddish soils, and a *karstic* erosion resulting from the infiltration of water and entire streams in the thick mass of permeable and soluble limestone. Narrow gorges in canyon forms, caves, and sudden large springs are abundant here.

The same belt of limestone continues northward circling around the middle of the Paris Basin; but here one passes from Burgundy to Champagne, a province whose name indicates the predominance of flat, dry, open plain. This name has gained world-wide fame from the reputation of the sparkling wines produced at the foot of a limestone cliff on a narrow belt of soil sloping eastward. The vineyard stretches mainly between and around the towns of Epernay and Reims, both great centers of winemaking. Immense caves in the limestone have been used as cellars to age the wine. Reims (168,000) long ago outgrew Troyes (114,000), the historic capital of Champagne. Both towns had great fairs on the road from the Mediterranean lands to Flanders; both invested capital in flocks of sheep grazing on the meager pastures of the limestone plains; both have since maintained active woolen industries. Reims, a dynamic community, seat of a new university, took advantage of a rich wine industry and of a better reclamation of the chalky land that stretches to the east of the *côte* (the cliff and vineyard) area—a plain that was called the "lousy Champagne" *(Champagne pouilleuse)* because it was so poor. In the twentieth century, with heavy fertilization from the spreading of all the refuse of the neighboring towns on the soil, it developed a successful agriculture; and a gay pattern of fields, dotted with large villages, now covers what was an empty land for sheep alone. Farther eastward the altitude increases slowly, the climate gets rougher, and vast stretches of wood and heathland expand again. So one enters the province of Lorraine.

In this northeastern section of France, because the layers have a steeper slope on the rim of the Parisian Basin, the alternation of hard limestone plateaus and lower damp depressions becomes more regular, and the contrast between the wooded heights and the rich soils in the depression grows sharper. On the best soils of Lorraine, at the foot of the escarpments, cattle raising is gaining over the old three-course crop rotation that stressed the production of grains. The habitat is concentrated in large villages, although the tillage rules of the community have been weakened by modern evolution and many fences are being erected to enclose the cattle grazing on the open fields demanded by old tradition. The village farm is a low building, oriented in depth, with its barn frequently on the street façade, while the lodging quarters open on the orchard in the back. A heap of manure usually occupies a large part of the sidewalk. A similar kind of habitat, but with more scattered farms and a greater emphasis on cattle, extends over the hilly parts of Lorraine, northward in the hard sandstone bar that made the small range of Argonne stick out on the landscape and in the forested crystalline plateau of Ardennes. Eastward the landscape becomes really mountainous in the Vosges, an oval-shaped mass of Hercynian rock raised between the Parisian Basin and the big trough of the Rhine. The trough subsided after the mountain had been uplifted, and the two slopes of the Vosges are very different: the westward slope is Lorraine, purely French territory, with a gentler gradient, deep valleys, and a more temperate and humid climate; the eastern slope is Alsace, much steeper, with more continental influences in climate as well as in population and a general orientation toward the Rhine. In the north the Vosges are lower, covered with a hard stratum of sandstone; in the south, under the push of the Alpine surrection, they reach higher altitudes, and the granite outcrops widely, forming rounded heights called *ballons,* the highest of which rise to 4500 feet.

Forest and pasturage in the highlands, agriculture with scattered industries in the depressions and valleys—here, as in Normandy, craftsmen worked on the farms and in the small towns to manufacture linens, woolens, and articles of wood, including musical instruments. In the nineteenth century, heavy industries invaded Lorraine and developed on a large scale. The main specialty of Lorraine today is iron and steel. In its northern part the province boasts the richest European deposits of iron ore west of Russia — more than 4 billion tons are to be found at small depth — ore of easy extraction by European standards but of a low grade (25 to 40 percent iron content) and rather phosphoric. A small area between Metz and Thionville had metallurgical works as early as 1800; here was founded the fortune of the family De Wendel, one of the leaders of French industry. This iron ore was in the section of Lorraine (department of Moselle) that, with Alsace, was annexed to Germany from 1871 to 1918. After 1880 large-scale mining started, owing to the development of the Thomas and Gilchrist methods of steel making, which permitted the production of high-grade steel from phosphoric iron ore. Thomas steel and, even more, pig-iron manufacture became the specialty of a vast industrial district stretching from the Luxembourg and German borders down to Nancy in the south. The mining now has moved westward into the area of Longwy and Briey; the output reached 55 million tons in the peak year 1929; it dropped to 21 million tons in 1948, to soar to 67 million tons in 1960 as the consumption of European iron and steel industries swiftly expanded. By 1966, it had again dropped to 54 million tons, as European steel mills used more high-grade ores from overseas. Though much of this iron ore, the *minette* of Lorraine, is consumed on the spot, large quantities are being sent to the French blast-furnaces in the north and center of the country or exported to Germany and Belgium.

The nearby coalfield of Lorraine, an extension of the Saar coal basin westward, in 1966 produced 15 million tons of coal, one fourth of the French production. The conjunction of coal, iron ore, and limestone in the area favored the erection of vast iron and steel plants and associated chemical industries. They have expanded greatly since 1947. Huge manufacturing systems have filled many of the narrow valleys, separated by still rural, quiet ridges; the valleys are teeming with the activity of heavy industry and mushrooming towns, full of smoke and traffic, while wagons loaded with pinkish ore smoothly glide along cables overhead. At night the sky is rhythmically set afire by the powerful red glow of emptying ovens, which provide visions of "hell with the lid taken off." Industrial Lorraine had in the 1950s a full scale boom; the population of the departments of Moselle and Meurthe-et-Moselle rose from 1.1 million in 1946 to 1.6 in 1962; the newcomers count among them many North Africans, Italians, Belgians, and Portuguese. Small towns are overflowing, and impressive housing developments begin to rise on the ridges' edge above the smoke and noise of the valley; such an extension of the town of Briey has been designed by the architect Le Corbusier. Two central cities dom-

Suburban sprawl invades a rural area in the French Jura. *(French Cultural Services)*

A large new mill at Carling in Lorraine. *(French Cultural Services)*

inate the area and grow one toward the other. In the North, Metz (160,-000), capital of the Moselle area, was under German rule from 1870 to 1918 and still has some German-speaking population around it. Long a border stronghold, it is now a prosperous center for a conurbation of over 250,000. To the south is the historic capital of French Lorraine, Nancy (258,000), still shining with the elegance of its eighteenth-century monumental section, built when the exiled king of Poland Stanislas Leszcinsky held court there. A major hub of rail and waterways, Nancy has a great variety of industries, a large university and many government offices. It serves as a regional capital for the country of iron to the north as well as for the more rural country to the east and south with its substantial industries making pottery and ceramics, working the salt rock deposits near Dombasle, and carrying on the textile and printing traditions of the region.

The people of Lorraine have always been proud, patriotic, hardworking, and conservative. Their metallurgy had in the recent half-century dominated French industrial management, often to the point of stifling developments that might compete with them. The Coal and Steel Community, then the Common Market, has forced competition and large-scale expansion on them. The canalization of the Moselle River provides a better and cheaper way to ship ore to the Ruhr, in exchange for the coal and metallurgical coke the Lorraine mills need. Despite its own present expansion, Lorraine can hardly prevent more French steel mills from moving seaward, as the new plant in Dunkirk already indicates. Still, north of Nancy, the prosperity of Lorraine depends too exclusively on mining and steel; the postwar boom may be over and economic diversification is needed. A planning authority has been established at Pont-à-Mousson to work out a regional program for an expanding future.

Alsace is another hotly disputed section of the former Lotharingia. It consists of the belt between the watershed of the Vosges to the west and the course of the Rhine to the east, thus forming the western half of the Rhine trough; it is all mountain slope and valley bottom. The slope is steep and picturesque, covered with beautiful forests and dotted with old castles and monasteries, and the deep valleys that penetrate it enjoy quite a reputation with summer tourists. They also group lines of factories, particularly textile mills, which at first used the power of the rapidly flowing rivers. The bottom of the valley consists of terraces that the Rhine has cut into the mass of alluvials filling in the depression. The upper terrace is drier and bears the vineyards producing Rhine wines; the lower terraces have intensively cultivated fields when dry enough, and meadows when damp. A string of cities that have known great medieval prosperity and still benefit by the thoroughfare of the Rhine follow the river, preferring the upper terrace sites. Most of these cities, with their beautiful old sections and churches, are small towns established at the opening of the valleys descending from the Vosges. Colmar (60,000) is the most important and typical of them.

Two major urban developments arose at the extremities of the valley, at the place where the north-south route of the Rhine crosses east-west roads that pass through depressions at the two extremities of the Vosges range. In the north, Strasbourg is the capital of Alsace. It has a large port on the Rhine, from which a canal sweeps westward through the Saverne Pass to join the Marne River and the Seine basin; the railroad to Paris follows the same route. Its bridge over the Rhine is the route of the Orient Express, the most direct from Paris to Munich, Prague, Vienna, and Budapest. The present city of 335,000 people—more than 400,000 with suburbs—has been one of the important crossroads of Western Europe for centuries; its beautiful old section has many features in common with other cities of the Rhine thoroughfare, from Zurich to Flanders and Holland. French for 200 years, German for 48, then French again since 1919, though actively "Germanized" during the occupation of 1940–1944, Strasbourg has become a symbol of the Franco-German struggle, and its population is still divided into factions. Both countries favored it while they held it, and the city, its port, university, hospitals, and other services are better equipped than most of its neighbors on either side of the Rhine. The German-speaking element now looks to Basel and Zurich rather than to Bonn. The Council of Europe set up headquarters here. A substantial industrial development, especially in food and leather industries, has grown up; recently mechanical and chemical industries too have been built. In a way Strasbourg has acted as an intermediary between diverse regions; it is also the junction of the Rhine with the canal that comes from the Saône and Rhone through the valley of the Ill River; a pipeline along this route brings oil from Marseille. But the heavier industries are in the south of Alsace.

There several cities share the function of the crossroads at the elbow of the Rhine and the Gate of Burgundy, between the Vosges and Jura ranges: Mulhouse (200,000); Basel in Switzerland; and several smaller towns on the French side. Mulhouse is the second city of Alsace and long an important French trading center; its position on the Rhine-Rhone waterway is well worth remarking. A free city until the end of the eighteenth century, it asked to join France during the Revolution. By then it already had an important industrial development, and its fairs had for a long time been a center of redistribution for the cotton piece goods brought from the Orient, especially from India, and called the *indiennes*. One day the local merchants decided to import the undyed cloth and put on it whatever colors they thought their customers would like; later they imported the yarn, and finally the raw material. Each time they developed the corresponding industry (dyes, weaving, spinning) in the neighborhood. All the valleys of Alsace and several places on the Lorraine slope of the Vosges work the cotton fibers for Mulhouse. The city itself has specialized in engineering: it builds machine tools and equipment for textile factories. This specialization has spread to other towns of the Gate of Burgundy and of the foothills of the Jura: Tagolsheim, Altkirch, Belfort, and, farther, Montbéliard and Sochaux were parts of this most diversified center of engineering that has developed production of loco-motives, turbines, diesel engines, motorcars, electrical machinery, elec-tronics, and typewriters. A large deposit of potash salts is mined in the area. This corner of France already has deep affinities with Switzerland: it is at the contact of the Rhine and of the Jura, and its Protestant elite is related to the Swiss.

The Jura range does not belong to the Paris Basin at all; it is one of the advanced ranges of the Alpine zone which are inserted among older and flatter Hercynian massives. A regular folding has affected a mass of limestone layers, creating a topography of narrow parallel ridges sepa-rated by winding valleys; this winding aspect, not unlike that of the Ap-palachian structure, is caused by occasional breakthroughs of a valley by a gap called *cluse* across a ridge or *mont*. The main push having come from the south, there is a more tabular topography with a few ridges to the north and on the plateaus a typical limestone or Karstic relief with closed depressions, deep canyon valleys, the disappearance of certain streams underground and their reappearance in huge springs, such as happens to the Doubs, a major tributary of the Saône. In the south the Jurassian type of topography is better achieved as the folding gets more intense and the uplifting higher. Well-forested ridges alternate with grassy valleys. Timber and cattle have been for a long time the main resources; hydroelectric power from the streams brought in some in-dustrialization. Paper and pulp are produced and some textiles worked. Besançon is the old capital of the Franche-Comté, standing on the edge of the tabular Jura. A picturesque and expanding city of about 120,000, it manufactures watches, man-made fibers, and hosiery. An industry of rock-salt extraction centers on Salins; articles of briarwood, especially pipes, are made around Saint-Claude; and watches around Pontarlier. All these trades, together with summer tourism, help maintain a rather high standard of living. Still the main resource is the dairy production, especially butter and *gruyère* or Swiss cheese, manufactured in coopera-tive plants. Two industrial centers attract the surplus of the mountain population: the engineering plants of the Gate of Burgundy area and the wider urban development of Lyon to the south.

The eastern half of northern France is thus more diversified and endowed with sharper contrasts than the western part. People from

Lorraine and Burgundy have played a large part in the formation of the French nation; those from Lorraine are known for their rigidity, which shows in their stubbornness, austerity, and patriotism; people from Burgundy are quite different; tall and handsome, jovial and witty, they are considered to be one of the smartest groups in the nation. And perhaps they have carried to their optimum the arts of living, cooking, and enjoyment of life. Perhaps because of its position at the crossroads, Burgundy seems to have achieved a happy synthesis of north and south.

## SOUTHERN FRANCE

The southern half of France is decidedly different from the northern. Physically it is higher land, with a much warmer summer climate and the penetration far inland of Mediterranean influences, as demonstrated by the vegetation. In its natural aspects it is also much more varied. Southern France is still predominantly rural, and its industrialization, although progressing rapidly, is more recent and scattered. The main industrial districts and population clusters are all in northern France. In the south regional life is somewhat stronger, growing with the distance from Paris. Provincial centers such as Marseille, Lyon, Bordeaux, and Toulouse were able to develop, and four out of five of France's cities with populations between 400,000 and 1,000,000 are in the southern half of the country. Still there is no sharp dividing line between north and south, and recently both have been changing fast. The south had been less destroyed by the war and more affected by the migration away from the farms and a low birthrate. But in the 1960s it was helped by the settlement of many of the French who moved from North Africa and preferred its sunnier climate. Many industrial plants (chiefly electronics and chemicals) have also come to the southern cities.

The structure of southern France, the antithesis of the northern basin, is that of a wide, low dome with two big walls, the Alps and Pyrenees, framing it to the east and south. It is possible to divide this area into six main regions—the central plateau in the middle, the Aquitanian basin in the west, the Pyrenees to the southwest, the Mediterranean coastland to the southeast, the Rhone corridor and the Alps to the east—and we shall review them in this order.

The central plateau (*Massif Central* on French maps) is a vast area of plateaus and hills made out of a large Hercynian peneplain faulted in many parts and uplifted, particularly in the southeast where there must have converged the pressures originated in the upbuilding of the Alps to the east and of the Pyrenees to the south. These pressures caused great tensions in the rigid mass of old rock; while the southeast was lifted, other sections sank. These faultings, happening on a tremendous scale, were accompanied and followed by volcanic activity. The volcanoes are now dead, and some of the craters are occupied by picturesque circular lakes, but a chain of conic summits retains their imprint on the topography. Vast lava platforms were formed at their feet; in the center, the radiation, outlined by the hydrography in the Cantal area, shows that Mount Cantal once was a volcano of tremendous size, comparable to the most impressive structures of today, which probably blew up, and fluvial erosion reshaped its ruins. The volcanic alignment, called chain of the *Puys* (the local name for the extinct volcanoes), follows a north-south orientation along the western edge of the big trough of Limagne. The Puys mark approximately the heart and the highest crest of the central plateau, with several summits rising above 6000 feet. The slope northward is gradual, penetrated by deep tectonic depressions; westward a gentle slope through Limousin leads toward the Atlantic lowland; in the south a large sunken compartment has preserved thick strata of limestone that fill up the depression and create the dry plateau of Causses. The eastern border is the most complicated; as a result of the pressures applied to it, it was broken into small mountainous compartments with deep valleys or depressions between them, making traffic easier and preserving in the depressions several small coal deposits on which industries were established. The proximity of the Rhone thoroughfare also helped the economic development. In other sections of the plateau's periphery also, small coalfields led to industrialization. There is quite a difference between the interior of the plateau and its periphery.

The cattle economy predominates in the interior of the central plateau. Meadows cover the gentle slopes and the damp bottom lands. The weathering of the crystalline rocks gives a deep and damp soil; the climate is rainy, especially in the west and center, yet vast areas of meadows are systematically irrigated to provide for a speedy and regular growth of grass; the bocage dominates the landscape. The cities are mainly markets for the beef cattle and their by-products. Limoges, capital of Limousin, is famous for its porcelain made of local clays and stones, but its largest industry is that of leather and shoes. From its station, cattle trains leave regularly for Paris. With its 120,000 inhabitants, it is the only important town of the western section of the central plateau. This western section is also the flattest part of the plateau, consisting of two levels of peneplain—the higher level, which is above 1500 feet bears the names of *Montagne* or, significantly, of *Plateau de Millevaches* (thousand cows).

As the altitude slowly rises eastward, the foot of the Puys volcanic range is reached. This is Auvergne, the province that is the heart of the central plateau and probably the richest in the area. On the average the altitude of the hills rises above 3000 feet, volcanism makes the topog-

Cork trees are grown with the pines producing pit props and resin. *(French Cultural Services)*

Once the shepherd on stilts walked across the marshy wilds that have now been reclaimed by reforestation and drainage. *(French Government Tourist Office)*

graphy bolder, and deep depressions contrast with the heights. A beautiful forest, in which the chestnut tree plays an increasing part, covers the slopes, while the summits are summer pastures for the cattle; the depressions have been filled with rich alluvials and are intensively cultivated — some of the best soils of France are in the Limagne. The climate becomes more extreme, rather continental in the sheltered troughs and on the barren heights. In the Limagne also some areas are irrigated. Meadows for fattening cattle or raising some well-selected dairy cows of the Dutch breed, some grain crops, and extensive orchards are the chief concerns of the Limagne through which flows the Allier River, a tributary of the Loire. South of it a few smaller depressions are found; to the east the upper valley of the Loire follows another string of depressions.

The Limagne concentrates many of the towns, among them several famous spas such as Vichy, one of the largest health resorts in France and the provisional capital of the country under German occupation in 1940–1944. Other spas are scattered on the slopes or in the valleys — Royat, Bourboule — for hot mineral springs are remnants of extinct volcanic activity. In the south of Limagne stands Clermont-Ferrand (170,000), the regional capital, a city with a university, monuments, and a large industry. Curiously most of the French manufacturing of rubber is concentrated here, in the firm of Michelin — only sheer luck brought the rubber industry to an isolated town amid hills and pastures. Farther south volcanic heights give way to granitic ridges.

One must reach the limestone plateau of the Grand Causses to find a different landscape and economy. The Causses are the driest landscape of France, as a result of the permeability of the ground where water disappears in depth. Karstic erosion sculpted curious landforms, gorges, and canyons, in places resembling the ruins of a town. Sheep graze the heath and the poor grass; their milk is gathered by the *Société de Roquefort* which makes the famous cheese, and their skins are worked in the leather factories of Rodez and Millau, the latter town specializing in glove making.

The eastern periphery of the central plateau is the most broken up and the most lively. Here old trades have thrived with the help of through traffic, small local mineral deposits, and lumber and charcoal from the forests on the hills. While textiles are more a specialization of towns inside the plateau, such as Tulle, Aubusson, and Le Puy, they are also present in the eastern depression, though overshadowed by metallurgy, recently given an increased importance by the development of coalfields. The industrial series begins almost in Burgundy, south of the Morvan, with the metallurgy of Autun, and especially Le Creusot, where the Schneider works has specialized in the high-quality heavy steel machinery, especially artillery. Farther south, as satellites of the Lyon industry, Roanne and Tarare work delicate textiles and make silk goods. Then the coalfield of St. Etienne (330,000) gives rise to a "black country" ribbon with an industrial avenue following the depression; here textiles are associated with the chemical industries and the finishing stages of metallurgy and engineering. The St. Etienne area makes dyes and silken goods, bicycles, and bridges; small towns scatter in the hills, like Annonay with a group of paper making and printing plants. Southward the mountainous border of the plateau has a greater continuity and massivity, and also becomes more barren as the dry Mediterranean influences increase. These are the Cévennes ridges, a land of tough mountaineers and the last refuge of the Protestants in France in the seventeenth century. The hills are planted with some forest; in the valleys, the mulberry tree was the basis  of the silkworm raising, though little is done now. Heavy industry developed in the Alès depression, where a coalfield yields notable quantities of coal (around Grand Combe), and metallurgical and chemical plants have been built. The first French nuclear power plant was built at Marcoules.

The range of the Cévennes and the whole border of the central plateau curves westward from there on, and the average altitude lowers. Depressions were dug out on the periphery at the contact of the crystalline rocks with sedimentary strata, where softer materials, marls, or clays outcropped. In these places some carboniferous layers let collieries appear on a small scale, and industries were established on them; in the south, Mazamet is a center for treating sheepskins and has some woolen industries; Castres has some engineering works; Decazeville and Brive have metal finishing industries and electronics and build electrical machinery; on the northern edge of the plateau, the group of Montluçon-Commentry support metallurgy and chemical industries, especially ceramics, glassware, and rubber. Such is the industrious rim of the old Hercynian hills owing to a scattering of coalfields.

Between the plateau and the Atlantic coast rolls a plain area, generally called the Aquitanian basin. Structurally it is a triangle sloping toward a median line, the Garonne River valley, and sloping also toward the west, that is, toward the Atlantic coast. The coastal lowland is rather flat. A gently rolling bocage land gradually rises from the coast toward the Limousin plateau in the northern section. Here the coast is often rocky and fringed with large islands. The two ports of La Rochelle and Rochefort were important until the eighteenth century; now they have lost much of their activity. The hinterland is mainly rural with sleepy market towns,very provincial in character, such as Angloulême. Along the Charente River some vineyards gave rise to the famous brandy industry centered in the town of Cognac. Further inland the bocage produces butter and cream, standardized and marketed through cooperative organizations of the Danish type.

The sea penetrates deeply inland through the wide estuary of the Garonne, called the Gironde bay. At the head of it, as far as oceanic navigation can go, stands the city and port of Bordeaux (555,000) now attempting large-scale renewal with a manifold industry that has developed on its trade. Bordeaux, which for a time belonged to the king of England, heir to the Aquitanian duchy, has close ties with England. For centuries its famous wines, from the grapes grown on a nearby sand-limestone ribbon of land, have been exported to Britain, where they killed off all local winemaking. From the pine forest to the south, it ships pitprops for English coal mines and receives coal in exchange. But the port of Bordeaux (which handled 7.4 million tons of goods in 1966) also has an important colonial past: its merchants developed the west coast of Africa and actively participated in the West Indies trade. Even now a good part of the tropical imports of France come to Bordeaux, which has large oil-pressing mills (especially for peanut and palm oil), soap factories, a great variety of food and chemical industries, and petroleum refineries. Most of the large plants, including an iron and steel mill, are scattered downstream along the water's edge. Bordeaux is an important cultural center, but as capital of southwestern France it yields now to the more rapidly growing Toulouse.

South of the Gironde, the coastal plain widens; it is sandy and bordered by a line of dunes. Pushed by western winds, the sand crept rapidly inland gaining in depth to form a hard impermeable crust, the *alios*, which kept the waters from infiltrating and transformed all this area (called *Landes*) into swamps and sands. In the 1870s reclamation through drainage was started and pits pierced through the alios. The Landes were turned into the largest French forest of pines, with some addition of cork oaks, and the area exported large quantities of pitprops, resin, and cork bark. The shoreline became a string of sea resorts; Arcachon, on a bay famous for its oysters, is the best known of these beaches. During World War II the forest and drainage system were not adequately maintained and too-wide areas were cut over; new reclamation measures were applied after 1947 to save the forest, but it was devastated again by terrible fires in 1949. Recently oil was found near Arcachon, and about 2.5 million tons of crude oil was obtained in 1966.

Inland to the south and east the Landes give way to a more rolling landscape: here develops the arc of valleys between hills on a vast fan-like mass of alluvials brought down by erosion from the Pyrenees range towering southward. Horse and sheep raising with some vineyards (producing the Armagnac liquor) cover the light, sandy soils. Rich and diversified agriculture occupies the heavier alluvials in the valleys. A set

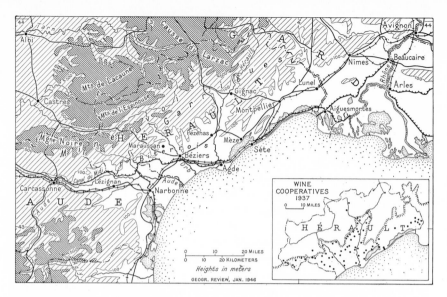

Map of Bas Languedoc, based on the *Carte Aeronautique de la France*. The inset shows the location of wine cooperatives in the department of Herault in 1937; the hachured line marks the edge of the uplands. *(The Geographical Review)*

Sulfur mine near Narbonne in Mediterranean Languedoc. Notice the classical farm, or "mas," and the rows of vines around and beyond it. *(French Cultural Services)*

of streams gathering to form the Adour River flows to the Atlantic and empties at the port of Bayonne, which has some industrial plants. Most of the drainage goes northward to the Garonne River.

The depression drained by the Garonne between the Pyrenean foothills and the central plateau is a gently rolling plain made of soft material with some stretches of hard limestone plateaus to the northeast. The limestone areas have a moderate Karstic topography, reminding one of the Causses; sheep are raised and agriculture is concentrated in the valleys. This is a manifold polyculture with grains, fodder crops, and much vegetables and fruits. Each town has its special product which is sent all over France and abroad: truffles around Cahors, tomatoes at Marmande, plums at Agen, mushrooms at Villefranche, so it goes. It is a prosperous country of small farmers who also raise poultry, cattle, and pigs. For centuries they have kept a remarkable stability in the population figures through systematic birth control; rather underpopulated in the 1920s and 1930s, this area has lately received a steady immigration of Italian and Spanish settlers. Toulouse is its capital, at the contact of the Garonne plain with the Pyrenean foothills and the Mediterranean area that widens eastward. The historic capital of Languedoc, guarding the passes leading to the Mediterranean or to Spain, Toulouse has become the sixth city of France (440,000) and benefits by an industrial development based on the hydroelectric power of the Pyrenees and the abundance of natural gas in its vicinity. It has large electrical engineering plants and makes airplanes (including the Caravelle and the Concorde), fertilizer, synthetic ammonia, and agricultural machinery. It commands, in fact, a part of the central plateau and the whole range of the Pyrenees.

"High are the Pyrenees," says an old French dictum, as the lofty range erects its formidable barrier from the Atlantic to the Mediterranean shores. And they are a continuous line of summits, a complicated bulky folding around a central nucleus of uplifted crystalline rocks. This crystalline central part makes the barrier more effective: a line of peaks rising above 10,000 feet cuts off France from Spain and leaves open only some passes on the sides. The slope is steep and the crestline closed, but many valleys, widened by the glaciation period, penetrate inside the mass. The French slope, facing northward, is well watered by abundant rainfall from the Atlantic, especially in its western and central sections; it is arid only in the east, where Mediterranean influences predominate. Elsewhere the slopes are covered with forests and the higher levels are excellent summer pastures: herds of cattle roam up and down the slopes according to the season. The bottom of the valleys has rich, intensive agriculture, mainly geared to a cattle economy. Harnessing the rapid flow of their steep rivers has brought power and industrialization to these valleys; several of them, especially those of the Ariège and Garonne rivers, have become lines of chemical and metallurgical factories. In the foothills of the range two new developments promise progress: a large deposit of natural gas was discovered near Lacq, and a large scheme of irrigation for intensive farming was started in the Gers area. The gas of Lacq comes out of deep wells at high temperature and with a high sulphur content. Special plants cool off the gas and remove the sulphur, then the gas is sent through a network of pipelines which brings it as far as Paris, and to many cities of western France; 5.2 billion cubic meters of gas were produced in 1966, and the sulphur thus obtained has turned France from an importer into an exporter of this valuable chemical. Chemical and aluminum industries surround the gas wells, and the new town of Mourenx houses their personnel.

The Pyrenees are famed for their grandiose sites and, in winter as well as in summer, attract crowds of tourists. Only two railroads cross the mountains, on either side of the central crystalline highest section: the Puygcerda railroad in the east and the more important Somport Pass railroad in the west, leaving from the beautiful town of Pau (110,000), a former capital of ancient Navarre. This kingdom was established on both slopes of the western Pyrenees and had for its foundation the original old Basque nation, settled there long before and speaking a language different from any other in Europe. Similarly Catalonia expanded on both sides of the eastern Pyrenees. These regional units were broken up when absorbed by the larger French and Spanish realms—and the opposition of these realms made the Pyrenees higher. And yet in a high basin inside the mountain the little country of Andorra remains independent and lively, supervised jointly by the French government and the Spanish Bishop of Urgel. The political autonomy of this mountainous country (191 square miles, population 14,000) dates back to 1278. Situated entirely above 3500 feet of altitude, it is a picturesque corner of Mediterranean highland, with some irrigated lands and an active trade; its capital, Andorra la Vella, is just a vast shopping center for tourists.

The main traffic between France and Spain passes along the two narrow coastal sidewalks at the extremities of the range. The two areas are in sharp contrast: the humid, forested Atlantic shore with large sea resorts (of which Biarritz is the largest) and the dry, barren, wind-swept Mediterranean cliffs built up in terraces planted with vines. The traffic toward Spain is not very active, besides tourism, and the better-developed part of the Pyrenees is the central section with its abundance of power.

A few hilly areas establish an interrupted link between the Pyrenees and the southern part of the central plateau. The Pass of Lauragais leads across the hills from Toulouse eastward and opens up near

Carcassonne on the coastal plain of Mediterranean Languedoc. And from the Pyrenees to the delta of the Rhone this flat plain is an immense vineyard, producing the big bulk of the common red wine of France. After the French vines were blighted by the *phylloxera* in the 1860s, the vineyards, restored with American plants, were organized as a solid area of small landowners grouped into cooperative associations: the farmer brings his grapes to the cooperative and later gets his check. This organization also controls the whole area politically and is quite influential as far north as Paris. The cities of the plain are local markets: Perpignan, amid its orchards; Carcassonne with its medieval *cité;* Narbonne, which still retains a Moorish imprint from the days when it was under Arabic rule; Béziers and Montpellier, both principal wine exchanges—but Montpellier (171,000) is an old city, with a great cultural tradition and a university that disputes Paris for the title of oldest in Europe; finally Nîmes (123,000), with a surprising array of well-preserved Roman monuments, and Arles on the Rhone—the Arles that used to be the Rome of the Gauls and remains one of the best museum towns of Europe.

The shoreline of this plain is a fresh one, swampy and sandy, constantly enriched by the silt of the Rhone brought by a westward coastal current. Narbonne, which was a port in the Middle Ages, is now several miles from the water's edge, and maritime navigation cannot reach much above Arles, on the main branch of the delta. Fleets of Crusaders left from Aiguesmortes in the thirteenth century, but now that walled town is well inland. This rapid advance of the delta has developed a low marshy plain, the Camargue—malarial until recently, dotted with lakes, the last corner of wilderness in France. Reclamation works have been progressing in the area—as well as raising bulls as it still does, the Camargue now has irrigated rice fields, along the lines of the Louisiana delta, and large vineyards, but also a national park.

This coastal plain is truly Mediterranean in character. There is only a short cold period with few days of frost, and the summer is dry; July and August are almost rainless, and the sunshine is abundant. The vine, the olive, and the mulberry all used to be the chief resources until the vine took over and irrigated hay and truck farming developed on the lower Rhone. The maritime life is not very active on the silted coast: the only important port is in the middle, Sète, built in the seventeenth century by Marshal Vauban at the Mediterranean entrance of the "Canal of the Two Seas," linking it through the Garonne valley to Bordeaux on the Atlantic. A great project, this canal has had only a local role. Sète imports timber and much wine from abroad to be blended with the local production, and has an oil refinery. The bulk of the trade and industrial activities are attracted to Marseille.

Agriculture in the Conflent: a typical farm in a high valley in the Mediterranean part of the Pyrenees. Notice the variety of crops and the importance of fruits and vegetables. *(The Geographical Review)*

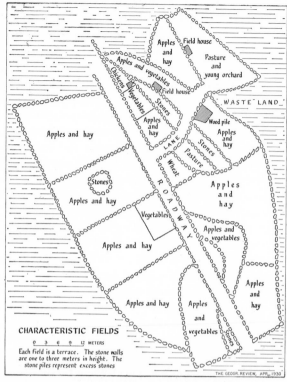

A village high in the Alps near Nice. *(French Cultural Services)*

East of the Rhone the landscape changes. The topography rises; hills come directly to the seashore; low limestone hills, then an old crystalline massif, the Esterel and Maures ranges (remnants of the blown-up and sunken old platform to which the present islands of Corsica and Sardinia originally belonged); and, finally, the Alps themselves. Thus the slope of the coastland increases eastward; and always the coast is indented, fringed with little bays and peninsulas, but with variations. As the coast veers to the northeast and mountains grow higher, it becomes a typical *riviera*, the name given to the steep Mediterranean slopes along the sea looking eastward. This is one of the most beautiful sections of France and Europe; it enjoys a drier and warmer climate owing to its eastern orientation and has been thoroughly organized for tourism. Nice (400,000) is its capital, with famous hotels, some industries, and an increasing number of retired persons from the north as permanent residents. As the central city for the Riviera, Nice has developed an impressive business district and attracted industry, particularly electronics. It has a new university and is growing fast. Cannes (213,000), a famous beach, quite select, has a good roadstead where a few liners call. A rocky corner of the coast, the principality of Monaco (370 acres, 25,000 inhabitants) remains an independent state, associated with France in matters of foreign affairs and tariff policy. Its town of Monte Carlo is one of the gambling capitals of the world; but the prince of Monaco collects more money for his budget from taxes on hotels and the sale of stamps. Monaco is a remnant of a feudal state that once was large and powerful; it is still famous for its oceanographic museum and the maritime explorations of the late Prince Albert.

The industrial section of Mediterranean France lies between the Rhone and the Riviera, close to the great corridor that stretches inland to the north. Surrounded by an amphitheater of barren hills stands the city and port of Marseille: a conurbation of about 1.2 million people, it is the third largest in France and its port one of the largest in the whole Mediterranean basin. Established in ancient times as a Greek colony, Marseille was long overshadowed by Arles, until its location away from the silt of the Rhone gave it a clear advantage. The creek called the Old Port was all that there was until 1848; then, with the development of French interests in North Africa and the new colonial empire, and with the opening of the Suez Canal in 1869, putting the Mediterranean again on the main roads of international traffic, Marseille had its great rise. Handling close to 64 million tons of goods in 1966, Marseille is the home of a large section of the French merchant marine and the largest French seaport; a pipeline links it to Strasbourg and Karlsruhe. Marseille has huge sums invested in Africa, the Near East, and the Far East and many foreign lines call here. The specialty of Marseille has always been that of the imperial French port, and its industries are built on tropical goods: it makes sugar, edible oils, soap, and also cement and machinery. A new port with twelve miles of piers was built from 1855 to 1930; still too small for the traffic it handled, Marseille then annexed to its facilities the vast water space of the Etang de Berre, a bay between the Rhone delta and its own roadstead, where a whole industrial area of oil refineries and chemical and engineering industries has sprung up. A canal tunneled through a limestone ridge links it directly to Marseille. The city is beautifully planned with large new residential sections. It is very lively and picturesque, a crossroads between East and West, with many Levantine influences, a real gaiety, and remarkable dynamism.

To the east, Marseille has a string of satellites on the coast, with shipyards and diverse industries, as far as Toulon (340,000), the major French naval base. In the small plains behind Toulon active truck farming has developed to supply the cities. Around Brignoles the main French deposit of bauxite, one of the richest in Europe, is exploited, the ore being sent to the valleys of the Alps to be processed into aluminum. Off the coast, in the open sea, the large island of Corsica (3360 square miles, 168,000 population) is French territory and strongly linked to France. It gave her the Emperor Napoleon and many distinguished civil servants. Still divided by the feuds of the local clans, Corsica is truly traditional Mediterranean territory with granitic soils, a hilly interior, and a xerophytic low kind of forest (the *maquis*). It lives largely off the tourist trade and emigration to France, where Corsicans are reputed to be able administrators.

A curious thing about the development of Marseille is that this leading French port has little hinterland of its own and little to export other than the manufactured goods of its own industry or of northern France. The Mediterranean coast of France is turned mostly toward the domestic market, and Marseille is a sort of *sui generis* development. Only rail, pipeline, and road link the great port to the industrial districts of St. Etienne or Lyon, for the great route of the Rhone northward is not yet a navigable one. The question of the Rhone's canalization has come up several times and was much disputed; it may be soon completed as a corollary to the works that harness the hydroelectric potential of the river. Marseille is now the regional metropolis of the Mediterranean seaboard of France, the only substantial region that is growing fast by net internal inmigration besides the region of Paris. This area also attracted in 1962–1963 a large proportion of the French Algerians who then migrated to France; also, it is benefiting by the increased affluence of the whole nation, the longer vacation periods enjoyed by tens of millions, many of whom come south in search of sun, sea bathing, etc. A bold plan to develop a string of new seaside cities between the lower Rhone and the Pyrenees adds to the future prospects of this region.

The corridor of the Rhone between the Alps and the central plateau presents an alternation of narrow and wider sections. The narrowest part, practically a gorge, is called the "Faucet" of Donzère; a huge dam has been built there for waterpower and another at Montélimar. Downstream the valley is wider and definitely Mediterranean; upstream northerly influences are more felt, and the bottom plains remain small as the Alps push closer.

The southern, or Mediterranean section, is still full of Roman influences, ancient or even more recent: Avignon was for a while the residence of the Pope during medieval troubles. This plain of the lower Rhone Valley has been greatly developed in the last hundred years, after a period of decline, and irrigation from the Durance River brought to the stony plain of Crau an intensive agriculture. A green country sprang up, producing fodder and vegetables, with screens of trees protecting the crops against the wind. Truck farming brought fortune to the area as large quantities of early vegetables could be sent by rail or truck to Lyon, Paris, and other northern cities. What had been for centuries a poor and abandoned land is one of the richest agricultural districts of France! Avignon (140,000) is the local capital which cans tomato juice and a variety of vegetables. Its Palace of the Popes and many other monuments still attract tourists who admire the contrast of the grassy lowland with the rocky and barren hills framing it: to the marvels of ancient architecture the landscape adds its own architecture which Mediterranean erosion and the proximity of the Alps make quite impressive.

Northward less agriculture is found along the valley; truck farming and orchards are still the main source of crops, until the bottom widens and vineyards clothe the lower slope of the Cévennes, producing the wines of Côtes du Rhone and Chateauneuf du Pape. The towns are the relays of the old route, and each has its industrial specialization: Montélimar makes sweets and nougat; Valence, at the opening of the Isère valley, manufactures textiles; St. Rambert d'Albon works hides and skins; Vienne makes woolens. None of them has taken great importance, for the shadow of Lyon extends far southward.

Lyon stands at the meeting of the Rhone and the Saône rivers. Several natural depressions radiate from its site, making of the place the main crossroads of eastern France. Its importance was recognized early, and the Romans treated it as the Gallic capital. As a center of trade and by its regional influence, Lyon is second only to Paris in France. Its population of 1.1 million in 1968 (with suburbs) decreased between the two World Wars, but since 1946 the conurbation has been developing again. Lyon's

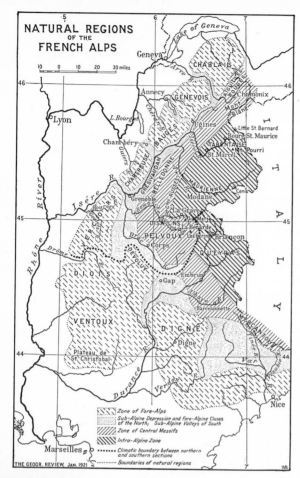

### NATURAL REGIONS OF THE FRENCH ALPS

10 0 10 20 30 miles

Lake of Geneva

Geneva

CHABLAIS

Annecy

GENEVOIS

Chamonix

Lyon

L. Bourget

Ugines

Little St Bernard

Bourg St.Maurice

Cham béry

TARENTAISE

St.Marcel

Mt Pourri

CHARTREUSE

BAUGES

BELLEDONNE

GRESIVAUDAN

Grenoble

MAURIENNE

Modane

Cenis

La Grave

DIS ... NS

St.Mert

La Berarde

PELVOUX

Le Bourg

Briancon

Corps

QUEYRAS

DEVOLUY

Embrun

D I O I S

Gap

VENTOUX

Barcelonnette

Plateau de St Christobal

D I G N E

Digne

MERCANTOUR

Durance

Verdon

Var

Nice

Marseilles

THE GEOGR. REVIEW, JAN. 1921

Zone of Fore-Alps
Sub-Alpine Depression and Fore-Alpine Cluses of the North; Sub-Alpine Valleys of South
Zone of Central Massifs
Intra-Alpine Zone
Climatic boundary between northern and southern sections
Boundaries of natural regions

*(The Geographical Review)*

**La Mer de Glace glacier in the Savoy Alps.** *(French Cultural Services)*

annual fair is the most important in France. Having filled the bottom of the valley, Lyon sends its residential suburbs over the surrounding hills and avenues of industrial plants along the main north-south road. In the nineteenth century, after a long fight with London and Milan, Lyon became the world's main market of raw silk and silken goods. The Chamber of Commerce explored part of China, and local craftsmen devised special looms to win this silk supremacy. In the twentieth century some decentralization began, greater mechanization produced cheaper silk, and the crafts of Lyon became too expensive. But the city fought to retain some of its markets, though cut off from the rest of the world in World War II. To silk, rayon was added, and a large chemical industry making fertilizers, dyes, pharmaceuticals, films, cameras, and sulfuric acid has grown up. Parallelly, a variety of engineering plants manufacture electrical machinery, mechanical goods, automobiles, and other machines. This variety of industries made full use of the presence of enterprising capital and skilled manpower. In fact, Lyon has colonized the surrounding regions as far as St. Etienne and Grenoble with factories working for it; it has invested large sums in the development of the Alps and elsewhere; the powerful French banking concern, *Crédit Lyonnais*, originated here; and large capital savings earned in trade have been constantly reinvested. Lyon is perhaps the only French city boasting some independence from Paris. Its business circles have a reputation for efficiency, reserve, stubbornness, and austerity — more than any other town in France, Lyon has something of a puritanical imprint on it, although it had few links with the English-speaking world. The center of the city now seems crowded and narrow; new, modern sections are expanding to the east; the railroad station and the airport are busy hubs, and the university is a great center of learning. Geographical position was a decisive factor, but much else was added by the tradition and character of the people.

North of Lyon, the corridor widens as the Saône depression expands between the plateaus of Burgundy and the Jura. To the northeast, the flat part of the depression is strewn with lakes that have been converted into fishing ponds. Farther north, the truck farming, poultry, and cattle-raising economy of Bresse takes over. This land resembles the north of France and is part of Burgundy. Lyon has always kept up its links with this area, but its more recent expansion of influence has been to the east, in the Alps.

The Alps form a higher and deeper barrier between France and Italy than the Pyrenees do to the south. And the structure of the range is somewhat different from the latter. Here again a crystalline central belt of higher massives constitutes the core of the structure, but an advanced belt of sedimentary layers, mostly limestones, has been folded and projected forward on the outside of the arch — that is, toward the west and northwest, or toward France. As a result the French slope of the Alps is much more gradual than the Italian one, and the range seems to open up in France while it tightly encloses the north of Italy. Fractures and valleys existing since the time of upbuilding have been deepened and widened by the icecap which is credited with having cut down to less than one half the height of the whole range. U-shaped valleys with steep slopes, bold peaks, and sharp crests with glacial cirques abound in the Alps. Because of altitude and geological formation, the greatest difference is between the inner crystalline compartments and the outside or border ranges. There are also substantial differences from north to south, for the higher summits are mainly in the northern half and climate changes southward, with a greater aridity in the vicinity of the Mediterranean.

The higher parts of the Alps are the domain of vast forests or, above them, of summer pastures *(alpages)*. The lower parts, in the valleys, are tilled; agriculture is dominated by orientation, because slopes looking to the east or south receive much more sunshine than those facing north or west. The former slopes will be cultivated to a higher level, while on the latter the woods will extend lower. Meadows generally occupy the bottomlands. The economy, though producing some grains or vegetables for local consumption, is oriented toward cattle and dairy products. Pastoral life is therefore extremely important, with seasonal migrations varying in type from range to range.

The principal valleys divide the whole system of the Alps into several ranges or massives, so that it is simpler to consider them as the southern, central, and northern Alps. The southern Alps are definitely Mediterranean. Sunny, made of complicated folds in which limestone strata dominate, they are barren, with many valleys reduced to gorges. Towns are few and are concentrated in the main valley of the Durance River or in the foothills near the Mediterranean where the culture of fruits, flowers, and vegetables can develop. This is the poorest section of the Alps, badly in need of reforestation and even of repopulation, as emigration has been considerable.

The central section is that of wide crystalline ranges like those of Pelvoux and Belledonne. The summits frequently reach elevations above 11,000 and 12,000 feet. Every valley is a little country by itself and has a name of its own—Oisans, Maurienne, Grésivaudan. The central Alps extend farther westward than do the others and have a developing cattle economy and a growing industrialization in the main valleys as the waterfalls are harnessed. A large valley, which marks the end of the high massives, develops along an axis oriented northeast-southwest, obviously following a structural line of fracture. The central ranges come up to it but do not cross it. The River Isère follows the valley, which at its widest part is called the Grésivaudan. This median furrow is the richest agricultural land of this section and concentrates much of the population of the mountains. A string of industrial towns follows a terrace above the river. Here hydroelectricity—what the French call "white coal"—was developed and applied for the first time on a large scale.

The junction of the Grésivaudan with several other valleys opens roads to traffic in all directions, and here stands Grenoble the old capital of the province of Dauphiné and the capital of economic development of the Alps. In its circle of green hills, Grenoble is a beautiful and active town (332,000 with the suburbs). The capital of tourism in the Alps, it is also a center of trade and industry that is more independent from the old domination of Lyon. With its 600-year-old university, its museums, its many chemical, mechanical, and food factories (which are clean because they use electricity instead of coal), Grenoble is a proud capital. It has always had a stubborn spirit of liberalism and attachment to democratic tradition, and also has always claimed to have its say on national problems whatever Paris decided—the Dauphiné was the land of the Dauphin, the heir to the throne, a condition which carried certain privileges, and Grenoble does not wish to forget this even in a republican regime. It had a brilliant record of resistance during World War II and has shown dynamism in reconstruction. It also has a large nuclear research institute. Specializing in research and services to institutions Grenoble has a variety of laboratories, particularly in fields related to electricity and hydraulics. In the Alpine area Grenoble is the only sizable city, with industries scattered in long strings along the rapid streams, and these industries are manifold. Though chiefly metallurgical, engineering, and chemical in the higher valleys, there are many textile mills and food industries scattered throughout the lower ranges and hills between Grenoble and Lyon or farther northward. The only other important regional center in the central Alps is Briançon, to the east in the heart of the central ranges, the capital of defense along the Italian border.

The northern Alps are the province of Savoy, once a part of the kingdom of Piedmont-Sardinia and united with France only in 1866. Savoy voted by a large majority to become French, and it not only looks thoroughly French but is more integrated in the national whole than many provinces that have been part of France for centuries. This section of the Alps is the most broken up by deep valleys and passes—along the Maurienne and through the Mont Cenis Pass or through the Tarentaise and St. Bernard Pass runs the age-old route to Italy that the French have traveled so many times. Though Savoy has some large crystalline masses, with Mont Blanc (15,782 feet) the highest summit of Europe, it is open mountain country, quite deeply humanized, with a rich cattle and dairy economy—a land of butter, cream, veal, and Swiss cheese, a land also of trade, with some of the best French resorts, such as Chamonix, a ski resort in the heights, or Aix-les-Bains, a spa in the valley. There are deep lakes due to fractures widened by the glaciers and rapid streams providing power. It is also a densely populated country which sends emigrants to Lyon and Paris. With the variety of industries, especially mechanical ones, spread through its small towns, such as Annecy and Chambéry, Savoy is closely related to Switzerland. (See map of traffic through the Alps, p. 388.)

Such is the variety of the French Alps. The ranges come up to Lake Geneva, but the French shore on the lake faces northward and is cold and windy in winter, making quite a contrast with the warmer, densely populated Swiss shore. The Rhone valley separates the Alps from the Jura: the Rhone is still a rapid torrent here, and its power has been harnessed by the big dam of Génissiat.

With the recent industrialization of the Alps and with the prosperous districts of Lyon, Marseille, and the Riviera, the southeastern section is the most prosperous in southern France. Still it cannot compare with the north in industrial and commercial might: it is more rural and more provincial on the whole. But in many ways it plays an essential part in the nation; as the saying goes in France: "The north pays the taxes, and the south runs the politics." Actually both combine their influences, nicely balanced, in national politics, and both admire and distrust Paris.


PARIS AND ITS REGION

The French capital has a greater concentration of the reins of national life than any other capital of a major power. It is, of course, situated in a favorable position—in the middle of the Paris Basin, amid the richest plains, with a convergence of valleys and navigable streams that made it a natural hub of traffic and at a point in the valley where the Seine is easy to cross because of the islands. Still these local advantages do not explain the extraordinary development of one of the largest cities in the world. There is no important source of fuel or raw material in the vicinity; it has no large seaport as in the case of London or New York, yet the present population of the whole conurbation, with the arms it extends in several directions, comes to about 10 million people. Paris owes its importance to the kings who in the tenth century chose it as their capital and proceeded to build on it a vast kingdom, then a vast empire. Its political function has been decisive. The site and the means of transportation were adapted later to the needs of the city; and the rail, canal, and highway systems of France that today appear to be focused on Paris were all achieved by government decision and sometimes at considerable expense.

Paris grew quickly in the Middle Ages. About 1200 King Philippe Auguste gave it a circular wall, some remnants of which are still standing; he paved the streets and even thought of some sewage system. So Paris advanced its position in Europe. By this time its university was already a great center of learning. With the huge fairs, the trade function grew, and Paris had about 300,000 inhabitants by 1400; its population must have reached the 500,000 by 1700 at the great time of Louis XIV. By then France dominated Europe. Versailles was built in the suburbs; canals were started around the city. By 1800 the Revolution had cemented the work of the royal dynasty and concentrated all the political and administrative power in the capital; in the nineteenth century the city grew still more. In the twentieth century decentralization from the old nucleus began, and outside rings and tentacles developed, following especially the main rivers and chief railways radiating from the old town. The City of Paris proper remains within the limits of the last belt of fortifications, built in 1840 and replaced by a ring of apartment houses in the 1920s. This older city is losing population steadily, for it groups the business and administrative sections; the Latin quarter of the university, some industry and only a few residential sections. As is usual in large European cities, the best residential district is in the west and the more populous and poorer sections in the east. Yet the Seine is followed by an alternation of both — while the most expensive modern apartment houses border the river on the cliff of Passy, the large automotive Citroen works stretch on the flatter bank opposite. Paris has a mixture of very old quarters, still filled with history (and often with luxurious mansions), and modern sections, built either for residence or business. It also has long monotonous rows of workers' residences, but every section can boast some large avenue and interesting monument.

No other city in the Old World has such an array and such a diversity of monuments and historical buildings, running the gamut of styles from the Roman amphitheater of Lutèce to the very modern Unesco building. The surrounding hills, chiefly edges of the limestone plains over the valley bottom, add diversity to the perspective. The suburbs have become an essential part of the city, from the palaces, with Versailles as a kind of shrine to national greatness, to the many ugly but teeming industrial towns that make up what was called the "Red Belt" when the political orientation of the workers' masses was opposed to the more conservative spirit of the dwellers in the old city. Its beauty, intellectual activities, and artistic splendor have made of Paris an extremely cosmopolitan city, a melting pot of ideas and of active business trasactions. Its banks and stock exchange control all the French economy tightly, in Europe and overseas. Its industries have developed to the point where, for the finishing stages, Paris is certainly the largest manufacturing district of France and one of the largest in Europe.

In the city of Paris proper are concentrated mainly the offices of financial and industrial management, of government and mass-media. Here also are all the establishments belonging in the entertainment function of the big city as well as much of educational and research functions (though some of the institutions in the latter categories have started to move out to the suburbs). The city aggregates, too, a whole world of craftsmen, specialized laboratories, and small manufacturing establishments working on order for a restricted clientele or a special market. All these industries and crafts are linked to their market and to the caprice of fashion; Paris is by far the largest concentration of luxury consumers in Europe, and it is a place that sets the fashion for France, and in the case of certain luxury products (such as women's clothes, perfumes, jewelry, and so forth) for a much wider international market.

Such specialties, often called "articles de Paris," employ only a fraction of the industrial labor force in the metropolis. Almost any kind of finishing manufacturing can be found in the Greater Paris area, from antibiotics and automobiles to zippers and zwieback. The heavier types of industry, requiring more space and easier access, have moved out to the suburbs or even farther, although some such large-scale plants can still be found within the limits of the central city. Increasingly Paris and its metropolitan area attract the plants that need the abundant and skilled manpower found there, the proximity to the regional market, or the proximity to other manufactures already located there.

For a long time Paris has been known as the most beautiful city in Europe, in terms of architecture and urban design; but it is also terribly crowded: the city proper has the highest density of residents of any large city in the world. This is due not only to the fact that for almost a century it has been built to a high average level (of about six to seven stories as a rule), but also to its rapid growth at a time when new building has not been adequately provided, either for housing or office use. In 1861 the City of Paris had a population of 1.5 million, the metropolitan area of 2 million, and the whole of France of 37.4; in 1962, the City counted 2.81 million (slightly less than in the period 1911–1931), but the metropolitan area rose to about 8 million while the whole country increased to 46.5 million. The difference between the populations of France and Greater Paris thus seem to have remained the same (that is, 35 million) a century apart, as if the latter had absorbed all the growth of the former. The actual picture of migration within France has of course been much more complex; several other cities and industrial areas have attracted migrants, but no other comparable growth has developed. The provinces tended to feel that Paris' growth had emptied the rest of the country of its substance and made it a "desert" in terms of initiative and opportunity. This feeling grew especially strong in the relatively stagnant

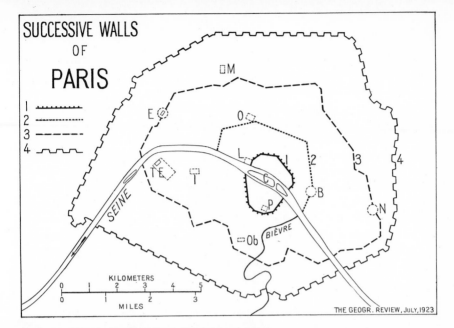

SUCCESSIVE WALLS OF PARIS

1 ·····
2 ·····
3 ----
4 ~~~~

SEINE

BIÈVRE

KILOMETERS
0  1  2  3  4  5
0  1  2  3
MILES

THE GEOGR. REVIEW, JULY, 1923

The successive walls of Paris: 1, wall of Philip Augustus, thirteenth century; 2, wall at time of Louis XIV, seventeenth century; 3, wall of 1789; 4, wall of 1840; B, Place de la Bastille; C, Cité; E, Place de l'Étoile; I, Invalides; L, Louvre; M, Montmartre; N, Place de la Nation; O, Opéra; Ob, Observatory; P, Pantheon; TE, Eiffel Tower. (*The Geographical Review*)

The park-and-museum pattern of the famous Champs Elysées, from the Egyptian Needle to the Arc de Triomphe. (*French Government Tourist Office*)

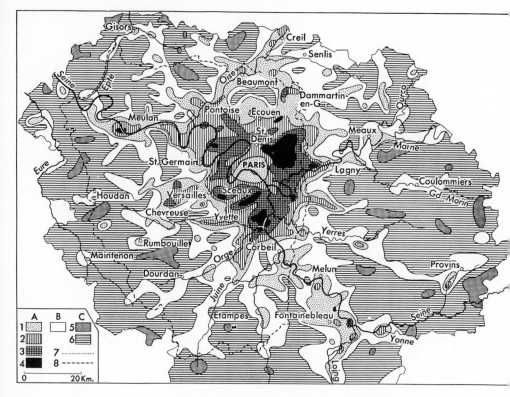

Growth of Paris from 1876 to 1936, a period of rapid industrialization.

Shades A indicate areas that have increased: A-1, from 25 to 100 percent; A-2, from 100 to 400 percent; A-3, from 400 to 1000 percent; A-4, more than ten times.

Shade B (in white) indicates stable population; that is, less than 24 percent increase or less than 10 percent decrease.

Shades C indicate decrease of population: C-5 decrease of 10 to 40 percent; C-6 decrease of more than 40 percent.

All figures indicate the changes in 1936 compared with the population in 1876. Observe the rapid expansion of the urban zone and the tentacles advancing along the main waterways and railways. *(Libraire Armand Colin)*

economy of the period 1920–1950, and the French Parliament adopted a series of measures aimed at limiting the development and encouraging new building in Paris and its immediate suburbs, where the over-all density of population reached 30,000 per square mile in 1962 — as compared with 15,600 per square mile in London and Middlesex counties, which aggregate an equivalent population, or 25,000 per square mile for New York City. It has only been from 1955 on that active building in and around Paris has developed with support from government funds, and the metropolitan region has expanded by leaps and bounds.

The French authorities feel, with reason, that Paris has much to preserve that belongs to the architectural treasures of Western civilization, and that stringent regulation must be applied to make sure that the coming expansion neither spoils the landscape nor devours too much of the valuable farmland that surrounds the present urban district. Here again the museum curator's state of mind may induce excessive caution, stifling proper action; for Paris would not have become a marvel of urban design without the ruthless renewal and redevelopment projects that followed the plans of Le Notre and Mansart in the seventeenth century or of Haussmann in the nineteenth. Not everything in today's Paris is worth preserving and some sections of the city, especially to the east, need a good deal of slum clearance. The office industry has not been able to develop as fast as it should for lack of space and restrictions on new office buildings in the center of town: what could not find space there did not go to French provincial cities, none of which offered the necessary organization; instead, the restrictions imposed in Paris benefited such international centers as Geneva, Brussels, and even Amsterdam and Frankfurt. In 1960 the policy toward Parisian development on the part of the French government and Parliament began to change: new plans for renewal of the central city and the rapid expansion of the suburbs were approved; the first large skyscraper was authorized; the central market of Les Halles, which redistributes food supplies to a good third of the French nation, was scheduled to be moved from the center of the city to peripheral locations; and a new urban district was recognized by law in 1961 to facilitate metropolitan administration.

In recent years, the suburban expansion has been impressive, and entire new cities quite comparable to the English "new towns" have been rising along the major valleys or railroads within a fifty-mile radius of the central business district of Paris. Most of the new housing, however, consists of large groups of high-rise apartment buildings, rather than of one-family detached units. This saves space, materials, and funds. The outer ring of the metropolitan region is still well provided with recreational space owing to the national forests that remain around the former royal and lordly palaces and châteaux (such as Versailles, Fontainebleau, St. Germain, Chantilly, Rambouillet) and today serve as public parks. On the plateaus surrounding Paris is still found the best soil and most intensive farming in the country, and this rural space must be defended against too much suburban encroachment for economic as well as for social and esthetic reasons.

Legislation restricting the growth of Paris may have caused more chaos and congestion in the metropolitan region, but it did not prevent growth. As it became obvious that more urbanization was to come, purely restrictive policies were abandoned in the 1960s and a new policy of a more constructive character, prevailed; it aimed at providing for future

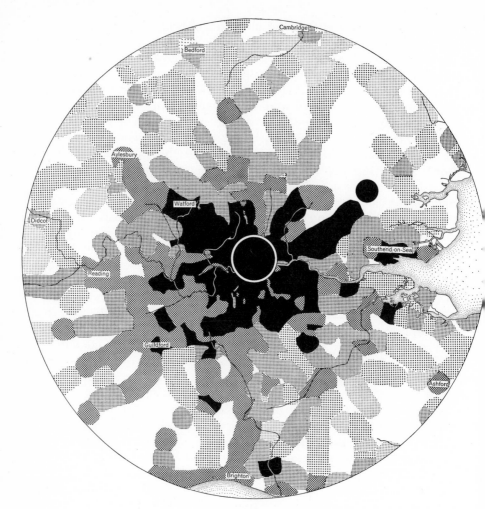

## LONDON

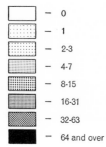

Number of trains per 16- hour "day"

- — 0
- — 1
- — 2-3
- — 4-7
- — 8-15
- — 16-31
- — 32-63
- — 64 and over

Frequency of passenger-train service for London *(above)* and Paris *(opposite)*. From David Neft, "Some aspects of rail commuting: New York, London, and Paris," *The Geographical Review,* vol. 41, 1959, pp. 151–163.

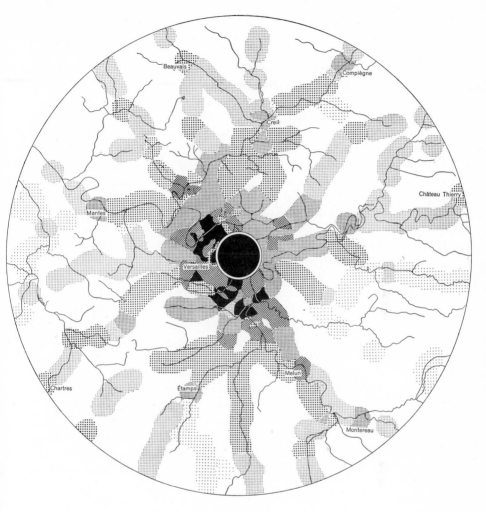

**PARIS**

MILES

The inner circle is the area within
5 miles of the center of the city

growth in an orderly, planned, and publicized fashion. The new law of 1961 authorized a new metropolitan type of regional government. What was first called the "district," then "region" of Paris, was defined to include the former three departments of Seine, Seine-et-Oise, and Seine-et-Marne. To facilitate local administration, the former two departments were replaced by a new redistricting, creating seven smaller departments, one of which coincides with the city of Paris proper. The whole *region* of Paris, an area of 4,700 square miles, inhabited by 9.5 million people (according to the census of 1968) was put under the authority of a Regional Prefect, assisted and supervised by a Regional Council, to provide planning, coordination, and enforcement thereof at the regional level.

The first head of the new metropolitan region was appointed in the fall of 1962. In 1965, he submitted a master plan for his region, to direct its growth and redevelopment until the end of the twentieth century. It was a comprehensive plan, attempting to forecast the growth of the whole as well as its diverse functional and geographical aspects; it aroused a great deal of discussion; hearings about it were held first by the Regional Council, and then by the French Parliament. A large and detailed atlas of the Paris region was prepared, under the aegis of the metropolitan authority, to inform all concerned about the available data and the regional trends. By 1968, implementation of the master plan had begun. This plan (called *Schema Directeur*) foresaw that the population of the region would rise to about 14 million in the 1990s. During this growth, the purchasing capacity of the population was expected to increase fivefold, the consumption of services sixfold, the number of motor cars threefold (reaching 5 million); the number of housing units should be doubled, therefore, in the next thirty-five years; floor space for housing use should be multiplied by four, for industrial use by two, and for office use by three.

Such growth in the very limited area could not be allowed to develop without strict and careful regulations as to where the various new equipment would be located. Only then could the various services be provided that would be required for traffic and transportation, proper water supply and sewage, schools, and other amenities. The essential expression of the master plan was a large-scale map setting forth the pattern of the development anticipated; the usual radial distribution of new towns was abandoned in favor of two main east-west axes along which habitat and economic activities would be concentrated, one of the axes passing to the north of the present conurbation and the other to the south of it; both would converge westward toward the valley of the Seine downstream from Paris, and it was suggested in the master plan that further growth beyond the present limits of the metropolitan district be concentrated in a corridor along the lower Seine, from the Paris region toward the sea, a corridor already marked by a number of towns and cities, particularly Rouen and Le Havre. Along the two axes concentrating the suburban growth, half a dozen sites were chosen for the development at each of them of a new satellite city of a size varying between 250,000 and 500,000 residents. Each of these new cities was to be planned under supervision of the regional authority to have enough economic function and a large enough central business district to serve a total population of at least a million in its own sector of the metropolitan area. Cities and sectors of such size should have a large enough local market to create actual decentralization from the far-too-congested center of Paris, which presently serves a population of more than 8 million besides functioning as a national and international center. The first satellite city in this category, to be located at Evry, to the south of Paris, was started in 1967.

This metropolitan-region experiment will be interesting to watch. No other urban district of comparable size in the free world has yet been endowed with a similar governmental unity and a master plan. The plan recognizes the need to provide for unavoidable urban expansion; this had been disregarded by all the previous legislation, which aimed at decentralization, limiting growth—as if a city such as Paris could remain indefinitely the size it had achieved, say, by 1960.

In many ways, Paris has outgrown the limits of France. In the whole of Europe only London and Moscow are metropolitan centers of comparable size and influence. For many centuries, it has played a leading cultural role on the continent. The great city is extremely well situated, in the middle of the Atlantic façade of Europe and in a rather central position in the EEC. The central headquarters of the EEC and of NATO are now in Brussels, and traffic between Brussels and Paris, mainly by rail, is intense. The mass-media market for French-speaking peoples is still heavily concentrated in Paris, which is perhaps, after New York, the largest international market of artistic talent. It cannot claim, nowadays, an economic or financial part as great as those of Moscow or London, but it is still the largest center in this category within the EEC. Despite the ordeals of the past, a troubled history, and a revolutionary tradition, Paris has kept its reputation for charm and taste, for a free and beautiful mode of living that has often been described in literature. The visitor often thinks of it as an artistic center set up for tourists. It is, in fact, a large concentration of hard-working, conservative masses of people who distrust in general change and luxury but have a traditional liking for spectacular events and a long-standing tradition of artistic perfectionism in daily work. Since the huge operation of urban renewal conducted in 1852–1868 by Baron Georges Eugène Haussmann, when a beautiful city was rebuilt with multistoried apartment buildings organized for expensive middle-class living, the central city has been in Paris the best residential part of the metropolitan system. Haussmann aimed, on the morrow of the revolution of 1848, to push the working crowds and the new industrial development to the periphery of the metropolitan area, farther away from the centers of power and wealth located in the historic core. He succeeded, and a century later the distribution of functions in the Paris region still reflects this planning. It gives to the growth of Paris, which is, in this respect, similar to that of many other large European cities, a general pattern very different from the American urban pattern of growth in this century. The concentration of the better elements of services in the old core has led to a widespread desire among all the inhabitants of the region to live as close to the center as possible. In the suburbs more high-rise, massive apartment buildings have been built recently than was authorized in the city proper. The conurbation has thus developed with a concave profile, achieving high residential density.

Further growth needed, indeed, new ideas in planning and design. The master plan of 1965 may have provided for the orientation needed. There is no doubt that Paris will continue adding people and economic activities, although the latter will be more in the category of services than in manufacturing production. But Paris is not the only large metropolis to flourish in France. A good deal of metropolitan development is occurring in other parts of the country, particularly in the south.

## THE FRENCH ECONOMIC STRUCTURE

Among the Western European countries, France has a wide reputation for economic stability. She has survived many crises with less reduction of the standard of living; unemployment in the 1930s, even the food shortage after World War II were on the whole less prolonged than in other neighboring countries. What could be termed the "elasticity" of French production is partly based on the size of the territory (212,000 square miles) and its variety—interior and coastal plains, low and high ranges of mountains, Atlantic and Mediterranean climates—but the principal factor is still human stability.

First of all, France was formed into a national unit many centuries ago and matured earlier than other European nations. As a way of conserving resources and as a way of life, the population figure was kept relatively stable: about 20 million people in 1700, 27 million in 1800, 39 in 1900, 50 in 1968. The increase was much slower than in most of the European countries; since 1900 the density of the French population has come up from 190 to 230 per square mile, remaining close to the average for Western Europe. Thus France has more agricultural resources per head of population than most of its neighbors. These rural riches are of course largely man-made and capable of further improvement or expansion. The stabilization of the number of people was due to a common unwritten decision to distribute the national income among a not-too-large group. Developing this income was thus certain to increase everyone's share. Parents wanted their children to have at least as good a life as they had and believed that the best way to do it was to keep down the number. The natural increase was thus very slow, and France was bled white during World War I; a wave of immigration helped to maintain some stability between the two World Wars. After 1940, for the first time in centuries, the French felt insecure; the common man and the government agreed that population figures had to be increased, that youth was needed, and that children were perhaps the best possible investment, even better than shares of Russian railways or Suez Canal. In the period 1946–1960 a natural increase by excess of births over deaths gave France 300,000 more people annually, despite the difficult material conditions of the postwar period.

This demographic change brought momentous shifts in the French economy. The age pyramid of the nation had an unusual shape by 1960: the low natality of the years 1914–1944, underscored by the deficit years of the two World Wars, gave France a population more massive than usual in the children and old-age sectors, while the sector of productive age (20 to 64 year old) was reduced to 56 percent of the total, instead of the 59–60 percent as it was in the years 1920–1940. A heavier burden fell on a smaller labor force; in the ages above 40, women outnumbered men. But the gradient of change in the future is going to be steep: the natural increase of the population stood at 357,000 in 1964 and 325,000 in 1965. The more numerous generation born after 1946 reached the age to enter the labor force in the middle 1960s. In fact, the total civilian labor force remained approximately stabilized around 18.8 million from 1954 to 1962, two census years in France. But since 1963, the labor force has increased, reaching 19.2 million in 1964 and 19.7 in 1965. The stability of the labor force in 1954–1962 was maintained owing to the importation of foreign manpower; there were 1.8 million foreigners living in France in 1962 (650,000 Italians, 430,000 Spaniards, 69,000 American citizens, etc.) and 335,000 Algerian Moslems then enjoying French citizenship. After 1962, the labor force expanded owing to the immigration of Frenchmen of European stock from Algeria, and also through absorption of the more numerous young generation into the labor force. The annual number of French people reaching the age of 20 remained around 500,000 until 1965, but rose to 750,000 by 1967, and is expected to remain above that figure every year until 1985.

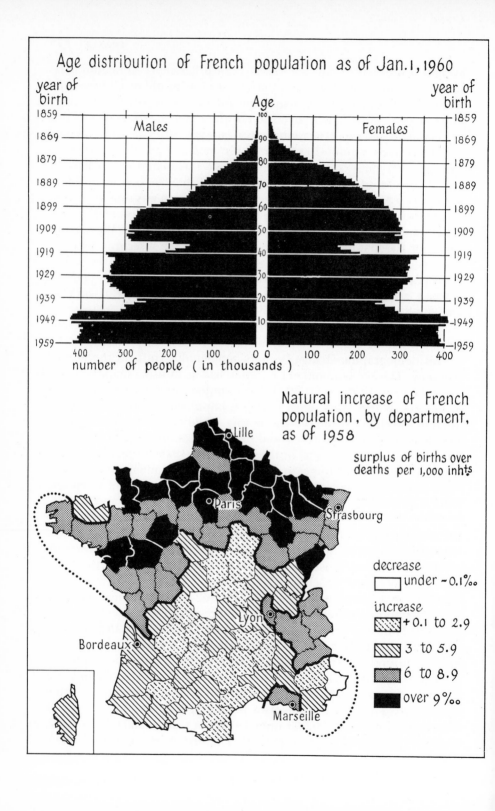

# Age distribution of French population as of Jan.1,1960

year of birth

Males

Age

Females

year of birth

1859 — 1859
1869 — 1869
1879 — 1879
1889 — 1889
1899 — 1899
1909 — 1909
1919 — 1919
1929 — 1929
1939 — 1939
1949 — 1949
1959 — 1959

100
90
80
70
60
50
40
30
20
10
0

400   300   200   100   0   0   100   200   300   400

number of people ( in thousands )

## Natural increase of French population, by department, as of 1958

Lille

Paris

Strasbourg

surplus of births over deaths per 1,000 inhts

Lyon

Bordeaux

Marseille

decrease
☐ under ~0.1‰

increase
▨ +0.1 to 2.9

▨ 3 to 5.9

▨ 6 to 8.9

■ over 9‰

Even if immigration had stopped by 1966, which was not the case, natural increase alone would bring the French total population to about 54 million people by 1980; with a net balance of total migration projected from the recent past, 2 million more could be added.

In the 1960s, therefore, the nation's economy is acquiring a momentum that it has not known for at least a century. If present projections hold true, France will be, in the 1970s, one of the fastest-growing countries of Europe in terms of both population and employment. This expansion is not developing, however, along the same occupational lines or along the same geographical pattern as it did in the past.

The distribution of the demographic increase is variable; the major difference is to be found north and south of a line running from Nantes to Dijon; in the south, the more urbanized regions of the southeast (around Marseille, Lyon, Grenoble, and in Savoy) are the more fertile, though the Riviera, with its high proportion of retired people, is a negative pole, as is most of the Massif Central (see p. 374). Thus the differences between north and south will sharpen, all the more so as the north has shown greater propensity to accelerate its rhythm of urbanization and industrialization in recent years. To this regional differentiation is being added another, less well realized in the country itself, between east and west on the two sides of a line approximately followed by the railway from Calais to Paris, Lyon, and Marseille. East of that line industrialization and urbanization have picked up much faster than in the largely stagnant west. In fact, most of the large industries of France have been for some time in that eastern part, and economic policies have favored it for at least eighty years; the northern industrial basin, the metallurgy of Lorraine, the commercial interests of Lyon and Marseille — and more recently of Strasbourg, Grenoble, and Nice — the rapid industrial and tourist development of the Alps and the Riviera have all been pulling the country's center of gravity eastward, balanced only by the growth of the Paris region. Since 1957 the position of the eastern provinces closer to the other members of the Common Market has attracted there a greater number of the new establishments that aim at more than just the French consumer. Though a few cities in the west have shown good progress, especially Rennes with its new automobile industry, Toulouse with airplane building, and the area of Lacq with its natural gas wells, most of western France seems underdeveloped compared to the eastern provinces.

Such a difference may also be noticed on the map of agriculture (p. 322), which is more stable than the map of industry. Although here, too, the more striking contrast is between north and south, there is some difference between east and west: the west has more small farms of a marginal type. Still, French agriculture has been evolving at a relatively rapid pace: the basic change is in the steadily increasing yields and productivity, especially on the larger farms. The agricultural output has been rising and producing substantial surpluses, not only for wine, a traditional French specialty, but also for wheat (over 10 million tons annually in the years 1957–1966, and 14.2 in 1965, making France share with Canada the third rank among producers of wheat, after the USSR and the U.S.A.), barley (over 6 million tons a year), corn (2 to 4 million tons chiefly in the southwest), sugar beets (11 to 17 million tons), and even rice (a heavily protected crop of the Camargue, about 130,000 tons a year). Livestock has multiplied too, counting in 1965 20.6 million heads of cattle, 9 million sheep, and 9.2 million pigs: livestock had increased by about 20 percent in the 1950s. The production of fodder and hay on one hand, of milk, butter, cheese, and meat on the other have followed the same trend; by 1960 France claimed to be the largest producer of foods of animal origin in Europe, second only to the United States in the rest of the world. Despite the high level of the people's consumption of such foods, the country had, of course, large exportable surpluses, and was capable of producing still larger quantities once the trend toward larger farms using more scientific and mechanized methods of farming could be accelerated.

That such an acceleration is needed there is little doubt. The small farmers who own their lands used to be the backbone of French politics. They elected to Parliament the middle-of-the-roaders who commanded the balance between the more extreme parties of Right and Left usually elected in the more industrialized areas and in the cities. In 1956 there still were 2,268,000 farms in France, only 21 percent of which had more than 50 acres of nonwooded land, though they cultivated 60 percent of the farmed area. By 1967, the number of farms had dropped to 1.7 million, of which 30 percent had more than 50 acres each. During the intercensal period of 1954–1962, agricultural employment declined by 1.3 million—a decrease of one fourth of the total farm population in eight years. During the same period, manufacturing employment increased by about 300,000, and employment in the services by about a million jobs. These figures show the rapid shift occurring in the French economy from the former emphasis on farming to a new industrialized and urbanized economic structure. As usual, the decline in the number of hands employed in farming does not mean a decline but, on the contrary, a rapid increase in the quantities produced. The French farms are producing more grain and dairy products than ever; in the 1960s they have had some difficulty increasing the production of meat, especially beef, as called for by official policy. But farm modernization progresses rapidly; it must be completed soon to be able to meet the competition of the farmers of the other countries of the Common Market in the 1970s.

The greatest changes are to come in the western region, south of the Seine River, where most of the small-scale farming is still located. These trends are becoming obvious to the local people, causing some political unrest.

Postwar reconstruction was a task of considerable magnitude in France; many of the cities, especially in the northern half of the country, had been more than half destroyed (especially seaports such as Dunkirk, Calais, Boulogne, Dieppe, Le Havre, Brest, Lorient, and St. Malo; but also inland cities like Amiens, Tours, Orléans, Caen, and Rouen); bridges and railways had been wrecked; most of the industrial equipment plundered or damaged. Reconstruction therefore caused the first resurgence of activity in an economy that had been rather stagnant since the 1900s. Then came the stages of modernization and expansion spurred on by the opening up of the national borders to outside influences, goods, and competition. Besides the foods produced by domestic farms, France has substantial national resources in raw materials: about 50 million tons of coal, 20 million tons of iron (in metal content of the ore), 2.6 million tons of bauxite, large quantities of potash and salt, and small quantities of tungsten, lead, zinc, and even uranium are regularly mined; waterpower is abundant and well developed (13 million Kw, or 40 percent of total installed electric capacity); natural gas from Lacq has become important; sulphur is obtained from that gas and pyrites in large amounts. Petroleum and textile fibers are the chief deficiencies in the French economy, as well as a variety of metals of which few countries have the whole gamut. Even in the case of petroleum, France has found some in her own ground; the largest oil field is at Parentis, near Arcachon, but other wells are worked in various parts of the country, especially the recently drilled shallow wells southeast of Paris. The present output of 2.5 million tons is only 5 percent of domestic consumption and 3 percent of the country's refining capacity; petroleum products are indeed the most costly and most bulky item of French imports.

The industries of France run the whole gamut of modern manufacturing. Metallurgy is an especially important part of heavy manufacturing, as could be expected from the third iron ore producer in the world (but only the sixth steel producer, with 20 million tons in 1967) and a substantial producer of bauxite (about 420,000 tons of aluminum, mainly primary, were produced in 1967). Textiles are traditionally second among the groups of industries. They still employ about 400,000 workers; but they have been less rapidly developing than either the mechanical or the chemical industries. The automotive and airplane building industries have developed fast, although they show great sensitivity to the moods of the export markets: in 1966, France's automotive industry built 1,764,000 passenger cars and 263,000 commercial vehicles;

Cables pulling cars to high summits go through a small cloud above the Alpine resort of Chamonix in France. *(French Cultural Services)*

France was competing with Britain for fourth rank among motor car producers and for third rank among airplane producers. The chemical and electronic industries, many of them owned by or with the participation of American companies, are developing on a large scale. French manufacturers can look to a rising number of yet underequipped consumers in the domestic market, and they should develop fast in the coming decade.

However, most tariff barriers for manufactured goods have been removed in 1968 within the Common Market; competition between the various firms in the EEC is bound to grow and to exert a powerful influence on European manufacturing, inciting them to regroup themselves, to mechanize and rationalize their means of production, and, in many cases, to specialize. Few of the French manufacturing firms are yet of a size to stand up well to open international competition. Many mergers are taking place, and there is other evidence that concentration of control of industrial production is now developing. The trend may mean the concentration of large industrial plants in some areas of the country at the expense of the existing picture of relative scattering. Moreover, expansion of production will not necessarily be accompanied by an increase in the number of production workers employed by manufacturing industries. The main growth of employment, similarly to what has recently occurred in the United States and in Britain, will be found in the services and in the nonproduction sectors of manufacturing employment (managerial, technical, and clerical jobs). These growing categories of employment tend to be concentrated in a small number of select urban areas.

During the 1960s, all the regions of heavy industry, particularly the northern industrial basin around Lille and industrial Lorraine, have shown slower progress than some new locations that attracted more modern economic activities. Partly, this trend may be ascribed to the legislation decentralizing industry from the Paris region and providing incentives for it to move to the less developed areas of western and southern France. However, the main growth in both services and manufacturing has been rather localized in a few areas. The most impressive growth was the southeastern corner of France, chiefly the Mediterranean seaboard from the lower Rhone Valley to the Riviera around Nice (with spectacular electronic establishments, mainly American-owned, coming to the vicinity of the latter city). In the southeast, too, the city of Grenoble has been developing fast, acquiring several new research centers. In the southwest, Toulouse has seen spectacular progress, largely due to its airplane industry and related research.

After the results of the 1962 census were analyzed, French economic planning had to give up the wishful thinking previous legislation had expressed about the possibility of keeping the old distribution of population over the provinces, either on the farms or in smaller towns and cities. Metropolitan planning for the Paris region expressed acceptance of the idea of continuous growth for the capital and major economic metropolises of the country. At the same time it was recognized that such planning may give advantages to Paris over the rest of the country, and to prevent this it was decided to establish a new governmental bureau to foster regional planning outside the Paris region (aménagement du territoire). Besides the usual decentralization measures, this new agency applied a new concept: a few cities or conurbations were to be selected as "regional metropolises" and provided with public authorities to plan for their growth and with priorities to obtain budgetary funds and other means for execution of the plan. The actual selection of these metropolises was a hard political operation: almost every city with a population of more than 50,000 asked to become a metropolis. It was decided to limit the number of these to less than ten. A public opinion poll was conducted to find out to which city the Frenchman would prefer to move if he had to (Paris being excluded); four cities came out of this poll with much higher popularity than all the others: Nice, Grenoble, Toulouse, Rennes. This showed the public's taste for amenities and for economic dynamism: these cities had promising industrial specializations; three of them had highly reputed universities, and Nice a new young one.

Significantly, the cities finally selected as metropolises were those where the largest conurbations already existed: Lyon-St. Etienne, Marseille, Lille-Roubaix-Tourcoing, Bordeaux, Toulouse, Strasbourg, Nantes, Nancy-Metz-Thionville. Without being called a metropolis or a conurbation, the valley of the lower Seine, below Paris, with Rouen and Le Havre, was given advantages similar to those given a regional metropolis, to help prepare for its growth as an adjunct of the Paris region. These planning decisions showed that the main pressures of growth or of stagnation were expected to develop in the larger cities, which were now given some instruments to provide for their future. This experiment of officially establishing and planning for a hierarchy of cities within a large country will be worth watching.

THE INTERNATIONAL POSITION OF FRANCE

France had struck a rather "happy balance" in the elaboration of her personality: the balance between maritime and continental interests. More than any other western European power, France is continental—more than Sweden certainly, as there is some insularity about Sweden that is completely absent in France. In the hub of European structure, history, and traffic, France is deeply dependent on the continent and reacts to every European event in a lively way.

French overseas interests have always been considerable. Through her Mediterranean and Atlantic interests, France has participated in every stage of the European expansion overseas. In 1946 she was still the head of the second largest colonial empire, which had demonstrated remarkable loyalty while the French mainland was occupied by the Germans in World War II. She had assets spread over all the continents: her private interests participated in many international concerns; and a long standing tradition of world-wide cultural relations had to be upheld. For fifteen years France has been undergoing a long and painful process of divesting herself of the political and military controls she used to exercise in various parts of the world. A protracted war in Viet-Nam (1946–1954), where the French forces held a Western position against communism, was followed by another war in Algeria (1956–1962), even more painful because closer to the mainland and involving the destiny of a million French citizens, mostly born in Algeria.

Almost all the other countries of the former French empire had been granted independence, most of them remaining members of a French Community, loosely organized on the model of the British Commonwealth of Nations. A few small territories scattered around the world remained French, having become distant lands integrated in the French national and governmental unity (islands such as Martinique, Guadeloupe, Reunion, New Caledonia, Tahiti, and others in the Pacific; and French Guiana on the South American continent). To the former dependencies France was still bound to supply economic aid and skilled personnel. There was a wide area of French-speaking peoples scattered throughout the world, an important part of which was the French-speaking population of Canada.

The present French attitude is perhaps more turned toward domestic problems than it has been for a long period. The country in the hub of Western Europe is tired of so many wars, bloodsheds, and occupations. If some over-all authority could offer to France for the coming hundred years a future such as has been the destiny of Switzerland or Sweden for the past century, the French people would probably accept it with enthusiasm. They feel that their troubled past endows them with greater experience for handling human relations and assuming an intermediate and compromising position. Their geographical position puts them exactly at the heart of the present world problems. But this geographical position at the crossroads is not an asset only: the privilege carries with it great responsibilities and certain dangers.

Financially, France experienced a long period of instability and successive devaluation of her currency until 1958. Then the sharp upturn taken by the national economy helped establish a better balance of trade and payments. In fact, the French are a much richer nation than their gross national product or the international standing of the franc may indicate. A hard-working people, the French in the nineteenth century developed the habit of investing most of their savings abroad or of keeping these in the form of gold and foreign currency, which was even worse for the flow of capital in the national economy. It was said that in the 1880s cab drivers in Paris were shareholders of the Suez Canal and Panama Canal companies and bondholders of the Russian railroads and the Turkish Treasury. With the exception of Suez, these ventures did not long prove profitable to the French as a whole. Still, as long as the feeling of lack of growth and therefore of gain at home persisted, the French savings went largely to fertilize foreign grounds. It has been estimated that in the late 1950s French private holdings in the United States and Canada might be close to 15 billion dollars, and that about half of the foreign deposits in the Swiss banks, a substantial source of international credit, were French. Since 1958 some of this wealth has been repatriated, while a good deal of the gold privately held in France has come out of the stockings and washing machines where it was said to be hid. The French are acquiring some much needed confidence in their own economy.

To bolster its balance of payments, France has had "invisible exports" other than these assets abroad, so much of which were out of the official statistics and control. There is perhaps no more classic trip for foreign tourists to take than to visit France (and also Italy); about 10 million of them come annually. In recent years, however, at least as many French people have traveled to foreign countries, something seldom done before. As she establishes broader relations with the outside than she has had for a century and a half, however, France also finds herself using more foreign patents and licenses than she exports. Thus the "invisible exports," valuable as they are, may not be of as much help as one would expect to the French economy. The country has also had to bear the heavy burden of a series of colonial wars, first in Indochina, then in Algeria. Since 1963, only has France known real peace; and military expenses have still diverted substantial public funds that could have gone into the country's equipment and modernization. It may be asserted, however, that among the many changes the 1960s will bring to France, there will be also a renovated position in world politics.

After 1964, the French began showing more confidence in themselves. Enjoying peace, the economic expansion of the EEC, much American capital investment, and the first benefits of an expanding demography, they turned under the leadership of General de Gaulle into the "*enfant terrible*" of the Western World. Without formally leaving the North Atlantic Treaty Organization, France requested all foreign troops and bases to be removed from its territory. It also refused to adhere to the treaty on nonproliferation of nuclear weapons. In financial matters, it criticized the international monetary system founded on the dollar and the pound sterling as reserve currencies and insisted on a return to an international gold standard. In these several ways, the French government seemed to assume a role of leading the Western European countries, particularly those of the EEC, toward formation of an integrated European power that could stand up against American leadership. In fact, the French people have well realized, since 1940, that they are too small a nation and an economy to rank as one of the greater powers of the world. But a people that has been a great power and a leader among nations for 800 years does not give up easily. Now their hopes and plans are pinned on the slowly growing feeling and machinery for European unity. They also hope that by being more neutral they may enhance their influence in the underdeveloped world and among the East European countries which are restive in the alliance imposed upon them by the Soviet Union. Basically, however, the French know well that they are both European and Atlantic and that they have always been both.

The village of Bremgarten, Canton of Aargau. *(Official Information Bureau of Switzerland)*

# 9

## Switzerland

Switzerland is a small country (15,944 square miles) established on the watershed of the Alps, in the central part of the range. It is usually considered to be part of Central Europe, as it is on the north-south road from Germany to Italy and as its way of life has much in common with Austria and other Central European areas. But most of Switzerland is to the northwest of the Alps and to the west of the Rhine. Moreover, in its social and economic life Switzerland offers the very essence of the Western European picture; though continental and without any territorial contact with the sea, it has actively participated in and remains integrated with the overseas expansion and activities of the Western powers.

Another traditional idea explains the role of Switzerland in Europe as that of a central crossroads on the continent, due to the Alpine passes on its territory. It is indisputable that Switzerland assumed such a role several centuries ago; but it was not the physiography of the mountains that gave it this important function. The Swiss did it through a historical process in which the natural facilities were utilized to the maximum. Here once again there was no simple determinism.

### THE PERSONALITY OF SWITZERLAND

The Swiss state arose in 1291 when the three cantons of Uri, Schwyz, and Unterwalden entered into a league to defend themselves against domination by the Holy Roman Emperor, whose domain included Germany and Austria. These three cantons or *waldstätten* had developed in the valleys deep inside the mountains as autonomous rural units like the free cities of Flanders or northern Italy. The mountain, buried for a long while under the icecap and then re-covered by a dense forest, was

385

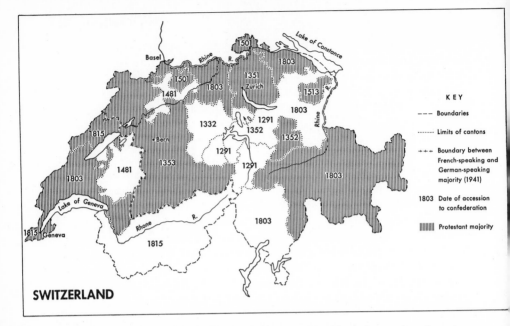

**SWITZERLAND**

K E Y

– – –  Boundaries

..........  Limits of cantons

+ + +  Boundary between
French-speaking and
German-speaking
majority (1941)

1803  Date of accession
to confederation

||||||  Protestant majority

Sketch map showing the development of the League of the Three Cantons into the present federation and the distribution of language and religious groups.

Sainte-Croix, a small town in the Swiss Jura, has a large, modern mechanical plant. This is a typical example of the scattering of Swiss industries today amid a semirural environment preserved over the centuries. *(Swiss National Tourist Office)*

penetrated and slowly occupied by settlers progressing upward, clearing bottoms and lower slopes, creating a pastoral economy that took the cattle from the lower meadows to the summer pastures of the high *alps* and down again every year. Two cultural and racial elements met here, the one coming up from the Mediterranean countries and the other from the Hercynian area dominated by the Germanic tribes – the Roman civilization with its system of law, peace and order, and the Barbarian dynamism, more attached to tribal solidarity and to fundamental freedoms of the individual. Like the Belgians in the Lowlands, the Swiss benefited by the synthesis of both influences. But these were not low-lying lands of easy traffic; they were a lofty and yet little-known mountainous range with a few passes between the valleys.

A central knot in the structure and in the hydrographic network of the Central Alps is the St. Gotthard massif from which deep valleys radiate in all directions, leading toward the major valleys and waterways of Europe. Here the Rhine, the Rhone, and the Ticino rivers have their springs and start to flow toward Germany, France, and Italy. The St. Gotthard Pass establishes easy communication between the north and south slopes. A road through the water tower of Europe, this pass was the keystone of trans-Alpine communications, and the approaches to this pass were held by the League of the Three Cantons, which in 1332–1353 was joined by several more cantons: Lucerne, the town at the entrance of the large valley; Zurich and Bern, larger cities, ruling the foothills and controlling the eastwest route that followed the foot of the high range; Glarus and Zug, neighbors in the hills. Thus in the middle of the fourteenth century unity was achieved in a small territory, where city and rural groups cooperated to maintain freedom at a major crossroads.

Among other principles, the Swiss League guarded the freedom of communications from north to south and from east to west in a feudal Europe, where lords ransacked or held for ransom the caravan trade across the continent, where the royal and imperial authorities had begun to strengthen themselves by taxing whoever was under their domination, and where most of the important trade was in the hands of free cities or guilds, claiming autonomy from these feudal or sovereign controls: Venice, Genoa, the Lombard bankers in the south, the cities of the Rhine, Flanders, or of the Hansa in the north. Holding the keystone to the communications in the area where they were the more difficult, therefore, was another free League, built on the same principle.

Difficulty of approach was instrumental in bringing early independence to the Swiss, for certainly they would have had much more difficulty in achieving and maintaining it had their country been flat and open. Switzerland was erected on a solidarity of valleys and slopes and on isolation as much as on through traffic. The other routes across the

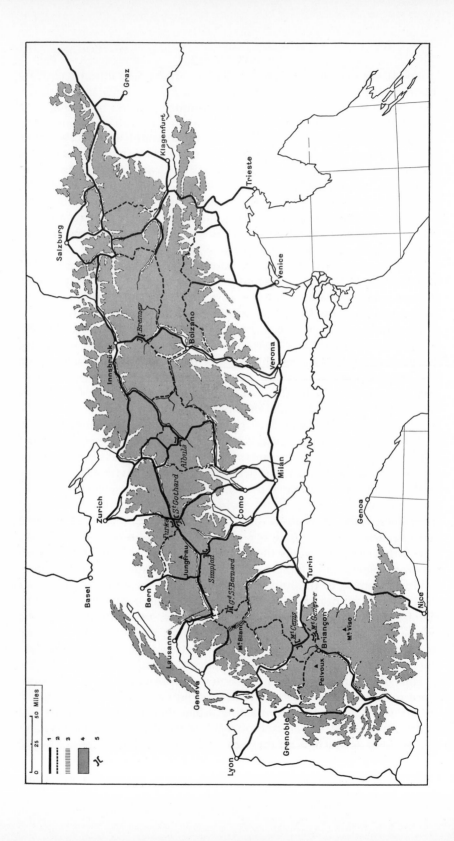

Salzburg · Graz · Klagenfurt · Trieste · Venice · Brenner · Bolzano · Verona · Innsbruck · Zurich · Albula · Milan · St Gothard · Como · Jungfrau · Furka · Genoa · Bern · Simplon · Turin · Nice · Basel · Lausanne · Gd St Bernard · Mt Blanc · Mt Cenis · Mt Genèvre · Mt Viso · Briançon · Pelvoux · Geneva · Lyon · Grenoble

0  25  50 Miles

1
2
3
4
5

Alps were also much traveled: the Mt. Cenis Pass between the French and Italian Alps, leading from Turin to Savoy and Lyon, was very important and was perhaps easier to travel than the series of passes in the Swiss Alps. But in the nineteenth century, the Swiss gained full advantage when they invested the considerable capital saved through centuries of trade and manufacturing in a network of railways and tunnels that is without competition in the Alpine belt and even throughout Europe. Because of this gigantic work, Switzerland became the hub of European communications, or more exactly a plexus, for it was not centered but consisted of an intricate network.

This small federation also quickly gained the respect of the world. In the beginning of the sixteenth century, treaties with France and Austria guaranteed perpetual peace and neutrality, but the fighting spirit of the Swiss was not extinguished: the country furnished renowned soldiers to form elite guards for many neighbors, particularly the French kings and the Popes whose Swiss guard polices the Vatican. Every time war has developed close to its boundaries Switzerland has strengthened the defense of its borders and called men into its army. Even during World War II, the Swiss endeavored to demonstrate their readiness to defend their land dearly. Again the topography is a solid foundation for the tradition of freedom, but it would not be worth much without the determination of the people.

This same determination to live together in peace is demonstrated by the fact that, while four languages are spoken on four different slopes within Switzerland, linguistic variety has not wrecked the national unity over the centuries. In Central Europe the linguistic map has been transferred to a racial map, and national unities or minorities have put their languages at the basis of their solidarity. Linguistic tolerance and the possibility of different cultures coexisting without national stratification and disputes is an essentially Western concept: in Switzerland in 1960, 69.3 percent of the population was German-speaking, 18.9 percent French-speaking, 9.5 percent Italian-speaking, and some 0.9 percent spoke Romansh. The official language of nineteen cantons is German, of five, French; in Ticino it is Italian and in Grisons (Graubünden), Romansh. And this variety survives in one of the oldest and best-welded

---

*(Opposite)* Pattern of trans-Alpine traffic. Key: 1, itineraries followed by railway and highway; 2, itineraries followed by highway only; 3, highway tunnel under Mont Blanc opened in 1965; another such tunnel is under the Grand St. Bernard; 4, areas above 3200 feet altitude (that is, over 1000 meters); 5, main passes used by modern trans-Alpine traffic (whether on the surface or through tunnels). Highways of secondary importance for trade traffic are disregarded; they were never important trade routes. The highway in the French Alps from Briançon to Nice is an example; it is more intra-Alpine than trans-Alpine. Such intra-Alpine highways have been built for strategic and tourist purposes in many parts of the French and Swiss Alps.

nations of Europe. Similarly, the people are not all of one faith: 53 percent are Protestant and 46 percent Roman Catholic. Although there is
some geographical concentration of each faith, there is also interpenetration, and in the canton of Geneva, John Calvin's citadel, the Protestants account for only 51 percent. Each Swiss is strongly attached to his
faith, his language, and his canton, yet all live happily together within
the national frame without much difficulty—few people have such an
art and skill in compromise and balance maneuvering as do Swiss politicians. The country has a well-knit personality, sharply differentiated
from all its neighbors, but founded on a combination of isolationism and
cosmopolitanism. It is unique indeed.

## THE ALPS, THE PIEDMONT CORRIDOR, AND THE RHINE

Switzerland is a mountain country. The Alps take up three fifths of the
territory, and the rest is occupied by low hills of the Alpine piedmont
or of the southern and eastern rim of the Jura. The structure of the
Alpine ridges is perhaps more complicated but better studied here than
elsewhere. This central part of the arch is the most fractured by tectonic dislocations, the most violently sculpted by glaciers and streams.
Here the crests, towering to more than 10,000 feet with their glaciers
and snowfields, come close to the range's edge. In many places the slopes
draining toward the North Sea and those draining toward the Mediterranean are not separated by high walls. The range is only eighty miles
wide between Lucerne and Lugano. Folds have piled up one on the
other, and few depressions are left between the synclines. Valleys following the axis of folding are few and short; but transversal valleys have
developed widely, penetrating deep into the ranges with the help of a
tremendously active erosion.

After the glaciers melted, the outline of this network of valleys opened
the way for flora and fauna species deep inside the range. The network
helps the exchange of air between heights and bottoms, creating a regular alternation of breezes as along a seashore; it also channels the
southern wind, called *foehn*, brings air masses from the warm Mediterranean, heated and dried by the descending movement on the northern
slope. Here the foehn accelerates the thaw of snow and ice, the flow of
rivers, and the ripening of the harvests. The outline of the transversal
valleys also led men deep into the range and opened the way toward the
passes.

The glaciers contributed a great deal to this "opening" of the mountain, although the main flow of the ice tongues must have followed a
pattern already set by fractures or fluvial erosion long before the Ice
Age. The imprint of glaciers is present everywhere through the digging
in the mountain and the moraines in the piedmont. Over-digging by

the glaciers at the outlet of the valleys led to the formation of the famous sub-Alpine lakes, adding more beauty and variety to the landscape. Elsewhere the bottom of the valleys was filled with fertile alluvium. Vast snowfields or glaciers still crown many summits; their lower level varies with orientation and glaciers expand more easily in the northeastern section where the Jura no longer screens the Alps from the northwestern winds bringing moisture. Orientation and screening vary the climate considerably: nowhere is the habitat more sensitive to the shadows projected by the high crests on the lower lands; nowhere does one observe so rapid an increase of aridity as the valleys penetrate inside the range and are sheltered from the circulation of outside air.

There are thus two main regions in the Swiss Alps: the northern outside front region and the internal region of which the axis is the deep depression followed by the upper courses of the Rhone and Rhine. The northern front has a complicated structure that favored the irregular design of the valleys that break it up. The penetration is particularly easy in the central part around Lake Lucerne—that is, around the Four Cantons, for the first four members of the Helvetic League were disposed around the lake. To the northeast the mountain is less high but more massive; the Säntis dominates the scenery, rising to 8200 feet, a common altitude in the central section. To the southwest the scenery has been affected by an unusual development of narrow valleys, following the axis of the folds and emptying by narrow gorges into the much wider and much lower transversal valleys. These two tiers of valleys, and therefore of settlements, are the result of the glacial overdeepening of the main channels. The same glacial action has strewn all the valleys with lakes reflecting the steep cliffs and snowy heights that surround them. In summer the whole area is a symphony of shades of green with a few white touches along the crests: the deep green of the woods, the clear green of the meadows, the blue-green of the lakes and streams, and a light sky that also varies from green to blue. The variety of the scenery in the different sections of this Alpine front has made it a famous tourist attraction in Europe. Few areas in the world have been endowed with such great comfort and facilities for visitors—the Swiss are past masters at getting the maximum out of their splendid land.

But crowds of tourists in summer as well as in winter (about 5 million of them annually) should not make us forget the other aspects of the Swiss economy that have provided some of the means to achieve such an organization of the area. Agricultural pursuits are centered on dairy cattle, as meadows in the valleys and tiers of pastures on the slopes provide the grass and hay. It is a very modern and scientific pastoral life, making full use of the local resources as well as of those offered by modern technique and science. Industrial techniques also have spread among the farmers who have had long periods of enforced leisure during the winter, especially at higher altitudes and in the northeastern section where the snowfall is heavier. Textile fibres and articles of wood are most frequently worked, but the area of St. Gallen and Appenzell is well known for its linens and laces. Recently these industries have been integrated. Waterpower brought more industrial possibilities to the mountains, but their economic life has to be considered as a whole, for there is no real break between the northern front and the internal Alpine regions.

The internal section of higher and more massive mountains takes on a majesty and a grandeur of landforms quite different from the more delicately chiseled outside rim. Sharp contrasts shape both the wild, inaccessible heights and the wide-open, verdant, densely settled bottoms of the main valleys. Nature is grandiose but violent amid the lofty peaks and crests with their glaciers, snowfields, and stormy winds. The height, mass, and power of the Alpine range reaches its climax in the St. Gotthard knot, a hub of tectonic efforts as well as a water tower in the hydrographic network. The Jungfrau is the most famous and most frequently visited summit of the massif, but many others average 13,500 feet. This is a resistant block of such proportions that it can be likened only to the Mont Blanc massif in the north of the French Alps, but the St. Gotthard has been more strongly sculptured by erosion. Still the pass through it has some narrow gorges that have long frightened travelers. Other ranges radiating between the major valleys around the St. Gotthard also are high and bulky, although they do not achieve such mass or such a towering position. Formidable escarpments overlook the valleys penetrating inside the heart of the range.

The Valais, followed by the upper Rhone, is the widest and richest of these valleys, and its rich soils are intensively cultivated. Sunshine is abundant where the shadow of the slopes does not extend too often; the climate shows a trend to aridity in this well-sheltered trough and can be very warm in summer. Fruit trees, vines, and vegetables are the chief crops; grains and meadows are important too, but in many parts irrigation has to be practiced during spring and summer. Every alluvial fan has its village or little town to which hydroelectricity brings some industrialization, especially metallurgical works (aluminum). The cattle go up and down the steep slopes according to the season, with a greater range in altitude and variety in pastures than on the northern front ranges. Here are famous mountain resorts such as Crans, Montana, and Saas-Fee. North of the St. Gotthard, the Rhine, flowing in a direction opposite to the Rhone's, continues the central furrow. Its valley, less deep and wide, is interrupted in several places by recent enormous landslides down the steep slopes. The river has cut narrow gorges across them, especially across the enormous mass that slid down at Flims. Here

Amid the Swiss peaks. In winter crowds come from all over Europe to ski on the snow-clad slopes near St. Moritz in the upper Engadine. *(Swiss National Tourist Office)*

No effort is too great to till a field atop a precipice, and old-fashioned farming goes on near fashionable resorts such as St. Moritz. *(Official Information Bureau of Switzerland)*

grains, cattle, and timber from the forests are the main resources. More valleys stretch to the south and east of the median depression; a network of high basins and narrow valleys, interconnected by gorges, has developed in the resistant crystalline rocks of the high ranges to the east. A poorer agriculture of rye and potatoes and the raising of beef cattle predominate in this higher world of the upper Inn River, which flows down to the Danube, or in the Grisons. The tourist business has revived this country around centers such as Davos and St. Moritz. Finally southward, the Ticino River flows toward the River Po and the Adriatic Sea. The valley here is much lower, sunny, dry, and the Mediterranean influence predominates, replacing the steep-roofed wooden houses with high stone buildings. Vines, almonds, and fig trees, with the olive tree and fields of corn, tell of another world, adding to the infinitely varied beauty of the small but well-organized Switzerland.

There are no large cities in the Swiss Alps. The largest, Lucerne (75,000), is already in the piedmont at the extremity of its lake valley, and other main urban centers are tourist towns like Interlaken and Zermatt, with populations that are mainly seasonal. A few places have expanded owing to some industry—Sion in the Valais or Chur and Schwyz. None of them has over 30,000 inhabitants. The bulk of the Swiss population and industries has been concentrated in the sub-Alpine corridor to which a steady flow of emigration from the mountains carries still more men.

This sub-Alpine corridor extends from southwest to northeast between the foot of the Alpine ranges on one hand, and the edge of the Jura and the Rhine on the other. This is a land of damp low hills and rolling depressions, with many swift-flowing rivers, of which the Aar, a tributary of the Rhine and also coming from the St. Gotthard knot, is the main collector. Many lakes of elongated shape dot the corridor; the two largest are at its two extremities: Lake Geneva to the southwest and the Lake of Constance (or Boden See) to the northeast. Glacial erosion and accumulation shaped this sub-Alpine gutter, and men settled here early, but the main function of the area in ancient time was the transit from Central Europe into eastern France. Clearing and drainage were performed in the Middle Ages, and now this region supports a density of population of about 800 to the square mile. It is still very picturesque, with small rounded hillocks capped with woods, fields and vineyards along the sunny slopes, meadows in the bottoms, interesting wooden villages scattered in the folds of the land, and many large cities, richly studded with historical monuments and kept clean in a way that seems almost incredible to the Westerner as well as to the Southerner.

Most of the corridor has a rather damp and severe climate, for the continentality of the depression, opened chiefly toward the north and northeast, is felt. Green, blue, and gray shades make up the often-

Rural scene in the mountains. *(Official Information Bureau of Switzerland)*

Settlements in relation to the noonday shadow areas at the winter solstice in a portion of the upper Rhone valley, Canton of Valais. Black patches or points indicate villages or scattered farms. *(The Geographical Review)*

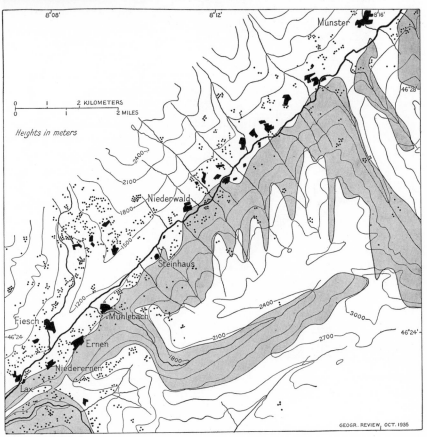

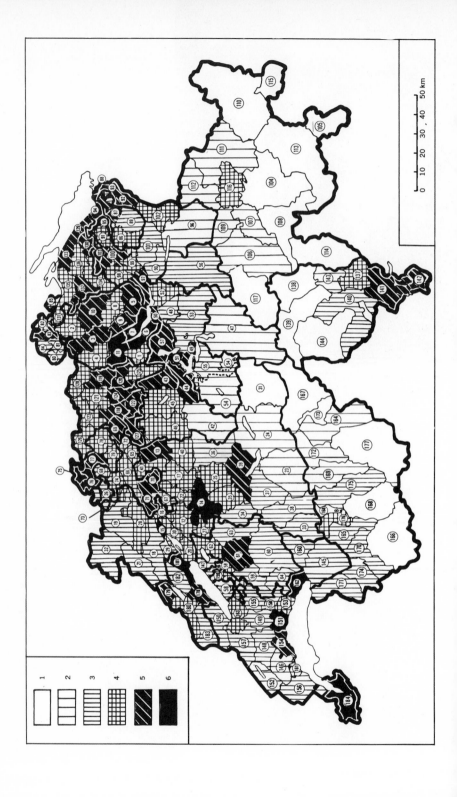

attractive scenery. But it is quite a shock to get out of the tunnel of Chexbres, the small ridge separating the grasslands of Fribourg from Lake Geneva—on the southern slope above the lake, the air is lighter, sunny, a pinkish coloration radiates, almost blinding the traveler used to the darker shades in the rest of the corridor. A long vineyard clothes the hills along the lake, reminding one of the French south. Here a country of Mediterranean texture and drainage comes so nearly together with another of definitely northern kind and drained to the North Sea, that the Swiss lowland appears by itself to have two orientations—the road along the foot of the Alps was, of course, an east-west one, but the route along the foot of the Jura, from Geneva to Basel, was a north-south one. Once again the crossroad's function is stressed, but independently of the Alpine passes.

Most of Swiss agriculture and some cattle-fattening activities are concentrated in these lowlands; but much more important, here are urban and industrial pursuits. The main industries are on the periphery of the depression; the country is much more rural around the old towns of Fribourg (40,000), which is proud of its old Catholic university, and Bern, the national capital. Bern is the fourth largest city of Switzerland, with 170,000 inhabitants. It lies in a green berth, surrounded by small hills, with the Aar flowing swiftly at the foot of the cliff on the edge of which stands the House of Parliament. It grew up as a crossroads, a large fair town, and the political center of the Federation. Today it is primarily a residential town, with a large diplomatic and administrative section. Although growing rapidly, Bern has kept its old quarters very much alive, with vaulted arcades along the streets and charming fountains ornamented with flowers in the midst; visitors and residents pay regular visits to the Bernese bears, ancient symbol of the canton. Few capitals are as quiet and attractive as Bern. As the Swiss economy grows, Bern also acquires a small but bustling business district; it is worried by the impact on the nation of the rise of Zurich as a dominant economic metropolis.

Extending like a pincer at the head of its narrow lake, Zurich counted 390,000 inhabitants in 1950, 500,000 by 1965; the city, with its suburbs, is not far from amassing one sixth of the Swiss nation. What is more important in a country founded on a principle of decentralization,

---

(*Opposite*) Population density of Switzerland, 1960, by administrative districts. Notice the concentrations in the northern corridor between the Alps and the Rhine and around the main cities, particularly Zurich. Key: 1, less than 60 inhabitants per square mile; 2, from 61 to 125 inhabitants per square mile; 3, 126 to 250; 4, 251 to 500; 5, 501 to 1250; 6, over 1250. (George Lobsiger and Société de Geographie de Geneve; after the map in "Quelques aspects de la population suisse," *Globe*, Geneva, no. 166, 1966)

This old section of Zurich along the left bank of the Limmat River serves as a picturesque façade for one of the busiest and wealthiest central business districts in the world. The Swiss have been able to preserve old framework and quaint charm in the center of their economic metropolis. The city extends far beyond the limits of the photograph into the valleys behind the wooded ridges. *(Swiss National Tourist Office)*

the commercial and banking growth of Zurich overshadows any other in Switzerland: its stock exchange and insurance companies begin to rule the market. Winterthur (90,000) looks like a distant suburb of Zurich. By an evolution similar to that of Mulhouse, Zurich started with a cotton-goods trade, acquired cotton manufacturing, and passed on to machinery building. Some of the largest and best factories making delicate precision machinery, engines, turbines, railroad equipment, and electrical engineering are at Zurich or near by. Winterthur adds leatherware and shoemaking to engineering and cotton. This concentration has ruined the textiles spread through the Alpine farms and has even shrunk the activities of St. Gallen (75,000), which manufactures linen and laces. Zurich is also an important center of learning, and its Polytechnicum is one of the most famous engineering schools in Europe. It is indeed a kind of metropolis in Switzerland. Its growth was enormous in the period from 1850 to 1910, when the population rose from 35,000 to 192,000. Growth began again in 1925 – and now the other cantons are worried: the canton of Zurich had over one million people in 1966, while the next in population size, Bern, had less on four times as much land, and the third, Vaud, counted only 488,000. The growth of Zurich and Bern is largely responsible for the increased weight acquired by the German-speaking element in the Federation.

The other main towns and industrial areas are located along the edge of the Jura. In the northwestern corner of the country, at the elbow of the Rhine, where the great river becomes navigable, and at a point where France and Germany touch, Basel was erected, the second city (240,000) and industrial center of Switzerland. Rock salt deposits had led to early chemical works, but the determining factors were the fairs and the trade of the Gate of Burgundy. With textile work spreading in the Vosges on one side and developing in Switzerland on the other, Basel started to make dyes. It is the capital of the Swiss chemical industry, especially of dyes and pharmaceutical products (it is the home of the firms *Ciba* and *Hoffman-La Roche*). Textiles, particularly silk, and machinery are fairly well represented. Basel is at the head of the Rhine navigation and the chief port of Switzerland. About one fourth of the Swiss foreign trade goes by water – and that means through the port of Basel. A whole fleet of river boats flying the Swiss flag goes up and down the Rhine from Basel, where also were registered the ocean-going ships owned by Switzerland. The city has a whole group of satellite towns making textile goods, chemicals, and machinery: Liestal, Rheinfelden, and Olten. The influence of Basel radiates far along the Rhine, and a twilight zone is shared with Zurich near Schaffhausen (37,000), the only parcel of Swiss land north of the Rhine; there the rapids of the river have been harnessed to produce power.

At the other extremity of the Jura's border, on a famous lake over-looked by majestic Mont Blanc to the south, stands Geneva. This city was the largest in Switzerland until the middle of the nineteenth century, and today, with its 300,000 inhabitants, it has a fame and a role all out of proportion with the figures. The city of John Calvin and of many historical events, Geneva is the symbol of the international role of Swit-zerland in other fields than banking or manufacturing. Here was created the International Red Cross, and its headquarters are still here. After 1920 the city was the seat of the League of Nations; it still houses in splendid modern buildings the International Labor Office, the World Health Organization, the World Council of Churches, and the European headquarters of the United Nations. Its university and Institute of Inter-national Studies have a wide reputation. Many conferences are held here, and crowds of tourists come to a place that unites historical impor-tance with a beautiful setting. It is a lively and dynamic city, looking southward and belonging to the playgrounds of Europe; but it is also an important center of trade and the capital of Swiss watchmaking, for watches are one of the leading export specialties of the country.

Geneva has been growing very fast in recent years; by 1966 the city counted 190,000 people, and the canton, which is in fact its conurbation since the farm population represent less than one percent of the in-habitants, 310,000. With the moves toward European economic integra-tion, Geneva has acquired still another role, bringing yet more offices and new residents, for it has attracted much of the international man-agement of business conducted in several countries by industrial or financial concerns. Some one hundred American firms had their Eu-ropean offices in Geneva in 1961; the central headquarters of the EFTA were located there, Switzerland being one of the Outer Seven; and many European firms and Middle Eastern oil magnates had established an office or villa in the city or near by. As more international conferences were held, the political function of Geneva as a meeting place was also expanding; whether it was atomic armaments, Laos, or Algeria that required discussion, much of it was taking place in Geneva. The largest European nuclear research center was built in its suburbs (CERN). All these white-collar activites were giving an extraordinary momentum to Geneva's expansion; the crowding in the city caused some overflowing toward neighboring cities, especially Lausanne, only 40 minutes away by train.

The influence of Geneva is felt deeply in the folds of the Jura, which begin almost in its suburbs. There, amid a rural scenery oriented mainly toward livestock and the dairy industry—this is the country of the Swiss cheese—are the towns manufacturing the watches for the great firms centered in Geneva: La Chaux de Fonds (45,000), Neuchâtel (40,000), and Le Locle are in this French-speaking country. Here, too, farming and craftsmanship have long been associated, the small towns making the delicate mechanisms. Along the edge of the mountains, marked by long lakes, Neuchâtel and, even more, Biel (70,000) have gone into machinery building; Yverdon (15,000) makes typewriters, chocolate, and cigars.

Along the shore of Lake Geneva a string of towns developed, many of them being famous resorts: this is a Swiss riviera, in many ways similar to the French Mediterranean coast. But it is also a very Swiss country, with the trade and manufacturing to be expected. After Geneva Lausanne is the main center (140,000), built on a steep slope, very lively, a railway hub, the center of a large foodstuffs industry, and varied manufacturing. To its east stands Vevey, a small town, but the headquarters of the huge industrial and chocolate firm of Nestlé. Chocolate, like watchmaking, is a Swiss institution and Nestlé one of the the largest European corporations.

From Geneva in the southwest to St. Gallen in the northeast the sub-Alpine and Jurassian sections of Switzerland are sprinkled with medium-size and small cities, each with some manufactures, occasionally of substantial scale, which produce, amidst the farming preserved over the countryside, a pleasant symbiosis of the urban and the rural. Large industries are carried on in a landscape that looks, for the most part, open and green. The decentralization of industries has successfully organized the whole area into something about as close to the nineteenth-century Utopian dreams of garden cities and greenbelt towns as exists in Europe. In this scattering it would be difficult to show where the orbit of Zurich is replaced by the orbit of Basel, or to describe exactly the "hinterlands" of Geneva and Lausanne. The coalescence of the orbits of these major centers helps the unity of the whole, and the scattering of urban activities sustains the distribution of political influence among the cantons.

The cities of Switzerland and the Alps together make up the two essential parts on which the country is built, an association of burghers in the plain and rural mountaineers. They have made of the country not only a crossroads of the world but a major center of banking, manufacturing, and culture. Perhaps because its proportions were modest, the Swiss economy has stood up better than that of any other Western European country against the decline of the continent's international role.

## AN ECONOMIC MARVEL—ITS FUNCTION IN THE WORLD

In the economic field Switzerland has achieved a unique position based more on a special "know-how" than on its crossroad's function. Transit trade is not very important in normal times compared to the importance of the Swiss banking, insurance, and export income. True, the country has been saved from the ordeals of the two World Wars. Stability might have been more difficult to maintain without such a long spell of neutrality—and stability is a priceless asset for inspiring confidence in investors. Switzerland has become the savings bank of Europe, and the number of depositors in its banks is much greater than the total population of the country. This banking function is a considerable source of invisible exports, and the Swiss franc has been with the United States dollar the "hard currency" of the century.

To banking, the Swiss have added a world-wide insurance business; they specialize in reinsurance, and a variety of operations. Then the revenue from foreign assets and investments ($140 million) and tourism ($500 million) adds to the services through which Switzerland balances its foreign payments. But the major part of the many imports needed by a highly specialized and rich economy are covered by the revenue from exports.

The Swiss production is varied: 9 percent of the labor force are occupied in agricultural pursuits and 38 percent in manufacturing. Whatever is produced has to be of high quality: the dairy products, the textiles, the machinery, the houses, and the consumer goods. Because of the quality and reasonable prices, a number of specialties are exported—Swiss dairy products, chocolate, watches, engines, electrical equipment, precision machinery, as well as many, varied gadgets. The Swiss have early succeeded in exporting to the United States such typically American goods as typewriters and sewing machines. They have used the reputation of certain firms and of Swiss patents to establish related companies in all the major consuming countries that can produce locally, the Nestlé or Ciba products being examples of such operations. To Europe they export watches, diesel engines, military weapons, electrical machinery, and even locomotives. No other country has managed to have such an export expansion without any of the necessary materials or fuels at home.

Switzerland imports from all over the world. Its strong financial position makes it a hard bargainer on the selling markets. If Egypt asks too high a price for its cotton, the Swiss will buy in Chile; if German coal, long the lifeblood of Swiss industry, does not come up the Rhine (as was the case in 1944–1949), Switzerland receives Polish coal by rail. If navigation on the Rhine is interrupted by blown-up bridges or other difficulties, Swiss imports and exports will use some free port and obtain a special corridor through France or Italy. Although continental, Switzerland manages to remain in touch with the maritime economy. Since 1942 it has been forming a merchant marine on the high seas. If asked about European solidarity, many a leading Swiss will answer that he feels more related to the United States or Australia than to Hungary or Lithuania.

Rapidly growing Geneva at the west tip of Lake Geneva has suburbs scattered amid woods and farmland. The view is taken from a foothill of the Alps on French soil. Notice the small lake harbor marked by a high fountain rising from it *(center right)* and above it the white mass of the large Palais des Nations, a United Nations building. The Jura range (in the background) is the location of the largest and best watchmaking industry in Europe. *(Swiss National Tourist Office)*

Watch factories such as this one at Biel are scattered in many small towns in the hills. *(Official Information Bureau of Switzerland)*

Dependent on the rest of the world for the supply of most of its food and practically all its fuels and raw materials, the Swiss economy is, of course, a fragile structure. It rests on the stubborn confidence the Swiss have kept in their financial and economic skill, in their ability to keep prosperity and peace. In many ways Switzerland reminds one of Sweden: it is a neutral country, with a high standard of living, almost no poverty, a country where all the gadgets work, where everything is of real and enduring quality. In anxious Europe, the Swiss have succeeded in maintaining an island of happiness; like a Scandinavian miracle, there certainly is a "Swiss miracle." Still, one cannot help wondering if Swiss prosperity could be divorced entirely from the situation on the continent and whether it is not founded on the existence of an active international free-trade system.

The Swiss currency has remained throughout this troubled century the strongest in Europe. At the end of 1965, gold holdings of official Swiss agencies were estimated at $3,044 million; no other nation could boast so high a per capita gold reserve. Switzerland could thus afford to buy anything anywhere as it pleased its customers. There was no attempt to produce too much at home; however some agricultural products were in excess of consumption, such as the local wines. As in any other Western country, there is some indirect protection or subsidy to domestic agriculture. Industries have gone essentially into the manufacture of delicate precision machinery or high-quality products, chemicals or foods. The textile industry is important, too, but Switzerland imports large quantities of all kinds of manufactured goods, and almost all kinds of foodstuffs and raw materials. For a nation of 6 million people, it is an important industrial power. By 1960, swelling deposits in Swiss banks and the country's extraordinary prosperity caused the Swiss to worry about the "overheating" of their economy!

Their devotion to free trade has not made the Swiss great admirers of the schemes for European organization. Being a small country, Switzerland prefers to deal with a world partitioned into a great many small national units so that more competition can be created between the possible suppliers and customers. While playing on the international competition which constantly animates the world arena, the Swiss have stayed systematically neutral, that is, have remained outside of all the major international organizations which may mean political involvement on any one side of the fence; they want to remain free to deal with everybody at any time. This was one of the essential reasons for locating so many international headquarters and conferences in Switzerland, particularly in Geneva. But Switzerland is not a member of either the United Nations or of NATO. It has been participating in the OECD and in the EFTA, both economic organizations which require little discipline from the member nations. If European integration were to take on an accelerated rhythm and a larger scale, especially if Britain and the Scandinavian countries joined the Common Market, then the Swiss might reconsider their traditional secluded neutrality. They have shown great adaptability to varying conditions and will find their place, which will be an important one, in the reorganization of Europe.

In recent years, the Swiss economy has remained prosperous and expanding in an uninterrupted way. Economic growth has also accelerated the growth of population. From 5.2 million in 1958, the total population of Switzerland rose to 6 million by the middle of 1966. At that time, about 14 percent of this total were foreigners. The latter represented also about one third of the total labor force. By the end of 1964, when the number of foreigners employed in Switzerland went over 720,000, the great majority of them being Italians, the Swiss became concerned about the developing situation. In some cantons, the percentage of foreigners in the total population reached threatening proportions (31 percent in the canton of Geneva). The proportion of Italians in the total population of the country had risen from about 3 percent in 1940 to close to 10 percent in 1964, and the Italian workers indispensable to the Swiss economy were asking for the right to bring in their families from Italy. In the delicate balance of languages and religions on which the Swiss political system rests, this rapid increase in the number of Italians, particularly in certain cantons, could have given them a role requiring a reshuffling of the whole political structure of the country. After long negotiations and an attempt at agreement in 1964, the Swiss parliament refused to allow an increase in the number of Italians admitted to Switzerland. New legislation required Swiss enterprises to reduce the number of foreigners they employed. The foreign manpower decreased from 721,000 in August 1964 (of whom 475,000 were Italians) to 648,000 in August 1966 (of whom 433,000 were Italians). There was also an endeavor to diversify the nationalities represented on the foreign labor force; to the traditionally predominant element, Italians, Spaniards, and Germans, were added Austrians, French, Greeks, Portuguese, and others.

Still, industries and services in the cities require more manpower, and Switzerland must allow for more immigration in future years; the forecasts place it at about a 29,000 annual average. But the main increase of the urban labor force now should come from the rural areas remaining in Switzerland. One may foresee that the farm population, especially in the mountain areas, will rapidly decrease in the immediate future.

Thus the Swiss population will continue to be concentrated mainly in the two more urbanized parts of the country: the northern triangle, Zurich-Bern-Basel, and the southwestern corner of the shores of Lake Geneva. These two areas are already quite congested. Rather chaotic, suburban sprawl has developed between the major cities, creating a complex symbiosis of urban and rural. Until recently, the Swiss could rightly pride themselves on the high quality of their housing and on the efficient management of their environment. Present trends indicate that more new legislation and regulation appear necessary to preserve the quality of the Swiss environment, especially in those areas where an increasing majority of the nation lives. The skill of the Swiss in organizing their environment has been one of their major assets. Their continued prosperity is bound to bring about more congestion in the more prosperous parts of the country. The Swiss way of life is characterized by a world-wide network of transactional relations, by the excellence of their industrial and commercial organization, and by the reputation and efficiency of Swiss banks and technicians. It has been enhanced by the traditional hospitality which has made of this small land-locked country an essential center of international transactional activities. The ways and the means the Swiss will apply to the protection and improvement of their domestic environment under the present pressure will be worth studying. Once more, Switzerland is faced with a geographical challenge that should lead to notable progress.

# Part III

## Mediterranean Europe

The setting of the old town of Antibes on the French Riviera is typically Mediterranean.
Surrounded by barren, eroded rocks, the town, built upward, is seen against the lofty
crestline of the Alps with scattered habitations in the foothills. *(French Government Tourist
Office)*

# 10

---

# Three Peninsulas
# and Many Islands

To the south of Europe three peninsulas stretch toward Africa. Each of them has a distinct outline on the map. To the west the Iberian peninsula, occupied by Spain and Portugal, separates the western basin of the Mediterranean from the open Atlantic by its bulky, quandrangular shape. In the center the Italian peninsula, with its famous "bootlike" shape, separates the western Mediterranean from the eastern, and three important islands complement it: Sicily and Sardinia, which are parts of Italy, and Corsica, a part of France. A number of smaller islands are scattered between Italy and Spain throughout this western Mediterranean. To the southeast the third and last European peninsula is the Balkan one, attached to the continent by a large basis directly to the south of the Danube River. Here are several nations, the organization and boundaries of which have shifted so often and have brought so many worries to the rest of the world that *Balkans* has become a synonym for Europe's political complexity, and almost for "international headache." The Balkan peninsula has a triangular shape, with a much-scalloped contour at its southern tip, and is surrounded by swarms of small islands, particularly to the east.

Each of the three peninsulas has a different geological and political structure. Each of them had its period of greatness which marked a crucial stage in the history of civilization: Greece opened the series with several centuries of domination of the then-civilized part of the West; Rome and Italy organized the Mediterranean world and left a political heritage that still endures in many parts of Europe; Spain and Portugal discovered the rest of the world and divided it between themselves at the end of the fifteenth century.

Natural as well as historical factors seem thus to differentiate sharply the three peninsulas. There is, however, a Mediterranean unity extending over all these lands. The features making up this unity create a contrast with the lands to the north, for Mediterranean Europe is a special area; it is different from the rest of the Mediterranean world as well as from the rest of the continent. The unity of these countries is largely determined by a common milieu consisting of the sea, the climate, and an historical evolution. The maritime tradition and modern evolution have once more brought them closer to Western Europe.

## THE CLASSIC SEA

No sea has ever been as much described or dreamed of as the Mediterranean. It has been the cradle of Western civilization, and the most momentous fights in history were fought out on its banks. Even during World War II, which involved all continents, it played an outstanding part in grand strategy. The Nazi's retreat started when it became clear that their armed forces were unable to keep a foothold on the southern shores of the inland sea.

Mediterranean means *amid the lands*. The interlocking of land and sea space is better achieved here than in any other part of Europe or the whole world. The European peninsulas are the main divides breaking up the sea's unity and separating the different basins from each other: the western and eastern basins are separated by the protuberance of Tunisia, the large isle of Sicily, and the Italian boot; the eastern basin pushes two large bays northward into the European continent: the Adriatic Sea (between Italy and the Balkans) and the Aegean Sea (between the Balkans and Turkey), leading toward the Straits and through them to the Black Sea.

The scalloped coast is generally mountainous; the crestline hugs the coast, isolating the sea from the interior of the surrounding lands. Nowhere are the mountains and the sea more interlocked and, at the same time, more opposed. In between the high peninsulas or islands, the sea is generally deep. To balance the uplifting of the lands, depressed compartments were sunk deep; depths of more than 3000 feet are everywhere close to the water's edge. This gives to the water mass of the Mediterranean a considerable volume. The total area of the sea covers about 1,100,000 square miles, and this whole mass is warm and saline. The deep basins probably have kept the water since the time when, before the Alpine foldings, they were in open contact with the vast ocean to the west.

But for a surface circulation, the Mediterranean is thus a string of deep isolated basins. It communicates with the Atlantic through the

Strait of Gibraltar, which is not deep, for about 700 feet below the water there is encountered a crest linking North Africa to the Iberian peninsula. The exchanges of waters through Gibraltar are complemented by those through the Dardanelles and Bosporus straits with the Black Sea. The man-made Suez Canal does not have enough depth for any appreciable flow. All these communications with the outside do not much affect the whole mass of this inland, almost isolated, sea. It is almost self-sustaining, although if at any time its level began to sink a compensating current coming from the ocean would fill it in.

The Mediterranean is almost tideless; oscillations of the water's edge, even at the equinoctial periods, are slim. But violent storms agitate it often and have made navigation on it rather difficult; it was a good school for the seamen who later sailed on to the remote transatlantic lands. The beginnings of navigation were helped by the division into basins and by the multitude of islands. One could go from any corner of the Mediterranean to another without losing sight of land or having to make too-long detours. The shape of the Mediterranean and its opening in the west on the broad Atlantic spaces may well have something to do with the westward movement of centers of cultures from ancient Egypt and Palestine to North America. The whole history of mankind might have been quite different had the classic sea been open in another direction.

Though a remarkable waterway, the Mediterranean is not a very rich sea so far as fishing goes. Mediterranean people went fishing early, and dried or salted fish has always been an important item of their diet. But the abundance of life in the Mediterranean waters cannot, however, be compared to what has been described as present in the North Sea or in the Bay of Biscay. It seems that the deep basins with a fairly homogeneous water mass are not as prolific as the mingling of diverse waters in a shallow sea. Some biologists have ventured the opinion that the Mediterranean is an "old and exhausted" sea, meaning that the fertile elements seem to have been used up. There still are migrations of fishes around the Mediterranean and through the Strait of Gibraltar between the sea and the Atlantic. Sardines, anchovies, tuna, and eels are the main species fished. Sardines took their name in ancient times from the island of Sardinia.

The beauty of the Mediterranean scenery has been so often described — and these descriptions have been classic for so many centuries — that it seems useless to insist on the features of such a glorious landscape. One should keep in mind that the combination of the deep blue of the sea with the rugged mountains surrounding it and with an exceptionally sunny climate have been the main factors in the colorfulness of the area. Nature has indisputably contributed to the extraordinary destiny of the Mediterranean; but it did not make it an easy country.

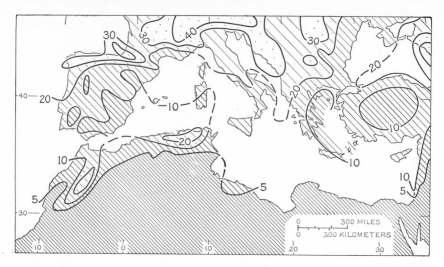

Aridity map of the Mediterranean, redrawn from a new world map of aridity by Jean Gottmann under the direction of Emm. de Martonne. The index of aridity used is a refinement of that presented by de Martonne in 1928, and the new (1939) formula is $Y = \dfrac{A + a}{2}$ where $A$ is the mean yearly index and $a$ the index of the most arid month; thus account is taken of the unequal distribution of rainfall.

Dubrovnik on the Dalmatian coast is situated on a promontory of the hilly, scalloped shore. The newer suburbs of the older walled city have begun to extend up the slopes. *(Yugoslav Information Center)*

## THE MEDITERRANEAN CLIMATE, "IDEAL" BUT ROUGH

Of all the components of the Mediterranean environment, the climate has been the most described and discussed. It has often been described as an "ideal" climate in which man lives better and enjoys himself more than in any other. According to another opinion this most enjoyable climate weakens the inhabitants and lacks the stimulating quality of the northerly climates. Let us have now a brief factual description.

"Mediterranean" climates are found in subtropical latitudes — that is, somewhat above the Tropic, on the western shores of the continents. Outside Europe such climates are known in California, central Chile, the Cape area of South Africa, and southwestern Australia. They never extend far inland, and the widest development is found around the European Mediterranean, owing to the penetration of that sea inside the continental mass. The chief characteristic of this climate type is the division of the year in two main seasons, one hot and dry, the other cool and rainy. This divorce of heat and humidity is exceptional over the globe; in almost all other cases the maximum of precipitation coincides with the warmest season. The existence of these climatic belts in specific positions with respect to the Tropics and to the continents is explained by the movement of the sun in the celestial sphere, which determines the oscillation in latitude of the high-pressure zones situated around each of the two Tropics to the west of the continents. In the case of Europe and Africa, it is the anticyclone centered on the Azores which pushes northward following the sun in summer and falls back southward in the winter. When it extends to the north, the anticyclone covers the Iberian peninsula and the Atlantic west of it; it closes the Mediterranean to the eastward traveling cyclonic depressions, which usually bring with them humid air masses and rain. Summer is dry, and the length of the drought (or xerophytic period), during which plants have to adapt themselves if they want to survive, varies from two months in Mediterranean France to almost six months in the southeastern corner of the inland sea.

Whatever the annual film of rain — and it is usually below 20 inches — its concentration during the period of lower temperatures leaves unwatered the period of the highest evaporation. This evaporation may reach considerable force. The mean temperature of the warmest month reaches 71° F. in Lisbon but 80° in Athens. The humidity occasionally falls below 10 percent in summertime. The average relative humidity in July ranges from 55 percent in Montpellier (France) to 46 in Athens. Great variations in temperature as well as in humidity are customary within the year, as well as from year to year. A substantial range of temperatures is even observed between day and night. The Mediterranean is not an area of averages but rather of extremes. The sea here is largely under the influence of the continents, which to the south and east are deserts. In many respects the Mediterranean offers sharp contrasts with the North Sea environment.

The concentration of rainfall in less than 100 days in the year and the dry summer help to keep the nebulosity low and the sunshine abundant. The dry, clear atmosphere adds to the beauty of the scenery and contributes to the attraction the Mediterranean has always had for people of northern and more cloudy climates. Navigation is also supposed to have been much helped by the steady summer winds blowing from the west and northwest (the so-called Etesian winds). Other winds, however, are so strong and blow with such force that a special defense against them had to be devised. Such are the northeasterlies in winter over the Balkans. The Dalmatian coast is famous for the *borah,* and the French coast for the *mistral* or the *tramontane,* which bring polar air masses from the frozen highlands down to the cyclones passing over the sea with such force that trees may be uprooted and trains derailed. In summer the hot *sirocco* wind from the south may be quite unpleasant. In many cases the winds have had to go over a mountain range; when they have gone down the slope, the up and down movement has left them hot and dry; this kind of wind is similar to the *foehn* of the Swiss Alps. The suddenness and force of these winds, blowing hot in summer and cold in winter, are characteristic of the Mediterranean and result from the contrast between land and sea, increased by the mountainous topography of the coastal areas.

The broken-up topography and the proximity to the oceanic humidity cause a great variety of local climates around the Mediterranean; whatever moderating influence the sea may provide is limited in its extension inland by the first crest of heights. On the two slopes of every range contrasts are easy to observe. More variety is found in altitudinal zones and in internal basins. On westward-looking slopes, maritime influences are better felt; while continentality is stronger on the eastward-looking ones. All along the Mediterranean coastal ranges of hills, long stretches of the shore oriented toward the east or southeast are called *rivieras.* The most famous riviera is the French one, along which the Alps come in contact with the sea and a steep mountainous slope faces southeast. Other rivieras are in Italy, one of them even oriented toward the southwest, which is exceptional. The southeastern coast of Spain, land of rich irrigated agriculture, could also be classified as a riviera. The rivieras are famed for their scenic beauty and for their warmer and sunnier climate, due to their orientation; they usually have much warmer winters than the neighboring lands that do not enjoy a similar position.

The Mediterranean climate is more moderate—that is, with a shorter

summer dry period and with less extremes in the variations of temperature and humidity—in the west than eastward. It is also more extreme
inland, especially in closed depressions, than on the coasts. The western
coast of Spain and Portugal enjoys an almost oceanic climate with some
Mediterranean trends; but the Greek peninsula, especially in its northern, rugged part, has a more extreme shade of the same climate, and
interior areas, such as the central plateaus of Spain or the Po Valley,
may be termed definitely continental. The climate role of the classic sea
is felt more in winter than in summer. The warm mass of water remains
a reservoir of heat during the cold season, being more than six degrees
warmer on the surface than the land on the shore. Moreover, the sea
creates a zone of instability and evaporation throughout a vast area,
most of which would probably be occupied by a northerly extension of
the Sahara if it were land.

As it is, the Mediterranean climate is wonderful indeed for tourism
and intensifies the feelings produced by scenic beauty and regular clear-
cut lines. It may well have had something to do with the birth in this area
of the Western fine arts, of the logic of the Greeks, of the architecture
of the Greeks, Italians, and French. But it is certainly not an easy climate
in which to live and work. It is rough—by its heat in summer, by its quick
changes of temperature, by its strong winds, by its violent downpours
and frequent storms at intermediate seasons. Mediterranean populations have always been faced with challenges from the climate, ag-
gravated by the design of the topography.

SLOPING AND DISCONTINUOUS LANDS

The topography divides the Mediterranean lands into a multitude of
cells separated by hills, mountain ranges, or valleys, so that regionalism
is fostered and communication by land is difficult. Irregularity is here the
rule. Even mountain ranges are seldom continuous over long stretches,
and their structural features and average altitudes change often. Plains
are a rare occurrence around the Mediterranean, especially in Europe,
but there are a few stretching rather widely: the Po plain in northern
Italy, the Languedoc plain in France, the lower Guadalquivir plain in
southern Spain. Everywhere else the terrain on the peninsulas and islands slopes; often the slope is steep, for most of the lands are above 600
feet in elevation even when close to the seashore.

The sloping quality of the land has several important consequences.
First, it makes erosion stronger all around, and the surface soil layer is
carried away quickly. Secondly, it renders more torrential the rivers
that already have such a trend as a result of violent showers during the
rainy season. Thirdly, it increases the calorific power of the sun's rays,

which always reach the soil in an oblique way and are closer to the vertical over a southward slope than over flat territory. To assess fully the importance of the slope in Mediterranean environment one must follow a rather involved system of natural conditions. The steepness of the slope makes the soil slide into the depressions. A great deal of it is carried away by the swift run-off of waters. The streams deposit this silt where the slope decreases sharply—that is, in the coastal plain or the interior basin. The fertility of the land is thus swept away from the slopes and accumulated in the form of deep, recent alluvium in the low-lying areas. One could speak of a concentration in space of Mediterranean fertility. But the streams, depositing their silt, become lazy, wander endlessly through the flat, almost slopeless plain, or, in many cases, are stopped in their rush toward sea level by some topographical obstacle. A line of hillocks fixing the shoreline bars the drainage toward the sea; a gorge may be cut through the barrier, but it will not be wide enough for the flood-time gauge; sometimes a river crosses a basin inland and has difficulties getting out of it through narrow gates to reach the coast. In all such cases, the floods will be held back upstream from the gorge, and the low-lying rich soils will be flooded during the heavy rains, turning into marshlands.

Marshes breed mosquitoes. In the warm climate of the Mediterranean, swarms of *Anopheles* are thus ready to distribute the virus of malaria over the swampy lowlands and their neighborhood, and the plains become thus a difficult area in which to live. They can be developed only when the drainage is well organized so that the spread of malaria can be prevented. Partly because of the threat of the *Anopheles*, and partly because there was not much low flat ground altogether, the Mediterranean habitat went up the slope and most of the rural populations established themselves at moderate elevations. A favorite belt of occupation is observed between 600 and 1500 feet. As the slope is often steep, men had to fight erosion and to build an infinity of terraces with stone-protected edges, so that enough leveled ground could be provided for crops and the soil kept from sliding down. The maintenance of these preserved slopes, one of the oldest human large-scale works in soil conservation, requires a great deal of labor. If this environment is abandoned to itself, malaria may again rule the plains and the fertile terraced slopes will be quickly eroded and reduced to barren rock. The Mediterranean peoples live in a fragile environment.

The slope has more positive functions. When a summit reaches high enough, it condenses humidity, which it then stores in the form of snow in winter. During the hot drier period this humidity is liberated and flows down to irrigate the rich lands along the foot of the slope. Snow-capped mountains, overlooking barren slopes and rich fields or mead-

The lower Var valley in the Alps near the French Riviera. Steep slopes and strong erosion have resulted in the silting of the lower parts. *(French Cultural Services)*

ows at their feet, are not an infrequent sight in the Mediterranean lands. But the slope bears fruit only when the streams are harnessed to production on the lower lands with good drainage and frequently with irrigation. The same harnessing may provide water power. The topography compensates to some extent for the climatic aridity.

The mountainous topography makes transportation and traffic harder by land than by sea. The Mediterranean peninsulas are thus divided up into areas facing the sea toward which the slope leads them. Opposed slopes sometimes communicate more easily by sea — although this may involve lengthy navigation — than by land, though the latter would involve a much shorter distance. Railroads need large investments and many engineering works to span Mediterranean lands, and continuity of such transport has been established only on the richest areas. Regionalism and political organization have been much affected by that topography, and it has been said that the Mediterranean political map is naturally one of many small units. But we should not forget that this was the first area in which a vast empire was erected rather early in Western history. The unifying function of the sea thus compensates to some extent for the breaking-up effect of the slope.

## GRANDEUR, DECLINE, AND REJUVENATION

In ancient times, the Mediterranean area was the civilized world. Outside that region, of course, the Chinese area was also important, but Chinese influence over world history cannot be compared to that of the cradle of Western civilization. Greece, Rome and Italy, southern France, and Byzantium, not to speak of the African and Asiatic parts of the area, were the guts of the world. In the Middle Ages this supremacy was weakened and slowly disintegrated; trade with the Mediterranean, however, remained an essential factor of the European economy. The Arab expansion dealt a terrible blow to the slowly declining Mediterranean system established by Rome. The Moslem rule was a brilliant and a most advanced one; it gave great momentum to Spain, where there flourished one of the brightest cultures of the Middle Ages; but it cut the Mediterranean world in two. Between the eighth and the eleventh centuries, people of Moslem faith were not admitted into Christian countries, just as Christians were not welcome in the Islamic empire. Only a few Jews were able to go across this religious border, and the historian Henri Pirenne has suggested that their specialization as middlemen may have started at that time. Trade between the two areas was reduced to a trickle. The Crusades attempted to re-establish a Christian Mediterranean unity without success. Later the new Caliph, the Ottoman sultan, attempted a circummediterranean conquest also without success.

At the end of the Middle Ages some commercial relations had been re-established. A few Mediterranean cities, especially the great Italian ports of Venice, Genoa, and Pisa, had commercial maritime empires linking West and East, bringing into Europe luxurious silks and jewels as well as the indispensable raw materials of that time, such as spices, which were a basis of the pharmaceutical and food-preservation industries. At the beginning of the Renaissance period in the middle of the fifteenth century, Italy was again the hub of European trade because of its central Mediterranean position. The Renaissance meant the spread of a cult of the ancient Mediterranean cultures; but it meant also the start of transoceanic navigation and the discovery of lands that could be reached by the sea lanes without touching the Moslem-held Mediterranean east. The currents of trade deserted the classic sea; the Mediterranean countries became a sort of backyard of Europe, and the prosperity and culture of the Moslem countries south and east of the sea decayed rapidly.

At the time of the Romans the Mediterranean had been beautifully developed within the limits of the technical means and economic needs of the day. Some other areas benefited by the Moslem or Byzantine rule. The Mediterranean environment requires constant toil and increasing investments to be kept in good shape — when it does not pay, the people stop making the effort and the land reverts to wilderness, or at least misery. This happened over vast areas throughout the Middle Ages and even more in the seventeenth and eighteenth centuries. Whether it was the lack of security resulting from wars, piracy, and monopolies or the lack of economic incentive as a result of little attention from and little commerce with the more powerful nations to the west and north, everything concurred in bringing about a situation of poverty and decay. Swamps and malaria spread; monuments changed to ruins; large cities shrank to the size of small villages agglomerated atop a hill for defense or at some crossroads where no more traffic passed. Then the situation began to improve in the nineteenth century, slowly, gradually. Napoleon reopened the Mediterranean when he made a daring expedition to Egypt. The British and French élite began touring the Mediterranean countries: Byron, Shelley, and Chateaubriand wrote about them. Russian expansion southward gave more animation to the Black Sea and the Straits area. The weakening Ottoman Empire opened up to Western influences and trade. New nations appeared on the European map, such as a renewed Greece and, later, Italy. Rivalry between France and Britain added some life to the Mediterranean activities. After 1830 France began colonizing North Africa. In 1869 the French opened the Suez Canal, linking the maritime navigation of the Mediterranean with that on the Red Sea and creating a new road, shorter and surer, from the Western world to the Indies and the Far East. The Mediterranean found itself again in the heart of international economics and politics. After the opening of the Suez Canal, the old Mediterranean nations began growing young.

Rejuvenation took on different aspects. The political map began to break down. In Moslem countries, the most affected by the sclerosis of conservatism, movements of "Young Turks" and "Young Egyptians" appeared. In the Christian countries on the peninsulas, old and new nations were claiming independence or unity: Greece, Italy, Bulgaria, Yugoslavia, and finally Albania became independent nations. Many of them in their nationalist impulse claimed authority, order, and expansion. Italian fascism was one of such manifestations. Mediterraneans did not want to be a sort of colonial territory for greater European powers, nor would they accept being treated as museums and loved for their past services and greatness. They intended to be real and modern. This often led them into trouble, but they seemed ready to face it.

These political developments fostered a quick economic recovery. Drainage and irrigation works reclaimed the lowlands; waterpower was harnessed; mineral resources were opened up and put to use. And much more rapid than the development of resources was the rise in population figures. It may be suggestive to stress recent figures: in 1937 the total population of the three peninsulas accounted for 104 million people; in 1948, after all the devastations and massacres of World War II, it was estimated at 113.5 million, and 135 million by 1967, — that is, an increase of about a million a year, despite massive emigration from certain areas. The increase was due chiefly to the crude birth rate, which used to be everywhere above 21 per 1000 inhabitants, but which is now decreasing and has come down to 18 per 1000 in Italy and 15 in Bulgaria. Population pressures develop and underscore the economic and social problems.

MEDITERRANEAN AGRICULTURE

The traditional Mediterranean rural economy is based on a threefold foundation: extensive cultivation of grains, intensive cultivation of trees, and finally transhumant sheep raising. In terms of resources, the basic items have been wheat, barley, olives, grapes, mutton, and wool. To some extent one should also mention the mulberry tree, on the leaves of which silk worms have been raised, adding another raw material to the regional economy.

Grains are well fitted to the Mediterranean environment, but they give variable yields according to the weather conditions. In years of drought the harvest is meager. Famine has always threatened with a series of drought years, and the Bible, written on the shores of the Mediterranean, put famine in the form of the lean and fat cows in Pharoah's dreams, which Joseph interpreted. Even clearer was his second dream: "Seven ears came up in one stalk, full and good; and, behold, seven ears, withered, thin, and blasted with the east wind, sprung up after them: and the thin ears devoured the seven good ears" (Genesis 41:22–24). Buffer stocks were the remedy Joseph suggested with such success, but stock piling on a large scale needs the possibility of capital immobilization for several years, warehouses, and other factors. It needs a great deal of human toil and organization to make of the Mediterranean a land where milk and honey flow.

The first improvement in land use was the introduction of the biennial rotation: one year grain, one year fallow. During the fallow year the soil can store for the next year a part of the rain that percolates. (The western American system of dry farming turns out to be simply an elaboration of the age-old Mediterranean system. Similarly, terracing the slopes was the ancestor of contour ploughing.) During the fallow year flocks of sheep grazed the fields and enriched them with their manure. Sheep raising was from many standpoints an important complement to tillage in the Mediterranean area; it also increased the meat supply, which was usually short, and even added some milk and valuable raw materials: wool and leather. The shepherd was given a divine rank by the Mediterraneans, and the bishop's crook is nothing else but a shepherd's tool used for centuries to catch a sheep and take it out of the flock. Shepherds in the mountains of the Balkan peninsula still use the crook to catch a sheep's leg and immobilize it.

Most characteristic of Mediterranean agriculture is the large-scale cultivation of trees. The tree, with its long roots tapping water tables deep underground and with its thick bark, can weather better than smaller plants the droughts and storms of the Mediterranean climate. The olive tree is the most typical of the Mediterranean. Throughout the year it keeps its silvery leaves that glisten, showing an adaptation to lesser evaporation, therefore to xerophytic conditions. The vine is another much smaller tree well fitted to the region; so are many fruit trees such as the fig and all the citruses. In the more oceanic parts of the Mediterranean the cork oak is frequent. Everywhere there are pines and cedars of local varieties. On the deforested slopes a low brush of thorny and odoriferous bushes spreads, called *maquis* or *garrigue*. But the Mediterranean farmer has given to the tree plantations some of the best soils of the area. The tree often provides the cash crop, and the *plantation* long was a

Langadia in the Peloponnesus. Orchards of olive trees surround a hillside village on the edge of the Arcadian Mountains in Greece.

Mediterranean system before becoming typical of the "tropical" countries. Vineyards cover the plain of Languedoc in France, the gently rolling country around Asti in northern Italy, and the hills around Xeres and Alicante in Spain and behind Oporto in Portugal. Citrus plantations predominate in many of the Spanish *huertas* (such as Valencia and Murcia) and around Naples and Palermo in Italy. Thick olive-tree plantations are to be found in parts of Spain, Italy, Greece; cork oaks are found in Portugal and Spain.

There has been a transposition of the trees by man around the Mediterranean. The mountain slopes, originally wooded, have been largely deforested, but the more arid plains have been often covered with tree plantations, some of which are carefully irrigated. On the best soils, which are not widely spread, the Mediterranean endeavors to get the greatest possible harvest: the warm climate almost all year on many lowlands insures a permanent fertility, if an adequate water supply is provided. In between the rows of trees other crops are cultivated, usually vegetables of some sort, sometimes even grains. There an intensive gardening is organized on small areas of good soils and abundant irrigation. Such areas, called *huertas* or *vegas* in Spain, are also found in other parts of the Mediterranean, for instance in the famous *Conca de Oro* (or Golden Shell) of Palermo in Sicily.

Altogether Mediterranean agriculture requires a great deal of organization. It cannot be successful in periods of political or economic instability. It blossoms chiefly when large-scale marketing can be set up, allowing the specialization of the most productive regions. Such possibilities existed at the time of the Roman Empire, extending the *Pax Romana* to a vast area. They have been true only sporadically and for rather short periods since. Brighter horizons opened up with the growing industrialization of Western and Northern Europe, with the expansion of the rail network and of rapid transportation by steamer on the sea. The Mediterranean lands specialized immediately in their natural function as the orchard and for certain months as the truck-farm area of Europe. But only small areas, thickly populated, were able to fit such a specialization. Over the rest of the area the old small-scale agriculture carried on, trying to insure self-sufficiency within a narrow local frame with rather backward but cheap means of production. This poorer kind of agriculture has been called the "traditional" one in the Mediterranean. It is no more traditional in fact than the rich specialized plantation of an almost American or Californian type. Both have traditionally coexisted in the Mediterranean, but the plantation type was linked so tightly to marketing conditions that it has been somewhat unstable.

The Mediterranean peninsulas are indeed a region of contrasts: clusters of booming activities are separated by stretches of almost empty desert; wasteland, though not always hopeless, is intermingled with intensive gardening spots. A great Mediterranean geographer, Professor Jules Sion, wrote that the Mediterranean is "the land of the *discontinuous* in space as well as in time." This lack of continuity in all respects is striking; it may seem paradoxical in an area that "invented" the method of logic and is so attached to tradition. Nature and history cooperated, however, to make it such a land full of interruptions.

In the twentieth century the Mediterranean countries seem to be fighting successfully the isolation that strained their activities. Agriculture, too, has been rejuvenated: better transportation facilities, more water made available, great estates broken up, more capital poured into the land, especially for drainage purposes—all these were factors. The malarial situation has been considerably improved by water control, public health measures, and better food—an old Tuscan dictum says: "The remedy to malaria is in the dishes." There could be no doubt as to the too-low standard of living, the traditional undernourishment, and the general weakening of the bulk of the Mediterranean peoples for many centuries. Recovery cannot be achieved very quickly. Public health is being improved, and already shows in a lower mortality, especially infant mortality, than a few decades ago. The ordeal of the Civil War in Spain, of World War II in Italy and the Balkans, had set progress back. The spirit of rejuvenation is still there and reconstruction proceeds apace. Much could be done to widen the agricultural basis and increase the production of foodstuffs or the exports which might be exchanged for more imported food. Water is the number-one problem throughout the area, which is still very far from full utilization of the available resources.

Social problems are also acute in the rural areas. The population pressure is considerable on the farms, and the control of the local resources, especially landownership, used to be concentrated in a small number of hands—*latifundia,* or large estates, have been a regional characteristic since Roman times. They are still far from being broken up everywhere. Agriculture around the Mediterranean needs considerable reclamation and expansion; it is all the more essential because the Mediterranean economy was chiefly rural and is urbanizing fast.

## INDUSTRIALIZATION AND ECONOMIC EXPANSION

In the nineteenth century, the Industrial Revolution and the opening of the Suez Canal brought back intensive maritime traffic to the Mediterranean, and railroads spread through the peninsulas, following the valleys, piercing the mountains with long tunnels. No longer were these countries the best endowed with roads: the Roman heritage of famous

The Bosporus. Here Europe meets Asia, and the Mediterranean joins the Black Sea. *(Three Lions)*

paved highways was no more than a relic, for road-building had developed since the eighteenth century in Western Europe. The airplane brought a last impulse to Mediterranean transportation: it was particularly helpful as it crossed land and sea, torrents and lofty ranges, with the same ease, saving many detours and transshipment operations.

Transportation being better organized, the development of local resources became easy. But with the modern merchant marines it does not pay to send bulky goods by the shortest route if that route involves transshipments and rail hauling. The Mediterranean ports did not handle much transit traffic toward northwestern Europe, for instance; ships went around the continent to the North Sea and even to the Baltic. Even Switzerland received a great deal of merchandise through the Rhine instead of by rail from the Mediterranean ports of Marseille or Genoa. The old system of trade on which the fortune of Venice had been founded could not work any longer. Although a hub of navigation, the Mediterranean has had to rely more on local resources. Mining was the chief one aside from agricultural products; important deposits of metallic, nonferrous ores are known and worked on the peninsulas: lead, copper, zinc, sulfur, bauxite, and pyrites are the most common. Some iron ore is also exported.

For successful large-scale industrialization, the peninsulas lack power. Coal is rare and almost absent. This is a major weakness, especially as no appreciable oil deposits could compensate the deficiency. Waterpower development has been pushed actively in certain areas, such as the Spanish Pyrenees, the Italian Alps, and the Balkans. The necessity of importing most of the source of energy in the form of coal or oil products remains a major weakness in the industrialization of Mediterranean Europe. However, deposits of natural gas have been discovered and are increasingly used in Italy. The abundance of coal and oil on the world markets and the promise of the forthcoming cheaper energy from nuclear sources are encouraging prospects. The countries on the Mediterranean peninsulas began industrializing in a modern way a century ago. However, most of the industries were concentrated in only a few corners of the whole area, particularly northern Italy, Catalonia, and a few seaports. The first industries to develop were textiles (an old Mediterranean specialty due to local wool and silk), food processing or refining, and some chemicals and shipbuilding. It was only after World War II that serious planning and investment went into the development of large-scale industries on an international scale.

Italy, as the more advanced of the Mediterranean countries and as a member of the EEC, led the way. In the Common Market, it is often remarked that Italy was the main beneficiary of European economic integration. Indeed, among the major countries of the world, the Italian rate of growth in the last fifteen years has been second only to that of Japan. Obviously, Italy would not have been able to build up the substantial iron and steel industry it now has without the help and opportunity brought by the Coal and Steel European Community. Portugal has been a member of the EFTA. Turkey, Greece, and even Yugoslavia have asked to become associates of the EEC. Spain has greatly benefited from active and generous American aid. All these countries directly profit by the greater affluence and economic expansion of Western Europe to the north of their lands.

The demand for more labor which the rapid expansion of Western Europe created in the 1950s and early 1960s caused a steady current of migrant workers to move north from the Mediterranean peninsula. About 1960, American observers could jokingly remark that instead of the traditional American saying, "Young man, go west," the contemporary European trend could be formulated as "Young man, go north," at least insofar as Mediterranean people were concerned. Population-pressure problems in the peninsula were relieved substantially as a result of the migration north and northwestward of several million young men and women: the Italians went mainly to Switzerland and France, then also to West Germany and Belgium, and some even to Britain, the Netherlands, and Sweden; Spaniards went to France, West Germany, and Switzerland; Portuguese, to France and Belgium; Greeks, to West Germany and Switzerland; Albanians, to Yugoslavia; Turks, to West Germany and France. Many of these migrations were temporary, but they brought a steady flow of money, sent or brought back by the workers, from the richer northern countries; Western Europe largely replaced America as the general outlet for Mediterranean emigration. It helped increase the interweaving of European interests and the gradual coming together of European nations. Some emigration overseas continued, chiefly to the United States, Canada, and South America.

Still, the overabundant supply of manpower cannot be absorbed by the other countries. The solution to the economic backwardness of the Mediterranean peninsulas must be found on the spot through domestic economic expansion in each country concerned. To catch up with the West, the Mediterranean countries must do more than build manufacturing plants, attract tourists, and develop agriculture. They must prepare for the postindustrial revolution social system, which requires much change in the traditional Mediterranean way of using the environment.

The political regime in recent times has been quite a hindrance to economic progress. Until the end of the nineteenth century large parts of Mediterranean Europe were "dependent territories" of large empires centered at some distance. The national revenue went largely to areas outside the peninsulas, and the population of the latter felt that great efforts were not very worthwhile—they would not benefit anyhow. In the fully independent countries local aristocracies or heads of party organizations (as was the case in Fascist Italy) kept most of the national revenue for themselves. Such situations were not very encouraging to the hard-laboring peoples, used to difficult life in an environment that nature has made beautiful but fragile. The natural environment, however, has been made responsible for too many trends in Mediterranean history. The Iberian and Balkan peninsulas are not among the least endowed sections of Europe in terms of soils and minerals. All the Mediterranean countries have abundant manpower, and a low-cost manpower by Western standards. When they have migrated to other parts of the world, these people have proved to be a valuable asset to the economies of the lands where they settled. Why should they be a liability, a burdensome surplus in the sunny lands of southern Europe?

The answer is not provided by physical or ethnic data. It is to be found rather in the inheritance of a difficult past: in a social structure that does not foster progress or fluidity; in a lack of certain types of technical education; in a lack of capital assets that could be invested in worthwhile development; in a lack of faith in the possibility of improving the situation. The last deficiency is perhaps the worst. This century, however, has brought some hope to the Mediterranean shores. Rejuvenated faith often meant adherence to some extremist ideology in politics. Such trends are easily understood in countries where there is so much resistance to change. With increased fluidity, the peninsular peoples should achieve a better life even if they cannot make good all their dreams of grandeur.

In the last twenty years considerable progress has been achieved. As the wounds left by the war were healed, new trends began to work. Large scale urbanization developed, such as these lands had not known since the Renaissance. Industries, heavy and light, were scattered around the beautiful countryside. These trends did not necessarily entail the classical forest of stacks spouting dark fumes; much of the recent development has been due to the virtues of the Mediterranean environment: crowds of foreigners use their increased time and means for leisure on the shores of the midland sea, enjoying the sunshine, the landscape, the souvenirs of the great past, and the gaiety of the people. The geography of amenities begins to play a part in national and international economics. Still, the three peninsulas are altogether the poorer, less developed part of Europe. In the present era of rising expectations and rapid expansion of opportunity, the promise of the future is thereby made even greater.

As the Mediterranean nations are growing younger and beginning to acquire more confidence in the opportunity that opens up for the mass of the people, new signs of ferment and unrest also appear. The stability of the existing political systems, many of them authoritarian and very conservative, is being questioned. Within the communist camp in Europe, Yugoslavia led the dissent against Russian domination, and Albania was the first of the former Russian satellites to shift to the obedience of Communist China. Greece was deeply divided by civil strife in the late 1940s, as Spain was devastated by civil war in the 1930s. Although the same people have been at the helm in Spain and Portugal for more than thirty years and political stability has been great in Italy and Yugoslavia for more than twenty years, there is a great deal of ferment in all these nations. All of them (with the exception of Albania and Bulgaria) have greatly benefited by the intensification of North Atlantic relations. They have participated in the Marshall Plan and the OECD. American military presence in the Mediterranean was reinforced after World War II and has remained as a dominant "umbrella" over the Mediterranean basin. Since 1967, however, Soviet naval power, coming in through the Turkish Straits, has been building up. In recent times, the Suez Canal was twice closed for navigation, first in 1956–1957, then again, and for a longer period, after 1967. The transit traffic through the Mediterranean, due to the importance of Suez, has been considerably jeopardized, as other sea lanes are being preferred as more secure. But it was not on the advantages of the transit trade that most of the rejuvenation of the Mediterranean peninsulas was based in recent decades. It was due to the reshaping of their internal structures which these nations have undertaken and which they should be allowed to pursue in stability and peace.

A street in Barcelona, in the beautiful ancient section of the city. Narrow, dark streets, usually crowded with people, are typical of Mediterranean towns. *(Spanish Tourist Office)*

# 11

## Spain and Portugal

The westernmost of the three southern peninsulas stretches between the Atlantic and the Mediterranean and is occupied by the two countries of Spain and Portugal. It is remarkably bulky. A continent in miniature, it is cut off from the rest of Europe by the lofty wall of the Pyrenees.

### THE MASSIVE IBERIAN PENINSULA

An almost regular quadrangle, the Iberian peninsula is formed of rather high land, and only in the southwest does land below 700 feet extend somewhat inland, Portugal occupying most of this more open façade. Elsewhere, according to the usual Mediterranean landscape, mountains come close to the seashore and small coastal plains are dominated by towering crests. The highest ranges are on the periphery of the peninsula: in the north, the Pyrenees and Cantabrian Mountains; in the south, the Betic Mountains. In the interior, tableland forms predominate at levels between 1600 and 3500 feet, with deeply eroded hills rising occasionally above them. A few depressions are followed by the main valleys draining the whole peninsula. Many aspects of it remind one more of African scenery than of other parts of Europe. This is indeed a wide bridge between the two continents, and the Strait of Gibraltar dividing Spain from Morocco is only a narrow and shallow trench.

Iberian massiveness contrasts with Italy or the Balkans. It creates inland an isolated country, very continental, although surrounded by the

431

sea on three and a half of its four sides. Mountains and plateaus are not easily accessible from the outside, that is, from the sea. Looking at the topographic map, one understands why the maritime expansion may have been only a brief episode in Spanish history — the country is not oriented to the sea by nature. Access to the interior is difficult for maritime influences of all kinds, including the climatic influences. The bulky peninsula, acting like a little continent, develops in winter a small high-pressure area on the central tablelands; the summer is dry, owing to the Mediterranean pressures' system. Spain finds itself under anticyclonic influences for local causes in winter and for general causes in summer. Most of it gets rainfall at the intermediate seasons. The interior is decidedly arid; though high, the tablelands and even the slopes of the mountains are dry and covered mostly by a *steppe*. Air masses coming from the west and northwest discharge most of the humidity on the coastal highlands. Those in the north act as a screen for the current incoming from the Bay of Biscay: the Pyrenees are verdant on the French side but rugged and brown on the Spanish one. Only the western coast, all along the open ocean and with a lower and more broken relief, is truly maritime. Eastward the Mediterranean does not supply much humidity, and whatever moderating influence it may provide is restricted to the coast by the topography.

There exist therefore a double set of contrasts in the Iberian peninsula: one between interior and coastland, the other between west and east; the greatest climatic contrast opposes the northwest to the southeast. There are three main regions in Iberia: the Mediterranean mountain coastland; the steppic continental interior; the humid Atlantic west and northwest. They belong to different climates, different topographical zones, and the geological structure explains a great deal. This structure is extremely complicated and varied. Here a knot has certainly been tied by the tectonic axes: ancient Atlantic ranges, Hercynian orientations and peneplanations, Alpine ranges, Mediterranean curving chains, and African tablelands mingle in the quadrangle between Europe and Africa, Atlantic and Mediterranean. The great system of tablelands, often called the Iberian *Meseta*, belongs to the great Hercynian system of highlands. The hypothesis has been advanced that the Hercynian folds here had to mold their orientations on an older resistant mass of the Caledonian Age. Then these ranges were planed and partly submerged by seas at various periods. The period of Alpine surrection brought substantial changes, rejuvenating the topography, giving to the peninsula its present main features. At a more recent time the present coastline was established. The remarkable straightness of the Atlantic coast, cutting through all lines of the structure, seems to indicate that Iberia is a remnant of a vaster land, which stretched westward and continued southward in Morocco. The famous legend of Atlantis, swallowed by the ocean's waves, seems current in the dim recollections of Mediterranean peoples, but geological evidence points to a much older, Pliocene disturbance. The southwestern part of Iberia is still somewhat unstable and has been ravaged several times within recent centuries by severe earthquakes.

Quaternary glaciations affected the Iberian landscapes; northern and western ranges show U-shaped valleys and other signs of glacial erosion, but no ice sheet seems to have covered the whole of the peninsula—it was too arid. Local ice accumulations left their imprint on the heights; some morainic traces have been found. Since the thaw of the glaciers (only a few small ice tongues remain on the highest crests of the Pyrenees), normal erosion has been very active, for the slope was often steep. But if the action of running waters has been predominant in the Atlantic areas of Spain, the drier regions have known, especially in the drought years, an almost desert kind of erosion with the winds playing an important part. In the center of Iberia certain landforms take on a pre-Saharan, quasi-desert aspect as a result.

The topography and the climate combine their influences to outline a mosaic in which three main systems (the Atlantic, interior, and Mediterranean zones) exist and which is repeated on the hydrographic, soil, and vegetation maps. Iberia is truly Mediterranean, as it stretches a transition from the humid Atlantic to a subdesert environment, and this transition proceeds more by local contrasts than by gradual changes.

## PAST GREATNESS AND MODERN PROBLEMS

History has added to the diversity and complexity of the Iberian peninsula, and the population of today is a complicated mixture. Ancient Greek and Latin writers told with amazement mixed with admiration of the old Iberic tribes, different from the rest of the European peoples, frugal and independent, hard-working and proud, fighting bitterly for their beliefs, often violent and intolerant but ready to endure almost with gaiety the worst ordeals. Few peoples seem so disposed to collective or individual martyrdom. We do not know much about the actual origin of the old Iberian peoples, but some remnants may be observed, for instance at the western tip of the Pyrenees where the Basque people speak a strange old tongue. Many racial and cultural layers have been laid upon the ancient foundations: Celtic influences, Greek and Phoenician colonies on the coast, Carthaginian, then Roman domination; then the successive Germanic tribes, crossing or visiting the peninsula and leaving over most of it for two centuries a Visigothic domination that ended at the beginning of the eighth century with the Moslem conquest.

The Moslem domination, which lasted seven centuries, opened in 711 a great period of Iberian history. The Moslem world in medieval times had a brighter, more advanced culture than the Christian West dominated by the Barbarians, and the advantages of that culture were brought to Iberia by armies of Arabicized Berbers, generally natives of northwest Africa. A remarkable civilization, heir to both Rome and the eastern Mediterranean, developed in Iberia and to a lesser extent in Morocco — it was far away from Arabia and different enough from the Middle Eastern countries to take on a distinct personality — and a Western caliphate was established at Córdoba, and transferred later to Fez in Morocco, opposing controls from the East. The Iberian Moslems have been called the *Moors* to make a clear-cut distinction between them and the Arabs. The Moors found an already prosperous country, especially in the south of Spain, and helped develop its resources, introducing new plants and methods of cultivation. In Spain Ibn-al-Awam wrote a *Book of Agriculture* which was a standard treatise of agronomical science; irrigation techniques were introduced and improved. Local architecture was influenced by Eastern style, and some buildings of medieval Spain are still models of art and beauty. The work in leather and metals also showed Eastern influences from then on. The Moorish rule was a liberal one on the whole; it allowed non-Moslem people to live and work almost normally, and the Jews played an important part in the cultural and economic development of medieval Iberia.

The religious zeal and spirit of independence of the Iberian people, however, could not accept ultimate Arabization. Led by the Visigoths, Christian peoples had fled to the northwestern hills, which the Moors could never conquer. From this base the famous *reconquesta* started in 718, was conducted with extreme daring and stubbornness, and achieved success when the Moors were definitely expelled from southern Spain, seven centuries after they had arrived. Granada was taken in 1492. It removed the Moslem barrier in the West to European trade and navigation forty years after that barrier had been strengthened in the East by the fall of Constantinople to the Ottoman Turks. The same year Columbus sailed westward, and the Portuguese had already begun ringing Africa.

The completion of the *reconquesta* marks the rise of the West in Europe. To the nations who achieved this feat, it gave great unity, impetus, and self-confidence. Portugal and Spain opened the modern European expansion overseas; they divided the world between themselves, and the sixteenth century was indeed a period of Spanish world supremacy. During the religious wars Spain stood up as the firmest champion of the Roman Catholic Church; few peoples have given so many and such great martyrs and saints to the Church as the Spaniards, from St.

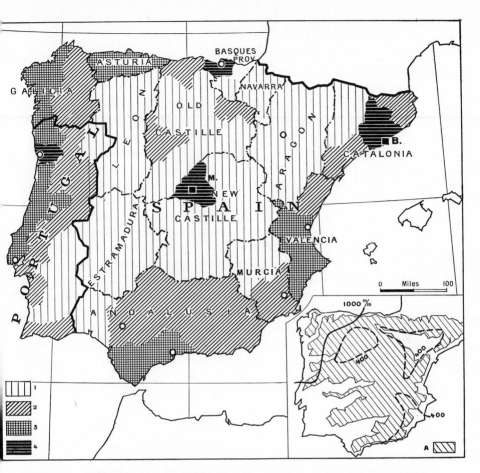

Distribution of population on the Iberian Peninsula, 1965. Key: 1, less than 150 inhabitants per square mile; 2, from 151 to 300 inhabitants per square mile; 3, from 301 to 500; 4, over 500. Black squares show cities of more than a million inhabitants each; there are two such cities, identified by their initials: M for Madrid, B for Barcelona. Circles indicate cities counting a population of 250,000 to 1,000,000; there are eight such cities (among which are Lisbon and Oporto in Portugal). Notice the striking contrast between the densities of population in the interior of the peninsula and along the maritime periphery. It would seem that the seashore has attracted the people and emptied the interior, where only Madrid, the Spanish capital, succeeded in agglomerating an important nucleus of population. Solid lines show national boundaries; broken lines show the limits of the provinces, the names of which also appear on the map, although densities have been mapped on the basis of smaller administrative subdivisions.

The inset map (*lower right*) provides a rough sketch of the physical conditions of the peninsula: the shaded area (as in A) shows the land at an elevation above 1500 feet; the other lines show the rainfall: the solid line divides the two parts of the peninsula receiving annually more or less than 1000 millimeters, that is, 40 inches of rainfall; the broken line shows 400 millimeters, that is, 16 inches. Topography seems to have had more influence on the distribution of the population than the climate, as rainfall has been supplemented by irrigation in the lowlands for many years.

Theresa to St. Ignatius of Loyola. Catholicism spread to the overseas territories colonized by Spain, and the Church is still quite influential there as it is in the peninsula.

The great expansion overseas brought incredible riches to Spain and Portugal, but the absolute monarch ruling in Madrid did not invest very much of it in the local economy. When its naval power was ruined by the Dutch, the English, and the French and its continental military power seriously threatened by the French, the Iberian peninsula began to lose one territory after another. In the nineteenth century the Spanish colonial empire fell apart. All the gold of Peru and all the silver of Mexico appeared to have been vaporized. To develop its own mines Spain needed capital investments from abroad, and British, French, Belgian, and German interests controlled a great deal of its mines and transportation. Portugal was in somewhat better shape. The question has often been asked whether Spain had not been "spoiled" by its too rapid success, political and economic, coming right after the hard fighting of the *reconquesta*. The Crown was ruined by many long wars, the country itself was swept by foreign armies during the Napoleonic period and divided by internal strife, but other countries of Europe have known a history as troubled as the Spanish and have come out with greater assets. The rapid decline of this great power is puzzling but positive. A bitter civil war in the years 1936–1938 disrupted whatever national economy had been organized, and recovery was slow until recently.

Spared the ordeals of the two World Wars, the Iberian peninsula seems still overwhelmed with its present problems, as it is the most backward and least evolving part of Europe west of the "iron curtain." Regionalism is very strong too, and the unity established by the absolutist monarchy after the *reconquesta* is tempered by local trends toward autonomy. As usual in the Mediterranean area, people are passionately attached to their province or even city of origin. Still, Portugal and Spain are both old nations strongly welded together, as their history has shown in many instances. Spain has by far the more complicated structure, and its present problems are far more acute than is the case in smaller and more prosperous Portugal.

## PORTUGAL, THE ATLANTIC FAÇADE

No country of Europe is so typically a maritime façade as Portugal. Even Norway has more continental highlands. Portugal has an area of 34,254 square miles, plus some islands in the Atlantic and territories in Africa and the East Indies, remnants of the great colonial empire of olden times. Stretching along the western coast of the peninsula, Portugal is widely opened to oceanic influences: its territory has the shape of a rectangle limited by the Atlantic to the west and south. A coastal low-land, which is rarely flat but does not rise much above 600 feet in elevation, follows the seashore and extends inland in the southern half of the country. Wide, flatbottomed valleys penetrate eastward among the higher lands.

The Portuguese territory extends over the western fringe of the high tablelands of central Spain. These come closer to the sea north of the Tagus River; in that area narrow but high ranges of mountains rise above the average altitude (around 2000 feet) of the plateaus. Most of these ranges are oriented southwest-northeast, a common direction along the European shores of the Atlantic, and the main valleys follow a similar axis. The relative proportion of high and low land determines the substantial difference between north and south of the Tagus valley. The climatic conditions vary also from north to south, as the drying up effect of the Azores anticyclone are felt more regularly and for longer periods in the south.

Northern Portugal can be defined as the lands between the Minho River (the lower course of which serves as boundary with Spain) and the Mondego River. A more important river crosses this area from east to west, and its valley has become a major thoroughfare; this is the Douro, which empties into the Atlantic at Oporto. The interior is rough country: a land of granite and schists, deeply eroded by swift streams. Wide stretches of the plateaus extend above 3000 feet with isolated mountains rising to 4500. In the heart of the northern massives, the climate is severe, the annual temperature averages 50° F., and snow falls occur frequently in winter on the highlands. The average altitude decreases and the climate warms up when one comes closest to the Douro valley. The land is here densely populated, intensively cultivated, with the vine playing an essential part on the well-exposed slopes but fully terraced, above which are forests of pines and oaks. Toward the east and south the aridity begins to show, and Mediterranean trees, bearing olives, almonds, and figs, begin to appear. The general slope leads westward, toward the coast; lower hills surround the old town and religious metropolis of Braga (41,000 inhabitants) around which the density of population surpasses 550 per square mile. The land use here is reminiscent of the *bocage* along the French Atlantic coast: lines of trees enclose small fields in which fruit trees are scattered; and intensive cultivation of corn, hay, beans, vines, and many other crops is carried out, utilizing the available soil to the utmost. The summer harvest of corn and beans, introduced from the New World, allows the dense population to avoid famine.

But the most intensive activities are concentrated at the mouth of the Douro, around Oporto (or Pôrto), the second city and port of Portugal and the capital of the famous port wine country. The district of Oporto in 1964 had 1400 people to the square mile; the city accounted for 315,000 inhabitants. Since the eighteenth century the port has grown, exporting its excellent wine (grown upstream along the Douro; see p. 439) chiefly to the British market. Most of the trade is still in British hands, and the longstanding association of Oporto with English interests has endured to the advantage of the area. An advanced harbor had to be built outside the Douro proper to avoid the irregularities of navigation in the estuary. The city is beautiful with its old sections and the picturesque commercial activity along the river. Its business district resembles cities of northern England. Some modern industries have developed. The hinterland mountains are richly mineralized and some ores are being mined; they may constitute the foundation of more industrialization in the future.

South of the Douro the lowland widens, then a wide depression drained by the Mondego River penetrates deeply to the northeast. Here one enters central Portugal, a more truly Mediterranean country, with the usual groves of fruit trees, patches of irrigated land scattered all around, and some threats of drought. Central Portugal has a high spine in the form of a line of ridges of ranges, extending from the Serra da Estrella in the northeast to the hills of Sintra in the southwest. Some of these hills are well mineralized, and tungsten ores are being mined. The northwestern slope, better watered, runs down to the Mondego valley and the coastal lowland. Coimbra, the old university town, is the local provincial center, with 50,000 inhabitants. South of the spinal ridge, the slopes overlook the verdant and rich depression of the Tagus. Here is the richest plain of Portugal, with intensively cultivated fields, intermingled with rice fields, orchards and cork-oak woods.

The Tagus widens before emptying into the ocean in a large depression where, on a large and well-sheltered basin, stands Lisbon, the national capital. Lisbon, a city of almost one million people, suburbs included, is an impressive capital. Its active port is one of the most beautiful sights in the country, with gently rolling hills surrounding the expanded Tagus, while white red-roofed buildings interspersed with churches cover the hills. In some respects, when seen from the southern bank of the Tagus, Lisbon reminds one of Constantinople on the Bosporus. Inside it is a most animated city, unusually clean and quiet for a "Mediterranean" town. The variety of its architecture, the houses often decorated with tiles of vivid colors, has great charm. The Avenida de Liberdade is a beautiful avenue going up the slope toward the circle of the Marquess de Pombal, who directed, in the eighteenth century, the reconstruction of the modern economy of Portugal. Downtown the narrow Gold and Silver Streets run parallel amid the buildings of banks and maritime

Harvesting grapes in the port-wine region. The famous wine comes from vineyards concentrated in a small area on the Douro upstream from Oporto. *(Casa de Portugal)*

The peaceful town of Penela in the Beira region near Coimbra. On the slope are olive trees. The white buildings of the town, with their red tile roofs, are dominated by the ruins of an old castle built by the Knights Templar in the twelfth century, guarding the road to Coimbra and the south. *(Casa de Portugal)*

trade toward the Praça de Commercio on the river, recalling certain monumental aspects of Stockholm. The whole city has a kind of quiet and cheerful dynamism which combines many of the qualities of the Mediterranean and the West. Warehouses follow the Tagus upstream, while factories spread downstream toward Belem, the historical palatial town, now a suburb, and farther toward the beaches and summer residences of Estoril and Cascais. Lisbon has had a troubled history. Earthquakes destroyed the city in 1575 and 1755, and almost all of it has been rebuilt since 1755. It has rapidly expanded in recent years, benefiting by the better organization of the national economy. A new industrial, suburban area has grown up on the south bank of the Tagus, around a large steel mill and other plants.

South of Lisbon the climate dries up; annual rainfall remains below 20 inches; summer temperatures are above 70° F. (Lisbon averages 71 in August.) Lower hills, gently rolling, are less thickly populated than the valleys up north, and sheep raising is important. Great estates stretch widely, but some plains have been colonized recently as the estates began to break up. The south is a sort of frontier for modern Portugal. Moorish influences are often apparent, and hills are crowned with the walls of the "Moorish castles," actually the well-defended sites to which the population fled during the insecure period of the reconquesta, only to empty them and rebuild towns in the lowland when peace and order again prevailed. Few towns are important: Setúbal (45,000) is a fishing and canning port; Évora (25,000) is a local center inland; Faro (18,000) is a small port on the southern coast at the foot of the mountain range of the Algarve. The Mediterranean environment, with its brush, rugged hills, perfumes, flowers, and fruits, is fully achieved in this southern province of the Algarve. A number of small fishing ports hide in the bays on the coast, sending their craft all over the tropical Atlantic. New dams commanding irrigation projects are being built and others planned. This area, if and when developed, could greatly increase Portuguese production of food.

Although a maritime façade and the pioneer of the European expansion overseas, Portugal is today chiefly a rural country. Its maritime activities are mainly in the field of fisheries: Lisbon and other ports send a fleet every year to the Newfoundland banks as well as to Iceland and the western coast of Africa. A catch of about 450,000 tons is landed annually. The Portuguese merchant marine (700,000 gross tons) is modest in relation to the part the country has had in the history of navigation. Perhaps it was the disappointment at being so quickly robbed by the Dutch and others of the advantages achieved in the first stages that has kept the Portuguese only moderately interested in sea trade. At any rate, trade has remained a great specialty of the Portuguese, and

A sailboat on the Douro River, with rocky, well terraced slopes in the background. *(Casa de Portugal)*

The highway to Lisbon in the city's suburbs. *(Casa de Portugal)*

one they have been able to carry on actively in full cooperation with British interests. Portugal is sometimes called the oldest ally of England or the British pier of debarkation on the continent, a part it assumed during the Napoleonic Wars. Trade and fishing cannot, however, account for the solid foundations of the national strength: these lie in the efficient organization of their land that the Portuguese have achieved.

Numbering 9.2 million people, the Portuguese form a rather homogeneous group. In old times they were a mixture of Celtic and Germanic elements with the older Iberian layer, with a substantial Semitic addition of Phoenicians, Moors, and Jews. Old rivalry with the greater neighbor Spain has united them, and regionalism is weaker in Portugal as a decentralizing force than in most other Mediterranean countries. Also the whole country is not large, and it has not known the same variety of relations and attractions as the much larger Spain. The Portuguese culture and temperament have many similarities with the Spanish, yet are still quite distinct. The people do not have the same fiery and fanatical attitudes; their behavior is definitely of a more moderate, milder kind. They are better diplomats and deal more easily with strangers. In many ways they are more orderly than most Mediterranean people are reputed to be. It can be said indeed that among Mediterraneans the Portuguese are the Atlantic shade. Their cultural association has been more with France and Britain, and it is also with those countries that they have traded most.

The change in landscape when one crosses the Spanish-Portuguese border going westward is often striking. To the rugged plateaus, little cultivated, with a few poor and shabby-looking villages, is opposed on the Portuguese side a more verdant, carefully cultivated country, with more prosperous populations, lighter shades, white houses decorated with tiles, a simpler and less tense atmosphere. The contrast particularly strikes the traveler on the road or train from Madrid to Lisbon. Portugal has certainly been better developed. It has substantial surpluses of olive oil, cork, and wine (chiefly port and muscatel) to export, and it sells large quantities of canned fish (sardines, tuna).

Agriculture still provides the livelihood of the majority of the population, although its share in the gross national product is being rapidly reduced by steady industrialization. In 1965, this share shrank down to about 21 percent. In 1965 Portugal produced 472,000 tons of wheat; 600,000 tons of corn; small quantities of rye, barley, and oats; 180,000 tons of rice; 1 million tons of potatoes; about 14.6 million hectolitres of wine; and 41,000 tons of olive oil. Forests provide substantial resources: they cover some 6.2 million acres, about half of which are in pinewoods and almost one fourth under cork oaks. Portugal produces over half of the world crop of cork bark; the cork and cork products rank usually as the main item on the list of Portuguese exports (about 180,000 tons are annually exported); sardines and wines take second and third place by importance in value on the export list, while the fourth place is occupied by the products from the pine forests (resin, turpentine, and pit-props). The only important exports not provided by farming or forestry are minerals: wolfram, the tungsten ore for which Portugal is one of the major world producers (996 tons of tungsten in 1965 made Portugal the first producer in Europe and eighth in the world), and some pyrites. The country has also some deposits of tin (about 600 tons mined annually), copper, manganese, molybdenum, antimony, lead, gold, beryl, iron ore (100,000 tons in metal content), and coal (428,000 tons in 1965). The more valuable minerals are mainly exported, the more ordinary ones are increasingly used in the gradually developing manufactures of Portugal. But mining production is declining altogether.

Industrialization is still in its infancy by modern standards; progress has been quite notable, however, through the 1960s. The larger industries, and the first to be developed, were the traditional ones: food-processing industries, fish canning (especially the famous sardines at Setúbal, Matozinhos, Portimão, Vila Real de San Antonio, and Olhão), cement (over a million tons produced, especially at Maceira do Lis, Alhandra, Torres Vedras), glass and ceramics (especially the colored tiles of Sacavem which decorate gaily the outside and inside of so many buildings). Recently waterpower has been greatly developed: 5 billion kwh. were produced in Portugal in 1965, 90 percent of which came from hydraulic sources; more dams are built and equipped, especially in the north, in the basin of the Douro River. Textiles have also been expanding, particularly the manufacture of cotton yarn around Oporto. Chemical plants are making fertilizers, refining sulfur, producing soaps, oils, and rubber goods; they are concentrated largely in and around the two main cities. The new mills near Lisbon produced 270,000 tons of steel in 1966. These industries are beginning to export to the Portuguese dependencies in Africa; but they still have to expand a great deal before they may be able to fully supply the domestic needs. Foreign trade is particularly active with Great Britain, the Common Market countries, and the United States. However, the African colonies represent an essential market that takes about one fourth of the exports and supplies some 14 percent of the imports.

While proceeding with some industrialization and modernization, the government of Premier Salazar has been cautious and conservative on this track. It seeks both to avoid inflation of the currency and to preserve the existing social structure and ways of life of Portugal. About 20,000 new jobs are created annually, although the labor force increases by at least 50,000 people every year. Thus the "surplus population" swells in threatening manner. Many of them emigrate if they can (mainly to France, Brazil, other Latin American countries, and also to Canada). A more significant long-range trend towards a solution has been the steady decline of the crude birth rate, which came down from about 33 per thousand in the 1920s to 26.7 in 1948 and 22 in 1967; it still is, however, one of the highest in Europe and this trend's effects are somewhat delayed by a parallel decline of mortality rates (from 13 per thousand in 1948 to 10.8 in 1966). This surplus population is the chief national problem. Part of it takes the form of crowding in the cities, chiefly in and around Lisbon. The density is growing very high in the districts of Lisbon (about 1300 per square mile), Oporto, Braga, and on the island dependencies of the Azores and Madeira (populated by some 600,000 inhabitants with scant means to make a living). Growth of manufacturing around Lisbon may lead to modification of the old saying about the three cities, that "in Lisbon people have fun, in Oporto they work, and in Braga they pray." The fun has been moving farther away, especially to Madeira, which has become an important center of international tourism. The vast territories of Angola and the Mozambique in Africa seemed to offer a possible frontier for expansion; the recent political unrest in Angola darkens the horizon for this goal. In Europe, Portugal has been a member of the EFTA, following its long-standing policy of alliance and economic association with Britain; it is reluctant to turn towards a continental system.

For a quarter of a century Portugal has enjoyed a period of peace and stability. A neutral ocean front in Europe during World War II, it has benefited by the flow of refugees through it as well as in a variety of other ways. The clever financial administration of Professor Antonio de Oliveira Salazar, its authoritarian prime minister, has made its currency strong. In many respects the contrast with Spain is striking. Portugal, however, is in great need of improvement in the economic and social fields—all the more as its population is expected to increase by 14 percent from 1965 to 1980, even if emigration continues at a rate of 40,000 per year.

## NORTHERN AND CENTRAL SPAIN

Spain is as continental as Portugal is maritime. It has isolated itself from the continent physically and morally to live alone behind the barrier of the Pyrenees. The efficiency of the Pyrenees as a barrier has been proverbial among the French for centuries—"to build castles in Spain" means to them to indulge in the most fantastic kind of wishful thinking. The Spanish slope is less steep on the average than the French one, but the lofty line of summits above 10,000 feet tower over more highlands averaging 6000 feet in the south. Massive, high plateaus descend slowly toward the Mediterranean in the eastern section of the range; the slope is sharper and more sculpted by erosion in the west. But even there it is quite arid: brown and yellow shades predominate instead of green and gray ones as soon as one crosses a pass and begins to go down the Spanish slope.

The Mediterranean section of the sub-Pyrenean area is the old province of Catalonia. Westward the land belonged to the kingdoms of Navarre or Aragon before the *reconquesta* created Spanish unity. Although the Pyrenees are lower and less massive toward the Atlantic, their crests are crossed by few practicable passes. The main thoroughfare follows the narrow coastal sidewalk along the shore of the Bay of Biscay. Then a railroad from Pau in France to Jaca in Spain crosses the high range at the Somport Pass (border station of Canfranc). The high valleys are dead ends, with a sleepy, marginal life, backward equipment, and small scattered villages. Amid the scanty brush covering steep limestone cliffs or heights, these valleys lead to the long and deep furrow in which flows the Ebro River. Almost parallel in direction to the general axis of the Pyrenees range, the Ebro valley widens as it approaches the Mediterranean but cuts through the coastal chains by narrow gorges. The valley has a steppic climate; in winter the cold northerly *cierzo* blows down from the high summits, freezing the land; in summer the sun burns the deep trench. This furrow follows the contact of the central plateau or *Meseta* with the sub-Pyrenean hills. As soon as the bottom of the valley widens enough to form a plain, the waters of the stream and its tributaries are used to irrigate the steppic but fertile land. Around Saragossa (350,000 people) a rich irrigated agriculture has thus developed: fields of wheat, tomatoes, alfalfa, and sugar beets alternate with orchards of cherry, pear, peach, and apricot trees. An oasis in the midst of rugged hills, this rich plain is a *huerta,* an example of the Mediterranean concentration of fertility in space. It could be extended farther if adequate water supply were provided. Saragossa is an active city, rapidly expanding with food and other industries, and is the main rail hub of northern Spain. The Ebro valley links Mediterranean Catalonia with the Atlantic section of Spain to the west.

The Atlantic area of Spain is situated along the north and northwest coast of the peninsula. It is a mountainous country consisting of the Cantabrian ranges and of the Galician massif. The structure of these highlands is rather involved. They were uplifted and folded between the deep trough of the Atlantic and the resistant block of the Meseta. Erosion has been active, for this northern façade is abundantly watered. The slopes facing west record the highest precipitations in Spain: more than 35 inches in general and up to 60 inches in places. The maximum rain-

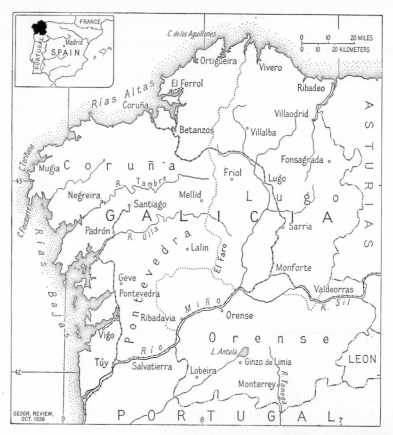

Sketch map of Galicia. *(The
Geographical Review)*

A street in Orense. *(Spanish
Tourist Office)*

fall occurs in Galicia in winter, according to the Mediterranean rule, but in the eastern section in autumn. Santiago de Compostela, the famous medieval pilgrimage in Galicia, at an altitude of 886 feet, has an average temperature of 45° F. in January and 66° in August, with an annual rainfall of 65 inches. This is a mild and damp country, so different from the rest of Spain. Luxuriant vegetation spreads on the slopes: oaks and chestnuts are the old native trees; the pine and the eucalyptus have been recently introduced in large numbers. Apple trees are scattered in the meadows, where fat cows graze; rye, corn, and potatoes are widely grown; the farm is often accompanied by a small silo built on pillars, the *horreo*. There are many things that give this Atlantic region of Spain a kind of Norman or Irish imprint. This impression fades away rather quickly as the mountain crests are passed toward the interior. The coastland is rich, better developed, thickly settled, while the interior is much poorer, especially in Galicia. South of the first ranges screening the maritime influences in the eastern section, aridity and continentality take over, and a topography of badlands or clayish and gypsum outcroppings is not uncommon. The complicated topography of the hills helped make of them a shelter for the Christians fleeing before the Moslem conquest and later a springboard for the *reconquesta*.

A number of notable towns are found along the coast. In Galicia deep bays, invaded by the sea, penetrate inland and shelter excellent roadsteads. These *rias* are studded with ports such as Corunna (200,000), El Ferrol, and Vigo (145,000), famous for the galleons that brought to it the treasures of the New World. Eastward the main ports have risen at points where transportation inland was easy—that is, the mountains were lower and the Meseta pushed closer to the shore. Such are the cases of Santander (125,000) and of Bilbao (325,000). The latter is the actual regional capital, largely owing to the proximity of high-grade iron ore mines. In the vicinity of Santander large-scale zinc ore mining is carried out, while farther west, around Oviedo (135,000) is found the principal coalfield of the peninsula. Iron and steel industries have sprung up as a result of this combination, especially at Bilbao and Oviedo. The Atlantic coast is not only the best watered in the whole country but also the best endowed with minerals. East of Bilbao the Basque country has some French imprint, and the town of San Sebastian (150,000), close to the border, attempts to serve as the Spanish Nice and attracts tourists in summer.

All this Atlantic section of Spain feels some population pressure. Emigration has long been important, Galicia supplying hard-working, poorly educated people from its backward small peasantry and the Basque country sending out to the large cities and overseas much more active and efficient elements which have been important in South Amer-

A typical ox cart in San Sebastian in the Basque country. *(Spanish Tourist Office)*

Fields and olive groves in Guipuzcoa in northern Spain. *(Spanish Tourist Office)*

ica. Much could be still accomplished to improve the lot of the local populations. Redistribution of part of them could also be considered, as much land seems to be open just south of the Cantabrian Mountains on the Meseta.

The Meseta constitutes central Spain and the main bulk of the peninsula. From the Ebro to the Guadalquivir and from the Cantabrian to the Betic ranges, the Meseta covers two thirds of the total area of Spain. It consists of a group of high plateaus, higher on the periphery than in their middle, almost entirely above 1500 feet, divided into two main tablelands — New Castile and Old Castile — by a line of mountain ranges. The Sierra de Guadarrama, with peaks reaching 7600 feet, is the loftiest and longest of these central ranges, which follow on the whole the south-west-northeast axis. The Meseta is a difficult country; its vast horizons suggest a sadness which is reflected in the melancholy and violent temperament of its proud people. The lower pleateaus are steppic, covered with reddish to yellow soils. The higher lands along the rim and the central line of ridges have forests and pastures. All are permeated with austerity and even despair. Old Castile, to the northwest of the Guadarrama, does not, however, look so hopeless to the naturalist: there are no apparent reasons why, an adequate water supply being provided, these lands would not bloom. Along the rivers the greenery of the *vegas* (or gardens) testifies to that end. The problem of irrigating vast expanses of dry land with few streams crossing them may not be easy to solve, but much could be done to make parts of Old Castile blossom. Some cities, ornamented with beautiful buildings and monuments of old times, such as Burgos (94,000 inhabitants), Salamanca (95,000), Valladolid (182,000), or even much smaller León (79,000) and Palencia, seem to be remnants of a past prosperity. Yet they are still very active, and have grown in the recent decades. When the spring is rainy, the darker soils give rich yields of grain. More scientific approach to land use may well turn this area into one of the richest agricultural sections of the Mediterranean.

Southeast of the central ranges New Castile has been so called because it was more recently reconquered from the Moors. It is better shielded from the northwestern humid influences and closer to the warmer and drier Mediterranean. The steppe is therefore lower; in the center of the plateau, La Mancha is a subdesert area, reputed to be one of the poorest of Europe. On the fringes of New Castile some centers of great rural and urban activity have flourished: all the Meseta is crossed by lanes of cattle and sheep migrations which take the herds from one pasture to another, from the lower and drier lands in winter up into the mountains in summer. Here was first developed the famous breed of the Merino sheep, which was later brought to the Argentine, Vermont, and elsewhere. Along the Tagus River a line of rural districts has successfully developed around some old towns with Toledo (41,000), which has been a capital for the Visigoths, the Moors, and New Castile, as the most picturesque. The fertilizing waters of the river and of the tributaries coming down the slope of the central ranges are responsible for this prosperity.

At the foot of the Guadarrama stands the national capital of Spain, Madrid, where all authority and riches have been so well centralized that even in modern times no other important city has been able to develop on the Meseta. Its political power alone can explain the fortune of Madrid: 3 million inhabitants are crowded in the city. The elegant section of the Prado, with its parks, museums, and mansions, contrasts sharply with the misery and filth of the workers' sections. No other capital in Europe gives such an impression of "surplus mankind," of crowds of children begging in the streets. Madrid is a beautiful city, large parts of which are devoted to the political and administrative functions of the capital, to big business, and to luxury industries. It is the central rail hub of the peninsula. Large-scale manufacturing could hardly be developed in such an isolated position, without any important resource, except for the local market itself, in the vicinity. But Madrid claims to be the first industrial city of Spain, at least by the number of manufacturing establishments and their variety. Within the great variety of small plants finishing consumer goods of all kinds, Madrid also has substantial works building machinery (railway rolling stock, elevators, some motorcars and motorcycles) and electrical and communications equipment, making clothing, shoes, and leatherware. Madrid is also a great cultural center for the whole Spanish-speaking world and its role as a center of tourism has been considerably developed in recent years. The regime of Generalissimo Franco has strengthened its central function over that of Barcelona, which used to be the economic and cultural metropolis.

## THE MEDITERRANEAN FRINGE OF SPAIN

Spain deserves to be classified in the Mediterranean area if only as a result of the importance that its southern and eastern coastal regions have in the whole national structure. This is a rugged coastland, with a truly Mediterranean, dry climate and little area of lowland. But the rainfall is still more abundant than in Madrid or Valladolid and slightly more regular. Its annual 12 to 22 inches are supplemented by the waters of many streams coming down from the highlands towering above the plains. In the southeast, where aridity is greatest, the sierras (mountain ridges) too are loftier and therefore better watered: the Sierra Nevada reaches 11,000 feet and has some permanent snowcaps. In the north the Pyrenees are helpful. But smaller mountains keep supplying appreciable amounts of water once streams are dammed and reservoirs maintained.

In this partitioned area, stretching in length, many local nuclei have developed; specialization and local patriotism are stronger here than in other parts of Spain, organized around certain cities. Between the eastern tip of the Pyrenees and the lower Guadalquivir River, one finds one city of more than a million people and ten others of more than 100,000. Barcelona is the capital of Catalonia, the chief port and industrial center of Spain with 1,665,000 inhabitants in 1965; capitals of huertas are Valencia (525,000), Seville (470,000), Málaga, (310,000), Murcia (261,000), Granada (154,000), Córdoba (210,000), Alicante (128,000), Cartagena (128,000), and Jerez de la Frontera (132,000). Cádiz, the other great port of the galleon fleets, is smaller today (125,000). Valencia and Murcia are famous for their oranges, Málaga, Alicante, and Jerez for their wines. This is a truly Mediterranean economy: each huerta a large oasis, most of them on coastal plains, exporting their products to far-off markets. The tree crops are essential too: grapes and citrus fruits, olives and cork bark, almonds and figs. But in between the groves and sometimes even between the lines of trees, other crops grow: rice is one of the specialties of Valencia; truck farming is prosperous; grain, clover, and alfalfa cover a substantial acreage. This development of urban life amidst purely rural areas seems also a Mediterranean feature. It goes back quite far in history. Many people who till land live in the cities or their suburbs; moreover the social structure and the low standard of living help explain such agglomerations of population.

Two main regional entities deserve mention, at the extremities of this lengthy fringe: Catalonia in the north and Andalusia in the south. The former expanded for a while on both sides of the Pyrenees. The Catalan people are somewhat less austere and are better businessmen than the average Spaniard, and their section is the best developed of Spain. On the tributaries of the Ebro, such as the Segre River, huertas have been tilled; the rapid streams have been harnessed up in the hills and yield a substantial amount of hydroelectric power. Textile and chemical industries run on that power in the valleys and in the suburbs of Barcelona. The city has specialized in cotton trade and manufacturing. It is a cosmopolitan center, with a legend of adventure and suspense pinned on it by history and literature, somewhat as on Marseille in France. Like most of the Spanish cities, Barcelona lives largely at night, when the heat of the day has subsided; unlike most of the other cities, it is largely industrial and very dynamic with 1.7 million people.

Despite Madrid's claim to more industrial establishments, Barcelona with its satellite cities forms a greater metropolitan area with a larger manufacturing output. It has steel mills and large mechanical shops;

most of the textile industry of Spain is concentrated in Barcelona and the nearby towns of Sabadell and Tarrasa. There are also rubber and tire plants in Barcelona, Villanueva y Geltrú, and Manresa, as well as chemical industries in and around the Catalonian metropolis, including artificial fibers at Badalona. Barcelona has been and still is, despite Madrid's progress in this field, the largest Spanish printing and publishing center. To the northeast of Barcelona, in the bays, creeks and on the promontories of the coast, has developed the *Costa Brava*, a new, fancy riviera, attracting crowds of vacationers in the summer.

Andalusia, in the south, reaches from the Mediterranean to the Atlantic shores. It is centered on the rich valley of the Guadalquivir River, a triangular plain, the largest lowland of Spain. Part of it, along the lower course of the river, is swampy and needs reclamation; but most of it has been organized in rich huertas surrounded by an olive tree "forest." Here the Phoenician and Roman colonizations were most successful, and the Moorish culture had its brightest development. In the Middle Ages cities like Córdoba and Granada were among the greatest centers of art and learning as well as of trade and industry. Here also the Spanish people are more subtle and mild tempered than on the Meseta or in the Pyrenees. Andalusia is a country of great charm and remarkable scenic beauty. The sharp crests and lofty peaks of the sierras tower over the wide lowland and the blue sea. Tourists come to admire and to ponder over such masterpieces of Moorish architecture as the Alcázar and the Alhambra. Córdoba had its own caliphate; Seville, still a seaport on the wide tidal river, still the regional capital, is full of the memories of El Cid Campeador; palms and xerophytic trees announce the proximity of Africa and of the Sahara. Granada, alone of the large cities, is in a high basin, up in the hills amid towering peaks. It was the last Islamic capital and redoubt in Iberia and keeps the Moorish imprint well in evidence. The coastland between Catalonia and Andalusia is an irregular string of huertas, of which Valencia is by far the most important. The considerable size of the city (about 600,000) is explained by the fact that a large part of the rural population lives in the town and does not have to go far from it to attend to the irrigated fields and orchards. Valencia, as well as Seville, has some engineering works, ceramics, glass, and leather plants. Habitat is very concentrated all over southern and eastern Spain. Off the eastern coast, Spain includes the Balearic Islands, an archipelago famed for its scenery; on the three main islands (Majorca, Minorca, and Ibiza) the same huerta system prevails around the hills. Palma de Mallorca, the main town, has 210,000 inhabitants. In the Atlantic, to the southwest, Spain possesses the Canary Islands, with a dense population and large banana groves. Another long string of seaside resorts has developed along the southeastern Spanish

Salamanca, the old university city, with an old bridge and the cathedral. *(Spanish Tourist Office)*

A busy intersection in the center of Madrid. *(Black Star)*

CATALONIA

0    10    20    30    40    50 MILES
0  10  20  30  40  50 KILOMETERS

GEOGR. REVIEW, APR. 1938

*(Above)* Place names are in Spanish, not Catalan. *(Below)* The distribution and respective zones of influence of market towns in northeastern Spain. *(The Geographical Review)*

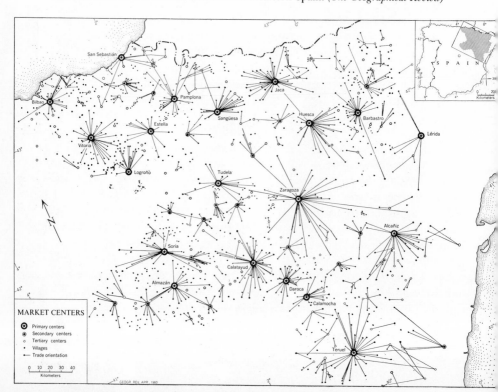

MARKET CENTERS

⊙ Primary centers
◉ Secondary centers
○ Tertiary centers
· Villages
←— Trade orientation

0   10   20   30   40
Kilometers

GEOGR. REV. APR. 1960

coast: this *Costa del Sol* attracts millions of Europeans, especially Germans, every year. An urban ribbon begins to link together the old, large cities of this seaboard.

Near the southern tip of the peninsula, where Europe comes closest to Africa, a small peninsula jutting southward is not Spanish territory. Linked by a sandy narrow path to the mainland rises the Rock of Gibraltar, converted since 1704 into a formidable fortress by British naval might. It is through the control of straits and narrow channels on which fortresses were established that Britain founded her political and military control of sea lanes, the road to India, and the maritime approaches to Europe. At Gibraltar, the Rock stood guard at the gate of the Mediterranean, keeping it open or shut according to the needs of British policy. With an area of 2.5 square miles and a population of 25,000, Gibraltar remains an important British naval and air base, despite periodic claims by Spain.

## THE UNDERDEVELOPED ECONOMY OF SPAIN

Four centuries have not yet elapsed since the court of Madrid considered itself as ruling most of the known world. Now very little Spanish authority remains overseas: on the other shore of the Strait of Gibraltar, Spanish territories in Morocco have been reduced to a few towns (Ceuta, Melilla). Spain controls also a piece of the western Sahara, the Rio de Oro territory, and a small colony in Guinea. In Spain the contrast between past and present is one of the most striking of history; such is also the contrast between the past and present trends mixing in the landscape. The country was terribly devastated by the Civil War in the 1930s, but long before that date a slow and continuous decline had set in. The absolute and intolerant state that came out of the *reconquesta* rose for a century with extraordinary brilliance. It seems to have been a magnificent display of fireworks, and the country seems to have gone to sleep after such excitement and such an overwhelming success.

In modern times Spain appears backward in its economic development and in its social structure. The country has put patriotic concern for its independence above all. Traffic is difficult anyhow across the Pyrenees, but it was made even more so by Spanish railroads, which used a gauge slightly wider than that of France (the standard European gauge) in order to make it less easy for the French to invade their land again. Maritime activities are restricted, although a merchant fleet of 2.3 million tons flies the Spanish flag and the annual fish catch approximates 1.4 million tons. With its specialized economy, small amount of industry, and its population concentrated chiefly on the maritime periphery, Spain has had to trade a great deal with foreign countries. Its usual role is that of a typical underdeveloped country: Spain exports certain foodstuffs (mainly wines, olive oil, citrus fruits, early vegetables in the spring) and raw materials (such as iron, copper, lead, and zinc ores, pyrites, mercury, and some potash, cork bark and hides); imports are much more varied and consist of foods, raw materials, and manufactured products of all kinds.

A considerable effort has been made since the war to improve this situation and develop agricultural production as well as industrial activities. What was achieved by 1968 remains, however, just a beginning. The textile industries, centered in Barcelona, are now satisfying the scanty requirements of the domestic market. Iron and steel have been pushed, particularly in the area of Biscay. In the 1960s, Spain produced annually 14 million tons of coal, more than double its average output in the 1930s. About 1.8 million tons of lignite were added to the coal. The installed capacity of waterpower plants reached 9 million kilowatts, six times the figure of 1949. The total per capita consumption of energy is also estimated to have risen to 1100 kilograms of coal equivalent in 1966 – double the figure of Portugal. As some 2.8 million tons of iron content in the ores were extracted in 1965, the iron and steel industries produced 2,400 tons of pig iron and 3,460,000 tons of steel.

Mineral resources are in fact quite abundant in Spain. In 1965 in various parts of the hilly country different ores were mined besides the iron of the northwest: small quantities of manganese, copper, bauxite, antimony, silver, magnesite, and substantial quantities of mercury (Spain was the first world producer of this metal in 1965 with 3,100 tons in Almadén), lead (59,000 tons chiefly in the Sierra Morena), zinc (40,000 tons, in the Basque country and near Santander), tin, and tungsten. Important quantities of salt and sulphur are also mined as well as potash in Catalonia. Most of these deposits could be greatly developed if a good domestic market existed for the output. At present most of the minerals extracted on a large scale are for export. In 1959, largely under pressure from American economic advisers, the Spanish government launched a plan of industrialization and development. Some results were achieved from 1960 on, inducing an expansion of exports, mainly towards the Common Market countries (which took about 45 percent of the exports while supplying only 1 percent of the imports). This trend helped temporarily the strengthening of the peseta, but could not last long. Increased industrialization would help, but Spain is moving only slowly and almost reluctantly in this direction, which may entail shifts in its social structure. The country has not adhered to any of the European economic groupings but the OEEC. Some actual help came in recent years from the building of American Air Force bases in Spain and of a naval establishment used by the United States Navy at the port of Roda near

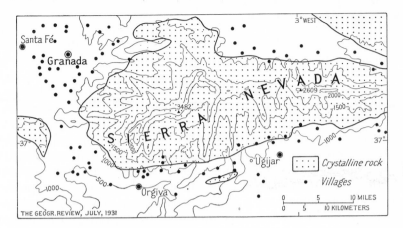

Distribution of villages in the Sierra Nevada. An upper limit to village sites is not enforced by altitude but by bed rock, with its attendant problems of relief, soil, and ground water. The shaded portion represents crystalline rock; surrounding rocks are sedimentaries (*The Geographical Review*)

A courtyard of the Alhambra at Granada. (*Spanish Tourist Office*)

Cadiz; a pipeline was built to carry petroleum from Roda to Madrid. American financial help has also been significant. The steady rise of many statistical indices has not yet brought Spain into a position to catch up with the times; in fact it is one of the few countries west of the "iron curtain" that does not actively participate in the recent economic expansion of Europe. Spain has to make up for many generations of backwardness: at present it gives the foreign visitor (and the tourists flock in large crowds to the seaside resorts and to the Balearic Islands, 15 to 17 million of them annually) the impression of popular misery and of being as overpopulated as Portugal or southern Italy. The Spanish average density of population is only 170 per square mile, while Portugal averages 260 and the whole of Italy 460. It is paradoxical that next to the booming countries of the Common Market, the backward economy of Spain, both underdeveloped and underpopulated by European standards, still claims a surplus of manpower.

With some 33 million inhabitants on an area of 195,000 square miles, Spain has a relatively rapid demographic increase, as the crude birth rate stands at about 21 per 1000 and the death rate at about 9 per 1000. Some of the demographic pressure has been eased from 1960 to 1965 by substantial emigration northward. But much of this labor is migratory and comes back after a few years abroad. In 1966, as the labor market in Western Europe tightened, although about 130,000 Spaniards went to work in other European countries, there was no net emigration, the first time since 1960. Obviously, Spain needs a profound overhauling of its economy.

Economic production has been expanding fast in recent years. At times, this expansion caused inflationary pressures, requiring tightening measures and in 1967 a new devaluation of the peseta. Some of the increase in production greatly helps the national consumption, though production is still characteristic of a developing economy as the growth sectors are largely in the basic and heavy industries: electricity, iron and steel, cement, petroleum products, and construction. But agricultural production has expanded mainly for wheat and wine, building up costly surpluses that can be marketed abroad only at a severe loss. The agricultural labor force is slowly moving from the farms toward the cities, to be employed in construction, manufacturing, and the services. The movement, however, is slow and little skilled manpower is available in Spain, or in Portugal, to help develop the more profitable sectors of manufacturing. The rural areas of Spain still demonstrate, by their lack of mechanization and the frequency of antiquated methods of cultivation and the use of draft animals, how human labor is wasted in this country. The resulting attraction it offers to tourists does not compensate in the long run for the losses and pressures on the national economy.

Spain should be one of the richer nations of Europe. Reality is quite different. Spain seems to have lagged behind the other Western European powers, chiefly as a result of her lack of social evolution. The large Moorish and Jewish bourgeoisie was replaced by a small number of aristocrats who concentrated in their hands all the enormous revenue of the empire, in so far as it was not kept by the crown and the Church. The national revenue is little divided among the people. Large landownership still prevails. Nationalization of certain enterprises, such as the main railways, has changed little. The Spaniard is certainly a hardworking man on the average, but he has seldom the feeling of toiling for his own good.

Recent history has recorded many remarkable trends in Spain. There was no lack of momentous impulses. The general line of evolution seems to have been well symbolized by the classic work of Cervantes: the Spanish people have been torn between the proud, uncompromising theoretician Don Quixote, who tilted with windmills, and the more modest and more realistic Sancho Panza. But Don Quixote was the master, and he kept riding the lean Rosinante — the condition of this legendary steed may well have been a hint as to the way of life of the bulk of the Spanish nation.

Rome. Beyond the Tiber River are St. Peter's Basilica and the Vatican. (*Three Lions*)

# 12

## Italy

No other national territory in Europe is as plainly defined on the physical map as is Italy: it covers the whole peninsula and is bounded on the continent by the high crest of the Alps. Only to the northeast is there no clear-cut topographical line to separate Italy from Yugoslavia. Such a well-defined area needed a geographical term to describe it, and for long centuries Italy remained no more than that. It was not until after the ideas of national unity, based on the people's will and natural boundaries, had been imported from the French Revolutionary armies and the Napoleonic Empire, that Italian patriots began to worry about the fact that Italy was merely a geographical expression. Their aspirations and endeavors succeeded in establishing national unity and independence and in making of Italy one of the important European powers of the twentieth century.

### THE BOOT-SHAPED PENINSULA

The Alpine folding seems to have taken care of shaping the whole of Italy. Its large arch surrounds it to the north and northwest, then smaller ranges, more or less of Alpine age, curve from the southern tip of the Alps eastward, then south and southeastward, building up the Apennine ranges, the spine or structural framework of the peninsula. Some limbs continue into Sicily to make the picture more complete. As a result Italy is essentially a mountainous country, dotted with peaks and crests but also strewn with small internal basins or coastal plains on the periphery. The only large plain develops in the north, inside the big bend of the Alps. Drained by the Po River, this plain is one of the largest on the Mediterranean shores; it adds an important aspect to the great variety of Italy.

461

Unity of the whole with great variety in the internal details resulted from the topography as well as from the history of Italy. The great Roman heritage was rooted in that country, but since it remained politically disunited after the disintegration of the ancient empire, Italy saw the rise of powerful regionalisms. With all its lands sloping down to some sea—and there are three of them around the peninsula—and with an elongated design, diversity was unavoidable. Differences arose from the extension in latitude, from the more maritime or continental location, from one slope to another. Italy is not isolated from the sea like Spain by a rim of highlands; on the contrary it is oriented almost everywhere toward the sea, but it may be toward the western or the eastern basin of the Mediterranean, toward the more open spaces to the south and west, or toward the more continental Adriatic in the east.

The variety of the outside relations has been very important in shaping these regional aspects. A country of difficult transportation, Italy has lived mostly through its network of crossroads: its history could almost be written in terms of the background of its seaports and the inland centers of traffic. At any period of history, Italy has had some regions living an isolated and almost self-sufficient existence while others indulged in large-scale international trade. The latter were centers of prosperity and power. When, at the end of the nineteenth century, Italy emerged united and independent from the period of Mediterranean decline, few of its cities had more than local importance.

The Italian recovery in the beginning of the twentieth century proceeded rapidly: a merchant marine was developed; a dense network of railroads and roads was built to unite better the diverse parts of the peninsula. Travel on the Italian railroads makes one clearly realize how difficult is the environment: for long stretches the railway disappears into tunnels; often it crosses gorges on long bridges; only in the Po plain does the rail cross land in a "normal" way.

"Normal" Italian conditions are as tough as the environment. While the topography has a dividing effect on the country, the climate tends rather to unify it. It is a typically Mediterranean climate, with a continental shade in the Po trough and with a milder quality in central Italy. The range of temperature between the coldest and hottest months reaches 43° F. at Alessandria in the north plain and drops to 26° at Palermo on the Sicilian north shore. It is always above 25°, which is a serious amplitude. In July averages throughout the whole country remain around 75°; but in January Alessandria records 31° and Palermo 50°. The temperature thus marks a clear difference between north and south, as the severity and duration of the winter vary. A similar contrast exists in altitude—that is, between coastlands and mountainous interior. The rainfall is on the whole abundant: 30 inches at Palermo, 40 at Milan,

52 at Genoa. But the dry period of the summer extends over at least three months (June–July–August) south of Rome, when the heat is highest. Plants require special adaptation or irrigation to survive such summers. The north plain gets a better distribution over the year. The continental quality of its climate helps the rain to fall in showers after very hot days. Although it is deeply maritime, Italy may get continental as a result of the topography screening certain areas from the sea. In the south of the peninsula and in Sicily, the rainfall increases inland quickly, and averages of 20 inches occur even on the plains.

The inconveniences of the climate are repaid in part by the famous Mediterranean luminosity: in Italy the sky dispenses a mild light which gives special beauty to the landscape. Fogs are, however, a common occurrence in winter at the bottom of the Po depression or in interior basins such as the depression of Florence. In the summer the colors are extremely bright and contrasted in the south, delicately graded in the north. The sunshine during the warm season has been taken advantage of chiefly in the irrigated plains, which are not very extensive.

The division of Italy in three main regions appears imposed by the physical environment: the north, center, and south. This last southern region includes the two large islands of Sardinia and Sicily; called in the Italian term *Mezzogiorno,* this sunlit south had a somewhat different history from the north, and the social structure and the cultural links are of a more purely Mediterranean kind.

## NORTHERN ITALY

The region of Italy north of the 44° latitude can be described as the depression of the Po and its mountainous rim. This rim consists chiefly of the Italian Alps and of the northern ranges of the Apennine Mountains. The Alps rise in the form of an enormous and magnificent amphitheater, enclosing the valley. The slope is steep everywhere but particularly so to the west and northwest; here the Alps of the province of Piedmont are often made of relatively soft schists, but culminate in the great crystalline massives of the French and Swiss border, including Mont Blanc. These western Alps are the highest section of this immense curving wall. In the central province of Lombardy the Alps are lower, and the slope is moderated by the appearance of limestone sub-Alpine massives which widen eastward, developing into a mountainous system in depth, whereas it has mainly height in the west. Long, ramified lakes extend their blue mirrors between the sharp crests in the Lombardian Alps. These lake landscapes are famous for their warm and mild climate and for their beauty, for here Alpine and Mediterranean nature mingle intimately. Tongues of the icecap dug them out and deposited the moraines barring

The Italian Alps. Cogne in the upper valley of Aosta in the western Alps and Lake Como.
(*Italian Government Travel Office*)

the drainage to the south. Thus were formed Lakes Maggiore, Lugano, Como, and Garda. Small inland rivieras have developed along their western shores.

From the vicinity of Lake Garda eastward, the Italian Alps widen, and immense limestone masses are divided up by deep and wide valleys along which the southern influences penetrate far northward. Of easy access and strange sculpture, the Dolomitic range looks like a gigantic staircase, resulting from the erosion of alternately soft and resistant layers. The large valley of the Adige River pushes north toward the great passes of the Austrian Alps, especially toward the Brenner. Italy obtained the area around Trento and Bolzano after 1919, though Austria and later Nazi Germany considered it German land, for part of the population of Bolzano spoke German.

Farther east the Alps break up into small ridges and hilly plateaus: the Julian area disputed between Italy and Yugoslavia offers no clear topographic boundary. Italian influences have penetrated far in a country where the bulk of the population was Slovene, that is, Slav. The peace treaty of 1947 left unsettled the question of Trieste, the chief port and city at the head of the Adriatic Sea; it was returned to Italy in 1954.

The steep slope of the Alps helped erosion to cut valleys and passes. The two main railways and roads leading into France cross along the seashore and through the Fréjus Pass at Modane. Old roads went through the two St. Bernard passes farther north, from which the Val d'Aosta or valley of the Dora Baltea River winds down to the Po. The Aosta area still has a French-speaking population, witnessing the close ties between the two slopes. The kingdom of Piedmont was until 1860 united to French Savoy, sitting astride the loftiest Alps. The Simplon and St. Gotthard passes lead into Switzerland from Lombardy. The main road to Central Europe passes farther east, via the Val d'Ampezzo and the Adige valley, to reach the Brenner Pass. Here in 1867 was opened to traffic the first railway crossing the Alps (see map, p. 388).

Owing to the deep furrows dug by the glaciers the Alps have not greatly isolated the lands to their south. Men crowded early into the valleys, and links were made from one slope to the other. Roman colonization went beyond the Alps; later the Barbarians flowed into the peninsula through the same passes. Italy has usually been invaded from the north, across the Alps. Conquests coming from the south, as in 1943, were exceptional. Italy stayed under the domination of trans-Alpine authorities for centuries.

The mountain used to be always densely populated, but in recent times overcrowding has caused emigration to assume large proportions. The mountain exodus has been stronger in the western Alps. The attraction of the rapidly developing industrial cities at the foot of the range has probably been very strong. The Alps remain however a source of riches in three ways: their forests supply timber; their summer pastures readily complement the meadows in the plain for the numerous cattle in the region; and last, but not least, the torrents and streams supply power, on which the industrialization of the plain is largely based. More factories are being built in the valleys, to be closer to the dams, as they are in France. When the hydroelectric potential is more fully harnessed such trends may bring new life in the heart of the Alps, already enlivened by the recent growth of tourism and skiing.

The north Italian plain covers 15 percent of the total area of the country. It is a sunken area and was a gulf of the Adriatic Sea. It was filled up chiefly with the debris brought down from the surrounding mountains. It is not a flat area but slopes gently toward the central gutter followed by the Po River; recent erosion has sculpted the rolling landscape outside the valley proper. The sub-Alpine zone of low hills is drained by rapid streams and needs irrigation; the low central furrow has over-abundant waters and needs drainage to avoid marshiness. Big springs surge through the alluvial fans at the foot of the mountains: they are called the *fontanili,* and their gauge is regular, being fed by deep underground aquifers; they help to irrigate the meadows of Piedmont and Lombardy as well as to maintain the flow of the streams in low-water periods.

Born as an Alpine torrent, the Po River flows swiftly into the plain. A series of alluvial fans, expanded by its tributaries coming down from the Alps, pushed the Po toward the foot of the Apennines. Having little slope to descend after Piacenza, the Po meanders lazily through a flat and damp area. Mud banks rise along its course and, approaching its delta, the river flows in an elevated channel several feet above the surrounding plain, which is constantly threatened with submersion. Owing to the Alpine amphitheater, the Po is an abundant river with terrible floods in the early fall. The Apennines' tributaries have low waters in the summer and floods at intermediate periods; the Alpine rivers have on the contrary high waters from spring to late summer. Both combine in October in the lower course of the Po. This variety of feeding helps maintain the minimum gauge, and the Po is navigable from Pavia downstream. A system of canals complements it but is used chiefly for irrigation purposes, especially in Lombardy, around Milan, and in the coastal area.

Men had to struggle in the plain first against the density of the forest, then against the unbridled waters; and every important city had a water-control policy. Venice promoted large works all along the main rivers in the seventeenth century. Earlier wars had sometimes been fought between cities because of "river conflicts." It has been said that the Po

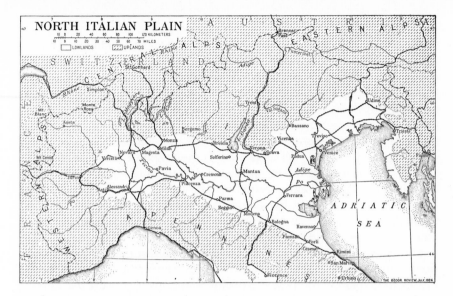

Sketch map showing the chief cities of the north Italian plain. (*The Geographical Review*)

Isotherms for January and July in the north Italian plain. (Temperatures are given in degrees centigrade.) The climate of the Po basin is comparatively extreme. Note, for instance, the greater range on the western shores of the Adriatic in comparison with the eastern shores. (*The Geographical Review*)

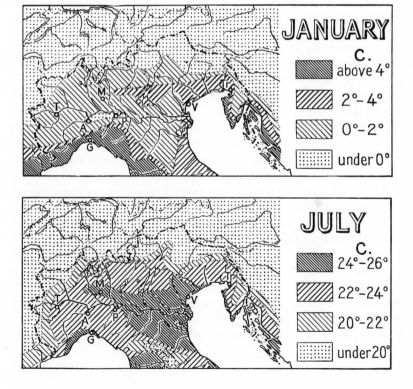

valley "is not the mother but the daughter of its inhabitants." The old way of life, founded on the growing of wheat and flax and the trans-humance of sheep, evolved into an intensive, specialized agricultural system: corn fields, mulberry trees in the east, olive woods on the well-exposed slopes in Venetia, rice in the damp bottom lands, hemp close to the Adriatic shore; and the vineyards that furnish the wines of Asti clothe the hills of Monferrate. A few volcanic hills add variety to the topography and to the soil map: such is the origin of the isolated peaks of the Euganean hills to the southeast. On this man-made soil is con-centrated most of the agricultural wealth of Italy. Such an organization has been made possible by investment in the land of capital earned through trade in the cities. The main urban and industrial develop-ment of Italy is found in this same plan.

The cities of northern Italy were among the main centers of civiliza-tion in the Middle Ages; they were largely responsible for maintaining in this dark period the best European traditions and, with the Renais-sance, preparing for modern expansion. In the western part of the plain, largely at the foot of the hills, strings of towns group most of the large-scale Italian industries. Turin, the capital of Piedmont from which the House of Savoy set forth to achieve the crown of unified Italy, is a major center. The city accounts for a large part of the rayon and cotton textile industries, builds automobiles (the Fiat car), and electrical machinery and equipment. Its population (1.1 million in 1965) has a reputation for wisdom and stubborn energy, reflected in the somewhat severe aspect of the central section. To its south, Asti makes wine and Alessandria man-ufactures felt hats and textiles and acts as a regional capital for a rich rural area. Other satellites of Turin in the Alpine valleys are the elec-trometallurgy of Aosta, the woolens of Biella, and the office equipment of Ivrea, the home of Olivetti.

However, the actual capital of the plain is Milan, in a more central position. The second city of Italy, Milan (1,670,000 in 1965) is its finan-cial and economic capital; its stock exchange is more influential than the Roman one; most of the leading industrial concerns, such as the Mon-tecatini group, have their head offices in Milan, for Lombard bankers taught financial science to Europe before the Scots entered the field. Milan rivals Lyon as chief market for silken goods in Europe. Its fac-tories build varied machinery, from ploughs to airplane engines, weave silk, cotton, and linen, and make electrical and electronic apparatus and precision instruments as well as steel, copper, ceramics and drugs. The conurbation counts 3.5 million people. With its famed cathedral, many basilicas, palaces, theaters, museums, and universities, Milan is also a cultural center of great repute. It is a very lively and tense city, and its moods weigh heavily on the political destiny of Italy. Recently,

A low standard of living prevails in these overpopulated hills, where the land has been cleared and tilled for centuries. (*Three Lions*)

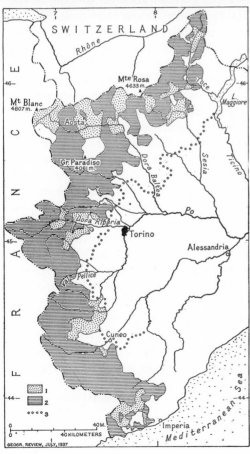

Depopulation in the Ligurian and Piedmontese Alps. The zone of "mountain depopulation" is shown by ruling (2); other areas in which population decreased between 1871 and 1921 are shown in stipple (1); the dotted line (3) shows the limit of the zone studied. (*The Geographical Review*)

that mood has been optimistic and expansionist. Milan has built a new subway, the most automated of Europe, a new airport, and many sky-scrapers. Numerous satellite industrial towns are grouped to its north in the area of Lecco-Sesto-Calende-Varese-Legnano-Gallarate. Other cities like Pavia, Mortara, Lodi, and Mantova are chiefly centers of food and dairy processing. Novara has large printing and chemical plants; Como, Varese, and Bergamo work the textiles. Eastward, Brescia (194,000) with its textile mills and mechanical plants is still a satellite. Then the Venetian domain begins.

Venice is indeed the capital of the eastern plain. This extraordinary city, with its 363,000 inhabitants now crowded on the small islets in a coastal lagoon, still attracts tourists by the architectural magnificence left by its past wealth and power. From what began as a shelter for refu-gees, screened by a sand spit from the sea and separated by water from the continent, the Venetians made in the fifteenth century the economic capital of most of Europe. The mariner of those times, entering the port amid so many palaces and basilicas, must have felt an awed admira-tion comparable to what the modern traveler feels on looking at the skyline and lights of New York City. Venice almost monopolized for a while the direction of Mediterranean trade, controlled northern Italy and the trans-Alpine roads, colonized the Adriatic shores, and directed Crusades. In the fifteenth century its population is believed to have reached 200,000; then, with the decline of Mediterranean trade, it fell around 1800 to less than 100,000 — by that time most of the Venetians lived off the tourist trade, the others off public charity. The twentieth century brought a rapid development of tourism and revived some in-dustries, such as the manufacture of glass at Murano, and sea navigation. Venice is again an important port, the second of Italy in 1965 with 14 million tons of goods loaded and unloaded, a major gate of the Po plain. Trieste is the main gate to Central Europe from the Adriatic shores; its separation from Italy in 1947–1954 helped Venice regain more port activity.

Trieste was developed as the Mediterranean seaport of the Austrian Empire to break the trade monopoly of the republic of Venice. Links with Greek merchants were established in the eighteenth century, and railways across the eastern Alps made Trieste the port of Vienna and Budapest, even to some extent of Munich. The port developed quickly but soon had to fight the extension inland of Hamburg's hinterland. Given to Italy in 1919, Trieste lost some of its advantages in the Danubian basin. It developed industries: iron and steel, shipyards, jute and cotton mills, oil refineries, engineering and food processing. Claimed by Yugoslavia in 1945, it was constituted as the *Free Territory of Trieste* by the peace treaty of 1947 and occupied by an international force. It reverted to Italy in 1954; the population in 1965 was estimated at 280,000. In 1965 the port handled 5.3 million tons of goods, and 291,000 passengers. Part of the traffic was to or from Austria and southern Germany.

Inland from the Adriatic coast several important cities, with expanding economic activities, scatter in the southeastern section of the plain. Through this area passes the main rail and road traffic between Milan and Venice on the one hand and Rome, Florence, and Naples on the other, as well as the Adriatic coastal routes from Bari and Brindisi toward Milan and farther north. Amid beautifully cultivated land stand Padua (214,000), Verona (245,000), and Vicenza (106,000), all cities of great art treasures and stages on the Venice-Milan road, guarding the approaches to the valleys of the eastern Alps; Verona especially, at the gate of the Trentino valley leading to the Brenner Pass, had a great medieval past and used to be the first large Italian city on the main road leading the German tourists south. On the Po, Ferrara (158,000), long a sleepy local market, now has important industries. At the foot of the first Apennine ridges, where the plain meets the hills, one finds another chain of cities, ones that played a notable part in the Renaissance period: Parma (163,000), Reggio nell'Emilia (123,000), Modena (156,000), and, truly the metropolis of this area and the first south of Milan to have its own orbit and province, Bologna (480,000). Famous for good food and gaiety and for the university that started here in the eleventh century, Bologna is also an important market for wheat, hemp, and hogs, a major rail hub, and one of the more rapidly growing cities of Italy. In 1936, Bologna counted 281,000 inhabitants; in 1951, 339,000; and in 1958, 420,000; by 1960 Florence was shocked to discover that Bologna had outdistanced it in size. This growth reflected rapid manufacturing expansion in the city and its suburbs: to the traditional food processing, leatherware, and ceramics industries have been added the more modern mechanical, electronic, and pharmaceutical plants that make it a booming place. The general expansion of the whole area helped, of course, the growth of the regional capital. Part of Emilia, to the northeast, is an immense "polder" with a checkerboard of canals draining the damp coastal plain. The silting has progressed rapidly here: Roman and Byzantine fleets once used the port of Ravenna, a regional marketplace with famous Byzantine monuments and mosaics, now several miles from the sea and rapidly expanding too. A whole industrial city, almost doubling the size of Ravenna (the population of which jumped from 91,000 in 1951 to 126,000 by 1965), grew there at the terminal of natural gas pipelines, with large petrochemical plants making synthetic rubber and other products. In Ravenna, however, one reaches the edge of northern Italy, and the south seems close.

The slope of the Apennines above the plain is dry and steep. Rivers

An old section of Bologna with medieval towers that were erected by the merchants. (*Italian Government Travel Office*)

The Grand Canal, Venice. (*Italian Government Travel Office*)

have dug narrow valleys cutting gorges through barren sandstone folds; such is, for example, the landscape in the hills south of Bologna and Ravenna. Only in the west does the range become lower and easier to pass. The hills of Liguria establish the link and the transition from the southeastern Maritime Alps to the northwestern extremity of the Apennines. Coming close to the seashore, these hills create a riviera which continues the French one. San Remo, Bordighera, and other sea resorts along the coast have in winter the clearest sky of Italy. Horticultural farms produce here two thirds of all the commercial flower crop of Italy. The coast curves around the Gulf of Genoa presenting its front to the southeast, the true riviera direction, then to the southwest. In the hills olive trees and vineyards thrive; on the shore tourism maintains some wealth. But at the end of the gulf, the city of Genoa (850,000) concentrates all the major industrial and commercial activities. Genoa attempted to rival Venice in the Middle Ages; in the twentieth century it disputed Marseille for the first rank among Mediterranean ports. Its hinterland is almost all the Po plain and the Alps. Part of the Swiss trade with the Mediterranean goes through its piers. Industries have little space in the port on which to develop, for the city is built on a steep slope, with several stories, and funiculars are almost as important as streetcars. Hard hit by several severe bombings in World War II, Genoa has gone to work again. It is the maritime tip of the Turin-Milan-Genoa triangle in which is found most of the heavy industry of Italy; its port handled 30 million tons of goods and 537,000 passengers in 1964. It is a bustling city, which recently added a large iron and steel industry and mechanical and chemical plants to its seaside suburbs. The conurbation counts over a million people.

Northern Italy thus plays an outstanding part in the national system. Here are the main industries, the most intensive and most modern agriculture, and the chief source of hydroelectric power. Here also are concentrated the urban working masses; this section of the country suffered from Allied bombings but was spared the destruction wrought by a campaign sweeping the territory. Northern Italy has always been hard working, and it claims a decisive voice in national affairs. It does not always get it—and the French saying that "the North pays the taxes and the South runs the politics" may also apply to Italy.

## CENTRAL ITALY AND ROME

The peninsula considers itself the main base of all national trends. The peninsula has a north and a south, divided approximately by a line passing immediately south of Rome and of the Abruzzi Mountains. In the northern half the Tertiary range of the Apennines curves in an arch, the convexity of which bulges eastward. The spinal range is thus closer to the Adriatic shore. To the west, groups of hills of different structure stretch between the main crests and the Tyrrhenian Sea. A winding line of deep valleys follows the contact of the Apennine with these hills. The main railroad from Florence to Rome passes along this structural furrow. The Apennines do not reach very high over most of their length; most of the crestline remains below 6000 feet. Only in the center of the peninsula, in the section known as the Abruzzi Mountains, do the highlands widen; crests above 3000 feet take in width over a half of the peninsula, and the Gran Sasso d'Italia rises to 9600 feet.

The Apennines form a ribbon of highlands deeply eroded by the quick and violent Mediterranean torrents. It is a country of difficult access. Railroads are few in the mountain and have been built at considerable expense. The new line from Bologna to Florence pierces the whole range in one tunnel twelve miles long. Many towns in the hills are difficult to reach even by automobile: they communicate with the outside by dirt roads. Every depression that is not too narrow is tilled and produces some olives and grapes. An old resource is the seasonal oscillation of sheep herds which go down to the plains in winter. Here are produced some local cheeses, including the hard *pecorino*, which is exported abroad. Sheep and goats have generally overgrazed the slopes; men have savagely deforested them. Reclamation of the hills is a necessity, but it is an immense task to start and difficult to carry out in isolated corners of an overpopulated range.

The eastern slope is sunnier, drier, steeper, and therefore much more eroded. South from Ravenna the coastal plain narrows to less than a mile in many places. No great center has arisen here: amid deeply rural districts, some ports, of which Ancona is the most important, carry on fishing and trade in the Adriatic. From the Marina di Ravenna to south of Rimini extends on the coast an almost continuous stretch of seaside resorts, recently developed, but already bristling with sky-scraper hotels that in the summer attract hundreds of thousands of visitors from all over Europe. The small and quiet town of Rimini (106,000) is being enlivened by this new function; north of it, an isolated hill is occupied by the picturesque independent republic of San Marino (23 square miles in area, 17,500 inhabitants), which issues its own coins and stamps. In central Italy, the Adriatic slope is just a narrow sidewalk lined with barren hills; the major part of central Italy looks westward.

The Tyrrhenian slope is complicated by both its structure and its history, but it is one of the most remarkable lands on the Mediterranean. A puzzle of hills is strewn with large depressions. At the intermediate elevation, the Mediterranean habitat has found its optimum. The landscape of Tuscany, especially around Florence, has been often cited as a typical instance of the Mediterranean "environment"; but in

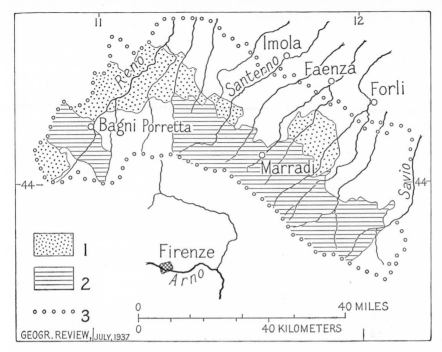

Depopulation in the Apennines of Emilia, Tuscany, and the Romagna. The zone of "mountain depopulation" is shown by ruling (2); other areas in which depopulation decreased between 1871 and 1921 are shown in stipple (1); the dotted line (3) shows the limit of the zone studied. (*The Geographical Review*)

The Pineta of Ravenna in Emilia. Note the old system of fishing. (*Italian Government Travel Office*)

fact it is rather exceptional. The scenery even nowadays remains similar to what we see in the paintings of the famous Florentine school of the Renaissance. The same lines of lean cypresses, the same artistic scattering of vines, olive trees, white red-roofed houses standing on hillocks in the shade of a cluster of Italian pines—this is a classic picture indeed. It is, of course, entirely man-made, arranged by the local people with great labor according to traditional rules and a delicate taste. Few rural regions elsewhere show a similar concern for appearance.

Commanding a large basin and the valley of the Arno River, Florence is the chief town of the area. Owing to the agricultural wealth of the surrounding land and to the trade in sheepskins, Florence early built up a zone of influence. It started working the wool and skins of the sheep, treated silver ore from the hills, and made fine jewelry. Its craftsmen and merchants made of it the capital of the woolen industries in Italy during the Middle Ages; many of the Renaissance trends started here; here was the home of the greatest school of painting; and its family of bankers, the Medici gave popes to Rome and queens to France. Today it is a shrine of medieval and modern architecture, a city of extraordinary charm, but it is also an important industrial, intellectual, and political center. Although a part of it was damaged in World War II, Florence, with 455,000 inhabitants, remains a regional capital of importance. Its medieval rival, Siena, higher up in the hills, has not kept up in similar fashion with the march of time. On the coast, Pisa (100,000) with its leaning tower and the Camposanto, has given up its port activities in favor of Leghorn (170,000), where heavy industries are rising. Tuscany is a prosperous rural country of small farmers: since the coastal swamps have been drained, part of the population came down from the hills to settle here. They are a lively and very civilized people, who always intend to have a say in national affairs. The area has taken advantage also of some mineral deposits in the hills: iron ore and magnesite are extracted, as well as the famous marble of Carrara from a limestone which gives sharp crests and promontories to the hills north of Pisa.

Several islands fringe the coast of Tuscany. One of them, the Monte Argentario, has been linked to the coast by two sand causeways, witnesses to the rapid silting of the area. The isle of Elba, with a rugged topography, is the most important one and was made famous by the brief period in 1814 when it was given to Napoleon as a token of his broken empire. Iron ore is mined on Elba.

South of Tuscany the topography rises, and the land looks more rugged. Some plateaus stretch at mean elevation, marked by lakes and volcanism. In Umbria, the limpidity of the air adds to the scenic beauty of the hills. This is the land of Perugia (120,000) and Assisi, of olives and cattle. The extinct volcanoes did reach impressive size, and earthquakes are not infrequent still in the peninsula, especially as one ad-

Florence, divided by the River Arno. (*Italian Government Travel Office*)

Siena and the plateaus of Tuscany, with farms amid terraces and fruit groves. (*Italian Government Travel Office*)

vances southward. Low brush, sheep pastures, and some fields in the depressions are the general aspect on approaching Rome. Then the mountains break up and a wider plain, the famous *Agro Romano,* opens up. Since the time of its ancient prosperity, the *Agro* has known terrible decay: a small number of Roman barons, about two dozen families, owned almost all the land and let it return to swamps and winter pastures for sheep. Malaria allied to large land ownership was ruining the country until the present century; recently reclamation has started, imposed upon the owners by the government. The hills around Rome were going almost wild and lacked schools, medical care, even priests. The Vatican felt at the end of the nineteenth century the necessity to take measures in order to "Christianize" the neighborhood. Few instances demonstrate better than this paradoxical destiny of the Roman country how far decay went on the Mediterranean shores. Since 1910, and particularly in the interwar period, considerable progress has been made on the *Agro* through drainage and public health measures. Grassy meadows maintain cattle; fields grow cereals and alfalfa. The calm and regular outline of the landscape now reflects recent organization and resettlement.

Throughout the vicissitudes of history, Rome never ceased to be a metropolis. When the imperial function was lost, it stayed a spiritual capital, but the material splendor of ancient times disappeared rapidly. The Emperors had accustomed Rome to live off the whole Roman world, at least the whole Mediterranean basin. The Eternal City was well situated in the middle of the basin, but had no natural advantage, nor did it develop special resources that could serve as a local base. In the fourteenth century, while Venice, Florence, Pisa, and even Naples were great centers on the international scale, Rome was reduced to a population of about 17,000 people, most of them ill with malaria. The city survived because of the past, the heritage of the Caesars and the Apostles. The Holy See made it sacred and brought crowds of pilgrims every year, and this spiritual function made the Romans feel that their past role of leadership was still maintained. When Italy was unified, Rome had to be its national capital, and it regained a political and administrative function that increased its population from 244,000 in 1872 to 1,695,000 in 1951. Tourism developed on a tremendous scale. As Jules Sion wrote: "The Forum earns more dollars than many factories." Archeologists are constantly finding new historical treasures in the soil of Rome, and the development of the government's authority over a more unified and expanding economy is bound to expand the capital city. The growth and improvement have been extremely rapid since 1870. It has accelerated since World War II; in 1936 the population was 1,180,000 only, about equal then to that of Milan; by 1965 it reached 2.5 million, more than 3

Map of the Agro Romano and adjacent regions as of 1928. Key: 1, boundary of city of Rome and suburbs; 2, boundary of commune of Rome; 3, railways; 4, tramways; 5, chief roads before reclamation; 6, chief roads built subsequently; 7, roads under construction; 8 to 11, population centers of varying degrees of importance (outside of the Agro Romano only the principal centers are indicated); 12, *borgate rurali;* 13, chief new agricultural centers; 14, principal *casali;* 15, hut villages. (*The Geographical Review*)

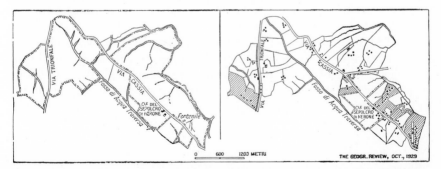

On the left is a great estate of the Roman Campagna in 1908: a single property 6.73 square kilometers in area, the economy of which was predominately pastoral. On the right is the same estate subdivided in 1927. About the old *casale* is an agricultural center of 0.68 square kilometers; the remaining area is divided into 32 farms, each with a farmhouse; the obliquely shaded areas are divided into small lots with 70 cottages. (*The Geographical Review*)

million with the suburbs. The more rapid growth of Rome in recent years is to be explained by the attraction of industrial management to the national capital, by an expansion of the city's academic, scientific, and international activities, by the attraction it has had for certain industries such as precision instruments, electronics, and communications equipment, pharmaceuticals, the movies, and, of course, printing and food processing, which increases to supply the local market. Rome is also the seat of the headquarters of the United Nations Food and Agriculture Organization and a meeting place for many international conferences.

With the incorporation of the Papal States, covering 16,000 square miles, into the Italian kingdom during the years 1859–1870 the unsettled question of his temporal independence lead the Pope to retire to the Vatican Palace. A treaty was signed in 1929 settling the problem of the temporal power of the Holy See: the Italian government renounced its sovereignty over Vatican City, which from being a section of Rome was raised to the position of a distinct political unit, with its own postal facilities, coinage, and radio. The Holy See got an area of 109 acres, to which must be added some buildings outside, including the Papal villa of Castel Gandolfo. The Vatican is therefore exterior to Rome in legal terms, but it continues in fact to be the very heart of Rome. Owing to the presence of the Pontiff, Rome has survived the period of decline and has accumulated monuments and palaces of all epochs since the fall of the Empire; because of its spiritual function, Rome remains a world capital and carries an authority widely transcending the boundaries of Italy.

Central Italy owes to Rome and to Tuscany the important part it plays in the nation. It is by its nature and its historical background a complicated area of high and low hills, internal basins, and coastal plains, of well-watered and dry slopes. It served as headquarters for a giant empire and later housed many small regionalisms. Near Rome there are large estates and around Florence, small peasant holdings; Tuscany has a carefully maintained and slightly archaic but streamlined landscape, while areas close to Rome are barely emerging from centuries of wilderness. There is more variety than in the areas to the north and south; there is certainly less prosperity than in the north and less misery than in the south.

## THE MEZZOGIORNO

The Mezzogiorno is Italy's greatest problem. The southern parts of the peninsula and the two large islands of Sicily and Sardinia are the most overpopulated and the least developed sections of the country. It has not always been so; the magnificent Greek ruins, the unearthed remnants

Two views of St. Peter's Square, Rome. (*Above*) The square as seen from the basilica, with the famous colonnade designed by Bernini in the seventeenth century and the avenue leading to the Tiber. Beyond the river, amid the roofs of Rome, is the low round cupola of the ancient Pantheon. (*Italian Government Travel Office*) (*Below*) The famous basilica designed by Michelangelo, with the Pope's apartments in the buildings to the right above the colonnade. (*Three Lions*)

of Pompeii, some Norman basilicas and abbeys testify to a great prosperity in old times when the south of the peninsula was indeed in the center of the Mediterranean world. The decline that set in with the Middle Ages cannot be explained by climatic changes or weaknesses of nature; it was human endeavor that changed the course.

South of Rome and of the Abruzzi, the heat and aridity of the summer gain rapidly. The ranges of the Apennines here curve slowly to the southwest, and the main crests are closer to the Tyrrhenian shores. Hills and plateaus develop therefore on the Adriatic side. The crest-by-crest advance of the Allied forces in their 1943 campaign, with a front sweeping the peninsula from the area of Naples northward to Rome, gave to the forces in the field a full taste of the sharpness of the Mediterranean topography; it was made worse by the torrential erosion that cut narrow deep valleys and filled them suddenly with mud and pebbles when the rain came. Limestone ranges mingle with sandstone and marls, especially abundant on the Adriatic side. A few old crystalline blocks surge amid the folds, such as the large horst of Calabria, where the massive La Sila expands its high tableland over 3000 feet within a few miles by airline from the water's edge.

The complicated structure of this southern half of the peninsula has not yet quite settled down. Earthquakes are frequent, and every decade an earthquake destroys entire towns; some of them caused thousands of deaths and started epidemics. Volcanism is active; the biggest volcanoes of Europe are here: Mt. Vesuvius towering above Naples, Mt. Etna reaching 10,700 feet in Sicily, and Stromboli on an island between the great island and the peninsula. In the middle of the nineteenth century an isle suddenly appeared above the Mediterranean waves, causing a conflict between Britain and the kingdom of the Two Sicilies as to sovereignty. Before any serious action was taken, however, the isle was swallowed up again by the sea; it reappeared later for too brief a period to cause any political excitement. The instability of the land has sometimes been blamed as one of the causes for the backwardness of the area, but it should be observed that in the vicinity of Etna and Vesuvius, where the ashes and lava of the volcanoes supply natural fertilizer, the land is among the most densely populated and most intensively tilled lands of Italy. Notwithstanding the constant deadly threat of the mountain that buried Pompeii and Herculaneum in A.D. 79, villages cling to the foot of the Vesuvius. A challenge to the inhabitants, the volcanism does not frighten men away, as do malaria and other fevers that weaken the internal resistance of the people.

Malaria has worked terrible havoc in all this area, and as a result the plains and lower hills returned almost to desert and wilderness. The Pontine Marshes south of Rome were reclaimed, drained, and irrigated

Density of population in Italy, 1951. Key: 1, less than 200 inhabitants per square mile; 2, from 201 to 500 inhabitants per square mile; 3, from 501 to 875; 4, over 875. The black squares show cities of more than a million inhabitants each; there are three such cities, identified by their initials: M for Milan, R for Rome, N for Naples. The circles show the eight cities counting between 200,000 and 1,000,000 inhabitants each. Limits of provinces are shown, although the densities have been mapped on the basis of smaller administrative subdivisions. Notice the scattering of nuclei of high densities, often situated close to the less populated areas; such contrasts are characteristic of the Mediterranean. Compare with the map of population density in Great Britain (pp. 266–267) and the similar map for the Iberian peninsula (p. 435).

in the 1930s, and this achievement will remain the main positive deed of the Fascist government. New towns were created, such as Latina, Nettuno, and Porto d'Anzio. Their settlement was begun by the people coming down the slope to the lowlands, now made more secure but for over a thousand years an area where men lived under the threat of malaria and pirates.

The only large city and important economic center in the southern section of the peninsula is Naples. A city of 1,250,000 people, it is often named as the *summum* of Mediterranean scenery. With a large mass of white red-roofed buildings clothing the slope around a semicircular bay dominated by sharp crests, with Vesuvius adding its conic elevation, illuminated ofttimes by the plutonic activity, this landscape has undeniable beauty and grandeur as a whole; the destruction wrought by the war, which badly hit this area has now been fully repaired. Seen from the inside, Naples is an extremely lively but poor city. While to its west, along the bay, extends some rich residential sections, most of the town is inhabited by crowds who live in a misery and filth rarely encountered in other parts of the continent. There is something momentous and tragic in the opposition between the great reputation of Naples and the reality of its slums. Every large city has its blighted sections, but the proportion here is frightening. The city proper is one of the most crowded in Europe and one of the least well equipped in terms of housing. For quite some time Naples did not experience any in-migration to speak of; the central city's population grew through natural increase alone. In recent years, out-migration seems to be taking over, though slowly. The conurbation extends much beyond the central city's limits; the province of Naples aggregates a population of 2.6 million at an average density of about 5700 per square mile. In fact, the metropolitan area extends to the whole region of Campania, populated by 5 million people in 1965, with an average density close to 1000 per square mile. The densities in and around Naples are much higher than in the case of either Milan or Rome. It is a painful situation, plagued by constant underemployment, and the gap between Naples and the cities of the north recently has been widening.

In 1800, Naples was one of the four cities in Europe with a population in the range of half a million or more (the others being London, Paris, and Constantinople). It was a great center of banking, business, and industry. But the Industrial Revolution seems to have bypassed it. Some industries did develop: chemical, mechanical, food, and shipbuilding. After World War II, great hopes were pinned on the last, but no large-scale growth materialized. The city and the various satellite cities in Campania (Salerno, Benevento, Caserta, Avellino, etc.) need much more economic development to provide adequate employment for the present population. Naples and its region have been clamoring for more government attention, help, and investment. In 1967, they were promised a large new automotive plant, government supported, Alfa-Sud, which should provide 30,000 new jobs in Campania—a substantial figure but still far from the necessary total to solve local problems. The port of Naples is the third in importance on the peninsula, handling 9.3 million tons of goods in 1964, with a transit of 2.2 million passengers, many of them on the short ride to Capri. Now the great southern city realizes that it has little chance to attract soon enough manufactures to supply all the jobs it really needs. It hopes, instead for a substantial development of the services, particularly in the research and cultural area, offering the amenities of its glamorous location, warm climate, and central Mediterranean position. Could such a large metropolis jump the stages of the Industrial Revolution into the white-collar era of the late twentieth century? The Neapolitans used to be quite pessimistic about their chances of catching up; some regional awakening is now developing.

The area around Naples is a plain enriched regularly by the ashes or the lava from Mt. Vesuvius. Its gray and dark soils are very rich and intensively farmed: citrus groves, tomatoes and other vegetables, and some cereal too. For good yields, irrigation is necessary, but over much of the Campania the peasants have to carry buckets of water from their shallow wells to the foot of the trees. Irrigation systems exist for only a small section of the rich plain. The province of Campania, which extends eastward over a large area in the hills, has landscapes of great beauty.

The misery and backwardness of the population increases as one proceeds higher up into the hills of Lucania or Calabria. The tourist who has seen the classical island of Capri and the little riviera of Sorrento and Amalfi occasionally goes to Paestum for a look at some of the most perfect works of Greek architecture, but he is not invited to proceed farther south. The scenery is worth it, but these lands are still a back yard of Italy, half abandoned, and even the national pride rebels at showing a blighted area of such magnitude to the foreigner. Emigration has slightly decreased the pressure of population, but it has little improved conditions. Housing is reduced to a medieval promiscuity; Professor Jules Sion noted around Potenza that if any building had a somewhat better aspect, it belonged to a peasant who had returned from a stay in America. "Around 1900," he remarked, "New York had more people from Basilicate (Lucania) than its two most important towns." Calabria is even worse. In lean years, people have to eat acorns and nettles; in summer the towns seldom can get water more than a few hours a day. There are still high summits and crests on which rain falls and deep underground watertables that could be tapped. Some of the

Contrasting views of Naples.
(*Above*) The noble setting of the
city with Vesuvius towering in
the background, numerous great
monuments, and the main docks
of the port (upper right). (*Below*)
A miserable and overpopulated
street. (*Three Lions*)

hilly areas recently needed to be "re-Christianized." This is the region described in the 1940s by the Italian writer Carlo Levi in his best-selling novel *Christ Stopped at Eboli.* It would need the rebuilding of a whole vast country, and too little has as yet been done.

The Adriatic coast is lower on the whole, with a better soil that had a great reputation of fertility in antiquity. But aridity is greater. In Puglia an aqueduct, about 1400 miles long, brings some water to the towns from the Tyrrhenian slope of the ranges. It is, however, inadequate to the need. Many houses have cisterns, gathering every drop of rain on the roofs. Rocky limestone plateaus and marshy, feverish lowlands cover most of the southeast of Italy. Some areas, however, have been maintained as rich orchards by the tenacious efforts of a dense population of small landowners tilling their lands. A tremendous olive grove follows the coast from Bari to Brindisi; almonds and vines mix with olive trees. Wheat and beans grow in places in between the lines of trees. Orchards also surround Otranto. The pressure of population forces the inhabitants of towns to go miles away from their home to plant in rocky ground the trees they will care for. Here again an organized, large-scale effort is needed to overcome the hardships imposed by a difficult environment. Bari (335,000) is the main Adriatic port south of Venice; it has a noted annual fair and varied industries. Brindisi is a port of call of liners going to the eastern shores of the Mediterranean. Taranto (210,000) is the capital on the gulf inside the heel of the peninsula. The population of these cities, though urban, does not indicate much industrial or commercial activity, as it would in France or England; it is largely a crowding of populations that do not have any prospects in the rural districts. Taranto is now developing: a large modern steel mill has been built there.

A picture similar to that of the southern peninsula is found on the large islands off the coast. Sicily is the richest: 4,850,000 people live on its 9925 square miles. The rugged hills of the interior have an austere grandeur, but they are barren and sleepy. In the summer the sun burns all the interior, where wheat and beans are the main products of large estates belonging to a small number of noble families. This interior presents a sharp contrast to the coastal area; more than half of the total population is found along the shores, concentrated around the main cities where rich orchards of citrus trees and vineyards are irrigated with trickles of water coming down from the hills. Palermo, in its Conca de Oro, groups 635,000 people. It is the richest huerta and the main port, which has regular links with Naples, Genoa, Tangiers, and Tunis, builds ships, and wants to become a major relay on the trans-Mediterranean route. Catania (400,000) is another huerta at the foot of Mt. Etna. Messina (265,000) on the strait separating the island from the peninsula, also has orange groves and active rail traffic. Syracuse and Agrigento, famous at the time of the greatness of Greece, work the land and maintain the ruins marking their ancient prosperity.

Sicily needs more water—that is, a better supply—which could be obtained if the necessary investments were made. Every important visitor from abroad is being asked the question: Will he help get dams built and make more water available? Emigration to the Americas can solve only part of the problem. The low prices offered on the international market for the citrus fruits and for sulfur, the two cash exports of Sicily, have made life harder. The exports of sulfur picked up after 1949, supplying about 150,000 tons annually, which remains below prewar figures. With the development of aviation, Sicily hoped at the end of World War II to become a hub of airlines and perhaps an "American aircraft carrier anchored in the middle of the Mediterranean." It wishes for a situation that would no longer leave it a "marginal" land of the Western world. In fact, the influences of the Near East are notable here, partly left by the Greeks and the Arabs, partly resulting from the backward economy and a feudal social system. The social problem is one of the main hindrances to the rapid development of an island which could put many resources to work. The discovery of oil on the island led to new hopes and even the suggestion of secession from Italy; the main oilfield is near Ragusa and produces annually about 2 million tons brought by pipeline to a refinery at Augusta.

Sardinia is about the same size as Sicily with 9300 square miles, but with 1,470,000 people it is much less densely populated. It has the well-earned reputation of being the poorest and least developed province of Italy. In the middle of the much-traveled western basin of the Mediterranean, Sardinia remains isolated, with few relations even with the Italian mainland. A land of shepherds and archaic peasantry, the island has some good soils and more plains than Sicily; the topography is complicated but rather open. The variety of the geological structure, partly of an old crystalline planed horst, has made the island known for its mineral wealth since ancient times. Today Sardinia ships out cattle and sheep, lead and zinc ores, and coal: the main coal basin of Italy producing close to 400,000 tons is situated in the southwest of the island, near the new town of Carbonia. Irrigation schemes have been started, with two dams built to store water and provide power. A large power plant has been built at Porto Vesme, with a capacity of 600,000 kw, to use the local coal and stimulate the island's industrialization. Cagliari, in the south, is the capital (206,000), and Sassari (100,000) is the largest center in the north. Some orchards surround each, but the sleepiness of Sardinia contrasts with the activity, almost exuberance, of Sicily. On the Sardinian shores, European developers recently dis-

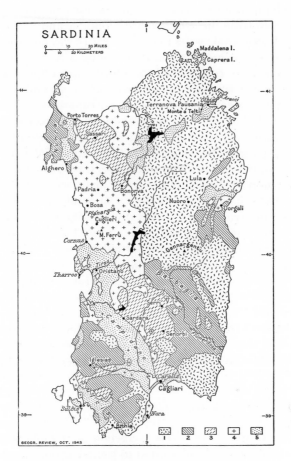

Map of Sardinia showing principal geological divisions. Key: 1, granites, crystalline schists; 2, pre-Tertiary; 3, Tertiary hills; 4, volcanics; 5, alluvial plains. The important reservoirs are in solid black. *(The Geographical Review)*

covered hundreds of miles of beautiful sand beaches; some touristic development has been started.

The Mezzogiorno is a problem indeed. In 1948 the Italian government created a special cabinet post of minister in charge of this problem. But the pressure from the area is more economic and moral than political. The south as a whole votes in a conservative way and follows without much discussion the instructions of its priests. Northern and central Italy are much more restless and therefore require more attention. As Italy, having lost a war and been destroyed by it, endeavors to stand firmly on her feet again, only the more pressing problems can to some extent be attended to. The southern problem, however, becomes more and more pressing as population increases rapidly without finding even the outlet of large-scale emigration. Campania, Calabria, and Sicily remain the major areas of emigration overseas. The frugal and hard-toiling population of the south should be made more of an asset, but as yet it is chiefly a liability. The urgency of a solution is greater in the cities where the crowds, increased by immigration from the rural districts as well as by a high birth rate, do not have even the possibility of growing a few olives and onions for subsistence.

The south has been more destroyed than the other provinces by the war; yet in a way it benefited by it. Measures taken by the United States military authorities have greatly improved the malarial situation; for the first time large-scale public health measures have been applied—the whole area seems to have been awakened from its sleep by the invasion. The future will show the psychological consequences of the shock, but in any event reclamation of the south is a tremendous, long-range enterprise.

ECONOMIC AND POLITICAL OUTLOOK

Italy is an old country which was awakened by the nineteenth century and which the Fascist regime wanted to put all at once in the forefront of the great political and economic world powers. But it is dangerous to speed up history. The Fascist regime may have precipitated certain positive processes, large public works especially, which had been conceived and in many cases started before Mussolini's march on Rome. The push for power led to a policy of prestige and aggression: much more could have been achieved to equip the country with the money swallowed in military expenditure, the conquest of Ethiopia and then Albania. Italy suffered from having sided with Germany in World War II and having attacked France and Greece. The treaty of peace signed in 1947 has meant a loss of territory in Istria and Dalmatia, reparations to be paid, and the loss of the former colonial territories. Fifteen years after V-E

Day, the scars of wartime destruction had healed and the country was engaged in much faster economic growth and evolution than it had expected.

Italians have to struggle against two main odds. The first is exterior and technically easy to overcome—the natural environment, with its topography and aridity. The second is the historical heritage of having been, for at least a few centuries, in the Mediterranean backyard of Europe and having to catch up in popular education, social organization, economic development, and capital accumulation to compare with the Western European countries. And Italy wants to measure up as a Western power. It is largely because the people from the west and the north of Europe treated the Italians as "Mediterraneans," "picturesque lazzaroni," who bask lazily in the sun among the beautiful ruins of the past, that the Italians revolted in their own way and preferred the hardships of the Fascist regime. Ultranationalism was prompted by the contemptuous attitude of the Western powers and even more by that of the tourists who came to admire the scenery and the monuments. The Italian felt he was treated like a nonentity in the midst of such beauty and almost asked to get out of the picture so that it could be better admired. Such a situation was unbearable to an active people who had had a great history and had just recently achieved unity and independence.

The psychological factor is always powerful in human affairs, and it drove the Italians to disregard their own material foundations. These foundations have been little improved, with respect to what the West has achieved, since the Renaissance. Therefore, before it can step definitely among the leading nations of Europe, Italy will have to rebuild that base. And in the Mediterranean environment this is not easy; it requires more capital and more labor than in the north. Italy can supply labor in large quantities, and cheaply, but almost every plain must be drained, then irrigated; almost every river of the Apennines has to be reshaped in its upper course and dammed in many places; almost every mountain range has to be reforested. Italian reclamation is too big a job to be achieved by one generation. The last fifty years have not been lost entirely, but the rhythm must be accelerated as time goes on.

A basic weakness of the Italian economy and a source of political trouble could be found in the fact that in the midst of a rapidly evolving Europe, the rate of population growth in Italy was faster than its rates of economic growth and capital formation. The years since World War II have greatly improved the relationship between these rates, however. Population increase has been slowing down: the crude birth rate averaged 30.1 per thousand in 1921–1924 and 24.5 in 1930–1934; it was 18.1 in 1951 and averaged 19 in 1960–67; the *net natural increase* (that is, natality rate less mortality rate) stood at 12.6 per thousand in the early 1920s, 10.4 in the early 1930s, around 9 in the 1960s. Although in 1947–1948 the Italian population was said to be increasing "at a speed of forty-five per hour," this slowed down substantially by 1960. The more rapid economic expansion that has taken place and is now being carried on provides for more employment within the country, but there are about 350,000 people added annually to the labor force and the growth of the number of jobs in industry and the services has not yet reached such a figure. Moreover, a steady flow carries people from the rural areas, especially from the mountains and from the south, toward the cities. Thus the crowds grow in the urban centers though they have little opportunity to make a living.

The natural increase by excess of births over deaths is unequally distributed over the country. Professor Aldo Sestini has stressed the fact that while this natural increase is strongest in the Mezzogiorno (where it is everywhere above the national average of 9 per thousand annually, and more than double that in Calabria, Basilicate, and southern Sardinia), the actual increase in population in the 1950s has been strongest in the metropolitan districts of the five largest cities of Italy (Rome, Milan, Naples, Turin, and Genoa); it was also much greater than the natural rate of increase in and around Palermo, Bologna, and Florence. Between 1951 and 1957 about 54 percent alone of the whole increase of the Italian resident population (some 2,400,000 people) was added to the population of the six largest cities, all counting already over half a million each; this proportion would be much higher if the growth of the six metropolitan areas were taken into account. This continued in the 1960s for the ten largest cities. Strong currents of internal migration continue to displace the Italian population, in particular carrying people from the Mezzogiorno, the Abbruzzi Mountains, and Venetia toward the larger metropolitan districts. These currents mean greater concentration around the six main centers, but also a gradual shift northwards and westwards.

The existence of so many large cities in Italy, a country which is still relatively little industrialized, is a striking feature. The population of Italy by 1967 had reached 52 million, a little less than that of the United Kingdom or West Germany and a little more than that of France. But Italy counted six cities of more than 600,000 and 37 in the category between 100,000 and 600,000; in 1961, Great Britain counted only six cities of more than 500,000 each and 46 in the next category: and it was the most heavily industrialized and urbanized of all the major nations of Europe; West Germany counted in these two categories eleven and 38 cities; France three and 23 (suburbs of Paris excluded). The size of the large Italian cities does not seem to correspond to their actual industrial or commercial strength; urban modes of life are different in the

Mediterranean countries. Families survive when only some of their adult male members have genuine jobs; these few support the whole group. Moreover, service occupations employ many more personnel to do a given piece of work than would be needed north of the Alps: intricate subcontracting helps to refine the division of labor to an extraordinary degree in order to divide the profit and achieve wider distribution of a scanty income.

Such techniques, reminiscent of underdeveloped economies, are not in the long run a solution for a nation that is rapidly becoming modernized and integrated in the advanced and expanding system of the Common Market. For Italy is one of the "Inner Six" and the treaty of Rome that established the EEC stipulates free movement through the whole area of both labor and capital, besides goods. As their partners in the EEC experienced manpower shortages, the Italian workers took advantage of the opportunity to migrate and work, and eventually, for some of them, to settle in the European countries to the north. Until 1930, large-scale emigration was a substantial help to the problem of Italian overpopulation, and most of the emigrants went to the United States and South America. When the immigration laws began to limit access to the United States, the currents of migration from southern Italy turned toward the cities of northern Italy and Rome, while from northern Italy emigrants went on to France, Switzerland, and, for a while, to North Africa. In the 1950s, Europe became definitely the main outlet of Italian emigration, particularly Switzerland, France, West Germany, and even Britain and the Netherlands. Italian manpower was highly competent for construction work and employment in the hotel industry. But Italians also went to the regions of heavy industry and to the large cities, where they looked for all sorts of jobs. In the 1960s, the emigration toward non-European countries stabilized around the annual figure of 50,000; the net balance of this overseas migration remained, however, in 1960–1965, at an annual average below 40,000, as there were people regularly returning to Italy to retire in the old country with a little capital saved in North or South America.

But the major current went toward Western Europe. About 200,000 to 330,000 Italians left for European destinations every year in the early 1960s; as most of them went on short-term contracts, the net balance of this migration came to only some 30,000 people a year. This was approximately the number of Italians who settled in European countries, but about 200,000 were revolving between the Italian labor market and the countries to the north on the Continent. Thus, in 1964, 112,000 Italians left for Switzerland and 94,000 reentered from Switzerland. Switzerland was, in recent years, the largest recipient of Italian out-migration; Western Germany came second, with a similar arrangement but for figures oscillating between 80,000 to 60,000 a year. France came third, and the United States or Canada fourth and fifth among the countries of destination. From South America, more people were returning than going. A new current was carrying about 10,000 Italians a year to Australia. This emigration helps build a network of relations abroad, thus developing new commercial ties, a market for Italian exports, and it provides financial support for relatives left behind.

The present rate of emigration helps to keep down the net increase of the Italian labor force, but it cannot provide any long-term solution for the pressure of population existing in Italy. Even during the booming 1950s and early 1960s Italy was the only important country of Europe unable to enjoy full employment. Since 1964, with the restrictions on foreign labor promulgated by Switzerland, with the more numerous young generation coming on the French labor market, and with the reduction of economic growth in West Germany, the prospect for the Italian emigrant narrowed. Obviously, the solution for Italian problems must now be found through domestic economic growth, technical modernization, and a better redistribution of the national income. These targets require long and stubborn efforts, a great deal of change and reform. To proceed with this program, Italy, considerably helped by both European integration and American investment, has accelerated the expansion of its production and undertaken various reforms of its social and economic structure.

In 1966–1967, the Italian economy was still booming, while expansion was slowing down in the rest of Europe. Still, unemployment was rather high (about 4 percent of the total labor force) and has been rising because the movement away from the farms continues at a rapid pace, while employment in manufacturing remains rather stable, owing to the progress in labor productivity and automation in industry. In 1966, of the total civilian employment, 24.5 percent was in agriculture, 10 percent in construction, 30 percent in manufacturing, and 35 percent in the services. The last category has been the only one increasing percentagewise in recent years; this is a healthy sign for a well-developed economy, in which production is expanding, too. In 1966 the gross national product grew by 5.5 percent, and the industrial share of the national production by 9 percent. As some of the indispensable reforms modernizing the Italian economy are being carried out, they also cause new problems, as they reduce employment in several sectors while increasing productivity.

The first and most obviously needed reform, long overdue in Italy, concerned the redistribution of land ownership. The *latifundia* held by absentee landlords are still common in the southern half of the peninsula and on the islands. In 1930, while 4.2 million farm holdings covered 65.7 million acres (an average of 15 acres per agricultural holding), some 3500 of them were estates exceeding 1250 acres each and aggregating 21.4 percent of the whole land area in farms; moreover, 36 percent of the cultivated land was held by 0.5 percent of the private landowners. Agrarian laws aimed at breaking up the large estates were passed in 1950. By May 1959, two million acres had been acquired for allocation to peasants, and three quarters of these lands had been allocated to 108,000 farmers; these new holdings averaged close to 15 acres each. While in other Western countries the trend was to increase the average size of farms, because more mechanized and scientific methods of production require larger units, Italy was not yet ready for this process. From 1947 to 1955, the number of farms in Italy increased by 10.6 percent, while it decreased by 4 percent in France and by 6 percent in West Germany; still, agricultural output kept rising in Italy about as it did in France and Germany. The agricultural census of 1961 counted 4.3 million holdings covering 65 million acres. Fifty-five percent of this area was in farms directly farmed by their owners. Still, 18 percent of the landowners held 45 percent of the land, using hired labor or share croppers to till it. There still was much reliance on cheap human labor and on draft animals in the Mezzogiorno.

The richest agricultural areas are still to be found in the plain of the Po. In 1966, Italy produced substantial quantities of a variety of crops: 9.7 million tons of wheat, a crop distributed over the whole country, but with higher yields in Emilia, Lombardy, and the region of Venice, and poorer yields in the south and on the islands; 3.3 million tons of corn, chiefly in the Po plain and around Rome and Naples; 530,000 tons of oats and smaller quantities of barley and rye; 480,000 tons of rice, mainly in Lombardy and the Piedmont; 3.5 million tons of potatoes and large quantities of other vegetables; 9 million tons of sugar beets, mainly in the Po plain but also in Puglia and Calabria; 10,000 tons of hemp, some flax and linseed (largely in Puglia), and cotton (mainly in Sicily). Italy has also a large production of truly Mediterranean crops: olive oil (417,000 tons, one third of which is now produced in Puglia and only small quantities in Tuscany, which ships most of the oil exported); citrus fruits (1 million tons of oranges and 0.5 of lemons, grown mainly in Sicily, Calabria, and Campania); a great variety of other fruits and, of course, the products of the vineyards, which cover 8.4 million acres and produce 68 million hectoliters of wine and 675,000 tons of table grapes, mostly in the Mezzogiorno, although the vineyards are spread all over the country and some of the more renowned wines come from the north or from Tuscany.

Agricultural production on the whole has been increasing in volume.

Italy is indeed the southern Mediterranean garden of the European Common Market; the gradual removal of tariffs and quotas for farm products among the Six is opening to Italian agriculture great prospects northward, particularly for fruits, vegetables, olive oil, and wine. The production of grain has been, however, somewhat on the decrease, with the exception of wheat, which is heavily subsidized. The livestock economy has been rather stationary through the 1960s despite a certain increase in the consumption of animal products in the country: in 1964, Italy had 9 million head of cattle, 7.7 million sheep, and 5 million hogs. The production of milk and cheese was still important but did not show much progress; in this area, the total Common Market production seemed to be larger than the demand, and the countries to the north better fitted for this sector of the economy. The major emphasis of Italian economic policy in recent years was on the expansion of in-dustrial and commercial activities, for the cities had to absorb the steady flow of labor coming off the farms.

Besides agricultural products, the natural endowment of Italy does not provide many industrial raw materials. Food industries are there-fore quite important in Italy, which disputes with France the first world rank for the production of wine and the same rank with Spain for olive oil. Italy is also the third world producer of cheese, after the United States and France. In the mineral realm, however, Italy seldom ranks among world or even European leaders, except for mercury, for which it is the second producer in the world after Spain; its mines supply small quantities of iron, zinc, lead, manganese, pyrite, bauxite, fluorite, and coal. Some oil has been located in different parts of the country, par-ticularly in Sicily but also in the Po plain; little production has been yet developed (2.6 million tons in 1964, but only 1.8 in 1966). Italy has been more successful with natural gas, of which it was the main European producer east of the Soviet Union until 1967 (about 10 million cubic meters a year). Water power is abundant in the mountainous country, and the total output of electricity reached 90 million in 1966, about half of this from hydraulic sources chiefly in the Alps. The demand for electricity is increasing very fast and the proportion of it supplied from thermal power stations using coal or petroleum products is rapidly increasing. Italy is a heavy importer of petroleum, and its government-controlled oil company, ENI, has been hunting for concessions on oil fields around the world. Because it is so dependent on imports of oil and coal for its energy supply, Italy has been greatly interested in the commercial production of nuclear energy, and is building stations for this purpose.

Traditionally, Italy has been a leading producer of textile manufac-tures and leatherware. The cotton, woolen, and silk industries have been substantially expanded since 1946. In 1966, Italian looms consumed 217,000 tons of cotton, almost as much as the British textile industry. Its woolen industry consumed, in 1965, 86,000 tons of wool, about half the British figure. Italy also has been very active in the field of man-made fibers (rayon, nylon, dacron, etc.), of which it is the fifth producer in the world.

Recently, Italy has considerably expanded its engineering industries; its exports of machinery have been quite important all over the world. Italian cars are popular throughout Europe, and the firm of Fiat won the much-disputed contract to build the first large Western-style motor car plant in the USSR. Italian typewriters, calculating machines, and electronic equipment have been quite successful on the international market and even in the United States. Italy also has achieved considerable recognition in the pharmaceutical and optical fields, and in precision instruments. To support the expansion of the mechanical industries and to better equip itself, Italy has built up its iron and steel industry; it has been the main beneficiary of the Common Market in this field. In 1966, the output of pig iron and ferroalloys rose to 6.4 million tons, and the output of crude steel to 13.5 million tons, both figures being double those of 1960 and four times those of 1954. Most of the iron and steel development is due to large new plants built on the sea coast (especially near Genoa and Taranto) to receive both the coal and the ores they need from overseas. The growth of the chemical industry has been about as rapid, both in output and variety of product. In their desire to achieve as much self-sufficiency as possible, Italian technicians have put to use, in spectacular fashion, the plutonian forces in the Arno Valley of Tuscany; special drilling and piping have channeled steam and hot fluids of volcanic origin from their underground labyrinth toward a plant at Larderello where steam is transformed into power and a variety of chemical products are extracted from volcanic fluids and gases.

Last but not least, Italy offers many services to foreigners in order to help balance the normal deficit of its foreign trade. Italy has to import large quantities of raw materials and grain (particularly corn from the United States), and like any other well-developed country it must also import a variety of mechanical equipment and other consumer goods. The main exports of Italy are fruits and vegetables, textile fabrics, leatherware, machinery and motor vehicles, plastic materials, and petroleum byproducts. The imports normally exceed the exports, leaving an adverse balance compensated by receipts from shipping, tourists' expenditures, foreign investment, and remittances from Italians abroad. Thus, the balance of payments may be, as it recently was, finally in favor of Italy. Foreign investments are, of course, a very irregular factor in the balance. Remittances from Italians abroad have been more steady and rose to a total of $326 million in 1965, but this level can hardly be long maintained. The profits from shipping activities may be more permanent. Italy had a merchant marine of 5.9 million gross tons in 1966, coming after the fleets of Britain, Norway, and Greece among European flags.

International tourism is a considerable resource; Italy receives some 24 million visitors from abroad per year. Only Canada has a greater number of foreign visitors annually (over 30 million). Italy can offer a remarkable array of amenities: long, beautiful seashores along a warm sea, well-fitted for nautical activities; mountain and ski resorts, especially in the Alps; and an unmatched range of art treasures, historical monuments, and beautiful landscape. Most of the tourists come from Western Europe; in 1965, the leading nationalities were West Germans (5.5 million), French, Swiss, Austrians, British, Americans (1.1 million), Dutch, and Belgians. The importance of the Roman pilgrimage enhances the significance of this world-wide attraction of Italy to foreign visitors.

The progress achieved in the last twenty years should not overshadow the acute problems the Italian people must still face. The economic and social lag of the Mezzogiorno remains a basic weakness in the whole picture. Optimism is more warranted by the change developing north of Rome than by what recently has been attained to the south of the capital. To a large extent, the long-range trends will depend on the improvement of education and the ability of Italy to train large masses of highly skilled labor. The Italians have always had a brilliant, but numerically small, elite, in the sciences, the arts, and the advanced sectors of technology. The modern competition between nations requires large numbers of highly qualified workers in all these fields. Other reforms are needed to provide a wider base for the mass consumption of both food and manufactured goods, which could be achieved only with a more equal redistribution of income throughout the country. The gradual integration of Italy into the Western European Common Market should provide favorable conditions for such an evolution, in which the relative backwardness of today's popular masses may be turned into a great resource for the future.

Since 1945, Italy has enjoyed peace and political stability. It has been a faithful member of NATO and of the EEC. It has participated in most of the select groups of nations making decisions for the economic policies of the Western world. Its relations with its neighbors have been, on the whole, quite satisfactory. Tensions with Yugoslavia have been resolved with the settlement of the question of Trieste. New tensions have arisen recently in the upper Adige basin in the Dolomitic Alps, particularly around Bolzano, where a German-speaking minority is being claimed by Austria as part of their Tyrol province. Some terrorism occasionally has flared up in the 1960s in that area, but it has not led to a situation causing international concern. Italy has been able to re-establish good relations with the African lands over which it had extended its colonial empire in the early part of this century. Indeed, its main problems remain economic and social on the domestic scene. The Italian fight for industrial and economic progress so as to catch up with the Western European nations to its north has scored considerable successes. The West could not afford to let these endeavors fail. Italy is now humming with activity, the most bustling country of the Mediterranean. Its people have hope and are regaining faith in the future, which is a basic factor of a people's progress and happiness.

## MALTA

In the very center of the Mediterranean Sea, directly south of the southeastern tip of Sicily, a small group of islands became, in 1964, the most recent addition to the list of independent states of Europe: Malta was granted independence by Great Britain, and while remaining a member of the British Commonwealth, it entered a new era of its political life. Like most lands of the Mediterranean, the new state of Malta has had a turbulent past. It was held in succession by Phoenicians, Greeks, Carthaginians, Romans, Arabs, and the kings of Sicily, who gave it to the Knights of St. John in 1530. The Knights were dispersed by the French revolutionary armies under Napoleon after the conquest of Italy in 1798, but the Maltese revolted against the French and asked for the protection of the British Crown in 1802. They became a British colony in 1814.

The total area of the state is 121.8 square miles, consisting of the larger island of Malta (95 miles) and the two islands of Gozo and Conino (see map, p. 500). The population was estimated, in 1966, at 370,000; about 12,000 less than in 1960, as a result of emigration. The capital and main city and port is Valletta, standing on a beautiful roadstead on the east shore of the main island. Its central Mediterranean position and the ruggedness of its topography made Malta a natural fortress commanding the central part of the Mediterranean and a perfect naval base for British control of that sea in the nineteenth century. Malta's economy has been dependent on British military installations, which were by far the main employer of the archipelago. In 1964, they employed about 12,000 persons, while the whole population of Valletta was 18,000. With independence, the British commitment in the islands was decreased; Britain has agreed to provide, for the first ten years, capital aid for the development and diversification of the Maltese economy. The Maltese

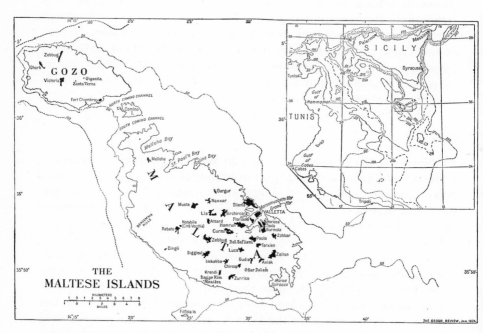

Map of Malta and Gozo showing the chief settlements. Important archeological sites are indicated in antique lettering. Inset is a map showing the situation of the archipelago with reference to the European and African shores of the Mediterranean and the basin of that sea. Depths are in fathoms. *(The Geographical Review)*

nation is one of the most remarkable melting pots of the Mediterranean, in which elements from many parts of Europe and the north shores of Africa have been mixing for centuries. English and Maltese are both official languages. The cultivated area covers 35,000 acres, the main farm products being wheat, barley, and a variety of fruits and vegetables. Goats and sheep make up most of the livestock. Private industry employs about 40,000 people, and plans are being drawn to develop engineering and chemical plants and the cultivation of flower seeds and cuttings. A new power station is being built, which will also desalt sea water for the public water supply. It is hoped that tourism may be developed, and Malta may become a tax haven for international corporations.

The highlands of Montenegro. A deep canyon penetrates inland from the seashore amidst barren limestone hills, fields, and a town along the shore. (*Yugoslav Information Center*)

# 13

---

# The
# Balkan Peninsula

The easternmost of the three peninsulas is the least massive. Jutting southward with a triangular shape, it is more firmly attached to and more opened toward the continent, for it is attached to the mainland by the valleys of the Lower Danube and its tributary the Drava, instead of by high mountains. The Balkan peninsula is quite bulky and continental in its northern part, but then it suddenly narrows down to a thin peninsula, deeply penetrated by the Aegean Sea from the east and the Ionian Sea from the west, breaking up into promontories and islands.

There is thus a contrast between north and south, between the more continental and somewhat Central European northern section and the more maritime and definitely Mediterranean southern one. Settlement and all the pageant of history have stressed this division further. The southern country is Greece, one of the oldest nations and participants of history; the northern country is the domain of the southern branch of the Slavic family of peoples, newcomers to the west and to independent national life. The two zones of civilization are quite different, yet they have lived together as neighbors for so long that interpenetration has been considerable. One of the results of this has been the creation of a belt of greater instability at the contact of the two zones, to the east in the area known as Macedonia, to the west in a new entity recently born as the independent state of Albania. To the extreme east the peninsula extends a narrow stretch of land, between the Aegean and the Black seas, toward Asia Minor. This corner of Europe has remained a part of Turkey, the bridgehead that the Turks keep as a vestige of the great em-

The Balkan Peninsula. General outline map showing main rivers, railways, towns, and political boundaries (with solid lines except on the sections where boundaries follow the course of major rivers). The dotted areas correspond to lands more than 1600 feet in altitude, making obvious the predominance of highlands in the Balkans. Main ranges are shown only by the names written along the main axis of the range.

pire they once ruled on the continent extending over all the Balkan peninsula and even farther north.

## A RUGGED TOPOGRAPHY

The Balkan peninsula owes its name to the mountain range which rises in its northeastern part. This range is perhaps the only relatively simple feature of the peninsula's structure, and can be related to the Carpathian system. On any topographic map of Europe, one sees the Carpathians curving through southeastern Europe, outlining a sort of giant inverted S. The main part of the curve is in Rumania and circles around the Transylvanian basin. It comes down to the Danube and is interrupted there by the river's gorge at the Iron Gate. South of the Iron Gate a range of mountains stretches, curving to the east, south of the Lower Danube: this is the Balkan range or, as it is called in Slavonic, *the Stara Planina*. As the Danube near Vienna divides the Alps from the Carpathians, so the mighty river separates the Carpathians from the Balkans at the Iron Gate.

The structure of the Balkan range is different from the Carpathian. The northern slope descends steeply to the low and flat Danubian plain, but the southern slope melts into a complicated system of highlands and ranges that occupies practically the whole Balkan peninsula. The Stara Planina could be considered a southern limb of the Carpathians, but to the northwest the Balkan lands are occupied by ranges and plateaus which seem to be an offspring of the Italian Alps. The ranges along the Adriatic Sea often are called Dinaric Alps, and the name is found farther to the southeast where some crests are called the North Albanian Alps. Whether a continuation of the Alps or of the Carpathians, the Balkan highlands are different in structure from either of these ranges.

The Dinaric folds have been erected slowly, through a complicated history beginning with the Secondary period. They have been affected by the Alpine uplifting and by the sinking of the Adriatic basin on the one hand and the Aegean on the other. One can still follow the main orientations of the Dinaric chains throughout Greece, in the alignment of the Aegean Sea islands down to Crete, which seems to mark the southern end of the structure. The sinking of these two neighboring areas had led the sea to invade the periphery of the highlands, and the 1500-foot line circles close to the shoreline all around the peninsula. The plains along the coast are reduced to small patches of lowland overlooked by steep and high cliffs. Inland the altitudes between 1000 and 2000 feet stretch along the depressions, valleys, or basins, while plateaus above 4000 feet extend widely and many crests rise above 6000.

The topography of the highlands is one of great irregularity. Some parts of the Balkan system are calcareous and others made of more resistant crystalline material; some volcanic intrusions remind one of the fact that, as in Italy, the peninsula is an area of instability where the tectonic moves have not yet come to rest. The steepness of the slope has favored an active erosion, and the highland is deeply indented and sculpted by valleys and internal depressions. The chief valleys or longer depressions appear to follow lines of faulting or other structural contact zones. For instance, the major, winding, north-south depression followed by two rivers (flowing in opposite directions), the Morava, a tributary of the Danube, and the Vardar, which empties into the Aegean, clearly marks the contact of the folds oriented from northwest to southeast, the Dinaric major axis, with the highlands stretching from west to east, an orientation which predominates in the Bulgarian and Macedonian structure.

Such depressions crossing the highland zone are few; on the whole the Balkan area is one of difficult traffic. In the northwestern parts communications are particularly difficult in view of the mass of the highlands and of the special character of the plateaus of the *Karst,* a name that has been adopted as typical of the landscape resulting from erosion of thick limestone layers. Water filters rapidly downward due to the permeability of the limestone. This permeability results chiefly from the solubility in water of carbonate of lime, which is one of the principal elements in the constitution of limestone. Owing to its cohesion, the limestone does not dissolve entirely on the surface: the waters work mainly underground, creating caves and a network of channels through which the streams circulate at some depth. Every so often the roof over such caves or channels thins out and falls in, creating surface pits, narrow gorges above deep valleys, and finally closed depressions called *dolines.* A doline has usually a circular or oval shape and some red soil at the bottom, the clayish residue of the solution of limestone; when several such dolines unite, a large interior depression develops, still floored with red earth or *terra rossa.* Limestone areas are frequent around the Mediterranean, and the red earths are a common occurrence. In many Mediterranean languages the red color and the earth are designated by words derived from the same root. Terra rossa has been considered typical of Mediterranean soils, but it is in fact only frequent in areas of weathered limestone. Before it is decomposed, limestone is generally gray or even white. Under the dry conditions of the Mediterranean, limestone rock begins by showing a great density of cracks and fluted sharp ridges that make walking very difficult on such terrain: this landform is called *lapies* and is found on vast areas of the Karst plateau and other dry limestone regions.

Whether of karstic topography or of more-rounded crystalline shapes, the Balkan countries are rugged. They enjoy also a variety of Mediterranean climate which the high elevation and the isolation from the sea, as a result of screening by coastal ranges, render more continental — that is, extreme in temperature and in the seasonal contrast of aridity. The position of the Balkans farther east decreases the chances of humid Atlantic air masses reaching the peninsula, while the greater proximity to Asia and the winter high pressures of Russia lead to an inflow of cold, dry air from the northeast in that season. The shores of the Adriatic are famous for the violent wind called *bora* that sweeps them, blowing from the northeast when a winter depression is over that sea.

The Balkans have a rough environment indeed; it is truly Mediterranean, with a continental shade that makes it sharper, and the ruggedness of the topography adds to the additional problem of difficult communications. The Balkan highlands have lived as a tissue of isolated cells, preserving archaic forms of life and resisting to the best of their abilities the multitude of influences and external interferences that have swirled across the peninsula throughout history.

## THE ETHNOGRAPHIC PUZZLE

In Europe the Balkans have a strong reputation for political complexity. This is quite natural when one considers the number and variety of dominations that have extended over all or part of the peninsula: the Greek and Macedonian empires of antiquity, followed by Rome, then Byzantium, and the Turks, the last domination retreating through the nineteenth century and the beginning of the twentieth as it yielded to local nationalisms, and also to the Austrian push toward the southeast and the Russian expansion to the southwest. Italian influences have been present continually along the Adriatic shores, where Venice ruled an empire and where Fascist Italy, not contented with a series of establishments on the coast, conquered Albania for a while. French and British influences have also been important in the cultural, political, and economic fields, but generally through indirect action.

None of these influences or dominations was able to unify the peoples on the peninsula. They successfully resisted assimilation into any one of the different cultures, yet they were somewhat marked by each of them. The rugged topography and the difficulty of access to many parts of the country played a part in favoring the resistant attitude of the people. This attitude was quite in line with the traditional European regionalism, and the diversity of dominations only strengthened the partitioning into many political units. The basis of this regionalism is the original complexity of the ethnographic map.

In the south the ethnography appears relatively simple, for the

Greeks were recognized as a distinct political group very early in history. Their cultural unity kept them distinct throughout the millennia. But they mixed with many other peoples of the eastern Mediterranean, and they colonized areas outside the peninsula from which they also received some immigrants. Their association with Turkey was particularly close; on the eastern shore of the Aegean lived many Greeks, and Smyrna (today Izmir) used to be one of the largest Greek cities. Some Greeks were assimilated by the Turks; others, who stayed loyal to their culture and religion, were treated as an unwelcome minority in the Ottoman Empire and exchanged in the early 1920s for Turkish residents of Greece. This exchange of populations, reputedly a model for such operations, greatly improved the relations between the two countries, for it removed the main cause of conflict—the ethnographic map of the areas concerned was somewhat simplified.

Ancient Greece was united under a single political authority with the Macedonian expansion, which culminated with the empire of Alexander the Great. But who are the Macedonians? In ancient times, when they subjugated the southern part of the peninsula, they were certainly regarded as foreigners by Athenians and Spartans. Macedonia is an ill-defined area to the north and northeast of old Greece; the Macedonians were less sea-minded than the southern Greeks, but they had a genius for continental organization which was unique. From Alexander's conquests on, Macedonian rule became the champion of Hellenistic culture. Greek was the language of the empire, and the civilization stemmed largely from Athens. The Greeks were certainly justified in 1918 in claiming historical and national (that is, mainly cultural) association with the Macedonians. But the Macedonians have also mingled with their neighbors to the north, the Bulgars and, to a smaller extent, the Serbs, as well as with the Turks to the east. This explains the claims of some of these people, particularly the Bulgars, as to their association with Macedonia. Whether Macedonia is Greek or Slavic (and particularly Bulgar) remains an extremely complicated and delicate problem. It might require a study, valley by valley and village by village, to form a definite opinion. But the boundaries throughout the peninsula have been set recently after deliberations in which non-Balkan powers participated and, in fact, usually had the deciding voice. Some boundary decisions reflected, therefore, the general European political situation rather than the views of the people on the land concerned.

To the north the Balkans are divided chiefly between two groups of people: the Bulgars to the east and the Yugoslavs or Southern Slavs to the west. The Bulgars seem to have been racially related to the Hungarians and Finns in ancient times; in the last millennium they were thoroughly assimilated into the Slavic culture and the Orthodox religion.

Their language is closer to Russian than to any other Slavonic tongue outside Russia, and they managed to keep such associations although they remained for a long time under Turkish rule. They claim as Bulgar several areas outside their present boundaries, Macedonia, especially along the lower Maritsa River, being the most important one.

The Southern Slavs are a more complex group. Three main peoples who compose it are, from east to west, the Serbs, Croats, and Slovenes. Although their vernaculars differ but little, the three groups have had different backgrounds. The Serbs stayed under Turkish domination from 1389, when they were defeated at the battle of Kosovo, until 1878, when the Russian victory over the Turks opened the way to independence. They are chiefly an agricultural people, linked to the mountains, and somewhat backward as a result of this history. The Croats are centered on the valley of the Sava River, oriented toward the Danube, and were for centuries under Austrian rule. They are therefore more familiar with Western culture and had a more advanced economic development. The Slovenes, closer to Trieste, have also been under Austrian rule, but their chief association was with the Italian bourgeoisie from Venice and other northern cities. To be quite precise one would have to mention also the Bosnian, Herzegovinian, and Montenegrin peoples, who are slightly different from the Serbs, and lastly the Dalmatians. No one was astonished early in the twentieth century by the claims to independence of the Albanians; more affected by the Turkish rule than were the Southern Slavs, they had yet managed to remain a different group, although situated within the zone of rival Greek and Southern Slav influence. Albanians have long had a very high birth rate and have migrated to surrounding regions, thus increasing the cultural, religious, and political puzzle of the peninsula's geography.

The diversity of the old basic settlement has kept the map diversified, although through history the main associations have altered. The fact that these peoples rarely had the chance to administer themselves, to have an independent national life, helped to harden their regional frames. The most individualized among them are certainly the Greek people, who had in ancient times a great period of national and cultural expansion. It is possible that in its general outline the present division, if it lasts, will bring about nations adapted to their territorial frame. And the process is going on right now, because Bulgaria, Yugoslavia, and Albania have had less than a century of independent existence in modern times. Regionalism has been favored also by the topography and the relative backwardness in which foreign domination left the masses. Lack of education is obviously the reason why none of the dominating cultures has been strongly implanted.

The topography also played an understandable yet curious part in the shaping of the nationalities of the Balkan peninsula. To rise as a nation, an ethnic group had to emerge from the mountains and establish a strong foothold at some point from which it could control the neighborhood but also at which there was enough good soil to permit a denser and more intensive occupation of the land. These two conditions were achieved only in the depressions, particularly in those that were open to the outside. Therefore the foundation of the political map lies on a triangle of crossroads, the location of which had been determined by geological structure.

The main line of traffic across the peninsula is the corridor followed by the Morava and Vardar rivers, leading from the Danubian plain to the Aegean Sea. At the two extremities are Belgrade on the Danube, the capital of Yugoslavia, and Salonika on the sea, the main port and economic center of Greece and the capital of Macedonia. From the central part of the corridor, another structural depression branches eastward, stretching between the Balkan range to the north and the ranges of the Rila and Rhodopes to the south; as it develops eastward, this depression becomes the valley of the Maritsa River. It forms the heart of Bulgaria, of which the Maritsa is the national stream, and Sofia, the capital, stands in the high basin linking the Morava valley to the Maritsa depression. Every nationality in the northern part of the peninsula is thus based on a thoroughfare; to the south, in peninsular and insular Greece, the sea becomes the chief highway.

The opposition between the old civilized country of Greece and the relatively "barbaric" Slavic countries to the north has led to several conflicts. None perhaps was so serious as the early postwar conflict that took the form of civil war in Greece but in fact constituted an active front between the forces that are for the East or for the West in Europe. Local rivalries are tenacious and fierce in the Balkans, where the feudal system has not yet been fully liquidated. It is easy for outside influences to play with internal conflicts—it is surprising that there have not been more conflicts in the troubled contemporary period.

YUGOSLAVIA

Yugoslavia, stretching over the northwest of the peninsula, is the greatest of the Balkan powers. It is also the most complicated and diversified. Its area of almost 100,000 square miles was in 1967 populated with 20,000,-000 inhabitants. The present republic was first constituted in 1919 as the Kingdom of the Serbs, Croats, and Slovenes, under the Serbian Monarch. During World War II the country was overrun by German armies, and the royal dynasty fled abroad. After liberation in 1945 Yugoslavia found itself in the Soviet zone of influence in Europe, and a government was formed, headed by Marshal Tito (Josip Broz), who had led the resistance against the German occupation. Yugoslavia was proclaimed a federal republic and the members of the royal family were deprived of their nationality. For their remarkable fight on the Allied side in the war, the Yugoslavs by the peace treaty with Italy in 1947 received the major part of the former Italian province of Venezia Giulia and the town of Zara (now Zadar) with the adjacent islands. They were given also a share in the reparation payments and most of the Free Territory of Trieste but not that city itself.

In the peace settlement of 1919 Serbia (the war had started in 1914 with the Austrian armies invading the small state) received a favorable boundary to the east at the expense of Bulgaria, who had sided with the Central Powers. Yugoslavia has thus gained on all sides. It controls most of the crucial Morava-Vardar corridor, a large part of the southern Pannonian plain, and a long coast on the Adriatic from Trieste to the Albanian border. The largest part of its territory, which includes even the southeastern foothills of the Alps, is made of the rugged and massive plateaus and ranges of the Dinaric system. Thus is created a certain contrast between the central highlands, poorer, less developed, isolated from the main currents of European traffic, and the more open, diversified, better developed periphery. Yugoslavia is bound to have a variety of orientations: it is Danubian, that is, Central European, for its richest parts and main cities are in the Danubian area; it is also Mediterranean and Balkan; and it has a stronghold of isolation in its center that helps to keep united a too-versatile organization.

Four languages are officially recognized in Yugoslavia: the Serb and Croat languages, which serve as the main *lingua franca;* Slovene, important in the northwest; and Macedonian, important in the southeast in the countries of the Vardar. Bulgarian is not recognized, although the Bulgars claim a substantial minority in the southeast. There are many minorities in Yugoslavia: Albanian, German, Hungarian, Rumanian, Italian, and Turkish elements are still present, although many of these aliens fled from the reborn and strongly nationalistic state after 1945.

Yugoslavia therefore presents a mosaic of natural and human regions. It could be the foundation of a well-balanced economy but as yet the resources have been used in only a simple way; it is a sound economy, with many "colonial" features that are encountered through the whole country. It was badly hit by the disruption and the destructions of World War II, and the heroic resistance of the Yugoslavs decreased the population figure by 1.5 million from 1940 to 1945. Since 1948, under Marshal Tito's regime this country has adopted the role of a buffer between East and West, in particular as a leader in political neutralism and nationalistic Communism.

A calm lake at the bottom of a depression in the rugged Yugoslav highlands. (*Yugoslav Information Center*)

Ljubljana, the Slovenian capital. (*Yugoslav Information Center*)

Three main regions can be distinguished in Yugoslavia: the Danubian north, the eastern Morava-Vardar country, and the Dinaric highlands.

For its larger part the Danubian north is drained by two tributaries of the great river: the Drava and the Sava, both coming from the eastern Alps. In the northwestern section, Slovenia is rather mountainous: a few high ranges, such as the crystalline Pohorje and the limestone Karavanke, are in fact Alpine foothills. They enjoy Alpine climate, with an average temperature for January of around 30° and for July of only 65°. The rainfall comes chiefly in summer and fall; forests on the crests and meadows on the valley floors are the usual scenery. Fields and orchards cover the lower hills of the alluvial fan. The Sava, to the south, winds across a severe highland, concentrating the population and the activities; the Slovene capital, Ljubljana (200,000), has been a relay since the medieval period on the road from Vienna to Trieste. The city has mechanical, chemical, and food industries and an active university. The highlands have attracted tourists; here, on the shore of scenic Lake Bled, was the summer residence of the kings.

To the south and southeast stretch the plateaus of the Karst with their characteristic topography, but to the north and northeast, low Pannonian lands extend, with a few ridges of hills, predicting the flatness of the nearby Hungarian plain. At the contact of the mountainous and lower lands, Zagreb, the capital of Croatia and the second city of Yugoslavia, groups some 820,000 people. It is an important economic and financial center with a well-known university. An intermediary between the plains of the Danube and of the Po, Zagreb had famous fairs; it suffers now from the decreased traffic between East and West and also from the increased centralization in Belgrade of the national economic management. Its industries include flour mills and breweries, leatherware and paper making, textiles and vegetable-oil mills; recently cement, glass, and mechanical works have been added, spurring on the city's growth. But Zagreb cannot drain off all the rich agricultural population of the plains around the Danube, where wheat and cornfields expand, mingling with orchards, vineyards, and fields of flax. On fodder crops and meadows stock raising maintains numerous cattle and many hogs. Large villages are often marked by the wells that remind one of the *Hungarian puszta*. It is truly Pannonian landscape that prevails in the flat Bačka region between Danube and Tisza, where Subotica (122,000) and Novi Sad (162,000) are the main towns manufacturing farm machinery.

Standing at the meeting of the Sava with the Danube, Belgrade, the capital, had a population of only 700,000 in 1965. The relatively small agglomeration of the capital of Yugoslavia can be accounted for by the fact that until 1920 it had been only the capital of rural Serbia and one city among many along the Danube. It was a cosmopolitan crossroads in the seventeenth century, but was later ruined during the ebb and flow of war between Turks and Austrians. Its rise started with independence: the city counted only 60,000 people in 1890. Industrialization has started, and the organization of a centralized and planned economy since 1945 has enabled the city to repair rapidly the ravages of the war and to grow fast. It has now an important administrative and cultural function to perform and attracts new manufactures; the conurbation agglomerates about one million people.

To the south of Belgrade, the rich plain of Sumadija gently rises southward. It is the beginning of the Morava-Vardar country, the heart of Serbia. The rainfall is abundant here, and part of it falls during the hot summer. A century ago a dense forest of oak and beech trees covered the Sumadija and served the revolting peasants as a shelter from the Turks. Now little woodland remains. The land is intensively cultivated, wheat and corn occupying 80 percent of the area, the rest being chiefly under fruit orchards, hemp, or flax, and fat cattle are raised. The density of the population (about 250 per square mile) has quadrupled since 1840 and the rise goes on.

Toward the southeast the Morava valley narrows down to a corridor between high cliffs. The mountains on both sides are massive and thickly populated. Herds of cattle and sheep go up and down the slopes according to the season, and the peasants till patches of soil along the valleys and in the high basins. The population is a mixed one to the east of the Morava and in the valley. The thoroughfare has attracted them as has also the development of mines: copper at Bor and Majdanpek, pyrites, and some coal. The towns trade in timber and cattle, make wine, leather, and flour. Nish (95,000) is the crucial hub of intra-Balkan communications, as it stands on the Morava at the place where the Nishava valley begins, opening the way eastward toward the high basin of Sofia, and beyond it to the Maritsa and the Straits.

The upper Morava is commanded by another important city. Skoplje, capital of Yugoslavian Macedonia, stands on the banks of the Vardar and in a high basin that is truly Mediterranean: the summer is dry and the average rainfall low. A cold, but more humid, winter brings the strong and icy wind called *vardarac*, which descends from the snow-covered heights north of Skoplje. The town is frankly Macedonian, with a notable Moslem minority of Turks and Albanians—the mosques with their minarets tell of the proximity of the Middle East. Skoplje has an important railroad station, for the city is surrounded by passes across the massive ranges of crystalline schist. The hills have been deforested to make space for pasture, and here the shepherd reigns. Fields now surround the town, since the recent defeat of malaria. Farther downstream the valley of the Vardar is followed by orchards and fields of tobacco, which is exported to Western Europe. Skoplje was growing fast when, in July 1963, it was almost completely destroyed by a series of tremors which took more than a thousand lives and left 170,000 homeless. With international help, Yugoslavia is rebuilding Skoplje, according to a plan prepared by a distinguished panel of experts, to become a bigger and better city, with a population of 260,000 by 1971, with a steel mill, a cement plant, and a variety of light industries.

From the Karst plateaus to the Morava-Vardar furrow, the Dinaric highlands are rugged and backward. They are poor, too—only one fifth of the total area is arable soil. The wooded higher summits tower over grassy plateaus or, more often, over stony karstic expanse. Depressions lined with red earth follow generally tectonic lines of faulting which cross the highlands in several furrows of a north-south direction. The Kosovo polje (plain) marks the eastern furrow; the central network of depressions radiates around Sarajevo, famous for the murder of the Austrian archduke in 1914, which signaled the opening of World War I. Sarajevo is the central market of the Dinaric highlands and the largest city outside the Danubian depressions, with 220,000 inhabitants, about one fourth of whom are Moslem. Here are beech woods on the crests, orchards on the better exposed slopes, and cornfields supplying the *polenta*, the main dish of the mountaineer. To the north, approaching the Sava, the topography becomes lower, the soils better, and the resources more varied. Banja Luka (130,000) is an important market for grain and cattle, and mines of coal and rock salt are scattered around. These Bosnian lands are rich and well populated compared with the semidesert Karst, where water is so scarce and so needed as a beverage that dishes are washed in goat's milk.

The limestone plateaus rise in an impressive and complicated wall above the Adriatic. The coastal areas or Primorje have attracted considerable population. In Quaternary times the sea invaded a topography of parallel limestone ridges separated by wide valleys and created a coast with many bays and, particularly, a number of lengthy islands, stretching parallel to the shoreline and close to it. This Dalmatian coast was colonized by the Greeks, by the Romans, and then by Venetians. In the lower sections of the shore, men crowded on the good soils of the Flysch outcroppings, and active maritime life developed at Dubrovnik (40,000), Split (130,000), Šibenik, Rijeka, and Zadar. Split was more populated and much richer in the first century A.D. than it now is, for it was organized to be an important port. However, between the World Wars, the most important Yugoslav port by its traffic was Sušak, the Slav suburb of Italian Fiume. Now the Yugoslavs can use Rijeka, the former Fiume, with its 111,000 inhabitants, its shipyards and its mechanical plants, as one of their main harbors.

With a rapidly increasing population, dynamic, and full of confidence in the future they will shape for themselves, the Yugoslavs have started rebuilding a devastated economy. Before 1940 they exported agricultural products, cattle and hogs, and some ores. The large estates have been broken up by an agrarian reform started in 1924 and rapidly pushed ahead since 1945. The government headed by Marshal Tito applied Communist doctrine to the economy in a rough manner; but it may provide the melting pot so needed to unify a sound country made up of varied elements.

Some new geographical trends began to develop, however, as a result of this planning and are being pushed further each year. The most significant of these trends is the present government's endeavor to reverse an old tendency in Yugoslav history: for centuries the richest and best developed areas of this country were the lower lands, either on the Danubian side or along the Adriatic shores; the highlands were considered the least important section of the national economy; a steady flow of population went towards the rich plain to the north, depopulating the plateaus. Now the national endeavor is directed toward a better development of these highlands, which constitute most of the national territory in area. Railroads and roads are being built to open these regions difficult of access to easy transportation. Geological exploration looks for more materials to be mined. Factories are preferably built, when possible, in towns of the hilly country, such as Skoplje, Sarajevo, or Banja Luka. It is significant that the name of *Titograd* has been given to the small capital (40,000) of rugged Montenegro previously called *Podgoritsa*, rather than to a larger city in the plain. A steady stream of people are now leaving their homes in lower areas to settle on the newly developed lands in the hills.

The endeavor to develop the more backward and difficult central, mountainous parts of the country at the expense of the better-developed sections, where growth would be easier, has been criticized in the mid-1960s, and some reforms have begun, reorienting the emphasis of the former plans. Yugoslavia encounters some of the same problems that are now plaguing most of the European countries, that is, the concentration of economic activities in a few selected areas, while many regions are left lagging. The federal structure and recent unification of Yugoslavia still require that every region be given a feeling of full participation in the national system so as to avoid regional frustration which could be turned into political opposition to the existing regime. In 1964, it was estimated that agriculture supplied about 40 percent of the total national income and industry 26 percent; but the respective shares of agriculture and industry stood at 38 and 36 percent in Serbia proper (the region of Belgrade), 42 and 44 percent in Croatia, and 49 and 50 percent in

Sarajevo, in the heart of the calcareous plateaus of Yugoslavia. The slender minarets attest to the presence of the Moslem minority which remained after Turkish domination ended. (*Yugoslav Information Center*)

Cetinje, near the Albanian border, in a depression amid the barren karstic heights. (*Yugoslav Information Center*)

Slovenia. These were the best-developed parts of Yugoslavia; in the less-developed parts, these same percentages stood at 43 and 25 in Bosnia-Herzogovina and 40 and 22 in Montenegro. The latter two as well as Macedonia and the Kosmet region of Serbia felt they deserved special attention and input to enable them to catch up with the more advanced developed areas.

New great works have been undertaken to spur economic development, particularly in the lagging regions. Irrigation schemes and the reconstruction of Skoplje should help the economy of Macedonia. A railway is being built from the new seaport of Bar in the south to Belgrade via Titograd. A canal system is under construction, linking the Danube and Tisza rivers. Agriculture still remains the main resource of Yugoslavia, as it supplies close to one half of the national income. In 1947, the Communist regime headed by Marshal Tito introduced a policy of farm collectivization. The laws of 1953 limited private land holdings to 25 acres per farmer and provided for compensation to the expropriated large landowners. About one third of the total land area is actually cultivated or under tree crops; another third is classified as wooded, although much of this area is low Mediterranean brush; and about one fourth is pastures. Only 8 percent has been classified as hopelessly unproductive. But much of the farming requires painstaking hand labor of little productivity. In 1965, Yugoslavia harvested about 6 million tons of corn, 3.5 million tons of wheat, and small quantities of barley, rye, sunflower seed, hemp, tobacco, and a variety of vegetables and fruit. At the end of 1965, some 1900 peasant cooperatives counted 1.4 million members, using 18,000 tractors and 4200 threshing machines.

Mining is the resource of Yugoslavia next in importance after agriculture. The output of mineral fuels is rather small (1 million tons of coal, 28 million tons of lignite, and 2 million tons of crude oil). But in the field of metal ores, Yugoslavia ranks among the important producers of Europe; in 1965, its mines supplied 900,000 tons of iron, 4000 tons of antimony, 62,000 tons of copper, 106,000 tons of lead, 525,000 tons of magnesite, 129 tons of silver, 566 tons of mercury, and 1.5 million tons of bauxite. There is also some mining of chrome, zinc, and gold.

Manufacturing remains the weak spot of the Yugoslav economy, but it is expanding. The per capita consumption of energy reached, in 1965, 1192 kg of coal equivalent (an increase of 25 percent in the three years 1962–1965). This consumption is higher than that of Spain, Portugal, or Greece, but about 50 percent below the level of Italy. In 1965, the production of crude steel reached 1.7 million tons and that of cement 3.1. There were also basic chemical, metal refining, and textile industries. The government was working hard to develop more mechanical and engineering industries; despite the emphasis on the underdeveloped

Makarska. The steep cliffs of the karstic plateau overlook this Adriatic resort. (*Yugoslav Information Center*)

An electrical engineering plant. The brigade working in the plant has pledged to achieve 110 percent of the Plan. (*Yugoslav Information Center*)

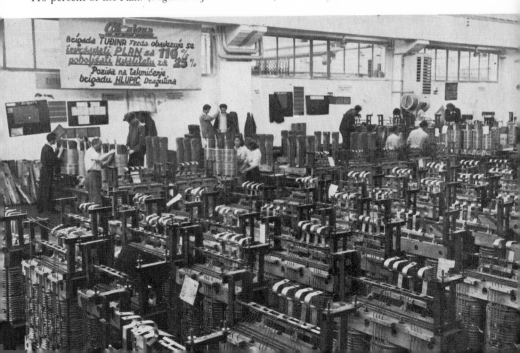

regions, the majority of industrial potential was concentrated in the northwestern part of the country. Yugoslavia still bears the heavy inheritance of centuries of Mediterranean economic backwardness. Its total industrial strength cannot compare with that of Czechoslovakia or even much-less-populated Sweden.

At the outcome of World War II, the Yugoslav regime, headed by Marshal Tito, was closely associated with the Soviet Union; but starting in 1948, it adopted a policy of "nationalistic communism," of greater independence from the USSR, and of economic cooperation with the West. Yugoslav trade was then oriented toward the United States and Britain; Yugoslavia accepted to benefit by the Marshall Plan in the 1950s, and in 1967, moved to become an associate member of the EEC. Its main exports (nonferrous metals, timber, and agricultural products) now go to the USSR, Italy, West Germany, Czechoslovakia, East Germany, and Poland. The main imports (a wide gamut of manufactured goods) come from the United States, Italy, West Germany, the USSR, and other East European countries. As the self-sufficiency of the Common Market tightened, Yugoslavia needed a special arrangement with it so as not to lose whatever position it had built up on the Italian and German markets.

Yugoslavia, as has been stressed, is continental and maritime, Danubian and Mediterranean. This duality of trends and also of heritage, which mixes the Greco-Roman elements with the Slavic and Germanic ones, may explain how a distinct original personality is being worked out for the country. This duality is reflected also in the conflicting trends of its political orientation. Under Marshal Tito's rule, Yugoslavia is about the only Communist country that insists on economic and political neutralism in international relations. This position may have seemed profitable for a while; it has brought to the head of the Yugoslav government greater international prestige, and to Belgrade more meetings of heads of neutral states. But it has not improved Yugoslavia's relations with the Soviet Union, and it may well cause serious economic difficulties at home.

## ALBANIA

One of the small countries of Europe, with 10,000 square miles and a population estimated in 1967 at 2 million, Albania stretches along the Adriatic shores, facing Italy across the narrow Strait of Otranto leading into the Adriatic. It is a mountainous country, between the Dinaric highlands of Yugoslavia and the ranges of northern Greece. A coastal plain, however, develops along most of its shoreline more widely than in most of the Balkan countries, but the plain is not well drained and is often feverous. The hills above are of difficult access and traffic, and the native population has been clinging to them with an admirable tenacity. For long years in the fifteenth century the Albanians resisted the Turks; finally they were conquered and solidly welded to Islam. About half of the population now is Moslem, but there is no state religion, since Albania has a Communist regime that keeps the country in the political orbit of the Soviet and of Communist China.

First proclaimed in 1912, Albanian independence waited until 1920 to become actually established. In 1927 Albania signed a treaty of alliance and economic cooperation with Italy. The Fascist government practically annexed the whole territory in the late 1930s, but local guerillas, with Yugoslav help, had cleared the territory of Italian and German forces by the end of 1944. A close alliance was later signed with Yugoslavia, but there may be some difficulties in applying it if the political orientations of the two countries remain different. A small state, little linked to the outside, Albania feels the need of a big brother's help to develop and to become modernized.

Most of the population lives in the interior basins amid the hills. It increases rapidly as hygiene measures are being introduced and as the bloody family feuds (vendetta) are being abandoned. Arable land is estimated to cover only 12 percent of the total area. This could be easily expanded with some reclamation and drainage of swamps, especially in the coastal plain. A variety of crops are raised, including tobacco around Shkodër (50,000) on the lower Drin, cotton in the plain, and a great number of fruit trees, the specialty of the central part of the country around the capital, Tirana (160,000), and Elbasani (40,000). Only ten towns altogether can boast a population of more than 10,000 each, and this gives the measure of the deeply rural character of the land, one in which a poor kind of forest occupies half of the total area, in which most of the population still wears clothing and footwear made in the home, and in which women herding cattle or sheep on the hillsides can also be seen spinning wool from a distaff. Still, a few industrial plants have been completed in Tirana and Shkodër, and the urban population was said to have reached about 30 percent of the whole nation by 1960. A few roads, railroads, and irrigation canals have been completed during the first two Five-Year Plans. About 17 percent of the land area is actually cultivated.

One of the main improvements achieved since World War II, under the Communist regime, has been the generalization of public health measures and a sustained drive against illiteracy (which was still prevalent by 1946). Albania granted to the Soviet Union a naval base in Valona (or Vlona), strategically located in a deep bay on the Strait of Otranto at the entrance of the Adriatic Sea and in the central section of the whole Mediterranean basin. The Soviet Navy built at Valona large submarine pens. Then Albania turned from the USSR to Communist China, whose influence became predominant by 1961, excluding Russian influence from the country. The main production of Albania that is industralized, and partly exported, is in the realm of raw materials: tobacco, petroleum (900,000 tons produced in 1966), and chrome ore. Roads are being built toward the mountain forests that could yield valuable timber; several hydroelectric plants are at work. On the whole, Albania remains the last large corner of wilderness left on the continent of Europe. In 1968 it authorized by treaty Red China to establish military bases on its territory.

The potential riches of Albania might be considerable once fully explored. The mountains are partly covered with impressive forests, of which there are few in the Mediterranean. It is estimated that about 17 percent of the whole land area of Albania is oak forest and about 12 percent elm woods; there are also pine and birch woodlands. The total timber reserve is estimated at 44.5 million cubic meters. The mineral resources are less well known, but it seems quite likely that they are considerable.

The Albanians have been working to modernize their country. Means of transportation have been improved; railroads now extend their network (about 100 miles in all), and the highway network reaches 2500 miles. Most of the foreign trade is carried on with Communist China, which took half of Albania's exports and supplied 70 percent of the imports in 1966. Trade with Western Europe did not amount to much more than 6 percent of the total.

Albania's major problem is the rapid increase of its population, by far the highest in Europe (3.1 percent annually in recent years, as the mortality rate has come down to 9 per 1000, while the birth rate remains close to 35 per 1000). This, however, indicates a lowering of the rate of increase in the mid-1960s as against the 1950s.

BULGARIA

As an independent state Bulgaria dates from 1878, and it became sovereign only in 1908. A peasant country also, it is much larger and more advanced than Albania, and its 42,800 square miles are inhabited by 8.3 million people. Bulgaria has been a cause of concern to the great powers and, before its appearance on the map, it was a cause of tension between Russia, who helped to liberate the country from the Turks, and Britain, who dreaded the territorial extension of this Russian satellite to the shores of the Aegean Sea and perhaps to the Straits. The conflict was solved by the Treaty of Berlin of 1878 by which Disraeli, with Bismarck's backing, gained a restriction of the expansion of Bulgarian territory southward. Since then a window on the Aegean has been a constant goal of Bulgarian policy, the key to its whole attitude toward the Macedonian problem, for Macedonian country stretches to the west of the Bulgarian border in Yugoslavia and to the south in Greece.

The structure of the country's topography is relatively simple. Bulgaria has a large mountainous area disposed in the shape of a C, its opening facing east—that is, facing the Black Sea. The northern arc of the C is formed by the Stara Planina or Balkan range; the western curve is centered on the massive Rila Mountains, where many crests of volcanic or intrusive origin rise to elevations of more than 6000 feet above a plateau with an average level of 3200. The southern arc of the C consists of the Rhodope ranges. Sofia, the capital, is established in a high basin piercing through the high tablelands of the C to the northwest leading to the Morava valley. There are two large depressions within the Bulgarian territory: to the north of the C, a gentle slope descends from the foot of the Stara Planina toward the Lower Danube; inside the C the depression drained by the Maritsa River opens, though with small ridges in its midst, toward the Black Sea coast to the east.

On the whole, Bulgaria is a cluster of closed cells, either massive mountains or more-or-less closed depressions. The Bulgarians are a proud and stubborn people. Under the Turks they lost almost all their aristocracy and elite, but as a nation of peasants, started recently on a new life, they have been doing fairly well—except for their mistake of siding with the wrong coalition in both World Wars, a mistake made partly because of their desire to regain the territory that had not been given them by previous peace treaties. Since 1945, they have been in the Soviet orbit.

The land has been put to intensive use, though with methods that are often primitive. The terraces dominating the Danube have been deforested and put under the plough. Rich black soil, watered by a summer rainfall, yields good harvests. Ruse (130,000) and Pleven (80,000) are the main towns, thriving amid rural prosperity. Since 1941 Bulgaria has regained a section of the Dobruja that had been annexed to Rumania between the wars. This has also favored the development of the port of Varna (180,000), renamed Stalin for a while, on the Black Sea, the maritime outlet for this Danubian section of Bulgaria. The other agricultural region is a string of basins descending from the higher area of Sofia to the valley of the Maritsa, of which Plovdiv (220,000) is the main center, and to the coastal plain of Burgas (110,000). Bulgarian agriculture was one of gardening: the peasant usually had a plot of land and tilled it with loving care. In the higher basins, fruit trees and potatoes are the main crops, especially around Sofia. On the lower lands wheat and corn are the main crops, but always the orchard is present, with the plum tree (which furnishes the *slivovica,* an alcoholic beverage, the staple drink of the Balkan peoples), the vines, and the almond tree. Tobacco and sunflowers are also important: the former supplies a major export item; the latter is the national source of fats. Some sugar beets appear along the Danube and some rice and cotton along the Maritsa. Nothing, however, is more characteristic of Bulgarian gardening than the vast fields of roses cultivated on an industrial scale. Bulgaria is the chief world exporter of rose essence for perfumery, although this crop lost in importance as chemical products swept the market. Still, the rose-oil industry, which became a government monopoly, produced 2 to 3 tons annually from fields in the Tundzha valley near Kazanlik and Karlovo.

The mountains are devoted to stock raising. There were in 1965 about 10 million sheep, 1.5 million cattle, numerous goats, and 2 million pigs. Little forest now remains, and that chiefly in the Rhodope range, of the former dense cover. The mountains also seem to be mineralized in many districts, but it was only recently—as, under Communist control, Bulgaria was also pushed toward industrialization—that mining began to develop to some extent. A search for fuels led to the extraction of coal (580,000 tons annually, mainly at the Dimitrovo field) and lignite (24,500,000 tons), which is used mainly for the generation of power. Some oil was recently discovered at Tulenovo, in the Dobruja: about 400,000 tons extracted in 1966 were taken by pipeline to Varna and exported crude, as no refining facilities were available yet but better quality oil has been found near Pleven. A refinery has been built at Burgas.

Other mineral resources include iron ore (585,000 tons of iron content mined in 1965), lead (100,000 tons), zinc (80,000 tons), and small quantities of copper, manganese, pyrites, and even uranium mined at Bulkovada. The iron and manganese ores are used, with imported metallurgical coke and more imported ores, in a modestly beginning iron and steel industry (in Sofia and on the coal at Dimitrovo) which produced only 700,000 tons of pig iron and 600,000 tons of crude steel in 1965; as this industry was practically nonexistent before 1954, the progress is rather rapid. The traditional textile and food- and tobacco-processing industries have been expanded and new manufactures of machinery, electrical apparatus and appliances, shoemaking, basic chemicals, cellulose, paper, and cardboard have been created and are steadily developed. The nonagricultural employment of Bulgaria rose from 710,000 in 1948 to 2,100,000 in 1966; at the latter date the country was still predominantly rural, as agricultural employment was estimated at 4 million, and the Plan for the 1960s foresaw transferring about 100,000 persons annually from rural to urban occupations, for the persistence of rural underemployment was recognized despite the active reform of agriculture.

Because the Turks had practically wiped out the large landowners in

Tirnovo and the valley the Jantra has eroded in the plateau.

Harvesting roses at Kazanlik.

Bulgaria and the average size of farms was down to 10 acres by 1939, the agrarian problem here was quite different from that of other Mediterranean and Danubian countries. The Communist regime collectivized the lands and gathered them in large units held by state or collective farms of the Soviet *kolkhoz* type. By 1959 only 4 percent of the agricultural land remained in individual farms. There were about 1000 large collective or state farms, with an average of 10,000 acres each. Thus scarce managerial and technical skills were more efficiently used, and mechanization could proceed apace. This process caused a notable reduction in the number of farmhands needed, and accentuated the obvious surplus of labor in the countryside. Production of grain was somewhat expanded and stress laid on the expansion of fruit, grapes, and vegetable (especially tomatoes) production. These crops have joined tobacco as major cash and exports crops. The Soviet Union and some of its satellites badly need fruits and vegetables, fresh or canned, and Bulgaria has been asked to supply as much as possible of these goods. About 2.5 million acres are now irrigated.

Similarly, much of the manufactures produced by the brand new industries of this country are for export, from shoes to electrical machinery, to other Communist nations. Bulgaria has increased the share of the free world in its foreign trade, but the Soviet Union alone still takes or supplies more than half of it. The Bulgarians, however, have been more respected and treated in a more friendly manner by the Russians than most of their other satellites. From the emergence of Bulgaria in the 1870s, the successive Russian governments have each felt more responsibility toward this small Slavic nation to the south. Although such attitudes are difficult to measure statistically, it seems apparent that Bulgaria has been somewhat better treated and allowed to keep more of its products for its own, rather modest, consumption, than have Rumania, Hungary, and even Poland; one could hardly draw any comparison with Czechoslovakia, long a much more advanced country, or Albania, a much more backward one.

A more interesting comparison would be with Yugoslavia, but the available figures do not allow for it easily. Yugoslavia is certainly a much richer and larger country than Bulgaria, and parts of it were much better developed before 1940. The average density of population is about the same in both countries, but this has meant greater pressure on the cultivated land in Bulgaria. Urbanization has proceeded faster, probably responding to this pressure, in Bulgaria, where the capital Sofia, with 800,000 people in 1965, was a larger city than Belgrade. Situated in an intermountain basin in the west of the country, Sofia is a major rail hub but lacks water transportation. It is a young and very active city (its population was only 16,000 in 1878), with a large university, vast residential sections (one of them grouping about 60,000 Gypsies who number in all over 150,000 in Bulgaria), and noisy, teeming industrial zones. Most finishing manufactures have been concentrated in or near Sofia; however, the dependence on supplies from and exports to foreign markets has spurred on the growth of industries in the seaports (especially Varna and Burgas) and on cities along the Maritsa River (Plovdiv, Dimitrovgrad). The greatest recent economic success of Bulgaria has been the development of seaside resorts on the Black Sea coast, attracting now crowds of summer tourists from all over Europe. Bulgaria has not forgotten the Macedonian problem, which causes a permanent tension between this nation and its neighbors Yugoslavia and Greece. This old problem induces Bulgaria to look south for the future—and outside the peninsula north for support.

## GREECE

Few countries of Europe have made such a contribution to mankind's common heritage as did ancient Greece. From the maritime periphery of this peninsular country came a civilization whose influence has endured for two thousand years, the civilization of a small group of people in a network of cities established in a restricted and rather difficult physical environment. But the "Greek miracle" did not survive the Roman Empire. A study of modern Greece is almost deceptive if it does not delve into history and archeology, but these are outside the scope of this volume. We must therefore limit ourselves to a brief account of present-day conditions and problems in a country with a most glorious past, but one to which its links have to some extent been severed by long centuries of Turkish rule.

Human endeavor in Greece was based on narrow and fragile foundations indeed. This is a typical Mediterranean country, and an extreme one in many respects, for its climate anticipates the eastern basin's conditions with its increased aridity and irregularity, with its rugged topography, and with the proximity of hills to shore everywhere. The deep penetration of the sea inland has left little continuity to any land feature. The ancient prosperity was founded on the sea and on a political and economic organization that did not last after the breakdown of Mediterranean unity. The Middle Ages brought terrible misery to Greece. Malaria swept the lowlands, and many of the population sought refuge in the rugged hills. Greece continued to be decimated by wars between people from the plains and people from the hills, by vendettas between families, and by sickness and periodic famines.

During those centuries many migrations and invasions also swept into the peninsula and contributed some changes to the ethnic map of

Greece. Conquered by the Turks in 1456, Greece became just another Ottoman province. Culturally and nationally, therefore, the continuity of the Greek tradition had been broken to such an extent that it seemed almost impossible to re-establish it. Yet a new awakening occurred in the nineteenth century, largely from Greeks established outside the peninsula throughout the Mediterranean and Black Sea shores. This Greek *diaspora* remained a staunch backer of the small kingdom of Greece, which gained its independence from the Ottoman sultan in 1830. The liberation of Greece for which Lord Byron fought was accomplished by pressure from the Western powers, especially France and Britain; it was one of the first signs of Mediterranean rejuvenation and of the coming breakdown of the Turkish and Moslem impact on the Mediterranean area.

In 1920 Greece received its present boundaries, but an attempt to enlarge a foothold in Asia Minor around Smyrna was frustrated by the sweeping conquest of Ataturk's armies—the Turks had been rejuvenated too. The Treaty of Lausanne settled the old Greco-Turkish conflict in 1924, fixing the boundaries and arranging an exchange of populations, and another exchange of populations was agreed upon with Bulgaria. More than 600,000 people left Greece, but double this number moved in, chiefly from Turkey. In 1928 it was estimated that about one fifth of the total population were refugees recently arrived. The settlement of over a million people within a few years was a major operation and cost much suffering and misery, but the operation gave Greece a homogeneous population, enriched with elements experienced in trade and industrial skills. Part of the refugees were resettled on the land, though on too-small plots (10 to 15 acres per family on the average), but the bulk of the immigrants crowded into the cities, which they greatly helped to develop. Greece did not achieve the almost complete encirclement of the Aegean Sea that it had planned in 1920.

The total area of Greece is 51,200 square miles and the population was 8.7 million in, 1967. War, occupation, and the famine that ensued in the years 1941–1944 led to a loss of several hundred thousand lives. Since 1945 the increase has been rapid, although northern Greece was for several years the arena of a deadly fight between government forces and pro-Soviet guerillas. Stable conditions have not yet fully returned to a much-disputed peninsula, which in a way commands access to the eastern Mediterranean from the European continent by the Vardar valley.

There are three main regions in the country: the north and northwestern regions are rugged mountains of a frankly Balkan type; central Greece is indeed Mediterranean; then the Peloponnese and the islands are a third region with a maritime Mediterranean flavor.

Northern Greece consists of two different structures: in the northeast, the Macedonian heights are old planed tablelands, rising between depressions of steppic landscape; to the northwest, folded ranges prolong the Dinaric system and are more wooded in a more humid climate. Macedonia in the east has a substantial area of coastal plain. The presence of malaria and of large estates prevented its development until after 1924, when the exchange of population led to efficient drainage work and expelled the Turks among whom were the landlords. The country has been transformed, although the struggle with malaria is not yet ended. Wheat, barley, and corn are the leading crops; the vine and the mulberry tree are common; and tobacco, although less important than before 1930, is still important in the Vardar valley. To the east of this valley tower the high cliffs of the plateau of Chalcidice, which advances in the sea as a smaller peninsula, sending three hilly prongs southward. At the tip of the easternmost prong stands the famous Mount Athos, a self-governing monastic community of twenty monasteries, grouped behind a high wall built to protect them against pirates. A tremendous mountain of marble, over 6000 feet high, towers above the monasteries, which are surrounded by cypresses and olive groves.

At the end of a deep bay, between the Chalcidice peninsula and the mouth of the Vardar, stands the city of Salonika (or Thessaloniki in modern Greek), the capital of Greek Macedonia and the southern gate to the Vardar-Morava corridor. The surrounding plain has been well drained and is intensely cultivated. A major crossroads, a dynamic city, cultivated, trading with faraway lands, its population of 260,000 in 1940 was depleted by the war (the conurbation counted 370,000 by 1961). Its position makes Salonika normally the maritime outlet of a large section of the Balkans. Its port comprises a free zone, part of which is assigned to Yugoslavia.

To the northwest higher ranges and fewer plains announce the proximity of the Dinaric system. In the rough and rugged mountains the humidity from the west makes the vegetation better and denser; forests appear, while vast olive groves stretch around the Gulf of Arta to the northwest and wheat fields predominate in the plain of Thessaly. In the ranges close to the Yugoslav and Albanian boundaries, Communist guerillas in the period 1945–1948 waged a civil war against the Athens government, which sided with the Western powers. The ranges are made of limestone or sandstone and schists (Flysch formations) and sometimes, as in the center of the Pindus range, belts of eruptive material appear. Sheep and goats graze up and down and slopes. There are some very good pastures and substantial forests in the Pindus Mountains; some timber is being produced and logs floated down the rivers. The plains of Thessaly, dominated by towering Mount Olympus, have been greatly improved around Trikkala and Larissa, but they still need further

Athens. A general view of the city, with modern buildings, as seen from the Acropolis. (*Three Lions*)

The Temple of Athena Nike on the Acropolis, with examples of the famous columns that have been duplicated all over the world. (*Three Lions*)

reclamation and better tilling methods to yield the rich harvests they seem capable of producing. The average density here was about 150 per square mile in 1961.

Central Greece is quite different. Here the Dinaric orientation meets a structural east-west axis that cuts across it, leading to a limitation of the southward advances of the continent. Calcareous dry plateaus replace the more verdant ranges. The dry and hot summers over a karstic land give a severe aspect to the cradle of the Hellenistic world. Contrasts are frequent and striking between well-wooded slopes and barren ones, between swampy and malarial plains and those covered with gardens and orchards. The Aleppo pine predominates, spreading its umbrella of thin needles over Mediterranean brush or olives, or vines. Here the Mediterranean environment appears to be naked, open to criticism and reorganization, though framed in landscapes of incredible beauty. Land and sea, high ridges and wide valleys intermingle here as often described in classical literature. In one of those valleys stands the magnificent site of Delphi, where the ancient oracle spoke. From Delphi to the sea a wide valley descends, densely planted with olive trees, like a silvery stream coming out of the rugged mountains. Toward the extremity of the southeastern peninsula the unexpected occurs, framed again between the steep slopes of barren heights: in a small coastal plain stands a large city, Athens, the largest urban agglomeration today of the Balkan peninsula and its surrounding islands.

The population census of 1961 counted 565,000 in the city of Athens proper, but 1,853,000 in Greater Athens; by 1967, the conurbation held over 2 million people. Not only has Athens been consolidated, for all practical purposes, with its seaport at the Piraeus, but the loosely scattering suburbs extend to Eleusis on the one hand, far out on the road to Sounion on the other, and in all directions around the central core as well. Where no organized development has been planned, squatting families have erected on empty plots of ground small cubes of cement as shelters in which to wait for the authorities to recognize them and bring them into the municipal water and sewerage systems. Athens for long centuries has been a great pole of attraction. Actually the site is of a common type in Greece, but this one also has the advantage of a central position on the Greek Aegean Sea. From the beginning Athens was entirely man-made, and its historic heritage has made the fortune of the city in modern times. The Turks had reduced it to a small provincial center: two centuries ago Athens was barely more than a small borough around the sites of the Acropolis, made into a fortress by the Turks, and of the ancient *agora*, the meeting place of the people. Modern growth was rapid, however, after 1830, when it became the capital of independent Greece. It is a brand-new town, largely rebuilt by architects from

Western Europe who did not take care to adapt it to its Mediterranean climate. Vast residential and administrative districts stretch out, surrounded by crowded and miserable suburbs where one can already notice some shade of Asia. The major warehouses and large factories are on the sea, at the Piraeus or near Eleusis. The memories of past glory occupy a small part of the city proper, but they stand for such a rich heritage, such a wealth of culture and wisdom, that they begin to attract large crowds of tourists—and they remain a heartening symbol for the Greeks themselves.

For the population of Athens needs to be heartened indeed. As any modern capital, the city concentrates a good deal of employment which could not be found on a substantial scale elsewhere in such a small nation. The government, business-management, mass-media, university, and cultural activities, the seaport and large airport (both used as NATO bases), and the organization of tourism form here a "mix" of economic activities offering more employment opportunity than could be expected in other parts of Greece. During the 1940s, because of the war and, later, the guerilla warfare in the hills, people streamed into Athens looking for some security; in the 1950s, with increased help from the United States and more active external relations, the attraction of the capital lasted. As in other large cities around the Mediterranean, family and "tribal" cohesion helps the newcomers; the redistribution of every small income through direct sharing and indirect subcontracting aids those less successful. Thus the labor market of the metropolis snowballs, and Athens keeps on growing.

Southern Greece consists of the Peloponnese peninsula, which is almost an island, for the narrow isthmus of Corinth has been cut by a canal trench. It is rugged and on the map resembles an outstretched hand with four fingers. Its mountains rise above 6000 feet in several places, and the orientation of the slopes is quite important, the west and northwest ones being much more rainy and better wooded than the rather desertic sections exposed to east and south. Here the population was dense and active in ancient times. On the isthmus, built on the slopes of a hill, stands Corinth, which has benefited little from its maritime canal and keeps on exporting the famous sun-dried raisins (known as *raisins de Corinthe* in French and *currants* in English). The vine, the olive tree, and the migrating sheep are the truly traditional Mediterranean products of the peninsula. Some orange groves are now developing. In one of the deep depressions to the southeast, Sparta used to be the warlike and puritanic rival of Athens, but today it keeps only the reputation of its glory. New Sparta is the regional capital of a rich agricultural valley. Other cities that have had a great past are now just small local sleepy marketplaces: thus Olympia, where the famous tradition of athletic

Olive groves near Sparta. (*Three Lions*)

A farmer of the island of Naxos. Notice the carefully terraced slope, the scanty vegetation, and the important role of the donkeys. (*Three Lions*)

games originated; Tripolis, in the center of the Peloponnese; or the small town of Megalopolis, founded by Epaminondas to be a great capital. Myceneae, the city of Agamemnon, is just a set of powerful ruins on a hill dominating the road from Argos to Corinth. More lively are the seaside towns, especially Patras (95,000), at the entrance of the Gulf of Corinth, or Nauplia (10,000), in a region rich in famous ruins, grouping tourist hotels and large jails, and dominated by a rock crowned with an enormous medieval fortress built by the Venetians.

Many islands complement Greece; scattered on all sides of the peninsula, they form more than one fifth of its present total area. Almost part of central Greece, so close is it to the mainland across narrow channels, lies Euboea, with another Mount Olympus towering in its center. The archipelago of the Cyklades (Andros, Tinos, Paros, and Naxos) prolongs the peninsula to the southeast. Larger and more important are the Ionian Islands, famous for their scenery, lining the western shore from Corfu to Zante. A number of other islands, large and small, along the Asiatic shores of the Aegean Sea recall the empire Greece possessed in Asia. And these lands are deeply Greek indeed, notwithstanding their proximity to Turkey. Some of them are still forested and could serve, if properly managed, as timber reserves for the country. To Mytilene (or Lesbos), Chios, Lemnos, Samos, and the Sporades, the Dodecanese islands, including Rhodes, that for a time had belonged to Italy were added in 1947. Finally, to the south of the Aegean, marking the end of the European lands to the southeast, the largest of the Greek islands, Crete (3200 sq miles with 500,000 inhabitants), stretches east-west, with high steep slopes above the sea to the south, an almost continuous and closed wall; the northern shore, looking toward the Hellenic sea, is more open and has some small plains. Crete was one of the war-devastated areas of Greece, isolated, a land of shepherds and pirates, and desolated by malaria. How could one of the earliest advanced cultures of mankind have been born here? Has the environment changed? That does not seem to be the case; instead Crete seems to be an extreme example of Mediterranean conditions, where human achievements are fragile and require a constant maintenance that does not always pay. It must be mentioned, however, that the island is at present fairly self-supporting in terms of food. Some rural areas look even wealthy compared to the average Greek countryside. Vines, olives, and citrus fruits are the main crops; some timber is produced, and grazing land is abundant. The problem of Crete has puzzled many historians. It prompted the Rockefeller Foundation to start a research project there, one which is also attempting to improve present conditions by public health and agricultural measures.

The story of Greece is approximately told by this rapid review of its regions. A rural country, Greece constantly needs to import foodstuffs, including wheat and meat. To pay for these, the country has exported chiefly tobacco and fruits, and some olive oil and cotton in good years. One wonders how such an economy could work in normal times. The services Greece can extend to the rest of the world seemed restricted to tourism and shipping. In recent years both have been better developed; in 1965, Greece received 800,000 tourists, and facilities to receive much more were being built all over the land; from 1956 to 1966 the Greek merchant marine rose from 1.3 to 7.8 million gross tons: such a quick rise was made possible by transfer to the Greek pavilion of ships owned by Greek companies under foreign flags, for some of the great ship-owners of the modern period are Greek though much of their business is conducted in other countries. But in the 1950s the Greek economy at last began a long-range evolution that should help the nation come out of the "underdeveloped" category.

The road will be long, however, and strewn with obstacles. Basically, this is still an agricultural country that must face difficult conditions of climate, topography, and soils. The centuries under Turkish rule have thoroughly ruined the soil on the slopes of this hilly land. Only 30 percent of the total land area is considered cultivable, and it supports 50 percent of the people. Surplus labor is evident all over the countryside, and one of the causes of Athens' rapid population increase. The classical Mediterranean crops are produced mainly for domestic consumption: the wines (especially the popular *resina*), olive oil (a small part of which is exported), grain, sheep (8.9 million), and goats (5 million) do not offer much for export. Although the output of wheat and the number of cattle and pigs have been increased, they are still not quite enough for local needs. Tobacco is plentiful but has suffered from the competition of the Virginia-type tobacco now favored on the world markets. Citrus fruits are being produced and their plantations expanded with the hope of exporting them (412,000 tons of oranges, tangerines and lemons were harvested in 1964).

Mineral resources are being explored and gradually put to use. Lignite feeds powerhouses (5 million tons in 1965); iron ore and pyrites are mined in Macedonia; there are also small quantities of lead and silver (at the Laurion mines), magnesite (in Euboea), chromite (in Thessaly), nickel, sulphur, emery, manganese, and, especially, bauxite (1,250,000 tons in 1965, chiefly from the mines of Eleusis near Athens but other deposits are known). With the participation of American and French interests, a corporation was formed in 1960 to expand the bauxite output and build an aluminum plant with connected water-power projects and produce some 50,000 tons of that light metal. A modest iron and steel industry has also been started, and Piraeus and Eleusis have active shipyards. Thus industrialization develops, as yet mainly in the vicinity of Athens. In 1961, Greece was made an associate member of the European Common Market: this holds a promise for widening markets for the export of tobacco, citrus fruits, and perhaps bauxite and aluminum. Later it might even bring in more capital investments from the Six and open more employment to the surplus manpower of Greece in the Western countries. Greeks have traditionally emigrated, and the country receives substantial support from about two million of its nationals settled in foreign lands, especially from the wealthy Greek colonies in the United States, Egypt, and Argentina.

In the 1960s, surplus Greek manpower emigrated to work in the Western European countries, mainly in West Germany. This outlet may not last, and although the natural increase of the Greek population is at present slow (the birth rate being around 18 per 1000 and the death rate around 8 per 1000), there is urgent need for an improvement in the domestic standard of living. The average per capita income has reached only $600 per annum, and the balance of payments is kept in workable shape owing to a constant inflow of money from the outside. Some balance is achieved as a result of aid and of revenue from activities of Greek interests around the world. For a large country with a stable domestic economy, a complement of "invisible exports" through services provided abroad can be a lasting solution. For the small and shaky economy of Greece, already threatened because of shrinking foreign markets for tobacco and currants, it becomes indispensable to develop new production capable of exporting industrial goods. In recent years some progress has been achieved in this direction, but considerable acceleration would be needed to take Greece out of its present backward economic position.

One of the major weaknesses of the recent economic development has been the high degree of concentration of modern industrial and commercial activities in the metropolitan region of Greater Athens, which has one quarter of the total population of the country and accounts for more than two fifths of the gross national product. This is how Athens has become the largest urban center of the Balkans. Meanwhile, northern Greece (Macedonia and Thrace) has been lagging badly. It is by far the most important agricultural region of Greece, supplying about half of the total commercialized farm output, but it has little else. Northern Greece was the main region of emigration in recent years toward Athens and overseas. To improve the situation and particularly to promote industrial activity around the stagnant conurbation of Salonika, an oil refinery and a steel mill are being built there. It is hoped that this will attract a variety of other plants and make Salonika the main port serving the Yugoslav portion of Macedonia and the reconstruction of Skoplje. Another project is directed toward the touristic development of the northwestern shores of Greece, one of the sunniest coastal regions of Europe.

The last of the Mediterranean countries we review in Europe has had the brightest "miracle" of ancient history and is nevertheless today one of the less developed among European nations. Greece has always had, in the shadow of the renowned Olympus, a rather difficult natural environment; to create a brilliant culture and a modicum of prosperity the Greeks always needed a great deal of organization and wit; it requires great stubbornness and a deep love of their land, which is beautiful indeed, to carry on the fight against both men and nature that has been their destiny.

## EUROPEAN TURKEY AND THE STRAITS

The eastern extremity of the Balkan peninsula, extending a double bridge toward Asia Minor, is still part of Turkey. Curiously enough, of all the political divisions of the peninsula it is the only one where low-lying land covers the major part of the area and where no high range rises. Most of the 9000 square miles that Turkey retains in Europe— some 3 percent of the total area of Turkey—are rather fertile and could be settled more densely than they are, with only 2.4 million inhabitants in 1965. But it is not the quality of the soil around Edirne (formerly Adrianople, 46,000 inhabitants) that makes this stretch of land important. This foothold on the European continent gives to Turkey the totality of the shores around the Sea of Marmara and the two straits through which this sea communicates with other seas: the Dardanelles to the south leading into the Aegean, and the Bosporus to the north leading into the Black Sea. The system of Bosporus-Marmara-Dardanelles, often called by historians simply "the Straits," is the road into or out of the Black Sea. It has had and it still retains an extraordinary political importance.

Since the eighteenth century the Black Sea has more and more turned from the Turkish "lake" it used to be into a Russian lake. The Straits are for Russia the way out of an otherwise closed, continental sea into the Mediterranean and perhaps into the oceans beyond. To Britain it has meant the threat of an immense continental power developing into a naval power and challenging the British on the high seas, while the British could not similarly challenge the Russians on the continent. To keep the danger away, Britain intended to keep the Straits closed to Russia. Several times Russia attempted to gain control of the area. She did not succeed in 1878, mainly because of British opposition. In 1914 she made the control of the Straits almost a condition of her entry in World War I on the side of the Western powers; the Russian Revolution of 1917 and separate peace with Germany set such a possibility aside, and it well suited British policy after 1919 to have Turkey, a hereditary foe of Russia and a small power nowadays, keep control of the Straits. This position on the Straits gives to Turkey a weight in the balance of international politics that otherwise she would never be able to keep.

On the Bosporus stands the great city of Istanbul. Under the name of Constantinople, it was the capital of great empires from the fourth to the twentieth century. Ataturk moved the capital in 1924 to Ankara. Amid the famous shoreline of marble palaces, beautiful gardens, and picturesque old residential sections, Ataturk in his desire for rejuvenation and modernization built coal piers and gas tanks. As in the case of Italy, the Turkish dictatorship waged war on the sources of Turkey's tourist reputation, considered a sign of weakness, but now this reaction has subsided. The Bosporus is still one of the most magnificent sites of the Mediterranean world. The city of Istanbul, however, has been substantially modernized and industrialized. Its population in 1965 was 1,750,000, about half of what it was a century earlier.

Istanbul and a good part of the Turkish power stand thus on a major thoroughfare, to guard it rather than to benefit by the traffic passing through. This traffic was modified as a result of the war, as most of the Danubian basin passed under Soviet predominance and oriented its trade relations eastward rather than westward. The Straits are one of the maritime highways of trade between Western and Eastern Europe and also between the Danubian area and the outside, and formerly this transit profited Istanbul greatly. The growing isolation of the East restricts the commercial role of Istanbul but may increase the political significance of its position. The city is still growing as a result of rural exodus from various parts of Turkey. The region of Thrace to the west has become the subject of attention and planning to help develop it. The success of the seaside resorts in neighboring Bulgaria has suggested similar plans to promote tourism on the Turkish side of the border. The present welfare of this rural region still depends on the migratory labor sent under contract to West Germany, particularly to work in mines and on the railroads. At this extremity of Europe one encounters, once more, the conflict of an emptying, lagging region with a sprawling metropolis.

As a result of controlling the shores of the Straits, Turkey assumes the part of doorkeeper of the Black Sea, which would be otherwise a Russian lake. Russian-Turkish relations therefore take on a special significance; on them hinges to a large extent the question of the access of Russia to sea power; on them depends to some extent also the weight of Russian influence in the Mediterranean. Many times, landlocked Russian power attempted to break through to open Mediter-

The Bosporus. Fifteen miles from Istanbul on the European side are the ruins of the Rumelhari castle, where the straits are narrowest, only 800 yards wide. A town nestles inside the old castle wall. Typical Mediterranean suburban landscape is seen on the opposite shore. (*Three Lions*)

ranean shores through the Balkan area. Several times Russian policy tried to acquire for its Bulgarian ally a foothold on the Macedonian coast of the Aegean. At present the possibility of outflanking the Straits held by the Turks rests on the control of Macedonia on the one hand and on the status of Russian relations with Yugoslavia on the other. The diplomatic puzzle resulting from the geographical layout of this part of the world makes of Turkey a Balkan power indeed and a European power as well. Now that naval strategy has been somewhat overshadowed by air power and rocketry, Turkey remains a staunch ally and an advanced post of the West's defense system. It has granted air bases to the United States and is a member of NATO and of the Central Treaty Organization, the headquarters of which are in Ankara.

The Straits and the Sea of Marmara cut through a kind of isthmus, a land bridge that brings together the Balkans and Asia Minor, Europe and Asia. There could be no better example of a natural crossroads. The importance of this site largely antedates the expansion of Russia. Under the names of Constantinople, Byzantium, and Istanbul, the city commanding the Bosporus has established a unique record by remaining for some 1600 years, from 330 A.D. to 1924, the capital of important empires; no other city in the world can claim so long and uninterrupted a record. Further back in history, Troy controlled the Dardanelles, and the Trojan wars remain to this day a classic and decisive episode of ancient Greek history. Few are the cases where a natural site has carried such permanent importance throughout the ages.

# Part IV

## Central Europe

The road between Aachen and Cologne, 1945. "Central Europe claimed for itself the position and role of the axis—generally it got the destiny of the buffer." Central Europe has often been partitioned into two or more parts. Such partitioning has seldom been so spectacular as the present "iron curtain." Bridges have been rebuilt but the "iron curtain" still divides.

# 14

## The Tidal Lands
## of Europe

The word central usually connotes an element of coordination, a node, a crossroads, but also a transition between extremes. The latter characteristic certainly is present in Central Europe as defined here for it encompasses very different countries, a wide gamut of ethnic diversity and of stages in economic development from West Germany to Rumania. But this central section of Europe has recently been more a rift than a bridge. Today West Germany is indeed Western by most standards and so is Finland, but other powers in the area are not.

The Central European powers have worked out for themselves an indisputable personality which often benefited by the many contacts it had with a diversity of neighbors. This personality was so linked to some of the surrounding areas that many times it attempted to dominate them, while a power that developed in any other part of Europe and expanded over the continent was bound to find the central section in its way. Thus throughout history Central Europe has been a land of ebb and flow, the most unstable part of the continent, and therefore should be defined as the area that lies between those parts endowed with more stability.

### THE DIFFICULTIES OF DEFINING CENTRAL EUROPE

As the word *central* indicates, this section of Europe is in the midst of the continent and in the midst of the surrounding influences and pressures. It is certainly a most important part of the continent, but very evasive—

543

the concept of Central Europe has shifted in longitude, and its boundaries have shifted even more. *Central* can be defined as the opposite of *peripheral*. Central Europe is east of the Western European countries of the Atlantic façade, north of the Mediterranean lands, and west of the Eastern region that borders on Asia. It has some features that can individualize its structure, but by physiography it is definitely a land of transition. Europe is not shaped like a basin or a dome, but is a complex of peninsulas stretching westward and southward, constantly swept by migrations or military fronts generally marching in an east-west direction.

The countries we have included in Western Europe are among the oldest nations formed in the Western world. They have expanded or retracted; some of them have known periods of domination over others; but they have all been clearly identified as distinct human groups for a long time. Regionalism is clearly a phenomenon belonging to the territories in the west, where nations are strongly rooted in their lands, although they have wandered more than others over the high seas and strange continents. In the east another kind of stability prevails, owing to the vicinity of the vast and rather empty spaces of the interior of Asia and to the fact that one main group of people, the Russians, have been living and expanding there for about a thousand years. Even in the Mediterranean peninsulas, open to access from several sides, there have been on the whole fewer tides of history than in the central section of Europe.

Accordingly the structure of this area warrants some attention. To the north, along the Baltic Sea, are mostly lowlands, open to traffic and with few topographical lines that could serve as foundations for "natural boundaries." A large part of Central Europe is made of the Great Plain of Europe, lying between the Rhine and some river in the East. Only large rivers flowing generally from southeast to northwest cut distinct lines across the gently rolling or perfectly flat lowland. South of the Great Plain the topography becomes more animated: here the Hercynian and the Alpine zones combine, interpenetrating and creating the most confused puzzle on the European checkerboard. These lands, most of which are drained toward the Black Sea by the Danube River, show a constant mingling of depressions—elongated, square, or rounded—and highlands of various structures and landscapes—old Hercynian raised blocks, higher ranges more recently folded and belonging to the Alpine system, or a combination of both. Nature has thus helped a struggle of east-west influences to develop over the whole area, for penetration is easy everywhere except in a few massive highlands. In the northern part there are no natural lines to which a nation could cling systematically for its borders; in the southern part, there are too many of them. In both cases a complicated mosiac developed.

We must define Central Europe, therefore, by the turbulence of its history, by the frequency of boundary shifts, and by the transitional and involved character of its regionalisms. We shall extend this notion of Central Europe to the countries situated between the Western powers, the Soviet Union, and the countries belonging to the Mediterranean area. A perfect division is impossible, as borders, of course, do not follow the limits of what would logically be Central Europe; there are sections of the Danubian basin, even rivers in Yugoslavia and Bulgaria, that are definitely more Mediterranean than Central. As we define it, Central Europe today consists of Germany, Poland, Czechoslovakia, Austria, Hungary and Rumania; Finland, a buffer between the Scandinavian area and Russia, should also be included. Whether the present western limit of the border of the Soviet Union represents accurately the limits of Central Europe eastward does not matter much for this study: Russia, wherever centered, has been for a long while the *Eastern power* par excellence; and the shifting concept of the *Central powers* relates precisely in a European's mind to what is between the Atlantic powers and the power of the East.

## GERMANS, SLAVS, AND OTHERS

Central Europe has been the arena in which was conducted not only the struggle between West and East, but also, and with greater acuteness, the struggle between the peoples established within the area and those pressing upon them from the outside. That pressure came from the west only in ancient times when the Romans held the Rhine, the Alps, and the Danube; then from Central Europe the great migrations of Germanic tribes swept westward and southward. Charlemagne brought about some stabilization, restoring the Empire in the Occident in 800; he Christianized the Germans and established his authority by terrible repression all the way eastward to the Elbe River. Soon, however, the Germanic world began to feel on the east the pressure of the expanding Slavic peoples, and for a thousand years this struggle between Germans and Slavs shaped most of the history of Central Europe. The Germans had an older, more advanced civilization; they considered themselves the heirs to the Roman Empire and dominated northern Italy for several centuries. But the Slavs proved to be demographically stronger; they were backed by the power of Russia and often allied themselves also with those Western powers that the central Germanic state was threatening.

This struggle between Slavs and Germans made political boundaries particularly unstable. Nothing illustrates this better than the vicissitudes

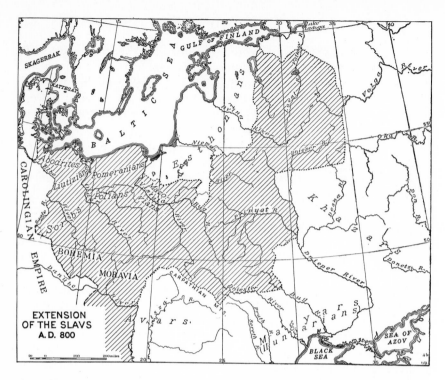

The spellings are those used in *The Geographical Review*, vol. 4, 1917. (*The Geographical Review*)

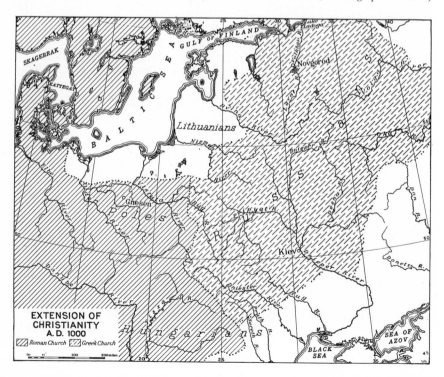

of the territorial history of Poland. A great country for several centuries in the Middle Ages, Poland at one time expanded across the continent from the Baltic to the shores of the Black Sea. In the eighteenth century a series of disastrous wars reduced it to more modest proportions, and in the 1770s, it was divided up among its three powerful neighbors: Austria, Prussia, and Russia. Poland then ceased to exist as an independent state for a century and a half, except for a brief revival, in union with Saxony, under Napoleon. In 1919, Poland, reborn, was assigned boundaries that it thereafter extended eastward through military conquest. Partitioned again between Germany and the Soviet Union in 1939, Poland was re-formed in 1945, this time centered farther west.

The boundaries of Germany itself have been just as mobile, expanding or retracting with the Holy Roman Germanic Empire, as the Hapsburgs, centered in Vienna, fought with other German princes, with the Turks, the French, or the Russians. With the rise of the power of Prussia under the Hohenzollern family, a new Germany appeared in the nineteenth century, centered in Berlin and becoming an empire (*Reich*) in 1871. This empire was not proclaimed in Berlin but in Versailles, after a victory over France, for the German government was too uncertain of the limits and destinies of its actual realm. Its area decreased in 1919, expanded again in 1937–1942 under Hitler, only to be crushed and divided up into zones of military occupation after World War II.

The instability of boundaries and the variety of influences that exerted themselves are even greater in the mountainous southern zone than in the northern plain. The Danubian basin was the arena of struggle between Rome, the Barbarians, and Byzantium and, later, between the Holy Roman Empire and the Turks. At the opening of the twentieth century, the Austro-Hungarian, German, Turkish, and Russian empires all vied for power there. The Germans and Slavs were not left alone; other peoples lived and mixed with them, some of them constituting strong enough nuclei to form the basis of nationalities. Such especially are the Hungarians and the Finns, speaking languages that have been classified in a special group, neither Germanic nor Slavonic but related to a group of Central Asiatic languages. Another special case is that of the Rumanians, in the southeast part of the area, who cling to an older Latin heritage and speak a Romance language, but one considerably influenced by Germanic, Slavonic, and Turkish vocabularies.

Thus Germany and Austria will form in our discussion one linguistic and cultural area in Central Europe, while the Czechs and Poles will form a Slavonic area; then three "miscellaneous" origins will explain Finland, Hungary, and Rumania. The linguistic map takes on a very special significance in this part of Europe.

## LANGUAGE + RELIGION = RACE

A tongue generally expresses the cultural background of the people who speak it. In Western Europe different tongues have not been considered an obstacle to the formation of a nation. Having three official languages at the same time has not prevented Switzerland from remaining for centuries one of the staunchest national individualities of Europe. Such a phenomenon is unthinkable in Central Europe. In an area where natural divisions are confused and where constant boundary changes have always brought different authorities, with different languages, political regimes, social ideologies, and religious beliefs, every individual and every community has felt the necessity for choice. They have generally chosen one culture and clung to it—openly if the ruling authority allowed it, underground if that authority sought to impose its own cultural pattern. Territories have changed hands so often that regionalism has not based itself on the land but rather on the culture, and especially on the tongue, the culture's vehicle.

Every independent state in Central Europe, as soon as it was able, claimed all the people speaking its language as its nationals. This trend became important after 1790 with the spread of the idea of nationalities developed during the French Revolution; it grew with the recognition of national minorities throughout the nineteenth century. Thus most of the Central European countries today are found to be a mosaic of minorities.

When political and legal situations change often, the individual is inclined to shift also, to some extent according to what favors his career or security at a given moment. A great many people in Central Europe, especially in its eastern parts, speak several languages fluently—it is much more convenient and almost necessary for doing business with neighbors. When the regime changes or the major influence in his area passes from one country to another, the individual may shift his linguistic allegiance. This is not only a demonstration of his versatility; it has political consequences and links him with the party of that language's culture and state. Thus, in the urban districts, statistics and even votes may show distressingly variable facts according to the political and economic situation of the moment.

Still every individual has to belong to some society, and only a few people can be versatile enough to hop from one to another successfully. Whatever his linguistic knowledge, the Central European comes from a certain circle: the important thing is the education he received, which taught him one principal language and one faith. This native tongue, together with a religion, will identify the individual or the community; they help define ideology, beliefs, social standpoint, and often temperament. And this pattern of culture, provided by the family and the school,

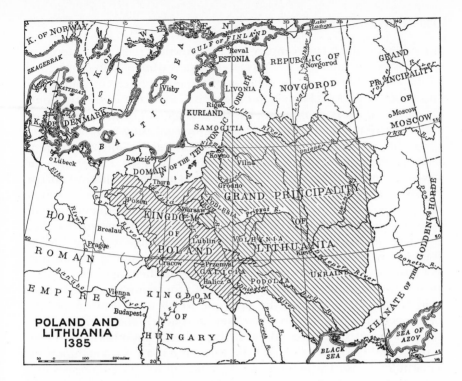

POLAND AND
LITHUANIA
1385

The spellings are those used in *The Geographical Review*, vol. 4, 1917. *(The Geographical Review)*

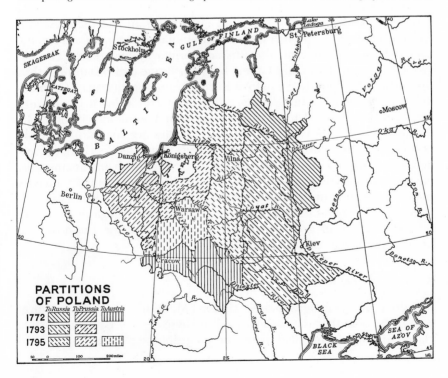

PARTITIONS
OF POLAND

| | To Russia | To Prussia | To Austria |
|---|---|---|---|
| 1772 | | | |
| 1793 | | | |
| 1795 | | | |

has since the nineteenth century and the growth of scientific materialism been given the name of *race*. No better demonstration of the supremacy of the cultural factor in the creation of regionalisms can be found than this belief of Central Europe in the formula that language + religion = race. Almost every community has been made out of such a variety of racial contributions that it would be highly confusing to admit it—one origin has to be chosen. And the choice is made mainly according to cultural features, especially since these can be changed if it becomes imperative—although race is in fact a biological and not a cultural concept.

Nowhere in Europe are regional feelings more subjective; nowhere else has the exchange of populations been applied so frequently and on such a scale in order to render certain areas more homogeneous. And nowhere else have national feelings been so easily built up to serve as the foundation for ambitious imperialisms. Empire in Central Europe does not express a situation of facts: it is considered the "right" of a certain people (recognizable by their language and therefore termed a race) to rule others. Here appears the principle which the Germanic peoples believed themselves heir to when they occupied Rome, and which the Slavs have felt they received from Byzantium—the inheritance of *imperium*. The German *kaiser* and the Russian *tsar* are variants upon the same title: *caesar*. Curiously enough, it was mostly in countries which Julius Caesar did not conquer that the tradition of his power left the greatest imprint.

Division among the Germans and even more among the Slavs was created by religion: the Poles were predominantly Roman Catholic, the Czechs largely Protestant, the Russians primarily Orthodox. The old division between Latin and Greek, between Rome and Byzantium, thus continues to complicate the map of Europe! Similarly northern Germans were predominantly Protestants, while Austrians were Roman Catholics—and that added to the rivalry between Vienna and Berlin. The divisions among the Central European peoples are rooted in very old history indeed and often in historical trends that neither originated nor developed much within the area itself; they were probably nurtured by the confused physiography and the lack of clear-cut natural divisions. A power originating in the midst of the Great Plain of Europe does not see limits to its horizons until the Atlantic shores or the Caucasus range are reached. This gives great personality to Central Europe, but it did not bring happiness to the local people.

AXIS OR BUFFER?

The great British geographer Sir Halford Mackinder has brilliantly presented the role that the eastern part of these central lands of Europe played in history. He called them "the geographical pivot of history" and

Reconstruction in Central Europe: A giant new stadium on the outskirts of rebuilt Warsaw.
(*Geographical Institute, National Academy of Sciences, Poland*)

The new aspect of the business center of Frankfurt-am-Main showing a few old buildings among many new ones. Vaguely seen in the left background below are the huge buildings of I. G. Farben Industrie, which housed American headquarters in West Germany after the war. (*German Information Center*)

proclaimed a much commented-upon formula that "he who commands Central Europe . . . commands the world." Mackinder actually wrote "Eastern" Europe, but he meant those tidal spaces between Germany and Russia which nowadays it is customary to call "Central" Europe. He noted the long history of the struggles and wars of Central Europe and the many problems settled by decisions reached after fighting in this area. As was natural for an Englishman, he was greatly interested in the relative importance of and the struggle between naval and military power. He believed that naval power could rule the world, but only on condition that no large continental power gained access to a large-scale maritime development. If such a situation occurred, the continental power could attack the naval power of maritime nations on the high seas without being reached in its heart, continental by definition, through any naval action. In practical terms he meant the old rivalry of Russia and Britain, the former pushing to the sea while the latter endeavored to keep it away from open access to the ocean. The basic problem, then, was the control of the territory between Russia and the Atlantic European shores—if Russia succeeded in dominating the German area, there would materialize what Mackinder, and many British strategists before him, considered a deadly threat to British power. Inversely, domination of the Russian continental area by Germany would be an equivalent threat to the power ruling the seas, particularly to Britain. Thus control of Central Europe might mean world political leadership.

Mackinder's theory and formula stress two essential characteristics of Central Europe as a whole: it is a *pivotal* area, and it is almost *landlocked.* It does reach the sea, of course, but mainly along the Baltic shores and along narrow coastal strips on the Black and North seas. The Baltic and Black seas are continental and communicate with the ocean only by narrow straits, easy to guard. The North Sea is more of an open window, and although the British Isles stretch between it and the open Atlantic, it creates many maritime possibilities. Still naval strategy cannot explain everything. It should be added that settling the age-old dispute between Germans and Slavs would, of course, put an end to one of the major sources of division inside the continent. The two groups of peoples united would probably constitute in Europe an overwhelming force, and they would complement each other in many economic and cultural aspects. The Western powers could not wish for such a development.

Central Europe has been therefore an arena of outstanding importance, closely watched from several sides. The fact that conflicts have often been settled there may qualify it for the title of "pivot," but people on the continent are constantly asking themselves: "Is Central Europe an axis or a buffer?" The Central powers felt they held a commanding position in the middle of things. As soon as they succeeded in building a strong political structure, their ambitions expanded quickly. Central Europe is in a way the Lotharingia of modern times: a territory dividing the continent in three main north-south belts. Since the ninth century the concept of Europe has greatly expanded eastward, and distances have been shortened. But minds remain focused on the same old ways of planning: Lothair, the eldest son, was given the central belt and the imperial title, with Italy; those who recently held the central belt of Europe, extending it to Italy, thought it would give them final supremacy; Hitler shifted the headquarters northward, but the Berlin-Rome Axis was only one more version of a very old plan.

Central Europe claimed for itself the position and role of the axis—generally it got the destiny of the buffer. Cut off from oceanic horizons by the Western powers, generally stronger, any Central power came to a terrible barrier in the Russian East. Expecting the world to revolve around it, Central Europe was simply presented with a two-front situation. The pivot has often meant only a meeting place between East and West. Other times it has become an iron curtain. Never perhaps has Central Europe more keenly felt its destiny of being a buffer than in the middle of the twentieth century.

There are some advantages in the position of a buffer, for one may count on the protection and economic help of at least one of the sides between which the buffer extends. The countries situated on the western side of the "iron curtain" have been well treated: Austria, since it is a neutral state and no more occupied, is more prosperous than ever; West Germany is quite prosperous, well rebuilt, the fourth greatest industrial power on earth, and assuming an increasing function in international finance; even Finland has been progressing well. The countries to the east have known a different sort of protection: economic development has been pushed there according to a general plan directed by Moscow and aimed at helping the Soviet Union more than the local people. Still reconstruction has been achieved and conditions improved from the all-time low reached during the immediate postwar period, when destruction and destitution were great and general indeed. The people have been far, however, from getting the abundance of goods and services they enjoy on the average west of the "iron curtain." Those who tried to rebel, as the Hungarians did in 1956 and the Czechs and Slovaks in 1968, have been repressed. The divided city of Berlin offers in its east and west parts a spectacular image of the two sides of the "iron curtain," and remains a symbol of the tension that surrounds it.

Several tides have been battering the buffer in this century. None of them succeeded in overrunning the whole area. The shifting balance is moving again in the 1960s: in the middle of the century, the division of Germany between Western and Soviet influences and the neutralization of culturally Western Austria and Finland left most of Central Europe within the Soviet sphere of control; now dissent is appearing among the governments that are members of the Warsaw Pact and in the political allegiance of Moscow. Rumania in 1967 and Czechoslovakia in 1968 registered disagreement with the Soviet Union and moved toward greater economic and political autonomy; they were rapidly restrained by the USSR; none of the nations of Central Europe has been, in the past, very friendly with Russian power. Traditionally, among the Slav peoples, the Bulgars and the Serbs were the more pro-Russian, perhaps because they were also more distant and located in the Mediterranean region. In Central Europe, the Soviet Union is playing a hard and tough game. A lasting tension here would easily become a threat to world peace. As so much could revolve once more around its inner conflicts, the buffer is also a pivot.

Finnish peasants harvesting. Scattered farms surrounded with meadows can be seen in the background. *(Finnish National Travel Office)*

# 15

## Finland

The Finnish nation is a newcomer among the independent nationalities of Europe. Groups of people of broad-headed Asiatic, non-Aryan stock lived throughout the northeastern part of Europe before the Slavs came there, and some of these peoples formed strong nuclei, retaining predominance in certain regions. These are the Ugro-Finnic peoples that live on both sides of the Gulf of Finland, to the east of the Baltic Sea. South of the gulf are the Esths, whose republic of Estonia is now part of the Soviet Union; north of the gulf are the Finns.

### THE NORDIC BUFFER

Finland was penetrated and colonized by the Swedes in the twelfth and thirteenth centuries and remained part of the Swedish kingdom until 1809, when Russia took over. Finland stayed under Russian rule until 1917, when independence was proclaimed; after 1904 the Finns had enjoyed some autonomy within the Russian frame. Thus Finland has been under the influence of both Sweden and Russia; Swedish culture is widely predominant, and the population shows a mixture of the older Finnish type with the taller, blond, "Nordic" type.

Although situated between the Scandinavian and the Russian area, Finland has been able to preserve some of its original traits and to build up a personality of its own. Both Slavic and Germanic influences are somewhat stronger here than in the Scandinavian countries. Finland is a country of the eastern Baltic and, of course, culturally and politically a buffer. During World War II Finland had a difficult time. After a war, started by the Soviet Union, in the winter of 1939–1940, it had to cede several stretches of territory to Russia. From 1941 to 1945 it participated

557

The picturesque design of morainic *ösars* amid the lakes. (*Finnish National Travel Office*)

The eastward march of the Finnish frontier and the location of the principal fortresses. The heartland of pure Finnish stock, in direct contact with Russian territories, was the buffer that resisted the impact of Muscovy. As the Swedish empire expanded eastward, the indigenous peoples were accorded increased security. The easternmost frontier was the one that lasted from 1920 to 1939. The treaty of 1945 reestablished the line of 1940. (*The Geographical Review*)

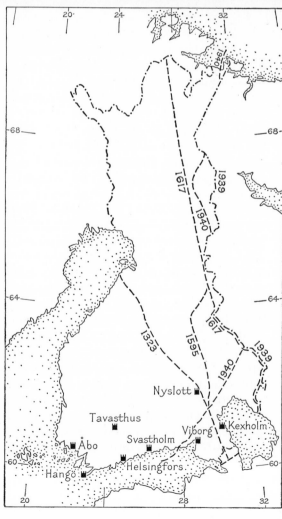

in the World War on the side of Germany and by the Treaty of 1945 had to admit final loss of even more territory, including the area of Petsamo, its narrow outlet on the Arctic Ocean, southeastern lands around Lake Ladoga, the city of Viipuri, and a stretch of territory on the eastern boundary between 68° and 66° north latitude. The Finnish people have endeavored to remain independent of both their large neighbors and on good relations with them. The attachment of the Finns to their motherland and to independence has been shown by their gallant conduct during the war and, even more perhaps, by the massive migration back to Finland of the vast majority of the population in the areas annexed by the Soviet Union.

The total land area, since 1945, is estimated at 118,000 square miles (some 18,000 less than in 1939) and supported in 1968 about 4.7 million people, of which about 91 percent declared Finnish to be their language; 8.6 percent are Swedish speaking; 92 percent of the population belong to the Lutheran Church. More than ever Finland is oriented toward the Baltic and the maritime spaces beyond. Although more continental than the Scandinavian countries, Finland has long known an urge to the sea. About one half of the navigating personnel of the Russian marine in 1914 was Finnish. Most of the population (and utilized land) is concentrated along the seashore.

## THE REGIONS OF FINLAND

The territory of Finland is a part of the great northern or Fenno-Scandian Shield of Europe. Old crystalline rocks make up the basis of the land, and the details of the topography show their variety: rounded backs of granitic outcroppings, bolder hills formed by quartzites. During the Tertiary period, the peneplain was faulted, and at that time the Gulf of Finland was probably sunk. Then came the glaciations, and the ice sheet planed the heights but hollowed out the valleys even more, leaving behind it an intricate network of lakes, some of which, like Lake Päjäne, were dug below sea level. While retreating, the glacier paused between the Gotiglacial and Finiglacial stages and accumulated in the south of Finland an immense morainic rampart—in fact a double amphitheater of hills, dissected in postglacial times by the erosion of streams. This morainic alignment dammed up the many lakes which filled depressions behind it; it forms the main topographic feature of Finland and bears the name of *Salpausselkä*. Rivers crossing it have rapids along gorges, and the Salpausselkä has become a "fall line" utilized for waterpower. North of it is the district of the lakes, south of it, a coastal plain. Some postglacial uplift of the land has been observed here, as in Sweden and Canada.

Urban Finland: (*Above*) Helsinki. (*Below*) The industries and modern buildings of Tampere, Finland's second largest city. (*Finnish National Travel Office*)

The whole of Finland is a rather low-lying land. A gentle slope from the north southward may be noticed. The land is slightly higher in Lapland, beyond the Arctic circle, but remains below 1000 feet south of it. Three quarters of the total area are below 600 feet, and most of it is covered with glacial drift—that is, boulder clay. The clayish texture of the soil adds to the difficulty of the drainage and to the dampness of the flat land. The Salpausselkä develops then as a major accident and governs a great deal of the drainage features. The boulder clay has been converted into fields and meadows by the Finnish farmers, the boulders being assembled in the stone walls that checker the plains and rise sometimes to five feet around small pieces of land.

The climate is definitely more continental than is Scandinavia's, although the whole country gives an impression of dampness. Practically every place is frozen from December to March; in July, Helsinki, on the southern coast, averages 62° F., but severe frosts are possible until June, and an Indian summer occurs in the fall. The rainfall is more abundant at the transitional seasons. The white carpet of snow covers the landscape for 120 days every year around Helsinki and 210 days in the north. The Baltic Sea freezes in winter along the Finnish coasts; in certain years the Gulf of Bothnia is solidly frozen, and in 1809 the Russian forces at war with Sweden crossed over on the ice from Vaasa on the Finnish coast to Umea in Sweden. Still, in the south the ice is not thick enough to stop ice-breakers, and the ports on the Gulf of Finland are open to traffic along channels maintained by them. To the southwest, in the middle of the Baltic, Finland owns the Aland Islands, an archipelago of great strategic importance on that sea, which, if controlled by a major power, would almost confer supremacy over most of the Baltic area. Neutrality of these islands, which enjoy a warmer and more moderate climate than the rest of Finland, is a question of utmost importance to the national defense of Sweden and also the Soviet Union.

The vegetation zones of Finland are quite similar to those of Sweden. Pine, spruce, and birch are predominant here too. The forests inland, with their damp and often peaty soils, have been for a long time an obstacle to traffic and settlement; some of the great forests of Finland were even occasionally known as "desert" country until very recent times.

As a whole, Finland is an homogeneous country, somewhat difficult to divide into regions—most of them are transitions. In any case, there is a considerable difference between the coastal areas of the south and west and the more forested and less populated interior, where the lake district has some individuality. The Salpausselkä and the southern and southwestern coast have attracted most of Finnish activities and population. The density falls from 250 inhabitants per square mile in Uusimaa (the department of Helsinki) to about 40 in the lake district, 19 in Oulu and 6 in Lapland.

Helsinki, the capital, built on a rocky coast, is also the main port of Finland. Its population rose from 4300 people in 1805 to 21,000 in 1850, 227,000 in 1928, and 510,000 in 1966. It has a regular plan, with many monuments and beautiful parks. There is about Helsinki a feeling of coziness that even the ordeal of war has respected. The city still has quite a sizable industry: sugar refineries, glass, china, and rubber factories, various food and chemical plants; Helsinki has specialized in mechanical industries, has shipyards, and builds engines, locomotives and railroad cars, and equipment for the timber, paper, and pulp industry. Two other important centers of population and industry are Turku, on the southwestern coast, and Tampere, on the Salpaus-selkä. Turku has a variety of industries (especially shipyards) and a population of 140,000 people. Tampere (145,000) is the largest of the string of industrial towns of the fall line. It is on this line that electro-metallurgy and electrochemistry thrive, as well as pulp and paper manufacturing. Here also are large textile mills and leatherware factories. In 1950, 32 percent of the Finnish population was urban, and in 1965, 44 percent.

## THE PRESENT POSITION OF FINLAND

Because of its association with Sweden for some 700 years, Finland had, for a country situated so deeply in the continent, an advanced civilization with some industrial and maritime interests. Those interests were developed to some extent within the framework of the Russian Empire, which was as a whole less advanced in the nineteenth century than Finland. Still the main economic rise came after independence was achieved.

The whole economy of Finland is centered on her two chief resources: the forest and hydroelectric power. The country is therefore geared to the export of forest products, raw or finished, and to some industrialization. Agriculture, although it testifies to a great skill in the tilling of poor soils, is secondary: the cultivated area covers only 8.5 percent of the land; hay and oats are by far the main crops, with rye, wheat, barley, and potatoes the other major ones. Cultivation has spread rather far northward, owing to the warm summer and long hours of sunshine in the subarctic region. Although farmers often own their land, there are few large holdings; most of the farms had, even before 1944, an area of between 10 and 60 acres; very few have more than 250 acres. The total tilled area, however, is slowly increasing as clearing of forests proceeds throughout the country, a process which has gone on for many centuries.

Since 1944 an actual agrarian revolution has developed in Finland, as nearly 35,000 rural families left their farms in territory ceded to the Soviet Union and were resettled elsewhere in Finland. All of them had found new holdings by 1951. The resettlement legislation passed in 1945 established two new types of farms: the so-called "warm farms," obtained through the partitioning of existing farmsteads so that every new establishment had at least some already-cultivated land; and the so-called "cold farms," from which "the yield at the moment of establishment does not exceed ten percent of the yield to be expected from all the agricultural land of the farm when in a condition ensuring full yield and on which no accessible buildings exist." This vast operation of resettlement meant both a great surge of pioneering in Finland and a further reduction of the average size of agricultural holdings in the country. Professor W. R. Mead concluded a detailed study of the cold farms in 1951 with these remarks:

> The objective of the displaced farmer is a balanced holding—the most economic combination of stock, cropland, and woodland. At the same time, the rural administrators of Finland aspire to a balanced economy. The creation of 35,000 new farms has necessitated a revolution in land division that has profoundly disturbed the established equilibrium. . . . For farmland is competing with woodland, and almost every displaced farmer (as well as many others) seeks an extension of his arable land. "Finland without woods is like a bear without a skin," runs a traditional proverb. The pioneer flays the softwoods at a time when timber prices are at a maximum. Life is ruled by wood, physically at the local level, economically at the national level. The displaced farmers of Finland are settled. . . . Their aspirations must be reconciled with a national policy that seeks to make the optimum use of a limited arable area and to conserve the principal raw material Finland offers to the world market.

The forest that covers 71 percent of the total land area of Finland is a tremendous resource, and remains such even after the cession of some richly wooded territory to the USSR. It is one of the main European reserves of softwood. The wood is usually cut during the winter; the trunks are floated down after the rivers thaw, as in Scandinavia, to sawmills established along the fall line in the Salpausselkä area, or at the mouth of the rivers. Kotka, a port to the east of Helsinki, has become an important center of sawing and pulp making. On the western coast such are also the functions of Kemi, Pori, Porvoo, and other towns. The different products of wood, from timber to paper, make up about 70 percent of the total exports of Finland. The rest comes partly from agricultural goods: butter, hides and skins, and meat. The crops best fitted to the

Rural Finland. (*Above*) The red-painted sheds along the waterfront of Porvoo date back to the fourteenth century. Much of the old town was destroyed by Soviet bombers. (*Below*) Logs are being floated down the river between forests and carefully tilled fields. (*Finnish National Travel Office*)

damp clayey soil predominant in Finland are fodder, oats, hay, potatoes, and, on the best developed fields, some wheat. Cattle raising is the chief agricultural occupation (about 2 million head of cattle and 600,000 pigs). Creamery butter of good quality is produced and part of it exported. Fisheries also have been developed since 1945 and the catch has reached 75,000 tons annually.

In order to build up a better-balanced economy, industrial development is being strongly pushed ahead in Finland. The main domestic resource is waterpower, even after the loss of the lower Vuoksi area to the USSR (with about one fourth of the developed power in 1944). Installed hydraulic capacity in 1964, about 1.8 million kilowatts, is thrice the figure for 1948. This is 70 percent of the estimated potential of the waterfalls (about 2.5 million horsepower). The largest dam is at Imatra (172,000 horsepower), where large paper and metallurgical works have been built. There are some ores, especially the deposits of copper and pyrites at Outokumpu (35,000 tons of copper content and 350,000 tons of sulphur content) and of magnetite-ilmenite ore found at Otanmakiin. Some nickel, zinc, lead, silver and vanadium are also being mined. The largest industries are those processing timber from sawmills to paper mills (5.5 million tons of woodpulp and 1.2 of newsprint were produced in 1965). Finland put to work the highly skilled manpower, which is probably her best resource, in textile, chemical and engineering industries, so that her economy resembles more and more that of her Scandinavian neighbors. Considerable progress has been achieved since 1950 in the industrialization and urbanization of the land. For the farms are too small and too many in Finland and the population pressure on the rural areas too heavy. Finnish styles and taste have opened new export markets to such products as glass, porcelain (made with imported china clay), wood objects, etc. Transportation equipment has become an important export. Finnish architects have a great tradition and have designed buildings and towns all over the world.

The Finns, still expanding their pulp and paper industries, hope to gain a better share of the expanding demand in Western and Southern Europe. They also develop their mechanical and electrical industries, as machinery and apparatus have accounted for over 15 percent of their exports. Foreign trade is most active with Great Britain, the Soviet Union, West Germany, Sweden, the United States, and France. In 1961 Finland became an associate of the Outer Seven (EFTA) but is still too close a neighbor of Russia to turn westward as much as the Finnish people may like.

The peace treaty of 1947 with the Soviet Union imposed a heavy burden on the small nation that had fought against the Allies in World

War II. But Finland paid all the reparations required by 1952, and the Porkkala military base in the south was returned by the Russians in 1956. By her culture, economy, and aspirations, Finland ought to be oriented westward. Recent history and her geographical position have not made that fully possible as yet. The courage and efficiency of the Finnish nation in this ordeal of the postwar years has won the admiration of many people in foreign countries. However, the buffer's part is seldom pleasant.

The Rhine River cutting through the old Hercynian platform. The mighty river has cut a deep winding path into the planed platform of the old crystalline surface; this view was taken in the spring near the small town of Pfalz am Rhein, in the so-called "heroic" section of the Rhine valley, dotted with medieval castles. The ruins of the old castle of Gutenfels are seen in the middle of the picture. Another fortified castle stands at the water's edge. These castles testify to the great importance of the river traffic throughout the centuries. Local feudal lords erected strongholds to defend their control of this area against outsiders who might wish to dominate the great thoroughfare. These lords also needed military power to control the river traffic and collect tolls on traffic. Notice the large barges being towed on the river. Woods cover most of the steep banks; fields and meadows predominate on the flatter areas that have been cleared from the forest. (*German Information Center*)

# 16

---

# Germany

The concept and the territory of Germany have changed many times in the course of history. The country presently described by that name was formed as a political unit in 1870, when the German Reich, or Empire, was proclaimed at Versailles after victory over France.

## THE GERMAN REALM

The territory of the Reich as of 1871 was much wider than that of Germany today; it included the annexed Alsace-Lorraine area in the west and eastward on the Baltic coast, Memel. The Reich's area was reduced the first time in 1919 by the Treaty of Versailles; it expanded again under Hitler, when Austria and then the Sudeten land were annexed, and covered most of Europe in 1941–1944. The military defeat of 1945 reduced it to its smallest size since 1871: its eastern provisional boundary with Poland follows the Oder and Neisse rivers. Moreover, all its territory has been occupied by military forces of the four major powers of the World War II alliance: the United States, Britain, France, and the Soviet Union. As no final treaty has been yet agreed upon by the former Allies, the situation remains fluid. Territorial extent and political and economic organization will not be settled until later, and the present "provisional" partition may last much longer than was expected. Never before has Germany felt so strongly the meaning of the buffer's destiny as in the middle of the twentieth century.

Indecision about boundaries is not unfamiliar to the Germans. Even when they were full masters of their situation, they rarely formulated a clear definition of their boundaries. There were, of course, the boundaries of the Reich, which did not coincide necessarily with the extent of the area populated and historically dominated by the Germanic peoples. Beyond the borders of the Reich was all the *Deutschtum*, all the Germanic realm, the concept of which neither was nor needed to be very stable. This included the populations speaking German or Germanic dialects; it included also areas of German culture and influence which were not populated by a majority of German-speaking people. It would be difficult to say, for instance, whether Bohemia with the majority of its people speaking Czech, a Slavonic language, was or was not included in the *Deutschtum*—it depended mainly on the amount of dynamism that the German Reich felt like demonstrating at a given moment. Farther on was the area around the *Deutschtum* which was less advanced in culture and less thickly populated than the German areas and which should therefore in the German view serve as a field of expansion for their dynamic culture and political organization. This encompassed the German "race." For almost 1000 years expansion toward the west found a strong, organized resistance from the Atlantic powers. Eastward and southeastward the resistance was less until the rise of Russian power in the eighteenth century and the claims for independence by the national minorities in, the nineteenth century made the Slavic dynamism at least as strong as the German one.

This special and highly mystical idea of what constituted their realm made it difficult to see what territory was properly Germany, but knowledge of the historical background helps to understand the German view-point and also the different shades of "Germanism" existing within the Reich. Germanic tribes came westward from eastern Europe a few centuries before the Christian Era. Their pressure was felt along the Rhine by the Celtic tribes and caused Julius Caesar to cross the Rhine and establish Roman military camps along the river. The pressure of the Slavic tribes from the east seems to have been sufficient from the fourth century on to cause a mass migration westward and southward. Breaking the *limes* (borders) of a weakening empire, the Barbarians crossed into France, Italy, and even sent some of their advanced columns into Spain and North Africa where the Vandals terminated a memorable march through Western Europe. In the fifth century no Germanic tribe remained east of the Elbe River; there the Slavic realm began. In the ninth century the Western countries reorganized themselves, and Charlemagne established a new Empire of Occident, carrying Christianity eastward to the Elbe. Then national feelings arose in the West, with the French and English kingdoms and with the Spanish struggle against Moslem domination. The Holy Roman Germanic Empire, formed between the Rhine and the Elbe and extending into Italy and along the

Danube, began a new offensive eastward from the Elbe in the thirteenth century, and the German frontier was pushed to the Oder River. Then, following in the path of the Swedes and the Danes, Germans established bases of operation on the Baltic coast for penetration into the Russian area—the military-monastic order of Teutonic knights made some of the most spectacular advances eastward in the Middle Ages. Then the German tide reached its maximum point, and Poland expanded; a new tide culminated with the successive partitions of Poland, and for a few years in the eighteenth century Warsaw was a German city. In the twentieth century the German tide receded again (see maps pp. 548 and 579).

The stable part of Germany that has been German for over a thousand years is the section between the Rhine and the Elbe. The countries of the Rhine bear the imprint of an older civilization, open westward, and are deeply interested in the West and maritime activities. Quite different are the lands east of the Elbe; those have been constantly swept by the human tides; they are for Germany a colonial land, an advancing frontier oriented eastward. Here was born, on the marches of medieval civilization, the state of Prussia, which finally succeeded in uniting Germany under its authority and in destroying the predominance of Austria, another base of eastward operations, which was born in the Ostmark but situated on the Danube and on the Alps, looking chiefly toward the south and southeast to the Mediterranean and Black seas.

Between the three poles of the Rhine, Prussia and Austria developed a complicated mosaic of regionalisms, sometimes organized in local political units, always penetrated by many influences from all three leading Germanic areas and from the outside. Here, too, the topography was more complicated, but a few important cities arose at the crossroads of this part of Europe. These were commercial and financial centers; some of them entered into associations, of which the Hanseatic League was the most famous. The Hansa went far afield from its original cradle in the northwest of Germany, where are Lübeck on the Baltic and Hamburg on the North Sea; and the Hanseatic domination of Bergen and Visby, London, Bruges, Cracow, and Danzig was at the foundation of the claims to "Germanic origin" of all these places. While the Hansa was primarily a commercial and maritime trust, at times it formed a political unit, but a unit opposed to the regional nationalisms that finally expelled it from many of its outposts.

The difficulties of regional organization in Germany stem from the variety of political and economic structures that brought them into being: the imperial policy, the city leagues, feudal domains, local developments, isolated crossroads, and many others. Upon that diversity inside the Reich, Prussia attempted to establish homogenization and standardization. It appeared necessary to build the Reich up as a base of further operations, to unify and expand the Deutschtum. Bismarck and Hitler were the two main managers of this German unity, and from 1940 to 1943, Hitler's Reich dominated the whole continent of Europe with a greater authority than any version of Germany had ever achieved. But it was a brief interim, preluding a military defeat and a postwar period in which the plight of the German realm seemed to be at its worst.

In 1945 Germany surrendered unconditionally to the Allies. New provisional frontiers were traced giving it an area of 136,000 miles, divided into four occupation zones under the authority respectively of the United States, Britain, France, and the Soviet Union. Moreover, the territory of Greater Berlin, divided into four sectors, was to be governed as an entity by the four occupying powers. The Allied Control Council ceased soon to function; by 1948 the three western occupying powers agreed on a central government for the three western zones. In 1949 the Federal Republic of Germany came into formal existence; in 1951 the Western Allies terminated the state of war with this new republic, usually designated as West Germany, with its federal capital at Bonn; and in 1955 it became a sovereign independent country. Since then it has been a member of the United Nations and of NATO; it also participates in the European Coal and Steel Community, the Common Market, and Euratom, that is, the Inner Six. In parallel fashion, in 1949 the Soviet Union organized its former occupation zone as a separate state, the German Democratic Republic, usually designated as East Germany, with its capital in East Berlin, the real powers of government being vested in the Communist party organization. East Germany has not been recognized by any non-Communist power as a separate and independent state.

In these tidal lands it is difficult to guess how long may last such boundaries as the new frontier with Poland and the line between West Germany and East Germany, today an essential part of the "iron curtain." Even in the west the boundaries of the Federal Republic underwent some minor shifts after 1949, as a few rectifications were carried out with the Netherlands, Belgium, and France. The Saarland, disputed with France for two centuries and given international status within an economic union with France from 1919 to 1935 and again from 1945 to 1956, was in 1959 fully integrated into West Germany, as one of its *Länder*.

The buffer finds itself still torn between East and West, a struggle especially obvious in the still subdivided and occupied Berlin, where the cultural and economic unity of the German realm survives. Since Berlin is isolated amidst East German territory, still heavily staffed with Soviet armed forces, the USSR has tried to take advantage of this situation to cut off Allied access to West Berlin, first in 1948, when an Allied air lift maintained the contact until normal relations were resumed, then again in 1961 by threatening to sign a peace treaty with East Germany and supporting the East German move to close the access from the west. Behind these efforts is the striking contrast in economic and political evolution which has developed in the two Germanies. A steady flow of migrants has been going from one to the other, avoiding "iron curtain" controls through Berlin, and its net balance has emptied East Germany at the rate of more than 300,000 persons annually. It is not practical, however, to study the present Germany along the shifting lines of an uncertain political map; more permanent are the sections resulting from the physiographic features and the recent historical past.

## NATURAL REGIONS OF GERMANY

The main difference that appears on a topographic map is between north and south: the north is primarily flat and low; the south is hilly and of complicated relief. A winding line that may be drawn from Aachen in the west, through Düsseldorf, Hanover, and Leipzig to Görlitz on the Neisse, leaves to its north only a plain, gently sloping northward, with almost no altitude above 700 feet. To the south of this line the altitude remains almost constantly above 700 feet and often reaches 2000. These heights of southern Germany belong to the old, planed system of Hercynian massives, and bold mountainous landscapes are found only along the southernmost boundary line that follows the first crest of the Alps.

The Hercynian zone and the northern plain divide Germany in two halves. Their contact is a belt of the utmost importance, because it has benefited from the exchange of products that are different in the two zones and because some of the best soils of Central Europe line this sub-Hercynian piedmont. The great glaciations explain some of the regional aspects of Germany. The Great Plain was almost entirely glaciated, but at its last expansion the ice sheet did not re-cover the southern or sub-Hercynian part of it. Thus the Baltic coastland has a more recent soil and hydrography, since it was under the ice at a time when man had already settled in the southern sub-Hercynian part of the plain.

The last extension of the northern icecap left its rim of morainic hills along the Baltic coast. This coast is low and sandy; its immediate hinterland gives the standard picture of the glaciated plain, with a "hesitant" drainage, a multitude of small lakes, linked together by slow, meandering streams. On the higher and better drained parts, heath and moorland still are frequent. West of the lower Elbe, the plain, which slopes toward the north and not toward the Baltic Sea, was glaciated at a more remote date than the area east of that river; still the drainage has had some difficulty in drying up the sandy land of the Geest. The North Sea coast, low and subsiding, has been reclaimed by a system of polderlands

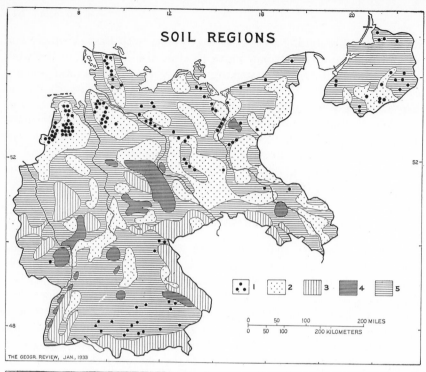

## SOIL REGIONS

1    2    3    4    5

0   50   100     200 MILES
0   50   100     200 KILOMETERS

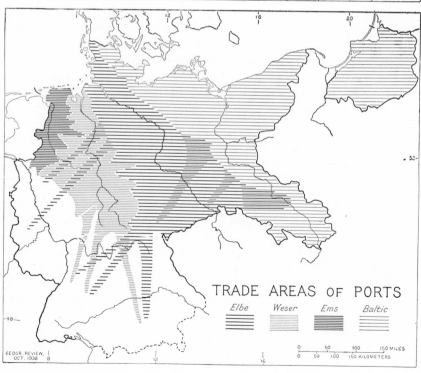

## TRADE AREAS OF PORTS

*Elbe*    *Weser*    *Ems*    *Baltic*

0   50   100   150 MILES
0   50   100   150 KILOMETERS

here called *Marschen*. Geest and Marschen recall the two main natural divisions of the Netherlands.

The Elbe serves as a natural frontier between two relatively different sections of the plain. Like the Weser and many other rivers of the plain, it flows in a general southeast-northwest direction. The main channels of drainage follow neither the northwardly sloping plain nor the foot of the Hercynian hills. It may be that their direction translates an old Hercynian orientation; but more probably the rivers follow the front of the icesheet at some stage of its retreat. This hypothesis explains most acceptably the approximate parallelism of all the main streams of the plain.

South of the glaciated area and north of the Hercynian zone, what we have called the sub-Hercynian belt has been endowed with wide patches of *loess* on a slightly higher and much better-drained level. The loess is here considered to be a soil formation enriched with particles brought by winds from the sandy beaches of the morainic areas; often it is dark, almost black, in color and is rich in humus. Man noticed the fertility of the loess areas early and started to till them long ago. The agriculture of loess has reached its widest extent and best integration in Germany between Hanover and Leipzig, in the area called *Börde*. The belt of loess is narrower, but better watered by abundant rainfall, in the west around Hanover; it widens eastward in Saxony, where the rainfall is less abundant.

The climate adds some slight differentiations to the various parts of the plain. It varies mostly with the gradual degradation of the maritime influence from northwest to southeast. Hamburg on the lower Elbe has an average temperature of 63° F. in July and 32.5° in January, while Leipzig records 64.8° and 30.6°; in the middle of the eastern section of the plain, Berlin has a 65.8° average in July and 31.5° in January, with a yearly range comparable to Leipzig's but a slightly warmer climate on the whole, although farther north and closer to the sea. The rainfall registers a similar transition: 28.5 inches at Emden, 27.5 in Hamburg, 25.2 at Hanover, 22.2 in Berlin; Leipzig has more rain than Berlin — 25.3 inches — owing to its position at the very foot of the Erz Gebirge northern slopes. On the whole these differences are rather subtle: the winter is definitely colder and a little longer eastward where the influence of the

---

*(Opposite)* Soil regions *(above)* and trade areas of German ports as outlined by the basins of their rivers *(below)* are shown in the boundaries of the 1920s. New borders have modified both land use and commercial networks. Key to map of soil regions: 1, moor soils; 2, sandy soils; 3, mountain soils; 4, steppe soils (black and brown soils); 5, mixed types, ranging from sandy loams to clay. *(The Geographical Review)*

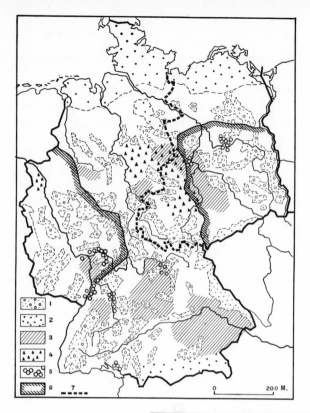

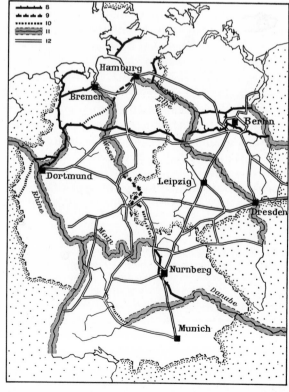

Russian anticyclone is felt more and where the Baltic warms the coastland less, being frozen north of Berlin for several weeks every year.

The transition is less regular and the continentality becomes stronger in some parts of the southern Hercynian section. Here, between the outlined limit of Aachean-Hanover-Leipzig to the north, and the Alps and the Rhine valley to the south, German topography is confused. Communications are difficult, and a dense forest cover made the country even more impenetrable until men cleared the plains and valleys. This hilly forest, *Hercynia silva* of the Latin authors, for centuries stopped the southward advance of Germanic tribes and efficiently protected the Roman lands. From this Latin expression, geologists took the term *Hercynian*, which is applied to an ancient system of planed and broken-up foldings. Many of the German massives in this area still are called *wald*, that is, forest, and the forest still is present, though with less thickness, on many of the highlands.

Perhaps the best way to disentangle the complexity of the area is to look at it as a triangle of mountains with a sedimentary filling inside. The triangle is formed by the edge of the Alps in the south and two Hercynian series of heights meeting somewhere in the vicinity of Hanover; the top of the triangle may be located at the northern extremity of the Harz massif; there two well-known orientations dominating the Hercynian folds and topography — northwest-southeast and the northeast-southwest — form a Hercynian V. In southern Germany the V appears upside down on the map, pointing northward, and the open side of the triangle in the south is closed by the Austrian Alps and the Rhine valley from Lake Constance to Basel. The eastern arm of the inverted V is formed by the Bohemian Forest (Böhmer Wald), the Thüringer Wald, and the plateaus north of them up to the Harz and to the hills along the Weser River. The western arm is much wider and consists of all the highlands along the Rhine; the Ardennes, Eifel, Hunsrück, and Taunus plateaus with the Black Forest (Schwarzwald) to the south and the Rhön pushing up to the Thüringer Wald to the northeast. This old southwest-

---

*(Opposite)* Agriculture and transportation in Germany (boundaries of 1947). Key numbers 1 to 7 apply to the map of agriculture *above*, numbers 8 to 12 to the map of transportation *below*: 1, main forested areas; 2, predominance of moors and meadows; 3, predominance of wheat cultivation; 4, predominance of sugar-beet cultivation; 5, predominance of fruit trees and orchards; 6, east and west limits of the area where potatoes are a major crop; 7, present boundary between Western and Eastern Germany; 8 main canals; 9, main canals built since 1950; 10, major canal being planned; 11, valleys of navigable rivers; 12, express highways. The railroads are of course a major means of transportation throughout Germany, but since practically all German territory is adequately serviced by rail, rail lines have not been included on this map. Waterways and express highways are a more localized feature and show the pattern of major transportation currents.

northeast orientation is also found farther eastward with the northern slope of the Ore Mountains (Erz Gebirge) in Saxony where the mountains are perpendicular to the Bohemian Forest.

Inside the triangle thus outlined, the average altitude is slightly lower than along the sides. While the resistant blocks of crystalline rocks (mainly schists, gneiss, and granite, with some sandstone cover preserved in spots) were raised and faulted, the sedimentary interior organized itself as a basin; limestone plateaus of a hard layer sloping toward the southeast determined a *cuesta* or scalloped and arched escarpment looking toward the northwest. The whole topography of this southern and hilly Germany has been modeled by the same convulsion of the earth's crust that built up the Alps, a piling up of folds that rose to more than 30,000 feet in elevation in the Tertiary era. Then the resistant blocks of the Hercynian system were broken up into smaller pieces and raised in a somewhat irregular way, so that they generally present a steeper slope toward the side of the Alps and a gentler gradient in the opposite direction. Big faulting at the same time caused the sinking of depressions and oriented the main valleys. The limestone plateau inside the triangle was slightly folded by the push and is sometimes called the German Jura (or rather the Swabian or Franconian Jura in its two parts west and east of a central depression). The southernmost section of Germany, at the foot of the Alps, is a plateau gradually sloping northward and was covered by the materials carried away from the eroded Alpine crests—a huge alluvial fan has thus developed, comparable to the one at the foot of the Pyrenees in southwestern France. A large part of the alluvium here accumulated is glacial morainic material. Terminal moraines of glaciers lobes and later fluvial erosion shaped the present topography in its detail. Rivers diverge fanwise toward the depression which follows the periphery of the fan and separates it from the Swabian Jura and the Bohemian Forest to the north; this depression is the valley of the Danube, which thus is fed mainly with Alpine waters.

The Hercynian highlands, the interior basin, the sub-Alpine plateau, and finally the Alps—such are the morphological components of a complicated region where landscapes are varied and contrasts frequent. The topography certainly helped the splitting up of the whole area into a number of political or administrative units. The depressions, with richer soils and an active traffic, attracted population. Especially important was the valley of the Rhine, and lands along it received a special imprint: a civilization zone was properly generated by the economic and political role of the great river. Another belt of outstanding importance is the contact zone of Hercynian massives with the Great Plain. At the foot of the old crystalline blocks, layers of the Carboniferous Period bear coal strata, and the richest belt of coal

Hallingenland in the Great Plain of Europe. (*Three Lions*)

Divisions of Germany and Austria into zones of occupation, 1945–1952. The Soviet zone of Germany became a separate state.

deposits in Europe follows this contact of the plain with the Hercynian highlands from the north of France to the south of Poland; some of the most important of these deposits are in Germany: the Ruhr and the Saxon coalfields. Thus two belts, the Rhine and sub-Hercynian one, have been the two main zones of population and wealth in Germany for centuries. At their intersection has arisen the Ruhr or the Rhineland industrial basin, one of the leading manufacturing centers of the world.

## REGIONS OF THE RHINE

The Rhine River has had a very special role in German history: it was the zone of contact of the German realm (a Central European area) with the western countries of the Atlantic and even of the Mediterranean. As a north-south section of the transcontinental route from the North Sea to the Mediterranean lands, the Rhine valley has elaborated a cultural zone of its own along its banks, quite different from the homogeneous colonial territories of Prussia. As a major thoroughfare, the river and the valleys branching out of it have given a solidarity to the different parts of the basin. Yet the eternal opposition between East and West made it a transition zone and also a zone of conflicts, illustrated, in the long centuries since the division of Lotharingia, by the struggle of France and Germany to dominate it.

The sources of the Rhine are in Switzerland and its mouth in the Netherlands, but Germany, of all the powers of the Rhine basin, possesses by far the longest stretch of the river's banks. From Lake Constance to Basel, the Rhine, flowing westward, serves as a boundary between Switzerland and Germany, except for a small section (that of the rapids) near Schaffhausen, where Swiss territory extends on both banks. Although it has been filtered and moderated by the large Lake Constance (Boden See), the Rhine is here distinctly an Alpine torrent, with a rapid flow and floods in late spring and summer when the snow and ice melt on the mountains. Upstream from Basel, the upper basin of the Rhine is quite Alpine: 20 percent of its area lies at an altitude of more than 5000 feet. At Basel the river turns northward and enters the flat-bottomed trough between Vosges and the Black Forest. The gradient decreases rapidly. Left to its own caprice, the Rhine meanders widely across the plain, but men have straightened and deepened its course: the nineteenth century made a "new" Rhine, artificial but easily navigable to Basel for large barges up to 600 tons. Larger boats come up to Strasbourg, and ocean-going shipping could reach Cologne but for the clearance height imposed on the masts by bridges over the river.

The navigability of the Rhine is greatly improved by the fact that from

Basel downstream the river drains a hilly Hercynian basin deprived of lofty ranges, where the tributaries have high waters in winter and early spring, when the run-off is greater owing to lack of evaporation and to the melting of snow on lowlands. This Hercynian regime, added to the Alpine contribution of the upper basin, gives a remarkable stability of flow to the Lower Rhine. Slack water rarely reduces the depth too far, and such a threat exists only during a brief period in the fall. A large canal follows the Rhine on the French side from Basel to Strasbourg; built to utilize fully the power potential of the river, it produces considerable amounts of electricity on the French bank, and there are plans of extending navigation up to the Boden See.

Navigation is easy on the corrected stream north of Strasbourg, where, having served as a border of France, the Rhine becomes German on both banks; it meets with the Main River at Mainz. Stabilized in so far as its regime is concerned, the Rhine then pierces through a narrow valley between high and steep cliffs, the high crystalline plateaus. From Bingen to Bonn, the valley is more picturesque. It has been called the "heroic Rhine" because of the many castles dominating it, because of the feudal rivalries between lords who levied tolls on the traffic and also because of the greater dangers of navigation—the famous legend of the Lorelei, the maid who by singing attracted sailors into dangerous spots where ships foundered, is a symbol of the "heroic Rhine," well known through the classic poem of Heinrich Heine. Near Bonn the bold forms of the volcanic heights of the Sieben Gebirge signal the tectonic strains that here interrupted the extent of the crystalline massives and probably imposed the general orientation of the Rhine valley across them.

Downstream from Bonn, the Rhine is a full and slow plain river, flowing past some of the largest cities and the biggest industrial agglomeration of Germany; it has received the contribution of the Moselle River, which drains a part of Lorraine and Luxembourg. At Emmerich the Rhine enters Dutch territory; its delta begins here, and soon it splits into several arms, some of which mingle with the Meuse waters. An old arm, maintained by canalization, leads to Amsterdam, but the modern main branch of traffic goes to Rotterdam or may direct shipping to or from Antwerp.

To many German historians and statesmen, the Rhine has been a symbol of German cultural greatness and domination of Western Europe. For centuries Germans strove to make the Rhine entirely German, even at times claiming control of its mouth. A waterway of such importance—indeed an "inland arm of the sea"—was of the greatest concern to many nations: the Swiss needed free through-traffic to link Basel with sea navigation; the Dutch needed the possibility of free upstream traffic to extend the hinterland of their ports; the Belgians needed

Sand dunes on the North Sea coast. (*Three Lions*)

Foothills of the Bavarian Alps near Munich. Note the recent reforestation in the foreground. (*Three Lions*)

the same freedom to give Antwerp a chance to compete inland with Rotterdam; the French needed the Rhine for easier communication with the sea for northeastern France. Until the end of the eighteenth century, a string of toll-exacting stations followed the great river, and certain cities or guilds held privileges for transportation or transshipment. The French Revolution introduced the principle of free navigation on the international rivers considered as "arms of the high seas," but it required a long struggle to insure the application of this principle in practice along the Rhine. It was stated again in the Treaty of Versailles, and between the two World Wars. A central commission, on which all the interested powers were represented, functioned, but always with difficulty, for the German government hinted several times at what it considered "foreign interference" in internal German affairs in so far as navigation was concerned on a river both banks of which were German for sections. Despite German opposition, the Rhine is still evolving toward the status of an open international thoroughfare. The German lands along the river have profited more than any others from the Rhine traffic. The volume of goods handled by Rhine navigation stood around 130–140 million tons in the early 1960s.

Industrial activities increase in scope and importance downstream along the Rhine. Along the upper course of the river, the main economic and urban developments remain on the Swiss or French side; on the German side, from the Lake of Constance to Karlsruhe, the Rhine goes around the mountainous block of the Black Forest, so similar to the Vosges, with higher rounded crystalline summits in its southern part and more tabular but still deeply dissected, less steep slopes on a sandstone cover in the north. A steep vaulted wall overlooks the Rhine plain, which is narrower here than in Alsace on the French side, and in the midst of which rises a small group of volcanic hills called the Kaiserstuhl (Imperial Chair). This plain of Breisgau is deeply rural; fields and meadows give an impression of solid, prosperous occupation; there are few towns: Freiburgim-Breisgau in the south and Baden in the north are only local markets; Kehl on the Rhine guards the bridge which crosses the Rhine at Strasbourg. Here the river flows quietly and has been more of an international boundary than in any other section of its course — before 1940, the two famous lines of underground fortifications, the Maginot Line and the Siegfried Line, faced one another on either side of the stream. It is peaceful and busy with commerce nowadays.

It is only at the height of Karlsruhe that more important urban centers and industrial activities appear: the Black Forest here becomes in places lower than 1600 feet; through the Pforzheim Pass the railroad easily runs eastward into southern Germany. German territory extends then

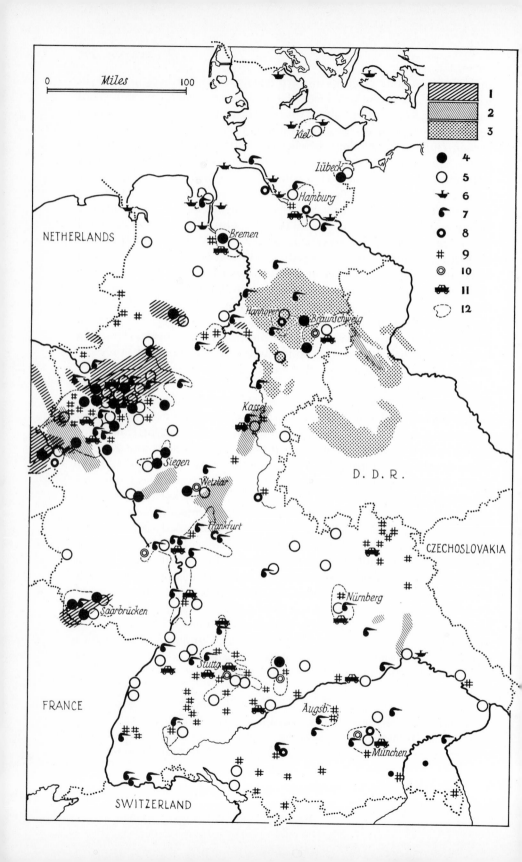

on the left bank of the river toward the Saar and Luxembourg. In the south the Black Forest was a wooded mass penetrated by narrow valleys with active agriculture. The northern and eastern slopes are the more settled; they have been for a long time the domain of a land-use system called *Reutberge,* with periods of tillage alternating with fifteen-year periods during which the land reverted to forestry. Small industries have scattered in the valleys and work timber, weave cloth, or make glassware. On the best exposed slopes vines have been cultivated. The valley of the Neckar drains most of that activity toward Stuttgart, the capital of Württemberg-Baden, a major crossroads where the countries of the Rhine come into contact with the checkerboard of plains and hills developing eastward in Central Europe. One third destroyed during the war, Stuttgart in the 1950s has taken a new lease on life. Much of the poorer, outlying sections were still waiting for better reconstruction in 1960, but the central districts and the suburbs have been excellently rebuilt and were sprawling out fast. The urban district of Stuttgart had some 500,000 inhabitants in 1952, which rose to 635,000 in 1965, and the major residential sprawl was beginning to develop beyond its limits, shaping a rather nebulous kind of urban structure entailing large-scale commuting to the business center and industrial zones. This growth was rooted in the old local tradition of mechanical industries; such famous firms as Daimler and Bosch originated here. Now many new plants have come here, some established by American firms and some having moved from East Germany; motor cars, various machines—and especially machine tools—electrical apparatus, and electronics are the major specialties of Stuttgart, although textile and chemical plants are important, too. A loosely built conurbation, partly scattered amid wooded land, encompasses a population of over a million. An ambitious urbanistic plan foresees here a huge "city amid vines and woods."

Almost symmetrically to the northwest of Karlsruhe (250,000), which specializes in transportation machinery (locomotives, railroad rolling stock, bicycles), across the rural and wooded plateaus of the Haardt, is located another bustling industrial region, the Saarland, until 1958

---

*(Opposite)* Distribution of industries in West Germany by 1960. Shaded areas mark major mineral deposits: 1, coal; 2, lignite; 3, potash salts. Symbols indicate the location of large manufacturing industries: 4, iron and steel (note concentrations in Ruhr, Saar, and the north); 5, metals and machinery; 6, shipyards; 7, chemicals; 8, rubber and tires; 9, textiles (mainly in the south); 10, optical and photographic industries; 11, automotive plants; 12, main manufacturing regions. It is interesting to observe how the rapidly developing chemical and mechanical industries appear scattered all over the land. The initials D.D.R. are the symbol in German for East Germany.

economically associated with France. The Saar's economy is founded on a rich coal deposit (13.7 million tons of coal extracted in 1966) and an early specialization in iron and steel (4.3 million tons of steel in 1966). It is part of the vast coal and steel belt that extends from Lorraine to the Ruhr, and the present functioning of the Coal and Steel European Community and of the Common Market enables the Saar, now separated from the French Lorraine, to exchange coal and iron ore with that region as conveniently as in the past. Over its 1000 square miles the Saarland has a density of population of about 1100 per square mile. Careful planning and zoning have preserved in a predominantly urban use of the land patches of woodland that give a rather verdant aspect to what would have been another "black countryside." The capital, Saarbrücken (135,000), has a substantial central business district and a lively university built amid the woods.

North of Karlsruhe, the Rhine flows in a flat plain dominated on both sides by the plateaus of the Haardt and Odenwald. The contrast is sharp between the multitude of large, prosperous villages in the plain and higher lands that frame it with wide expanses of woods and heath. Here are a few isolated large villages that make their living mostly from the products of cattle raising and forestry. The most active and densely settled part of this country is at the contact of the plateau with the plain. To the east this line of contact, called the *Bergstrasse,* is a string of properous rural centers, specializing in orchards and fruit growing. Some tobacco is produced around Bruchsal, and vineyards still surround Heidelberg, the old university town that stands at the entrance of the Neckar valley in the plateau. The main producing area for Rhine wine faces the Bergstrasse, spreading along the foot of the western plateau — as usual, vineyards prefer the bottom of east-facing slopes. The chief urban development of this area is located at the meeting of the Rhine with the Neckar; it is the double town of Mannheim-Ludwigshafen, which groups together more than 500,000 people. Mannheim is a great port on the Rhine and a center of transshipment. At first it made flour out of grain and cellulose out of timber, but now large mechanical and machine-tool works coincide with a great development of chemicals; in Ludwigshafen was born the *Badische Anilinund-Soda Gesellschaft* which became the nucleus of the *I. G. Farben Industrie,* the largest chemical concern in the world around 1914 and still a powerful trust until 1944.

Such urban development only announces the thriving group of cities that has established itself at the northern extremity of this depression. There the Rhine receives another important tributary, the Main, which forms an elbow and penetrates through a narrow valley into the crystalline plateaus to the north. Here an important crossroads developed as a result of the topography. While the Rhine provides a way southward or

The Black Forest is in a narrow valley, almost a gorge, cut in the midst of granitic hills. The slopes are clad with a dense forest of conifers; big blocks of granite have rolled down into the stream. (*Three Lions*)

A waterwheel is used to raise water for the leather tannery at Altmarkt in the Alz valley. At the right is a meadow planted with fruit trees. (*Three Lions*)

to the northwest, the Main opens a road eastward; a large tectonic depression opens a route straight northward toward Kassel and the northern plain, and to the southwest the plateaus of sandstone have been covered by tertiary sediments and rich loams, permitting the development of an intensively cultivated area of open fields. The importance of the crossroads, the rich grounds of the low-lying areas, and the variety of resources found on the surrounding higher lands have affixed here one of the main centers of wealth and commercial development of the German realm. The old city which controlled the navigation on the Rhine and Main for centuries stands at their meeting — Mainz (145,000), the golden city of the Middle Ages, with its old picturesque section, its modern mechanical and automotive industries, its shipyards for riverboats, its breweries and leather factories. But Mainz no longer commands the crossroads in the heart of which it stands.

The capital of all southwestern Germany, and of the American zone during the occupation, is near by on the Main River at the entrance to the Hessen-Kassel corridor leading northward. Frankfurt-am-Main (680,000 inhabitants) rose as a center of trade, and since the seventeenth century it has been an important financial city, particularly owing to a group of Jewish banks, such as that of the Rothschilds who began in Frankfurt. Its main development started in the nineteenth century and was accentuated with the railroads of which it became a hub: the Main River was canalized and linked by a small canal to the Danube. An industrial suburban ring manufactures beer, motorcars, machine tools and business machines, electrical equipment, printing machinery, furniture, and clothing; a number of satellite towns specialize in chemicals or leatherware, and Hanau in jewelry. Since 1945 it has served as the main headquarters of the American forces in Germany. If Mainz and the large and elegant spa of Wiesbaden (260,000) are included, the Rhine-Main crossroads can be said to agglomerate an urban population of nearly 2 million. For the last twenty years, American business in West Germany centered on Frankfurt, where the U. S. Army headquarters remained. Though badly destroyed by bombings, the city has been rapidly and extensively rebuilt (see p. 551) and has become one of the main business and financial centers of Germany, with the most active airport and center of international finance: thus the old banking tradition has been revived.

To the north stretch the wide and high plateaus of Hercynian crystalline rocks, largely schists. This is a land of contrasts between on the one hand the higher areas, with wide-open empty, wooded, or heathy spaces swept by winds and rains, and on the other hand the sheltered depressions, with better soils, dense population, and active traffic. The valley of the "heroic Rhine" is a teeming street of farms and towns, specializing in fruits and wines, and about one fifth of the population is engaged in commercial pursuits. The valleys of the Rhine, Moselle, and other tributaries are rather dry, especially in winter, while the heights are very damp and get most of the rain in the cold season. Three valleys of tributaries channel the traffic of the plateau area toward the Rhine and help to break up the highlands into compartments. The Moselle River comes down from French Lorraine; at the point where it meets with the Saar River stands the old city of Trier (Treves), which used to be quite a capital in the Middle Ages and is now only a regional center. The wide valley, cut into terraces, at the bottom of which the Moselle meanders, separates the heights of the Hunsrück to the south from those of the Eifel to the north. The Eifel is dotted with small lakes, some of which (called *Maare*) occupy little craters, reminiscent of extinct volcanism. On its right bank the Rhine receives the Lahn River, whose valley separates the Taunus from the Westerwald, then the Sieg River, which divides the Westerwald from the Sauerland.

Near the meeting of the Rhine with both the Moselle and the Lahn stands Coblenz (105,000), another old crossroads, now the capital of the Rhineland-Palatinate. None of the cities along the "heroic Rhine" has developed much in the past two centuries: greater freedom of navigation, competition from the railroads, and concentration of industry in large districts have rather emptied this section of the Hercynian zone, especially the plateaus. The blossoming centers of the Frankfurt-Mainz compact, and even more of the Ruhr industrial basin, were too close by.

As the resistant crystalline layers disappear, being covered by recent sedimentary strata, the Rhine comes out of its narrow stretch at Bonn, under the shadow of the volcanic Sieben Gebirge, to enter a gradually widening plain, funnel-shaped, opening to the northwest on the great northern plain. Bonn (about 150,000 people) has an old cultural tradition; founded by the Romans, an active port and a great university have established its reputation; its industry was helped by a lignite deposit near by. Too close to the metropolitan area of Cologne, Bonn has not become a regional capital, but it was chosen in 1949 as the seat of the government of the new Federal German Republic. A metropolitan region with a population of close to 600,000 has now developed around Bonn.

From here on the Rhine is a powerful and well-controlled stream, flowing slowly across a flat plain to the sea. It receives no more important tributaries but becomes one of the most active waterways on earth. Rural life teems in the plain around: fields and meadows have replaced the forests; scattered farms and hamlets announce the Dutch kind of land use; and wheat, rye, oats, and fodder crops bring high yields. The majority of the farms are of small (12 to 50 acres) or medium (50 to 250

The Rhine at Cologne. The view shows the rebuilt central district around the cathedral. (*German Information Center*)

The Rhine at Mannheim. (*Three Lions*)

acres) size, but there has been a trend toward larger farms with mechanization and the capital investments of industrial corporations in real estate. The development of cities in the nineteenth and twentieth centuries has favored a more intensive agriculture and an orientation toward cattle raising as the major production. The soils are rich here, owing to patches of loess signaling the sub-Hercynian belt, and farther north around Münster heavy marls give deep damp soils favorable to truck farming. The sub-Hercynian belt has never been purely rural: one of the main thoroughfares of Europe has followed it since early times, and this trade spurred urban growth. Recently the coal of the Ruhr gave it a powerful incentive again.

Cologne is the first large city encountered when going down the Rhine. It was founded by Julius Caesar as a military camp and later was a Roman colony, *Colonia Agrippina*, in A.D. 50. It early became the great city on the Rhine, with its monumental bridge on which the railway from Paris to Berlin used to cross the river, with its central section of narrow but busy and elegant streets, and with its many churches, dominated by a famous Gothic cathedral—the Archbishopric of Cologne was in the Middle Ages one of the most influential of the German realm. A member of the Hansa, Cologne was a great inland port, receiving ships which sailed across the North Sea; textile and metallurgical industries started as early as the thirteenth century. From the sixteenth century on a period of decline set in with the rise of the Dutch trade on the mouth of the Rhine and with the opposition of Catholic Cologne to a predominantly Protestant Germany eastward; its population in 1794 numbered only 50,000 people. A new and rapid growth opened up in 1870 when Cologne was included in the newly unified German Reich; from 80,000 in 1871, its population rose to 161,000 in 1885, 428,000 in 1905, and 772,000 in 1939. When World War II began, Cologne was the regional capital of the Rhineland, the fourth city of Germany, and a great banking and industrial center. The industrial ring of suburbs built since 1880 processes the grain, leather, and vegetable and mineral oils brought by the Rhine; many plants manufacture machinery, ships, metallic cables, and glassware. Its industrial importance, and even more its role as a hub of rail and water transportation, made of Cologne an indispensable target of strategic bombing. In 1946 the hard-hit city had a reduced population of 488,000 people. It was one of the large German cities that suffered most as a result of the war, and it may be unable to regain its former leadership on the Rhine, since the chief centers of the Ruhr have been better preserved. However, as reconstruction proceeded apace, the population rose to 780,000 again by 1961, 845,000 in 1965 and the metropolitan region, reaching up toward Düsseldorf and Gladbach, counted 1.5 million.

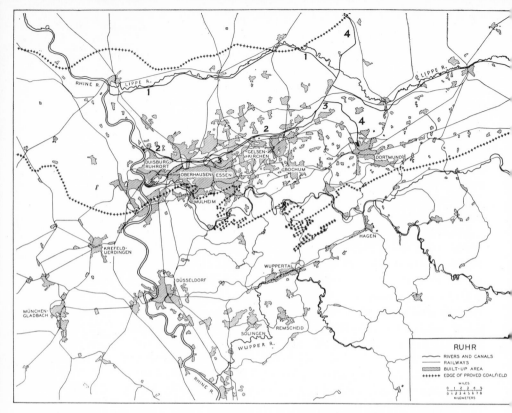

Built-up area and transportation system of the Ruhr. The canals are: 1, Lippe Seiten; 2, Emscher; 3, Rhein-Herne; 4, Ems-Dortmund. *(Chauncy D. Harris)*

Loading coal on a canal barge at Ruhrort near Duisburg. *(Three Lions)*

To the west of the Rhine basin, two important industrial districts have developed on small coal basins: to the southwest the Saarland, and also to the west the Aachen (or Aix-la-Chapelle) district, which stretches in the sub-Hercynian belt between Liege and Cologne. Aachen (177,000) produces over a million tons of coke per year; it makes steel, machinery, and woolen cloth and works in lead and zinc, of which some ores are found in the vicinity. Both these centers announce in only a very modest way the tremendous agglomeration of people, cities, and plants of the Ruhr.

In 1960, the Ruhr was indeed the largest industrial district of Europe west of Russia, and probably the best integrated one. Its structure was erected rapidly, chiefly between 1870 and 1913, on the local resources of fuel (coal along the foot of the Hercynian plateaus and lignite along the Rhine from Bonn to Cologne) and on the commercial traditions of the Rhineland. These traditions did not consist only of the natural advantages of the waterway of the great river and of the land traffic along the sub-Hercynian belt; they brought also an old network of international relations and substantial capital accumulated by the regional banks, as well as an undeniable spirit of enterprise and an art of management, both of which developed fully in the wide and ambitious framework of a German Empire striving for European domination.

Coal is at the base of the Ruhr industries. Coal mining in this section started along the Ruhr River and developed northward, tapping deeper seams. The output rose from 12 million tons in 1870 to 60 million in 1900 and 114 in 1913, although it fell to 50 in 1946, it rose to more than 125 million annually from 1954 to 1965; it declined slightly in 1966–1967. At such a rate of extraction the explored reserves may last 200 years more. The greatest variety of qualities of coal is found here, with vast quantities of the coking coals that are lacking in most of the other coalfields on the continent. Lignite is also being largely utilized. Water is available in large quantities from the rivers descending the plateau's slope toward the Rhine: the Ruhr, the Emscher, the Lippe. The Ruhr is by far the most important feeder, controlled by a series of dams, while the Lippe and the Emscher evacuate the waters polluted by the factories and the cities.

For centuries metallurgy was widespread in the valley of the Sieg (Siegerland), along the Rhine upstream, and in the Sauerland plateau; local iron, lead, and zinc ores were smelted with charcoal and worked in many towns. All these activities were concentrated on coal; blast furnaces of the Siegerland rapidly exhausted the local ores; but all the German attempts to tap, for self-sufficiency reasons, the poorer deposits still could not supply the huge ore needs of the Ruhr metallurgy. These ores or metals came from abroad, largely by the Rhine: iron ores from Sweden, France, Spain, French North Africa, and recently from Canada; nonferrous ores and manganese from all over the world. Similarly the textile fibers were imported, and so was most of the food consumed by the crowded population. It has been calculated that during the 1920–1940 period well over one half of the materials consumed in the Ruhr and of the production of the area came from and went to countries outside Germany. The Ruhr was one of the workshops of the world and lived much more off international trade and military orders than from regional or national markets.

The Ruhr differs primarily from other European industrial districts in its thorough integration. It is a complete industrial region where metallurgical, mechanical, textile, and chemical manufacturing are all largely represented. The Ruhr was the first section of Europe to develop on a large scale the *vertical* integration of all stages of production from the coalfield to the finished metallic or chemical product, as well as the first to develop the *horizontal* concentration of all large manufacturers engaged in the same kind of production and united in one big concern. With the help of—and, during the Nazi regime, under the control of— the Reich government, the industrialists of the Ruhr erected such a strongly welded structure of varied industries from coal to the most intricate engineering that the Ruhr became indeed a marvel of business administration. All kinds of measures were applied to give it a privileged position. For instance, German transportation rates were lower for iron ores than for coal, so that French and Swedish ores could come more cheaply to the Ruhr than Ruhr coal could go to the foreign areas producing these ores. This helped greatly the concentration of manufacturing on coal rather than on ore, although ores had to be transported in larger quantities than coal per ton of steel obtained. But the Ruhr then made more steel than the ore-mining areas, which lacked coke.

Much more important, however, was the favorable effect on the Ruhr and some other German industries of the organization of industrial management into large cartels during the second half of the nineteenth century. From a national level it spread to an international level, as German concerns fanned out of the Ruhr and associated with many groups from Britain, France, Belgium, and elsewhere to control and direct most of the large-scale industrial production in Europe, particularly in the fields of metallurgy and chemicals. So ramified and widespread were these networks of industrial and managerial interconnections that they seemed to lose all geographical meaning. Still they carried considerable importance for the distribution of industrial activities, because through cartel organizations they planned the trends of production in the different countries and favored definitely certain areas rather than others.

Integration did not prevent certain specializations in different parts of the industrial district. In the south, along the Ruhr River, are the out-croppings of the coal-bearing layers which were mined first. This older part of the Ruhr is the one grouping the finishing industries and the larger cities. Still in Sauerland, south of the Ruhr, stands the chief textile city of Wuppertal (a conurbation of 500,000 with its suburbs), weaving cotton, making cloth and clothing mainly from yarn imported from nearby München-Gladbach or from Belgium and France. An industry of dyes has been added to earlier pharmaceutical products, and Wuppertal also produces machinery for textile mills. The integration has been with textile centers on the west side of the Rhine, such as München-Gladbach (150,000) and Krefeld (220,000), where the immigration of refugee French Huguenots in the seventeenth century started the silk industry. Farther south the group of Solingen-Remscheid (300,000) carries on the traditional finishing metallurgy of the Sauerland, and Solingen has had a great reputation for its cutlery, hardware, arms, and weapons.

The heavy modern industries developed more directly on coal are north of the Ruhr River. "Black-country" scenery, an almost continuous urban area, stretches from Duisburg to Dortmund. This section is indeed the heart of the Ruhr, and it becomes more and more crowded with industries and housing, despite the persistence of wooded patches; saturation here seems close. Essen is the capital of steel, and its monumental central business section built anew is in sharp contrast with the endless residential quarters of workers that have developed around it. Essen is the home of the famous Krupp iron and steel empire, and it is the seat of the coal-mining administration and of the *Ruhrsiedlungsverband,* the authority for land-use planning in the district. Its population rose from 470,000 people in 1925 to 667,000 in 1939 and, even after all the bombings, was 725,000 in 1965. Dortmund (650,000), like Essen, is mostly an immense iron and steel center; it is also one of the main hubs of canals and rails in the area. Bochum (360,000) and Gelsenkirchen (370,000) have seen their impressive metallurgical plants overshadowed by the chemical works of more recent construction. Gelsenkirchen was the home of Stinnes, another empire builder of the Ruhr. Other large towns have sprung up eastward with a migration of both coal pits and industries toward the Rhine: thus Oberhausen, Hamborn (where were erected Thyssen's steel works), Mülheim, and finally the leading Rhine port of Duisburg-Ruhrort. The Duisburg conurbation, which has annexed Ruhrort and Hamborn to form one city called Duisburg-Hamborn, accounts for 500,000 people. Before 1940 it boasted the largest river port in the world. Different groups of basins specialize in imported ores, petroleum, grains, or shipments of coal. All kinds of heavy industries along the piers produce millions of tons of steel, flour, cement, cellulose and paper, glass and brick, and a variety of chemicals. Duisburg is more of a business and industrial center; Ruhrort is a suburb devoted entirely to coal; the group of ports centered on Duisburg make up the largest Rhine port. On the world scale of inland ports, only during World War II did Pittsburgh, Pennsylvania, reach a higher figure, not to mention the Great Lakes ports.

On the Rhine, about halfway between Duisburg and Cologne, stands Düsseldorf (700,000), another city with a powerful business section that for a while was the commercial capital of the Ruhr though it is not a part of the Ruhr district proper. Despite a ring of industrial sections specializing in engineering (machine tools, locomotives, equipment for mine pits and steel mills), Düsseldorf is an elegant city, away from coal and with extensive shopping sections, theaters, and museums. Most of the business transacted here relates directly to the huge industrial and urbanized region extending around it in all directions. The city is also the political capital of the North Rhine-Westphalia, the largest, richest, and most populated of the *Länder* of West Germany. Although it is smaller than either Cologne or Essen as a city, Düsseldorf also has substantial industries. But its main role is increasingly to attract governmental, managerial, and financial offices, and to develop as the capital of the Greater Ruhr area. Since the 1800s, when Napoleon I began replanning and beautifying Düsseldorf, it has been a sophisticated city, but it is now assuming the leadership of this extraordinary region.

There are now five cities in the half a million to a million size in the Ruhr and the adjacent section of the Rhine valley, and at least eighteen ranging in population between 100,000 and 500,000. From Bonn in the south to Münster in the north extends one of the densest urban constellations in the world, aggregating today over eleven million people. It has a nebulous structure, but on the whole it offers over a long area the most impressive concentration of heavy industries one can see on the continent: the European who sees the Ruhr for the first time cannot fail being strongly impressed and often amazed by such industrial might. Only in some parts of the northeast of the United States and in the Tokaido region of Japan could one find comparable manufacturing power over similar areas. The Midlands-Lancashire industrial complex in England has been now surpassed by the Ruhr in several sectors of activity.

The Ruhr has recently been producing more than 20 million tons of crude steel a year and transforming a good deal of it into every kind of machine and tool possible, from locomotives and turbines to needles and pocket knives. Almost every other important category of modern manufacturing is represented there by substantial plants, although there is a definite emphasis on coal, steel, and heavier industries. Although the

A large coal mine at Gladbeck, near Essen, in the Ruhr. (*German Information Center*)

Main plant of the Volkswagen motor car company, at Wolfsburg, near Braunschweig. (*German Information Center*)

Rhine has been its major artery, the Ruhr now needs and has every possible means of transportation by waterway, rail, highway, airlines, power lines, and pipelines. It has pioneered in building a pipeline to carry pulverized coal over several miles, thus attempting to rescue coal—the markets of which have been recently shrinking in Europe—from the victorious competition of the more easily transportable petroleum products, gas, and electric energy. A constantly improved network of canals and railroads carries to and from the Ruhr the mass of goods consumed or produced here in every possible direction.

In the years 1880–1945 the Ruhr had a growth yet unprecedented in Europe. Its enormous industrial potential was not affected very much by the physical destruction of the war. But this potential used to be geared to serve the economic and military expansion of Germany. After a brief postwar eclipse, the Ruhr has pushed its production, in volume and variety, higher than ever to serve this time the peaceful aims of the growing demand of Europe and in countries overseas. Its coal output may be somewhat decreasing but never had the industrialists of the Ruhr dreamt they would be making as much steel and machinery as they did in 1960. After a period of deconcentration of the major industries, under Allied pressure, the management of the Ruhr has been reconcentrated again and seven concerns produced, since 1960, 99 percent of the Ruhr's huge output of steel. In the economy of the Inner Six the Ruhr is playing a central role, and it benefits from its central geographical position in the very middle of the northern, best developed half of the territory covered by the Common Market. The expansion of the Ruhr has played a great role in the whole recent boom of the West German production; some signs of saturation can be detected, however, and the surest of them is the remarkable rhythm of growth of other West German centers, though less well endowed in terms of either fuel resources or water transportation. The Ruhr is still based on the heavy industries such as coal, iron and steel, basic chemicals, which now employ less personnel. If European economic development proceeds at the same pace in the coming decades as it has in the recent one, the Ruhr will probably cease being such an exception on the continent; but from such a powerful base the great concerns born here may set out to dominate more of the new European industry.

## SOUTHERN GERMANY

To the east of the Rhine countries stretches the hilly southern half of Germany—the Alpine and Hercynian sections, with the Swabian-Franconian basin in the center, which we described briefly among the natural regions of Germany. This area has always had an especially important part in Germanism. Here, in the old forests cleared by a steady advance of the Germanic tribes southward, one may perhaps find the roots of German mysticism even more than on the Rhine. It was from a *burg* on top of a hill that the rise of the Hohenzollern started, leading to their downfall in 1918; it was from Munich that Hitler began his rise to power, and at Munich that the international agreement was signed surrendering Czechoslovakia to the Nazis. It was in Nuremberg that some of the major speeches of the Nazi period and the racial laws were proclaimed. Southern Germany is perhaps more purely German than any other part of the Deutschtum.

In the south, the Alpine crests divide Germany from Austria. This is an area of summer resorts, where Germans like to go to gaze at the mountains with their bold crests and a few peaks. The only spot where German territory penetrates slightly inside the range to include a corner of truly Alpine scenery is the very southeastern corner of the Reich's territory: here stands Berchtesgaden, where Hitler made his inaccessible headquarters above the calm mirror of the Königsee. From the Alps to the Danube then develops the slope of the Bavarian pre-Alpine hills and the sub-Alpine plateau. Bavaria is a land of woods and pastures; the mountaineers are attached to their hills, and few of them emigrate although the country is not rich. Traditions of long standing are preserved in the villages as well as the towns — Oberammergau is famous for its medieval religious plays. Trade crossing the Alps has been channeled through a small number of main valleys, and important commercial centers have controlled these routes. In recent times the harnessing of the swift and abundant rivers has helped the industrialization for which the old trading habits prepared the main cities.

Augsburg was a Roman creation and owed to this origin a high standing and connections with Italy in the Middle Ages. In the fifteenth century it was quite a capital of trade, but its wealth was destroyed in the Thirty Years' War. Its rich bankers tried to rebuild it in the Italian style, but commercial predominance passed to Munich. In the nineteenth century, the railroad brought some new activity and industries, but Augsburg (210,000) remained a satellite of the Bavarian capital. Munich is now the third city of Germany (1,215,000). It is built in one of the largest cultivable plains of the sub-Alpine region, but its fortune was due — once Augsburg was ruined — to the political power of the Bavarian kings. Munich developed first as a residential, administrative, and political town; after 1880 its growth became miraculous, and in fifty years the population increased threefold. This could not be explained without a speedy commercial and industrial development. Munich manufactures a variety of goods: textiles, clothing, foodstuffs, furniture, electrical equipment, motorcars, locomotives, rubber tires, optical and precision

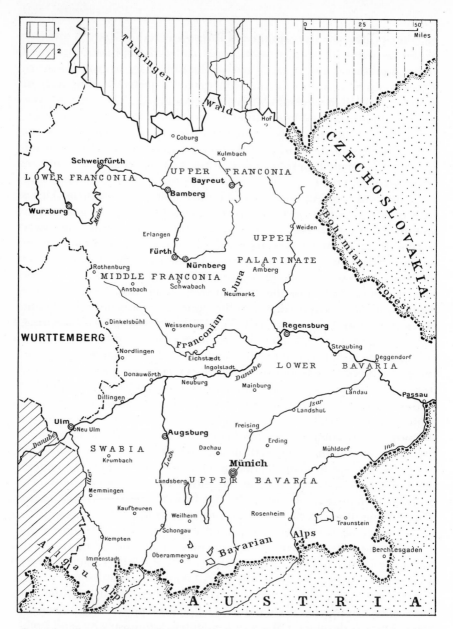

General outline map of Bavaria in southern Germany. Key: 1, adjoining area under Soviet occupation (the German Democratic Republic); 2, adjoining area under French occupation in 1945–1953. Bavaria is the largest in area (28,000 square miles) and second in population (10 million) of West Germany's *Länder.* It can be termed also the most mountainous and rural. The population is 72 percent Roman Catholic.

instruments. Its rise has prevented the development of any other sizable urban center in the south of Germany. Ulm and Regensburg in the Danube valley are purely local centers. Munich has greatly benefited by the fact that it was the largest city in the U. S. zone of occupation. Its population increased by more than 100,000 between 1946 and 1952, and by 200,000 in the years 1952–1960.

North of the Danube the internal basin shapes its arched contours, with sandstone and limestone plateaus opposed to the verdant depressions in the clayey layers. Soils are better and the climate is milder to the west, toward the Neckar valley, in Württemberg. The chief city, Stuttgart, belongs indeed to the Rhine region, and only small local towns have developed in the loamy depressions: Heilbronn weaves cloth and produces chemicals, owing to local salt and gypsum deposits; Tübingen has a university of repute. Eastward, Franconia offers a more severe aspect: the climate is more continental and the soil either too damp, as in the Steigerwald, or too calcareous and rocky, as in the Franconian Jura; woods and meadows predominate. The country is mostly rural without dense population, and the valley of the Main and its tributary, the Regnitz, have concentrated the human activities. Nuremberg (470,000) is the only important city here. It was a major crossroads and a great center of trade throughout the Middle Ages and the Renaissance period. Its role in German history has been a significant one as a meeting place of north and south, and until World War II it still retained a beautiful old section enclosed by high medieval walls around which a new and important industrial city had developed. Metallurgical and electrical plants surround the old town. The end of the Hitler era gave it a new historical importance — badly bombed during the war and partly ruined, having lost more than 100,000 people, Nuremberg in 1946 became the seat of the international tribunal for war criminals. Again, Nuremberg reigns over the vast region where Amberg, Bamberg, and Würzburg (120,000) are largely local centers. Diversified industries, often linked with local agricultural production, are scattered through these towns. Bayreuth to the northeast is famous for its industries of wood and even more for its Wagner festivals. Here we touch the large Hercynian massives of central Germany.

Once more the first impression of the Hercynian section is of the contrast between the verdant depressions and the forested heights to the east. Germany occupied the outside slopes of the Bohemian Forest and of the Ore Mountains, these two ranges enclosing the Slavic world of Bohemia. Both ranges are covered with a rich coniferous forest, one of Germany's chief reserves of timber. The Bohemian Forest has little else to offer, and it has not been thickly settled. Much more curious are the massives to the north: their importance, mass, and degree of industrialization is much greater in the east than in the west.

Munich along the Isar River. (*German Information Center*)

The Burg Markt, near Augsburg, stands over the ancient battlefield of the Lechfeld. It was an ancient trading town bought in 1514 by the famous banking family of Fugger, who reshaped it as a castle; the buildings are now used for farming. (*German Information Center*)

The western section of this Hercynian zone continues the plateaus of the Rhine. It has been faulted and affected by volcanism. It consists of a few wooded plateaus of sandstone, small volcanic ridges like the Vogelsberg or the Rhön, and small ridges of hills lining the Weser. In the depressions are concentrated the people and the wealth: a low corridor stretches from Frankfurt to Kassel lined with the rich fields of the Wetterau, with towns of which Kassel is the important rail crossroads, and with locomotive building and textiles. The valley of the Weser is another such depression between ridges; Osnabrück (140,000) is the local center.

Quite different is the economy of the eastern Hercynian massives, the Harz, the Thuringian Forest, and the Ore Mountains, looking toward the Elbe and drained by its tributary, the Saale. Since 1945 these areas have been part of East Germany, under Soviet control. Thuringia is a remarkable example of development of such old areas; its economy could be likened to the eastern section of the French central plateau. Some iron ores were smelted on charcoal in the hills during the Middle Ages. With the clearings directed by monasteries and some iron works controlled by the local lords, a dense settlement thrived; many small towns became important exporters of finished metallurgical goods; and Schmalkalden earned a reputation in ironmongery. Although devastated during the religious wars and having exhausted its ores, the region remained industrial; with the railroads, coal and raw materials were brought in, and the same towns kept on manufacturing hardware and weapons, but added such products as electrical equipment, typewriters, clocks, thermometers, and tools for laboratories. The story of the Thuringian Forest has been repeated on a smaller scale on another Hercynian horst, the Harz, where some copper ore is still extracted and where finishing industries and industries based on the forest (matches, paper, furniture) occupy a ring of small towns.

Between the two horsts the depressed basin of Thuringia shows the usual checkerboard of wooded sandstone or limestone heights with fields and meadows on marls. These fields are fertile and intensively tilled, but they are not very extensive. Here one enters East Germany, beyond the "iron curtain." A few towns of about 50,000 inhabitants have played the part of small capitals; each has a bright cultural tradition and some delicate finishing industry: Erfurt alone reaches 190,000 and manufactures ceramics, machines, and chemicals; Gotha is famous for its printing and map-making plants (the Justus Perthes geographical publishing house); Jena is an academic city but with precision optical industries (such as the Zeiss plants) and chemical factories. Weimar is mainly a residential town.

Finally a major industrial district has developed in Saxony along the slope and foot of the Erz Gebirge (Ore Mountains). This Saxon slope of the Erz Gebirge is the most densely populated of all the Hercynian massives; the forest cover has been better cleared, largely in order to utilize the mineral deposits to which the name of the range testifies. In postwar years the Soviet authorities have actively pushed the mining of some uranium ore near Aue. Industry long ago deeply penetrated the mountain, and the discovery in the foothills of important coal mines led to a large-scale modern industrial development. But in this area, far away from the sea and from any intensively traveled road, the quality of the manpower was, with fuel, the chief resource. Metallurgy is not predominant and remains limited to mechanical plants, mainly at Zwickau (130,000). Textiles are predominant at Plauen (terribly destroyed by the war), Chemnitz (which with 300,000 people claims the title of "German Manchester"), now named Karl-Marx-Stadt, Freiberg, and even at Dresden, the historical capital of Saxony.

An elegant residential city, with famed theaters and museums, Dresden (630,000 in 1939, 510,000 in 1946, 508,000 in 1965) had a variety of mechanical, chemical, and optical as well as textile factories. It was the real capital of the line of industrial cities at the foot of the hills from Plauen to Bautzen. Dresden was built on the Elbe River and therefore at the gate of the main valley crossing from the northern plain to the interior of the Bohemian Hercynian stronghold. Like Munich and Stuttgart, Dresden owes its position to its kings and its political function. This upper section of Saxony looks toward the plain and especially toward its regional metropolis of Leipzig. It used to be linked with the Ruhr, which supplied a part of the semifinished materials that were worked into the final product by the skilled manpower; the relative importance of this district was increased during World War II, for it was less bombed, enjoying a more central position. But it has been included in the Soviet zone of occupation, and therefore has found itself suddenly oriented toward the Eastern powers and severed from the Rhine countries.

THE NORTHERN PLAIN

The sub-Hercynian loamy belt and the seaboards of the Baltic and North seas frame the wide-open, sandy, and empty expanse of the German section of the Great European Plain; from Rhine to Oder similarly there is a considerable difference between west and east, particularly on both sides of the Elbe River in its section from Hamburg to Magdeburg.

In the west, the plain north of the Ruhr is rather poor. The sub-Hercynian belt of loamy soil is narrow, as the Hercynian hills push northward with the Harz and the Weser ridges. The rich agriculture has been further complemented with some ore deposits: iron, manganese, and some petroleum, developed especially under the self-sufficiency pro-

Cassel, one of the gateways to the northern plain. *(Three Lions)*

A rural scene near Hanover in the Weser valley though mechanization rapidly replaces old techniques. *(Three Lions)*

gram of the Nazi regime. Hanover (560,000) and Brunswick (240,000) are the principal centers, with a variety of metallurgical and chemical industries. This is one of the main motorcar building areas of Germany, especially at Wolfsburg (see p. 597). But if one progresses to the north or to the northwest, the rich and densely settled scenery is quickly replaced by a less attractive tableau: the glaciated plain opens with its poor and damp soils. West of the Weser, the land of Oldenburg is all peat bogs or *Geest* with polders *(Marschen)* along the coast. It is a Dutch landscape, but closer to its natural state than the more reclaimed territory of Holland. Poor agriculture with a predominance of cattle raising was the rule, with more intensive occupation in the Marschen. Between the Weser and the Elbe stretch the Lüneburger Heide, a better drained (because slightly higher) zone of sands, heaths, and some woods. These poor lands have been rather depopulated by the exodus of rural people before 1940. North of the lower Elbe, in Schleswig-Holstein, the same damp plain continues with many peat bogs amid patches of beech woods. This is a particularly oceanic country, the beginning of the Jutland peninsula between the North Sea and the Baltic. The Kiel Canal, uniting the two seas across German territory, has brought some animation to a part of Schleswig, but the aftermath of World War II brought more with the resettlement here, in the cities or on improved farmland of 2.5 million refugees from East Germany. They increased by 40 percent the population of Schleswig-Holstein.

Here, on the shore of the North Sea, are the two large ports on which Germany hoped to base its overseas expansion. Hamburg is the largest German seaport and the second largest river port, after Duisburg. Hamburg is situated on the Elbe sixty miles from the sea and is kept open to large oceangoing ships by dredging. Huge docks have been dug in the river banks. From the twelfth century Hamburg was one of the leading members of the Hansa, but large-scale modern development did not begin until after 1840, taking on a new tempo with the unification of the Reich. An association with Berlin was greatly to Hamburg's benefit; in 1938 the great port handled 71 percent of the German imports by sea and 57 percent of the exports. Until 1888 Hamburg was a great emporium, a free port and city, and after its integration in the customs of the German Reich, it remained a free port, in which the redistributing trade, important for certain tropical goods such as coffee and wild animals, could be carried on without payment of taxes to German customs. It was the home port of the Hamburg-Amerika Line, of the Kosmos Lines to South America, of the *Deutsche Levantlinie,* and of others. The variety of world-wide traffic was great, and in the 1930s Hamburg handled about 20 million tons of goods annually and served some 600,000 passengers—for calling liners a speed port was built at

Cuxhaven on the mouth of the Elbe. In 1937 the conurbation of Hamburg was organized to include the suburbs of Altona and Harburg-Wilhelmsburg. Its total population thus reached 1,700,000 in 1939, but was reduced after heavy wartime bombings to 1,400,000 in 1946. In the reorganization of 1946, it was formed into the *Land* and free city of Hamburg and constituted the largest unit of industrial and commercial activities outside the Ruhr in West Germany. In 1965, with a population again of 1.8 million, Hamburg handled a port traffic that cleared 20,000 vessels with a total tonnage of 34.9 million tons; but by the volume of goods handled it was only the largest port in Germany, still far behind Rotterdam and a dozen other ports in the world. The general hinterland of Hamburg used to lie eastward, along the Elbe and the canals leading to Berlin, or Dresden. The "iron curtain" has cut the great city off; it is not yet well connected by waterway to the Ruhr; its main feeder is the railroad, especially the newly electrified route southward to Munich and Frankfurt. But Hamburg is a proud and stubborn city, still the largest in Germany besides Berlin. It has developed its own industries, an impressive concentration of shipyards, metallurgical, chemical, and engineering plants, and oil refineries, with a new accent on electrical machinery. The city generates itself a large part of its port's traffic, unloading much more than loading, of course.

Despite wartime destruction, Hamburg is a spectacular city, with an active and more impressive central business district than in most German cities. It handles about one tenth of the securities operations in West Germany, and a good deal of its foreign-trade transactions. Links with Denmark and the Baltic have been developed. The city is also the great shopping center for a large section of northern Germany. It has some beautiful residential sections for the wealthy, bearing a Victorian imprint; and its Hagenbeck zoological park has once again become the largest market for wild animals in the world. New glassy towers have risen, testifying to the importance of the office function in the city. Hamburg must work hard, however, to counterbalance the increasing attraction for the German economy of the seaports in the Rhine-Meuse delta, and even to compete with two other neighboring ports: Bremen and Lübeck.

Neither of these has the actual majesty that Hamburg has managed to retain. Much smaller, though still notable, is the port of Bremen on the Weser. In olden times it used to be more important than Hamburg, but it lost out in the competition. The Weser is a less wide and deep waterway than the Elbe, and the advanced port of Bermerhaven had to be built downstream. Bremen specialized in relations with South America and the Far East. It was the great port for the importation of cotton, rice, and jute, and it evacuated millions of European emigrants leaving

Downtown Hamburg, viewed from the city hall. (*German Information Center*)

View of the central port area of Hamburg. The business section is across the river, where the steeples rise. (*German Information Center*)

Germany or Eastern Europe for overseas. Still the hinterland of Bremen is normally smaller than that of Hamburg, and it is further reduced by competition with the smaller port of Emden on the mouth of the Ems River. The Ems-Dortmund Canal did not replace the Rhine for the Ruhr, but cut into the hinterland of Bremen. After the war, Bremen benefited by serving as the American military port in Germany, and it was therefore favored over Hamburg in the establishment of connections with southern Germany, which was the American zone of occupation. The city's population rose to 600,000 by the end of 1966, and the *Land* of the free city, which extends downstream to include the advanced speed port at Bremerhaven, totaled 742,000. Large industries are at work, including iron and steel and chemicals. The plain to the south and southwest of Bremen is not yet very much cultivated, though forests and meadows are important, but oil wells have been drilled and are working, and natural gas has been explored.

To complement the maritime network centered on Hamburg and Bremen the Kiel Canal was dug, uniting the Kiel Bay of the Baltic with the mouth of the Elbe. It helped Hamburg and its free port to become one of the gates of the Baltic Sea, rather than Copenhagen. The traffic of the canal, which has a depth of 35 feet, was very active until 1940; some 40,000 boats (of which one half were sailboats) passed through in 1938, representing a tonnage of 22.5 million tons. Timber and ores went from the Baltic to the North Sea, while coal, grains, and iron and steel goods were coming the other way. But the port of Kiel (270,000) on the Baltic entrance has benefited little from the canal traffic and has remained a naval and regatta center, although it is the capital of rapidly developing Schleswig-Holstein. The canal has helped the Baltic trade of Germany; however, the West German shores on the Baltic are now reduced to little, and the national role of the Kiel ship canal is only regional. Still further to the east, West Germany includes the port of Lübeck (240,000), another industrial center with a steel mill, shipyards, and engineering plants. Lübeck was also an active Hanseatic city and has kept some interesting Gothic buildings. This area of Schleswig-Holstein has developed fast, accommodating many of the refugees from the east. The resettlement policy has thus stimulated a part of northern Germany which would have otherwise suffered more from being cut off from the neighboring areas behind the "iron curtain."

The "iron curtain" follows very closely to the east the canal from Lübeck to the Elbe, then extends southwards passing just east of Brunswick. Beyond it, the eastern section of the Great Plain opens—humid and sandy, strewn with lakes, bearing the fresh imprint of the last glaciation, and since 1945 under Soviet rule. The lands of Mecklenburg and Brandenburg are flat and covered with forests; the boulder-clay sections in the north are more arable and carefully tilled. The traditional crops are rye, oats, and potatoes. After 1875 the large holdings were broken up, and an evolution started toward more cattle and horse raising. Large use of fertilizers and systematic reclamation improved the yields. A particularly difficult area, swampy and boggy, covered with dense pine woods, occupied the central section of the plain between the Elbe and the Oder: this was the German march of Brandenburg, a base of operations eastward. The old Slavic settlement cleared the hillocks; then the Germans cleared the valleys and drained a part of this plain. Here the Prussian kings decided to fix the seat of their capital, and Berlin rose in a curiously unfavorable environment. The former capital must be studied separately because of its present special status.

The *Länder* of Brandenburg and Mecklenburg are relatively forested (over 32 and 20 percent respectively of their land area), chiefly with pine and spruce. In Mecklenburg there still is much heath and poor open land. On the Baltic, the only important port of East Germany is Rostock (184,000), which is also its only city north of Berlin with more than 100,000 population. The contrast remains strong between north and south in the northern plain of East Germany.

If any regional considerations could be found to explain the artificial but stupendous rise of Berlin, the principal factor might well be the wealth of the plain south of the capital's area. There, in the angle between the Harz and the Erz Gebirge, is the richest section of the sub-Hercynian belt. The *Börde* section of the Great Plain is covered by rich soils, mostly loess of black coloration. Here, with an involved crop rotation, the highest yields are obtained to make the *Börde* indeed the granary of Germany. Large farms, highly mechanized, make this plain resemble to some extent the Beauce south of Paris. The usual rotation is a six-year cycle: two years of sugar beets, two years of cereals (wheat or oats), and two years of potatoes, beans, or fodder crops. The fattening of cattle and hogs is added to these cultures. The manpower came from the east and was in large part Polish. Mineral resources are also important here, especially potash (Stassfürt, Halle), rock salt, and lignite on a large scale.

On such wealth, both agricultural and mineral, large cities were built early. Magdeburg (267,000 people in 1965) is a great port on the Elbe and so well situated at the contact of the plain and the Hercynian hills that its choice for capital may have been more logical than Berlin. It suffered greatly in the religious wars, and its population was decimated in 1631. In the nineteenth century its rise started again with the canalization of the Elbe and with heavy industry encouraged by the Krupp metallurgy and by potash. Beer and sugar are two important products resulting from the surrounding rural country. Still, Magdeburg was too close to Berlin, and the capital of the south had moved on to Leipzig. Halle had a similar story; with its 280,000 people, it is chiefly an important manufacturing center.

The capital of this rich area, and to some extent of the industrial Saxony farther south, is Leipzig (595,000). Built amid swamps and forests, Leipzig in the twelfth century established fairs that made its reputation and fortune. Until recently these were the most important fairs of Central Europe. At the end of the seventeenth century, when Augsburg, Magdeburg, and Halle were ruined by religious strife, Leipzig attracted the Protestants fleeing from France, the Low Countries, and the Rhineland. It became the first trade center of Germany, especially for textiles and books—during the Seven Years' War its population of 25,000 paid a ransom of 12 million thalers without being ruined. In the twentieth century the Leipzig Fair was still a great event, especially for machinery, books and printing equipment, furs, and optical articles. A vast ring of industrial suburbs had surrounded the old trading center. Leipzig was indeed a remarkable development, and it disputed Breslau for the role of one of the commercial gates to the Eastern Slavic world. It still is but this time on the east side of the divide. While the area of Leipzig-Halle used to be a leading center of machinery production, which was shipping a variety of it to all the other parts of Germany and even beyond, now it makes it for shipment to the Soviet Union and its satellites, hungry for all the tools of industrialization. The shortage of manpower is constantly becoming worse, mainly as a result of the people's flight to West Germany. Leipzig's population was smaller in 1965 than in 1946. That city remains the leading East German center of manufacturing and trade. Its fairs still attract customers from various countries; but the major printing and publishing fair of Europe is now held at Frankfurt-on-the-Main. The latter's namesake, Frankfurt-on-the-Oder, which finds itself now the East German's border city on the railroad from Berlin to Warsaw and Moscow, has only 58,000 inhabitants, despite a large iron and steel mill started here to take advantage of the connections by waterways. East of the Oder one enters the present territory of Poland and another cultural area.

## BERLIN

The former capital of Germany by the summer of 1968 was still under the occupation of the four powers of the victorious World War II alliance; in fact it was divided between West Berlin, a *Land* of West Germany, electing representatives to the Federal Parliament in Bonn, and East Berlin, the capital of East Germany. The division of this large metropolis, aggregating by 1967 3.3 million people (2.2 of whom live and work in the western sector where the central business district is located), caused grave tensions in 1961, for the Soviet government threatened to cut off either directly or by turning over to the East German Communist government the control of access to Berlin. A major factor contributing to the tension was that the interpenetration of the two Berlins made possible a constant flow of refugees from the East to a western territory from which they could be flown to West Germany. This migration bled white the East German economy, precluded the expansion of production, and demoralized the people altogether. Another reason was the desire of the East German authorities for recognition by the non-Communist powers, and their main asset in the strategy of international relations was that their territory surrounded Berlin. Since 1961, it became impossible for East Germans to cross over to West Berlin; a high brick wall isolated the latter, reinforcing the "iron curtain."

Berlin is perhaps the most artificial of all the large European capitals. Out of a small village of Wende fishermen on an island amid swamps and lakes, the princes of Brandenburg made an impressive capital. In 1650 it was still only a small town, but in the eighteenth century, with the growth of the kingdom of Prussia, a more rapid development started westward along the central avenue, *Unter den Linden*. French Huguenot refugees brought with them some small industry (jewelry, silks) and organized truck farming in the section of Moabit. Mainly a city of officials and soldiers, Berlin had some 100,000 inhabitants in 1780 and grew to 500,000 by 1865; but the boom began after the proclamation of the German Reich in 1871. In 1890, the city had 1,680,000 people, in 1925, 4 million: Greater Berlin reached 4.6 million in 1939, still had 3.2 million in 1946, 4.2 in 1955 and again only 3.3 million in 1967.

The imperial capital organized the German rail net around itself. With the growing centralization of economic life, officialdom and the roles of the local banks, stock exchange, and law courts increased rapidly. Industries gathered in the suburbs; all aspects of metal finishing were represented in Berlin: motorcars and tractors, machine tools and engines, pumping equipment, and, above all, electrical engineering. Between the two World Wars Berlin tried to become the world capital of electrical machinery. Two great concerns had entire towns of workers and plants in the suburbs: the *A.E.G. (Allgemeine Elektrizitätsgesellschaft)* and the *Siemens-Schukert* group, the latter with its *Siemensstadt* built among the pine woods. From electric clocks to electric engines and turbines, every possible kind of machinery run by electricity was built in Berlin. Telephonic equipment and electronic industries were recently added.

Like all large industrial cities, Berlin has also had a large clothing-manufacturing and a powerful printing and publishing industry. Large

The Kurfürstendamm, main business artery of West Berlin in 1960. In the background is the damaged steeple of a church, kept as a memory of wartime destruction. (*German Information Center*)

Reconstructed West Berlin: a park, new residential buildings, and, in the background, manufacturing plants. (*German Information Center*)

plants processed foodstuffs and produced the beer, sugar, oil, margarine, flour, and chocolate consumed by the city. And all this varied industrial function was supervised by the most important commercial organization Germany has ever had, controlling in the 1930s even Hamburg, Bremen, and a great deal of the Ruhr. The totalitarian system of the Nazis was bound to give Berlin a crucial role in the integrated economy of Europe that that system attempted. It was a moment of greatness and of great danger. Hard hit by the war, Berlin was taken by the Soviet armies after fierce battles. It not only lost then more than one million people who fled or were killed during the operations, it also lost its commanding role in Germany and knew a period of misery worse than the inflation period that followed in the wake of World War I.

The 340 square miles of Berlin were divided in 1945 among the four major Allied powers. The Western powers in Berlin had to face a blockade that necessitated the famous air-lift operations of 1948–1949. Largely because of American air power, it was possible to save the Berlin population by flying in enough supplies even during the period of bad winter weather to feed and heat a city of over 2 million inhabitants. This unprecedented experiment started with the landing of 250 tons of supplies for the civilian population on June 28, 1949; within the thirteen months that followed, the air lift delivered a total of 2,230,000 tons of food, coal, and other goods to the blockaded city. During the spring of 1949, 8000 tons were flown in daily until reduced schedules were instituted in August 1949, as land traffic was resumed. No other large city has ever been supplied for so long a period by air. Still this record could not make happy a city whose historical role had led it to such a situation. Berlin means much to German unity and its recent history. The fact that the East German Republic created in the fall of 1949 under Soviet auspices had its capital in Berlin was a source of serious concern to the Western powers. By 1953 West Berlin had been restored to decent living conditions through the efforts of the Western Allies; but the contrast was still sharp with the misery in the eastern section, although many of the residents of the eastern sector worked in the western sector.

Amidst Communist-dominated territory, West Berlin is, of course, a show case of Western democracy. It is bustling with activity and has been almost completely rebuilt, often with luxury. The large city is linked to the West only by one railroad line (via Eisenach and Bebra to Frankfurt-am-Main), two highways, and three air lanes, each 20 miles wide. German commercial traffic can use other routes also, but these are the only routes of access for Western military use and are therefore the access claimed by the Allies under the former treaties with the Soviet Union. Still, Berlin received from the West 8 million tons of goods in 1960. The manufactures produced in West Berlin in 1959 were sold within West

Berlin for 25 percent of their total value, while 61 percent went to West Germany, 12 percent were exported to the non-Communist countries, and only 1.8 percent went to the countries of the Communist bloc. Many of the factories and offices of German firms previously located in Greater Berlin have moved out to West Germany, even though they may have left a branch office in West Berlin. This migration profited several large industrial centers in the Federal Republic, especially Stuttgart, Munich, Frankfurt, and Hamburg. On the other hand, Berlin kept some business for itself, and in 1959 negotiated 6.7 percent of all West German transactions in securities. It is remarkable indeed that despite its isolated position West Berlin managed to become more prosperous than East Berlin, which benefited from its governmental functions in a country whose industrial production was expanding. Both East and West Germany were pushing their output of a variety of industrial goods; but Berlin showed quite clearly how much each government was doing on its side of the fence for the local people.

Since the crisis of 1961-1962 and erection of the Berlin wall, a feeling of tension has permeated the local situation and dampened economic progress. The supply of manpower commuting from the surrounding areas of East Germany was cut off. For a while an immediate threat seemed to be hovering over West Berlin. President John F. Kennedy then made a state visit to West Berlin and stressed the determination of the American government to maintain the integrity of the place, in the speech in which he declared, "I am a Berliner." From 1964 to 1968 the relative thaw in Soviet-American relations helped restore the confidence of West Berlin in its security, but along the wall tension remains constant. In the coalition government of West Germany, formed in 1966, the mayor of West Berlin, Willy Brandt, assumed the post of Minister of Foreign Affairs. From 1962-1966, the population of West Berlin has remained about stationary. Growth would be difficult in such besieged conditions. Tension flares up periodically, interrupting the flow of traffic along the corridors to West Berlin.

## THE EXPANDING ECONOMY OF WEST GERMANY

After the defeat suffered in World War II, the whole of Germany appeared heavily ravaged by the destruction of the war. But the pace of reconstruction has been in many ways amazing. The actual "boom" and prosperity that developed in the late 1950s and early 1960s in West Germany seemed quite miraculous for a country that started reconstruction only fifteen years ago. This prosperity is, of course, only a relative one. The average standard of living remains far below what it is in such countries as the United States, Canada, and Switzerland, or even Great Britain and Sweden. The mass of the labor force receives somewhat less in terms of wages and benefits than in several other European countries, but the West Germans are gradually catching up. To begin with, their industrial output has caught up and surpassed every other nation but the United States, the Soviet Union, and Japan. That West Germany with an area of 95,400 square miles and a population of 58 million in 1967 was the fourth largest manufacturing power on the globe, and also an important producer of agricultural goods, is a matter to be pondered.

True, the industrial potential had been gradually built up for at least a century and had risen to great heights in 1940–1943 in order to supply the war needs of Hitler's Reich; but the destruction of the physical plant was great by the end of 1945, and even more disruption resulted from the cutting off of the whole German area east of the "iron curtain," except for West Berlin. Never before had the land now in the Federal Republic produced as much as it did by 1965. The size of the expansion achieved is impressive, but the pace is even more so, for though many other countries in Europe and elsewhere have also been growing in the same period, none has sustained as rapid a development, with the probable exception of the European part of the Soviet Union and Japan.

The local supply of raw materials in West Germany is great only for coal, potash salts, and, though to a much lesser degree, for lignite and lowgrade iron ore. In 1965 the mining output reached 135 million tons of coal, 102 million tons of lignite, 2.5 million tons of iron (in metal content of the ore), 2.8 million tons of potash, 6.8 of salt, 7.9 of crude oil, and small quantities of sulphur from pyrites, lead, zinc, natural gas, and barite. Only for potash was West Germany the first world producer, and only for potash and coal did it have exportable surpluses of mineral raw materials. To expand manufacturing the country had to put to the best possible use its main resources, an abundant and not expensive skilled labor force and a remarkable "know-how" in industrial management and commercial organization. The most profitable kinds of manufacturing were therefore those needing the greatest amount of skilled labor; these are categories of goods for which detailed comparative statistics are less available on the international scale than for more massive production of heavier goods. Germany has traditionally been, however, a great producer of the more expensive kinds of delicate machinery, of equipment for a variety of industrial plants, and of precision and measurement instruments. Such types of production in recent decades have flourished in several other countries, for techniques easily cross national boundaries nowadays. Still, Germany may have overemphasized the role of heavy industry and manufacturing for export. The year 1967 did not show any growth.

As a result of war and defeat, after 1945 Germany lost most of her merchant marine, civil aviation, foreign assets, and international patent rights. Some of these were being rebuilt again in recent years, as the Lufthansa airlines reappeared on international routes and the Federal Republic's flag flew over 5.7 million tons of registered merchant ships, surpassing the merchant fleet of Germany in 1938. Still the volume of West Germany's foreign trade made it more dependent on services tendered by other countries. But defeat had also brought in its wake substantial financial advantages to West Germany: for years after 1945 the Germans were disarmed and therefore spared the large expenses of military defense and of research for the costly new types of modern armaments, thus leaving more funds for investment in domestic economic development; also Germany had to be protected by the Western Allies against the threat from the East, and large numbers of Allied troops, mainly American, were stationed on West German soil. The members of the U. S. Armed Forces and their dependents, who resided for periods in West Germany, numbered most of the time half a million people; even though a large part of the supplies of this military population (to which smaller numbers of British and French troops should be added) came from the outside, they were also consumers of some German goods and of many services. The presence of large numbers of Allied forces constituted a very sizable "invisible export" helping the German balance of payments.

Realizing the temporary nature of such resources, and their dependence on a shifting condition of international relations, the West German authorities adopted policies aimed at bolstering their economy in more permanent fashion. On the one hand, they stressed the production at home of basic agricultural and mineral goods; on the other hand, they did not encourage too much the growth of the German's individual consumption; last but not least, they favored measures attracting foreign investments and broadening foreign markets for their products. Economic cooperation with foreign countries developed successfully, largely owing to West Germany's participation in the Common Market and to the flow of American capital invested in Germany.

Endeavors to diversify domestic production outside manufacturing, in order to attain greater self-sufficiency, have been a significant and steady trend in the 1950s. In the mining field, as indicated above, the results were important but limited. Still, the petroleum output is reaching a substantial figure, though the consumption of petroleum products has been rising faster than this output in recent years. More important is the prospect for natural gas production in and near the North Sea. A large network of gas pipelines is being laid through the country. Even if the major deposits are found outside German territory (as was the case in Groningen), the new framework recognized for economic planning must now be that of the EEC, with the probable addition to it later of other West European countries.

In the European arena, West Germany had offered the advantage in the 1950s of combining a skilled, disciplined, expanding, and moderately paid labor force with rather advanced and efficiently managed industrial equipment. This still gives it some advantage in the Common Market, but other countries are catching up in Europe and elsewhere. In 1958, West Germany lost to Japan the third rank among countries producing television receivers; in 1964, the third rank among steel producers; and in 1967, the second rank among producers of motor vehicles. Manufactures scatter around the world and gather in new regions of concentration. Germany had to reorganize its economy after 1946 to rebuild its cities and accommodate millions of German "expellees" who immigrated from areas east of the "iron curtain," where they had lived in territories now assigned to East Germany, Poland, Czechoslovakia, the Soviet Union, etc.; a second stage in reorganization came after 1958, enforcing gradual integration into the Common Market.

The influx of immigrants from the east has been customary in the German realm since the 1860s, when many workers were brought from the Polish provinces to the mines and plants not only of Silesia and Saxony, but also of the Ruhr. The recent migration to West Germany at first caused grave resettlement problems in a country still suffering from the destruction wrought by World War II, but by swelling the number of workers and consumers it subsequently forced on West Germany, and made possible, rapid economic expansion. By 1958, the total number of expellees was estimated at 9.6 million, or 7.6 percent of the total population. Despite this considerable increase, West Germany imported, in 1959–1968, more workers, at least on temporary contracts, mainly from Mediterranean countries (Italy, Spain, Greece, and Turkey). The lowering of tariff barriers within the EEC and the rise of new modern industries in many foreign countries brought about a competitive situation in which West Germany felt the need to straighten out its domestic economy, which was not booming any longer. Automation and rationalization of production on the one hand, a slump on the markets of steel and a slight recession in European consumption during the mid-1960s on the other hand, have now restricted the expansion of the labor force and caused some durable unemployment despite a goodly surplus in the balance of foreign payments.

To better fit itself into the framework of the EEC, West Germany has substantially streamlined its agriculture since 1958. The total employment in agriculture and forestry represented, in 1966, about 10.5

percent of the labor force, and it was still declining in relative as well as absolute figures. The tilled land area in the Federal Republic extended over 19 million acres; meadows and pastures covered about 14.5 million acres. There were enumerated, in 1965, 1,451,000 agricultural holdings, of which half had less than 12 acres each and only 2700 were over 250 acres. The major crops were wheat, barley, rye, oats, potatoes, and sugar beets. The production of grain was still below domestic consumption, and West Germany was a heavy importer of grain. But the livestock economy had been successfully expanded, particularly in the dairy field; at the end of 1965, West Germany had 13.7 million head of cattle (half of which were milch cows), 17.7 million hogs, and some sheep and horses.

Forestry has long been important in Germany; the forest area covers 16 million acres in the Federal Republic. Government supervision controls the management, cutting, and reforestation of the woodland. Despite the high density of the population, agricultural pursuits remain an important part of the economy and more so by volume of production than by number of people engaged in them. The expansion of farm production was achieved largely by means of subsidies offered by the federal government, which are among the highest subsidies in any country of Europe. As the Common Market regulation is being extended to farm products, it may become increasingly difficult, especially for the smaller German farmers, to compete with the French, Dutch, and in some respects Italian farm producers. German agriculture has put a heavy emphasis on dairy products, and there already is a large annual surplus of such products, particularly butter, in the EEC as a whole.

The employment dependent on construction and manufacturing has remained, in the 1960s, rather stabilized around the figure of 9.8 million jobs, that is, about 35 percent of the labor force in 1966. Of this total, construction occupied about 1.5 million, the mechanical industries about 1 million, electrical equipment almost as much, textiles and clothing about 900,000, and transportation equipment (including motor vehicles) about 500,000; the most rapidly expanding sector of manufacturing employment was in the chemical industries, which rose from 500,000 jobs in 1962 to more than 900,000 in 1966. Still, as mining and heavy metallurgy declined in importance, while textiles and heavy machinery did not show much progress, the present slackening of employment in the Ruhr area can be easily understood. There is some outmigration of workers from the Ruhr toward other centers of industrial activity specialized in more expanding sectors, such as exist in the metropolitan areas of Hamburg, Munich, Frankfurt, and Stuttgart. The Ruhr remains by far the largest German conurbation and manufacturing center, but its relative weight within the nation may have passed its apex.

There is, however, little doubt that as European economic integration proceeds, the West German economy will remain very prosperous, although it may soon begin to look like one of the older economic regions of the European system in which the younger centers may have more impressive growth rates. Perhaps Germany has been holding its own domestic demand down too rigidly in order to keep the foreign balance of payments and its currency stronger. In this respect, Germany has followed the same general line of fiscal and monetary policies as most of the other West European countries, and an early resumption of economic expansion in all those countries would of course add impetus to the German economy as well, particularly so because of the large export potential of German industries.

German foreign trade is one of the largest among the countries of the world: exports reached a total value of $20 billion in 1966, while imports rose to $17.2 billion. The imports, consisting chiefly of foodstuffs and industrial raw materials, come mainly from the United States, France, the Netherlands, Italy, Belgium, and the United Kingdom. West Germany's partners in the Common Market now supply it with twice as much as it buys from the United States and the United Kingdom put together. This integration in the EEC is even more striking as one looks at the main markets buying German exports, which rank by importance as follows: France, the Netherlands, the United States, Belgium, Switzerland, Italy, Austria, Sweden, and the United Kingdom. Like most of the West European countries, the Federal Republic has been importing much more from the United States than it has been exporting to it.

However, Germany has had a very favorable balance of payments in dollars, due partly to the general surplus of its trade balance and partly to American expenditures in Germany—a result of keeping troops on German soil or of capital investment in German industries. Financially, the West German economy is very closely linked to the American one. But in recent years it has taken a more European course. It is also trying to develop business relations with the other countries of Western Europe beyond the "iron curtain." A great deal of the planning and present policies of the Federal Republic is dominated by the question of its relations to East Germany. The hope persists that the recent thaw in East-West relations on the European level may lead to a resumption of more normal relations with the section of Germany that remains in the Soviet orbit. The contrast, however, between the two economies and their standards of living has rather widened recently, and the Communist authorities in East Berlin as well as in Moscow are not likely to reopen any gates for more escape of the Eastern Germans to the West.

## THE PROBLEMS OF EAST GERMANY

East Germany counted on an area of 41,000 square miles a population of about 17 million in 1967. Due to migration westward, it was 1.5 million less than it had been in 1950, despite an average rate of natural increase of the population. In 1944–1947 this section of Germany also received a large number of expellees from east of the Oder-Neisse line, and from the Central European countries that used to have large German national minorities (especially Czechoslovakia, Hungary, and Rumania). By 1950 the number of these expellees living in the Soviet zone of occupation was estimated at 4.5 million; they have therefore caused East Germany grave problems of resettlement, employment, and housing—in an economy that did not have the elasticity of West Germany; in the poor province of Mecklenburg alone, the expellees formed over 40 percent of the population in the years 1946–1950.

Under Communist rule, the economy of East Germany has been strictly planned and directed from Moscow. In the postwar period and to this day so great has been the hunger of the Communist countries for almost every kind of farm and industrial products that an area like East Germany, already well developed and industrialized before the war, with a numerous and skilled labor force, represented for their vast empire a considerable asset to be fully utilized. In the former German economy these eastern regions, besides their rich agriculture in the south and their forests in Brandenburg and on the Hercynian ranges, were mainly producers of machinery and chemicals, which were shipped to other parts of the country. The chemical industries had developed on a large scale owing to the local resources of lignite (250 million tons per year, the greatest lignite output of any country in the world), potash (2 million tons), and salt (1.9), and to the presence of specialized skills. The machinery industry used to be fed the iron, steel, and other metals, as well as the coal it needed, from the western areas of Germany, such as the Ruhr and the Saar, but since 1946, it has been fed from the Soviet Union or Poland. A pipeline bringing Soviet oil to Leuna, near Halle, was completed in 1967.

After a first postwar stage of looting any industrial goods and equipment they could obtain for the Soviet Union, the Russian planning authorities found it useful to re-establish in East Germany its traditional specializations in order to supply machinery and chemicals, this time, to the Communist bloc. Thus the output of lignite from the great deposits around Merseburg, Leuna, Bitterfeld, and Skopau was pushed, the powerhouses using the lignite rebuilt and expanded (half of the equipment had been taken away to Russia), and the whole field of chemicals encouraged to develop. Synthetics and fertilizers are quite important:

in 1965 East Germany produced 95,000 tons of synthetic rubber, and large quantities of synthetic textile fibers (112,000 tons of rayon and acetate staple and 19,500 tons of noncellulosic fibers).

Even greater was the effort made to develop the output of machinery. But East Germany produces only small quantities of low-grade coal (2.2 million tons) and iron ore (about 490,000 tons in metal content annually). The over-all planning of the COMECON in Moscow decided to develop in East Germany an iron and steel industry large enough to supply the needs of the machinery industry. In 1936 the area now in East Germany produced only about 8 percent of the German steel (that is, around one million tons). In 1946 this production was down to about 150,000 tons. By 1966 it had climbed up to 4,120,000 tons of crude steel and 2.4 million tons of pig iron and ferroalloys. The rate of growth of this industry, steep from 1948 to 1957, has been slow more recently, for it is an industry difficult to run in highly artificial conditions. The main new establishment was set near Frankfurt-on-the-Oder, at an upstream location where the new town of Stalinstadt has been built. The iron and steel plant of Stalinstadt receives its coke from Polish Silesia and its iron ore from the Krivoï-Rog desposit in the Ukraine. The location on the navigable Oder and near its junction with the Oder-Spree canal was important to transport by water of many of the raw materials and products. The iron ore, however, arrives mainly by rail. Most of the pig iron produced is shipped to the steel mills at Hennigsdorf and Brandenburg, farther west, and nearer to the mechanical industries of Magdeburg, Halle, East Berlin, and Leipzig. Another center of pig iron production has been built at Calbe on the Saale, using the poor quality iron ores of the Harz mountains and coke made from lignite; this almost experimental plant demonstrates the difficulties of keeping the East German iron and steel industry going on a large scale without the normal connections that could bring to it the necessary supplies.

The mechanical industries are working as fully as the supply of metals and skilled labor permits. The latter has recently become more deficient. As the major German firms moved from East to West Germany, and with the boom the mechanical industry has been undergoing there, technicians know that they can find easy employment in much better conditions by moving to West Germany. Many did so, and East Germany has been desperately trying to accelerate its automation in order to compensate for the flight of qualified manpower.

Another problem has been the lack of easy maritime linkages with the outside. The small ports on the Baltic coast of East Germany were not adequately equipped for a whole country's foreign trade. In 1965 the overseas trade of East Germany amounted to 8.8 million tons, most of which went through its own small ports, that is, Wismar, Rostock, Stralsund; but much had to transit through Hamburg and the now Polish port of Szczecin. To give this separate economy more autonomy, and its own merchant marine, Rostock was chosen to become the main port. On the estuary of the Warnow River, this old Hanseatic city had shrunk in recent centuries before the winning competition of Stettin, Lübeck, and Hamburg; it is now being revived. At the former naval base of Warnemünde, its advanced speed port, a large shipyard has been started, with related engineering plants, to build a new East German merchant marine (it had one million registered gross tons in 1966) and also more ships for the Soviet Union, from whom the steel is imported. A fishing port and processing plant have been built at Rostock's suburb of Marienehe. Rostock is the city in the north of East Germany which has grown the most in the 1950s; the plan foresaw there a city of 200,000 by 1965, and it reached 184,000, with a port handling a traffic of 6 million tons.

To fulfill their industrial goals the Communist authorities have to drain to the cities all the available manpower, and critical shortages of personnel have therefore developed in farming. Increased mechanization of agriculture is indicated by the rise in the number of farm tractors (60,300 in 1959) and a high consumption of chemical fertilizer (46 percent higher in 1959 than in 1951). But even on the rich soils of East Germany socialized agriculture has not been able to achieve the kind of expansion recently observed in West Germany and Western Europe in general. The yields of the state farms showed better averages than those of the cooperative farms, but stayed below those of individual private farms. The cattle density per acre of farmland was higher in East Germany than in any of the Communist countries in Europe, and it seemed to be mainly due to the higher share allowed to individual farms in the total agricultural output. There were 4.7 million head of cattle in 1965, 8.8 million hogs, and 2 million sheep. To obtain deliveries, the authorities had to increase substantially the prices paid to producers.

On the whole, of course, East Germany, with its relatively high population density and urbanization, is a food importer, especially of grain, meat, fruits, and vetetables; it exports some sugar, as here, too, the sugar beet crop has been expanded. The production of grains has been about stable in recent years (about 1.8 million tons of wheat, 1.9 of rye, 1.6 of barley, 0.8 of oats). No clear progress can be observed through the 1960s, except for the sugar beets (5.8 million tons in 1965). In the case of farming, it is the socialist system of control rather than the shortage of personnel that seems to be responsible for the failure of production to grow. A trade agreement concluded in 1959 ensures that at least 46 percent of the foreign trade is transacted with the USSR and over 76 percent with all the Socialist bloc.

There is little doubt that East Germany's great economic problems, arising from its recent evolution, demonstrate how little adaptability Communist rule has brought it. The contrast with West Germany is the contrast between the two economic and social systems that have divided Europe between them. The political differences have also played their part. East Germany certainly wishes for reunification of the whole German area at least as much as West Germany; but on this score the prospects remain as yet rather dim.

The monumental rebuilding of Warsaw, which was terribly destroyed in World War II. In the center the skyscraper is the House of Culture, which is very reminiscent of the main building of Moscow University. Notice the vast squares and open spaces, the endeavor to create large perspectives. *(Geographical Institute, National Academy of Sciences, Poland)*

# 17

## Poland and Czechoslovakia: Link and Buffer

No part of Central Europe shows better the instability of boundaries and national units, characteristic of the whole area, than the two countries that form a Slavic wedge driven westward into the heart of Europe. Poland and Czechoslovakia both developed out of the early medieval advance of Slavic peoples into Europe, when they occupied all the territory east of the Elbe and north of the Danube. Later in the Middle Ages, after the eleventh century, the Germanic peoples again pushed them back eastward from three main centers of operation: the Teutonic knights had their bases on the Baltic shores and in the lower basin of the Pregel and Niemen rivers; Brandenburg arose in the midst of the Great Plain; the *Ostmark*, later *Österreich* (the Eastern Reich) or Austria, was created on the Danube. From these three districts the Germans fought for the domination of the eastern countries. But two areas remained stubbornly Slavic and did not permit themselves to be assimilated by the German cultural or political organization: in the midst of the Great Plain, the Poles occupied the basin of the Vistula River between Brandenburg and the Teutonic fortresses; in the hilly Hercynian area, between Brandenburg and Saxony to the north and Austria to the south, the Czechs held Bohemia.

While the eastern Slavs or Russians were being weakened by the invasions of the Mongolian hordes who destroyed the Dnieper state, Poland and Bohemia knew a period of greatness. For a time at the end of the Middle Ages, the kingdom of Poland extended across the continent from the Baltic to the Black Sea shores, only to recede rapidly until it disappeared entirely in the eighteenth-century partitions. The kingdom of Bohemia was an important participant on the European scene until the Czechs were utterly defeated in 1620 at the Battle of the White Mountain and submitted to Austria. After eclipses of 150 and 300 years both nations acquired independence again with the defeat of the German and Austrian empires in 1918. Poland and Czechoslovakia, reborn, managed to expand substantially to the east: the Czechs formed a unified country with the Slovaks and the small Carpatho-Russian group, extending along an east-west mountainous axis; the Poles then defeated the Red Army in a brief campaign which gave them a large section of previously Russian territory to the east.

The military expansion of Nazi Germany eastward started with the occupation of Bohemia in February 1939, and World War II opened on September 1, 1939 with the German invasion of Poland. Both countries were again divided up between their neighbors and ceased to exist independently but for governments-in-exile that resided in London. In 1945 both countries regained their national status. Czechoslovakia obtained the same boundaries as in 1919 but lost its easternmost sub-Carpathian province, which was annexed to the Soviet Union by the Treaty of Moscow of July 29, 1945. Poland did not regain the Russian territories to the east but was compensated with some German territories to the north and to the west. The two countries have now a long common frontier following the crests of the Carpathians and the Sudeten range, and both have been brought under tight Soviet control.

The destinies of these two Slavic countries thus seem to parallel each other, but relations between them have not always been good. At the time of the weakening of Czechoslovakia by the Munich Agreement of 1938, Poland hastened to increase its territory in the vicinity of Teschen in Silesia. The peoples of the two nations are very different indeed. The Poles are mainly oriented toward the Baltic and have always been a more rural nation. The Czechs have older links with Western Europe: in the thirteenth century Bohemian kings studied at the University of Paris; later Bohemia participated actively in the commercial civilization and the industrialization of the Hercynian and Alpine belt of Europe— it used to be referred to as the westernmost province of the Austrian empire. Poland was mainly a buffer in the broad open plain; Bohemia, with its partner of Slovakia, used to be a link between east and west.

THE NEW POLAND

According to the decisions of the Allies at Yalta and Potsdam, the eastern boundary of Poland is the famous *Curzon Line* (suggested by Lord Curzon in 1918 as the limit of the territory populated with a majority of

Poles), and its provisional western boundary is the Oder-Neisse line, leaving to the Slavic country Pomerania (with the port of Stettin or Szczecin) and the whole of Silesia. This area has 121,130 square miles and is one fifth smaller than the prewar territory. Its population, by 1967, numbered 32 million people; this figure is hardly comparable with the 35 million inhabitants of the 1939 area. The German occupation was a rough administration for Poland: the numbers of the population were reduced, especially through the extermination of the Jews (there were over 3 million in prewar Poland) and the slave-labor practices applied to the Poles. Then with the change in territory most of the Poles living east of the Curzon Line were repatriated to the new area and settled mainly in the provinces taken from Germany; Germans in these territories were expelled west of the Oder-Neisse line. These transfers of populations were made in order to avoid constant national minority claims and difficulties. They meant a great many miseries for the people involved, but they may prepare a less troubled future for a more homogeneous people, if the geographical position allows it.

As it now appears on the map, Poland has a well-rounded shape. As indicated by the general direction of the main streams draining it, the Vistula and the Oder, it is a vast plain, gently sloping toward the northwest from the Carpathians to the Baltic shores. In the south the Hercynian zone melts with the sub-Carpathian plateau providing a slightly more animated topography; north of 52° latitude, the plain would be perfectly flat but for the hills erected by the morainic accumulation of the last glaciation. Here in the territory which was formerly East Prussia, the moraines reached their highest development, piling up to more than 800 feet in places—around Gdańsk (formerly Danzig) the layers deposited by the glaciers are more than 450 feet thick. The drainage of this area has been difficult, and it is not yet quite dried up: many lakes and swamps dot the plain, especially eastward in the swampy district of the Mazurian Lakes.

In this northern and low section of the plain, the climate is severe, although the Baltic is near by. The average temperature of January is below 30° even on the coast; in the interior the snow lies on the ground for seventy to eighty days every winter. A thick forest of coniferous trees covers the land: pines on the sandy soils, spruce on the more humid clay. The spruce woods have been largely cleared, and the boulder clay has been tilled and to some extent reclaimed by the German settlers in recent centuries. It still is a land of poor agriculture and scattered occupation, with large holdings owned by absentee proprietors until World War II. Pomerania and East Prussia were the classic lands of the Junkers who supplied a large proportion of the officers in the German armies. The lands were cultivated to produce potatoes, rye, and hay, and many herds of cattle were raised on them; the pine woods were also systematically

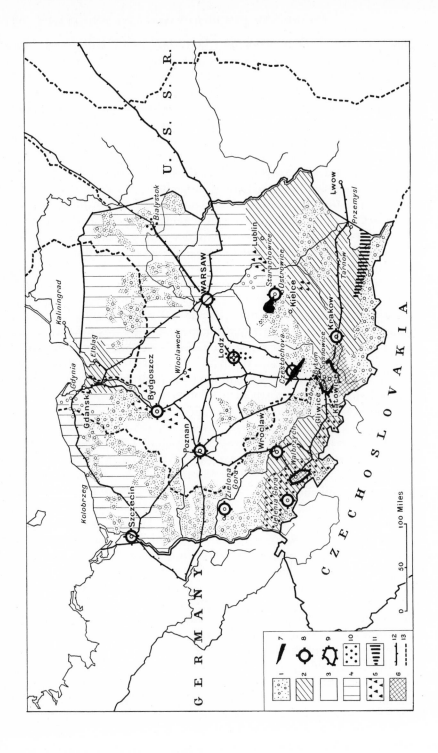

U. S. S. R.

GERMANY

CZECHOSLOVAKIA

Kaliningrad
Gdynia
Gdansk
Elblag
Kolobrzeg
Szczecin
Poznan
Bydgoszcz
Wloclaweck
Bialystok
WARSAW
Lublin
Lodz
Zielona Gora
Walbrzych
Jelenia Gora
Wroclaw
Czestochova
Gliwice
Zabrze
Bytom
Sosnowice
Katowice
Kielce
Starachowice
Ostrowiec
Krakow
Tarnow
Lwow
Przemysl

0    50    100 Miles

1  2  3  4  5  6  7  8  9  10  11  12  13

exploited and brought an appreciable amount of timber. This was a difficult land, and changing hands has meant some temporary setbacks in maintenance.

The seashore always attracted most of the towns and urban activities. Poland often fought for an exit to the sea. Gdańsk, having become the Hanseatic city of Danzig, was strongly Germanized; as it guarded the entrance to the Vistula, in 1919 it was made a "free city," independent of both Germany and Poland. But the dispute over it continued, and Poland built near by its own national port of Gdynia, linked by rail to the hinterland. Now this low, sandy coast, with its hooks or spits of sand enclosing lagoons (or *Haffen* in German) slowly being silted by rivers, has several important towns: on the estuary of the Oder, Szczecin (315,000 in 1966), the former German city of Stettin, was badly destroyed in World War II and had to be rebuilt; such is also the case of Gdańsk, built near the mouth of the Vistula (or Wisla), the population of which was 324,000 in 1966; finally, there is Gdynia (165,000), built north of Gdańsk in the 1920s to give to the then almost landlocked Poland its own seaport. In its present borders Poland has a wide Baltic seaboard and two important maritime gates. Gdańsk is now the main port, rebuilt and repopulated since 1946, coordinated with its former rival and now partner, Gdynia. The latter has specialized in passenger and long distance speed traffic; most of the scheduled lines call there, while Gdańsk is the industrial port, with large food processing and timber working industries, and it ships out most of the Silesian coal that makes up about one third of the total value of Polish exports. The nearby seaside resort of Sopot, in summer, attracts crowds of tourists from abroad. Gdynia has regular lines linking it to the Americas as well as to Shanghai and Haiphong in the Far East. Szczecin, also rebuilt and resettled after the war, drains the basin of the Oder River, on which navigability has been improved. Besides the Polish traffic in port, a special section handles the Czechoslovak transit trade, and some trade from or to East Germany also goes through this port, which builds ships, makes cement, machinery, and clothing, and works wood. This

---

*(Opposite)* Economic map of Poland. Key: 1, main forested areas (chiefly on sandy soils); 2, black soil belt of intensive farming with predominance of wheat; 3, areas of poorer agriculture with predominance of rye and potatoes; 4, predominance of meadows and moors; 5, main areas of sugar-beet cultivation; 6, Silesian coal basin; 7, iron-ore deposits; 8, major industrial centers; 9, the two main concentrations of manufactures (both in the Silesian region); 10, textile industries; 11, petroleum-bearing area; 12, main railways; 13, boundaries of Poland between the two world wars (as of 1924–1939). Notice the concentration of resources in the south and west of present-day Poland.

Baltic coast finds at her back the poor country of the morainic heights, the main resource of which is forestry.

Farther south, in the central part of Poland, the soil is somewhat drier, the drainage is better organized, and an early settlement made for denser populations. In the midst of this area the capital of Poland was a center from which colonization was directed actively. Here are more big villages and small holdings. Wheat and sugar beets are added to rye and potatoes. Some large cities have developed: Bydgoszcz (255,000) and Toruń (110,000) stand at the point of contact with the higher moraines and work the timber floated down the rivers and canals; Poznan (436,000) is a more important center of industries (mills, breweries, ceramics, pottery, agricultural machinery). The city has long been the capital of the western section of Poland, annexed to Germany in the nineteenth century. Its industries are varied and oriented toward the finishing of consumer goods, for the main local resource—besides abundant and relatively skilled manpower—is the proximity to rich lignite deposits, a source of energy and a raw material for the production of chemicals.

The two largest cities of Poland are situated in the most central district of the country, amid the richest soils: Warsaw and Lodz have had a very rapid development for half a century, largely owing to an active Jewish population which formed about one third of the cities' population in the 1930s. The Jewish communities were almost completely exterminated by the Nazis under the German occupation in the period 1939–1944. Both cities suffered greatly from bombing and fighting, and Warsaw, the historic and political capital of Poland, was rebuilt according to a monumental plan fitted to the traditions of the beautiful and elegant city. The new plan gives special emphasis to open spaces within the central district of the city and to monumental buildings for mass culture and recreation, considerations which the Communist dominated regime claims to give priority to (see maps p. 634 and photographs pp. 626 and 633). The suburbs have sprawled more widely in starlike fashion, and a variety of industries have been rebuilt or established anew; to the older specializations in machinery, ceramics, and clothing have been added the manufacture of electrical apparatus, the paper and printing trades, and a variety of food processing plants. In 1939, Warsaw had 1.2 million inhabitants; in 1946 there were only 500,000 in the city proper; in 1966 1.2 million again, but more than 1.6 million in the metropolitan area.

Lodz, which had not been destroyed by the war, also saw its population reduced from 670,000 in 1939 to 497,000 in 1946 to rise to 750,000 by 1966; but the metropolitan area, which includes a whole constellation of industrial satellite towns, reaches a total of about 900,000. Lodz is the

A major thoroughfare in the rebuilt Polish capital. (*Geographical Institute, National Academy of Sciences, Poland*)

Rural Poland. Notice the importance of horse traction (some 2.5 million horses in 1965, with 77 inhabitants per motor vehicle). The long wagons and simple harnesses are typical of Slavic countries. (*Polish Research and Information Service, New York*)

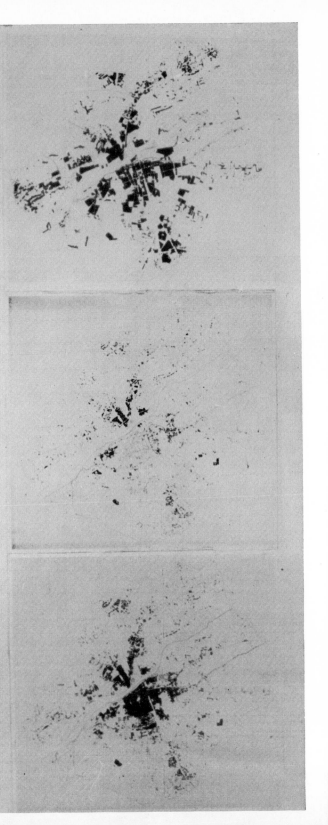

WARSZAWA W LATACH

1939     1945     1955

"Polish Manchester," the largest textile center of the country, now concentrating about two thirds of Poland's cotton manufacturing and one third of its woolen industry. It is a creation of the nineteenth century, and developed quickly at first for the large Russian market. Further developed by Poland between the two World Wars, it also began manufacturing electrical machinery and leatherware. After 1946 a good part of its production was again destined to the Russian market. Despite its growth, Lodz remains basically an industrial city, with many outdated manufacturing plants, its main buildings reminiscent of Victorian-style capitalism, but also a lively university and planning for an expanding future; still in many ways a distant satellite of Warsaw, where the cultural life continues to be concentrated. The planned economy of recent years has caused the growth of the administrative function and the centralization of authority in the national capital.

The southern part of Poland is the highest in elevation and the richest from all standpoints. Here Poland gets a chance to form the basis of a strong and well-balanced economy. The boundary follows the crests of forested mountains: an Alpine range (the Carpathians) and a Hercynian-raised block (the Sudeten). At the foot of these mountains stretches a sub-Hercynian area through which still crop up a few small Hercynian blocks, such as the ridges of Lysa Gora near Kielce. This sub-Hercynian belt has rich, well-drained, loamy soils with a rainfall of about 30 inches annually. Such is the country of "Little Poland" around Kraków (Cracow) and the newly acquired plain of Silesia around Wroclaw (Breslau). Sugar beets, wheat, rye, and potatoes are the chief crops. On either side of the former German-Polish boundary the rural system was very similar, with rather large holdings and a not-too-modern agriculture. Silesia was the last part of Germany to mechanize its agriculture, for Polish manpower was abundant, cheap, and administered almost like serfs by the German management of the large farms. In the 1930s it almost seemed as though the Polish side was progressing better in agricultural practice. Now equalization has been achieved. But most of the manpower is not being utilized on the land; the industrial development is paramount.

This industrial rise occurs mainly in the coalfield area of Silesia. The two main cities are at some distance from it: Kraków (530,000 people), a

---

*(Opposite)* The three stages in the recent history of Warsaw: the city's profile before the destruction of World War II in 1939 (the blackened regions indicate built-up areas); then in 1945, what was left standing and usable of the former capital; and the proudly rebuilt city and capital as it stood in 1955 when reconstruction, though not quite completed, was well advanced, especially in the central part (see photos pp. 626 and 633). *(Geographical Institute, National Academy of Sciences, Poland)*

great historic center, is probably the most intellectual and most Western city of Poland, although its elite was decimated by the German occupation. It has food and mechanical industries and is preparing for the role of regional capital that may become essential. Around the old historical city, still dominated by the royal castle atop a hill, a new conurbation is forming, the main element of which (now included in the municipal limits of Kraków) is the new huge industrial suburb of Nowa Huta centered on a large iron and steel plant around which mechanical industries are being expanded. Thus Kraków has been tied more closely to the vast industrial complex developing on the coalfield to its west.

In Upper Silesia, at the contact of the sub-Hercynian and Alpine zones, one of the richest coal deposits of Europe has most of its total extension now in Polish territory. This field was divided among Russia, Prussia, and Austria in the nineteenth century, among Poland, Germany, and Czechoslovakia after 1919, and is now almost entirely in Poland, though a section is beyond the Czech border. Most of the pits are less then 1000 feet deep, and extraction is easy. True, not all of the coal extracted is of the best quality and only part consists of good coking coal. But the reserves are tremendous, probably more important than those of the Ruhr, and the quality would be better if deeper layers were tapped. The mines were equipped by large investments of foreign capital, partly French and partly British. The same area also offers zinc and lead ores and, at the very foot of the mountains, a string of small oilfields. Some iron ore is extracted, especially in the escarpment of Częstochowa. Natural gas is exploited for heating the cities or plants and is processed into gasoline, with 400,000 tons of crude oil and 1380 million cubic meters of gas being produced in 1966 chiefly around Jaslo. The output of coal reached 122 million tons in 1966, still rising while it was now decreasing in the Western countries.

A large industrial development has sprung up on the coal, utilizing the other available resources. Large-scale metallurgy and chemical industries have developed, financed by French, German, and American capital. The Polish government from the beginning took some direct interest in the plants. Thus a large industrial district that strives to become a complete organism with a variety of activities has developed in Upper Silesia and has actively pushed ahead since 1946. And a "black country" scenery surrounds the chief centers of mining and manufacturing: Katowice, Królewska Huta, Myslowice, Sosnowiec, Chorzów, Zabrze (formerly Hindenburg), Gliwice (Gleiwitz), and Bytom (Beuthen). Katowice, with 288,000 people, called for a while Stalinogrod, has become the main center of the industrial district and the main rail hub, from which a direct railway (completed in 1938 with the help of a French loan) conveys the coal and industrial exports toward the port of Gdynia

A coal-mining center in Lower Silesia. (*Polish Research and Information Service, New York*)

A state railway car factory at Wroclaw. (*Polish Research and Information Service, New York*)

Gdańsk. The main hindrance to a larger development of Upper Silesia is still its lack of good means of transportation, especially by water. It is a continental area, and it looks toward its continental neighbors the Czechs for a partnership that may help to build up an impressive industrial area in a region where recently a backward rural life reigned. The compactly urbanized district of Upper Silesia agglomerates some 2 million people.

Practically the whole of Silesia is now Polish territory; since 1945 Lower Silesia has been severed from Germany and given to Poland. The coalfield and industrial basin of Upper Silesia is therefore united with the industrial area that developed in the nineteenth century on the Lower Silesian coalfield and around the great commercial city of Breslau, now Wroclaw, largely with labor from Poland. Once more rebuilt and resettled with a purely Polish population, Wroclaw is developing again, now as a manufacturing city. It once was the chief center of German trade and penetration eastward in this sub-Hercynian plain; it was famous for its banks and fairs, its market of furs, skins, and timber. From 630,000 inhabitants in 1939, its population fell to 171,000 in 1946, when the Germans were expelled, then reached 480,000 by 1966. Its industries are varied: Wroclaw is the second most important Polish textile center (after Łódź), working wool rather than cotton, and one of the main centers of engineering and heavy mechanical production.

It indeed seems that almost all the new Poland's industries have been concentrated in the western half of the country, and chiefly in the southwestern quarter. The successive Six-Year and Five-Year Plans of the Communist government have also attempted to establish more industries to the north and east. The lignite deposits around Poznan and the general maritime development of the Baltic ports should help the move northwards. Toward the east a prewar scheme has been actively revived to build up a "Central Industrial District" around the confluence of the Vistula and San rivers, taking advantage of water transportation and of a position about halfway between Kraków and Warsaw. North of Kielce (100,000) a new industrial area has arisen specializing in engineering and chemicals (particularly munitions) in such growing towns as Starachowice (40,000) and Ostrowiec (40,000); a steel mill has been built at Stalowa Wola. However, still very little industry is found east of the Vistula. The largest city there is Lublin (200,000), the regional capital of the southeastern quarter, amid relatively rich agricultural land. In the northeast, Bialystok (138,000) has a similar regional role but in much poorer farming area, where the forests occupy most of the land.

There is a striking contrast between the eastern and western sections of Poland. As a general rule, east of the Vistula the land is poorer, less developed, more rural, forested; the southeast is not as poor, in terms of quality of soils, as is the sandy, morainic northeast, but the southeast is more densely settled, and this density of rural population on small farms and with little new resources that can be developed in the area causes the southeast to be the region of gravest concern to the planners in Warsaw. In the *voyevodstvo* (district) of Lublin, the density reaches 200 inhabitants per square mile, which is almost equal to the density of the *voyevodstvo* of Warsaw; but the latter encompasses a conurbation of 1.6 million, grouping two thirds of the population, while the agglomeration of Lublin accounts for only 250,000, or just one eighth of the district's total. The situation is even worse farther to the southeast, in the district of Rzeszow-Przemysl, where the average density of population approaches 250 to the square mile.

The eastern regions are thus the lagging parts of Poland. The great effort put in the reconstruction and rehabilitation of Warsaw, Gdańsk, Poznan, Wroclaw, etc., and the input in the development of Silesia and the Baltic seaports, all benefited mainly the western half of Poland. The eastern regions, having their back to a poor section of the Soviet Union, will remain a serious problem: some of their population must be moved west, and at the same time from the farms to urban activities, for which they are not prepared. There are many difficult regional problems in this country, besides its national economic and social planning.

## THE PROBLEMS OF A REJUVENATED POLISH ECONOMY

The Polish economy has evolved rapidly since World War II. It has done so under the worst possible auspices: the country was thoroughly devastated in the war; the nation was left numerically reduced, its territory shifted between new borders, its political and economic status that of a vassal of the Soviet Union. The German occupation on the one hand and the Soviet Communist conquest on the other had largely beheaded the Polish people, not only quantitatively but also qualitatively, by destroying many of the élite and of the skilled population. One of the worst problems still plaguing the Polish economy and society by 1960 was the lack of a skilled labor force. Immediately after 1945, things improved slightly because of the return to Poland of relatively large numbers (several tens of thousands) of skilled Polish workers who had lived and worked in France in the 1930s and who came back to help rebuild a new and better Poland. Still, the situation remains difficult to this day; the 1960 census showed considerable progress, for instance, in the Polish nationwide fight against illiteracy: the complete illiterate represented then only 2.7 percent of the population over seven years of age, but the percentage rose to 83.8 percent in the population aged fifty years and over.

The building up of a large-scale modern economy in a not-too-advanced and largely rural country is always difficult and lengthy. The Polish nation, to be sure, has long wished to achieve just such a reconversion. To do this under Russian auspices and Communist rule brought upon the Poles a hard and paradoxical pressure: for this is a devoutly Roman Catholic nation and a people whose history for the last 200 years has been largely a long struggle against Russian domination. The Poles dislike Russian rule as much as German rule; the Russians know it, and while they sponsor the industrialization of Poland, they do not make it easy for the Poles. Still, in the last twenty years considerable progress has been achieved in training the manpower, in the education of the mass of the younger generation, and in the expansion of industry and a variety of commercial services. This process did not proceed without arousing constant resistance and new difficulties. Poland is still largely a rural, agricultural society, but it is evolving. In 1950, almost half of the total labor force was employed in agriculture and forestry; in 1960, the percentage had dropped to about 40, and, by 1967, was estimated to be around 20 percent. The urban population meanwhile rose from 39 percent of the total population in 1950 to 50 percent in 1966. Also, one third of the urban population was now concentrated in cities of more than 200,000 inhabitants each, meaning big-city modes of life. The process of urbanization is now coming to cause a crisis of the small towns. These are not fitted for the large-scale industry that Polish planning is endeavoring to develop. The small-size enterprises in those towns are usually noncompetitive and cannot expect help from a centralized and socialized planning system. Only administrative centers of some size or small cities attracting tourists (either on the seaside or for winter sports in the Carpathian Mountains) have good future prospects. Modernization brings about a rapid concentration of population and economic activities in a small number of selected spots.

Agriculture has also been affected, but in a special way. At first most of the land was collectivized according to Communist theory, but met with ruinous passive resistance from the peasants. Softer measures introduced in the 1950s let the majority of the 50 million acres of agricultural land remain in private hands (about 85 percent of this total by 1965). About 7 million acres are the property of the state and cultivated by 6500 state farms. A new approach to collectivization is being tried by organizing "agricultural groups" and "rural housewives groups" to obtain some cooperative action by the small farmer. The basic difficulty of present farm policies in Poland is that the average size of the farm in private hands is still very small. In 1960, the farm population totaled 10 million, of whom 8.2 million lived and worked on private farms of less than 25 acres each. The small farms could not support the cost of modern equipment and tilling methods in terms of fertilization, seed selection, etc. To improve the productivity of the land, agricultural policy was faced with the need of heavily subsidizing the small private farmer or removing him from the land to help the formation of large holdings that would still remain in private hands. Both were against the principles of a socialist economy, and one is thus faced with the difficulty built into the Communist system of improving farm output. And this contrasts with the high rate of growth achieved by the European countries west of the "iron curtain," which are not afraid of large-scale agricultural capitalism.

The main crops in order of importance in the area they cover are rye (about 8 million tons a year), potatoes, wheat (about 3 million tons), oats (about 2.5 million tons, as horses are still an essential part of rural transport), barley, sugar beets, etc. An attempt to grow corn has been abandoned. The livestock seems to be stabilized around 10 million head of cattle, 13 million pigs, 3 million sheep, and 2.6 million horses. Agriculture remains the poor relation of the five-year plans. These have systematically emphasized industrial and urban growth.

The forests are an important part of the Polish economy, bridging the gap between farming and industry. They cover 20 million acres (see map, p. 644) and supply a variety of resources, from firewood for the poor rural people to raw materials for large-scale industry and export; the forests are even becoming a special source of foreign exchange: they still are replete with wildlife, including relatively large game, and this attracts a category of tourists from the West, who like to go hunting. Thus, an invisible export develops besides the traditional more concrete exports from the Polish farms and forests: timber, flax, sugar, and the world-famous Polish ham.

In the field of industrialization, the results achieved twenty years after the devastation of the war are quite impressive. The most precious asset of Poland in this area is the Silesian coal. In the lean postwar years of 1946–1950, Poland was the only European country ready to export sizable amounts of coal. Before the war the coalfields now in Poland totaled an output of 66 million tons, kept down for lack of markets. In 1946 about 48 million tons were mined, and in 1948, 70 million. The coal output kept growing every year, though at a slower pace: 84 million in 1952, 95 in 1956, 122 in 1966. Every year since the war coal has been the main item on the export list (21 million tons exported in 1965). Foreign markets, however, have been shrinking west of the "iron curtain." Through Gdańsk, Polish shipments still reach the Scandinavian countries, and some go much farther; but the glut of coal on the international markets of the West in recent years has restricted Polish prospects. There still remain important and increasing needs to be satisfied among its neighbors in Europe under the same rule. For its own production of energy, Poland also mines lignite (20 million tons in 1965, of which one fourth was exported).

The other mineral resources are rather scant: iron ore (800,000 tons in metal content), small quantities of lead, zinc, nickel, copper, and magnesium, and large quantities of salt (2.2 million tons). Nevertheless, the industrial development of such a country has been impressive: 3.7 million people are now employed in manufacturing; the textile industries consume 150,000 tons of cotton and over 20,000 tons of wool; the output of electric energy reached 48 billion kwhr. in 1966, fivefold the 1950 figure; the iron and steel industry produced 5.8 million tons of pig iron and ferroalloys and 9.8 of crude steel, for which much of the iron ore must be imported—largely from the Ukraine. The engineering industries, especially heavy machinery, are a specialty of Poland and supply substantial exports of railroad rolling stock. Poland also built 30,000 passenger cars and 37,000 commercial vehicles, a very small output for a country of this size.

Although the cities have been rebuilt and the industries expanded, Poland still maintains an average individual consumption that is quite low in comparison with other European countries, especially those around the Baltic. If in the last twenty years the Communist rule has achieved part of their economic plans, the country still has a long way to go before achieving full prosperity. Its living conditions were so wretched through the 1940s, however, that the 1960s marked undeniable progress.

The foreign trade of Poland testifies to the political orbit in which the country must revolve. The most active commercial relations are with the Soviet Union, East Germany, Czechoslovakia, the United Kingdom, West Germany and Hungary. Curiously, for a nation which experiences just the first steps of massive industrialization, most of the exports besides coal and sugar are finished industrial products including railway rolling stock, cement, and ships. Poland is becoming a maritime power with a merchant marine of 1.2 million tons. This association means, of course, paradoxically enough, a social and economic evolution which could be termed a "Westernization" of the Polish structure. It would mean bringing Poland closer to the Western countries' pattern of an industrialized economy and an intensive agriculture with machinery. In one way, the rapid urbanization of Poland should also help solve its difficult rural population problem. This remains the heaviest burden the rejuvenated Polish economy has inherited from the past, and is a characteristic common to all the countries with a backward, underdeveloped recent history. In view of its means at the time, Poland had a surplus population even after the terrible bleeding of the war. Now, with some help from the West, despite its Eastern appurtenance, the

Polish nation works hard at raising the quality of its people by mass education and technical training, instead of losing them through emigration, the main outlet for population pressure in the past.

## THE CZECHOSLOVAK STATE

As its name suggests, the republic of Czechoslovakia was born in 1918, with the breakdown of the Austro-Hungarian Empire, of the union of two closely related Slavic peoples, the Czechs and the Slovaks. Born again after the ordeal of 1938–1945, liberated from German and Hungarian domination by the armies of the Soviet Union and the United States (though its sub-Carpathian Ukrainian section was amputated), the Czechoslovak state stretches from west to east — from Bavaria to the Ukraine. But it is not a "buffer" in one sense, for it is certainly not a physical transition. While Poland has a shifting and vague boundary in the midst of the flat, almost amorphous Great Plain, the Czechoslovak state is deeply rooted in a mountainous area which has a very clearly defined individuality in the topography and in the strategy of European settlement and traffic. The Czechs occupy the interior of the Bohemian Square, a quadrangular system of Hercynian massives with a depressed basin in the center; the Slovaks occupy the western Carpathians and, especially, an almost round system of ranges in the center of which rise the Tatra Mountains. Czechoslovakia is thus a double stronghold: the western fortress being of Hercynian structure, more massive but with ample living space inside, and the eastern bastion being a high dungeon surrounded by lower lands. Between the two a depressed corridor, populated mainly by Czechs, opens a road through the mountainous state and constitutes one of the main communication arteries of Central Europe.

The strategic importance of this fortress country is obvious when one looks at the map. There is another old saying which goes "He who holds Bohemia commands Europe." Past history does not always bear it out, but cases of decisive events that relate to the area do abound: the victory of Austerlitz in the Moravian corridor, in 1804, gave to Napoleon the command of Central Europe, and the Munich Agreement of 1938, dismantling the Bohemian stronghold in Germany's favor, opened the way to the expansion of Hitler's empire over most of Europe. Slovakia complements well the Bohemian position: it covers the weaker, Moravian side of it and insures a territorial continuity between the advanced Slavic post in Bohemia and the predominantly Slavic Eastern Europe.

Thus the queer layout of Czechoslovakia on the map of Europe means a great deal. Here is a fortress country, surrounded by peoples who did not wish it well and who were much stronger and very different: Ger-

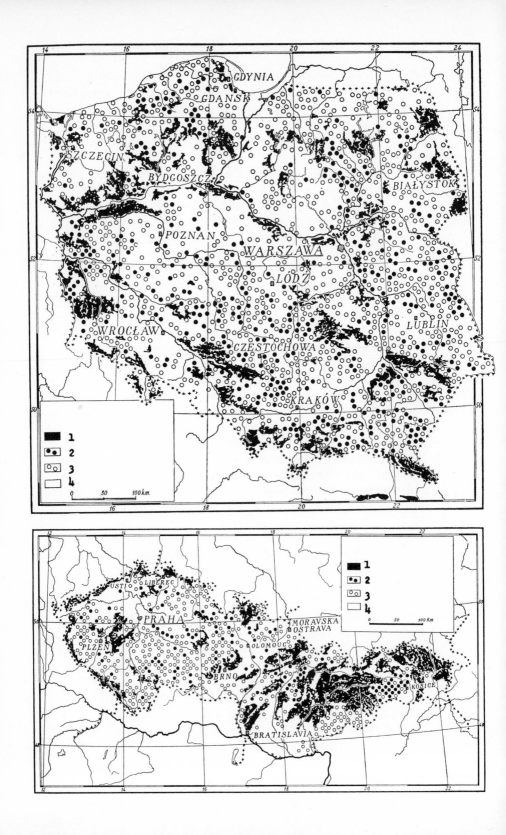

mans, Austro-Hungarians, Russians, and even Poles, with the Turks in the background for several centuries. In their mountains the Czechs and the Slovaks were able on the whole to preserve their personality and moral independence. They regained a genuine political independence under the leadership of one of the greatest personalities of this century in Europe, Professor Thomas Masaryk, president of the Czechoslovak republic from 1918 to 1935, and the true father of Czechoslovakia. Indeed, he conceived the role of his country as that of a link between the West and East in Europe: Slavic by race but Western by culture, united historically with both Russia and France, neither of which had ever dominated it directly up to that time. The political constellation of the powers formed out of the breaking up of the Austro-Hungarian Empire in 1918 was called the Little Entente, and grouped together Yugoslavia, Rumania, and Czechoslovakia, the latter being the essential keystone. In a way, the economy of Czechoslovakia also shows a combination of Eastern and Western elements: Slovakia is a more rural and mountainous province; Bohemia is a more industrialized and urbanized one. There was in Thomas Masaryk's philosophy a great devotion to general moral principles and to the idea of serving the unity and peace of Europe: he lived and taught in the United States for a part of his life and believed in the possibility of peaceful cohabitation of free peoples, however different they might be. After his death came the great crisis of Czechoslovakia, and World War II caused considerable changes.

Although Czechoslovakia kept almost all of its territory of the prewar period, it has been faced with a grave problem of resettlement. Within the boundaries of the state, especially in Bohemia, there was a considerable German minority. The Bohemian Square has been besieged by German settlement, which long ago gained predominance on the outward slopes of the three main ridges—Bohemian Forest, Erz Gebirge, and Sudeten. Some infiltration started early inside the square, with German nuclei of settlement being formed on the inner slopes of the peripheral ridges and with strong German elements established in the cities of Bohemia. It was an important element, and one which contributed to the commercial and industrial development of the area; but this was not an isolated minority: it was the advanced spearhead of the massive German push against the Slavs. The political problem was measured by statistics and by the pressure again rising from the Reich: the

---

*(Opposite)* Distribution of forests in Poland *(above)* and Czechoslovakia *(below)*. Key to scale: 1, main forested areas; 2, areas with much scattered woodland; 3, areas with little woodland; 4, areas without forests. (After maps published in *Le Monde Forestier*, vol. 1, *L'Europe et l'U.R.S.S.*, by the U.N. Food and Agriculture Organization, Rome, 1957)

The Tatra Range, with high, bold peaks and on the gentler slopes forests of conifers. In the foreground is a resort. (*Czechoslovak Consulate General*)

census of 1930 recorded a total population of 14 million on the present territory, of which 9.7 million were Czechoslovaks, 3.3 million were Germans, and 597,000 were Hungarians. The Germans were concentrated on the periphery of Bohemia-Moravia, the Hungarians on the southern periphery of Slovakia; in Bohemia about one third of the population was German. Thus arose the conflict of the so-called "Sudeten Germans" and the cession to Germany of those areas in which they claimed majority, brought about by means of the Munich Agreement with the consent of Italy, Britain, and France, when the latter powers expected to gain a longer peace in Europe at the expense of the Czechs. It was also the end of any possible Czechoslovak resistance to the German advance, for in this way Germany penetrated inside the natural Bohemian stronghold. To avoid repetition of such conflicts, Czechoslovakia, with the consent of the Potsdam Conference in 1945, transferred to the American and Soviet zones of Germany all its German minority, and the border areas thus depopulated were resettled with Czechs. In 1950 the total population of Czechoslovakia amounted to 12,340,000 people, a decrease of 2.3 million from the 1939 estimates.

A similar exodus of Hungarians from Slovakia and the severance of sub-Carpathian Ukraine left Czechoslovakia a more unified nation than it ever had been, so far as language, race, and culture are concerned. By 1967, the population reached 14.3 million, gradually catching up with the figure reached thirty years ago; about 9 million were Roman Catholics; and there were left small national minorities of 400,000 Hungarians and 150,000 Germans. At the same time a gradual political evolution tied Czechoslovakia closely to the Soviet Union. The predominance of the Communist party in the government was decided; the proximity of the Red armies was important, but one should not underestimate in the Eastward trend of the Czechs the psychological weight of the shadow of Munich. The nation has lost, at least temporarily, its function as a link, a function which is hard to maintain in the split-up Europe of today.

## BOHEMIA AND MORAVIA

The country of the Czechs is the essential part of the whole political and economic structure. The Bohemian Square is formed by a large Hercynian system with the two classical directions of the "V" orienting its four sides: southwest-northeast or southeast-northwest. The whole mass was uplifted when the Alps rose, and it has a general northward slope that appears in the drainage toward the Elbe of most of its interior. This interior has been fractured and sunk: sedimentary layers have thus been preserved in the middle of the Hercynian ridges, forming a closed basin

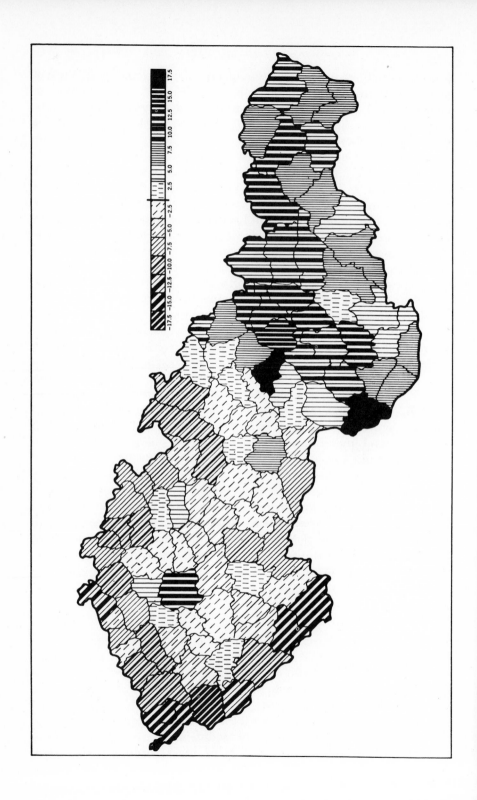

with limestone plateaus and clayish depressions at the foot of the escarpments. As in the central plateau of France or the Rhineland massives, this uplifting and faulting has been accompanied by volcanism, signs of which are still obvious in the geology and in the hot springs on which famous spas were built.

The classical schematic outline of the square is not quite achieved in reality. Three main ranges form a high rim of forested mountains to the southwest, northwest, and northeast; the fourth side, toward the southeast, is more open; an alignment of hills, or, more accurately, the top of a plateau called Vrchovina Ceskomoravska (the Czecho-Moravian heights), limits it above the Moravian-Silesian corridor. The whole of Bohemia is a mosaic of hills and depressions, of ancient granitic and gneissic substratum, covered in places by more recent sandstones, limestones, or marls. The highest summits rise at almost 5000 feet, but most of the area is below 1500 feet in elevation.

The elevated rim makes the interior more continental. A dry winter with clear skies is typical of the area; Prague has a January average of 27° F and of 67° in July; the rainfall, of about 20 inches, occurs mainly in the summer. The crests of the surrounding heights, especially to the west and northwest, are much better watered and covered with an abundant carpet of snow in winter. The winter can be very severe; at times when the "barometric dorsal" crosses Central Europe, the thermometer sinks below zero in the heart of Bohemia. Men have cleared the low-lying soils and the valleys; the heights remain covered with the thick growth of the predominantly coniferous forest.

The Ore Mountains (called locally Krushné Hory) have steep inward slopes. Here is a beautiful hilly country with a few small mining towns, among which Jáchymov is the most famous because of its radioactive pitchblende ore from which silver, radium, and uranium are extracted. In the depressions are scattered some lignite deposits, old centers of textile and chemical industries, and some famous spas, in particular Karlovy Vary and Mariánské Lázně. The main industrial centers are Teplice-Sanoy (52,000), where the famous Bohemian glass and crystal are made, and the iron and steel center of Chomutov (37,000). The Elbe River cuts through the Hercynian barrier to reach the Great Plain in Saxony: its deep valley has always been a main street, with large villages and rich cultures, especially vast orchards. Ustí (72,000) is the main town, with a long line of plants making glass, cloth, and machinery.

---

*(Opposite)* The change in the number of inhabitants of Czechoslovakia, 1921–1961. The scale denotes both decrease *(left)* and increase *(right)*, giving the annual rate of change per mil and per administrative district. *(Czechoslovak Academy of Sciences and Vlastislav Häufler)*

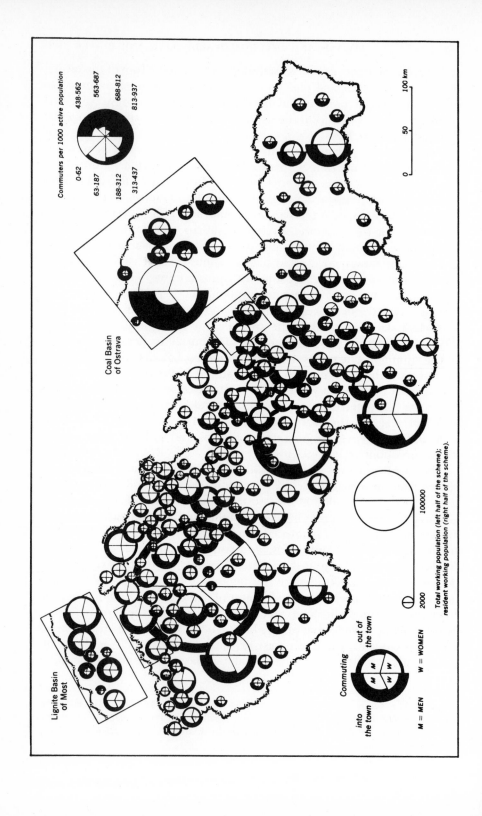

Commuters per 1000 active population

0-62     438-562

63-187     563-687

188-312     688-812

313-437     813-937

Coal Basin
of Ostrava

Lignite Basin
of Most

Total working population (left half of the scheme);
resident working population (right half of the scheme).

Commuting

out of
the town

into
the town

M = MEN     W = WOMEN

0    50    100 km

100000

2000

A similar economy of industrial small cities scattered among a country of forests, meadows, and small patches of fields covers the inner slopes of the Sudeten and of the Bohemian Forest (the latter bearing the names of Šumava or Česky Les). In the Sudeten, Liberec (71,000) makes cotton cloth, Trutnov weaves linen, and Yablonec (30,000) maintains an industry with a world-wide reputation for colored glass and crystal. The Šumava remains closer to the forestry industries, making all kinds of articles out of wood, from pitprops and furniture to matches. This slope oriented toward the northeast is the oldest and most windy. A depression cuts across it, letting Budějovice (70,000) guard the road to the Danube at Linz and make ceramics as well as pencils (the Hardtmuth industry) with local graphite.

The main wealth of Bohemia is concentrated in the center. The Polabi, or Plain of the Elbe, is a rich industrial district, but two small depressions shelter the chief urban and industrial agglomerations. Plzen (Pilsen; 141,000) is in the middle of a rich agricultural district where barley, wheat, and oats are rotated with sugar beets on the loamy soil. Industry started here owing to a small coalfield which was soon exhausted, but the industries kept developing—the famous breweries, the Skoda steel works (one of the chief arsenals of Central Europe), ceramics, machinery, and paper making. Few cities give such an impression of being entirely formed of workshops and large plants. But the main industrial development rings the capital.

Prague (Praha) has a population of over one million. It is a great historical center of administration and learning, with many monuments and beautiful residential sections. Its name means *a ford:* the River Vltava passed here over resistant bars of quartzite which made it shallow. Until 1850 the city had less than 100,000 inhabitants, mostly foreigners, particularly Germans. The railroads and modern industry, using the coal of the Kladno field, made it a large city—300,000 people in 1878, 400,000 in 1910, 921,000 in 1947, 1,025,000 in 1966. The industrial function, spread among the suburbs, is varied: iron and steel finishing industries and engineering make up its core; anything that can be made out of steel is produced here, railroad rolling stock, automobiles, electrical machinery, and machine tools playing a great part. Textile and leather industries are well represented, as are chemical manufacturing and, of course, glassware. The concentration of certain branches has a sort of

---

*(Opposite)* The commuting intensity of Czechoslovak towns. In most cases the commuting is from rural areas into urban centers. For Prague, however, there seems to be almost as much movement out of the city as into it. Commuting is very active in Slovakia. *(Czechoslovak Academy of Sciences and Josef Hursky)*

Residential buildings in the Prague suburbs. (*Czechoslovak Consulate General*)

Prague: view of Hradcany castle as seen from the Charles Bridge. (*Czechoslovak Consulate General*)

monopolistic trend: one central bakery supplies almost all the bread that the city eats. Its role of political capital greatly contributed to the blossoming of the city and increased particularly its commercial and banking activities. Although far from the center of its national territory, Prague makes its influence felt all over. No other city in Czechoslovakia reaches even one third of its population.

The whole of Bohemia-Moravia had a population of 9.8 million in 1966; Bohemia's density of 310 to the square mile was still below that of the Moravia-Silesia corridor, which reached 365. This corridor, a tectonic depression between the Hercynian Bohemian block and the Alpine range of the Carpathians, stretches from the Hungarian to the Silesian plains across the highland belt. Most of it is drained toward the Danube by the River Morava; the northern or Silesian section is drained by the Oder toward the Baltic. At the watershed a pass called the Moravian Gate channels the traffic. The Gate is a forested area, but south of it a wide depression is covered with rich loamy soils that have yielded some of the richest European harvests of sugar beets. Cities spread through it, like Brno (330,000) and Olomouc (77,000), have concentrated the population and the industries, helped by the proximity of Silesian coal. Brno, the Moravian capital, has the largest national textile center, specializing in woolens, as well as many food industries.

But it is north of the Moravian Gate that, in the corner of Silesia populated by the Czechs, the mass of heavy industry concentrated and developed a "black country." A string of cities has developed on the coalfield — such as Ostrava (265,000), with the mines and furnaces around it, Kravina, and Bohumin — an almost continuous agglomeration of more than 500,000 people. Heavy metallurgy and chemical industries are the specialities of the area, which sends its coal to Brno, Prague, and Pilsen and even farther to Vienna and the Danube. But most of the production is consumed, and the nation is becoming industrialized so rapidly that it needs Polish coal. The average density of population in Bohemia-Moravia, even after the evacuation of the Germans, is quite close to the average for Switzerland. Without the financial and tourist resources of the Swiss, the Czechs have resorted to manufacturing.

## SLOVAKIA

Slovakia is definitely different: it is a mountainous and mostly rural country with an average population density of 215 over an area of 19,000 sq. miles. The province does not quite make up a natural region: the northern slopes belong to Poland, while to the south Slovakia extends over a fringe of the Hungarian Plain at the foot of the hills, and the Danube serves as its southwestern boundary on a long section. Most of it still is a rough mountain: fields and meadows clothe the slopes up to 2000 feet only; then the forest covers the mountain up to a level of 4500 feet, above which barren rock or Alpine summer pastures prevail. Although there are low passes in the heart of the ranges, Slovakia has remained an isolated bastion; traffic and settlement went around it. It required the formation of Czechoslovakia to bring about the building of a road and a railroad in the 1920s, chiefly following the valley of the Váh from west to east to establish a continuous internal link with the easternmost sections of the national territory.

Political domination by Hungary maintained until the middle of the twentieth century an agrarian regime of great landlords, and the peasants' condition had changed little since the days of medieval serfdom. A high birthrate maintained the density of the population and led a stream of emigration toward Hungary and farther on toward America. In the interior the villages are lines of small thatched houses; the livestock often lives under the same roof with the family. Ancient crafts exist on these farms, as do also refrigerators and modern television sets. Slovak people are rather isolationist; they are also conservative, devout Roman Catholics, and they would prefer following the leadership of their priests rather than the instructions of the Czech officials. In 1945 Slovakia was provisionally granted self-government within the Czechoslovak republic; regional matters are settled by a Slovak National Council in Bratislava, but local commissioners are responsible to Prague.

Small towns are scattered in the mountain, working local timber, clays, and other resources. Most of them are in the long valley of the Váh, above which towers the high range of the Tatras, culminating at Masaryk peak (8500 feet). A crystalline and volcanic protuberance along the River Hron has been known since old times for its ores: some iron and manganese has been mined, as well as gold. Somewhat richer is the agriculture of the Danubian Plain, based on grains, but to which the Czechs introduced beet and fodder crops. Here are also the main cities. Košice (106,000) has been a regional capital, developed mostly by Hungarians and Jews, where wood, pulp, and textiles are being worked. The economic capital is the port on the Danube, Bratislava (272,000), a thriving city to whose older sugar and flour mills has been added the modern heavy industrialization of oil refineries, chemicals, and sulfuric acid plants. Notwithstanding this, Slovakia, a marginal province of the former Hungarian domain, remains in sharp contrast with Bohemia, which used to be the workshop of the Austrian Empire. Every year about 100,-000 Slovaks migrate to Bohemia-Moravia to swell the expanding industrial labor force of the western province. Such a lasting division of labor is not all to the liking of the Slovaks, and they are industrializing too. Besides the rapid growth of Bratislava, other developments are taking

The town of Klatovy in Czechoslovakia. (*Czechoslovak Consulate General*)

place. In 1961, Košice began building a large new suburb around a new iron and steel mill boasting to produce ultimately five million tons of crude steel annually (as much as the whole of Czechoslovakia in 1956!), with coal from the Ostrava mines and ore from Krivoï-Rog. Another desperate scheme it would seem, but one that may work on a smaller scale than was planned.

## THE CZECHOSLOVAK NATION BETWEEN EAST AND WEST

In its Bohemian-Moravian provinces, the Czechoslovak republic has a stronghold of economics as well as strategy. It is a rich country, in normal times one of the important European exporters of sugar and of delicate manufactured goods, from pencils and crystals to locomotives and electric turbines. The Czechs learned many lessons during their life with the Germans. Their richer soils are as well tilled as those of Western Europe; their industries are almost as strongly integrated as those of the Ruhr. On the whole, less than one fifth of the Czechoslovak population depends on agriculture, which is a very low ratio east of the Rhine. The rural country has suffered from too large land holdings, and an agrarian reform was started cautiously between the two World Wars. Pursued more brutally since 1945, 2,600,000 acres were confiscated from German or Hungarian owners and redistributed to small farmers. With the Communist party in power, larger lands were assigned to communal or cooperative ownership, and most of the important industries were nationalized. In 1952, about 30 percent of all arable lands was tilled by collective farms and 14 percent was state owned and operated. The total proportion of farmland in the "socialist sector" reached officially 82 percent by 1959. However, most of it is in cooperative rather than entirely collectivized farms. The cooperative farms seem to have been well accepted in this country, even by the Slovak peasants.

As the proportion of the labor force in agriculture decreased to 25.5 percent in 1950, 20 in 1965, and further since, serious labor shortages have often developed at harvest time. The farm output has been increasing only very slowly; in the 1960s it recorded annually 1.9 million tons of wheat, 1 million tons of rye, 500,000 tons of corn, 1.5 million tons of barley, 0.61 of oats, 6.3 of potatoes, and 7 of sugar beets. The livestock counted 4.3 million heads of cattle, 5.3 million pigs, 600,000 sheep, and 200,000 horses; the numbers of cattle and pigs had not changed much since 1955. But the main endeavor of economic planning has been here, too, in the field of industrialization.

The industrial raw materials found within Czechoslovak territory are substantial but not large enough to produce surpluses. The forests, which cover 35 percent of the land area, supply large quantities of timber. The mines are rich mainly in coal (28 million tons in recent years), lignite (70 million tons), iron ore (0.8 million tons in metal content), some copper, lead, and rock salt, and more significant quantities of uranium, radium, silver, and graphite. The manufacturing industries, the total output of which was tripled from 1948 to 1959, require greater supplies in fuels and raw materials, much of which comes from the Soviet Union (such as iron ore) and Poland (chiefly coal).

At the end of 1957 it was estimated that the total gross value of industrial production was distributed as follows among the main industries: construction, glass, and ceramics — 4.4 percent; fuels and energy — 9 percent; metallic mines and metal processing industries (including heavy iron and steel) — 9.8; light industries (such as textiles) — 18.3; chemicals — 6.8; food processing — 22.5; and machinery building — 29.2. Thus again in Czechoslovakia the mechanical industries were the most important and those whose expansion was the more actively pushed, another proof of the great demand in the present world. Most of these mechanical industries were located in the northeastern section of Bohemia-Moravia. They had begun to invade Slovakia in the valley of the Váh River, near the great steel mills of Ostrava. There were also large concentrations of machinery making plants in and around Brno, Prague, Plzen, and Olomouc. The crude steel output of Czechoslovakia reached 9.1 million tons in 1966.

Most of this production of machines went to the Soviet Union and its satellites; two thirds of the Czechoslovak foreign trade was with the Communist countries (37 percent with the USSR). But substantial exports of machinery, including machine-tools, went to Western countries, especially to underdeveloped lands undergoing industrialization. The Czechs have specialized in the mechanical industries for a long time and they feel that they should continue, although they do not neglect textiles and chemicals. But how large a raw material base will they be able to build up? To deal with this concern, as well as with a similar source of anxiety in East Germany, there was talk in the 1950s of an "Eastern Ruhr," uniting the mineral and human resources of Poland and Czechoslovakia around the Silesian coalfields. Although they possess only a minor section of the coal deposit, the Czechs may contribute greatly to such an ambitious project with equipment, goods, and skilled manpower. They are particularly advanced in terms of technical and managerial skills often lacking in the other Slavic countries. But the Czechs are not numerous enough and their rate of natural increase has been rather slow (it was down to 5 per 1000 in the 1960s). The Slovaks, on the contrary, have a fast rate of increase (16 per 1000) and a much younger population; but they would like to see this new Ruhr expand also to their territory, which is still mainly rural.

The transportation problems of this landlocked economy are considerable. The Oder River is not the Rhine; the Moravian corridor could open the road to a migration of plants toward the Danube, but this is not so good a waterway as the Rhine is, and it is a long way from Bratislava to the sea. Czechoslovakia already boasts one of the denser railway networks in the world (it is second in density only to those of Belgium, Britain, and Germany); it may soon be overworked.

Both Poland and Czechoslovakia present the interesting picture of two nations which saw their population decreased on the whole from prewar levels and two areas in which large resettlement operations have taken place. They are industrializing fast and experiencing serious labor shortages in both urban and farming activities, although in different ways. The two nations are rather different in temperament, and their historical pasts have not always oriented them in the same direction. Czechoslovakia had never known Russian domination before 1945 and was feeling more friendly toward her Slavic "brothers" than she was toward the Germans, under whose yoke she has spent recent centuries. There is some economic complementarity between the two countries, and it may cement more permanent relations between them. Still, after twenty years of Communist rule, both countries were restive. Because of its better traditional relations with the Russians and because of its more advanced economy, Czechoslovakia dared, in 1968, to change its government and embark on a series of economic reforms leading to a liberalization of the regime. For some time the Czechs have tried to avoid being only a buffer; they have been selling their machinery, particularly their machine tools, to Western countries and have even gone into partnership with private capital in a few industrial firms in the developing countries. All this looked like a timid beginning, a thaw in the Soviet sphere of influence in Central Europe. Such trends were first felt in the areas that have had a long tradition of being links between East and West. But in August 1968, Soviet forces occupied Czechoslovakia and imposed more orthodox Communist policies.

The Danube at the Iron Gate. (*Yugoslav Information Center*)

# 18

---

# Countries of the Danube: Austria, Hungary, Rumania

No part of Europe better deserves to be called the "tidal lands of history" than the Danubian basin between Bavaria and the Black Sea. The Danube, like the Rhine, served as a *limes*, a border of the Roman Empire, and to guarantee its security, Roman legions crossed the river often, establishing strong colonies to the north. The Barbarians who pressed on this *limes* were of many origins: Germanic and Asiatic tribes (of the Ugro-Finnish or Sarmatian and later Slavic origin). In the Middle Ages the German or Holy Roman Empire established a strong base of operations eastward on the Upper Danube: that was the Ostmark, which developed into the Austrian Empire. Soon Byzantium, heir to classical Greek and Roman culture, Austria, the Turks, and the Slavs were fighting for control of lands in the basin. Then the retreat of the Turkish Ottoman Empire, the "sick man" of Europe, in the eighteenth and nineteenth centuries led to advances by the Austrian or Russian empires and also to the emergence of regional national entities which soon developed into independent states. A new map was created by the Treaty of St. Germain in 1919, officially ending the Austro-Hungarian Empire. By it Poland and Czechoslovakia benefited in the north, Italy and Yugoslavia in the south, and three countries situated entirely in the basin received new shapes: the "residual" states of Austria and Hungary, remnants of a vast political structure, and Rumania, a new nation formed in the nineteenth century, which was considerably expanded in area in 1919.

Several times before World War II the problem arose of the reorganization of this whole area on a regional scale. If one eliminates the possibility of the domination of the whole basin by any one power, a Danubian "concern" would have formed a sizable whole within the European framework, and it should have been able to restore larger economic horizons without infringing upon the political independence of the participating powers. Since the end of World War II similar proposals for a Danubian regional organization have been brought up again by distinguished scholars and statesmen. There are at least seven different political units along the Danube, but only three of them are essentially "Danubian": Austria, Hungary, and Rumania. Germany controls the upper course of the Danube down to Passau, but this is the least important section of the river and plays a third-rate part in German economic assets or worries. Czechoslovakia, Yugoslavia, and Bulgaria have sections of the course, at least on one bank. But Czechoslovakia is still based north of the river, and on the whole its orientation is more toward the Elbe or toward the Oder basin. Although the Danube is an important waterway, particularly for Slovakia, the Czechoslovak economy still is not mainly Danubian. Similarly Bulgaria is based on hills and basins with few links to the Danube; its national stream is the Maritza, flowing to the Mediterranean. The river's role is greater for Yugoslavia, the capital of which is Danubian. But Yugoslavia is a Mediterranean country in many respects, with a variety of interests definitely more Balkanic than Danubian.

Thus we come to a narrower delimitation of the purely Danubian realm. The river, at least, is a subject of great international concern, all the more so since the return of Bessarabia to the Soviet Union has meant that a power more important than the other riparian countries now occupies the northern bank of the Danube from its meeting with the Prut River down to the sea. How much this great river links together the countries it crosses will appear in a brief review of its role as a waterway.

## THE DANUBE AS A WATERWAY

By the length of its course and the area of its basin, the Danube is a greater stream than the Rhine, although it cannot compare with the Volga. It is indeed the river par excellence of Central Europe; as Emmanuel de Martonne has observed, the Danube starts in its upper course as another Rhine and ends in its lower section as a minor Volga.

The Danube has its springs at Donaueschingen in the Black Forest and flows eastward across southern Germany, changing its orientation at Regensburg to follow the foot of the sub-Alpine plateau. In Austria it continues to flow between the Alps and the Hercynian massives; in the vicinity of Vienna, where the Danubian valley is narrow, both groups of highlands come almost in contact and there is the threat of rapids. Then the Danube enters a steadily widening plain, the large Pannonian depression of Hungary. At the middle of the northern section of this plain, it veers sharply to the south and crosses the remainder of the plain in this direction. In Yugoslavia it turns eastward again and after receiving several important tributaries reaches a new gorge, the Iron Gate, a narrow pass between the Transylvanian Alps to the north and the Balkans in the south. Beyond the Iron Gate a new flat plain widens, through which the Danube flows eastward, with a northward section, before emptying with a large delta into the Black Sea. Its course has thus three clear-cut sections separated by the narrows of Vienna and of the Iron Gate, and each section has a different regime, owing to the streams which feed it.

The Upper Danube, in Germany and Austria, is an Alpine stream. Curiously enough, although born in a low Hercynian mountain, the Danube immediately is fed much more by its right-bank tributaries coming from the Alps, such as the Iller, Lech, Isar, than by its Hercynian left bank. Most of the Hercynian area and the basins with it have a general slope northward because of the Alpine push from the south, and the drainage has been established in this direction, toward the Rhine or Elbe. The contribution of Hercynian massives should not be discounted altogether, but it is minor, especially in winter when these heights, being more continental than those along the Rhine, keep their snow covers for a longer period. The Alpine contribution, on the contrary, is extremely important. At Passau the Danube meets the Inn, which drains most of the eastern Alps, and almost doubles in gauge. It is a powerful stream that flows through Vienna, but one with a distinctly Alpine regime with floods rising in the spring and early summer. At that season the Danube has all the aspects of a large torrent and often threatens to overflow its banks; at that season too there is no "Blue" Danube, for its waters are muddied with the silt taken from the steep slopes of the Alps.

Below Vienna the middle and second course opens. Through the Pannonian Plain there is little slope; the stream's gradient drops immediately, and the Danube becomes a lazy, winding river, dividing itself into several arms, losing much water by evaporation during the warm season. The farther the Danube advances across the plain, the greater is the contrast between its high waters in early summer and its low waters in early autumn. Slovakian tributaries bring some water with a lower mountain regime, but without much affecting the total flow. In Yugoslavia the Danube is joined by the Tisza, which drains a large part of the eastern Carpathians but has a yearly curve to its gauge similar to that of the Danube since both streams flow parallelly from north to south across the Pannonian Plain. More variety is introduced by the Drava and Sava, which also start from the Alps but drain a large basin that includes the Dinaric range and plateaus enjoying a Mediterranean climate of winter rainfall. The Sava has some regularizing effect owing to the big streams surging at the foot of the Karst limestone lands where water circulates chiefly underground.

Gathering all these contributions, the Danube passes the Iron Gate. The river has actual majesty in spring, with the abundant flow filling the narrow and impressive gap, but in the fall the thinner film of water lets the rocky bottom create rapids in places, and navigation is more dangerous for two to three months. Here ends the middle section of the course, and the lower one opens with a slow and again lazy but wide stream winding through the plain.

The Alpine contribution remains predominant down to the delta. Because of it the Danube can maintain a course and an adequate water-table throughout the summer in the dry and hot plains. Covering an area of 315,000 square miles, the whole basin is diversified and divided among many national and regional administrative authorities. Long ago the need for some coordination was recognized, with the result that navigation has been kept free and the channel greatly improved. But the Danube is still far from being the man-made waterway that the Rhine is. Some great works have been carried out along it, but many more would be useful. In the nineteenth century, Austro-Hungarian authorities blasted a deep channel through the rocky bars of the Iron Gate, forcing the river to flow into a narrow trench, but, though the depth now stays greater throughout the year, the speed of the current makes navigation upstream more difficult. If the upper sections of the tributaries were controlled in the mountains by a system of dams and reservoirs, much could be done to improve the depth and the regularity of the river, favoring navigation in the fall and avoiding inundation at floodtime. Such dams would also be an important source of power—it was estimated that, up to 1940, less than 5 percent of the total water-power potential of the Danube basin had been harnessed. The water from the river and its main tributaries could also generate agricultural wealth through irrigation of the Pannonian Plain.

Navigation, flood control, waterpower, and irrigation—all create the need for an international authority that would supervise the water problems of the Danubian basin. That is why a TVA project on the Danube has been suggested. Since 1856 a European Commission of the Danube has functioned in which not only the riparian powers participated but also those having special interest in Danubian commerce and navigation, particularly France and Britain. The Commission's main field of competence and worry has been the safeguarding of free navigation—it has

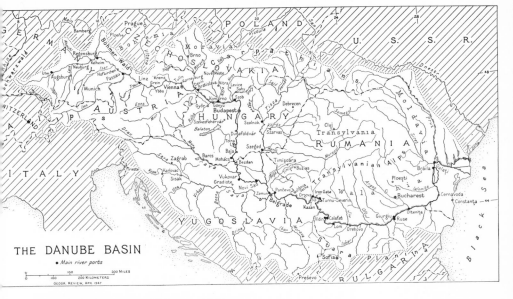

# THE DANUBE BASIN

● Main river ports

0  100  200 MILES
0  100  200 KILOMETERS
GEOGR. REVIEW, APR. 1947

The boundaries are as of February 1947.

Austrian town of Stein on the Danube. (*Austrian State Tourist Department*)

been more concerned with legal than technical matters. Re-formed in 1921, the Commission's membership was limited to Great Britain, France, Italy, and Rumania. In 1939 the ships of the Commission and many of its powers, including control of the naviation of the delta, passed to the Rumanian government. In 1948, an international conference meeting in Belgrade organized a new international commission but voted to exclude states which were not riparians of the Danube. The headquarters of the new commission were moved to Budapest. The restoration of the Soviet Union as a riparian state (and her greater influence among the Danubian countries) gave Russia a dominant position in the new international status of the river challenged only by the Yugoslav position. In June 1963, an agreement was signed between Rumania and Yugoslavia providing for the building on the Iron Gate narrows of a dam and hydroelectric power plant between Gura Vaii (Rumania) and Sip (Yugoslavia). Work on this huge project has started and should be completed by 1971; the installed power is to be 2 million kw, allowing for an annual output of 10 billion kwh. This project should help regulate the flow downstream and, therefore, improve navigability on the lower section of the Danube.

While some of the defects of the Danubian waterway may be corrected to a considerable extent by engineering, the severe winters will continue to close it to navigation during the period of frost. On the average the Lower Danube freezes for two months at least every winter. And during the thaw period, which lasts a fortnight more, navigation is not practicable either. The period of freezing and thaw plus the period of slack water considerably shortens actual use of the great river. Similarly, the lack of canals and canalization of some tributaries reduces its efficiency for traffic. The economic backwardness of Europe east of the Alps shows in the inadequate use to which the Danube has been put. But the means of transportation are still rather deficient in most of the area, and, notwithstanding its defects, the Danube remains a major link at least between the three purely Danubian countries.

## AUSTRIA, AN ALPINE "RESIDUAL" STATE

Austria, is essentially an Alpine country, quite comparable to Switzerland on the physical map of Europe but very different in other respects. Its territory of 32,400 square miles has for a backbone the northeastern ranges of the Alps, and these mountains occupy 70 percent of the total area. Sub-Alpine depressions stretch to the northeast and southeast; then, across the Danubian valley to the northeast, a section of the Bohemian Forest covers about 10 percent of the territory. Austria is more open and its territory wider only in the east; almost the whole of it is

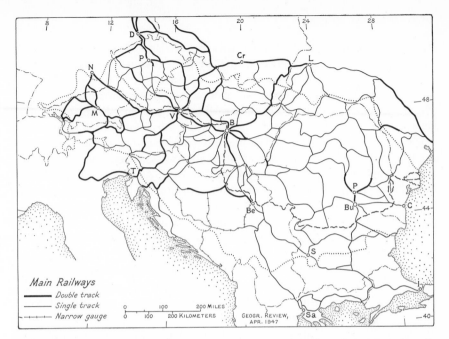

Main railways of the Danube Basin. The basin is delineated by a dotted line. Key: B, Budapest; Be, Belgrade; Bu, Bucharest; C. Constanța; Cr, Cracow; D, Dresden; L, Lwów; M, Munich; N, Nuremberg; P, Prague; S, Sofia; Sa, Salonika; T, Trieste; V, Vienna. (*George Kish and The Geographical Review*)

Mineral resources of the Danube Basin. (*George Kish and The Geographical Review*)

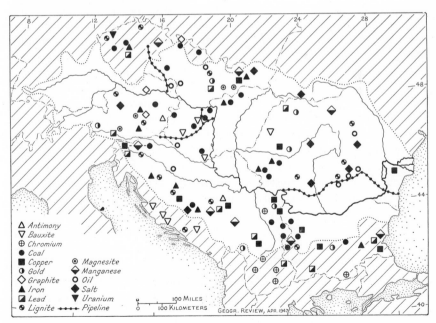

drained in the same direction, toward the Danube. Founded as the *Ostmark,* Austria is oriented eastward by its nature as well as by history, but the weight of that history is a heavy burden on the present state.

The Ostmark was so successful as a base of operations that it became the headquarters of the Holy Roman Empire, and that Empire endured as one of the chief powers of Europe until the French fight against the *"Maison d'Autriche"* achieved the disintegration of the Empire centered in Vienna. The two main stages of disintegration were marked by the 1804 treaty in which Napoleon I obtained the Austrian sovereign's renunciation of his old title of German Emperor to become Emperor of Austria and Hungary, and the Treaty of 1919 by which Austria-Hungary was broken up. Thus the republic of Austria came into being as a "residue" of what had been for several centuries one of the greatest powers on earth.

By its language and culture Austria belongs to the German area; historically it has looked eastward and southward and has been more associated with the Hungarians, Czechs, Croats, and Italians whom it dominated than with the Germans to the north. The latter had passed under the leadership of Prussia in the middle of the nineteenth century and rivalry left some lively feelings in Austria. Still, Austrian patriotism had little time to develop within the shrunken space left to it after 1919. On March 12, 1938, the Nazi armies took over the small republic by force and proclaimed *Anschluss*—annexation to the Reich. The Allied armies liberated Austria in 1945 and re-established its independence within the 1937 frontiers, but under Allied military occupation and supervision and divided into four zones of occupation similar to those of Germany. Once again the question arose whether Austria was or was not a "viable" state in so reduced a "residual" territory.

It seemed in the first postwar years that the moneys spent by the foreign occupying forces were the main resource of the country. But hard work and much help from the West improved the general economic condition. In 1955 a treaty signed by the four Allied powers and the Republic of Austria made the latter an independent, sovereign, and neutral state; all military occupying forces left. Deliberately turning its economy towards the West and participating in the general economic expansion of Europe, Austria began to enjoy a genuine prosperity, putting to better use much of its heretofore underdeveloped resources.

There are three regions in Austria, all very different one from another: the Alps, the sub-Alpine areas in which the small section of the Bohemian Forest may be included, and finally Vienna, the great city. The largest in area, the Alps in all respects form the most picturesque part of Austria. These are the eastern Alps, different by their orientation and structure from the western part of the system in France and

Switzerland. The general direction is east-west, with severely folded limestone ranges to the north and crystalline higher massives to the south. The deep trench of the Inn valley follows the southern limit of the limestone ridges; south of it, crystalline central ranges or schist crests extend almost to the Italian border; along this boundary some peripheral limestone ranges reappear.

The central crystalline massives are interrupted by a large gap through which passes the best road across the eastern section of the Alps — the Brenner Pass, opening a route southward from the wide valley of the Inn to the Mediterranean, Venice, Trieste, and beyond. The Brenner has been one of the major passes in the European network of trade and traffic, the gate to Italy from Central Europe and vice versa. The "guard on the Brenner" means to Italy defense from Germanism and from invasions of northern armies. Another gap, that of the Arlberg, establishes easy communications between the upper valley of the Inn and the valley of the Rhine in Switzerland; it is followed by the east-west road from Switzerland to Vienna (see map of Alpine passes, p. 388).

This disposition of valleys and passes made an "open" mountain of the western section of the Austrian Alps. The westernmost province of Vorarlberg is oriented partly toward Switzerland and Lake Constance, with lacework for St. Gallen and some textiles and food industries mostly for Swiss interests in small towns such as Dornbirn (28,000 people), Bregenz (21,500), and Bludenz. Farther eastward the mountain is steep and is the domain of classical Alpine economy: cattle ranging and forestry. Agriculture and population are cencentrated in the main valleys, that of the Inn being by far the most important. The Inntal has rich cultures and intensive dairy production. The foehn wind coming down from the south warms up the climate and maintains some Mediterranean plants on the southward-looking slopes. The valley is the heart of Tyrol, a province of simple, traditional, vigorous mountaineers. The capital is Innsbruck (the bridge on the Inn) built at the meeting of the Inntal with the Wipptal, which comes down from the Brenner. Since the twelfth century Innsbruck has been an important market and relay on the road from Rome and Venice to Augsburg, Nuremberg, and Vienna. In the seventeenth century, its activities began to decline as traffic by sea made the passes through the Alps less important, but a rejuvenation came after the railway crossed the Brenner in 1864 and the Arlberg in 1884, restoring Innsbruck (110,000 inhabitants) as a hub of trade, an important fair, and a great center of tourism and electrical industries.

East of the Tyrol the mountains gain in height and mass. In the center towers the lofty range of the Tauern, a crystalline continuous barrier with its bold peaks, wide cirques, and sharp crests, its glaciers and eternal

Sellrain valley in the Tyrol. (*Austrian State Tourist Department*)

Glimpses of the Silvretta Glacier on Piz Puin (12,000 feet) in the Austrian Alps. (*Austrian State Tourist Department*)

snowcaps. In the northern limestone ranges some valleys widen north-ward, and towns have risen at the points where they leave the mountain: thus Salzburg (112,000) on the Salzach, mostly a residential center until some industry was brought in, partly during World War II, and Steyr (38,000) on the Enns River, center of a small industrial region utilizing local iron ores and timber. Steyr, which makes tractors and ball bearings, is close enough to the heavy industry of Linz to belong to the latter city's orbit. Salzburg is a regional capital that greatly profited by the generous spending of the United States Forces whose headquarters for Austria were in the city. Moreover, located on the border with West Germany and on the main railway from Munich to Vienna, Salzburg has assumed the role of the main gate to Austria from the Western countries, and especially the gate to the touristic and winter skiing resources of the Austrian Alps. In the city of Mozart an annual music festival is now held and various summer schools have been established.

In the heart of the Alps, some small depressions harbor local agri-cultural market towns with meadows around them: thus the small re-gions of Pinzgau, Pongau, or the Gailtal, which is drained eastward by the Drava River. Two large depressions penetrate the southern border of the Alps and form the heart of the two provinces of Styria and Carin-thia. In the latter the basin of Klagenfurt, with its mixed Slovene-Aus-trian population, is an area of rich agriculture, with orchards, vineyards, wheat fields, timber, and pulp industries. Klagenfurt (69,000) is an im-portant rail hub and has some metallurgy. Much more active is the in-dustrial life of Styria, in the corridor of the Mur-Mürz rivers, where iron and magnesium ores are extracted and some coal and lignite have been found. Chemical and metallurgical industries were built, especially around Leoben (36,000).

Eastward Styria opens through an area of piedmont low hills into the Pannonian Plain. Here the sub-Alpine area of Austria melts into the fringes of a vast, flat plain. It is still rolling land on which clusters of chestnuts and linden trees scatter amid corn and wheat fields, orchards, and meadows in the bottoms. Graz, the capital of Styria, stands at the entrance of the Mur valley. The second city of Austria with 250,000 people, Graz has a calm residential section and a vast industrial section of flour mills, breweries, chemical plants, pulp and paper mills, and railroad rolling-stock manufacturing. An oil pipeline has brought an oil refinery here. Since Graz attracts all the urban activities in this area, a purely rural economy dominates the flatter and richer soils of the Burgenland, which stretches to the northeast toward the Basin of Vienna, a well-sheltered depression, filled with alluvials, covered with loess, and followed along its contact with the mountains by a line of thermal springs. A small ridge separates this depression from another occupied by Lake Neusiedler. Here vineyards, meadows, and truck farms are mixed with small but numerous industrial towns, spread in what is to some extent the metropolitan area of Vienna. Wiener Neustadt (34,000) is the only town of any local importance. The capital standing on the Danube is too close by for other cities to develop.

Vienna is at the contact of the Alps, the Danube, and the Pannonian Plain. Along the Danube upstream from the capital, a corridor forms the north of sub-Alpine Austria. North of the Danube, the Bohemian Forest's fringe is called by the peasants *Waldviertel,* where woods cover the granitic hills, or *Weinviertel,* where well-exposed slopes with some patches of loess favor fields and especially vines. South of the Danube, the foot of the Alps is richer in both its rural economy and its urban centers. Wels (41,000) has an old tradition of machinery building; St. Pölten (40,000) specializes in textiles and chemicals; but Linz, on the Danube, is the main city (200,000). Once it had only an old ford and bridge; then, with the railroads, it developed textile and machinery manufacturing. During World War II its industrial role was greatly increased, as many steel industries, machine-tool, and roller-bearing plants were brought there; Linz was well situated in an area between the two fronts, far from Allied bomber bases. Since 1945 the largest of these plants have been dismantled, but several major industries have been maintained and developed (iron and steel, machinery, plastics, glass, food processing). Still the greater industrial activity is concentrated in the capital.

Vienna has been a great imperial capital and also a great center of trade. Its administrative and political role dictated this, but its geographical position simplified everything. Few cities are situated at the meeting of three so different kinds of regions as the Alpine, Hercynian, and Pannonian and located on a major waterway as well. The central part of the city tells its history, with the circular *Ring* of parks and great, palatial government buildings that replaced the ramparts of 1703. The eighteenth century, definitely fixing in Vienna the main capital of the Hapsburgs, who had lost Spain, and the rapid advance eastward against the Turks, opened the great period of Viennese history. Around 1800 Vienna had 300,000 inhabitants; it was the largest European city after Paris, which it endeavored to rival, having built at Schönbrunn an Austrian palace in the style of that at Versailles. It expanded quicker with the urbanization push of the nineteenth century: 587,000 people in 1857; 2,030,000 in 1910. It was a cosmopolitan city, gathering elements from all parts of the empire—a beautiful city also, with its many castles, churches, and monuments, and a gay one at the time of the waltzes. The aftermath of World War I hit Vienna hard: a city of 2 million people found itself restricted to the framework of a nation totaling only 7 mil-

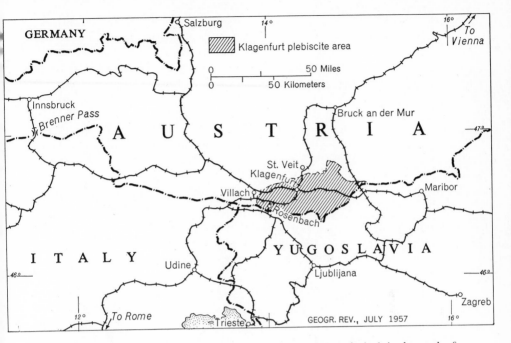

GEOGR. REV., JULY 1957

The area of Klagenfurt, once disputed between Austria and Yugoslavia, is in the south of Austria today (*above*); it is relatively well industrialized and has a variety of manufactures (*below*). (*Dr. Randall and The Geographical Review*)

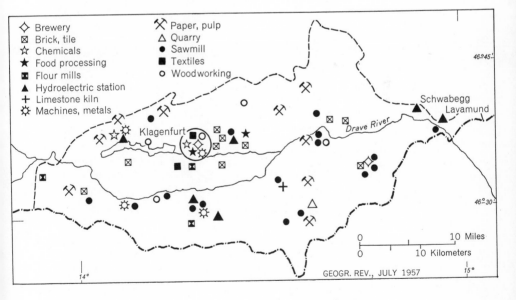

GEOGR. REV., JULY 1957

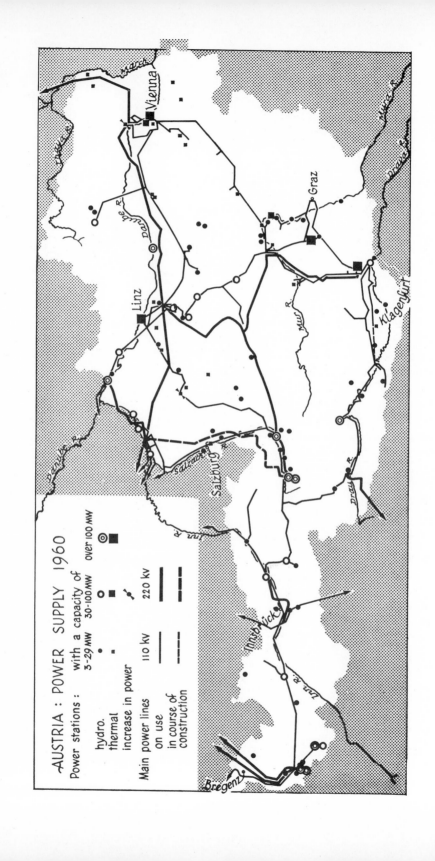

AUSTRIA : POWER SUPPLY 1960

Power stations :   with a capacity of
                   3-29 MW  30-100 MW  over 100 MW

hydro.             ●        ○          ◎
thermal            ■        ■          ■
increase in power  ✓        ✓

Main power lines   110 kv   220 kv

on use
in course of
construction

lion people altogether. A period of inflation and famine followed the war; then readaptation was attempted, and Vienna became a poor city, suffocating within a too-small marketing and administrative domain. World War II was even worse. Vienna was taken by the Red army after a bitter battle; like Berlin, it was divided into four Allied occupation zones until 1955; its population decreased to 1,616,000 in 1951; by 1961, it reached 1,627,000, and with suburbs, the conurbation approached 1.9 million by 1965.

The commercial role of Vienna could be difficult, for the city is in a sense situated on the border between the zones of influences of west and east in Europe. Used to looking eastward for its supplies and for marketing a large part of the products of its manufacturing (machinery and electrical equipment of all kinds, ceramics, paper, furniture, textiles), Vienna now may find itself cut off more than ever from an area dominated from Moscow, one of its oldest rivals. The specialization of many Viennese industries, like those of Paris, in the production of high-quality luxury articles has evolved towards a more diversified mixture of industries, aimed either at national mass consumption or at the import markets of the Western countries. Woolen, rubber, and food manufacturing, as well as musical instruments and printing are among the main Viennese industries. In the 1950s the capital has also concentrated within it many of the services needed by an expanding, although small, national economy; it has also attracted some international functions, particularly the headquarters of the International Atomic Energy Agency. Its opera and concert halls remain the very heart of the city, and the focus of night life. Large new public works have been undertaken to improve the urban features of a city whose monumental sections make it quite beautiful.

In our time of accelerated urban growth, Vienna does not appear any more as a too-big head for a small country. At the gates of Communist-dominated Europe, it has assumed a role of international crossroads that

---

(Opposite) The Alps endow Austria with hydroelectric potential estimated at 40 billion kilowatt-hours per year. About 12 billion were produced in 1959, plus another 3.2 billion kilowatt-hours from thermal powerhouses, needed to maintain a year-round output even during the winter slackening of the hydraulic production. This map shows the distribution of the equipment by mid-1960; "increase in power" denotes powerhouses where work was being conducted to increase capacity. Austria exports a great deal of electricity: up to 20 percent of the output in some years. These exports go mainly to West Germany, small quantities to Italy and Czechoslovakia. About 75 percent of the installations are state-owned; however, the Austrian Treasury does not have the means to finance the full utilization of the country's potential (though the output doubled in the 1950s). Some help has come from the World Bank. Several corporations are now being formed with the participation of German, French, or Italian capital to produce more power, mainly for export to the participating countries.

it hopes to develop. Still, even in 1960, the scars of the war, the occupation, and the impoverishment since 1914 were apparent. The population has kept up some pro-Socialist leanings, despite obvious hatred of the Russian occupation and its memories. Politically, the capital has often been opposed to the majority in this rural, conservative, devoutly Catholic nation. If more prosperity could be achieved and maintained, such differences would probably be lessened.

In the 1950s Austria made a new economic start. Although the treaties of 1955 have made it politically a neutral country, it has been increasingly bound with the Western world and has received much American help. For this small, Alpine, landlocked country a comparison with Switzerland seems unavoidable and fertile in conclusions. Austria is twice as large in area; its population of 7.3 million people is 20 percent greater; the density per square mile reaches 375 in Switzerland, but only 220 in Austria. The natural resources in fertile soils and availability of lumber, coal, and iron ore are greater in Austria, although they are not very considerable, with the exception of wood. Tourist assets are also comparable. Still Austria is rather poor and recently even doubted its ability to exist, while the Swiss have one of the better organized economies in the world. But the Swiss economy was organized on the Western model, on a world-wide basis, and with a view to supporting itself within a small national territory. Austria has never been satisfied with such a view; its system was a regional one, based on its domination of surrounding countries. The origins of the two countries are also different—the imperial marginal province as against the league of small mountain communities. Curiously enough it is the latter that succeeded in building the stronger and wider economic structure; Austria is not equipped to take full advantage of its resources. The organizational factor in economic geography is a fundamental one, and it appears in a striking manner when one compares the two Alpine countries.

To adapt itself, Austria needs now the will to do so; at bottom the Austrian problem is psychological: the nation will have a hard life so long as it will not accept its new status. A serious effort in this direction has recently been started. Domestic resources are being put to better use. The output of Austrian mines have been pushed, but they were extracting from small deposits in most cases and could hardly yield large quantities (in 1965, Austria mined 59,000 tons of coal; 5.4 million tons of lignite; 1.7 million cubic meters of natural gas; 2.8 million tons of oil; 1.1 million tons of iron ore in metal content; and small quantities of copper, lead, zinc, bauxite, tungsten, antimony, and salt). Mining output was significant chiefly for magnesite, of which Austria supplied half of the world production (1.8 million tons in 1965) and high-grade graphite (80,000 tons annually). Postwar finds of petroleum in the Soviet zone of occupation turned out to be disappointing, and Austria must deliver to Russia part of its oil production. Two basic resources, steadily put to better use, are waterpower (see p. 674), supplying an expanding amount of electricity, part of which is exported, and the forests, which yielded 11 million cubic meters of roundwood in 1965; accessible and productive forests cover about 10,000 square miles, close to one third of Austria's land area.

The agricultural production was also intensified and showed an increase of about 20 percent in the 1950s. The greater quantities produced of wheat, barley, potatoes, and pigs are mainly responsible for the progress. The development of tourism brings six million visitors annually to Austria, especially to the Alps (where Kitzbühel has become a fashionable international skiing resort) and to the musical events in Salzburg and Vienna. But Austria's best chance to establish a sound and prosperous economy lies in developing manufacturing: some primary industries have been developed (in 1965 the country produced 4 million tons of cement, 2.2 of pig iron and ferroalloys, 3.2 of crude steel, and 98,000 tons of aluminum); the main endeavor, however, has been to expand the output of machinery, electrical apparatus, measuring and musical instruments, woolens, shoes, and furniture. Progress on the latter articles has not been so striking as in other countries of Europe; but Austria is becoming industrialized; industrial employment surpassed 600,000 by 1960. The low-wage policy applied in Austrian industries has been easy to maintain because many of the plants have been nationalized since the war; it improves the nation's competitive position but decreases its domestic consumption, an essential foundation of lasting economic strength.

Austrian economic growth is largely due to American help. From Marshall Plan funds the small nation received the equivalent of $165 per capita, the highest such allocation in Europe. Austria is a member of the Outer Seven (EFTA), but most of its trade is with the countries of the Common Market; and now it is from these countries that investments are expected to come. However, Austria may not be quite ready to adapt itself and plan its economy according to its present status. Some territorial conflicts have flared up since the war, first with Yugoslavia concerning the Klagenfurt area (first settled by the plebiscite of 1920 and again guaranteed to Austria by the 1955 treaties), then with Italy in the Upper Trentino region, which has been Italian since 1920. Talk about a new union with West Germany is now precluded by the 1955 treaties and the neutrality status imposed on Austria. To achieve a stable balance within its present borders, Austria may have to learn more from the

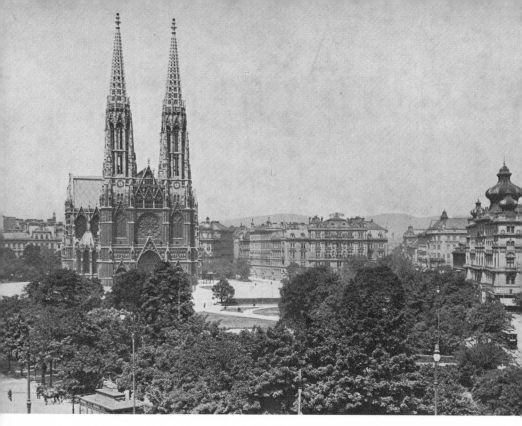

Vienna. (*Above*) Independence Square, formerly Maximilian Square. (*Below*) A fashionable street. (*Three Lions*)

Swiss model; but the differences of the historical backgrounds cannot be erased in one generation. The Austrians have not yet forgotten their "central position" in Europe and their Danubian past.

## HUNGARY

Hungary is another "residue" of the Austro-Hungarian Empire, but its status is much different and creates fewer problems than that of Austria. A country of 35,900 square miles, populated by 10.2 million people who used to dominate within the dual empire a territory three times larger, Hungary offers a strikingly different picture. The country is flat, for it covers most of the Pannonian Plain, a depression occupied by a lake that left flat sediments. The perfectly flat plain takes up two thirds of the territory, in the center and east; to the west a few ridges and hills remain, outcroppings of Miocene limestone or small volcanic thrusts. Hungary has thus two major regions: the plain and the hills. This present territory still represents the richest part of the former Hungarian realm: it has a considerable agricultural wealth and before partition was less dependent on its satellites. Moreover, the Hungarians or Magyars, although they have not forgotten the drastic reduction imposed on them, rely less on the past and have adapted themselves better than the Austrians to their modest status.

The hilly country to the north and west of Hungary has some heights reaching up to 2000 feet. This was a country settled early by man, for it has neither the difficulties of the high mountainous slopes or the insecurity of the open, broad spaces to the east. It is a gently rolling country with some patches of oak and beech woods on the ridges and verdant valleys in between. The depressions are not so swept by the cold winds of winter, and the elevation tempers the heat of the summer. In the wide valley of the Raba River many different colonizations have mingled since the Romans established their colonies, which developed into the towns of Szombathely (57,000) and Gyor (74,000). Wheat and sugar beets thrive on the rich Quaternary soils, between the grassy meadows in the flooded bottoms and the orchards and vines higher on the slopes.

The most impressive ridge of Hungary is the Bakony Forest, overlooking the lengthy Lake Balaton from an escarpment caused by faulting. Some granite and limestone outcrop in the ridge, and a few basaltic hillocks attest to the volcanism caused by tectonic strains. The lake is a shallow one and is being quickly silted. It is frozen in winter, but the slope of the ridge overlooking it, oriented to the southeast, is considered as a little Hungarian riviera with vines and villas. South of the Balaton, the land is lower, more open, riddled with parallel furrows of a south-north orientation. Extensive grain cultivation is carried on with a predominance of wheat and some cattle. A last group of hills appears in the Mecsek ridge, at the foot of which a dense population has concentrated around the town of Pécs (135,000), where ceramics and some metallurgy and mechanical industries are taking advantage of the existence of a small coalfield in the vicinity.

From the gorge of the Danube near Esztergom, where the river pierces a small volcanic massive before turning sharply southward, to the foot of the Carpathians extends an area of hills, mainly volcanic, under a cover of sandy or loess soils. Here the Matra heights reach 3300 feet in elevation. In the depressions large villages till the soil, raise cattle, and cultivate the vine. Miskolc (171,000 inhabitants) is the central market of northern Hungary, with vast silos, flour mills, and mechanical and tobacco factories.

Aside from this semicircle of hills to the west and northwest, Hungary is a monotonous plain, the Alföld. The southern section of this plain belongs to Yugoslavia, and the eastern reaches are Rumanian territory. Sweeping winds have accumulated some ridges of sand dunes in the central and northeastern parts of the plain; a wide patch of loess extends in the center and the main streams, the Danube and Tisza, regularly flood the flat bottomlands along their banks; and on the black loess soils, rich yields of grain are harvested. The habitat is concentrated in big villages resulting from recent resettlement. Most of the Alföld had been emptied of its population by the raids and campaigns of the Turks in the seventeenth century, but the Turkish retreat in the eighteenth century caused a large resettlement operation. Thus Slovak, Serb, and Rumanian groups have populated the fringes of the plain to the north, south, and east. It is only in the central section that the Magyars predominated in numbers; everywhere else colonization was conducted under the supervision of Hungarian or Austrian landlords who owned vast domains. In the nineteenth century the *puszta*—that is, the open steppe devoted mainly to extensive cattle raising with little cultivation— was slowly organized into a more thickly settled and better-used area. In the section between the two great rivers, the sand dunes restrict the arable surface, to about one half the total area; wheat is here associated with corn and rye. The puszta landscape still has been preserved in a section near Debrecen in the northeast, where large herds of cattle with long lyre-shaped horns pasture over a dry steppe, sandy and dotted with white alkali patches. Elsewhere the usual remaking of the soil by man has been progressing steadily. Struggle against floods along the main rivers has been a major task and was favored and directed by the government; the Danube flows nowadays between artificial dams maintained by riparian associations.

Hungary is thus a country of strong, recently organized, but on the whole prosperous, rural life. The climate is rather severe: Budapest records 70.3°F. as a July average and 28.2° in January; its range of mean temperatures thus reaches 42.1°, and Debrecen increases it to 45.7°; for three months at least its temperature remains below the freezing point, while the three summer months are hot indeed. The yearly rainfall averages 26 inches in Budapest and 21.5 in Szeged, most of it falling during the intermediate seasons. A Mediterranean influence makes August and September drier and the continental influence makes the winter drier. Still there is no month with an average rainfall below one inch, even in Debrecen or Szeged. The summer half-year receives over half of the yearly precipitation, and, with the thaw of the snow, the ground is kept wet enough for most crops to develop. But the yields could be made much higher and the harvest more regular if irrigation could be introduced on a large scale. Some works have been completed to this end by tapping the Tisza or the Danube.

Grains, rotated with potatoes and beets, and cattle ranging remain the two main kinds of agricultural activities. Well over half of the population depends on this agriculture, the resources of which could be considerably expanded by a more intensive land use. Urban life is very active too, concentrated in a few large centers. Debrecen is the regional capital of the eastern Alföld; like the other three cities of the plain, Szeged, Kecskemét, and Hódmezövásárhely, it is largely a dense agglomeration of villages. Urban and rural life are deeply intermingled. Debrecen (137,000 inhabitants in 1962) is a major market, especially for livestock; Szeged (116,000 in 1966) plays a similar part but is also a rail hub in the south of the plain, and the traffic developed industries (milling, breweries, sugar refineries, some machinery, and leather ware). The capital of Hungary still concentrates all the actually urban and large-scale industrial developments.

Budapest with its suburbs has 1,950,000 inhabitants. Although it lost a large part of this population during the siege by the Red army in 1945, it recovered by 1950 most of its prewar 1,724,000 people. Its role in the country is comparable to that of Vienna in Austria, with the difference that Budapest is the only large industrial center in the middle of a more agricultural country. It is in the natural center of the country and not an "excentric" head like Vienna. Few countries are as fully centralized in their capital as Hungary in Budapest. The city grew on the Danube at the contact of the hills with the Alföld. Bude, on a hill towering above the stream, was the citadel, symbol of authority; Pest, on the low eastern bank, was the plain's market. Their union describes the double political and commercial function on which the urban growth arose. A Turkish stronghold for over a century, Budapest was emptied by war and plague in the seventeenth century; in 1710 its population was 1000 at the most.

New rice fields in the "puszta" of Hortobágy, now irrigated. (*Legation of the Republic of Hungary*)

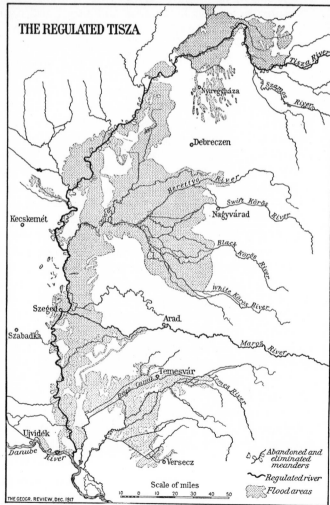

THE REGULATED TISZA

Tisza River
Szamos River
Nyíregyháza
Debreczen
Berettyó River
Swift Körös River
Nagyvárad
Kecskemét
Black Körös River
White Körös River
Szeged
Arad
Maros River
Szabadka
Temesvár
Bega Canal
Temes River
Újvidék
Danube River
Versecz

Scale of miles
10  0  10  20  30  40  50

△ ⌇⌇ Abandoned and eliminated meanders
⌇⌇ Regulated river
▒▒ Flood areas

THE GEOGR. REVIEW, DEC. 1917

Like many European rivers, the Tisza flows in a man-made channel. (*The Geographical Review*)

It grew, therefore, with the resettlement of the plain, to become a cosmopolitan city where all the peoples of Central Europe and of the Balkans mixed in the nineteenth century. Only about 1900, when the "Magyarization" of Jews and Slovaks was achieved, did it become properly the Magyar capital. A monumental and elegant city in the center, with famous palaces along and bridges over the Danube, Budapest takes on a more "frontier" look in its recent, mushrooming suburbs, especially to the east on flat terrain. Almost all the metallurgy and most of the leather and textile industries of Hungary are in Budapest; between the two World Wars, the city added large mechanical manufactures and chemical plants to the older specialties. In many ways Budapest is a complete industrial finishing center, as it is the only one in the nation and as it has kept an involved network of trade connections. Most of the commercial business of Hungary, interregional or foreign, was transacted here. The port on the Danube adds to the general activities. Budapest, like Vienna, had a hard time after 1920, but it regained greater prosperity before 1940. The siege of 1945 and the social reforms that followed were severe ordeals, but the city has picked up with a remarkable vitality. Even the rebellion against Soviet rule, roughly suppressed in 1956, affected it only temporarily.

In the present difficulties of Europe a rural country usually can take more easily the tests imposed upon it by political events than can an involved and therefore more delicate industrial and commercial economy. The whole history of Hungary has been one of trouble, and the work accomplished by a small people of Asiatic origin, isolated in the center of Europe between the Slavs and the Germans, indeed commands some admiration. Their cultural achievements gave to the Magyars a civilization of their own and some advantage over certain neighboring regions. Still the country has just recently ended its "colonial period"—that is, a period of resettlement and quasi-frontier economy. It is predominantly rural and is struggling for an improvement of its control of the physical milieu. One of the major problems has been the agrarian reform, steadily pushed forward after 1920 under the direction of such remarkable statesmen as Count Teleki, who was also an eminent geographer. About 8 million acres were distributed to small holders or to public communities (in the case of forested land) until 1945. Under Soviet influence a more rigorous breaking up of the large estates was carried out by the postwar regime. There was an important small-landholders party in the parliament elected in 1947. Having fought on the side of the Germans against the USSR in World War II, Hungary was a vanquished country, and the Red army has maintained an unspecified number of troops there to keep a tight control. A peace treaty was signed in 1947 with the Soviet Union, and Hungary remains in the zone of Soviet control.

This position of Soviet satellite is particularly difficult for the Magyars, who, since the Turkish retreat, have considered the Russians as their major foes in the east. Hungary is thus psychologically in opposition to an attitude that may be adopted more readily by Czechoslovakia or Bulgaria. Also the *bourgeoisie* or middle class, which had been developing in Budapest, was generally ruined by the new regime and its socialist trends. The peasants like the possession of their land, but as elsewhere, they quickly began disagreeing with government planning that called for large exports of agricultural goods. Hungary is experiencing in a way the same problems that were mentioned for Poland and will be found in Rumania as well. Then too, there has been the threat of collectively operated farm units, and the Magyars disliked that. The general planning of the Soviet-dominated Eastern bloc called for an increased agricultural production by Hungary and Rumania to complement the food and industrial needs of Bohemia, Silesia, and other industrialized sections. As production goals were not easily met, collectivization of farms started in 1949; by 1959, as a result of successive drives for collectivization, over half of the arable land area was farmed by collective or state farms. The major endeavor of the recent economic plans and again of the second Five-Year Plan, which ran from 1961 to 1965, has been to industrialize Hungary at a faster rate than agricultural production was being expanded; but given the great needs in food of the Communist countries, more agricultural products would be greatly welcome. The second Five-Year Plan called for a 65 to 70 percent rise for industrial production and a 25 to 30 percent rise for agricultural production; still targets for agriculture were not reached.

Since the 1950s the production of cereals did not increase much in Hungary: the wheat harvests in 1955–1964 were about equivalent to the average for 1948–1952 and about 10 percent below the 1934–1938 level; the bumper crop of 1965 reached 2.3 million tons; the corn crop was increased by about 50 percent (to 3.5 million tons in 1962–1965) as was the barley crop (1.1 million tons); oats and rye remained stationary, and the rice harvest very irregular. Potatoes and tobacco were slowly increasing in output; the livestock showed increases in the numbers of pigs (7 million) and sheep (3.4) and the cattle herd was stable, even decreasing slightly. Such inability to expand the agricultural output seems characteristic of Communist countries, especially where collectivization has been actively pushed. Formerly an exporter of grain, Hungary is now satisfied with concentrating on feeding its own population, which the country can easily do if too much of its harvest is not forcibly exported to other Communist areas.

Besides her active farming, Hungary has appreciable mineral resources. Coal is mined near Pécs (4.3 million tons in 1965), and large

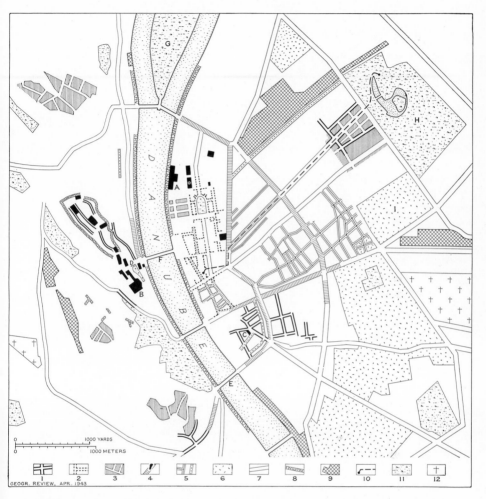

Distribution of certain functional areas in Budapest. Key: 1, former residence of titled nobles; 2, banks, financial institutions, and industrial corporations; 3, high-class residential areas; 4, better-class shopping district; 5, vice areas (official, unofficial); 6, slums; 7, notable street; 8, promenades; 9, railway stations; 10, subway; 11, parks; 12, cemeteries; A, House of Parliament; B, Royal Palace; C, University; D, cable line; E, Ferenc Jószef Bridge; F, suspension bridge; G, Margaritsziget Park; H, Varosliget Park; I, "Chicago." *(The Geographical Review)*

Budapest. *(Above)* Outlook on the Danube. *(Below)* A tractor factory. *(Legation of the Republic of Hungary)*

lignite deposits are mined near Salgótarján and Tatabánya in the north (27 million tons in 1965); small quantities of petroleum and natural gas are produced, mainly in the southwest near Lispe. A deposit of uranium was recently found near Pécs. But the main mineral production of Hungary is bauxite (about 1.5 million tons mined annually); the deposits at Gant and a few other places are among the richest in Europe, superior to those of France and Greece in terms of reserves. There is also a small output of iron and manganese ores. Hungary has not been manufacturing much aluminum (only about 50,000 tons of primary metal), as most of its bauxite is carried away to Russia and Czechoslovakia. The lack of energy resources is usually cited to explain the rather slow development of the aluminum industry in Hungary; the country's output of electricity increased fast, however, from 1954 to 1965 (from 4.8 to 11.2 billion kw-h). But great efforts have been applied at creating a large scale iron and steel industry and manufactures of machinery. In 1965 Hungary produced 1.6 million tons of pig iron and ferroalloys, and 2.5 of crude steel (a 75 percent increase over 1954); the main steel works are located at Salgótarján and Diosgyör, near the lignite, and in the new city of Sztalinváros (the former small borough of Dunapentele) on the Danube, south of Budapest, where the coke comes from the basin of Pécs and the iron ore can be brought up the Danube.

The iron and steel thus produced are mainly destined to the machine-building plants most of which are in Budapest and specialize in locomotives, railway rolling stock, turbines, tractors, electrical apparatus, and even motorcars (about 5000 trucks annually). Still more important in terms of employment is the older textile industry, also concentrated mainly in Budapest. The cement and construction industries have been among the fastest to expand. In a way, although on a smaller scale, Hungary has been included in the COMECON planning with the more industrialized countries, East Germany, Czechoslovakia, and Poland, where engineering has been most actively pushed, along with a supporting rise of the steel output. Although this trend is likely to be maintained as the hunger for machinery of all kinds is far from being satisfied in the Communist countries, more stress is being now put on chemical production. A large group of chemical plants has been built near the Tibisco, based on natural gas from Rumania brought in by pipeline.

Thus the industrialization of Hungary is proceeding steadily, largely through publicly owned manufacturing enterprises, which employed 802,000 persons in 1954 and 1,800,000 in 1966. While Hungary imports larger quantities of fuels and raw materials from other areas in the Russian orbit, it exports increasing quantities of machinery (mainly machine tools and electrical equipment and apparatus) in exchange.

The foreign trade with the USSR, Czechoslovakia, and Rumania accounts for more than half of all the Hungarian external transactions. Austria and Yugoslavia account for about 5 percent each. In 1960 a three-year Anglo-Hungarian trade agreement was signed and later extended to 1972 to develop Hungarian relations with Western Europe, Hungary purchasing British finished goods (machinery, textiles, radio and television equipment, motorcars, and chemicals) in exchange for foodstuffs and some manufactures (bacon, butter, fruit, vegetables, aluminum, and some chemicals).

On the whole the Hungarian economy is better endowed, more diversified, and better balanced than that of Austria. In some respects it is more convenient not to be cut off, as Austria is, from the Lower Danubian basin; but Hungary pays a very high price to maintain its links with the East. The Hungarian nation, especially since 1956, has fewer illusions left and no expectation of a larger frame in which it could be included. A distinct zone of civilization, the Magyars dislike equally a too-close association with either the Slavs or the Germans. Still their geographical position seldom leaves them any choice. The implications of this position were particularly obvious when, faced with a German ultimatum to take sides in the conflict in 1941, Count Teleki, then prime minister of Hungary, saw no solution open to him that was acceptable and preferred committing suicide to choosing either one of two ordeals. The individual solution saved the collective honor. The Hungarian people in their landlocked plain, surrounded by warring powers, have shown for centuries an extraordinary vitality and a great ability to survive. This is the first time in its history that its national destiny is to be dependent mainly on the great Slavic power.

## RUMANIA

More varied and again different is the country of the Lower Danube — Rumania. Its boundaries have been fluctuating constantly since it first appeared on the political map of Europe in the middle of the nineteenth century through the union of the principalities of Walachia and Moldavia under a common king, who claimed full independence from the Turkish sultan. A small kingdom between the Carpathians and the Black Sea, it became a much larger country in 1919 when it was granted new territories taken from the Austrian, Hungarian, and Russian empires. Further shifts in the boundaries occurred between 1940 and 1947, when a peace treaty was signed in Paris fixing the present boundaries: the major change consisted in the separation of Bessarabia and Bucovina, which went to the Soviet Union. Rumanian territory was estimated in 1965 at 91,700 square miles (instead of the 113,900 of

1939). It now extends over four major regions: the Pontic Plain (Pont is the old Greek name for the Black Sea), the Carpathians, the highlands of Transylvania, and the eastern periphery of the Pannonian Plain of Banat. In 1939 the population was approximately 20 million (of which about 70 percent were Rumanians); in 1960, it was 18.5 million (87 percent being Rumanian) and in 1966, 19.1 million.

The Rumanian people result from a very complicated mixture, beginning with the Romanized populations who were established on the Lower Danube to guard one of the imperial *limes* against northern tribes. Having first developed in the Pontic Plain, the Rumanians went looking for shelter in the highlands when Mongol raids made the open steppes insecure. They colonized the basin of Transylvania—that is, beyond the forests which covered the Carpathians—but later returned and reoccupied the plain, particularly in the nineteenth century, starting from the mountainous stronghold. Slavic, Magyar, German, and Turkish elements have certainly mixed with the original Rumanians to form the present people, who speak a romance language but who keep in their vocabulary influences of the penetration by all the elements mentioned. These people have increased rapidly. The population in the old provinces grew from 3.9 million in 1850 to 8.75 in 1930, but recent statistics are hard to evaluate, as some changes in numbers have resulted from the exchanges of populations which removed a part of the Magyar and German minorities (8 and 2 percent of the population in 1966), and also from the massacre of the Jews, who formed about 4 percent of the prewar total and 1 percent today.

The regions of Rumania may be divided into the central highlands and the plains around it. The best way to review these is by starting in the west and progressing toward the Black Sea shore. In the west the first region is the fringe of the Pannonian Plain, settled with Rumanian people in the nineteenth century. Vast alluvial fans at the foot of the Transylvanian Mountains occupy most of this area and are cut up by rivers going down to the Tisza. Towns that grew out of large villages, such as Arad (115,000), with many industries, especially rolling-stock and textile plants, Oradea Mare (112,000), a market for timber and cattle, and Timişoara (152,000) capital of the Banat, live off the produce and needs of this rich rural country, which raises cattle and cultivates tobacco, sugar beets, wheat, and the mulberry tree for feeding silk worms.

To the east, following the main rivers, one penetrates easily inside the highland stronghold of central Rumania. While the Carpathians form a semicircular barrier toward the Pontic Plain, the interior of Transylvania opens rather easily toward the west; it used to have sizable Magyar and German minorities, but the Rumanians were still in the majority and more linked with their brethren of the eastern plains. The Carpathians and the Bihar range form a rugged frame around the basin of Transylvania, in which erosion has sculptured hills, valleys, and wider depressions in sandstone, marls, and gypsum layers. The frame of higher mountains is made of peneplained, uplifted, and folded sections, where crystalline rocks outcrop on vast areas. Glaciation has also affected these mountains and contributed to the deepening of the valleys and sharpening of the high crests. On some parts of these Transylvanian "Alps" the regularity of many crestlines present a somewhat flattened top, with the same altitude within a certain area suggesting definitely the existence in older times of a leveled surface which erosion dissected after uplifting.

A thick forest cover remains on the heights with some Alpine summer pastures on the higher parts. Pastoral life animates the slopes, while the population remains concentrated in the lower areas. Vineyards and large orchards of fruit trees are the main cash crops. Local agriculture is of a rather primitive kind, producing wheat, corn, and a variety of vegetables. This is a country isolated from the main currents of traffic and unused to large-scale mechanical transportation. The exports are the rather light cargoes of high-priced fruits and cattle (which often walk long distances). The greatest resources that this area contributes to the outside are the minerals of the subsoil. Mining has long been conducted here—one of the Transylvanian ranges is known as the Ore Mountains. There is some coal and lignite, vast quantities of iron, copper, and lead ores, bauxite, rock salt, natural gas and gold. With the exception of gold, all these minerals are exploited to a small extent only, due to the lack of equipment and of means of transportation. It may be said that the Rumanian Carpathians serve as one of the ore reserves of Europe, the development of which has been postponed until some future date when it may be needed. Similarly the hydroelectric power potential was almost unused, and only a small part of the forests was systematically worked for timber. The highlands remain the part of Rumania where the future may bring, once adequate equipment is provided, greater prosperity to the nation.

The best-utilized resource of the Rumanian Carpathians is the rich petroleum field of its eastern foothills, the best in Europe outside Russia. This area was closer to the sea and within a short distance of the Danube, a major waterway. Europe has always been short of oil since the beginning; British, American, and French interests developed the field actively between the two wars, wells being scattered on the slopes amid a thick forest cover along a belt centered on the chief collecting city of Ploeşti. Both wars restricted the production. From 7 million tons in 1937, the oil output decreased to 3.6 in 1944; Allied bombers raided

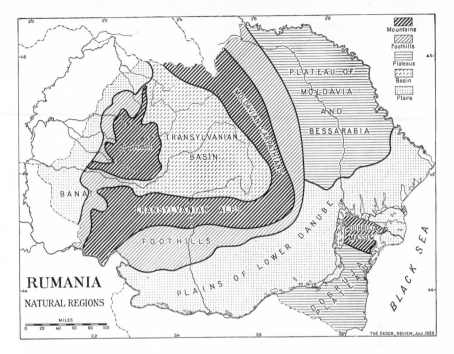

The boundaries of Rumania on these two maps are as of 1922–1939. (*The Geographical Review*)

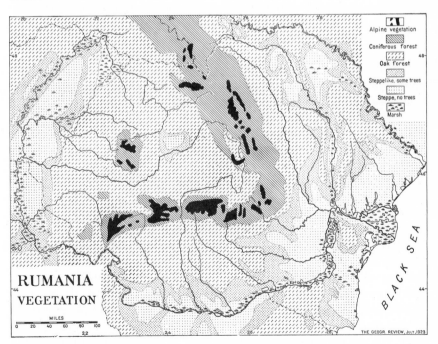

the field, and later Soviet technicians carried off to Russia a large part of the drilling machinery that had been available for German use. In 1967 the production reached 13.2 million tons. The natural gas (around 18 million cubic meters) is being used in the Bucharest area and a pipeline takes it to Budapest. The property of the oil wells and installations has been nationalized since 1945.

Urban life has been scattered throughout the highland area in a small number of cities, often well-endowed with historical monuments and guarding the main crossroads or gates of the interior basin. The chief city and capital of Transylvania is Cluj (168,000 people in 1966), a typical old rural provincial market, working the local products from grains and hides to timber and some steel, and residence also of many officials. Braşov (140,000) is at the foot of the mountain, commanding several passes; its plants make paper, furniture, woolens, and machines, refined oil, and tan leather. There are also specialized mining towns and the curious iron and steel center of Reşita (50,000) in the Ore Mountains. Ploeşti, the oil capital, is more important as a center of industry (with 140,000 people). There we reach the threshold of the Pontic Plain.

In Walachia and Moldavia the structure of the land is diversified. In Moldavia begins the series of old and low platforms that underlie most of European Russia, sloping gently eastward; in Walachia the Danube crosses a plain that, like the Pannonian, was occupied in recent geological times by a lake finally drained; but east of the Danube the Dobruja region shows a complicated structure of "plateaulike" hilly ridges to the north, around which the Danube skirts before opening up in a large delta, with all the lakes and swamps and arms of land that gain upon the sea. A new ship canal was built across this area, from the Danube to the Black Sea from Mediaş to Cernavoda. Some 40 miles in length, it shortens by 150 miles the access to Danube ports for ships of no more than 15,000 tons. Constanta is the new, rapidly developing capital and seaport (135,000) of the Dobruja; its metropolitan region agglomerates 200,000.

The Moldavian and Walachian plains are a domain of extensive grain cultivation. Corn is produced mostly for the peasants' food, while wheat is the chief cash crop. Before 1914, when Rumania was restricted mainly to these plains, its main function used to be wheat export. Brăila (122,000) and Galati (113,000) were the main ports where hills of golden grain were sucked out by pumps to fill the ships going to Western Europe. Little mechanization or fertilization was applied, and the prewar average yield of 16 bushels per acre was one of the lowest in Europe. Dr. Samuel Van Valkenburg has outlined an interesting comparison between Rumania and the wheat belt in the American Middle

West, showing how much more manpower was used and how much smaller was the share of each individual inhabitant, especially as rainfall in the steppic region of the Lower Danube was less regular than in the more humid Midwest.

Grains are not the only crop of the Pontic Plain. Fodder crops feed the livestock, chiefly cattle and horses, and the sunflower is cultivated on vast surfaces, as well as the recently introduced soya bean. Sunflower and soya furnish the much-desired vegetable oils, of which a severe shortage developed right after World War II, especially in the Eastern countries. Rumania took upon itself to increase its shipments of oil-seeds to Poland and Czechoslovakia, both of which needed them badly, from 1948 on, in exchange for industrial goods. Here, too, Communist governments have collectivized farming since 1949; by 1965 about 96 percent of the arable land was claimed to be in state or collective farms.

As in Hungary, urban life in Rumania is largely concentrated in the capital. Bucharest is a city of about 1.3 million people, the only one over 200,000 in the whole country. The metropolitan region, a separate administrative division, counted 1.5 million people in 1966. The city is not on the Danube but at an important crossroads in the plain, developed as such by the Walachian princes who chose it for their headquarters. Since the seventeenth century it has been a center of trade, a cosmopolitan town, with vast warehouses and many narrow little streets around a monumental central section. In the last century growth was rapid: Bucharest had only 70,000 inhabitants in 1830; with the railroads, the independence of the kingdom, and the large-scale export of grains and, later, of petroleum products, Bucharest developed to its present size. The industrial function is mainly oriented toward the domestic market and is less impressive than that of Budapest or Vienna. There is a sharp contrast between the elegant sections of the richer people and the surrounding poor sections of the workers. Financially and commercially, Bucharest concentrated all the business of the nation.

The sharp contrast in the capital is typical of the whole country. Rumania used to have a fashionable, refined elite, who possessed most of the nation's income, and the vast mass of the population showed little of the "old cultural" traditions claimed by the aristocracy. Almost a colonial country in a way, Rumania was bound to be a fertile field for Soviet propaganda. Its rural masses, of Greek Orthodox religion, were closer to prerevolutionary Russia, while the elite was closer to France in culture, though not in democratic spirit. Having taken from the French, as a severe judgment has said, "most of their vices and none of their virtues," the Rumanians were dominated by the Nazis from 1940 to 1945, then passed under Soviet control. The Soviet Union was granted by the peace treaty reparations in kind to the extent of $300 million. Navigation on the Danube and on the Black Sea was all placed under the management of the Soviet-Rumanian company Sovromtransport. Soviet occupation forces left only in 1958.

One of the most underdeveloped countries of Europe, Rumania perhaps grew too quickly without having had time to form indigenous cadres for the nation. Most of the important economic development has been handled by foreign interests throughout history. The picturesque embroidered clothes of the peasants, the musical talent of the numeous gypsies, the wealth rapidly acquired from some mineral resources, especially oil, could not make up for the low standard of living, the ignorance of the majority of the population, and the too-slow progress of agrarian reform. Rumania offers thus a third stage of underdevelopment among Danubian countries. Although its plains were less depopulated and better drained than the Pannonian one, they were definitely less well organized. Notwithstanding its relative high density of population, Rumania was the least "humanized" of the countries west of Russia, and it may remain for some time a "field of expansion" for stronger and better organized powers.

Like the other countries whose economies are controlled from Moscow, Rumania has been induced to develop much of its resources and to push its industrialization. The results are less obvious here, however, than in most other East European lands. Partly this was due to the lack of skill and of enthusiasm on the part of the Rumanians, partly it may have been deliberate on the part of Russia, in order to avoid giving to Rumania a greater share in the economy being organized and developed east of the "iron curtain"; for in a time of economic scarcity and rising needs, the Rumanian resources would have seemed a logical target for quick large-scale development.

The agricultural production has been somewhat modernized and mechanized, and on the vast expanse of rich soils of Rumania it did not need much to obtain substantially improved yields. In the 1950s farm products increased by more than 25 percent in the country and the sugarbeet harvest more than doubled. In 1965 Rumania harvested 6 million tons of wheat, 128,000 tons of rye, 124,000 of oats, 485,000 of barley, and 5,870,000 of corn; Rumania was the third largest corn producer in Europe, after the USSR and Yugoslavia, and the fourth of wheat after the USSR, France and Italy. Rice, linseed, and tobacco were produced in small quantities; sunflower seed, fruits, and vegetables yielded large crops. Livestock was important, too: 4.7 million head of cattle (a figure that, as in other Communist-controlled countries, could not be made to rise much), 12 million sheep, 6 million pigs, the last two kinds of animals increasing in numbers. Tractors were still few: about 90,000 by 1965, that is, less than in East Germany or Czechoslovakia for a much

A street in Bucharest. (*Three Lions*)

The oil fields near Ploesti. (*Three Lions*)

larger farm output. Supplies of chemical fertilizer were still meager: about 2 kilograms per acre of tilled land in 1959 (against 13 in Hungary and 40 in Czechoslovakia). Such figures hint at what the farm potential of Rumania could become if put to full use as in the intensively developed Western countries of Europe.

This margin between real and potential production is likely to be even wider for the mineral resources. In this area Rumania produced in 1965 6.1 million tons of coal; 6 of lignite; 12.5 of crude petroleum; 17.2 billion cubic meters of natural gas; 750,000 tons of iron ore (in metal content); 30,000 tons of manganese; and small quantities of bauxite, lead, mercury, silver, and gold. Large deposits of rock salt are mined. Rumania is, with Poland, one of the few Soviet satellites that can boast surpluses of energy resources. Just as Poland can export its Silesian coal, Rumania has enough oil and gas for serious export. Pipelines take the oil from the Ploeşti, Boldeşti and Piteşti fields to Giurgiu on the Danube, Constanţa on the Black Sea, and Odessa, the Soviet port. The abundance of mineral, natural gas, and waterpower resources in Transylvania has spurred on the growth of the main cities in that rich province (Cluj, Braşov, Sibiu) but also of a variety of new small industrial centers (such as Turda with glass and chemicals, Diciosânmărtin, and Mediaş). Braşov-Stalin is being made into the main Rumanian iron and steel center. As more gas fields are being tapped in Transylvania and the Banat, more possibilities for scattering industrial plants are open. A gas pipeline is crawling from there towards Hungary. New textile plants have been inaugurated at Iaşi and Botoşani. Galaţi is building a steel mill; Braila makes pulp and paper using reeds which are abundant in the delta; agricultural machinery is produced in Braşov. Bucharest, however, still gets the lion's share of the manufacturing of finished goods, machinery, textiles, clothing, shoes, and leatherware, as well as the food-processing industries. Lumber from the forests (27 percent of the total area) is another important raw material.

The major trade relations of Rumania are with the USSR and its Communist neighbors. The COMECON countries however took 85 percent of the total external trade in 1952 but only 75 percent in 1957 and 65 in 1965; some relations with Western countries are gradually being reestablished.

In the 1950s, Rumania was the most neglected of the countries of Central Europe vassalized by the Soviet Union after World War II. But in the 1960s, it worked hard to develop its industry and improve its agriculture, although it received less help from the COMECON organization than did the other countries in the Soviet orbit. By 1967, the government of Rumania began to show some independence toward its powerful neighbor to the north. Rumanian trade relations with West European countries were increasing (particularly with Italy and West Germany); the Soviet authorities became worried, and a five-year trade agreement was signed in December 1965 between Rumania and the USSR, according to which Rumania would deliver oil products, textiles, ships, and machinery in exchange for coal, iron ore, motor cars, and other machines. Still, in foreign policy, the Rumanian government continued to show increasing independence in 1968. A new breeze of freedom was blowing along the Danube until came new Soviet pressure and the occupation of Czechoslovakia.

## THE COUNTRIES ALONG THE DANUBE

The Danube River could indeed serve as an axis of Central Europe as we define it. It flows from its head springs in West Germany through Austria, Czechoslovakia, Hungary, Yugoslavia, Bulgaria, and Rumania. And it now touches Soviet soil before emptying into the Black Sea, which has largely become a Soviet-dominated lake. Only East Germany, Poland, and Finland remain outside the Danubian valley, while Yugoslavia and Bulgaria belong to the Mediterranean part of Europe. Still, the countries along the Danube form a distinct family of nations with many links between them as a result of history as well as geography. They have all been influenced by German culture at some stage of their development, and almost all of them still have a small German minority, even after the reduction of these minorities at the end of World War II.

The Danubian countries do not lack resources or population, but they were not able in the past to take full advantage of their potentialities. After World War II, they experienced a period of hardship and of profound reorganization of their economies and society. With the exception of West Germany and Austria, they have been brought under Soviet domination; their agriculture has been largely collectivized, and this reform has made it more difficult to increase production despite a considerable need for such expansion. Most of the industry and large-scale commerce has been nationalized, but this sector of the economy has fared better under the socialist regime. Substantial industrialization and urbanization is taking place, although much of the over-all planning in the framework of the COMECON has been directed to the policies and needs of the USSR.

The population migrations that followed World War II have considerably decreased the problems that stem in most countries of the Danubian basin from the presence of national minorities. The ethnic map, which used to be a very complicated puzzle, has been considerably simplified. The new greater unity of each nation should help it establish a more stable political system. However, under Soviet domination, the political process has been directed by the various Communist parties controlled from Moscow. Hungary was the first of the Soviet satellites in Central Europe to rebel, in 1956. This attempt at actual independence was crushed. In the 1960s, a more gradual evolution has led Rumania and Czechoslovakia to show greater autonomy and to re-establish more relations with the Western countries of Europe. Yugoslavia which among the socialist regimes, used to be the only one in opposition to the USSR has played the part of a buffer and a link between East and West. Now that common enterprises have been started by Rumania and Yugoslavia on the Danube (particularly the great Iron Gate dam and power development) and that West Germany has been made an associate member of the Danube Commission, one may hope for some softening of the effects of the "iron curtain" along the Danube. These countries of the Danube still keep a great underdeveloped potential, the development of which has progressed rather slowly under Soviet auspices. One should not, however, expect a too rapid evolution of the Danubian countries westward. Over all the expanse of Central Europe and the Baltic hovers the shadow of the giant neighbor to the east.

# Part V

## Eastern Europe: The Soviet Union

Moscow: A meeting on Red Square. *(Sovfoto)*

# 19

---

# Russia
# in Europe

Eastern Europe is almost as difficult to define as Central Europe, because its western limit shifts with the expansion or contraction of the area included in Central Europe. But to the east the limit is stable because it is purely physical: the Urals range and river, the Caspian Sea, the Caucasus range. The definition is simplified moreover by the fact that for several centuries the major part of this territory that runs to the Urals has belonged to one political unit: Russia. The boundaries of Russia have been shifting, of course, but the bulk of the eastern part of Europe has remained Russian. In 1917 a revolution transformed the Russian Empire into the Soviet Union, which became a federation of republics. Still the largest by far of these republics is the Russian one, which covers most of the European part of the Union. We are justified therefore in considering that the Soviet Union coincides with Eastern Europe, all the more so as the national philosophy of the Russians is largely of continental inspiration and is not purely European: the Soviet Union stretches eastward into Asia and its Asiatic territories are vaster than the European ones. This was also true of Russia for centuries before 1917.

Once inside the Soviet Union one feels in the climate as well as in the political "atmosphere" the proximity of Asia. The Soviet Union covers, within its 1946 boundaries, a total area of 8,708,000 square miles—that is, about one sixth of the land area on earth. Less than one fourth of this total is in Europe, but these 2 million square miles constitute a good half of the total area of Europe. And there is a striking contrast indeed between the two halves of the European continent: the Western half all

European Russia. This general outline map of the Soviet Union in Europe in 1953 shows boundaries of the main republics composing the federal union. The capitals of these republics are indicated by double circles, and their names are in bolder type. Main cities and rivers have been indicated. Names of Soviet cities are often changed; thus in the Caucasian area the name of *Dzaudzhikau* stands for the town known until 1953 as *Ordzhonikidze*, after an early important official of the Soviet regime. *Stalino* and *Stalingrad* were renamed again *Donetzk* and *Volgograd* in 1961 and *Molotov* reverted to *Perm*. All towns shown have over 100,000 inhabitants.

in peninsulas and islands, divided among many nations, and the Eastern half a continental mass little indented by the few bordering seas (the Black, Baltic, and White seas), united in one large political unit. This continental mass presents a uniformity in its topography and in its population which has little in common with the variety and partitioning of the Western, maritime half of Europe.

## THE GIANT OF THE EAST

Russia has been a giant in Europe for quite some time. For several centuries it was the largest political unit of territory occupied by relatively uniform populations. The British Commonwealth and empire were and still are much larger in area as well as in population than Russia has been or than the Soviet Union now is. But there is no continuity in territory among the British lands, and the peoples inhabiting them belong to many races and cultures. In Russia the periphery alone offers such a variety; internally it has uniformity, although imperfect, on a scale unknown in other parts of Europe.

The question then arises: why was it that Russia did not play a leading part in the world until recently? Size does not always confer leadership on a country—the whole history of Europe testifies to that. However, it should be realized that Russia has been a potent factor in European politics since the fourteenth century at least, and one of the Big Five in Europe since the beginning of the eighteenth century or, more precisely, since the defeat of the Swedes by Peter the Great at the battle of Poltava in 1709. In Asia, Russia has been one of the leading powers since the end of the eighteenth century. By mere size of territory, Russia played a notable part; but the population, spread so thin over so vast an area, was too busy with domestic problems to be active in foreign affairs, unless for reasons of self-defense. Russia was also an isolated country, the periphery of which was rather wild and desertlike, and Russian development proceeded for a long time almost in a closed world of its own. The great changes began to occur when Peter the Great went westward to understand this strange Western world better, saw his first ball in Königsberg, worked in the shipyards at Amsterdam, and studied government at Versailles. He learned what had made the Western nations strong and rich, and ever since the Russians have endeavored to make up for centuries of backwardness and to compare in all respects with the West. Applying Western methods and techniques on a Russian scale should have produced a tremendous power. Experience has proved that it was not easy. The opening of Russia to Western influence had at first the effect of endowing Eastern Europe with a "colonial" kind of economy, producing foodstuffs and raw materials for Western markets and importing manufactured goods. In its continental frame Russia was a giant but weak in so far as distant operations were concerned, because she was not participating either in the maritime expansion or in the financial development of Western civilization.

Isolation in trade, self-sufficiency within a regional framework, and suspicion of, even hostility toward, the accumulation of capital, especially when foreign controlled, are three basic points in the traditional Russian attitude. These have arisen largely as a result of the country's background: no outlet to the open sea, few transport facilities across the broad spaces of the national territory, and little national accumulation of capital, which has had to be borrowed from abroad, often at high cost. Russia might have become a tremendously powerful and rich country had she applied Western techniques to her vast open lands as was done in the United States. But the Russians were not able to do this because culturally their national heritage was different and, being landlocked, they were unable to play a part on the sea as had the Americans, who were heirs to the maritime, advanced culture of Western Europe. With an extraordinary stubbornness and a genuine mysticism, the Russians cling to their own cultural inheritance: it is for them a great force in time of crisis, but it is a weakness when performing the task of systematic Westernization of their techniques and methods.

The Eastern giant has therefore a considerable strength, but strength of a different nature than that of the major powers in Western or Central Europe. It would not be an oversimplification to explain a great deal of the difference by the continental outline of the territory: because few topographical barriers impeded traffic inside this continental area, it was normal for the different parts to look one toward another rather than toward the outside as might have happened had lofty ranges broken up the land continuity. Throughout the Soviet Union develops the great stretch of plains which has been called the *Eurasian* area, as it covers the eastern half of Europe and practically the northern half of Asia. Only the Ural range interrupts to some extent the perfect continuity of this plain. All the other (and much higher) mountain ranges of the Soviet Union are situated along its periphery, from the Carpathians to the ranges of the Far East, passing through the Caucasus and the highlands of Central Asia. The Eurasian area thus seems to be a closed world of easy inside traffic, with barriers of high, almost impassable, ranges and plateaus to the south and with the even more impervious barrier of the Arctic Ocean and its ice pack to the north. The Eurasian world opens only by narrow windows eastward on the Pacific shores, but broadly westward on Central Europe.

The European part of the Soviet Union is the most simple of the major divisions of the "sixth part of the world." It consists of one immense table-land, with some structural diversity along its periphery. Most of this has been "Russified" for at least a century, some of it for many hundred years. The uniformity is thus greater, although here again the periphery introduces some variety. The European part is more thickly populated, with 180 million people on 2.2 million square miles — that is, an average of 81 to the square mile as against an average of less than 10 on the thrice larger, Asiatic section of the Union. All the major cities, the larger industries, and some of the best-developed agricultural regions are in this European part. Its importance has been increased by the addition of new territories along the western border and by tighter relations with satellite countries in Central Europe and the Balkans. The main devel-opment of the Union in recent years has, however, taken place within the Asiatic territories. Population increase and economic development have been intentionally accelerated there. The Soviet Union is moving east, and this trend should gradually reduce the relative importance of the European part. But it will be some time before Siberia or Soviet Central Asia can rival in any appreciable way the economic and demo-graphic power of Eastern Europe.

Although it means describing one half of the whole continent in area, the main features of European Russia can be outlined rather briefly. The structural unity makes the distribution of topography, climate, and vegetation much simpler than in the other parts of Europe.

## NATURAL REGIONS: THE ZONES OF VEGETATION

The Russian tableland extends from the Arctic Sea in the north to the Black Sea and the Caucasus range in the south, and from the Baltic Sea and the Carpathians in the west to the Urals and the Caspian Sea in the east. It is on the whole a flat, gently rolling plain that appears to be a widening out of the Great Plain of Europe come to cover the full width of the continent. Over such an area the structure cannot be absolutely uniform of course; a few structural domes, with very gentle slopes, are separated by slightly depressed areas. The uplands, of which one is situated in a central-western area between the basins of the Volga and Dnieper rivers and the other along the Middle Volga, appear on the maps as still, flat plateaus, rising slightly above 600 feet and creating hilly aspects in a few places: thus the Valdai Hills to the northwest, or the Zhigulevsk Mountains, which are actually an eroded cliff at the edge of the plateau towering above the middle course of the Volga. In the northwest some hills were caused by morainic accumulation of the Qua-ternary icecaps; in the east the topography rises slightly in the Ural foothills. On the whole, monotonous, flat spaces prevail. The country is wide open to climatic influences that can sweep from one end to another without any local variety imposed by the topography (see map, p. 708).

The two dominant climatic influences are the influence of latitude, making the transition gradual from the northern shores of the frozen Arctic Sea to the southern shores along the Black Sea, which does not freeze much, and the influence of the continent—that is, of the tremendous land mass of Asia stretching to the east, increasing the extremes of temperature and the aridity throughout the whole year. To some extent one influence compensates for the other; because the continental anticyclone makes the winter dry, it favors the concentration of the bulk of the yearly precipitations during the warm season; this is important, for the vegetation growth, arrested by the frost during the winter, has to make up during the warm season for that period of rest.

In the south some Mediterranean influences reach the shores of the Black Sea. But to the southeast, European Russia borders on the vast belt of deserts which stretches across Africa and Asia from the Atlantic coast of western Africa to Mongolia in the Far East. The shores of the Caspian Sea and the lower basin of the Ural River are very dry, a threshold to the vast deserts of Central Asia. In the northeastern part of Russia, along the Arctic shores, another kind of desert, due to cold instead of aridity, develops. Thus in the two eastern corners of European Russia climatic extremes reach a point unknown elsewhere in Europe. The frozen Arctic does not greatly moderate the impact of continentality. To the northwest, however, warm tropical water masses from the Atlantic reach the northern shores of the Kola peninsula, making it possible for some ports to remain ice-free most of the year and warming up the climate somewhat.

Winter is cold throughout the whole Soviet Union. In the western outskirts Riga (in Latvia, on the Baltic) records an average of 24.3° F. in January and has four months below the freezing point; on the Black Sea shore Odessa records 26.4° in January and has three months of frost. Moscow, in the center of the country, averages 13.6° in January, and Chkalov (Orenburg), a gateway to Asia on the Ural River, shows only 4.3°. The average temperature remains below 32° for five months both in Moscow and Chkalov. In the very north, in Archangel, frosts last over six months and in Kola seven months. The summer temperatures range from 64° in Riga and 65.7° in Moscow to 71.6° at Chkalov and 72.7° in Odessa. The hottest month, July, is most felt on the shores of the Caspian, below sea level, with both Astrakhan and Baku averaging over 77°.

Over the greater part of European Russia the yearly precipitations average around 20 to 25 inches, of which more than one half falls between April and October; only the Crimea and the eastern shores of the Black Sea get most of their rainfall between November and March—the result of Mediterranean influences. This Mediterranean shade in the south somewhat varies a climate that otherwise is fairly even over the entire area. The length of the frost season is also a major differentiating factor; aridity begins to count as a determinant feature in the south and southeast. Thus a regular zoning of vegetation and soils in latitude has been obtained, the different belts shifting slightly northward as they approach the continental mass of Asia in the east.

The natural regions in European Russia are best described as vegetation zones, provided one remembers that *vegetation* expresses the climatic and soil conditions. This section runs the whole gamut of climates from the arctic to the subdesertic types, and following the well-known Russian geographer Leo C. Berg, we may review them from north to south: the *tundra,* the temperate forests, the wooded grassland, the steppe, the semidesert, and the subtropical area. To complement the picture it may be useful to add a last category: the higher altitude climates in the Caucasus and Ural ranges.

The *tundra* coincides with the Arctic zone. It is too cold an environment to allow for the development of trees. A rather low brush, largely made of mosses, predominates. The main climatic features can be described as follows: a long and severe winter; a brief, warm summer with prolonged light (owing to latitude), but an average temperature not exceeding 48° in the warmest month; frost occurring sometimes in the round; there is little rainfall and little evaporation, due to low temperatures; and the ground is frozen permanently below a certain depth. This last phenomenon, called *permafrost* (in Russian *vechnaya merzlota*) makes the ground as solid as a block of ice; the summer thaw affects only a superficial layer, which remains swampy, and thus the building of any heavy permanent structure in areas affected with permafrost is very difficult.

In its extreme form the arctic tundra, completely treeless and even devoid of brush, is almost absent from the European part of the USSR. It covers only some areas on the islands of the Arctic Ocean, of which Novaya Zemlya (New Land) is the largest. A large part of these islands is still covered with glaciers. The northern point of Novaya Zemlya is at 76°57' north latitude, but other islands reach latitudes above 80°. The typical tundra has no trees, but brush resulting from the degeneration of certain tree species such as dwarf birch trees. Peat bogs appear and spread. Vast areas are covered with mosses and lichens. Toward the west and the south the tundra loses its severity and trees appear, first following the rivers, then spreading between the valleys. We come thus gradually to a landscape of wooded tundra, where the peat bogs become

ARCTIC OCEAN

30°    40°    50°    60°

80°

SEA OF
BARENTZ

NOVAYA ZEMLYA

NORTH CAPE

POLAR
CIRCLE

FINLAND

WHITE
SEA

URAL MTS.

POLAR
CIRCLE

BALTIC SEA

Moscow

Warsaw

Kiev

ARAL
SEA

CASPIAN SEA

BULGARIA

BLACK SEA

40°

TURKEY

4

1    5

MEDITERRANEAN SEA

IRAN
(PERSIA)

2    6

30°    40°    50°

3    7

considerably developed. This is the case of the northern and central parts of the Kola peninsula in the northwest.

Farther south the transition from tundra to temperate forest of broad-leaved trees follows a gradation that we have already recorded in Sweden, but it occurs here on a much larger scale and with more shades of differentiation. The forest zone covers immense territories throughout the Soviet Union and over a half of its European section. It may be limited both in the north and the south by the boundaries of those areas where spruce *(Picea excelsa)* is found. The southern limit passes approximately along a line following Lutzk-Zhitomir-Kiev-Kaluga-Gorki-Kazan-Ufa, and then follows the foothills of the Ural range. The forest on the whole is predominantly coniferous (pines and firs), but trees with leaves increase in importance southward (birch, then oak). Peaty swamps occur frequently. The winter is still severe but the summer gets warmer. The yearly rainfall averages 20 inches here. The soils are rather leached, and the grayish, ashlike coloration of the top layer led to their classification as *podzols* (*zola* meaning ash in Russian). The classical type of podzol profile is gray at the top as the humus of rotting leaves, bark, or needles falling from the trees darkens the ground. Underneath there is a white level, completely washed out, turning at a greater depth to a yellowish-brown color where the soluble elements are deposited to form a clay horizon. This last clayish layer may form a crust that will interfere with the normal circulation of water underground. The main region of the podzols stretches through the median part of the forested belt. To the north the soil is too swampy and peaty for the formation of true podzols, and to the south broad-leaved trees mix in increased numbers with the spruce and pine, adding to the humus supply of the soil. The main extension of the podzols coincides thus with the purely coniferous forest.

One can therefore subdivide the forest belt into two main sections: to the north the *taïga*, almost exclusively coniferous, with a predominance of pines and firs, a thinner density of trees, and poorer or more swampy

---

*(Opposite)* Soil zones and vegetation in Soviet Europe (after the Soviet World Atlas; Mercator projection exaggerating areas northward).

1. Tundra—polar soil frozen permanently in depth.
2. Podzols—forests predominantly coniferous.
3. Wooded grassland soils with a touch of podzolization.
4. Black soils—steppe.
5. Chestnut soils of dry steppes.
6. Grey soils—deserts.
7. High altitude soils with alpine pastures.

See also the map of vegetation and land use in Europe, p. 434.

soils; to the south the mixed forest, with a mingling of oaks and firs, a denser distribution of trees, better soils, and of darker coloration on the whole, although podzols are still common. Leningrad lies at the contact of *taïga* and mixed forest, while Moscow is fully in the mixed-forest environment. The forest belt used to be well populated with an abundant fauna, including large mammals such as bears, deer, and small animals precious because of their furs (mink and ermine); now efficient hunting has so depleted the stock of valuable species that one finds them only in faraway corners of the land, where the woods have been little touched. Elsewhere wolves, foxes, and squirrels are still common, as well as a great variety of birds.

South of the limit of the forest belt just described, the wooded cover breaks up to be replaced by a checkered landscape of woods alternating with open, grassy areas; this belt is called the wooded grassland (in Russian, *lesostep*) and provides the transition to the open grassland or steppe. The gray forest soils turn gradually to the more or less compact black soils, characteristic of the steppe. Large areas are covered with thick deposits of loess, which is here much more than surficial soil layer and reaches a depth that led to its being treated by Professor Berg as an alluvial formation of a special kind, with a topography of its own. From northern Bessarabia to the south of the Ural range, the wooded grassland extends its irregular pattern; the oak is the typical tree of this zone. It seems that in recent times the woods have been steadily pushing southward, and the wooded grassland has gained on the steppe in many places. This southward migration of vegetation zones might be related to a similar trend noticed in Sweden and generally explained by a climate damper than in prehistoric times. Whatever changes may be happening, they are extremely slow and slight.

The southern and southeastern parts of European Russia show a definite trend toward aridity. Here extends the steppe: the almost treeless grassland, where narrow ribbons of woods appear only along the bottoms of the valleys. The soils are of dark coloration because of their high humus content. Over vast areas they are black—the famous *chernozem* or "black earth" of the Ukraine—elsewhere they are usually chestnut brown. The steppic belt enjoys warm and rather dry summers: the relative humidity of the June-July season around noon stays around 35 to 45 percent. The rainfall averages 12 to 18 inches a year, with a maximum in early summer followed by a dry spell; in certain years five to six summer weeks are absolutely rainless. If the June rains fail to moisten the ground, a drought will mean a lean harvest. Here we are in a semi-Mediterranean climate with the permanent threat of the lean cows alternating with the fat ones; and droughts are generally caused by the predominance of the eastern influences—as in Pharaoh's dream, the easterlies may burn the steppe. This occurs when the area finds itself (as sometimes happens in spring and even in summer) on the fringe of the anticyclone. Hot air masses, dried up by a descending movement, flow in to extend the desertlike landscape for a while.

The vegetation of the steppe offers two varieties, which correspond to the two main shades of soil. In the north, on the black soils, the grassy cover is made chiefly of a thick carpet of graminaceae; to the south, on the chestnut-brown soils the grass is thinner and contains many species with xerophytic adaptation. In winter most of the steppe is covered with snow; in spring various plants blossom, the steppe turns green, and is dotted with yellow and red or blue flowers. In May the steppe usually becomes silver-gray with red patches, but in mid-June, with the ripening of the grain, the steppe appears golden yellow as the flowers fade out; in summer the general coloration becomes more and more yellow-brown. Every year the grass cover dies out and serves as organic fertilizer for the ground. There has been much discussion about the origin of the steppe: according to certain authorities the grassy cover must have been much higher and denser before man burnt it periodically or utilized it in some other way. This view, however, has been frequently disputed, and it is possible that human action has less affected the steppic vegetation than has been thought at times.

Originally wild life seems to have been abundant on these open grassy spaces. Herds of wild horses were known here as late as the eighteenth century. Antelopes and stags were many; small mammals, especially the rodent species, were numerous and are still important because of their underground digging and soil-mixing work. Owing to their flat, open scenery, the steppic areas are ideal for large-scale livestock raising and for hunting, and such were the first activities that man developed early in this region.

While they have a high and dense cover of a prairielike kind to the northwest, to the southeast the steppes gradually become semidesert. The semidesert belt extends between the Volga and the Ural rivers south of Saratov, and along the banks of the Caspian Sea. This is a transitional area with a considerable variety of plants (all xerophytic grasses or bushes) and of soils (with a predominance of the light-chestnut shade). The yearly rainfall decreases; patches of saline soils are frequent; the soil is rather poor in humus but rich in soluble mineral elements; a salt-pan layer may develop at some depth with even underlying gypsum strata. The fauna is definitely poorer than in the steppe. The Lower Volga serves as a biological boundary, and many species do not cross it eastward. However, no actual desert occurs in the European section of the Soviet Union, although it covers a broad expanse east of the Caspian (see map p. 34).

The grassland stretches southward to the Black Sea and to the foot of the Caucasus range. Narrow areas along the Black Sea may claim to be subtropical—a Mediterranean riviera borders the hilly coast of the Crimea peninsula. Then a hot and humid stretch of land borders the Black Sea on its eastern shore, again at the foot of the Caucasus. Some tropical crops thrive in the vicinity of Batum. This last area is so close to Turkey and Asia Minor that it is hardly European, and indeed it has a very particular type of climate.

These zones of vegetation, coinciding approximately with soil belts, appear to obey mainly the law of latitude. Local climatic variations little affect this zoning; the topography rises high enough only on the periphery. The vegetation zones have been therefore the main factor orienting the organization of space. But through this immense territory another element of organization, extremely important to people because it served as a natural network of highways, has been the river system.

RIVERS AND DRAINAGE BASINS

Across the broad and flat expanse of the Russian lands, the rivers have always had an essential role. Owing to the uniformity of the topography and of climatic conditions, drainage basins could expand on vast areas, giving impressive size to the main streams. Nowhere else in Europe are the rivers so powerful and so important in every respect. All of these mighty streams flow, on the whole, from north to south; only a few rivers of smaller size take their course toward the Arctic Ocean in the north or the Baltic Sea in the west. The major rivers—Dniester, Dnieper, Don, Volga, Ural—empty into the southern seas—Caspian, Azov, Black. All the Russian rivers freeze for varying periods during the winter and have a longer period of navigation downstream, in southern areas, than upstream in the north. As they drain a rather flat, humid, and forested area (with the exception of their lower sections which cross the steppe), these rivers are generally well fed. The lowest gauge occurs during the winter, when they are frozen; the thaw combines its water masses with the spring rainfall to cause floods in that season, and high waters occur usually in the forest zone between March 15 and May 15. Since the slope is very gentle, the water level rises slowly, gradually, as the contributions of all the tributaries add to the main stream, building up its gauge and might toward its mouth, making it easier for the river to keep an impressive flow through the summer and the early autumn, when the heavy evaporation and the low rainfall cause the gauge to decline. From the spring floods to the autumn slack waters, the curve is rather simple and uniform throughout the country.

This abundant flow and the gentle slope make navigation easy when the river is not frozen. Few rapids interrupt the river transportation system; a major exception is the Dnieper rapids at Zaporozhe, now corrected by the Dnieprostroï Dam and a canal with locks. The river network constitutes a magnificent system of transportation, even though it is paralyzed in the cold season: its winding waterways cover almost the whole country rather thoroughly. Several waterways come close one to another, so that connecting them either by land portage or by construction of canals has not been too difficult. Any atlas will show this ramified network: the upper basins of the Volga, Dnieper, and Western Dvina come very close together in the Valdai Hills, which serve as a sort of central watertower of Russian hydrography. In a similar manner the upper basins of the Pechora, Northern Dvina (both drained toward the Arctic), and the Kama (a tributary of the Volga) come close one to another in the foothills of the central Ural range. At Volgograd, the Lower Volga comes quite close to the big bend of the Don. Interconnections have been built linking these mighty streams together to establish almost continuous waterways from the Baltic to the Black and Caspian seas and from the Arctic to the Caspian and to the Mediterranean basin.

The masterpiece of the whole system is the Volga River, often called the "Mother of Russia." Its 2325-mile-long course drains a basin 538,000 square miles wide. It is by far the biggest European river. The Ural and Dnieper each have a length of over 1400 miles; the latter's basin covers 200,000 square miles. The Don is of slightly smaller size. The Northern Dvina and the Pechora in the north, the Western Dvina and the Niemen in the west, and the Dniester to the southwest are all among the larger European streams, smaller than the Danube but comparable to the Rhine; the Neva, although not one of the great rivers of Europe, carries a powerful flow. Some of the Volga's tributaries, such as the Kama and the Oka, are great rivers in their own right.

The navigability of the network, however, remains subject to some climatic variations: the duration of the frost period is a major consideration; the Volga usually freezes for 140 days every winter at Gorki and 109 at Volgograd, the Dnieper for 93 days at Kiev; floods and possible drought periods have to be allowed for. The mighty Volga at Kuibyshev, in the middle of its course, carries approximately twelve times as much water in May as in September. As a general rule, the continental influences make the variations more extreme and capricious in the eastern parts of the country than in its western part. The Baltic streams, such as the Neva or Niemen, are the most regular, partly because of the climate and partly because the many lakes of their basins act as regulators. These lakes are due to glacial action and morainic topography not encountered in the drier and warmer parts of European Russia.

Glaciers, of course, have played a great part in shaping the present

A small village on the endless Russian plain. *(Sovfoto)*

The Dnieper River at Kiev. *(Sovfoto)*

topography and drainage of northern and western Russia. The main action, however, has been that of the icecap centered on the Fenno-Scandian Shield and the Baltic area. The same mechanism as was described in Scandinavia has been at work in the northeastern parts of Europe—it is only that here every phenomenon due to the vanished glaciers or to present cold is found on a larger scale.

## THE TERRITORIAL EXPANSION OF THE RUSSIANS

We do not know much of the early history of the peoples who lived in Eastern Europe in antiquity. The Scythian and Sarmatian tribes who occupied the Ukrainian area may be ancestors of the Slavs; certainly they were greatly influenced by the Greeks who settled all around the *Pont* or Black Sea. Many invasions came from Asia during the first millennium of the Christian Era, leaving layer after layer in the population of the steppe and perhaps also of the forest. In smaller numbers, but important for their cultural and economic role, were the Varangians from Scandinavia who gave their name to the *Russ*. There was little order and cooperation among the many tribes and clans that populated the area. A popular tradition holds that actual unity of an important group of tribes (every one being centered around a *gorod* or fortified town serving also as a trading center) came only in the ninth century when a delegation invited the Varangian Rurik to come and rule the Russians. "Our land is great and plentiful, but there is no order in it" was the description of his new realm given to the prince.

The first region to be opened to outside relations and trade was the transcontinental route from the Baltic to the Black Sea, following the Western Dvina and Volkhov rivers upstream and the Dnieper downstream. The Varangians came down this route, while the Greek or Byzantine merchants went up from the south, and their meeting favored the development of trade and urban activities. The capital of what has been called the "river state," as it became a political unit based on the rivers, was Kiev on the Dnieper at the entrance of the black-soil steppe. The site of Kiev probably benefited by the land caravan route passing across the steppe from east to west. Kiev was one of the major crossroads of European trade in the tenth and eleventh centuries; it was also a cultural center where Nordic and Mediterranean influences mingled, a more advanced and perhaps richer city than either London or Paris at that time. But the pastoral tribes of the steppe kept the river thoroughfare constantly under attack—this was not only the usual feud between nomads and sedentary people but also the push westward of populations which were themselves under pressure from other peoples arriving from Asia. In the southeast, around the Caspian Sea and on the Lower

Volga, another group of peoples had organized a relatively prosperous area. Those were the Khazars, said to have adopted the Jewish religion, and about whom we know chiefly from the writings of Arab geographers of the ninth to eleventh centuries.

A strong push came out of Central Asia toward the Black Sea areas with the Mongol expansion of the twelfth and thirteenth centuries, building up the empire of Genghis Khan. Nomadic hordes swept the open steppe, bringing to an end the prosperity of the Dnieper trade, taking and ransacking Kiev in 1240, destroying the river state, and practically chasing the Russians out of the steppe. The Russians fled northward into the forest, which was a good shelter from the Mongols, people of the wide-open steppes to whom the thick woods were strange and dreaded. This Mongol invasion marked a break in Russian development and a shift from an orientation toward Byzantium to an orientation toward the Baltic. At first Novgorod, one of the oldest Russ towns, on the Volkhov River, inherited the leadership lost by Kiev, for in the twelfth century the Novgorodians, led by a Varangian aristocracy, had founded establishments on the Upper Volga and on the Oka River, trading by the great riverway directly with the Caspian area. This trade suffered from the Mongol drive, but Novgorod continued to dominate a vast territory extending from the Oka River to the Baltic. It came to grips with the Germanic drive eastward from the west and with the Knights of the Teutonic Order, based at Königsberg, in a dispute over the Baltic areas and was forced to submit to them. Novgorod thus became a member of the Hanseatic League and remained a great trade center until the fifteenth century.

The position of Novgorod, however, was a fragile one as the city was on the fringe of the Slavic territory, close to the expanding Germanic or Swedish empires. No lasting peace could be established with the Teutonic Order, then Roman Catholic and attempting to win over the Russians of the Greek Orthodox faith. Thus the leadership of Russia shifted from the thoroughfare area along the rivers to isolated clearings of the thick, mixed forest, particularly in the area that is sometimes called the Russian Mesopotamia, between the Upper Volga and the Oka. Between the Mongols or Tatars to the south and the Finns and Lithuanians to the north, the real Russia rose amid forests, lakes, and swamps, clearing the land, and organizing a way of life as self-sufficient as possible to avoid outside domination.

In one of those clearings, away from any major stream, rose the power of Moscow and its princes. Appearing on the Russian scene in the middle of the twelfth century, Moscow became the capital in 1263. Its tsar Ivan III conquered Novgorod; then Muscovy achieved the status of a great empire when Ivan IV, known as the Terrible (1547-1584), conquered most of the basin of the Volga and western Siberia. In the seventeenth century, therefore, the territorial foundations of Russia's greatness were well laid. The tsar's authority was that of an absolute monarch, tempered only by the feudal privileges of the aristocracy of the *boyars*. Peter the Great embarked on a great enterprise of Westernization of the technique of living and of government. At the end of the eighteenth century, the western boundaries of Russia stretched approximately along the same lines as existed in 1949; the nineteenth century added only small areas to the south in Europe. The main expansion then took place in Asia.

The total population of European Russia was estimated at 17.5 million in 1724, at 55 million in 1859, 87 million in 1897, 162 million in 1959 and 185 million in 1968. Within the last hundred years the population within the Russian-dominated area has increased threefold without important changes in territory. The population of the Asiatic territories has increased many times; Europe accounted for 94 percent of the total population of the Russian Empire in 1859, but for only 75 percent of the Soviet Union in 1959. While noting the statistical expansion of the Russian peoples, we should not overlook the considerable numbers who were lost through emigration, not to mention wars and famines. The emigration which followed the Revolution of 1917 and the subsequent civil war was estimated at more than 2 million. Russian emigrants and contingents from the nationalities along the European periphery contributed substantial numbers to the settlement of the Americas. Finally, World War II cost the USSR losses probably approximating 20 million people, mainly young men. Few nations have had in the recent centuries an expansion, demographic as well as political, comparable to the Russian one. In 1940, when the Soviet armies were experiencing serious difficulties in their war against little Finland, Stalin was able to remark that "the Soviet mothers give to the Union one Finland every year." Soviet official statistics were scarce, but an annual figure of births of 4 million, about the population of Finland, seems quite plausible for 1940. The rapid expansion of territory after the sixteenth century helped to remove barriers between the groups, and racial distinctions are seldom clear cut in the European section of the Soviet Union.

Thus it may be said that there were four stages in the making of Russia: the first stage was that of the *river state* centered in Kiev, living from trade and transit; the second stage was the isolation in forest clearings and the gradual sweep from clearing to clearing, largely along rivers—Moscow was the capital of this second stage, during which national self-sufficiency was emphasized. With Peter the Great the third stage opened, Russia coming to the west, sweeping the steppes to its south and east, starting

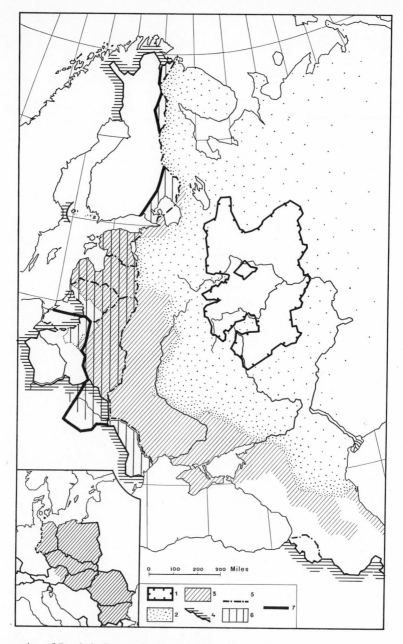

Expansion of Russia in Europe in the past 500 years.
1. The principality of Muscovy in 1462.
2. European acquisitions from 1462 to 1689.
3. European acquisitions from 1689 to 1801.
4. Western boundary of the Russian empire in 1914.
5. Western boundary of the Soviet Union between 1922 and 1939.
6. Areas occupied by the Soviet Union from 1939 to 1941.
7. Western boundary of the Soviet Union as established in 1945.
Inset map shows the territories controlled or occupied by the Soviet Union forces in Europe since 1945 and as of January 1954.

drives toward the open sea — St. Petersburg (Leningrad) was the capital, and the influence of the Western powers was predominant in government. The fourth stage opened with the Soviet Revolution of 1917: it returned to the capital to Moscow and the general direction closer to isolation, economically and culturally, with advances along the periphery but with a stubborn distrust of the West.

The Soviet Union today is in the middle of the fourth stage of Russian history. The variety of the past and the rapidity with which vast spaces were incorporated into Russian territory have made the assimilation of the diverse people inhabiting these lands a big job. The Soviet system is endeavoring to achieve homogeneity, a goal toward which the tsars had already made some progress.

## THE RUSSIAN "MELTING POT"

The problem of nationalities in the Soviet Union is one of the most intricate in Europe's human geography. In Soviet Asia there are groups of peoples who by their language, culture, and past differ from the Russian family of peoples. In Europe the relationships are more involved because they are closer. The Russians are a nation formed during the Middle Ages through the experience of life in common, along the same waterways, under the same rule, with elements which were certainly diverse at the start. They are the most numerous by far and for several centuries have been the best organized of all the nationalities in the Soviet area. The Russians number certainly over 120,000,000 — that is, well over one half of the total population of the Soviet Union — and constitute the largest unified national group in Europe. The unification may in some cases be recent and the racial origins may be diverse; but the unity is still indisputable, and foreign efforts to break it up have never succeeded in recent times. This Russian nationality is so much more numerous than any other in the Union that it dominates and assimilates easily. Moreover, it is the only one in Soviet Europe which has had its own great history and advanced culture. No other people within the Union can boast victorious campaigns throughout the whole of Europe and through Asia; none has a literature or an array of famous names in various walks of life comparable to what Russia can offer. It does not matter much for the purpose that some of these men were of Ukrainian or Byelorussian origin — they acted as Russians and earned their fame through their participation in the Russian system.

Such an advantage was gained partly as a result of historical developments, partly through the systematic policy of the tsars who tried to "Russify" the other peoples of their empire. Actually this policy of Russification was seldom applied, and until the beginning of the twentieth century very little was done to educate the masses of the people, the non-Russian nationalities being kept carefully outside all major cultural developments. The Jews were forbidden to settle inside Russia east of the area called the *Pale,* stretching along the western border, unless they had considerable fortunes or university diplomas. However, large numbers of Jews have participated actively in the Russian cultural development beginning at the end of the nineteenth century; in some instances they even spearheaded it. Attempts at Russification were directed several times toward peripheral nationalities, strongly rooted in their land, such as Finns or Georgians, with varying success. Some discrimination has existed. In the heart of central Russia the people of the Mordves lived until the 1910s in a half-wild condition, learning about the world behind the curtain of woods that surrounded them when sawmills began to penetrate their isolation; and the Mordves were a "nation" of about one million people (1,450,000 in 1939). Thus there remained a great variety of peoples in Soviet Europe. Although the variety was greater in Asia, about twenty distinct nationalities, numbering over 100,000 individuals each, were mentioned in the 1959 census for European territories.

In some cases, the tremendous extension in space of the empire has been the cause of regional differentiations. Thus arose a Ukrainian nationality—it could only claim the inheritance of the river state directed from Kiev, plus more recent "frontier" origins. For, from the sixteenth to the nineteenth centuries, the Ukraine was a frontier country indeed, as the meaning of its name in Russian signifies. The open steppe in the south attracted adventurous men, especially groups of serfs fleeing the serfdom of the large estates in Russia or Poland. Such people, looking for freedom, provided the first nuclei of the settlement of the steppe on the Don, Donets, and Dnieper. Organized in warlike associations, calling themselves Cossacks, led by elected chiefs or *hetmans* (later *atamans*), these settlers chased the nomadic Mongol tribes, fought the Turks, Poles and others. In many cases history put them down under the label of "bandits," for ruthless they were and outlaws too. But, as their lands grew, the Cossacks felt unable to defend themselves alone against large powers. They asked the Russian tsar for protection, accepted his sovereignty, and gave the Ukraine to Muscovy as a borderland. In exchange they were granted privileges and became in the south the guardians of the imperial interests. After the Soviet Revolution of 1917, independent *hetmans* reappeared, claiming a separate Ukrainian state. But they were only gang leaders. When the imperial power had gone, local trends began to develop, basing themselves on old traditions. Few of them succeeded. Such a Ukrainian drive is more a regional than a truly national venture. The same would be true of the White Russians or Byelorussians, another vestige of the river-state period. A nationality controlling the upper reaches of the Dnieper and Western Dvina as well as the basin of the Pripyat River, the Byelorussians have even less background to claim than the Ukrainians; they have been simply a buffer area between the Russians on one hand and the Poles and Lithuanians on the other.

These two nationalities are the only large groups claiming some autonomy in a truly political and territorial sense. Other nationalities in Soviet Europe are small groups, and they are either related to other nations outside the Union, such as Germany or Poland, or they are small and localized groups such as the Mordves or some Tatar clans scattered along the Volga or in the Crimea. The addition to the Union after World War II of the three Baltic republics of Lithuania, Latvia, and Estonia has created there a new regional pattern; but each of the three nations is too small within the huge Soviet system to be of considerable influence.

The Soviet regime adopted a policy for the nationalities problem much more favorable to all the small groups of people than any the imperial regime had ever had. This has been usually explained by the fact that Joseph Stalin himself was originally a Georgian and very much aware of the "minorities" or "nationalities" problem in Russia. His policy has been to give a federal organization to the Union and to grant cultural and administrative autonomy to all nationalities who could handle it. Some small groups, unable to evolve a culture of their own, have been helped to do so by ethnographers or historians assigned to that work by the federal authorities in Moscow. Was that a trend toward decentralization? It may appear so on the surface. Actually the autonomy thus granted was only a façade: educating Byelorussians or Mordves in their own "national" history and culture and teaching them at the same time something of the Russian culture and history could only give them an inferiority complex about their "nationality" and excite their desire for more active participation in the Russian system. A policy that boasts to have developed a modern Mordve and Tatar literature has probably done more to "Russify" these peoples than the "Russification" of the tsars could ever have achieved by waiting for the small peoples to come themselves to the imperial culture across the many obstacles that had accumulated in their way. The main advantage obtained is the feeling of all these smaller peoples that nothing is imposed upon them in this field and that they *may* stay away from the Russian culture if they choose to do so; very few, however, decide to estrange themselves from a much larger and richer whole, access to which is wide open. It must be noted that no substantial Ukrainian or Byelorussian national setup developed even under German occupation during World War II, although the Germans hoped for a long time to split the Russian unity.

Whether such a policy in the long run will not succeed in creating

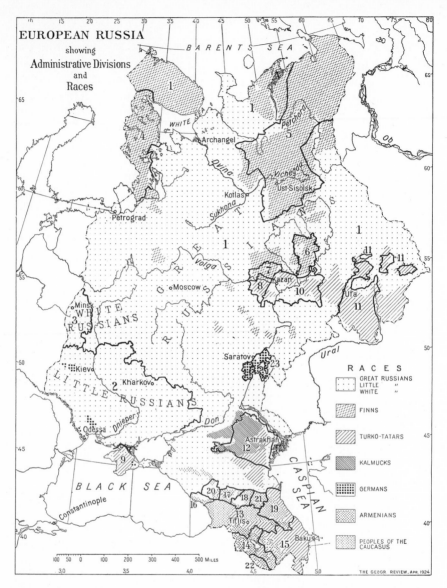

The principal ethnic groups of European Russia as of 1924. The numbers refer to the following administrative divisions: 1, Great Russia: Russian Socialist Soviet Republic (43 governments); 2, Republic of Ukraine (12 governments); 3, Republic of White Russia; 4, Workers' Community of the Carelians; 5, Autonomous Province of the Zyrians; 6, Autonomous Province of the Votyaks; 7, Autonomous Province of the Cheremisses; 8, Autonomous Province of the Chuvashes; 9, Tatar Republic of Crimea; 10, Tatar Republic of the Middle Volga; 11, Bashkir Republic; 12, Kaimuck Republic; 13, Republic of Georgia; 14, Republic of Armenia; 15, Republic of Azerbaijan; 16, Republic of Abkhazia; 17, Republic of the Kabards; 18, Republic of the Mountaineers; 19, Republic of Daghestan; 20, Autonomous Province of the Karachaevo-Cherkesses; 21, Autonomous Province of the Chechenzes; 22, Autonomous Province of Nakhichevan; 23, Workers' Community of the Germans. Since 1945, ethnic variety has been increased by the annexation of more territories westward. Migrations during World War II may, on the other hand, have accelerated the mixing-up process, especially in the Ukraine. *(The Geographical Review)*

stronger nationalisms is left for the future to observe. More people in the Ukraine are speaking Ukrainian now than a generation ago; more scientific and literary works are being published in Ukrainian. Perhaps the government in Moscow felt that such a regional development was bound to come anyhow and preferred to orient and to help rather than to see it emerge in opposition to the central authority. It is hard to say whether actual nations will or will not be created as a result of Stalin's policies in the peripheral lands of the Union. But the Soviet regime has higher ambitions than straight "Russification." It imposes on all the peoples of the Union a common political faith which appeals to the Russian tendency toward mysticism. It imposes a communistic economic and social structure, and it establishes solidarity through a common way of life. It creates through the Communist party a common hierarchy and a united direction of all important affairs that can run politics and economics, national or regional, because of channels that do not take into account national boundaries or administrations. In such a system it may be preferable to create some new nations within the truly Russian area, the fidelity and control of which are well secured, if it will make it easier for other nations on the outside to work with the Union and perhaps to enter it. The incentive of autonomy within a federal system is in line with the ultimate goal of communism and may well appear as a camouflage to more imperialistic ambitions than the tsars ever had. Meanwhile, through the economic and social leveling, rationing, and centralized planning of the Communist regime, the Soviet peoples become more and more thoroughly homogenized.

What may appear on the surface as a confused and complicated evolution covers a steady attempt, pursued with different methods according to the historical period, to achieve throughout the vast areas of the Russian or Soviet zone what the "melting pot" brought about in North America. Because of geographical and historical differences in the building up of the two nations, Russia and the United States turned out to be on the whole strikingly different nations. As early as the 1830s, Alexis de Tocqueville wrote this striking comparison as a conclusion to the first volume of his classic *Democracy in America*: "There are, at the present time, two great nations in the world which seem to tend towards the same end, although they started from different points: I allude to the Russians and the Americans. Both of them have grown up unnoticed. . . . All other nations seem to have nearly reached their natural limits, and only to be charged with the maintenance of their power; but these are still in the act of growth; . . . they are proceeding with ease and with celerity along a path to which the human eye can assign no term. The American struggles against the natural obstacles which oppose him; the adversaries of the Russian are men; the former combats the wilderness and savage life; the latter, civilization with all its weapons and its arts: the conquests of one are therefore gained by the ploughshare; those of the other by the sword. The Anglo-American relies upon personal interest to accomplish his ends, and gives free scope to the unguided exertions and common sense of the citizens; the Russian centers all the authority of society in a single arm: the principal instrument of the former is freedom, of the latter servitude. Their starting point is different and their courses are not the same; yet each of them seems to be marked out by the will of Heaven to sway the destinies of half the globe."

Curiously enough, a little more than a century after these lines were written, the conclusion of World War II brought about a political situation that Tocqueville seems to have forecast. His remarks underline an extremely important feature of Russian character and policy: the deep popular distrust of the stranger, the constant necessity of fighting other men. Kiev had to fight the constant attacks from the nomads of the steppe. Novgorod and Moscow, hiding in the forest had to defend themselves for centuries from the Tatars and the Teutonic Knights. Tocqueville wrote at a time when Russia was attempting to become permanently Westernized. Although foreigners from Western countries were organizing its government and economy, the struggle against outsiders was apparent to contemporary observers.

## RUSSIA AND THE WEST—MYSTICISM AND PLANNING

Psychologically the Russians have never been able to rid themselves of the dread-of-the-outsider complex that long centuries have imprinted. Metaphorically, the Russians are still hiding somewhere in the forest or anxiously guarding their territories recently acquired outside the familiar woods. They do not expect good to come from abroad. To live and carry on the fight in such a state of mind requires great hopes for the future—no morale could be maintained without such ambitious hopes. Every Russian or Ukrainian harbors them individually as well as nationally. About at the same time that Tocqueville wrote about America, another Frenchman, the Marquis de Custine, visited Russia and in 1839 wrote his impressions: "An immense inordinate ambition, the kind of ambition which can take root only in the soul of an oppressed people, and be nourished only on the misery of an entire country, is now astir in the hearts of the Russians. . . . In the hope of washing himself clean of his impious sacrifice of public and personal liberty, this kneeling slave fills his dreams with visions of world domination." (As quoted by Lewis Galantière, in *Foreign Affairs*, October 1949, p. 114.)

During the nineteenth century, however, the Russian people were emancipated and became more closely associated with Western culture, to which they contributed two generations of brilliant and refined *intelligentsia*. Then, too, the Revolution has occurred, reforming deeply the whole national system and changing totally its social structure. What deeply rooted forces the Revolution has unleashed in the Russian soul has seldom been realized. Marshal Tukhachevsky, one of the most influential and interesting leaders of the Soviet armies until he was purged in 1937, stated in his youth (as quoted in *The Red Army* by Michel Berchin and E. Ben Horin): "We Russians are all religious, the reason being that we have no religion. I am not a Christian. Moreover, I hate Vladimir the Saint who introduced Christianity in Russia, thus handing over Russia to Western civilization. We should have kept our crude paganism, our barbarism. But they will both come back."

In its association with the Western world since Peter the Great, Russia had been looking for the secret of Western might. In three respects at least she was to be disappointed: as practiced for two centuries, this association did not give to Russia the freedoms enjoyed in Western Europe by the mass of the people, or the industrial and technical development on which power and prosperity seemed to be so dependent, or the great maritime development that has been a constant Russian dream since Peter's trip to the West. On the first point, the Russians could hardly blame anyone except themselves for their internal political development: substantial progress had been achieved in the century preceding 1917, but it was slow, and patience was running out. On the second point, again the policy of the Russian government was to be blamed first: foreign technicians and capital were slowly developing the immense country, and some national interests were controlling large possibilities, but the backwardness and ignorance of the huge mass could not be overcome so quickly. As for the third, the urge to the sea had led the Russians to establish themselves strongly on the banks of the Baltic and Black seas, the latter being free of ice; Murmansk on the northern coast was also ice free, and important developments had been started in the Far East. In these developments, of course, the Russian pushes have encountered on their way the stubborn opposition of the leading maritime powers, which could not wish for such a rival to rise on the high seas. Britain, occasionally backed by France, has been vigilant to guard against Russia's gaining control of either the Danish straits or the Black Sea straits, which would have opened wider horizons to the Russian navy. Later a similar opposition arose in the Pacific from Japan. But no country can ever achieve the full scope of its national dreams. To bring about the kind of reaction that has developed since 1917, a challenge deeply entrenched in the people's mind was necessary; Custine's and Tukhachevsky's remarks may provide a key to it.

The Soviet regime, as organized under the leadership of Stalin, was in certain respects more absolute and deprived the Russians of more essential freedoms than the tsarist policy was ever able to do. The whole Union from top to bottom was enclosed in a rigid discipline bent on the achievement of one great aim. This aim, equally active under Stalin's successors, is not only world domination; it is also a promise of paradise on earth: all the freedoms will be granted and perfect material equality and happiness will be established . . . as soon as possible. And it turns out that the possibility may be remote because all the foreign countries, designated as "capitalistic" to recall the interference of foreign capital in Russian affairs and to fit the Communist doctrine, are doing all they can to prevent the Soviet Union from achieving the happiness for which at least the formula is provided.

The necessity is thus stressed of fighting the power and prosperity of the West, of which the Russians have been jealous for centuries. The responsibility for the final outcome of the Communist experiment is also put in advance on the shoulders of the hostile foreigners instead of being left to the Soviet government. The Russians have a deep mystic strain. They believe, more passionately perhaps than any other nation, in their mission on earth: this Messianic complex is at last satisfied with Communist doctrine, handled by the totalitarian authority of Stalin or his heirs. A great wall had been built around the Soviet Union long before the "iron curtain" was proclaimed in the West. Russia again went into the shelter of isolation to reform itself, and perhaps to prepare for a new sweep across the surrounding lands. This time the Russians were told that, because of the magnitude of both their task and the outside menace, a great preparation was necessary. They did prepare: the Five-Year Plans were aimed at entirely reshaping the country's economy and also at reinforcing its defense against possible wars. The wars came — and the Nazi invasion found the Soviet Union much more prepared than anyone in the West had expected. After World War II, reconstruction started, geared again to the same aims: to build up the country's potential for both economic and military power.

Many documents and books have described the sacrifices apparent in the low standard of living imposed upon the Soviet people. Public opinion is still fed more statistics of progress than meat and fats; some authors seem to believe that the Russians are queer people satisfied with mere announcements of an increase in production figures. Such results are achieved because these announcements sound to the Russian ear like one step forward on the hard way to achieving paradise on earth and making obvious the truth of their Gospel to the whole world.

Planning in the Soviet Union is precise, detailed, and imperative. All political authority and all economic power is centered in the single arm of the federal government. The logic of mathematics reigns through the economy of this sixth part of the world: a small group of brains at the top decides the aims of the over-all policy; their decisions, converted into figures and detailed instructions, are projected over the whole country and supposed to reach the remotest corner of it. To make a nation work like an assembly line would require transforming it into a mass of automatons. In its stubborn endeavor to achieve the hoped-for results, the Soviet government had to impose on the population forced labor for millions and a strict discipline for all. It is an ironic paradox that, in order to achieve the rapid development of a vast area, the Soviet brains have studied chiefly the American example. For long years the constant motto throughout Soviet Russia has been: "Catch up with America!" or "Let us outstrip America!" Such slogans were less heard for some years but, as economic growth is proceeding faster, Soviet leaders have again been announcing that they will catch up soon.

The main directives of the Soviet economic planning have had to follow paths quite different from those that brought success and prosperity to American development: collectivization of practically all worthwhile enterprises — agricultural, commercial, and industrial — was a first step, indispensable to give to the central authorities full control of every bit of property. Then the development of all known resources was pushed ahead. Finally decentralization of production was emphasized, partly in order to avoid too great damage to the whole system in case of invasion of one area, but also in order to make up for the difficulties of distribution over a vast territory through which means of transportation are still scarce or at least inadequate.

In the field of agriculture, Soviet planning has led to a speedy mechanization on large collective or state-owned farms. These kolkhoz or sovkho now use tractors and modern tools instead of the primitive implements of the beginning of the century. Mechanization, however, is far from being complete: vast areas have to practice the old backward kind of agriculture, and industries are not yet able to meet all the demand. The same situation holds for fertilizers. The collectivization of the farmsteads caused a severe drop in the figures for livestock in the 1930s — animals cannot be grown like grain by a few controlled and combined operations; they require a daily care and devotion. The peasants did not seem willing to provide either when they were forbidden to use the products of their animal raising. Several regulations, moderating doctrinal collectivism, have since authorized every peasant member of a kolkhoz to maintain some stock for his own use as his personal property. As a result the figures for livestock have gone up, and the production of milk doubled from 1950 to 1965 in the Soviet Union. The lack of

animals for traction as well as for manure used to be one of the demanding reasons for mechanization and the large-scale use of artificial
fertilizer.

The Russian yields for most of the crops seem to be among the
lowest in Europe, but the vast areas sown make up for it. Recent trends
have also favored the spread of food crops such as grains and potatoes
to almost every part of the Soviet Europe where they were possible. New
breeds of wheat and rye were devised by biologists in order to let the
fields go farther north. Yields in those areas on podzolic soils are particularly low; but some local supply is thus insured to areas that may be
cut off from the main producing belts (the Ukraine and western Siberia)
either by lack of transportation possibilities or by military operations. In
this way the threat of famines resulting from the droughts is also somewhat alleviated: most of the grain-producing areas are in the steppic
zone, on the subarid margin, where droughts occur periodically and
cause great trouble.

The building up of the industrial might of the country has been
pushed much more actively than the agricultural development. Similarly
new industries, such as metallurgy and chemicals, on which rests the
involved structure of modern industrial production, were favored as
against less "basic" industries of foodstuffs, textiles, and consumer
goods. The percentages of increase ordered by the Five-Year Plans
showed clearly this trend; and they also stress the preference given to
manufacturing over production of the raw materials that used to be a
specialty of the Russian exports, such as timber. The export of many raw
materials has ceased because of increased domestic consumption: oil and
manganese ore, for instance.

The main bottleneck of the Soviet economy was long in the realm of
transportation. Through the building of canals and railroads, the Soviet
regime has achieved considerable improvement of the pre-Revolutionary situation when the network was very scanty; navigation on the main
rivers has also been greatly improved. Transportation does not seem to
be in recent years as much of a hindrance to economic development in
the Soviet Union as it used to be. The waterways are carrying a good
deal of the traffic, particularly for bulky goods; pipelines are crawling
in various directions from the main oil and natural gas fields, helping
relieve the fuel load on the railroads or river barges. Most striking has
been the improvement of rail and trucking freight transport.

The war of 1941–1945 was a terrible ordeal for the Soviet Union: it
is not called there "World War II" but "the Great Patriotic War." Not
only has it caused enormous and widespread physical destruction over
the land, it has considerably decreased the total population. Estimates of
losses vary from lower (around 14 million people lost, half of them being

civilian losses) to higher evaluations (some of which set the losses at over 30 million). The Soviet census of 1939 gave the figure of 170.6 million for the total population of the USSR. After the annexations of 1940, which brought the boundaries quite close to their present line, the population was estimated at 191.7 million. The census taken in 1959 gave a total of 208.8 million, indicating an increase of about 17 million for twenty years or less than 0.5 percent as an average rate of natural increase. As illustrated by the quoted sentence of Stalin about the fertility of the Russian women, one might have expected from whatever was known of Soviet demography in prewar years a much higher rate of increase. In the 1950s, United Nations statistics set the natural rate of increase annually at 1.7 percent for the world, 1.8 for North America, and 0.8 for Europe without the USSR. One would have expected an increase of *at least* 1 percent for the Soviet Union, which would indicate a "deficit" of some 20 million people, a likely compromise figure for the actual wartime losses. This view seems also supported by the fact that the 1959 census acknowledged 20.7 million more women than men in the Soviet population (in the United States in 1960, for a total population of 180 million, the women outnumbered the men by about 2 million).

Such a terrible decimation, killing off at least one tenth of the people, caused a shortage of labor that has not yet been overcome, probably reduced the birth rate for the postwar years to an appreciable extent, and called on women to assume a variety of activities usually reserved to men. Planning had to take on a different character in postwar years: reconstruction and expansion of output remained the major concerns until about 1960. Economic policies were also affected by another political event: the death of Joseph Stalin, March 5, 1953. Soviet leadership evolved to come under the direction of Nikita S. Khrushchev, Chairman of the Council of Ministers and First Secretary of the Central Committee of the Communist party until 1964, when another team succeeded him at the head of the Soviet government. A gradual evolution of policies and even of the official doctrine ensued. Some harder line policies seem to have come back in favor by 1968, as witnessed by the tough line adopted toward Czechoslovakia, where liberalization was proceeding too fast for the Kremlin's taste.

While weakened by destruction and decimation, the Soviet Union in some respects emerged strengthened by the outcome of the war. It had become the second power in the world, one of the two "super-powers," and, either by military occupation or by the control of the Communist party organization, it seemed in 1950 to dominate one half of mankind. In Europe it had imperial problems and the economic planning decided upon in Moscow had to encompass the European countries east of the "iron curtain." The USSR reinforced its power position by developing

A machine-tool plant in Moscow. (*Sovfoto*)

Stalingrad destroyed. The city recovered from its ordeal during World War II and was later renamed Volgograd. (*Sovfoto*)

nuclear armaments and intercontinental missiles, by launching successfully its sputniks (1957) and luniks (1959) and by sending its cosmonauts orbiting around the earth (1961). These achievements could have given to the Soviet government and people a feeling of greater security, but they also convinced them of the force of their military power. The Berlin crisis of 1961 and the resumption of nuclear weapons tests by the USSR stressed once again that by that time only that country and the United States held in their hands the means of either opening or deterring a new world conflict. The Soviet Union had suffered too much from the war concluded in 1945 to wish for another round of terrible devastation. Its people are just beginning to enjoy the fruits of a somewhat liberalized administration and of a gradually better supplied economy. However, despite considerable progress achieved in this field in the last ten years, the standard of living of the Soviet Union remains much lower than in almost all the rest of Europe. Russia has achieved much better recovery and advance in the scientific and technological areas than in production and distribution. In the field of practical economics the Soviet Union has still a long way to go before "catching up with America."

## ECONOMIC EXPANSION AND ITS DIFFICULTIES

In 1967, the Soviet Union celebrated the fiftieth anniversary of the Bolshevik Revolution, which established the rule of the Communist party in Russia. Assessing the results achieved by half a century of Soviet regime, an abundant literature stressed considerable economic expansion and technological progress in this vast country. Although the Russian empire had begun to industrialize seriously in the first years of this century, it was still, in 1917, a backward, little-developed country. Though much more populated at the time than the United States, it did not have one tenth of the American industrial power. Now it has become indisputably the second economic and political super-power of the modern world, catching up with the United States in some sectors of industrial production, and still growing and planning more expansion in the immediate future. Technological progress has been enormous, as illustrated by Soviet achievement in space. However, the Soviet Union found itself in the 1960s still plagued by shortages of various goods and basically preoccupied with production. True, the European section of the USSR, which still plays the dominant role in the Soviet economy, had been terribly destroyed by military operations in 1941–1945; most of its essential parts had to be rebuilt and re-equipped after 1946 amid a great stringency of materials and labor. No wonder strict austerity had to be imposed on the Soviet consumer, who had never been spoiled in the past either. An official report claimed, by 1950, that gross industrial production had then surpassed the level of 1940; capital goods output was estimated at 205 percent and consumer goods output at 123 percent of the 1940 output. At that time war scars were still quite evident all over the land, and throughout the 1950s strict economic planning, enforced as a matter of principle as well as necessity in the Soviet situation of scarcity, sought essentially to provide the country with some basic equipment for production and transportation. It was not until 1958 that the production of consumer goods was given priority over capital goods in general economic planning. And that priority was slight until the mid-1960s, when the interests of the consumer came really into the limelight of Soviet policy.

Industrial expansion in the USSR, and particularly in its European parts, was quite successful in developing the production of mineral raw materials and goods produced by heavy industry. It lagged badly, however, in its endeavor to expand agricultural production. A great deal of attention and care were lavished in the twenty years following the end of World War II on the needs of agriculture, but the expected results were not achieved. Even in the field of industrial production, the Soviet planners felt that their resources warranted better results in terms of rate of growth than had been actually achieved. In 1965–1968, new ideas came to the fore in the Soviet debate on methods of economic management. A new theory designated as "Libermanism" (as it was expounded by Professor Evsei Liberman, an economist at the University of Kharkov) emphasized the need for incentives bringing profit to the producer. The Communist economic philosophy had previously rejected the principle of profit in the process of production being made by individual workers or individual producing establishments. The new philosophy would gradually lead to a liberalization of the whole Soviet economic system, bringing it much closer to Western methods, which used to be described in the USSR as "capitalistic." The Soviet administration expects that the new methods will foster greater labor productivity and provide incentives for a rapid rise in the output of goods and services of all kinds.

The bulk of both economic production and consumption in the USSR is located in its European sector, particularly in the southern two thirds of it; there, over a small proportion of the total land area of the Soviet Union, are found the great majority of the people and of the developed resources. Although more rapid rates of growth have been recorded in recent years in the Asiatic sector of the Union, the basic economic wealth now at work is found west of the Urals. And during the last twenty years, the European part of the Soviet Union has been considerably transformed. Following the general trend of urbanization now pre-

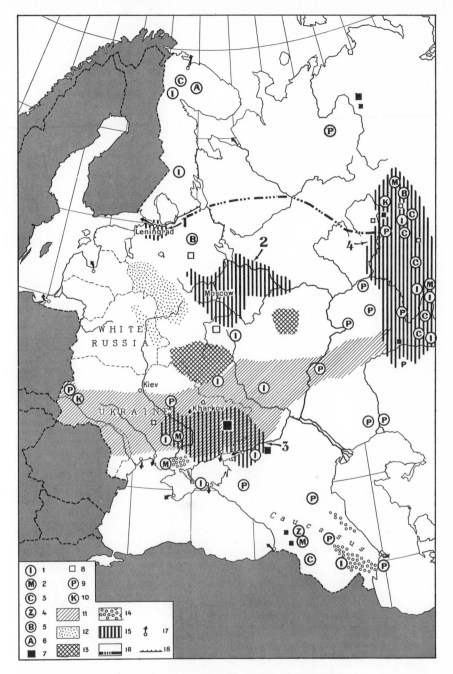

A sketch of the economy of the European part of the USSR. Key: 1, iron-ore deposits; 2, manganese ore; 3, copper ore; 4, lead and zinc ores; 5, bauxite; 6, apatite; 7, principal centers of coal mining; 8, lignite basins; 9, principal centers of oil extraction; 10, potash deposits; 11, main area of intensive cultivation of wheat and sugar beets (the black-soil belt); 12, flax-growing areas; 13, hemp-growing areas; 14, cotton-growing areas; 15, principal manufacturing areas; 16, northern limit of the zone of intensive agriculture; 17, principal maritime ports; 18, main canals.

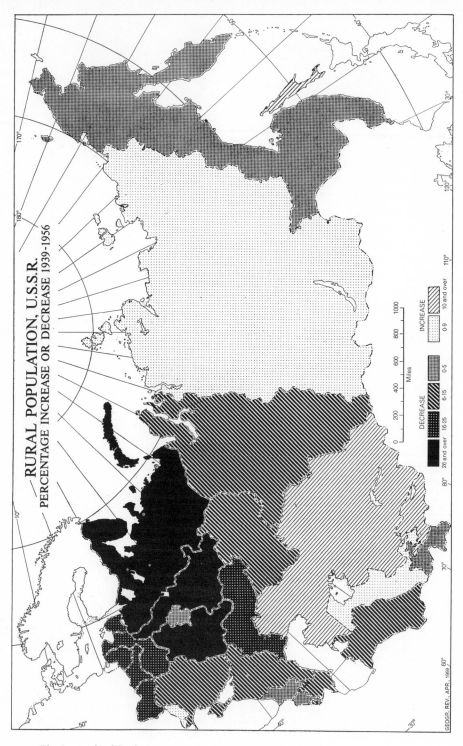

RURAL POPULATION, U.S.S.R.
PERCENTAGE INCREASE OR DECREASE 1939-1956

DECREASE

0-5

6-15

16-25

26 and over

INCREASE

0-9

10 and over

Miles

0   200   400   600   800   1000

GEOGR. REV., APR. 1959

*(The Geographical Review)*

dominant in the world, the reconstruction and development of the cities, urban facilities, and industrial equipment have proceeded better and faster than rehabilitation of rural areas. The last population census in the USSR was taken in January 1959, when a total of 208.8 million inhabitants was counted: about 100 million were urban and 109 million rural. By 1966, it was estimated that the rural population had declined slightly to 107 million, while the urban population had risen to about 125 million, and since then the urban total is increasing by 2 to 3 million annually. It is, therefore, in the 1960s that the USSR became, in majority, urban for the first time in history, and it must be remembered that of its eight cities of more than 1 million population, six are located in Europe and only two (Novosibirsk and Tashkent) are in Asia. Of the major groupings of large cities, the three most impressive are in Europe: the central industrial region around Moscow, the Donbass region, and the cities on the middle Dnieper. The concentration of equipment necessitated by urban growth worked mainly in favor of certain sectors of the European territories.

The 1959 census counted a labor force of 99.1 million people; only a minority already then, about 39 percent, were employed in agriculture, most of them on the collective farms. The members of the collective farms had been previously authorized to till small private plots of land and keep a few animals of their own; in the 1950s these trends were discouraged. Animal husbandry has long been an obvious weakness, almost a failure, of Communist farming; when forced to enter a collective farm, the peasants slaughtered most of the animals they were not allowed to keep as their own, and the livestock was considerably reduced in the process of collectivization. This decline in the herds was observed in the Soviet Union before 1940 and was again evident in the countries of Central Europe, where collectivization of farms developed after the war. In the whole of the USSR, there were about 56 million head of cattle in 1950, 80 million by 1960, and 97 million by 1968. The production of milk about doubled from 1950 to 1965, when it reached 72 million tons. Some progress has therefore been achieved, more impressive in dairy than in meat production; while in 1965 the USSR produced more milk than the United States and even more butter, according to the official statistics, meat production was much below the American level. Besides the cattle, the USSR counted, in 1968, 52 million hogs and 140 million sheep. These two categories of animals had declined in number as against the early 1960s. This decline may well have been due to a series of poor harvests, particularly of grain, which forced the USSR to buy wheat in large quantities (over 8 million tons in 1963–1964) from the United States, Canada, and Australia.

To improve agricultural production, the farms were increasingly mechanized, the use of mineral fertilizers and improved seed was greatly expanded (the consumption of mineral fertilizer was multiplied fivefold from 1950 to 1965), rural electrification was rapidly pushed ahead. Nevertheless, the 1960s showed only little progress of the actual harvests, particularly in the Ukraine and along the Volga, where great efforts had been made. The answer seemed to lie in the difficulty of getting collective farming to produce according to plan because of managerial problems. The Soviet authorities were, however, working hard to improve the technology of farming. New land was broken up and brought under the plow, particularly as a result of drainage of marsh land in the western sections of the European territory; irrigation also was expanded in the southeastern regions.

The state and collective farms grew into huge organizations, and they obtained more autonomy from central or regional planning offices than was the case during the Stalinist era. In 1959, each collective farm had on the average 830 acres of sown land in the Georgian republic, a mountainous area where the farmsteads were relatively small, 1500 to 2000 acres in the Baltic republic, 6000 acres in the Ukraine, and 10,000 to 12,000 acres in the Volga area and the Kouban, where some of the original giant grain kolkhozes were first established. The optimum size for a kolkhoz in the Soviet Union is now considered to be around 7000 acres of arable land, and even more in the dry areas of Asia. A good many of the state farms (or *sovkhozes*) are much above this average for the collective farm. Thus, agriculture takes on the aspect of large industrial production and needs to be mechanized and rationalized. The optimum and the practical size varies, of course, from region to region and according to the specialization of the farm.

Despite all this scientific organization, Soviet agriculture has not yet succeeded in assuring self-sufficiency in agricultural products, particularly foods, though this might have been expected from a great rural country once considered to be the breadbasket of Europe, and potentially, of the world. In 1965, however, farm output statistics were rather impressive: with 59.7 million tons of wheat, the USSR was by far the first world producer of this major crop (of which that year the United States harvested 36.1 million tons); the USSR also harvested that year 16.2 million tons of rye, 6.2 million tons of oats, 20.3 million tons of barley (leading all other producers for these crops), but only 19 million tons of corn (less than one fifth of the American harvest), and 580,000 tons of rice. Because of its failure to develop successfully the cultivation of corn, which had been one of the chief disappointments of the Khrushchev administration in 1958–1964, the USSR ranked second to the United States among world producers of grain. However, the statistics of production make one wonder whether all the output listed in official docu-

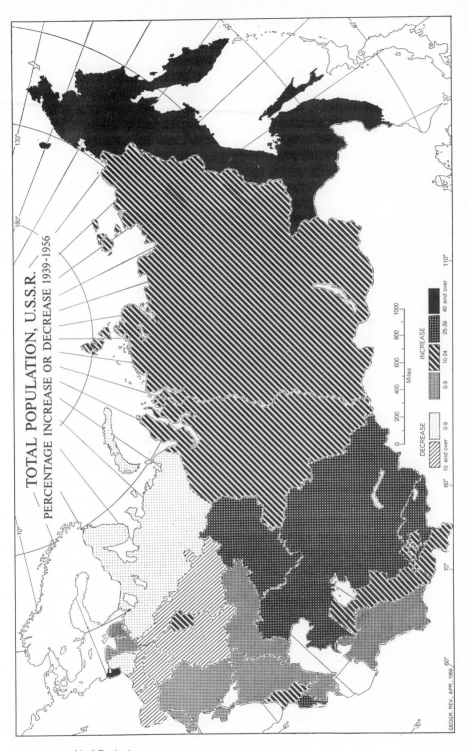

TOTAL POPULATION, U.S.S.R.
PERCENTAGE INCREASE OR DECREASE 1939-1956

DECREASE
10 and over
0-9

INCREASE
0-9
10-24
25-39
40 and over

Miles
0  200  400  600  800  1000

GEOGR. REV., APR., 1959

(The Geographical Review)

ments reaches consumers. With comparable populations, North America and Western Europe have been plagued with problems of agricultural surpluses despite smaller total figures of production. It is possible that the agricultural areas of the USSR are not yet equipped in storage and transportation facilities in a way adequate for the handling of their large harvests of grain; thus, a part of these harvests may be lost before it gets to the consumers. Also, a larger amount of grain and fodder is now consumed by the livestock, as considerable emphasis has been put on the production of milk and meat. The wool clip, which had doubled in the 1950s, remained in the vicinity of 350,000 tons (most of it produced in Asia), an amount insufficient for the needs of the USSR, which also imported a good deal of Australian wool.

With the exception of the larger state or collective farms, there seems to be little enthusiasm in Soviet rural country for farm work; all visitors agree on the rather sad look of the agricultural villages, with perhaps a few exceptions in higly specialized areas such as the wine growers in the foothills of the Caucasus. Too often, the agricultural labor force, made up in majority of women, does not benefit much from increases in its output; nor is it given much responsibility or praise for increases, both being allotted to planning officials in some distant bureau. The new trend aiming at a liberalization and decentralization of the economy, and introducing the incentives of profit, may help Soviet farming to catch up with the Western agricultural capability.

The Soviet regime has done better for the cities. These, like their counterparts elsewhere, are growing fast. In 1959, the census recorded that 37 percent of the labor force was employed in industry, mining, construction, and public utilities; 5.2 percent in distribution and government; and 10 percent in science, education, research, and health services. These percentages have increased in the 1960s at the expense of the proportion of the labor force in agriculture and forestry, which was, in 1959, far too high for a modern, developed economy. The USSR is still plagued in the 1960s by a manpower shortage due to the war losses and the low birth rate of the 1940s and early 1950s. Mechanization and automation in industry and transportation are being emphasized to some extent at the expense of the production of consumer goods. The rate of industrial expansion continues to be quite impressive, particularly in the output of basic raw materials and energy. Though statistics are not available for the production of military materiel, there is little doubt that considerable expansion was achieved in that sector of finished goods.

The general index of industrial production for the whole of the USSR rose from 23 in 1940 to 40 in 1950, 100 in 1958, 122 in 1960, and 184 in 1965. The rise was especially spectacular for "producers' goods";

the index went from 19 in 1940 to 197 in 1965, while in the same time the consumers' goods index went from 36 to 159. The most rapid rates of increase were observed for the chemical industries (16 to 245), metal products (15 to 237), and output of electricity (19 to 229). The average consumption of energy per capita is gradually reaching European levels: it stood at 3029 kilograms of coal equivalent in 1962, and 3611 in 1965. Still, it was below per capita energy consumption in Czechoslovakia, East or West Germany, Belgium, and Britain. In 1965, the Soviet rate of energy consumption was about equivalent to that of Norway, which is not a highly industrialized country; the great distances within the USSR increase the consumption of energy for transportation purposes; and the per capita figure is still only about a third of the average for the United States.

In 1965 the USSR produced 380 million tons of roundwood, 89 million tons of iron content in the ores it extracted, and 3.4 million tons of manganese content; for these three raw materials it was by far the largest producer in the world; in coal mining it came a close second to the United States, with 427 million tons. Still, in the production of iron and steel, the USSR was second to the United States, with 66 million tons of pig iron and ferroalloys and 91 million tons of crude steel. A large part of the Soviet production of iron and manganese ores, particularly from the Ukraine, was exported to the Central European satellites to feed their blast furnaces. The USSR achieved considerable success in exploring for oil and natural gas. Vast reserves were found in the Asiatic territories, but the major part of the present production comes from the Volga region, the Caucasus, and the Ukraine. The 1965 output of 242 million tons of crude oil and 127 billion cubic meters of natural gas put the USSR in the second rank among world producers, right after the United States. For lignite, it came second after East Germany. These figures show the progress achieved in the production and consumption of energy. But the USSR has also made a considerable effort to develop its water power resources. These are still considerable as a potential in Asia. In Europe, they have been already developed to a large extent, particularly by the construction of huge dams on the powerful rivers of European Russia. Both the Volga and the Dnieper rivers now flow downstream like strings of lakes formed by reservoirs behind the dams, some of these lakes taking on enormous proportions and looking like small ramified inland seas, especially on the middle Volga and the lower courses of the Dnieper and the Don. Besides helping provide electricity, these reservoirs are good waterways and constitute vast storages of water that can be used for multiple purposes.

Through the vast expanse of its land area the Soviet Union mines a great variety of minerals in varying quantities. There are very few ores in which this country is deficient; still the domestic production is not sufficient for some of them, particularly for bauxite, large quantities of which are imported from Hungary. The Soviet Union is still equipping itself and therefore cannot afford a rate of recuperating old metallic wastes and mining the by-products of its own consumption comparable to the rate of recovery of secondary or remelted metals now in operation in the United States and Western Europe. This source of raw materials is bound to develop, of course, with the mass of materials used either for capital or consumer goods in the future.

The USSR is still far from achieving an economy of abundance. It does not rate high as a producer of passenger motor cars, refrigerators, or television sets. Despite terrible housing shortages, its construction industry has not grown as fast as the energy or metal industries. A car or a decent apartment remains a great luxury even in the major cities. But Soviet resources are gradually coming to a point where concentration on the production of capital and defense goods is adequately assured, and government policy may authorize devoting an increasing proportion of the industrial capacity to satisfying the patiently waiting average consumer. The new theories admitting the principle of profit making and of some liberalization of the economy obviously point in that direction. A significant illustration of the change in attitude toward consumer goods was the recent decision to contract with the Italian firm of Fiat to build a large plant manufacturing passenger cars of the usual Fiat type at Togliatti, a city on the Volga named in honor of the late Italian Communist leader.

The Soviet Union has now had more than twenty years of continuous peace. It has developed a more advanced economy than it has ever had. It feels politically and economically more secure in the present world, and begins to look with some optimism toward the future. The gradual relaxation of the autocratic rule that prevailed under Stalin and even of the narrow interpretation of Communist economic doctrine (which begins to show in such theories as "Libermanism") have led to a more liberal attitude toward the individual consumer at home as well as toward more active economic relations with the outside world. Calling in the Italian firm of Fiat to build a large motor-car plant on the Volga was another sign of gradual "opening up." The political "thaw" that started soon after Stalin's death seemed to gradually develop until 1968. Then, however, it was sternly restrained when Czechoslovakia and Rumania showed signs of rapid evolution. It must be kept in mind that the Soviet economy remains closely coordinated with the economic program of the satellites to the west of its border. The Soviet output alone does not always reflect the actual situation on the domestic market of a good many manufacturing industries. In its relations with the smaller Communist-

Moscow at night. The Kremlin is in the upper right section of the view, and the towers of the new skyscrapers rise in the background. *(Sovfoto)*

controlled countries of Europe, the USSR has been following a rule rather unusual for a dominant economy: the satellites have been requested to supply large portions of the output of their manufactures to the Soviet Union, which, in exchange, provides them with raw materials.

This is a reversal of the usual relationship in an "imperial" trade situation, in which the dominant power was the principal manufacturing partner while the dependent countries, being less developed and expected to remain so, contributed foodstuffs and raw materials. The Soviet empire works the other way: the USSR exports to East Germany, Poland, and Czechoslovakia grain, cotton, iron and manganese ores, crude petroleum, and some other metals, and receives in exchange, machinery, textile piece goods, leatherware, electrical apparatus, and even some precision instruments. Manufacturing is developed in these countries partly for their own needs and partly to supply the great appetite for manufactured goods of all kinds in the USSR, which, in final analysis, has been using the labor of these dependent countries to satisfy some of its own needs. Similar relations exist in the foreign trade of the USSR even for food: grain may be exported to Poland in exchange for ham and meat; fertilizer may be provided to Bulgaria and Rumania, whence fresh or canned fruits and vegetables are imported. The Soviet Union has been, indeed, at the center of the programming of the COMECON and the main beneficiary of it.

In its long-range planning, the USSR could not have expected to remain indefinitely dependent on the contributions of its allies, or satellites. Its final target is, of course, self-sufficiency. The USSR is still far from being able to "catch up" with the United States in terms of the actual well-being of its people. It is difficult to ascertain at present how much the present evolution of the various Communist-controlled countries of Europe may mean to the Soviet rate of economic expansion in the future. Most important in the analysis of the dynamic evolution of the USSR are its internal achievements and difficulties at home and particularly in its European territories. Reviewing the different regions of Soviet Europe, we shall divide them into two groups: the marginal republics on the periphery and the Great Russian area as its central core.

The Dnieprostroï Dam. *(Sovfoto)*

# 20

## The Marginal
## Soviet Republics

In past centuries and in very recent years Russia has had a frontier turned toward the west and the south. In the south she undertook a "reconquest" of the steppe, chiefly against the Turks, heirs of the Mongols; to the west she struggled with the Germans and other Western nations for the tidal lands of Central Europe. Around the big bulk of Russian territory, mostly forested, there thus developed a semicircle of marginal territory where foreign influences have been more active and where remain alive some old historic memories that would have little meaning inside the country. These marginal lands have therefore had more national minority problems, either because of immigration and the mingling of outsiders or as a result of regional patriotism, such as we described in the Ukraine.

It may seem strange that such an empire, Russian or Soviet, would keep along its most vulnerable borders the big bulk of populations of questionable loyalty. More efficient "melting-pot" policies might have attempted assimilation inland by scattering the heterogeneous elements amid the wide purely Russian area. Such was not the tsars' strategy, nor does it seem to have been that of Premier Stalin during World War II. The traditional Russian strategy consists in trading space for time, slowing down the enemy's invasion by a slow, hard-fought retreat, using the invader's spearhead, forcing him to extend his lines of communications through little-known country, devastated by the operations and the Russians' scorched-earth policy. Then there is the severe Russian winter, to which no other European power is accustomed and which is the best possible ally for a nation that in the past used to hide in the frozen woods and strike back. Both Napoleon and Hitler were defeated in the same way.

With such a strategy it appears preferable to leave along the vulnerable border those populations which may be sacrificed more easily from the standpoint of national policy, and the Russians have generally done just that. In the past century, however, some of the chief centers of the national economy have grown up precisely within this marginal belt, increasing the whole country's vulnerability and making it less easy to sacrifice these areas. After World War II the margin of security was extended far westward and southwestward, as Soviet forces occupied a vast sector of Germany down to Lübeck, and as a number of "satellite states" were incorporated in the Soviet Union's system of defense. In the 1950s the first line of defense would have stretched along the famous "iron curtain" from Lübeck to Vienna and the Maritsa River in Bulgaria. Defense in depth is thus extended far beyond the actual borders of the Union, and the "marginal republics" may feel more secure. They were terribly devastated by World War II and needed a considerable amount of reconstruction.

It would be hard to state definitely whether World War II increased or decreased the acuteness of the nationalities problem in this marginal area. The Soviet view holds that there no longer is such a problem, since the nationalities have been granted full autonomy and have their own cultural developments. The question of loyalty to the Union remains: the Soviet considers the question to be one of loyalty to the Communist doctrine and party rather than one of federal patriotism. In fact, communism and Russia have been melted to such an extent in the Soviet Union that *nationality* and *patriotism* there no longer mean what they do elsewhere. Then, too, the German invasion caused a mass migration of the borderland population inland: a great part of the Ukrainian population went to Siberia; reoccupation of the land began behind the front as liberation progressed. There is no certainty, however, that the same people came to the same places: in the system of permanent and total mobilization practiced by the Soviet, such changes may occur unnoticed. In any case the war meant more mixing of populations throughout the Union. On the other hand, the population which stayed under German occupation went through somewhat different experiences than those in areas that were not occupied; the Germans encouraged all regional nationalisms and some seeds may have been left in fertile ground. Finally, certain areas that had ceased to be Russian-controlled between the two World Wars, such as the Baltic countries or Bessarabia, were incorporated again into the Union; moreover, some territories that had never been Russian politically (the sub-Carpathian Ukraine, Königsberg) were also annexed.

The geography of these marginal republics has therefore recently been reshaped. We shall review them by following the marginal arc from northwest to southeast. In that order one finds the Karelian Republic, then the three Baltic countries (Estonia, Latvia, and Lithuania), Byelorussia, the Ukraine, and the Moldavian Republic, then the Caucasus area.

## THE KARELIAN REPUBLIC

This republic was established in 1940 after the Soviet-Finnish War: it covers an area of 70,000 square miles, stretching between the Kola peninsula to the north, the White Sea to the east, Finland to the west, and Lake Ladoga and the Svir River to the south. The territories taken from Finland were added to the old "autonomous" republic of Karelia, with the exception of the Baltic seashore and Viborg. The population of this area results from many shifts, for most of the Finnish elements seem to have gone back to Finland, abandoning the land they once occupied, and resettlement has taken place in areas vacated by the Finns. In 1959 Karelia counted 619,000 inhabitants and 700,000 in 1966.

The whole territory of this republic belongs to the forest zone, predominantly coniferous with some admixture of birch. The landscape is similar to that of Scandinavia and Finland. We find here the fringe of the Fenno-Scandian Shield, and the topography results from morainic accumulation by the icecap, broken up by normal erosion in recent periods. Only low hills are found here disposed in a rather confused pattern. The glacier left behind it as usual a great many scattered lakes and an intricate drainage. Many rivers are, in fact, channels of communication between lakes rather than independent streams. The two largest lakes, almost small closed seas, are situated to the south of Karelia: Lake Ladoga to the southwest, which empties into the Baltic through the Neva River, the second largest river in European Russia by the volume of its flow; and Lake Onega to the southeast, which empties partly into the Ladoga by the Svir and partly into the White Sea by several channels.

A system of canals built in the nineteenth century (called the Mariinsk system) linked the Upper Volga to the Baltic through these two great lakes, the Svir, and the Neva. All these waters are frozen solid for several months in winter; during the siege of Leningrad in World War II, the Red army operated a railway across Lake Ladoga, built on the ice. The waterway system has been improved by the Soviet regime, and its importance increased through the digging of the great Stalin Canal, now renamed, from the Baltic to the White Sea.

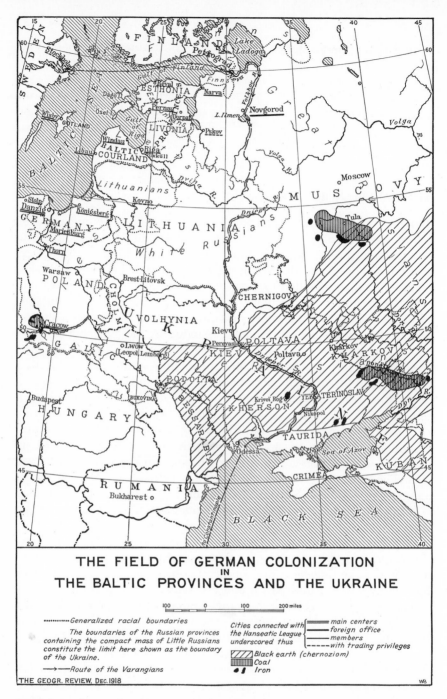

## THE FIELD OF GERMAN COLONIZATION
### IN
## THE BALTIC PROVINCES AND THE UKRAINE

100     0     100     200 miles

·········· Generalized racial boundaries

The boundaries of the Russian provinces
containing the compact mass of Little Russians
constitute the limit here shown as the boundary
of the Ukraine.

——→—— Route of the Varangians

Cities connected with
the Hanseatic League
underscored thus

▨ Black earth (chernoziom)
▥ Coal
● Iron

═══ main centers
═══ foreign office
─── members
⌐---- with trading privileges

For almost a thousand years German settlement tried to progress eastward and dominate Russia. The 1940s saw the tide come up to Stalingrad, and it was turned back. Most ethnic Germans have been expelled from the Soviet Union. *(The Geographical Review)*

The capital of the Karelian Republic is Petrozavodsk (135,000), built on the bank of Lake Onega by Peter the Great to make use of local iron ore and to manufacture arms and equipment for his imperial capital near by. Some metallurgical and mechanical plants are here at work, but the main industries of the area are timber, leatherware, pulp, cellulose, and paper. Hydroelectric power is being developed; a new large power station operates at Vygostrovo since 1961, and the improvement of the canal system has stimulated the regional activities. Some marble is being quarried, and mica is being mined. The southern and better-developed part of the republic remains within the economic zone of influence of Leningrad (formerly St. Petersburg), the great city of the Baltic area; to that city's market and to the transit trade from and to it, the republic owes much of its activity. The repopulation of the republic, mainly with Russian elements, has dissolved the national problem, but Finland continues to consider parts of it as *terra irredenta*.

## THE BALTIC COUNTRIES

To the southwest of Leningrad, the three republics of Estonia, Latvia, and Lithuania occupy a large sea front on the Baltic. They were formed as separate and independent states after World War I and were reincorporated in the Soviet Union in 1940. Each has its own background in medieval history on which to base its national claims, and there are also variations of culture in this Baltic area which make it quite different from Russia proper.

Estonia covers 17,600 square miles, with a population of 1,285,000 in 1966. Its capital, Tallinn, a port on the Gulf of Finland, has about 335,000 inhabitants. The Estonians speak a language and claim racial origins related to the Finno-Hungarian group. They possess deposits of oil shale from which gasoline and lubricants are extracted. Peat bogs also occupy vast areas. The exploitation of the forest (21 percent of the total area) and of the grasslands (about 36 percent) are the main activities; but fields of rye, oats, barley, and flax cover about one fourth of the arable land. The area under cultivation had been extended by 1965 to 1,930,000 acres, which was still only 80 percent of its extent in 1940. Cattle raising, however, is the main cash crop, and butter used to be the main export. In 1966 there were 610,000 head of cattle, 171,000 sheep, 600,000 pigs. The collective farms numbered 470 and the state farms 157. Although the amount of mechanical equipment on the farms was much greater than in prewar years, the general data about agricultural activity, including numbers of livestock, indicated a smaller output. The output of milk in 1965, for example, was 955,000 tons, compared to 782,000 in 1940; that of meat, 107,000 tons, compared to a 1940 figure of 106,000.

The industrial production seemed to be in better shape. The extensive forests provided materials for the saw-mills, for furniture, pulp, and match industries, and for basic fuelwood. Textile plants were at work in Tallinn and Tartu (85,000), the latter being the site of the main Estonian University, founded in 1632. The rich shale deposits of northeastern Estonia in 1965 produced 15.8 million tons of shale, much of which was converted into gas (513 million cubic meters that year) which was sent by pipeline from Kokhtla-Järva to Tallinn and Leningrad. In the neighborhood of Tallinn a deposit of phosphorite is being mined for the production of superphosphates. Power stations have been established on large peat deposits and a hydroelectric station was completed on the Narva River. A large factory making electric motors and other apparatus works at Tallinn, which is also the main seaport of the country. Thus Estonia is becoming industrialized while her rural economy is lagging.

Latvia is somewhat larger (25,200 square miles) than Estonia; of its population of 2,300,000, no more than 62 percent claim to be Latvians and 27 percent are Russians. Its capital of Riga, at the mouth of the Daugava River (which the Russians call the Western Dvina), was one of the chief centers of the monastic orders and Germanic influences in Russia. We are here at one of the Baltic ends of the "river state," and the relations of this area with Russia have for centuries been more developed than those of other parts of the Baltic countries. During the period of independence, Riga was one of the important centers still outside the Soviet Union of Russian-language culture and printing, publishing newspapers in Russian with a clearly anti-Communist slant.

A city of about 665,000 inhabitants, Riga was badly hit by the war, but has rebuilt itself rapidly. Its old traditions and remarkable vitality continue to show up well under Soviet domination, which plans to make a main Baltic outlet out of this port. During the period of independence Riga was developing industries to make up for the narrowing of its hinterland by the Soviet boundary. The Latvian economy was very similar to that of Estonia, but on a larger scale: timber and butter again were the main exports; textile and pulp industries flourished; and over 100,000 people were employed in the industrial plants in 1940. The country has large peat deposits and also gypsum; amber is found in the coastal areas. Industrialization has proceeded fast here, too. In 1965 industrial and office workers numbered 916,000, forming a clear majority of the labor force. There are large textile plants (50 million meters of cotton fabrics were produced in 1965, 10 of linen, 12 of woollens, and 10 of silks), cement and fertilizer plants, a steel mill (139,000 tons of crude steel in 1965), and industries making leather footwear, rolled metals, railway rolling stock, and electrical engines. Riga has also shipyards and

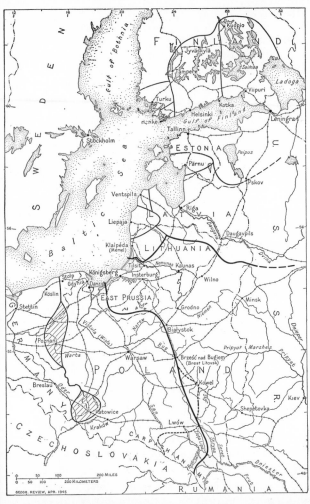

Map of the eastern Baltic, showing port hinterlands and prewar boundaries. *(The Geographical Review)*

The waterfront, Riga *(The Geographical Review)*

related engineering, as well as some electronics. Its harbor has the largest traffic among Soviet Baltic ports after Leningrad. The other important towns are Lepaya (84,000), which is a naval base, Daugavpils (87,000), and Yelgava.

Agriculture remains a very important part of the economy, but employs fewer people. After the war the large estates were broken up and distributed among the landless peasants, then the peasant farms were amalgamated into large collective farms (about 800 of them) and 187 state farms. The cultivated area (about 3.7 million acres) was mainly under fodder crops, rye, oats, potatoes, sugar beets, and flax. As in other parts of the Soviet Union, the livestock figures were, in 1966, somewhat below those of 1939; meat production has been slightly increased, but the output of milk has risen more.

Lithuania is the largest of the three: 26,000 square miles, inhabited by 3 million people. Its capital, Vilna (Vilnius in Lithuanian, and Wilno in Polish) had a population of 207,000 in 1937 when it was a Polish city. Its political and administrative functions have attracted more population recently, but Vilna has been much affected by the war. It used to have a large Jewish population and was sometimes called the "Northern Jerusalem" because of the cultural Jewish tradition and activities carried out there; almost all of this part of the population were wiped out under Nazi occupation, and Vilna started again with an almost new look under Soviet auspices in 1946; in 1966 its population counted 305,000. Kovno or Kaunas (276,000) was the capital of Lithuania during the period of independence and is still the second largest city. The same kind of economy, based on forestry (chiefly pine forests) and cattle raising with some grains, as in the other Baltic countries led to some prosperity before the war, which wrought terrible havoc through the whole territory.

Lithuania is the only one of the three Baltic republics that can boast a great past. For a while in the Middle Ages the Grand Duchy of Lithuania expanded across Eastern Europe, from the Baltic to the Black Sea. The Russians were poor neighbors and even paid tribute for some time to the Lithuanians. Then the Grand Duchy lost much of its lands to Poland, to Sweden, and finally to Russia. The feud with Poland was resumed as soon as both countries again became independent in the 1920s and centered around Vilnius. The Soviet authorities have given back the city and its surroundings to Lithuania, and have again provided the country with an outlet to the Baltic through the port of Klaipeda (Memel in German; 125,000 in 1966), which has been disputed by Germany. But Lithuania was not given another piece of German territory on the Baltic to its south, which was instead taken over by the Soviet Union.

Like the other Baltic republics, Lithuania is being rapidly industrialized; by 1959 practically all 400,000 peasant households had been incorporated in collective or state farms, while the number of industrial and office workers rose to 930,000 in 1965. Industrial output included cotton, woollen, and linen fabrics, leather footwear, timber, beet sugar, cement, heavy engines, bicycles, and ships. Peat was mined and used for power production. Agriculture was quite the same type as in Estonia and Latvia, with much emphasis on rye, oats, potatoes, sugar beets, and fodder crops. The livestock, in 1967, numbered 1.6 million head of cattle, 1,710,000 pigs, and 200,000 sheep. The forests, which cover about 17 percent of the land area, and are mostly made of pines, produced substantial quantities of timber. Arable and forest lands were expanded, owing to the drainage of some 2.5 million acres of swamps. Lithuania is the largest and most populated of the three Baltic republics, but it does not have an urban and industrial center of the size of Riga. On the Baltic shore to its southwest another large and now Russian urban and maritime center is growing.

Here the old city and important port of Königsberg, the capital of the Teutonic Order and of the German drive toward the northeast, was finally "Russified" in 1945. While most of the East Prussian territory was turned over to Poland, Königsberg and its vicinity were considered too vital a problem to be handled by either Lithuania or Poland: this area was attached directly to the Great Russian republic which covers most of the USSR. Although no territorial continuity exists between the big bulk of that republic and this small piece of land, its strategic and psychological importance was such that it was placed in Russian hands. Königsberg had a population of 372,000 in 1939. It was the largest city, manufacturing center, seaport, and naval base of the whole Baltic area; it meant also a great deal to the Russians as the historic headquarters of their German enemies—it would be the first place Germany would claim if it felt able to do so. For all these reasons the Soviet policy with regard to this place is easy to understand. Renamed Kaliningrad and evacuated of its German population, the city seems to have been resettled with Russians. There is small doubt that Kaliningrad will play an important part in Soviet planning for the Baltic: it is the best and most westward advanced port they have within their present territory on that sea; Lithuania and most of Byelorussia will probably be included in its hinterland. In 1966 the population of the Kaliningrad district counted 680,000, of whom 261,000 lived in the city.

The whole area of these Baltic countries, though divided in four distinct administrative units, has a considerable unity: physically it has the same forest, predominantly coniferous, covering the moraines left by the Quaternary icecap. Humid climate and soil favor grassland and livestock raising. Forestry and agriculture were the main occupations of the inhabitants, although some industrialization had been started before

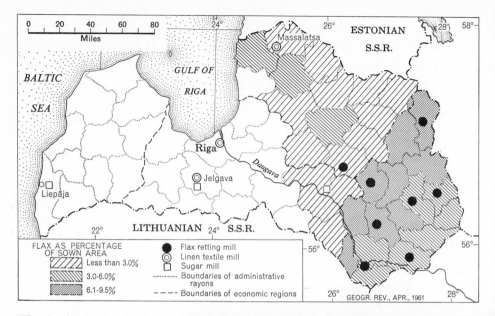

"Flax in the Latvian S.S.R. according to George A. Taskin, "The Soviet Northwest," *Geographical Review,* New York, vol. 51, no. 2, April 1961, p. 225. *(The Geographical Review and Dr. Taskin)*

Map legend:

FLAX AS PERCENTAGE OF SOWN AREA
- Less than 3.0%
- 3.0-6.0%
- 6.1-9.5%

- ● Flax retting mill
- ◎ Linen textile mill
- □ Sugar mill
- ⋯⋯ Boundaries of administrative rayons
- — — — Boundaries of economic regions

GEOGR. REV., APR., 1961

The reconstructed central square of Minsk, capital of Byelorussia. The inscription over the ornate groundfloor windows of the central tower says: "Restaurant the Rainbow." Next to the tower the large inscription proclaims a shoe repair shop. *(Aloys A. Michel)*

the war. The Soviet regime quickly introduced notable changes: the first step, by agreement in 1940 with Germany, was the evacuation of the German elements from the three republics. These Germans were not very numerous, but they were most important in the regional economy—the Baltic "barons" used to be great landlords and to control most of the local economic development. Since 1945 the economy of the three republics was rapidly brought into line with the Soviet general system, and that was done even more brutally in the Kaliningrad area. Divided among themselves, opposed to both German and Russian influences, suspicious of the Poles and even of the Swedes, the Baltic countries always needed outside protection. During the period between the wars, they were linked mainly to Britain, their main customer for timber, butter, and flax. Now they have returned to Russian domination as before 1917; their *de facto* integration in the USSR has been recognized by Britain but not by the United States.

## BYELORUSSIA

The Byelorussian Soviet Socialist Republic (or White Russia) was in 1919 one of the original constituent republics of the USSR. Its territory was cut down by the Polish advance eastward and then restored fully in 1946. Now it stretches to the Bug River in the West and encompasses a large part of the Dnieper upper basin and that of a tributary of the Dnieper, the Pripyat. A land of rivers indeed, it is extremely humid and swampy. A vast area of undecided drainage stretches west of the Dnieper, south of the main morainic heights. Here the divide between Black and Baltic seas passes through a flat plain, and the water has almost submerged it, helped by the podzolization that makes the soil less permeable in depth. Byelorussia could hardly be called a natural region, but the Pripyat or Pinsk marshes are one of the most striking natural regions of Europe: they are the widest stretch of unreclaimed, still feverous, marshland. Inhabited by a population of fishermen, the marshes are a practically impassable forest to those who do not know the few lanes on which traffic can safely cross the humid and dark woods. Modern armies have systematically by-passed and avoided this area. The rest of Byelorussia is safer and drier ground but not very much richer: sandy areas covered with pine woods to the north and some wooded grassland with denser population and better soils to the southeast on the middle Dnieper.

The unity of the region lies perhaps in its transitional character and in its indecision, formulated by the drainage. It is rainy in the warm season and frightfully cold in some winters: here Napoleon's Grand Army suffered one of its worst disasters in the French retreat of 1813, while attempting to cross the half-frozen Berezina River. Human features are

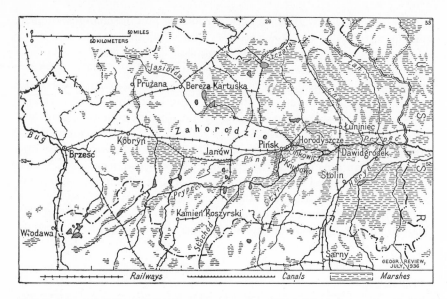

Sketch map of Polesia showing the waterways about Pińsk. Note the canals: the Royal Canal connecting the Pina with the Bug and the Vistula and the Oginski Canal connecting the Szczara and Niemen with the Jasiolda. This area is now part of Byelorussia. *(The Geographical Review)*

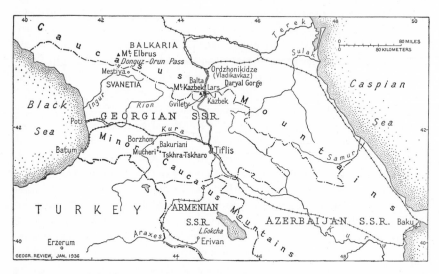

Location map of the Caucasus. *(The Geographical Review)*

most likely responsible for what unity there is: the population's language is very little different from actual Russian. Some regional patriotism is founded on medieval memories of the river-state period; many northern or western influences have been felt here. Muscovy never actually penetrated this area, to which the Russians came back only in the eighteenth century. To them Byelorussia was therefore a kind of poor, backward marginal land: no attempt was made to reclaim the Pinsk marshes; they were considered only good for defensive purposes. Jews who came from the west were allowed to crowd here, and it was they who were responsible for most of the economic development in this region during the nineteenth century.

The total area of Byelorussia covers 81,000 square miles; the population in this area, in 1959, numbered 8.1 million people, and in 1966, 8.6 million, about 80 percent of them Byelorussians and 8 percent Russians. Towns concentrated a large portion of that total. Minsk (717,000), the capital, was mainly important as a military headquarters, commanding a large part of the western border area. Other important towns are: on the Polish boundary, Brest-Litovsk (91,000); in the heart of the marshes, Pinsk; Grodno (72,000); Vitebsk (194,000), Orsha, and Mogilev (164,-000) in the northern forested part; and Bobruisk (117,000), Zhlobin, and Gomel (226,000) in the wooded grassland area to the south. In this difficult environment men had to live a modest life, as self-sufficient as possible. Some fields of grains (more extensive in the south), meadows, and forestry helped a rather backward country to make a living. The Soviet regime has started drainage and irrigation works on a large scale on some *sovkhozes*, with mechanization and considerable capital investment. The marshes, when drained and well-tilled, provide a very rich soil, giving high yields of grains or industrial crops. Fodder and cattle raising should be the natural vocation of this area. The vast woodlands yield substantial quantities of timber. In 1965 there were 15 million acres under cultivation; one fourth of this area was under fodder crops, one fifth under potatoes (the usual crop for poor, morainic soils around the Baltic), and about one half under grains. Flax was an important crop in the northern section of Byelorussia, while some hemp was produced in the south. Recently some experimental plantations of mulberry trees seem to have succeeded near Gomel, and silkworms are being raised in the Vitebsk region. The livestock in 1965 counted 4.7 million head of cattle, 3.7 million pigs, and 0.8 million sheep and goats. Practically all the tilled soil was in mechanized collective and state farms; however, by 1958 only one out of every three collective farms had electric power. In the vast Pinsk marshes, about 3 million acres of marshland have been drained, opening to agricultural use rich new lands that yield harvests of grain, potatoes, fodder, and other crops.

The number of industrial and office workers in Byelorussia at the end of 1965 reached 2,400,000, of whom 159,000 were specialists with higher education. There is obviously heavy employment in the government bureaus; but the industrial output is expanding, too, especially in recent years since the reconstruction of the cities and main plants has been completed. About one third of the industrial output is produced in the city and district (or *oblast*) of Minsk. In the Byelorussian capital are concentrated particularly electric production (powerhouses mainly fed with peat from nearby deposits), engineering plants, match, leather, and shoe factories. Woodworking industries are important, too, in Minsk, Gomel, and Brest-Litovsk. Gomel has also paper, pulp, match, and textile plants; Vitebsk is a textile and leatherware center; Mogilev produces chemicals and building materials, while Grodno makes paper, shoes, sugar, and foodstuffs. Among the main specialties of Byelorussian manufacturing are agricultural machinery, linen fabrics (57 million meters in 1965, especially at Orsha), rayon, and prefabricated houses. The output of electricity reached 8.4 billion kw-h in 1965. The Soviet regime, following its policy of waterway development, carried out through the Pinsk marshes the construction of a canal linking the Dnieper to the Bug and thus established a direct and easy connection from the Ukraine to Poland. Byelorussia is therefore being gradually equipped for a better utilization of its resources. But it still looks like a backyard of the rich Ukraine.

## THE UKRAINE

To the southwest extends one republic which should hardly be called "marginal," so important has its part been in the Russian or Soviet whole. The Ukraine has had a strange destiny. It started with Kiev and the river state, cooperating or making war with the seminomadic tribes of the Polovtzy or Pecheneg. Then the Mongol invasion rendered the steppe, with its characteristic open spaces, swept by nomads, unfit for sedentary occupation. The Russians, re-emerging from the forest, considered with awe this broad, open territory with no place to hide and with grasses so easily set afire over immense areas. They reached Kiev again only in the 1660s and began going down the Don River, organizing the colonies of Cossacks who, with their long leather whips called *knout*, seemed semi-agricultural military formations in themselves.

The Ukraine in the seventeenth century was still a headache and a problem: it seemed unlikely that this country could ever be decently organized at any time. Its very name *Okraïna* means margin, borderland. But when joint Russian and Cossack efforts had succeeded in pushing back the Poles from the west and the Turks from the east, it was decided that some occupation had to be organized—Catherine the Great offered all the land one could occupy to whoever among the Russian aristocracy would move colonies of serfs to the Ukraine. Settlement developed; the fertility of the black soil was discovered and put to use, and around 1800 a French *émigré*, the Duke de Richelieu, was appointed governor of southern Russia. He organized the country and built on the Black Sea the port of Odessa, around which a large city and market arose. In the nineteenth century the Ukraine became the granary of Russia, its richest agricultural area, rotating wheat with sugar beets and fodder crops. Then iron ore was found at Krivoi Rog, in the Dnieper bend, and coal along the Donets River. Combining these resources, a powerful industrial area, the Donets Basin (commonly known as *Donbass*), grew up in the twentieth century, and in the eastern Ukraine the recently grown-up city of Kharkov has become one of Russia's largest.

The Ukraine appeared in the 1920s as the most essential part of the Soviet economy by its concentration of both agricultural and industrial production. The aim of the Five-Year Plans was to increase this development, but at a slower rhythm than in other areas, newer and farther inland. In 1946, as a result of the Russian advances westward, vast territories were added to the Ukraine: the region of Lwów (ceded by Poland), northern Bukovina and part of Bessarabia (ceded by Rumania), and even Ruthenia or sub-Carpathian Ukraine (ceded by Czechoslovakia). With the latter addition, the Ukraine crossed the Carpathian range and extended its territory into a corner of the Pannonian Plain of Hungary. In 1954, the Crimea was also incorporated into the Ukraine. From the upper basin of the Tisza to the Sea of Azov, the Ukraine as now constituted covers 232,000 square miles; the population of this area in 1959 was 41,893,000—almost exactly the size of France, about one tenth smaller in area and larger in population. In 1966, the population reached 45.5 million.

The comparison with France is suggestive in many respects: right away it is easy to perceive the difference in "age," in historical development, in cultural contribution, and even in economic development; the natural factors would all be in favor of the Ukraine in such a comparison. The Ukraine is almost completely flat, with only a low range of mountains along its western border: the Carpathians; almost all its territory is covered with the richest soils of Europe; it is easy to cross, especially with the help of large navigable rivers such as the Dnieper, the Dniester, and the Bug (not to be confused with the Polish river of the same name). Its coal and iron deposits are easier to work and yield higher-grade materials than the French ones. The Ukraine has also important deposits of manganese ore, around Nikopol, some bauxite, and graphite. Yet with all these natural advantages, what a difference between the present economic wealth and standard of living in the Ukraine and in France. Such a confrontation should be suggested to those who think that they can explain history, economics, and power problems by environmental considerations alone.

As one piece of the huge might of the Soviet Union, the Ukraine should be able to develop its production and population rapidly. But it too was terribly destroyed during the war, when from 1941 to 1944 it was the major battlefield of the German-Soviet clash. Production rises during postwar years seem to indicate a higher rate of increase in the nondevastated parts of the Soviet Union than in the devastated parts. This would mean as a whole quicker development in Asia than in Europe and in the central regions of Europe (east of Moscow and north of Volgograd) than in the marginal regions, among which the Ukraine was by far the most important and the hardest hit. As a whole, the Ukraine was too essential a part of the Soviet system to be allowed to lag behind in its reconstruction, and by 1952 the output of its collieries and heavy industries reached the prewar level. But one must realize that, consistently with the policy of inland development, its relative importance within the Union is bound to be decreased.

Although the country is fairly united within one region, important differences can be observed from west to east, and the Ukraine should therefore be divided into four different parts: the western section, consisting of the newly attached territories; central Ukraine, the old country of Kiev, the Dnieper, and Odessa; eastern Ukraine, the land of Kharkov, the Donbass, and the Azov seashore; and finally, southeastward, the "Mediterranean" peninsula of Crimea.

In the western Ukraine the steppe has not yet begun: it is made of forested mountains and cleared plateaus sloping gently from the foot of the Carpathians. Patches of rich black loess surround Lwów (500,000), the largest city of what used to be a granary of Austria and later of Poland. This is deeply rural country compared with areas farther east: wheat, sugar beets, cattle, and hogs are its main products. At the foot of the Carpathians small oilfields have been developed. To the south, in Bukovina, Chernovitsy (175,000) commands the easiest passes across the Carpathians, which narrow down and lower their crests in this vicinity. A disputed point throughout several wars between Russia and Austria, Chernovitsy is now in Soviet hands as are the passes themselves and their southern approaches in the backward rural land of Ruthenia raising sheep around the small towns of Uzhorod and Mukachevo. At the foot of the northern slope of the Carpathians, around Boryslaw, oilfields are in operation. In Bukovina, some oil was also found, and gypsum, alabaster, and lignite are mined. A pipeline carries gas from Dashava to Minsk.

Kiev, the reconstructed capital of the Ukraine. *(Above)* Young Ukrainians pause at one of many bookstalls, which alternate with ice cream stands along Kreshchatik street, a historic artery. *(Aloys A. Michel). (Below)* A busy crossroads in the center of the city. *(Sovfoto)*

Central Ukraine is the historical and the agricultural heart of the country. It centers around Kiev on the most continuous stretch of black soil: a deep, fat, sticky earth, which after the thaw in the spring turns into such a mass of oily clay that it is hard to walk on. Mechanized equipment has had some difficulties on the black soil at times; tanks in wartime were stuck trying to get off the roads. But for over a century the richest agricultural area of Russia has been developed here. Large farms produced grains and beets and fodder, as on the loamy plains of Western Europe. The towns in the midst of this area grew quickly—Nezhin, famous for its truck farming; Konotop, Zhitomir (133,000) Berdichev, Kremenchug, (130,000) Vinnitsa (154,000)—each processing the agricultural production, milling grain, refining sugar, distilling alcohol, and pressing sunflower and other oilseeds. These cities have also been industrialized, making agricultural machinery, fertilizer, and other chemicals. The rich peasants put up quite a resistance to collectivization for a while, and in the early 1930s the spread of sovkhozes and kolkhozes threatened to disorganize the whole output.

Kiev, the old capital and the oldest large city of the Union, stands amid the fields and meadows; it has rebuilt the sections destroyed in the war. In 1966 the city counted 1,371,000 inhabitants and was proud of its eleventh-century monasteries, its monumental section of the eighteenth and nineteenth centuries, and its vast industrial suburbs manufacturing foodstuffs, chemicals, and machinery. The city has a southern charm, a vitality, and a humor that are not felt in many other capitals of the Union. Kiev is the seat of the Ukrainian government, which has an array of departments and its own representation in the United Nations. It is also the center of Ukrainian culture, with an important university and an academy of sciences. The destruction wrought by the war has been so great that a new city with a different plan has emerged from under the ruins. The Dnieper, although frozen three months in the year, gives to Kiev the role of an inland port. The city now has a subway and many green spaces and parks, and it expects fast growth.

Kiev stands today at the contact point of the more agricultural part of the Ukraine and of the large industrial area extending down the river. The iron of Krivoi Rog (500,000) and the manganese of Nikopol have been coupled on the Lower Dnieper with the power produced by the huge Dnieprostroï Dam built on the river's rapids. The rapids of Zaporozhe (570,000) were turned into an asset and doubled by a canal which prevents interruption in the navigation. Vast electrometallurgical and electrochemical industries have surrounded the Dnieprostroï, which, blown up by the Russians during their retreat in 1941, has been rebuilt since liberation. The city of Dniepropetrovsk (790,000) is the capital of this industrial area, in fact a prolongation of the Donbass westward to the Dnieper. The iron mines produce over 40 million tons of iron content annually, about half of total Soviet production, and more than any other single iron ore basin in the world.

On the mouth of the Dnieper, Kherson (220,000) has mechanical plants, a local market, and a transshipment point. The main ports of the Ukraine on the Black Sea are to the west of the Dnieper's mouth: Nikolaev (290,000) on the estuary of the Ukrainian Bug is a metallurgical center and has large shipyards; Odessa, the largest Black Sea port, 170 years old, had 750,000 inhabitants in 1966. Odessa is a cosmopolitan city, with a mixed population in which the Greek and Levantine elements have always been important. It recalls the ancient Greek colonization around this sea and the links between medieval Kiev and Byzantium. There is something truly Mediterranean in the joviality of the city, its colorfulness, its variety. The seaport has attracted a number of industries. The curious aspect of it is that Odessa, like Kharkov, is not linked to a river—this is almost exceptional in Eastern Europe, but both cities are creations of the nineteenth century.

This southern region of the Ukraine, along the Black Sea, is definitely steppic, treeless, and endowed with chestnut soils and a trend toward aridity in the climate. The growth of several towns, such as Uman and Pervomaisk in the immediate hinterland of Odessa, has been based on agricultural prosperity. Since 1946 the Ukrainian territory has stretched along the coast to the mouth of the Danube and now borders on the main arm of the mighty Central European stream at its delta. This small detail gives to Soviet naval patrols, based at Izmail, the possibility of controlling the entrance to navigation on the Danube.

Eastern Ukraine is the most recently settled and developed part of the the country. It is a drier steppe, and the extreme climatic influences of the continent are strongly felt here. But the main feature of this eastern area is its heavy industrialization, without par anywhere in the Soviet Union. This is the Donbass, which started first along the Donets on the coalfield and has expanded in several directions (as usually happens): westward toward the Dnieper and Krivoi Rog, from which iron and manganese ores come; northward toward Kharkov, which is the regional capital and main redistribution center; southward toward the Azov seashore, where navigation leads either to the Black Sea or up the Don River.

The Donbass suffered greatly during World War II as a result of both the Soviet scorched-earth policy and military operations. As Soviet statistics give little regional breakdown, it is difficult to estimate the actual importance of the present output; but before 1940 the Donbass coalfield annually produced some 75 million tons of coal, and it had risen to 180 million tons in 1965, or 42 percent of all the Soviet output, mostly of good quality. Around these mines were grouped about forty-five blast furnaces. The whole of the Ukraine (eastern and central) in 1939 produced 6.5 million tons of pig iron and 5 million tons of steel ingots; in 1965 these figures had risen to 32 and 37 million tons respectively. Numerous chemical industries were identified with the metallurgy in the area, many of them in the southern section of the coalfield and along the Azov coast, especially at the port of Zhdanov, formerly Mariupol (375,000), which used to be famous before 1914 as a grain-shipping point. The coal reserves of the Donbass are estimated at 35 billion tons, of which about one third is anthracite. Coupled with the hematite ores of the Krivoi Rog they constitute the foundation of Soviet power in iron and steel. The Donbass ships coal to the Moscow area. The densest network of railways of the Soviet Union covers the Donbass and its vicinity, and the railroad from the Donbass to Moscow carries the heaviest traffic in the Union. Stalino, renamed Donetsk in 1961 (106,000 inhabitants in 1926 and 825,000 in 1966), is the largest city and rail hub of the basin; Lugansk (340,000), Makeevka (410,000) Kramatorsk (136,000) and Gorlovka (340,000) are the other leading industrial towns. But the real capital of the industrial region, Kharkov, is on its fringe.

Kharkov certainly deserved in 1940 to be called the third industrial city of the Soviet Union. Between the World Wars it was the political capital of the Ukraine, but this function has moved now to the older and more central city of Kiev. Kharkov is sometimes described as the "Soviet Pittsburgh." By European standards, Kharkov is a "young city"; it grew up in the nineteenth century and developed with the railways. Away from the sea and any large stream, it began as a market and soon had also a large fair. Kharkov is conveniently situated at the point of contact of the industrial Donbass with the rich black soils to the west in the Poltava (177,000) area; it is also at the line of contact of the open, dry steppe to the southeast with the more humid grassland, crossed by small wooded ribbons, to the northwest. The former zone traditionally raised sheep, while the latter concentrated on cattle. Kharkov started as a market for grains, meat, leather, and wool in the middle of the nineteenth century. Kharkovian banks and the technical schools of the university were instrumental in the development of the Donbass: little by little the emphasis of its activities shifted to redistribution trade in foodstuffs, textiles, and timber and then to mechanical industries utilizing the Donbass steel. Before 1914 a large locomotive plant dominated the factories, stressing the rail-hub function; later it was converted into one of the largest tank and tractor factories of the Union. Machine-tool plants and electrical engineering came here under the Soviet regime, as well as the largest tractor factory and the first nuclear physics institute of the country. From 175,000 people in 1897, the city grew to 280,000 in 1913, to 417,000 in 1926, 833,000 in 1939, 930,000 in 1959, and 1.1 million in 1967. Hard hit by World War II, during which it was twice taken by the Germans and twice liberated by the Russians, Kharkov was rebuilt according to a plan that takes into account the "intellectual" and economic-directing functions of its downtown section and that aims at a scattering of specialized suburbs all around, with parks between them. Very few new cities in Europe have so quickly achieved such status in the hierarchy of managerial and brain-trust centers.

To the southeast of the Ukraine a large peninsula, in the shape of a lozenge, stretches between the Black and Azov seas, enclosing the latter and converting it practically into a Soviet lake which communicates only by the Kerch Strait with the Black Sea. Although in 1954 integrated into the Ukraine and therefore administered from Kiev, the Crimea has a striking and definitely marginal personality. It is attached to the Ukrainian mainland by only two narrow necks of land. Most of the peninsula is occupied by a dome of limestone, folded and faulted, particularly in the south and east where the hilly topography takes on a truly mountainous scenery and rises to 5000 feet. A sharp folding determined the steep slope overlooking the sea to the southeast: a Mediterranean riviera scenery and economy have developed there with sea resorts, famous tourist centers, fruit orchards, and vineyards. Tatar clans still hold the hills and the steppic stretches in the north and west of the peninsula.

At the southern tip of Crimea a large, well-protected roadstead harbors the port and naval base of Sevastopol (200,000). Twice this strategic city underwent long sieges: in 1854–1855 during the Crimean War between the Russians and the French and British; then in 1941–1942 in World War II. In both cases Sevastopol put up a gallant defense and was terribly devastated; in both cases it rapidly started rebuilding a large and beautiful city, which is one of the attractions of the Crimean riviera as well as the Soviet's chief naval base on the Black Sea. In the midst of the riviera coast, the town of Yalta, famous as a resort, was the site of a decisive inter-Allied conference, attended by Roosevelt, Churchill, and Stalin in 1945. At the eastern tip of the peninsula the town of Kerch (115,000) controls the entrance of the Sea of Azov.

This small peninsula has three towns, whose populations have each gone above 100,000: Sevastopol, the naval base; Simferopol (217,000), the regional capital and rail hub; and Kerch with its iron industries. The narrow strip of land leading to Kerch has rich iron-ore mines. The quality of the ores (about 40 percent in iron content) is lower than in the Krivoï Rog, but the reserves are at least as important and are estimated at over a billion tons of iron. Kerch and Krivoï Rog both send ores or pig iron to the Donbass and other industrial centers in European Russia.

The shores of the Black Sea in the Ukraine. *(Above)* The port of Odessa as seen in the summer of 1960 from the top of the monumental Richelieu stairs, so named in honor of the French duke who founded Odessa while he was governor of New Russia around 1800. *(Below)* The southern Crimean shore near Yalta, with rocky promontories, vineyards, and small woods typical of the Mediterraneanlike landscapes of this "Soviet Riviera." *(Aloys A. Michel)*

The Kerch ores are the most recent, geologically speaking, of the iron-ore mines in the Soviet Union, as they date from the Upper Pliocene only.

As a result of both its natural endowment and the development rapidly achieved in the last 200 years, the Ukraine remains — once the havoc wrought by the last war has been repaired — the richest part of the Soviet Union and indeed the main pillar of the whole Soviet economy. It used to be the breadbasket of the tsar's empire, and it has been converted into the main source of basic industrial materials of the Soviet empire. In the 1960s, the Ukraine contributed to the total Soviet output 40 percent of the coal, 56 percent of the iron ore, 40 percent of the manganese, 50 percent of the pig iron, 40 percent of the crude steel, 16 percent of the cement, 50 percent of the soda ash, 67 percent of the sugar, 30 percent of the tractors, 90 percent of the main-line diesel locomotives, and 50 percent of the trucks. Of all the major raw materials, only for oil, to which the small Ukrainian oilfields contributed barely 2 percent of the Soviet total, was this remarkable republic more dependent on the Great Russian area than vice versa. For some essential materials, such as iron and manganese ores, the Ukrainian mines of Krivoï Rog, Kerch, and Nikopol were the major suppliers of the iron and steel works of the East European satellites where so much steel, machinery, and other manufactures were produced, not only for local distribution but also for consumption in the Soviet Union. While producing such a large share of the Soviet industrial output, the Ukraine had only 2.7 percent of the land area of the USSR and 20.8 percent of its population. The concentration of economic wealth here was all the more remarkable since the Ukraine used to be by far the principal farming area and foodstuffs-producer among the various regions that make up the Soviet Union.

It still is an essential breadbasket, but its agricultural output in recent years has shown a trend that threatens serious decline. In his speech before the plenary session of the Central Committee of the Soviet Union's Communist party January 17, 1961, Mr. Khrushchev quoted disconcerting data: in 1960 the Ukraine delivered to the state warehouses only some 358 million *puds* of breadmaking grain, or 65 percent of the average quantities supplied in the period 1948–1958. In the 1950s the agricultural machinery of the Ukraine had been greatly improved and expanded: the number of tractors for ploughing went up from 14,000 in 1949 to 115,000 in 1960, the number of cornpickers rose from none to 19,500 in the same years. By 1960 the area sown with wheat had been decreased mainly in favor of corn, which covered 40 percent of all the sown area of the Ukraine (26.3 million acres in 1960). It was the corn crop that proved disappointing in 1959 and a failure in 1960. Mr. Khrushchev blamed the failure on the regional management's

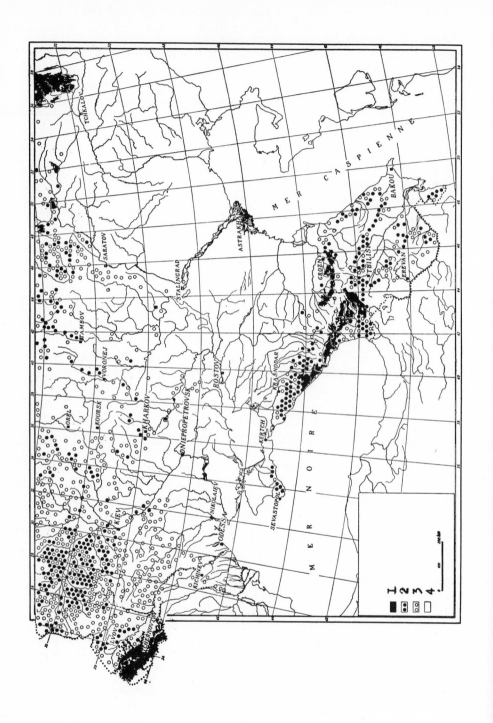

mistakes or irresponsibility. It may well be, however, that while such a massive reform of a large farming region requires some time to bring full results—and may easily be mismanaged in the first years—the basic difficulty was that the Ukrainian climate, quite different from that of the American Midwest, is not favorable to corn and often is the cause of crop failures. Whatever opposition exists in the Soviet Union nick-named Mr. Khrushchev "Nikita the Corn" (Nikita Kookooroozny). His overthrow, in 1964, was partly due to his administration's failure to develop agricultural production. Altogether, the agriculture of the Ukraine, like most of Soviet farming, has not evidenced the successful expansion of industrial production. The grain crop still varies a great deal from year to year and does not show great progress since the late 1950s. It supplies about one fifth of all Soviet output.

The Ukraine has been one of the main areas from which the Soviet planners thought they might be able to shift populations to the wide, empty areas of Siberia and Soviet Central Asia. These hopes have not much materialized. Although millions of people residing in the Ukraine before the German invasion went east during the war, most of them quickly returned after its liberation. Despite the hardships of the period before reconstruction was completed in the terribly destroyed land, they chose to stay in the Ukraine, partly, perhaps, because they liked that area better or believed more in its future and partly by order, for the recon-struction of the Ukraine was one of the most urgent tasks in the master plan of Soviet economic recovery. In the present condition of a man-power shortage in the Soviet economy, the government could hardly afford to depopulate seriously the very heart of Soviet production, agricultural as well as industrial. The emphasis given to the problem of nationalities under Stalin and the greater amount of economic self-government delegated to each republic's authorities by the 1958 reg-ulations could have reinforced the local nationalism of the Ukrainian people. However, most Ukrainians are of not so distant and often very recent Russian origin. More than any of the other marginal republics of the USSR, the Ukraine has risen to its present eminence and develop-ment as a result of Russian settlement and partnership. The Ukrainians are not actually regarded as different from the Russians in Moscow or Siberia, as many of the other peripheral nations are. The Ukraine may

---

(*Opposite*) Distribution of forests in the south of the Soviet Union in Europe. Key: 1, major forested areas; 2, considerably wooded areas; 3, small density of forests; 4, nonwooded areas. Notice the concentration of forests in the western reaches of the Ukraine and in the Caucasus ranges. The great treeless steppe extends from the lower Dnieper to the Urals. (After *Le Monde Forestier*, published by the U.N. Food and Agriculture Organiza-tion, Rome)

play a distinct part within Soviet politics, but separatist trends have seldom amounted to much, except during the short period of German occupation of the Ukraine at the end of World War I. Ukrainian nationalism exists, but as a possible trend towards secession from the rest of the Russian system, it seems to have been wishful thinking on the part of some foreign experts.

## THE MOLDAVIAN SOVIET SOCIALIST REPUBLIC

In its southwestern reaches the Ukraine's territory surrounds a small republic made out of lands that were formerly parts of the Ukraine or of Bessarabia. The Moldavian Republic recalls the existence of a people and a dialect of that name. It covers 13,200 square miles and in 1966 had 3,400,000 inhabitants. About 65 percent of them are Moldavians and 15 percent Ukrainians. Almost entirely rural, this republic specializes in the production of milk, fruits and grapes; cereals, sunflower, tobacco, and sugar beets are also cultivated. The processing and canning factories are largely concentrated at Kishinev (290,000), the capital, and at Tiraspol (90,000) on the Dniester River. The farms have been thoroughly collectivized and almost all the industries are state-owned, according to the Soviet rule.

## THE CAUCASIAN AREA

The wide isthmus between the Black and the Caspian seas is largely occupied by the lofty mountain range of the Caucasus. It is a mighty and complicated structure stretching more than 800 miles in length from the Kerch Strait to the peninsula of Apsheron on the Caspian. It is fairly continuous from coast to coast and presents a barrier comparable in many respects to that of the Pyrenees, but on an enlarged scale. Like the Pyrenees, the Caucasus lies between plains to the north and high, massive and faulted tablelands of semi-African structure to the south. Immediately to the south of the range a deep and narrow rift (the Ebro valley in Spain and the Dura valley in Transcaucasia) separates it from the tablelands. At the two extremities the intensity of the uplifting subsided, and the hills regularly decrease their height. The central section or "axis region" forms a high, uninterrupted wall, where many summits rise above 13,000 feet. Mount Elbrus reaches 18,470 feet in elevation; it should be considered the highest summit in Europe, as it surpasses Mont Blanc by some 3000 feet, but geographers do not all agree that the Elbrus is in Europe. The traditional boundary between Europe and Asia follows the main crestline of the Caucasus, and the high summits would therefore be just on the divide.

Soviet geographers have shown a definite trend to include their Trans-caucasian territories in Europe. Georgia, which is south of the main crestline, was the homeland of Stalin and several other high dignitaries of the Soviet regime. Moreover the Caucasus does not cut clearly through the isthmus from coast to coast; it has a northwest-southeast axis that makes it border in a tangential way on the two seas it divides. Still, one must recognize that, once across the first high crest of the range, one enters a different world: a complicated structure, an even much more complicated ethnography of many small and varied peoples hiding in the valleys. The climate is definitely warmer in the depressions, more humid on the Black Sea coast, and much more arid in the areas looking eastward. The Russians speak here of their "tropics"—humid tropics on the Black Sea slope, with such crops as tea and cotton grown without irrigation, and dry tropics requiring irrigation on the Caspian side. In-deed, this is no longer Europe; it cannot even be called Mediterranean; although transitional, this Caucasian world belongs to Asia.

The mountaineers of the Caucasus are famous for their many clans and the variety of their languages; their fierce spirit of independence led them to defend themselves stubbornly against any kind of outside pene-tration. The Turks did not control, properly speaking, most of the high-lands officially included for centuries in their empire. When, in the nine-teenth century, the Russian conquest penetrated the Caucasus, the new rulers came upon the same difficulties: on the northern slope the whole nation of the Cherkess (or Circassians) preferred to move out of the area in which they had lived for a long time rather than to accept Russian rule. Where field and meadows, villages and towns had existed, only idle wildernesses remained, and the rapid growth of the forest recovered these mountains with a dense vegetation, erasing the traces of the Cher-kess occupation. Transcaucasia had to be given special treatment, and until 1914 the tsars maintained a viceroy of Transcaucasia, thus grant-ing some autonomy to the area. The Soviet regime organized the region into a set of republics endowed with local self-government to some ex-tent. In fact, not until Georgians were important in the government at Moscow could real incorporation of Transcaucasia in the Russian realm be obtained. Some trouble developed there in the years 1954–1957 after Stalin's death, Lavrenti Beria's downfall, and Stalin's downgrading.

The Caucasus Mountains are highly mineralized and rich in water-power, and these resources are being steadily developed. Most of them are situated in what we consider to be the Asiatic part, but one essential resource is found at the foot of the northern European slope—oil. The foot of the Caucasus was the first large oil-producing area of Russia and of Europe. Until the 1930s its output represented at least 90 percent, if not more, of the total Soviet production; it must have supplied by far the better part of it until 1952. Three main oilfields are found along the Caucasus, of increasing importance as one proceeds from Kerch toward the Caspian.

Maikop is the first oilfield and the smallest. In 1942 it was taken over by the German army but only after its installations had been scrapped by the retreating Russians. It is situated in the foothills of the northwestern extremity of the Caucasus; now it has yielded in importance to the gas fields of Stavropol which are linked by pipelines with the central natural gas network of Russia. The next field is more important. Around Grozny the wells scatter in the foothills of the central, lofty part of the range. Two small ranges of hills stretch parallel to the west of Grozny as though protecting it on that side. The most advanced spearhead of the German forces reached these hills in the summer of 1942 but could not surmount the first crest—partly for lack of oil and lubricants, the German columns were stopped almost in sight of the oilfield they needed. The total reserves of this area are estimated by Soviet geologists at about 800 million tons, but these oilfields were reduced to a minor role by the discovery of much richer fields recently in other parts of the Soviet Union. Still more natural gas wells are now operating to the southeast, near Mahatchkala.

The largest of the sub-Caucasian oilfields is situated at the easternmost extremity of the range on the Caspian shore. Around Baku and on the Apsheron peninsula lies the oldest and best-explored major Soviet oilfield. Its reserves are estimated at 2.5 billion tons, but its production, having reached 21.4 million tons in 1937, seems since to have had increased difficulties. By 1965 its output was 21.5 million tons, supplying 9 percent of the total output instead of 15 percent in 1958. Baku has been a mushrooming city, growing on oil like cities in Texas, born around 1900 and with 1,165,000 inhabitants in 1967. It is the capital of the republic of Azerbaijan and definitely a threshold of Asia, where Russians, Armenians, Caucasian mountaineers, and Moslem Turks mingle and from time to time fight. A large refining industry and abundant natural gas have attracted chemical manufactures. Baku has also many food-processing plants, and it is a large fishing port, producing also canned fish and caviar. In fact, Baku is the economic capital of the Caspian basin. Two important pipelines leave from its oil fields: one of them crosses the isthmus following the Kura depression to the Black Sea port of Batumi. The main pipeline follows the foot of the Caucasus to the north, and, draining the Grozny and Maikop areas, carries oil to the Donbass. Specially built tankers carry the oil from Baku across the Caspian and up the Volga River.

The progress made by the production of oil in other parts of the Soviet Union has decreased considerably this function of the Transcaucasian republics, previously their main one in the Soviet economy. The elimination from the top command of the country and the Communist party of most of the persons who originated in the minorities of the Caucasian area has decreased the part played by that area in Soviet internal politics. However, the three marginal republics of Transcaucasia still have a great strategic role, since they border on Turkey and Iran, and considerable importance in the Soviet system of minorities and of relations with the non-Communist countries of the Middle East: there is an Armenian minority scattered through various lands around the Mediterranean, an Iranian province of Azerbaijan, and much interest abroad in the status of Georgia since the disappearance of Stalin and Beria.

Georgia is the second largest in area (27,000 square miles) and population (4.6 million in 1966) of the three republics. The Georgians, who in the Middle Ages had an interesting culture and art of their own, form about two thirds of the population; 11 percent are Russians and as many are Armenians. In its warm valleys dominated by snowcapped peaks, is found some of the most beautiful scenery in the European part of the Soviet Union. Its territory extends to the west to include the "wet tropics" of the Black Sea shoreland near Batumi (94,000), Poti (42,500), and Sukhumi (83,000), the latter a renowned seaside resort. There are rich agricultural areas in the valleys of Georgia, and on the coastal hills. In the Colchis area large marshes have been drained, yielding very rich soils, now intensively cultivated. Georgia produces some of the more exotic crops found in European Russia: the tung tree, for its oil; bamboo; high-quality oriental tobacco; vineyards and mulberry trees abound in Imeretia and Kakhetia, where wines, brandy, and silk are produced. There are also, high up, large areas of fine forests. Important manganese mines are found at Chiaturi; coal, baryte, gold, and other minerals are mined; but the main industrial center is at Tbilisi (or Tiflis), the capital of Georgia, a city of 825,000, and by far the largest center inside the Caucasus range.

Azerbaijan is slightly larger than Georgia (33,500 square miles) and more populated (4,735,000). Besides its capital, Baku, an oil-producing city and a port on the Caspian, it has notable cities at Kirovabad (170,000) and Sumgait (52,000). Georgia looks toward the Black Sea; Azerbaijan is oriented rather to the Caspian. There are some iron-ore mines and an iron and steel industry (producing about half a million tons of steel a year) and a variety of other mineral resources. The farms produce about the same crops as in Georgia but with more emphasis on long-staple cotton, grown under irrigation, and citrus fruits. There are synthetic rubber and plastic-fiber factories at Sumgait, working by means of the natural gas sent from Karadağ by pipeline. Armenia,

Oilfields in Baku. The wells on the Apsheron peninsula tap deposits under the Caspian Sea. The dome and minaret of this formerly Moslem area near the border of Iran rise in foreground. *(Sovfoto)*

In the mountainous Caucasus amid rugged hills, the Georgian Military Highway passes along an arid valley just north of the Krestovy Pass. *(Courtesy Prof. Aloys A. Michel)*

finally, is the smallest of the three republics (12,000 square miles with a population of 2,200,000). Its heart is the basin of Erivan (643,000), its capital and major industrial center, and the valley of the River Araks. The farming and industrial activities are about the same as in Georgia and Azerbaijan. Tourism is being developed in these spectacular mountain areas.

The Transcaucasian republics have indeed been incorporated now in the European Soviet system, largely by the personal policies and power of Joseph Stalin. They are less marginal and, in various ways, more "Russian" than the Baltic republics at the other end of the vast expanse of European Russia. They are also better treated and even more trusted in the present Soviet regime. There is little doubt, however, that some marginal republics, and the Transcaucasian ones especially, have played in the Communist party control of the Russian empire a much greater part than might have been expected after the Bolshevik revolution of 1917. In recent years the predominating Great Russian element seems to have asserted more actively its actual power in the government and in the general direction of Soviet affairs.

The Volga River in its upper course near Ivanovo. *(Sovfoto)*

# 21

## The Great Russian Area

The inner Soviet Europe belongs to the Russian Soviet Federated Socialist Republic (RSFSR), which also stretches over most of the Asiatic parts
of the Union. This is the old and vast area occupied (most of it at least
since Ivan the Terrible) by the Russian people or Great Russians, as
they used to call themselves, to differentiate themselves from the Byelorussians and the Ukrainians (who are also sometimes called the "Small
Russians" or *Malorossy*). This Great Russian area is great indeed but
fairly uniform; a study of it can be made rather rapidly, since it has
fewer territorial subdivisions than have more diversified parts of Europe.
It is also the part of the Soviet Union where minority problems or ir-
redentist claims are least likely to arise.

Physically the Great Russian area is a plain, gently rolling in parts but
immense and monotonous as a whole until the foot of the Urals or the
Caucasus is reached. For its greater part it is covered by woods. Trees
grow scattered in the north where, along the Arctic coast, a corner of
tundra develops; to the south the forest breaks up into wooded grassland and turns to the dry, open steppe that occupies a vast area in the
southeast. A large northern part of this area is drained toward the Arctic
and a small western corner toward the Baltic, but the big bulk of the
territory belongs to the Volga drainage basin. To the south the two much
smaller basins of the Don and Ural rivers frame the Lower Volga. It may
be convenient therefore to divide our regional review as follows: the
northern area, the Baltic region and Leningrad, the Volga basin and
Moscow, and the southern parts of Russia.

The physical uniformity is on the whole underlined by a human unity.

777

Not all the peoples of that area are, of course, of the same Russian ancestry. Many peoples have their "autonomous" republics, territories, or regions; none of them has either the numerical strength or the cultural development that could warrant an actually autonomous life. In most cases, the "autonomous" areas are the most backward and are being brought up, under Russian guidance, to the standards of modern civilization—the Mordves are one of the best examples of this category.

Throughout this vast and fairly uniform area, where the principles of the melting pot have been and still are being applied more strictly, there are three main sections along the western borderlands that have to be considered separately. One of them is much larger than the two others; it should be called the *Volga basin* and treated as the geographical heart of the Russian or Soviet system. The two others are almost marginal or peripheral lands: the northern section from the Baltic to the Arctic illustrates one form of the drive to the open sea, while the southern or, more exactly, the southeastern, almost Asiatic, section illustrates the other aspect of the drive toward the sea.

Moscow stands in the middle of this whole area, in the center of the upper section of the Volga basin. Since the thirteenth century all Russian history has revolved around it; even when the capital moved to St. Petersburg, Moscow remained the center of the internal domestic-settlement process. It merits a study by itself, having been for years one of Europe's great capitals. Most of the past and present geography of the Great Russian area could be told in terms of cities, following their development, shifts of interests, and their parts as crossroads. It is chiefly by radiation from some strongly entrenched and ambitious city that every one of the regions within the area was settled and organized. Many of these cities are located on the main rivers. They acted as crossroads of the more-or-less regular river trade with the less regular, but still important, caravan trade that went through the forest and across the more open grasslands. The cities rose as nuclei of power based on the wealth and strategic importance of fairs and markets.

## NORTHERN RUSSIA

From the Baltic, on which Leningrad is built, to the Arctic shores there stretches a vast area which has been Russian for many centuries but was little occupied or developed until the twentieth century. The 60° of latitude parallel, which passes in the northern outskirts of Leningrad, was considered for a long time the limit to agricultural activities and dense settlement. It still keeps this role, although the Soviet regime has endeavored to push the limit farther north. The development of the northern area was successful only in spots or along a few routes.

The region of Leningrad is rather different from the rest of this area because the city is situated in the southwest, close to the Baltic Sea. True, the Gulf of Finland of that sea freezes in winter, as do the large Lakes Ladoga and Peipus in the vicinity. The average temperature in January is 18.3° F., but the summer is warm (63.5° in July) and has long hours of daylight in June and July. Situated slightly farther north than Stockholm, Leningrad knows also the "white nights," when the sun does not go far under the horizon and the sky is lit up all around the clock. In winter the day is quite short. The environment is definitely humid: to the 20.6 inches of yearly precipitations, one should add the dampness of the surrounding marshy area, through which the Neva carries a huge flow of water, emptying into the Baltic the surplus of a vast basin drained toward Lake Ladoga. The site chosen in 1703 by Peter the Great for the capital of a vast empire that was to look westward was set in the midst of marshes—a confused topography left by the retreating glaciers and slowly modified by the fluvial erosion on the neck of land between the Baltic and Lake Ladoga. The Neva River was embanked with granite blocks; the land around was drained. The monumental city that arose immediately became the political and administrative capital of a vast and highly centralized empire as well as an important seaport. After a troubled history, it still is one of the most beautiful cities in Europe.

Like Stockholm and almost like Venice, Leningrad can claim to be a masterpiece of masonry. It is built on hundreds of small islands, and many canals still wind through the city. Some of these canals lead to the Neva and Lake Ladoga, where the Baltic–White Sea Canal then opens the way to the Arctic and the older Mariinsky system connects with the Volga and Moscow. It was by waterways that Peter's capital (then called Saint Petersburg, renamed Petrograd in 1914, and rebaptized Leningrad in 1924) communicated with the interior until the rail line to Moscow was completed in 1851. Excentric as it was, Leningrad could hardly remain the capital of a new regime, turned chiefly toward domestic reformation and stressing constantly the threat of outside intervention. But, under Moscow's leadership, Leningrad remains one of the chief industrial cities of the Soviet Union.

The population of the city, which approximated 2 million in 1914, fell to about 1.6 million in 1926, rose to 3.2 in 1939, and fell by at least a million people during World War II to rise yet again to 2,880,000 in 1959 and 3.6 million in 1966. This increase was achieved by the growth of industries. The old downtown section with its palaces and churches of very mixed architecture, Italian Renaissance mingling with Victorian or with traditional Russian styles, has been preserved as a museum area and performs administrative functions. Industrial and residential suburbs have sprung up since 1930 toward the south and the north. To the pre-Revolutionary metallurgical and ship-building industries have been added vast mechanical, chemical, and engineering works. These industrial suburbs as well as the palatial old summer residences around the city suffered severely during World War II. Leningrad was besieged by the Germans for two years; air bombings and artillery fire destroyed a great part of the city, while many inhabitants died of hunger and epidemics. Leningrad lost one million people by deaths from various causes during the siege. New, large-scale plans were prepared after 1945 and reconstruction went on; the city is now farther away from the border. As a seaport on the Baltic, Leningrad may come up against a serious competition from more advanced harbors, such as Riga and Kaliningrad; but at present it commands a wider area of which it will remain the central market and chief industrial agglomeration. It readily receives shipments of Polish coal. Leningrad is also the main naval base of the Soviet Union, and the second largest cultural center. It is also one of the chief transportation hubs of the country, with major highways, rail lines, and waterways radiating from it. The Mariinsky canal system linking it to Rybinsk on the Volga has been rebuilt and enlarged, carrying now large vessels, in less than three days from Leningrad to the upper Volga.

The economic region focused on Leningrad seems to include the Karelian and Baltic republics; but it also extends over an important area of the Great Russian region—the area between the Baltic and the Valdai Hills, where Volga and Dnieper have their sources. This is a morainic area of confused topography, with many lakes and streams interrupted by rapids. Along the Volkhov River a line of old cities—Novgorod (82,000), Staraya Russa, Velikie Luki—recall the "river state" and form a line of fortresses. Waterpower has been harnessed on the falls along the Volkhov, Svir, and Neva Rivers. The peat bogs supply fuel to powerhouses too. A belt of truck farming and dairy economy has developed around the large city, to the production of which can now be added the important agricultural surpluses of the Baltic republics. The abundance of relatively cheap power helped the spread of plants manufacturing pulp and paper, aluminum, cement, fertilizers, and wooden goods. Most of these plants follow the Baltic-White Sea Canal, which skirts around the Lakes Ladoga and Onega and from the northern extremity of the latter heads straight north.

The Karelian republic, which we reviewed with the marginal lands, stretches due north of Leningrad. Eastward in the irregular scattering of low hills it is difficult to determine exactly where the watershed passes between the Baltic and the Volga basins. But to the northeast the vast and rather empty spaces of what is properly northern Russia open up. Very few large cities are left in this section of the Union. Vologda

(166,000) may be considered as its gate—a rail hub from which lines radiate toward Leningrad, Moscow, the Ural area, and Arkhangel in the north. Then for several hundred miles there is no important urban center.

Two large rivers, the Northern Dvina and the Pechora, with the smaller Mezen between them, drain the whole area northward to the Arctic. Here the winter becomes particularly severe and long: the rivers stay frozen for 200 days a year, and the average annual temperature is rarely above 32°. A coniferous forest covers the land: pines predominate in the west, firs in the east. Soviet experts claim that there is much more timber in this area than in the whole of Scandinavia plus Finland. Practically all the settlement and development here was linked to woodcutting and floating of logs down the Northern Dvina and its tributaries. Where the Dvina empties into the White Sea stands Arkhangel, the regional capital and the chief timber-exporting port of Russia. Its population grew from 35,000 in 1912 to 308,000 in 1966 as the factories processing the lumber multiplied. Since 1930 lumbering has been mechanized, and plywood, pulp and paper, alcohol, and resin are produced in the area. As several towns increased in importance because of this industrialization along the rivers (for instance, Veliki Ustyug and Kotlas), an effort was made to supply them locally with some of their food needs. Thus agriculture was pushed above the 60th parallel, introducing potatoes, barley, flax, and meadows. Some wheat has also appeared as biologists in Leningrad worked for the development of seeds that would fit the short subarctic vegetative season.

The basin of the Pechora occupies the northeastern corner of European Russia; it is mostly covered by the autonomous republic of the Komis, or Zyrians, a backward local people whose capital is Syktyvkar (100,000). Some of them still live in huts, like the Lapps, and hunt fur-bearing animals. Lumbering has spread to this country. Large-scale reindeer-raising provides skins for the manufacture of suède leather. Large deposits of coal and oil have been ascertained in the Pechora basin and, although little worked as yet, are considered as one of the fuel reserves of the Soviet Union. Ukhta and Chibyu are new oil towns in the heart of the taïga. To the east, the altitude rises, and forest densely clothes the northern crests of the Ural Mountains, some of which reaches 5000 feet and more. Still farther north, the desolate frozen aspects of the tundra take over. In the Ural foothills, new coalfields have been developed near Vorkuta and Inta. A new lumbering center and seaport has been built in the Pechora delta at Naryan-Mar. The threshold of Asia is reached here. Most of the development of the Urals area has taken place farther south, in the basin of the Kama, a tributary of the Volga.

Northeast of Arkhangel the land as a rule is frozen permanently in depth and the taïga scatters, turning to tundra on the approaches to the Arctic coast. But a quite different economy prevails to the northwest, on a peninsula stretching between the White Sea (which is a big inland gulf) and the Barents Sea (a section of the Arctic Ocean). Here the Kola peninsula belongs to the Fenno-Scandian Shield; its old, resistant rocks, though polished by the ice sheets, display a higher and more diversified topography. The northwestern corner is reached by warm waters and kept ice-free throughout the winter, or almost so. Here Russia built the port of Murmansk to keep an Atlantic contact with her Western allies during the two World Wars. In 1914 the whole Kola peninsula numbered some 20,000 inhabitants: fishermen on the coast, Lapps in the interior. In 1966, Murmansk, founded in 1916, already had 280,000 people and the district of Murmansk about 700,000. A large port exporting phosphates, lumber, and furs in peacetime, importing all kind of supplies in wartime, Murmansk also receives some coal from the Russian-operated mines on the Arctic archipelago of Svalbard, which is Norwegian territory but under a Soviet threat. The coastal strip extended westward with the annexation of the Finnish section of the seaboard, so that the little port of Petsamo is now Russian (and called Pechenga) and the Soviet Union has established territorial contact with the Norwegian province of Finmark.

Murmansk has chemical industries and a fishing fleet, the chemical raw materials coming from inland. The peninsula has one of the richest phosphate rock deposits of Europe and, in old crystalline strata, a variety of high-grade ores—iron, copper, nickel, vanadium, titanium, molybdenum. Along the railway that, coming north from Leningrad, crosses the peninsula from Kandalaksha to Murmansk, several mining towns have been recently created. The main centers there are Kirovsk (56,000) and Bryanka (80,000), established amid the ore-extracting points and the waterpower stations. The rugged tundra that surrounds it has even been forced to produce some food crops that mature under the midnight sun. Reindeer and some cattle are raised on the peninsula. This development parallels in many respects what the Swedes have achieved in their Norrbotten.

Such is northern Russia, where the forest and mine economy remains predominant and where large-scale activities are localized around three main cities: Leningrad, Arkhangel, and Murmansk. Aside from the southwestern area of Leningrad, the rest of this vast region is somewhat "colonial" in character; a large part of its settlement was achieved through the establishment of forced-labor camps for lumbering and mining, and the technical problems raised by its development are still only partly solved. The population density remains around 5 in the basin of the Pechora River and around 8 per square mile in the Ark-

Traditional winter transport in the far north: A caravan of reindeer-drawn sleighs. Roads are few in the northern reaches of Russia. A railway branches out from the Moscow-Arkhangel main line toward Kotlas, Vkhta, and Vorkuta. But elsewhere the airplane or the sleigh are essential means of transport during the long winters.

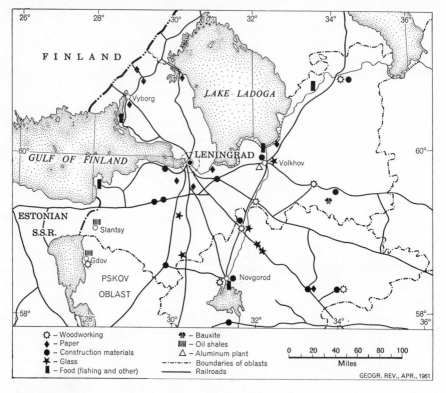

The main industries of the northwest—the Great Russian area around Leningrad. *(The Geographical Review and George Taskin)*

hangel oblast. A gradual transition leads southward to the basin of the Volga.

### THE UPPER BASIN OF THE VOLGA

It is helpful to divide the vast basin into an upper and lower section. To the north and west, extending widely, stretches a ramified network of tributaries, the two principal ones being the Oka to the south and the Kama to the northeast. The point where the Kama flows into the Volga south of Kazan may be taken as the dividing point between the upper and the lower courses. From that point onward the Volga turns south and flows directly to the Caspian depression, receiving no more important tributaries as it crosses open grassland or dry steppes. The upper basin is therefore the humid one, which feeds the mighty river, and it belongs to the forest zone with a wooded grassland fringe to the south and east.

The upper basin itself must be subdivided in two parts: the western part is the Volga-Oka country, centered around Moscow, more densely populated, better organized and developed; the eastern part is the Volga-Kama country, a more thinly settled region, but one which includes the European slope of the Urals.

The Volga-Oka country has sometimes been called the "Russian Mesopotamia." It was the heart of the Russian resistance in the medieval period and the springboard from which the imperial expansion developed. Nowadays it could also be called the region of Moscow, for almost all the cities within the area are in the immediate orbit of the capital. Moscow has such an importance as the capital of the strongly centralized Soviet Union that it cannot be adequately treated in the regional frame only. But constant reference to it is unavoidable in the Volga-Oka region.

Both these great rivers start from the Valdai Hills, this chief center of stream dispersion in European Russia. Their basin is geographically and politically the heart of Soviet Europe. It is also the mixed forest area; the soil is rather poor, and the natural resources scarce. The timber of the forest and the lignite basin that develops south of Moscow are the two main resources. Both are widely used, but they cannot explain the intense industrialization of the area, one of the main manufacturing regions of the USSR. Agriculture too has been pushed to some extent by the Soviet regime, but rural prosperity would require the remaking of the soil by man—the Russians, having vast areas of excellent soils directly south of these forests, did not need to perform such expensive work here. The clearings in the forest did not suit the large kolkhoz with its heavy mechanization, and villages still consist of the same *isbas* (cabins) built of logs and often miserably furnished inside. Potatoes, hay, and flax are the chief crops, although some wheat and rye are raised, and cereal cultivation has been favored by the Five-Year and Seven-Year Plans. But these rural activities cannot compare with the industrial development of the region.

To the south of Moscow, along the Oka and even south of that river around Tula, are located the heavier chemical, iron, and steel industries. The reason for this specialization is the presence of the lignite basin and also of some coal deposits. The coal is rather deep and of poor grade, and to avoid mining it, a new process was devised at Novo-Basovskaya to burn the coal in the mine. At a depth of more than 200 feet, the coal is burnt in its layer, a system of pipes carrying compressed air into the strata and channeling the gas produced by combustion to the surface. This gas is then utilized either for power or for chemical purposes in the plants built near the mine. Tula (375,000) also had some iron ore in its vicinity and used to smelt on charcoal in early times, manufacturing many goods out of steel. This was a cutlery center and

The forest, with some clearing, in the Moscow region. *(Sovfoto)*

one of the Russian arsenals for several centuries. Today, owing to the presence of cheap fuel and the proximity of the Moscow market, heavy industries have spread, particularly to the newly built satellite town of Novomoskovsk. Kaluga (176,000), Serpukhov, Kolomna (130,000), Ryazan (300,000), and Murom stand on the Oka as one goes downstream, all benefiting from the proximity to Moscow and Tula. Only Kaluga suffered much in World War II, for it was overrun in the German advance toward Moscow.

Several cities located to the west of Moscow were thoroughly destroyed. The front remained in the vicinity of Rzhev, for instance, for two years. As towns in this area were largely built of wood, only the structures of brick chimneys lined the streets when this area was liberated: all the buildings had been burned down. Kalinin (311,000), the next town on the Volga, was a more important industrial center than Rzhev. With it, located at the point where the Moscow-Leningrad railway crosses the Volga, begins the series of towns supplied chiefly by the traffic along the great river but also by a relatively dense rail network. The main industries here are rather light or finishing ones: textiles and engineering and mechanical works. Yaroslavl (486,000) and Kostroma (205,000) are textile and machinery centers chiefly. Ivanovo (400,000) and Vladimir (203,000) (which are not on the Volga but closer to Moscow) are also large manufacturing centers. At the meeting of the Volga and the Oka, Gorki (formerly Nizhni-Novgorod) has specialized in motorcar, airplane, and river ship building; due to its strategic location the city has always had an important commercial function, and its fairs used to be the largest in Russia. In 1966 the "Soviet Detroit," as Gorki is often called, had a population of 1.1 million; the first superhighway of the Soviet Union was built in the 1930s between Gorki and Moscow. The large city is surrounded by specialized satellites: Dzerzhinsk (200,000) makes synthetic fibers and rubber; Balakhna makes newsprint.

Increased by the addition of the Oka waters, the Volga flows majestically downstream, but the density of the cities and industries drops immediately east of Gorki. The Volga-Oka, a sort of central metropolitan region for the Soviet Union, hobnobs with little-developed areas, populated chiefly by some of the "autonomous" backward peoples—the Chuvash, whose booming capital Cheboksary, built on the Volga, had 83,000 inhabitants in 1959 but 170,000 in 1966, and south of the Chuvashes, the Mordves. Each of these two "autonomous republics" has about a million inhabitants. To the northeast develops the vast basin of the Kama, the largest of the Volga's tributaries. The powerful forest eastward has been but little penetrated as yet. Only along the main streams and the few east-west railroads leading into Siberia does settlement reach notable proportions. In the early nineteenth century this

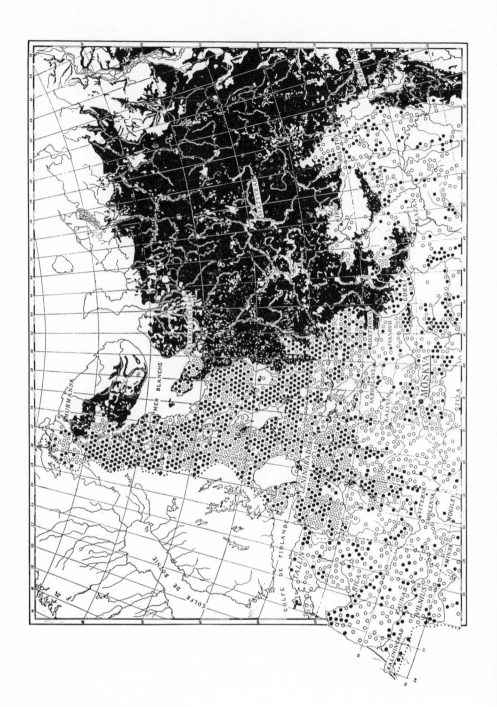

still was a region to which political convicts were sent in exile. Lumber is again here the major resource. Kirov (300,000) on the Viatka River rafts the logs from the surrounding fir forest down to the Kama and Volga. Factories working wood or making sawing machinery have been built in Kirov.

The upper basin of the Kama is more active, as it consists of the piedmont of the Urals. Here for centuries small iron works were spread through the forest, smelting local ores on charcoal. Several towns have now become notable industrial cities: Berezna, Izhevsk (360,000), and especially Perm (785,000), which is the actual regional capital, grouping metallurgical plants and processing local phosphates into fertilizer. Substantial oil deposits have been found in the vicinity of Perm, and these helped to develop the region. Moreover, this city commands the entrance to some of the easy gaps across the Ural Mountains toward Siberia and the industrial area of Sverdlovsk. Farther south, on another tributary of the Kama, the city of Ufa (683,000), capital of the Bashkirs, controls amid hilly country the rail lines leading to Chelyabinsk and to Magnitogorsk—that is, to the main industrial area of the Urals on their Asiatic slope. An appreciable oil production is now obtained from oilfields scattered around Ufa (Ishimbaevo, Sterlitamak, Belebei), to which the pipelines bring the oil and then continue towards Moscow. It is between this area and the lower Volga that a series of rich oilfields have been recently discovered. This find, described by some sources as equal in importance to the Koweit oilfields, caused, in the 1950s, a rise in the known reserves of the USSR from 1 to 4.5 billion tons.

The network of the Kama is well supplied with water, for it drains the slope of the mountain range and a vast area of damp forest. This majestic river, on which regular steamers travel for days in both directions, empties into the Volga just north of the 55th parallel, in a country inhabited by Tatar populations, a reminder of the medieval Mongol invasions. There has been much more cohabitation between Slavs and Mongols in parts of Russia than is usually realized. On the Volga, upstream from the meeting with the Kama, stands Kazan, the capital of the autonomous Tatar republic, which was built on a hillock above the area threatened every spring by the Volga floods. Kazan has an old *kremlin*,

---

*(Opposite)* Distribution of forests in the north of the Soviet Union in Europe. The areas in solid black show the extent of the massively forested land; the black circles indicate a dense proportion of woodland; the little circles left white indicate areas of scattered and less frequent woodlands; areas without any of these symbols are the nonwooded lands. Compare with the map of the southern parts of the Soviet Union in Europe (p. 768). The northern half is much more forested. (After *Le Monde Forestier*, published by the U.N. Food and Agriculture Organization, Rome)

the inner fortress of the Tatar princes. Wooded grassland extends around this city, which for a long time manufactured shoes and boots, soap, and candies. Tanning materials were brought from Japan and tallow from Siberia. Soviet industrialization has made of Kazan a large city (805,000) which dresses pelts, makes soap, leatherware, photographic films, machinery, and typewriters. It also builds ships for river navigation and processes a good part of the milk and timber produced in the surrounding area. Truck farming is carried on on the "dumping grounds" along the river. The agriculture of Tatary has been mechanized and is diversified. River navigation on a large scale starts at Kazan as the Volga downstream has been converted into a series of reservoir lakes by huge dams producing power.

The contrast between the relatively slight development achieved until recently in the Volga-Kama section with that of the Volga-Oka one is striking indeed. It may be explained by the tendency of Russian authorities in recent centuries to look chiefly westward or southward and to pay relatively little attention to the immense eastern reaches of the empire. The Soviet regime has to some extent reversed this trend, but the tremendous size of the work to be done imposes long delays. Industrialization has stimulated the growth of certain towns, and collective mechanization has been a drastic but quick way of modernizing farming methods and practices. However, the difference remains considerable between these yet little touched countries and the densely populated and long-organized European countries to the west.

## THE LOWER BASIN OF THE VOLGA

As the Volga flows southward after receiving the Kama, the wooded grassland turns gradually to the steppe on the eastern bank of the river, which acts in its lower course as a climatic and biological boundary. The population scatters more and more, the climate becomes more continental, and modern activities concentrate in a small number of large cities on the great waterway. As one goes down the Volga southward, the climate warms slightly but the rainfall decreases sharply: Kazan has temperature averages of $7.6°$ in January and $67.8°$ in July; Astrakhan, in the Volga's delta, records $19.2°$ in January and $77.3°$ in July. The difference in aridity is much greater: 16.8 inches of precipitation in Kazan annually and in Astrakhan only 6.4, which is a subdesert figure.

While aridity mounts quickly as one goes east from the Volga in this area, the western bank is still wooded. Beautiful forests, yielding a rich lumber output, cover the Mordovian Republic, or more specifically the Volga hills or Zhigulevsk Mountains, actually a deeply eroded plateau which does not reach more than 1100 feet in elevation. These hills overlook the low valley of the mighty river atop a cliff of several hundred feet: this topography has favored rapid erosion, which was tempered only by the wooded cover. This area, quite picturesque and almost exceptional in Soviet Europe, has been called the "Russian Switzerland." It offers scenery in sharp contrast with the flat and dry plain to the east.

Little development other than rural, however, has occurred in the hilly western part of this middle section of the Volga basin: Saransk, capital of the autonomous Mordves, had only 23,500 inhabitants in 1939 but 90,000 by 1959; Penza, the chief urban center, had 325,000 people in 1966 and mainly woodworking and food-processing industries. The important cities and industries are in the valley of the Volga. Four areas are notable along the great river, that of the Samara (Kuibyshev) bend and the cities of Saratov, Volgograd, and Astrakhan.

The Volga makes a curious meandering bend in the province that formerly was called Samara. The city of that name, renamed Kuibyshev, served as the Soviet government headquarters in the years 1941–1944 when the German armies threatened to reach Moscow. Kuibyshev is a most important relay on the Volga route; it is also a hub of railways going to the southern Urals. The railroad going west crosses the Volga at Syzran, where the river, having circled to form the bend, turns again southwards. In 1937 oil was struck at Syzran, giving to the area a new and increased part to play in the Soviet's economy. The bend is also utilized for water control purposes: it provides the best site for a large dam on the Volga. Work is now completed on a grandiose scheme damming the mighty river at the root of the bend and diverting a part of its flow through a canal dug directly across the bar of resistant material that caused the bend to develop. The great dam at Kuibyshev created a fall in the river course used by a large power station to generate some 2.1 million kw, the largest hydroelectric station in the world at the time of its dedication in 1957; moreover, the water behind the high dam was backed up quite far, forming an enormous reservoir that extended upstream above Kazan and into the lower valley of the Kama. This Kuibyshev sea was at the time the largest man-made lake in the world: it improved the navigation on this section of the Volga, helped to regularize the water flow downstream, and stored huge quantities of water for multiple-purpose uses. One of the uses would have been irrigation of the rich chestnut soils between the lower courses of the Volga and Ural rivers to the south and southeast, where summer droughts restrained the fecundity of the soil. This enormous project centered on the great bend of the Volga at Kuibyshev was a first and an essential part of an actual remolding of the course of the whole Volga to the benefit of both agricultural and industrial production along the river.

The city of Kuibyshev (960,000 in 1966) is rapidly developing into a regional metropolis of impressive proportions. Besides the old heritage of grain elevators, flour mills, and food industries, it has now large mechanical and chemical industries. The area around the bend and to the east has become the largest oil-producing basin in Europe, and it also produces large quantities of natural gas. While a network of pipelines carries some of this wealth westward to Moscow, Leningrad, and beyond, Kuibyshev also refines a large part of it and developed petrochemical industries. Mechanical plants are also springing up in old and new cities up river: Syzran (167,000), Ulianovsk (formerly Simbirsk, now 275,000 inhabitants), and the new cities of Zhigulevsk next to the big dam and Togliatti, where the Italian Fiat Corporation is building the first large plant of Western-like passenger cars to be set up in the USSR.

This middle Volga region, from the bend south, benefited during World War II from sheltering people, industries, and institutions evacuated from areas to the west invaded or threatened by the German advance. Now the oil and gas fields and the Volga waterpower and navigation have made it a region of great attraction for a variety of industries. Farther south on the river, after Volsk, a city specializing in cement and other construction materials, Saratov is the main center, standing amid a rich agricultural region also dotted with oil and gas wells. Saratov (700,000) used to be the site of the last bridge crossing the Volga, a high bridge of which Russian engineers were very proud. West of here, the escarpment that follows the valley of the Volga is lower and breaks up, making it easy to reach the upper Don or centers of the eastern Ukraine. A variety of factories in Saratov refine oil and beet sugar, make machines from tractors to ball bearings. Nearby, around the town of Engels, was located until 1941 the autonomous republic of the Volga Germans. Suspicious of the loyalty of these Germans during the war, the Soviet authorities evacuated them to Siberia, and the republic disappeared from the maps. Since the nineteenth century, several generations of German settlers had helped to develop in this area a rather advanced kind of farming, combining the cultivation of hard wheat and sunflower and mustard seed with cattle raising.

Now Saratov stands also on the upper reaches of another enormous reservoir lake formed behind the newer great dam across the Volga at Volgograd. The latter city stands at another sharp bend of the river where the Volga turns from its southward course to the southeast and heads for the Caspian Sea. The dam, reservoir, and power station (with a capacity of 2.5 million kw) are even bigger than those at Kuibyshev and their construction reflect the experience gained in building the latter. The city of Volgograd is becoming a focus of the whole Russian waterways system, as the canal completed in 1952 links the Volga here to the Don River on which another huge lake has been developed. Now

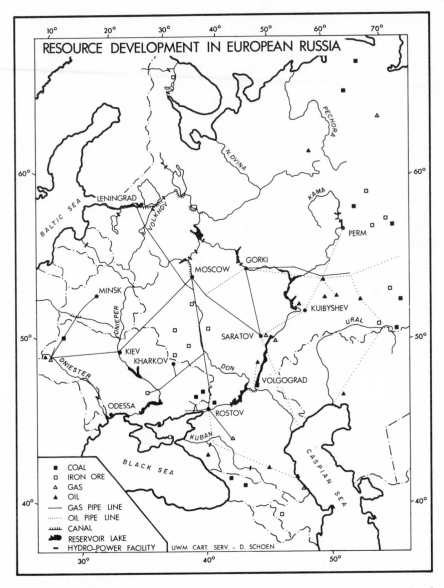

Basic natural resources are steadily developed, especially the great river network, oil and gas, coal and iron. Compare with maps pp. 733 and 788.

large steamers may come up from Rostov on the Don, an Azov seaport, by river, lake, and canal to Volgograd and proceed from here, either downstream to the Caspian or upstream to Kuibyshev and Kazan. Located on an elbow of the Volga, where its course comes the closest to the Don, this city developed originally as a point of transshipment and a portage on the way from the Caspian to the Azov sea by river. First named Tzarytzin (i.e., the city of the tzars), it also served as one of the main gates to the Central Asiatic steppes and deserts; camel caravans were not uncommon on the city streets. In the Middle Ages, it was a center of the Tatars' caravan trade, and it long kept something Asiatic in its personality. East of the city, saltpans and sand dunes make their appearance in the landscape in places; the summers are hot and dry; the annual rainfall averages some 14 inches but varies greatly from year to year. In 1920, Tzarytzin had 90,000 inhabitants; it was later renamed Stalingrad and developed rapidly as the metropolis of the lower Volga basin; by 1939, its population reached 445,000. Its strategic commanding position made it a target of the German advance into Russia in 1941–1942. Stalingrad achieved world fame in the great battle of 1942 when the German Nazi armies attacked the city, trying to cross the Volga, but were stopped, cut off, surrounded, and finally compelled to surrender. It was the first major defeat of Germany on land in World War II, a memorable blow to German military prestige, and a testimony to the stubbornness and resourcefulness of Russian resistance to the invader. In the battle, most of the city and its suburbs were annihilated. Reconstruction was rapid: the city counted 591,000 inhabitants in 1959 and 720,000 in 1966. Renamed once again, Volgograd, in 1961, it is a basic node of the Russian great rivers' navigation network. Plants line the Volga for some 30 miles: great tractor and mechanical works, oil refineries, synthetic rubber plants, shipyards, canning factories, and sawmills, which have been traditionally the major components of a very diversified industrial complex.

On both sides of the Volga, south of Saratov, the climate takes on a dry, definitely steppic character. The whole area down to the Azov and Caspian seas is periodically subjected to devastating droughts. After the local kolkhozes mechanized on a large scale, soil erosion took on threatening aspects. Whipping up sand from the dessicated soil, dry winds from the east and south have had the same effect on the Lower Volga steppe as on the Dust Bowl of the American Great Plains. The fight against the droughts was taken up early by the Soviet authorities: first, a program of soil conservation, resembling that applied by the U. S. Soil Conservation Service, was adopted; a reforestation program was started; screens of trees and a belt of woodland were planted around Volgograd. The long-range policy aims at irrigation of a large part of this steppe, insuring its regular fertility. The huge reservoirs on the Volga were planned in large part to supply the water storage for this irrigation project south of Kuibyshev, and perhaps, as far south as the river's delta. But the flow of the Volga although mighty is after all limited. Using more of the water upstream of Volgograd would leave little to flow onward to the Caspian, a shallow sea, the level of which is maintained largely by the contribution of the Volga. Serious threats to survival of the Caspian as a large sea arose as the ambitious engineering reshaped the Volga upstream. The future of the irrigation plans of the steppe may threaten all the lands and populations around the Caspian, unless Soviet engineering manages to increase substantially the amount of water flowing down the artificial stairway of reservoirs and channels into which the Volga and some of the other major streams are being converted. This work along the Volga axis has become one of the most impressive experiments of our time in recasting the physical environment of a large section of Europe to improve the opportunity of regional and national economics.

Turning to the southeast, below Volgograd, the Volga divides itself into several arms and ends with a wide delta at the Caspian. This large interior sea is kept from drying up largely by the water brought by the Volga. Though the level of the Caspian fluctuates from year to year, it remains always below sea level. A wide tract to the north and northwest of its shores is below sea level too; in fact the Volga already flows below sea level when passing Volgograd. Saltpans are more and more frequent, and the area is occupied chiefly by herds of sheep and seminomadic Kalmyks, an Asiatic people. The territory of Kazakhstan, a Central Asiatic republic of the Union, comes close to the Volga delta in the east. In the middle of the delta the city of Astrakhan (360,000) has gained world fame as a market of sheepskins of the black curly variety that thrives in the continental climate with the severe winters of that area. Astrakhan is also the main transshipment point between the Volga River and Caspian Sea navigation. Fishing is an important industry here, and large-scale canning is carried on at Astrakhan and in the nearby Caspian port of Lagan.

The Soviet government has begun to enact a program designed to settle the Kalmyks and convert them to large-scale cattle ranging. Irrigation is being developed between Volga and Ural. The Ural River, which drains the southern section of the range of that same name, flows down to the Caspian across semidesert territory. In the 1930s the northern shores of the Caspian near the Urals' delta acquired an increased importance as a result of the discovery there of important oil deposits. The many oilfields found and now developed in the area between the Volga and the Urals, a fairly vast area indeed, has given it a role somewhat comparable to that of Texas, in terms of oil supply, in the United States. At first Soviet geologists and economists spoke of a "second Baku" in the Emba region, north of the Caspian; then the fields discovered around Kuibyshev, Buguruslan, and Ufa brought forth hints of a "Soviet Koweit" in that area between the Middle Volga and the southern Ural Mountains. In the early 1950s it was realized that a vast oil-bearing area extended between the Urals, the Caspian to the east and the Volga, Don, and Azov sea to the west. About 200 million tons of oil and vast quantities of natural gas were obtained there by 1967. The USSR was assured of considerable surpluses for export.

Oil is not the only resource and industry of the European slope and foothills of the Urals. Much heavy industry has developed in the major cities of this area. Timber from the mountains is an important resource, and there are a variety of local ores. The main iron and steel and metallurgy works are on the Asiatic slope of the Urals or inside the range, but machinery and railway rolling stock are built on a large scale at Perm and Ufa.

We shall omit in this rapid review of Soviet Europe the major industrial areas of the Ural range which are on its eastern side. Cities like Perm, Ufa, and Chkalov have greatly benefited, of course, from this trans-Uralian development, as they stand on the main crossroads leading from Europe to western Siberia. The western slope of the Ural range does not seem to possess the vast resources of metallic ores on which was founded the industrial mushrooming of centers like Magnitogorsk and Chelyabinsk. But we should also mention the important copper deposit of Mednogorsk at the southern extremity of the range and on the European bank of the Ural River. Since World War II the general policy of the Soviet government seems to have been to develop or evacuate heavy industries beyond the Urals while reinforcing the finishing stages of manufacturing and the so-called light industries along the Volga axis.

## SOUTHERN REACHES OF EUROPEAN RUSSIA

Throughout the eighteenth and nineteenth centuries, the major drive of Russian power was perhaps oriented more southward than westward. One of the routes it followed was the Volga, but that area had been "Russified" earlier. More complicated was the push directly southward from the Upper Volga-Oka region: it involved fighting with the Turks, the Tatars, and many other nationalities. It led to the conquest and development of the Ukraine, and to the purely Great Russian area it added substantial parts. Many towns rose just along the land routes leading from Moscow to Kiev and Kharkov; such was the case of

Shipping at Volgograd (Stalingrad). The activity of this river port has increased as a result of the opening of the Volga-Don canal. One of the largest hydroelectric power stations on the Volga was completed at Stalingrad in 1955. *(Sovfoto)*

Orel (200,000), Bryansk (276,000), and Kursk (250,000), all hard hit during World War II. But more important perhaps as a historical trend was the drive down the Don. That large river drains the regions south of the Oka and west of the Middle Volga, down to the Sea of Azov. The Don has probably the greatest popularity among the Russian rivers, not counting "Mother Volga." Its upper course and tributaries drain principally a large part of the wooded grassland area. There Voronezh (590,000), on a tributary of the upper Don, is the largest city. It is on the northern fringe of the black-soil belt and an important railroad hub on the lines leading from Moscow to the Donets and lower Don. It has developed large mechanical and chemical industries, producing diesel engines, synthetic rubber, and the like. It also has large railroad repair shops; to utilize some of the iron ore from the deposits situated to its west, near Kursk, iron and steel plants have been built at Lipetsk (230,000).

The lower Don is a rich steppe dominated by the cultivation of grains. In the eighteenth century, when this Don area became the main basis of the Russian expansion along the Black Sea shores, it acquired a romantic reputation from the Cossacks of the Don. These Cossacks were semi-military, semiagricultural groups of people settled in a frontier area to occupy and guard it against outside attacks as well as against any internal disturbance. The Cossacks quickly became a sort of mounted military police as well as the spearhead of the Russian armies in battle. Even with all the modern mechanization, Cossack cavalry seems to have played a part in World War II, especially in wintertime. The Don Cossacks with their picturesque uniforms, their famed horses, and their "rodeolike" exercises, their terrible reputation in battle, and their singing during rest periods are known throughout the world, often for only one of these many activities. They played an important part in the settlement and the political organization of the Ukraine. But the lower Don is no longer a Cossack country. From the industrial agglomerations of the Donbass to the steep slopes of the Caucasus, vast steppes expand, where highly mechanized agriculture produces grains on black and brown soils. In Rostov, the main city at the mouth of the Don, July temperatures average 74.7° and yearly precipitations 18 inches. Farther to the southeast, at the foot of Caucasus, the rainfall increases to 25 inches and more. But these averages do not apply regularly. The steppes between the Don and the Kuban and farther east are subject to droughts just like those on the Lower Volga. Wheat, sunflower, and some sugar beets are the major crops. Near Rostov, in the Salsk steppe, the giant sovkhoz "Gigant" used to be cited before 1941 as the epitome of mechanization and standardization of Soviet agriculture (see p. 799).

The important cities are seaports or else those which line the foot of

Mechanized grain harvesting on the Gazursky state farm *(sovkhoz)* in the Stavropol region. *(Novosti Press Photo)*

the Caucasus, particularly in the oil-producing areas. Rostov-on-Don is the regional capital. Standing on the estuary of the river, this city has an old history for southern Russia. It started as a Cossack stronghold but developed rapidly in the eighteenth and nineteenth centuries. Around 1900 it had 120,000 inhabitants, but Kharkov had already outgrown it and had emerged as the capital of the Donets basin area. Rostov grew steadily, however, reaching 300,000 in 1926 and 737,000 in 1966. This rapid growth was not directed by adequate urban trends. An unhealthy and crowded town, it was partly destroyed during the civil war of 1918–1921, when the drought, added to the political disorder, caused terrible famines and epidemics in the Don-Kuban area. In World War II it suffered severely again. Reconstruction made Rostov a better-planned city with wide boulevards. Its position as a sea and river port, increased by the new Don-Volga Canal, and its proximity to the Donbass are promising for the future, all the more so as recent geological finds indicate the extension of rich layers of anthracite coal eastward from the Donbass, in the vicinity of Rostov. Thus heavy industry has been coming to the lower Don area, which previously was chiefly concerned with the processing of its agricultural products and the manufacturing of farm machinery.

On the Kuban River, which drains the northern foothills of the Caucasus toward the Sea of Azov, Krasnodar (395,000) is the regional capital, adding the proximity of the local grain production to the oil and to the mountain cattle economy. Most of the region's grain exports used to be shipped through the Black Sea port of Novorossisk, which now boasts the largest cement plants in the Soviet Union. Farther south Tuapse ships oil and marks the beginning of the hot and humid coast of the Black Sea where tropical fruits are easily grown.

In the large isthmus north of the Caucasus, between the Black and Azov seas to the west and the Caspian to the east, the Russians have for some time contemplated a ship canal. This would establish a direct link between navigation on the Caspian and on the southern seas bordering Soviet Europe. Work was started along the depression followed by the Manych River. Earlier an irregular canal for smaller craft had been built between the Lower Don and the Caspian shore. But the depressed Caspian level makes necessary an impressive stairway of locks. Moreover, the variations in the level of the closed sea complicate the situation. There are no prohibitive difficulties in the engineering, however, and it may be possible some day to see the Caspian open to ships coming from the Black Sea. One may wonder whether such a tremendous excavation task is worth while now, when oil, the main product of the Caspian shores, can be transported through pipelines at a low cost. Still the Russians have always, since the days of their "river state," placed special significance on waterways, and today they have linked the Caspian and the sea of Azov by the Volga, the Volga-Don Canal, and the Tzimlyanski reservoir on the Don (see map p. 793).

## MOSCOW AND THE VOLGA AXIS

If a thousand years ago the Dnieper used to be the main axis of Russian national life, then one can suggest that "Mother Volga" today is playing such a part. This is not new in Russian history. One could say that the Volga, with its tributaries, has been essential at every period of Russian isolation, each time that Moscow was the capital. The Soviet regime, intent again on isolation, gave great attention to the Volga as an axis of the national economy, at least in Europe. An intricate system of canals has been devised to link it better with other streams. Its upper course is linked with Lake Ladoga and the Baltic, its lower course with the Don and the Azov Sea. Large ships and hydrofoil "busses" are used on it for passenger traffic. Industrialization has been speeded up along its banks. The most stubborn fight put up against the German invasion was either on the Upper Volga (which may be explained as a defense of the vital Moscow region) or on the Lower Volga, where Stalingrad acquired a symbolic value in World War II similar to that of Verdun in France in World War I. The growth of cities along the great river and its main tributaries is remarkable: according to the census of 1959, out of the thirty-one cities in the USSR with a population of over 400,000, ten stood on the Volga or its tributaries. The dams and vast lakes now strung up along the Volga insure a huge supply of electricity and fresh water. Outside the Ukraine, the lands along the Volga, magnificently endowed by nature, have been those best developed recently by the Russians. Moscow stands on a small subtributary of the national river.

Moscow is perhaps the best possible instance in Europe of a great city arising in an environment and on a site where nothing seemed to favor it. This rise cannot be explained otherwise than by the skill of the princes who lived in the Kremlin in conquering the greatest continental empire ever brought under one rule and in centralizing this empire in the city. Even during the two centuries when St. Petersburg was the seat of the imperial government, Moscow remained the religious capital of Russia, the city in which lived most of the aristocracy of landlords who directed, much more than did the official administration, the agricultural economy. Moscow was definitely a more important cultural and economic center than was the official capital during the eighteenth and nineteenth centuries. It is from Moscow that the first canals, railways, and roads radiated, and this centralization of the transportation system has been increased by the Soviet administration: today the capital sits in the hub of the whole network covering the European part of the Union.

As the actual capital of a centralized and tightly directed economy, in

The Kremlin. The "Chiefs' town" of Moscow contains the palaces of the rulers, the cathedral of the Orthodox Church, the court of justice, and the arsenal. *(The Geographical Review)*

The Kremlin wall above the canalized river. *(Sovfoto)*

a country where rivers are the main channels of trade, the site of Moscow was paradoxical: the Moskova River flowing through the city was a small tributary of the Oka, no waterway at all. Engineering has taken care of that situation: the Moskova has been transformed into a large water terminal linked by a ship canal to the Volga. From the Upper Volga in the north, large river ships, after passing series of locks, reach the heart of Moscow. Several large and fast tankers were built, fitting exactly the Moscow-Volga Canal locks, to bring large quantities of oil up the river. From the Upper Volga the old but much enlarged Mariinsky system of canals leads into the Onega and Ladoga lakes and through the Neva to Leningrad and the Baltic. From Lake Onega, another canal leads into the White Sea and thereby to the Arctic Ocean. Another system of canals connects the Upper Volga with the Volkhov and Dnieper rivers. From there the way is opened to the Black Sea, or, through the Pripyat River and the new canal, to the Vistula and the Baltic or the German system of canals. Moscow claims now to be a port of five seas: Baltic, Caspian, White, Black, and Azov. The whole network was improved by the new water link between the lower Don and the Lower Volga opened in 1952. The new canal makes it possible to send Donbass coal to the Moscow area by water and the timber of the northern forests to the Donbass. A great deal of traffic between Moscow and the Donbass goes by rail, along several lines, one of which was the first in Russia to have a double track. The best highways of the USSR also radiate from Moscow, leading to Gorki, Kuibyshev, Saratov, Leningrad, Kiev, Kharkov, and Minsk.

Thus Moscow is by far the best-equipped Soviet city for communication with all the parts of the Union. It has grown rapidly in the last fifty years. In the eighteenth century, when it lost its function of political capital, Moscow grouped a population of about 150,000 around the Kremlin, a walled city of palaces and churches in itself. Most of the wooden houses of the outlying sections were burned in 1812, when Napoleon took the city and the Russians set it afire. In 1861 the population reached 380,000, but a rapid expansion followed, with industrialization attracting peasants liberated from serfdom and free to move into the town. In 1897 the population passed the million mark and in 1915 neared 2 million. The Revolution of 1917 and the civil war that followed reduced the size, but the curve went up again after 1924 with a steep gradient: about 2 million in 1926 and 4,137,000 in 1939. Such growth made for an acute housing shortage. People crowded into small apartments; entire families had to live in one room. In 1930 more than 60 percent of the houses were still made of wood, which is rarely the case in European cities. Although some huge blocks of apartment houses in a modern style had been erected, they were far from satisfying the demand. Government planning kept increasing the crowding without fulfilling the housing needs of the urban population. After 1945 a new plan of reconstruction along the best principles of urban planning was adopted. Entire sections of the city were to be razed and rebuilt in modern style with wide, airy avenues, but the blueprint was actually applied only to the very center of the city. Here the Kremlin remains the seat of the Soviet government and high command, the brains and heart of the Communist party and system. A monumental section extends around its old walls. But farther out the residential and industrial sections will have to undergo a thorough rebuilding before they take on a truly "Western" aspect. In 1959, the capital's population reached 5.03 million, and 6.5 million in 1967.

The Soviet authorities are determined to make Moscow a great, beautiful, and modern capital, the first city of the Union in all respects. They have an immense task of building and of sanitation ahead of them to achieve this goal. The Soviet capital has become one of the largest cities in Europe. Its outer ring has an impressive array of industries, mainly the manufacturing of finished goods and delicate machinery. More and more specialized cities enter in the immediate orbit of Moscow between the Volga and Oka. The whole Mesopotamia between these two rivers is indeed, as we noted earlier, a region focused on Moscow and directly dependent on it. Moscow is also one of the European capitals with the highest proportion of white-collar workers: they are all civil servants, in many different branches of the administration.

The territory of the Russian Empire was built up from Moscow and around it (see map, p. 718). The network of means of transportation was and still is being developed according to a pattern radiating from Moscow. The physical association of the city with the Volga by a ship canal is recent, but the association of the capital of all the Russians with the Volga axis is quite ancient. This historical association explains in part why Russia expanded so much and so successfully towards the east and the southeast. In those directions organized political resistance was weak, of course; but it has not always been so, and the peoples of the Soviet Union might have been less Asia-minded without such an association of the greatest river system of Europe with this artificially erected metropolis.

On the other hand, Moscow's predominance in the Russian tradition has greatly helped to keep within its European parts the big bulk of the emphasis of past development and therefore, today, the main weight of Soviet power. It was in order to make Moscow and the central part of Russia safe from Turkish threats that Russia expanded towards the Ukraine. It was in order to better supply the historical heart of the empire of the tsars that such emphasis was put on the agricultural development of the southern parts of European Russia. Under the Soviet regime, agricultural development for the normally forested areas around Moscow and north of it was stressed at first, and more grain crops were developed in the central Russian area in an attempt to make it self-sufficient. This aim has been abandoned with the steady growth of Moscow as a city and of the Central Industrial Region around it. This region encompassed in the early 1960s about one fifth of the total population of the Union, that is, somewhat over 40 million people; the population of the administrative district of Moscow, which covers 18,000 square miles, amounted in 1959 to almost 11 million—one of the largest metropolitan areas in the world.

In the 1950s, knowing its incapacity to build enough housing in a city already very crowded, the Soviet regime tried to discourage people from the rest of the country from moving to Moscow, even forbidding it. So great, nevertheless, was the capital's attraction that more people constantly flocked to it, settling if necessary on the periphery and outside city limits. Having thus grown to its present size and shape, the city of Moscow recognized its population expansion recently by annexing many of the suburbs on its periphery and establishing regulations based on a new urban plan for the Soviet capital. This plan surrounds the metropolis with a vast belt of green, about three miles wide, where existing buildings will be demolished, parks and fruit orchards planted, and only a few large new schools are to be built. In this way the city hopes to keep itself from sprawling too far in an ugly suburban way. New satellite towns, however, have been recognized and outlined on the plan, so that the expansion of population, industries, and trades may go on.

The Central Industrial Region around Moscow is by far the largest and most active manufacturing complex within the Soviet Union, especially for the finishing stages of manufacturing and "light" industries of all kinds. So great are the requirements of its supply that no attempt is made any more to make it self-sufficient. Besides all the power produced within the region, from peat or waterfalls (a large hydro-electric station works at Rybinsk, and others are on the Upper Volga), more is brought in from the great dams at Kuibyshev or even Volgograd; natural gas is brought by pipeline from the Middle Volga fields; pig iron and steel come from the Donbass and the Urals; a variety of machines and other goods are carried here from all directions, and many parts of the world. The local supply has in some respects been weakened by too rapid use, especially the forests which are greatly impoverished in a radius of over two hundred miles around Moscow.

It has been the endeavor of Soviet authorities to channel toward the eastern parts of the Great Russian area, and especially toward Siberia, as much as possible of industrial growth and the internal migration of

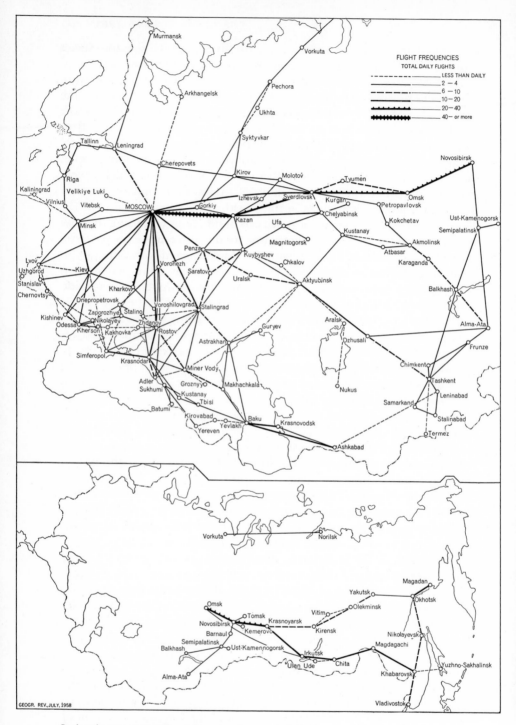

Soviet air transport. *(Above)* the extensive network in European Russia; *(below)* the routes linking the far east primarily via Omsk, Semipalatinsk, Balkhash, and Alma-Ata. *(The Geographical Review and George Kish)*

the population. The attraction of Moscow has nevertheless proven stronger than even the strict rules of the Soviet administration. In its present endeavor to improve the life of the Soviet citizen, the government could not but work hard at improving first of all living conditions in the capital itself. No Soviet industry has expanded more recently than the construction industry in and around Moscow. Many new buildings are obviously erected for show, including a vast, modern-looking new building within the Kremlin itself; but much housing is being constructed of various types: from high-rise, impressive—though Victorian-looking—apartment towers in the middle of the city to, in much greater quantities, cheaper but much-needed, ordinary housing projects on the periphery. In 1960, the housing units were built at the rate of 18 per 1,000 inhabitants annually. At this rate it will still require many years before the great backlog of housing demand that has accumulated in Moscow (and in most other large Soviet cities) since at least the Revolution of 1917 will be satisfied.

The city of Moscow has always had in and around the Kremlin a beautiful old nucleus for city growth. The Stalin era added an extraordinarily monumental subway but did little for actual embellishment of the capital. The Khrushchev era was more conscious of the prestige value of greater and more esthetic urban achievement in the capital of such a vast empire. The rapid expansion of construction is now aimed both at the embellishment of the city—because it must become an immense "showroom" of the regime's achievements—and at fuller satisfaction of the craving for better housing space that is still a very general wish and need. The esthetic and ethical progress that must ensue has been determined by obvious political considerations, and its rhythm is just as obviously restricted by the imperatives of economics.

The spectacular attempt by Peter the Great in the beginning of the eighteenth century to take away the leadership in Russia from Moscow and the Volga by erecting a new capital on the Baltic seashore did not have all the impact he seems to have expected. It did not break up the Russian tradition of isolationism; it did not make Russia look less towards Asia. Moscow remained the historic and economic capital during the two centuries of political administration of the empire from St. Petersburg. The Soviet regime found it "realistic" and popular to bring the political capital back to Moscow. Sites of great cities have often influenced the course of empires.

Moscow is not only a national headquarters but in several respects an international one. Like any national capital, it has a numerous diplomatic corps, which is crowded in the central part of the city under an unusually strict supervision by local authorities; diplomats are forbidden to go more than fifty miles outside the city without special permits. But the international role of Moscow is still wider, for it is the "Mecca" and the head-quarters of the Communist party throughout the world, a growing head-quarters for relations with satellite countries in Europe and Asia. For centuries, like the Russian emperors who took the title of tsar, meaning to be new Caesars, Moscow believed it had inherited the imperial func-tion from Byzantium with the fall of Constantinople to the Turks. Dur-ing the long struggle against the Turks and the expansion in Asia, the feeling was strengthened that Moscow was the "third Rome" (Constan-tinople or Byzantium having been the second one). When after 1917 communism began to coincide in a curious way with Russian national-ism and imperialism, the expression "third Rome" acquired a very spe-cial meaning: communism was also a new faith that even attempted to replace all previously existing religions. Although that attempt failed and the Soviet Union has allowed some revival, under strict control, of the Orthodox Church, the Kremlin remains an outspoken rival of the Vatican in the spiritual domain.

While the Soviet Union officially applies a federal constitution and works on reviving or promoting a number of small, backward local cul-tures, it has achieved a degree of centralization in Moscow which prob-ably no large power has ever had in its capital. Moscow has become not only a geographical name but also a political term, symbolizing different things that are different expressions of the same force in international affairs. That deep link of a city and an idea, both national and spiritual, is a rather unique phenomenon in the modern world. It has deep roots in Mediterranean history: some of the capitals of ancient Egypt, Jerusa-lem, Rome, and then the Constantinople of the Basileus and even more of the Moslem caliphs may have had a similar role. But the history of Europe would call such a cultural and political phenomenon oriental rather than European. Europe indeed is by its design a peninsula of Asia and a perpetual arena of struggle between the East, pressing on westward, and the West, resisting the continental pressure. This struggle was never simply a matter of political and military balance; it also took the subtler forms of cultural and ideological interpenetration.

# Part VI

## Conclusion

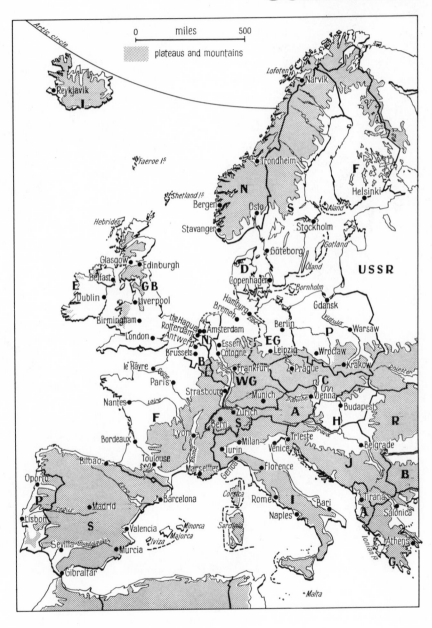

This scene in the Netherlands—the most crowded and one of the most comfortable countries of Europe—shows that while asking for more Europeans do not ask for very much. Along a canal in the center of the city of Utrecht, a terrace is used for a café, and an old bridge serves as a parking lot for bicycles. New modern buildings neighbor on old Dutch houses and a church. Careful landscaping gives great charm to an environment of brick, steel, and cement. *(The Netherlands National Tourist Office)*

# 22

## The Diversity
## and Unity of Europe

The variety of the small European continent is great: such is certainly
the general impression derived from this rapid review of the countries,
regions, and problems of Europe. Yet if one endeavors to reduce the
variety and the complexity of Europe to a small number of dominant
elements, there are two ways of simplifying and reducing the whole involved situation to the struggle between two influences. One approach
is to say that there is and there seems always to have been an East and a
West in Europe. The other one is to say that there has always been some
opposition between the maritime countries and the continental countries.
And both simplifications could be combined, especially in the middle of
the twentieth century when Western Europe considers itself primarily a
part of the "Atlantic community." Thus there seem to be two Europes:
one Western and oceanic, the other Eastern and continental; but the
reality at every step reveals more diversity.

The boundary between the two Europes is constantly fluctuating, and
the acuity of the opposition changes from period to period as well as
from country to country. The overwhelming fact remains that Europe
is territorially one continuous land; for ages it has lived a history whose
waves were constantly recorded, although in different ways, throughout
its whole territory. Above the duality there exists a general unity that
cannot be overlooked. But the relative parts played by these two factors
of diversity and unity vary greatly from period to period. In times like
the years following World War II, a duality prevailed on the two sides

of the "iron curtain"; but after twenty years of peace diversification develops and blurs the picture; yet the crisis in this century is general for Europe and creates some solidarity.

## ATTEMPTS AT INTERNAL ORGANIZATION

The idea of European unity is very old. In a way it was the Roman or, more exactly, the "imperial" idea of ancient and medieval times. But European unity was never actually achieved in political terms. Perhaps during the feudal period, when the Christian faith was the binding element of all peoples on that continent, as opposed particularly to the Muslim powers in Asia and North Africa, perhaps then Europe was more united than ever before or ever after: the authority of the Church was indeed the highest at that time, and sovereigns, even emperors, bowed to the spiritual power.

As absolute monarchies were shaped and nationalisms arose, the division into nations and coalitions stressed the diversity and, at times, the duality of Europe. The possibility of a united or federated Europe was treated as an idea and an illusion. Napoleon attempted to achieve it by force and diplomacy: soon he found himself facing an alliance of Britain with Russia. In 1814–1815 the Holy Alliance of the main powers that completely defeated Napoleon may have seemed an organization capable of dominating the continent, but agreement among the Allies did not last. In World War II Hitler tried to bring about European unity under his domination, but he too failed, and the countries he had occupied were left with a sour taste of propaganda in favor of Europe as one political unit. As soon as the German threat of domination was put out of the picture, East and West separated again, and the Soviet Union began organizing as her own orbit those countries either occupied by the Red army or having a traditional leaning toward Russia because of their Slavic origin. At the same time communism as a political doctrine was greatly reinforced in several countries of Western and Mediterranean Europe by the general impoverishment and the ordeals of war and occupation. The Eastern countries are coordinated by a system of pacts and committees that links them strictly to one another; in politics as well as in economics there is a strong centralization toward Moscow; the obedience of Communists participating in the different national governments of these countries is an essential factor in the system. Yugoslavia has been severing many of its connections with the Eastern bloc, after having been, during the period 1945–1948, one of the active participants; and its geographical position at a greater distance from the Soviet border as well as its maritime façade on the Mediterranean makes it easier for the Yugoslav government to show greater independence. In the 1960s, more of the Eastern countries began evolving away from strict obedience to the USSR. In 1968 this evolution was sharply interrupted by the occupation of restive Czechoslovakia, stressing once more Soviet supremacy.

The Western countries have been more divided. None among them had so overwhelming a weight within the group as the Soviet Union has had in the Eastern bloc. Moreover, the democratic system of government does not call for and is even opposed to any totalitarian discipline of the kind advocated by the Communist doctrine. Feeling divided and weak after the destruction wrought by World War II, Western Europe called on the United States for economic and political help, and an Atlantic community took shape, expressed in the North Atlantic military pact and the European Recovery Program. To take advantage of the help thus extended by the United States, the European powers had to cooperate. Several organizations were born during the years 1945–1949 which endeavored to establish closer coordination. Some of them were strictly regional, such as the group of the five powers created by the Pact of Brussels and bringing together Britain, France, Belgium, Luxembourg, and the Netherlands. But more important as operating machinery was the European Organization for Economic Cooperation, grouping all the countries that benefited by ERP or Marshall Plan funds. In 1949 a Council of Europe was formed, on which most of the maritime countries of Europe were represented, and met at Strasbourg. Whether these efforts will lead to a definite and lasting organization is not clear as yet, but the evolution toward a large economic integration was greatly accelerated in the last decade. In 1953, according to the "Schuman Plan," the European Coal and Steel Community was formed by six powers, which then organized after 1957 the European Common Market. The practical success achieved by these "communities" in developing output and improving the standard of living and general prosperity of the member nations was such as to surprise the critics and even the partisans of the scheme.

The economic and political consequences of the Common Market have been considered in detail in this book. That the venture was a success and a great promise was demonstrated when the United Kingdom, its most important critic, asked to join it. If Britain becomes a full-fledged and lasting member of the "European Economic Community," the main obstacle to integration of the countries west of the "iron curtain" would have been overcome. It may give to the whole a better balanced structure and avoid the threat of domination of the group by a single power. Grouping three large economic powers such as Britain, West Germany, and France, a European Community should be able to develop well and fast without becoming the empire of just one people or one financial concern. Whether political integration will ensue is another and more doubtful matter. Although the Common Market had decided to establish a "Secretariat" for the coordination of political action, it was only with reluctance and some suspicion that the member governments went into the experiment. British participation may slow down further the process of political integration but more coordination and and interweaving is bound to come in the wake of economic integration.

The trend toward economic unity was fostered after 1945 by the need for reconstruction—which was easier to accomplish when the resources each country could draw on were broader—by the feeling among the European countries of their great weakness when compared to the giant super-powers of the world that had emerged from the war, and by a good deal of regional complementarity. The various national economies of Europe were largely complementary for three reasons: a certain unity of culture (at least for the upper level of society, those who direct the consumers' taste; the general fact of proximity that has created habits of exchanging goods; and, last but not least, the concentration of heavy population densities and large-scale industrial areas in certain parts of Europe (chiefly in the West). These areas used to be consumers of foodstuffs and raw materials from other less industrialized parts of the continent, which in exchange bought manufactured goods.

This relationship of "old and young" economies between East and West works normally toward more commercial intercourse. But we must bear in mind that outside Western Europe there is a slowly rising feeling against the financial, economic, cultural, and political domination that that area had until recently over other parts of Europe. Most aggressive nationalist movements founded themselves upon national dissatisfaction, for which Western predominance can be blamed: fascism in Italy, nazism in Germany, communism in Russia must be partly traced at their origins to an anti-Western feeling in the people and the desire to become equals in every respect of the great Western powers. Industrialization is widely believed to be a panacea for weakness and poverty. A growing trend prefers to reserve to national use many materials that were previously exported. Moreover, agrarian reforms in the great agricultural areas, although long overdue, begin by disrupting the existing channels of production and trade. In many cases they induce the peasants who become landowners to keep more of their production for their own use. This may in the long run lead to a higher standard of living all the way round, but at the first stage it looks like a restriction of the output available for the market. The breaking up of large estates and the trend toward speedy industrialization create an economy in the eastern half of Europe oriented toward regional self-sufficiency rather than toward trade relations with the western half.

In fact the economy of whole sections of the European continent does not evolve rapidly; on both sides of what has been called the "iron curtain" a substantial amount of material remains to be exchanged between East and West. The general orientation, however, does not favor general European cooperation. Two particular problems will be especially hard to deal with in order to improve internal relations even among countries of good will. These two problems relate to Britain and Germany.

Britain is too much an island and too closely linked, both by culture and by economy, to non-European countries, particularly to the United States and the Commonwealth countries as well as her dominions overseas, to be able to participate wholeheartedly in a strictly European scheme. Former colonial powers, such as France and the Netherlands, may also have some problems to solve with their former dependencies, but none of them is dependent to a similar extent on these extra-European relations. If a choice had to be made, Britain seems closer to severing her connections with Europe than those with the rest of the English-speaking world. Fortunately no such choice has to be made, and all of Western Europe prefers to keep outside links one way or another. However, the attitude of Britain will remain a source of difficulties for any attempt to organize a strictly European scheme.

Germany is a quite different question. Defeated in the two World Wars, divided up into zones of occupation, and in the autumn of 1949 divided into two separate states between which passes the "iron curtain," Germany is a hard-to-solve problem in politics as well as in economics. Politically its central position makes it easy for Germany to play East against West and vice versa—it is the old balance-of-power game. But all the past history of Central Europe has taught us that this game cannot be played successfully by a country geographically situated between the two parties it aims at opposing to each other. The remarkable success of Britain in the balance of power on the continent has been largely due to her position outside the continent. It would be much more difficult now for any Western European country, including Britain, to play the United States and the Soviet Union one against the other, for instance, without suffering finally from the tension or conflict thus stirred up. The Soviet Union has been bent on keeping Germany divided and threatening the West with a new great war if the German problem was not solved according to Soviet policies. The Berlin crisis of 1961 symbolized this situation.

The reorganization of Western European countries is too often viewed from American shores as a counterpart to the strongly united organization that Soviet domination has given to the European countries situated between the border of the Soviet Union and the "iron curtain." It must be remembered that such a grouping together under foreign leadership is heavily resented in all countries that have at any time submitted to it. There are powerful seeds of weakness and deterioration in such an organization. Only in so far as the Western powers could make out of their reorganization a freely-accepted going concern would unity mean strength.

## POPULATION PRESSURE AND STANDARD OF LIVING

It is a common belief that some relationship exists between the density of population and the standard of living in Europe: the more people are crowded the less resources they are supposed to command, and the greater their need of expansion if they are to survive. There is no scientific basis whatsoever for this generalization, on which were based many claims of the so-called "have-not" nations between the two World Wars. It is true that some of the greatest crowdings of population in Asia, especially in India and China, coincide with areas of low standard of living and urgent need of improvement. But in Europe it has almost seemed that the lower the standard of living, the thinner the density. That appears obvious in any comparison of Russia with the Atlantic seaboard, for instance. Yet this does not hold in many places here either. The truth is that the greatest variety of relationships is possible: thinly populated Sweden is much better off than thickly populated Italy, but Sweden is not better off than the thickly populated Switzerland. Until the 1930s the Netherlands, Belgium, and Britain used to be among the richest countries, with very high standards of living, although they were among the most overpopulated in the world (compare maps on pp. 82, 88, and 100).

*Overpopulation* in this sense means that a population not adapted to the conditions of its environment *feels crowded*. Nomadic tribes feel crowded in any city or even village; a population which does not want or know how to use certain resources within its reach may feel crowded, while in the same conditions a more industrialized or technically more advanced group of the same size would experience a shortage of manpower. Almost every European country remembers a period when it felt "overpopulated" with half its present population or even less. The development of new resources, new trade relations, and new technology change entirely the value of the relationship of man to space. This may explain why Germany felt overpopulated and asked for more *lebensraum* when its density of population was below the British figure, although the local resources of Britain were less significant than the resources of the much larger Germany.

The sad thing about overpopulation is that it cannot be put into figures if one wishes to be realistic: a nation, not an area, is overpopulated when its people feel that they *ought to have more*. It is not always space they ask for: it may well be greater comfort, a higher standard of living. The comparison of Germany and Britain is significant in that respect: the German nation felt that it was entitled to the same prosperity, the same standards, and the same power in the world as Britain. It thought that territorial expansion would open the way to the attainment of those satisfactions that industrial and commercial expansion had not been able to provide. It discounted the centuries of toil, of blood, sweat, and tears, that the British had spent in building the prosperity and power they enjoyed. Toil had not been enough, of course—the rise of a nation depends very much on its internal affairs, its ability to manage its own social and economic problems, which usually become more acute with every step forward on the path of political might and economic development. That is why history cannot be avoided in any honest attempt to explain the facts and the figures of present-day geography. That is why empire-building, although it could not help do some evil, rested on solid foundations only when a greater endeavor toward good largely outbalanced whatever evil went into its texture. The geography of Europe shows curiously that a country gets the fate it deserves on moral grounds rather than on the stature it seems able to build on the bare material resources of its territory.

What precedes indicates clearly that every nation has had to strive to improve its condition, if any improvement were to be achieved. But it is so easy to avoid serious difficulties in internal politics by blaming all obstacles to progress on foreign affairs, on neighbors, and on the leading world powers. Most of the European governments have been doing just that—it increased international tension but decreased the internal pressure, at least for a time. The use made of the "outside threat" by the Soviet authorities in the USSR from 1917 to 1965 has been successful in many respects; the Nazi authorities followed the same pattern of propaganda—people prefer generally to blame their unhappiness on their neighbors rather than take the responsibility for it themselves, and the political geography of Europe has been, alas, governed by this principle for ages. It led to the simple belief that any internal pressures could be relieved if more space were available; to get more space, the most direct way was to get rid of the neighbors or to enslave them.

Climate, topography, zones of vegetation, and mineral resources have always been invoked to camouflage the truth—that is, the deeply rooted human instincts for better life, more comfort, and the pursuit of happiness. But these instincts are *human*, and they can develop without always leading to greed, bloodshed, and enslavement. Geographers, who have spent a long time studying the relations between society and environment, cannot allow their research work to serve as raw material for that kind of political camouflage. But neither can they achieve the full understanding of their own problems without always reckoning with the social and economic motives. There would hardly be any progress for mankind without these motives.

It follows, therefore, that the urge toward improvement of the environment (which is partly expressed in a higher standard of living) is both normal and desirable. But it is bound to create internal pressures, feelings that more ought to be achieved or gained. Some balance has to be found between the indispensable progress and the possible greedy trends. Such a balance will be in perpetual evolution: no stability for any appreciable length of time could be expected. The continuity of European history weighs heavily on the present: much is still determined in the politics and economics of this old continent by the memories of earlier days, by the shadows of ruined castles towering above the farms and the towns.

The population pressure and the urge for higher standards of living are "stubborn facts" in Europe. They are particularly acute after periods of privation and bloodshed such as World War II. Throughout the pages of this volume, we have briefly outlined the regional aspects and their trends. The general problem of Europe now is the achievement of a higher standard of living for the lower strata of the population throughout the continent. The success of the very diversified political platforms labeled "socialist," which vary from the truly democratic structure of Sweden to the totalitarian communism of the Soviet Union, has much to do with the urge toward higher standards. Curiously enough it is the American example and success that is largely responsible for the European efforts to organize more efficiently their own pursuit of happiness. The American model has long been in the headlines of the Soviet papers and constantly in the minds of Scandinavian reformers. Since 1945 it has had more influence than ever, whatever the official proclamations inspired too often by sheer national pride. In fact the "Americanization" of the way of life and of the economic methods is striking nowadays in most of Europe west of the "iron curtain." The diffusion of supermarkets, American-like equipment in the home, skyscrapers, television, and advertising are some of the symbols of this trend.

It may seem paradoxical to speak of higher standards in a continent that had been destroyed, left hungry and naked by the wartime ordeal. Reconstruction proceeded, however, with extreme rapidity, and on the whole, Europe produces today much more foodstuffs and raw materials than it has ever produced. The farming populations eat better, with the exception of some collectivized areas, than they have ever eaten. Collectivization was, even in Russia, to a large extent a measure aimed at preventing the agricultural producer from consuming too much of his own products at the expense of the growing city crowds. In a way the suffering of the war and postwar period may well have paved the way for better living conditions for Europeans, if the problems of distribution channels and the relationship of prices to wages are settled in a manner allowing due recognition of everyone's needs.

A dangerous trend of thought in Western Europe is seen in the asking of surprising questions: Is not the average standard of living of the producing population too high in these countries? Can they compete on outside markets with the younger industrial countries, and especially with the United States, if the cost of production remains as high as it is? The easiest way to decrease the cost of production is always to cut down the wages of the producing workers; but this leads unavoidably to a decrease in the purchasing power of the population, therefore to a shrinkage of the national consumption, the domestic market, and, of course, to a stiffening of political tensions. The over-all importance of foreign trade has dominated many European minds so strongly that the essential role of the domestic market is almost forgotten. They seem to assume that the domestic market will always buy all that it can but will not be able to supply itself without importing a great many materials. Thus we come to the basic question: Has Europe the ability to support itself within the continental or even within a regional framework?

## OPEN OR CLOSED ECONOMY?

The continental resources of Europe are substantial, but their relative importance in world production has been steadily decreasing for at least a century. This has affected Europe's role in international economics; the scalloped little continent has not retained its former predominant position, which was possible largely because of the astute management of world trade and finance by the Western nations. Since World War I and even more since the depression of the early 1930s, Europe has looked for a higher degree of self-sufficiency. The continent could probably feed itself without great difficulty, though a readaptation of the diet would be needed, making it less varied. But the whole land use of the continent would have to be reshaped before Europe could produce enough textile fibers for its needs. True, artificial fibers today may replace the natural textile materials — chemistry makes self-sufficiency much easier to achieve in almost all respects. But chemistry and transportation require fuel, and in this basic field Europe is not so rich as it thought it was at the beginning of the Coal Age. Coal and waterpower are relatively abundant, but little oil has yet been found outside the USSR. Natural gas is present and increasingly used. Some day the development of atomic energy for commercial use will change the entire picture, but for the present Europe will have to depend on other parts of the world for a variety of supplies.

If a totally self-sufficient economy appears hard to achieve without lowering the standard of living—and no one can reasonably wish to do that—how large should be the framework on which European planning ought to concentrate? Certain authorities have been advocating a Eurafrican system, in which Africa would complement Europe. In many respects Africa, most of which was so recently politically dependent on Europe, makes a substantial addition to the producing capacity of Europe, especially of agricultural products requiring hot climates and certain minerals (copper, graphite, phosphates, diamonds, gold, uranium). But it is doubtful that as a market for manufactured articles, Africa, inhabited by fewer than 200 million people of low standards of living, would answer the needs of European exports. To maintain and improve already high standards of living, industrialized countries need to trade more with countries willing and able to buy a variety of complicated man-made goods and machines, the production of which employs many skilled workers. In other words, a modern industrial country has greater need for an export outlet for articles suited to an advanced civilization than for supplies from abroad. It is easier to find new sources of supplies than to establish new outlets of that kind.

This correlation makes it imperative for Europe, and for its Western section especially, to keep and even to develop its economic relations with countries of the same culture and parent civilization: the Americas, Australia, etc. That is why the Atlantic-community solution better fits the situation, notwithstanding the considerable difficulties arising from the competition between similar productions, and occasionally surpluses, on both sides of the ocean. Africa, Asia, and Oceania are not excluded from such a scheme; on the contrary, they supply a valuable trade increase to the area of Western civilization. The more they develop their own cultural standing and their material needs, the more valuable an addition they will be, as a market for both Europe and America. The colonial powers of Europe used to believe that the more cheaply a colonial dependency produced, the more advantageous it was; colonial control aimed at keeping prices down to some extent. Nowadays it seems well demonstrated that the most helpful dependency is the one that consumes the more expensive goods and is able to pay for them—the original principle is thus reversed. Modern empires prefer to give a substantial amount of self-government to their dependencies, encouraging even protective tariffs if necessary to help the prosperity and therefore the purchasing capacity of the local market.

Obviously Europe's role in the world cannot become that of a closed, self-sufficient area. Reduced to such an extreme, Europe would probably develop such internal pressures that it would either quickly blow up or decay. A closed economy may be maintained for some time in the Eastern section, less densely populated and still keeping a wide margin of development possibilities. The West in Europe seems determined to remain open on the outside and simultaneously to fight for its happiness and a better integration in the world economy. It has been Europe's privilege for centuries to lead the material progress of mankind and to insure also a great cultural upheaval. Now prosperity and security may be achieved by striving to open wider and wider that relatively closed world which has participated actively in the working of European civilization.

The major strength of the European countries should not be founded on overseas markets, as, in fact, it never was during the periods of European prosperity and greatness. The basic strength of a nation is at home, in the organization of its resources, which may be primarily its human resources if there is not much granted by nature to the national territory. The case of Switzerland is typical of countries that manage to remain prosperous and influential without being well endowed by local resources. All countries cannot be other Switzerlands, of course, but there are very few on earth, and perhaps no other in Europe, so poorly endowed by nature. In the last twenty years, an active search for new resources at home has turned up more.

The search for an "open" economy is not separable from the endeavor towards a better life at home, a greater national income better distributed among the population. There is a great deal to be done in order to make European markets compare in their prices and in the purchasing capacity of the consumer to the markets of the United States, Canada, or Australia. The higher density of population is certainly no answer, for the time is not yet so remote when the densely populated countries of Great Britain and the Netherlands had much higher standards of living than almost any less densely populated country in the world.

Today, in fact, there are two great urbanized regions stretching on both sides of the North Atlantic Ocean, one of which has been called *Megalopolis* and extends along the Northeastern seaboard of the United States from Greater Boston to Greater Washington, D. C., the other framing the southern part of the North Sea and the English Channel and including most of England on one hand and a triangle from Amsterdam to Paris and the Ruhr on the other. These two very densely crowded urbanized areas contain the hundred million people enjoying the highest average incomes and standard of living of any group of similar size in Europe. These concentrations of people, wealth, and activity have been built upon several generations of the practice of an "open" and as world-wide as possible an economy and on a specialization in large-scale trade that helped the redistribution of income accumulated in these great urban regions.

In our time of rapid urbanization Europe, where such economic systems and the gathering of people in trading cities started long ago, remains the continent that can in the next fifty years achieve the greatest results in a drive toward economic progress. Europe may now be selling relatively fewer quantities of goods – although it ships as much and more in value – but they are goods that incorporate in a smaller volume greater amounts of labor and therefore of money. Europe may have increased its imports more rapidly than other continents, especially in volume, but this mainly reflects the greater use of petroleum products and the increased need for some other materials obtained at lesser expense abroad. The rapid recovery of the balance of payments in the 1960s of this recently ravaged continent demonstrates that the European capacity to produce is greater than ever; and the programs now being made foresee a continuation of this rapid expansion of both production and consumption. Curiously enough, it is where the numerical density of population is the smaller, where manpower shortages are more acute, particularly in the Soviet Union, that it appears more difficult to satisfy the needs of the average individual in terms of material conveniences as well as they are being satisfied in the more crowded countries of Western Europe.

PROGRESS IN EUROPE

European people consume more and ask for more. Even the more authoritarian governments have had to recognize these demands and promise to satisfy them "soon." The process of "catching up with America" goes on all over the small continent and means progress there. But most European countries are still far from being ready actually to catch up, even in ten years, even though their politicians may so promise. An enormous progress in the total volume of consumption, however, has been achieved, taking the per capita consumption of Europeans far beyond any previously known level, even in the "fabulous" times of prosperity in the late 1920s. Perhaps the 1960s will be recorded by history as much more "fabulous" and "booming" than any of the previous decades of recent times.

Part of the consumption may be achieved through military expenditure and will not benefit the consumers' market directly. The fact still remains that national products throughout Europe are on a rising curve much steeper than in the prosperous 1920s. The major problem that remains is therefore the redistribution of the national income among the various layers of the population. When it does not help improve the standard of living of the majority of the people, increased output does not serve genuine prosperity or political stability. Among economies, the great success of the middle of the twentieth century is undoubtedly the United States' economy. A geographer would betray his professional mission if he were to assert that the geographical distribution of minerals and agricultural soils is the determining factor of American wealth. The standard of living of the common man in America is the result of a social and economic organization that produced an economic system substantially different from those still prevailing on the continent of Europe.

Geography is a study of distribution, a study of regional differences. It makes one feel strongly the interrelations and the interdependence of the world. It cannot discount, however, the ancient and very-much-alive duality of Europe: East and West have two different ways of understanding their mission and of working for their own aims. There are many reasons for this; and the difference between maritime and continental regions seems woven into most of them. Why should the monotonous, infinite, gray line of the horizon at sea suggest different trends of thought to the human mind than the landlocked horizon? Perhaps there is no answer; perhaps this influence of the sea results from the special conditions it provides for traffic. The high seas have always been freer to daring navigators than the lands covered with a network of boundaries, tollhouses, and customs controls. Moreover, a continental power could trade only through the neighbor's territory, while across the maritime spaces direct contacts were possible with different, strange civilizations. This variety and the possibility of free choice were inspiring; perhaps the opening of space navigation may similarly inspire formerly landlocked nations. Whatever the answer, the scalloped outline of the small continent, the deep interpenetration of land and sea, and the tremendous impact of navigation on European history have each carried great weight for European destiny. The extraordinary change now in process is, in a certain equalization, what used to be defined as the potential of the geographical environment with its limitations and its opportunities.

Nowadays it seems that technology has liberated such advanced civilizations as those of Europe from the shackles that used to be imposed by the local environment. Geographical position loses much of its significance when technological progress makes it possible to dig ship canals into the continent and replace one source of energy with another chosen from three or four technologically possible solutions, when the airplane crosses land or sea with equal ease, when technological means making it possible to reshape the physical characteristics of a whole country are offered not only to the richer nations but even to the poor

The promise of spring blossoms at Delphi, near the ancient ruins of the famous temple of the Greek Oracle. *(André Bouquin, Athens)*

ones. To take advantage of all this opportunity, the various nations have to go through a social and political evolution, and this is the essential problem. It is not the physical environment or the lack of means to avail itself of modern technology that creates the inequalities and the diversity of present-day Europe. It is the inheritance of the past and the psychological attitudes determined by and expressed in local shades of culture, accepted social structures, political concepts, and other abstract systems that make the map of Europe look like a mosaic despite all the pressures suggesting unity or at least organization in two big realms.

The contemporary acceleration of change seems to increase regional variety over the small continent despite the steady diffusion of similar kinds of techniques and equipment. In 1945, observing the largely devastated world that looked to the United States for help, methods of technical and managerial organization, Wendell Willkie wrote about a forthcoming "One World." How strange this may seem today as one looks at the world of the late 1960s. A great deal of wishful thinking has been done by politicians and philosophers hoping for a unification that would solve the problems of a diversified world. The small continent of Europe has in some respects grown more homogeneous. The machinery used on the farms is rapidly growing uniform from the banks of the English Channel to those of the Don River; similar types of airplanes fly all over the continent and its bordering seas; similarly built ships ply around its shores; the same kind of "international style" architecture produces similar urban landscapes around the whole continent, and it may be difficult to distinguish the nationality of urban dwellers by the way they are clad. And while this process of apparent uniformization goes on, the various countries and regions of Europe keep on affirming their individuality. The way of life varies from region to region. Local and regional politics become increasingly vocal as the gradual process of economic integration and twenty years of peaceful coexistence decrease the weight of national administrations. Within the framework of general economic and social progress due to both peace and a new philosophy of rising expectations, local interests and cultural nuances attain a new and important role.

It would seem from recent trends that the present progress throughout Europe brings about simultaneously an apparent material uniformity and a greater cultural and perhaps even political diversification. What kind of balance will result from the working of these different trends within the European system is yet difficult to discern. It will be an interesting experiment to watch. Regionalism is taking on curious new shapes, some of which still seem to be rooted in the inheritance of a feudal medieval past. At the same time, Europe as a whole, particularly the parts of it that have, or may gain, independence from Soviet control, is working toward the elaboration of a role to play in the present world; a role that will be based on a wider resource base provided at home but a nonetheless intensified system of relationships with the other parts of the world.

Europe discovered the rest of the world not because it could not survive without overseas resources but because it felt a mission to go and explore what lay beyond the horizon. The Europeans are still like Ulysses, or the Viking, thirsty for exotism and adventure. They now want both peace and excitement. They are more mobile than ever and would be sadly bored if they had to organize their lives within the narrow space of their small continent. Europe must be open on the outside and remain an active participant in the general life of a diverse world.

# Suggestions
# for Further Reading

A complete bibliography on the geography of Europe would fill several volumes thicker than the present one. It is available, as readily as could be wished, in the fifty-odd tomes of the *Bibliographie Géographique Internationale,* published annually in Paris since the end of the nineteenth century. I certainly do not claim to have read all the materials mentioned in this annual bibliography – that would require more than a lifetime. The enumeration of the published materials that I read before writing *A Geography of Europe* and when revising it three times would, however, cover many pages and would not be useful to such a general study. Moreover, to the printed sources I have added in large measure the results of my own research and observations in the field. Therefore I shall limit myself to listing references to the truly important works that may be helpful to those wishing more detail or those looking for orientation in some studies of or research in geographical problems in Europe. I have mentioned chiefly materials available in English and of recent date; only classics or important recent works in foreign languages have been included. Statistical materials are of course a tool of the utmost importance for the geographer, and most of the countries of Europe publish annual statistical handbooks or yearbooks. There are also now national atlases for most of the countries of Europe. These have been used abundantly in the preparation of this book. Although they have not been enumerated in the bibliography, the student looking for more material will find it useful to consult them. For recent years the monthly bibliography in *Current Geographical Publications* (American Geographical Society, New York) is very helpful.

## PART I GENERAL FEATURES

There are several good books on the geography of Europe as a whole. Some of the other textbooks published in the English language on the subject can be used to compare, or, for some regions, to illustrate points made in this volume. The physical analysis of natural features has been recently enriched by many studies of local details rather than by general views of Europe as a whole. Economic studies have been, on the other hand, very numerous, and many of them have been encouraged by the trends to economic integration in attempting to present large-scale views of the matter, despite existing national differences. On the

827

physical features, Armin K. Lobeck's *Physiographic Diagram of Europe*, Madison, Wis., 1923, is a useful introduction. The volumes on Europe of *Handbuch der Klimatologie*, edited by Wladimir Köppen and Rudolf Geiger in the 1930s, are a standard source for climatological data. W. G. Kendrew, *Climates of the Continents*, New York, 1937, provides a handy summary. See also C. E. P. Brooks, "The Role of the Oceans in the Weather of Western Europe," *Quarterly Journal of Royal Meteorological Society*, April, 1930, pp. 131–140.

Any good textbook on the history of Europe or the volumes in the standard Cambridge Medieval and Modern Histories would illustrate many points made in chapter 2. On the recent economic evolution, the annual *Economic Survey of Europe*, published since 1947 by the United Nations Economic Commission for Europe in Geneva, is rich in information. The volume for 1952, entitled *Economic Survey of Europe Since the War: A Reappraisal of Problems and Prospects*, Geneva, 1953, is particularly valuable for the period of postwar rehabilitation. The important report by Ingvar Svennilson, *Growth and Stagnation in the European Economy*, Geneva, 1954, published by the same Commission (ECE), took a longer historical view and heralded the economic expansion of the years that followed. The ECE also publishes bulletins reporting on various aspects of the European economy, particularly on East-West trade relations in Europe. More statistics are found in the *Monthly Bulletin of Statistics*, published by the Statistical Office of the United Nations in New York. In many cases, the yearly *Statesman's Yearbook*, edited by S. H. Steinberg, New York, is also helpful to supplement the U.N. *Statistical Yearbook*.

Important information is also included in the following works:

Allix, André, "The Geography of Fairs," *Geographical Review*, October, 1922, pp. 532–569.
de la Blache, Vidal P., *Principles of Human Geography*, New York, 1925
Coon, Carleton S., *The Races of Europe*, New York, 1940
Dovring, Folke, *Land and Labor in Europe: 1900–1950* (*Studies in Social Life*, vol. IV) The Hague, 1956
East, Gordon, *Historical Geography of Europe*, London, 1938
Fitzgerald, Walter, *The New Europe*, London, 1945
Kirk, Dudley, *Europe's Population in the Interwar Years*, Geneva, League of Nations, 1946
de Martonne, Emm., *Traité de géographie physique*, 3 vols., Paris, several revised editions, the most recent in 1946–1950

The publications of the Research Group for European Migration Problems at The Hague are helpful on population trends. Many articles in the quarterly review, *Foreign Affairs*, New York, are most valuable updating sources.

Atlases such as *Goode's School Atlas* or *Oxford Advanced Atlas* supply many excellent maps. On a larger scale, the best research atlases now available are *The Times Atlas of the World*, London, 1954–1958, 5 vols., especially vol. II (Russia), III (Northern Europe), and IV (Southern Europe); the older international edition of *Stieler's Atlas;* the World Atlas of the Italian Touring Club; and the Soviet *Atlas Mira*, 2 vols., Moscow, 1935–1940 — also a smaller, revised one-volume edition, Moscow, 1954. Good historical maps can be found in the old *Atlas Classique Vidal-Lablache*, Paris, and the newer, *Atlas of World History*, edited by R. R. Palmer, New York, 1957; *Atlas van de Westerse Beschaving* by F. van der Meer, Amsterdam, 1951, presents in helpful cartographic form the cultural background of Western civilization, especially for Europe. Good economic maps are found in several of the above mentioned atlases and in the more specialized *Oxford Economic Atlas of the World,* Oxford, 1959 (2d ed.), *Oxford Regional Economic Atlas of the U.S.S.R. and Eastern Europe,* and *Atlas Général Larousse,* Paris, 1959.

Finally, mention must be made of a regional description which is nevertheless the best over-all source available to date on European geography and which remains a major source for all studies of that continent, the French series *Géographie Universelle,* edited by Vidal de la Blache and L. Gallois, Paris, 1926–1948. I have used liberally the wealth of information assembled, especially in the volumes by Albert Demangeon on the British Isles (an English translation is available, London, 1939), the Benelux countries, and the human and economic geography of France; by Emm. de Martonne on Central Europe and the physical geography of France; by M. Zimmermann on Scandinavia; by J. Sion, Max. Sorre, and Y. Chataigneau on the Mediterranean peninsulas; and by Camena d'Almeida on the Baltic countries, Finland, and the Soviet Union. A. Demangeon and Emm. de Martonne have been my teachers at the University of Paris, and I owe them much more than what was learned from their writings.

Additional reading material illustrating the material in chapter 3 on the utilization of resources will be found in the volume edited by F. J. Dewhurst, J. O. Coppock, and P. Lamartine Yates, *Europe's Needs and Resources* (Twentieth Century Fund) New York, 1961. On the matter of the European economic groupings, the authoritative study of Louis Lister, *Europe's Coal and Steel Community: An Experiment in Economic Union* (Twentieth Century Fund) New York, 1960, provides helpful discussion and data. Also, the various Communities periodically publish reports and statistical bulletins. The OECD in Paris has published many such valuable bulletins and statistics, much of which down to 1959 has been summarized in the above mentioned volume by Dewhurst, Coppock, and Yates, covering the European countries west of the "iron curtain." More OECD materials come out every year, including pamphlets providing annual reviews of the economy of every country west of the iron curtain.

## PART II  WESTERN EUROPE

On the decline of Europe, see the classical little work by Albert Demangeon, *America and the Race for World Dominion,* New York, 1921 (first published in French under the title *Le Déclin de l'Europe*). For the various countries, in the order in which they were taken up, the following are suggested.

### THE SCANDINAVIAN COUNTRIES

Chabot, G., Beaujeu-Garnier, J., and Guilcher, A., *L'Europe du Nord et du Nord-Ouest* vol. I, (in the "Orbis" series), Paris, 1958

Friis, Henning (ed.), *Scandinavia Between East and West,* Ithaca, N.Y., 1950

Kimble, G. T., and Good, D. (eds.), *Geography of the Northlands,* New York, 1955

Mead, W. R., *An Economic Geography of the Scandinavian States and Finland,* London, 1958

O'Dell, A. C., *The Scandinavian World,* London, 1957.

*Quarterly Review* of the Skandinaviska Banken, Stockholm

Andersson, I., and others, *Introduction to Sweden,* Stockholm, 1956, 4th ed.

de Geer, G., *Sverriges naturikedomar,* Stockholm, 1946

Höök, E., Elshult, A., and Risberg, H., *The Economic Life of Sweden,* Stockholm, 1956

*Atlas över Sverige,* Stockholm, 1953 ff
Osvald, H. (ed.), *Swedish Agriculture,* Stockholm, 1952
Streyffert, T. *The Forests of Sweden,* Stockholm, 1938
The Swedish Economy, Ministry of Finance, Stockholm, annual.

Adamson, Olge J. (ed.), *Industries of Norway: Technical and Commercial Achieve-ments,* Oslo, 1952
Knudsen, O., *Norway,* Oslo, 1961
Reusch, Hans, *Norges Geographi,* Oslo, 1927
Sund, T., and Sömme, A., *Norway in Maps,* 2 vols., Bergen, 1947
Stagg, F. N., *North Norway,* London, 1952; *The Heart of Norway,* London, 1953; *West Norway and Its Fjords,* London, 1954; *East Norway and Its Frontier,* Lon-don, 1956; *South Norway,* London, 1958

*Danish Agriculture: Denmark as a Food Producer,* Copenhagen, Danish Agricultural Organisations, 1960
*Facts about Denmark* (published by the Ministry for Foreign Affairs), Copen-hagen, Annual
*Industrial Denmark* (published by the Federation of Danish Industries), Copen-hagen, 1958
Skrubbeltrang, F., *Agricultural Development and Rural Reform in Denmark,* Rome, 1953

In addition, a number of interesting studies were published in 1960 on the occasion of the International Geographical Congress held in Stockholm; see listing in Wilma B. Fairchild, "The Nineteenth International Congress, Stockholm, 1960" in *Geographical Review,* New York, January, 1961, pp. 109–113.

## THE BRITISH ISLES

The annual Command Paper entitled *Economic Survey for* [year] gives an official analysis of trends in Great Britain for recent years. A great wealth of information is also available in the series of regional studies published under the direction of P. Sargant Florence of Birmingham for the Midlands and of G. H. J. Daysh of Newcastle for the north-east of England.

Best, R. H., and Coppock, J. T., *The Changing Use of Land in Britain,* London, 1962
Camps, M., *Britain and the European Community,* Princeton, N. J., 1964
Edlin, H., *England's Forests,* London, 1958
Freeman, T. W., *The Conurbations of Great Britain,* Manchester, 1959
Hart, J. F., *The British Moorlands,* Athens, Ga., 1957
Mackinder, Sir Halford, *Britain and the British Seas,* London, 1902
Mitchell, J. (ed.), *Great Britain; Geographical Essays,* Cambridge, 1962
Ogilvie, Alan G. (ed.), *Great Britain,* Cambridge, 1930
Smith Wilfrid, *Economic Geography of Britain,* London, 1949
Stamp, L. Dudley, *The Land of Britain: Its Use and Misuse,* London, 1948; and Beaver, S. H., *The British Isles,* London, 1954, 4th ed.
Watson, J. W., and Sissons, J. B. (ed.), *The British Isles. A systematic geography,* Edinburgh, 1964.
Zuckerman, S., "Food production in relation to the National Economy," *Journal of the Science of Food and Agriculture,* London, 1950, no. 9, pp. 255–263.
*This Changing Britain,* repr. from *Geography,* July, 1964

Charlesworth, J. K., *The Geology of Ireland*, London, 1952
Freeman, T. W., *Ireland: Its Physical, Historical, Social and Economic Geography*, New York, 1950; 2nd. ed., 1965
Gallagher, F., *The Indivisible Island*, London, 1957
Jones, E., *A Social Geography of Belfast*, London, 1960
McCarthy, A. J. P., "The Irish National Electrification Scheme," *Geographical Review*, October, 1957

Cairncross, A. K., (ed.), *The Scottish Economy*, Cambridge, 1954
Darling, F. F. (ed.), *West Highland Survey*, Oxford, 1955
Oakley, C. A. (ed.), *Scottish Industry*, Edinburgh, 1953
Struthers, A. M. (ed.), *Scotland's Changing Population*, London, 1948
*Agriculture in Scotland*, Command Paper, Cmd. 7717, London, 1949

Daysh, G. H. J., and Symonds, J. S., *West Durham*, Oxford, 1953
Florence, P. S. (ed), *Conurbation: A Planning Survey of Birmingham and the Black Country*, London, 1948
Fraser, M., *Wales*, London, 1952
House, J. W., and Fullerton, B., *Tees-side at Mid-century*, London, 1960
Simpson, E. S., "Milk Production in England Wales," *Geographical Review*, January, 1959, pp. 95-111
Thomas, Trevor M., "Wales: Land of Quarries and Mines," *Geographical Review*, January, 1956, pp. 59-67
Willatts, E. C., and Newson, E. C., "The Geographical Pattern of Population Changes in England and Wales, 1921-1951," *Geographical Journal*, London, 1953, pp. 431-454
Bird, J., *The Geography of the Port of London*, London, 1957; and *The Major Seaports of the United Kingdom*, London, 1965
Rasmussen, S. E., *London*, London, 1954, (abridged Pelican Books edition, 1960)
Centre for Urban Studies, *London: Aspects of Change*, London, 1964

*THE BENELUX COUNTRIES*

*Overseas Economic Survey: Belgium and Luxembourg* (H.M.S.O.), London, 1953; and annual surveys by OECD, Paris
*Le Problème des grandes agglomèrations en Belgique* (published by the Institut belge de Science Politique), Brussels, 1957

Demangeon, A. and 'Febvre, L., *Le Rhin*, Paris, 1935; Jean Ritter, *Le Rhin*, Paris, 1963
Dickinson, R. E., "The Geography of Commuting: The Netherlands and Belgium," *Geographical Review*, October 1957
Franks, H. G., *Holland as an Industrial Country*, The Hague, 1957
———, *Holland's Industries Strike Ahead*, 1961
Gay, F., and Wagret, P., *Le Bénélux*, Paris, 1960
Goris, J. A., (ed.), *Belgium* (United Nations Series), San Francisco, 1945
Gourou, Pierre, "L'agglomération Bruxelloise," *Bull. de la Société Royale Belge de Géographie*, I-IV, Brussels, 1958
*Agriculture in the Netherlands*, The Hague (official), 1962
Landheer, Bartholomew (ed.), *The Netherlands* (United Nations Series), San Francisco, 1943
Lingsma, J. S., *Holland and the Delta Plan*, The Hague, 1964
Maltha, D. J., *Agriculture in the Netherlands*, Amsterdam, 1947

Mulder, G. J. A. (ed.), *Handboek der Geografie van Nederland*, vol. I, Zwolle, 1949
van Veen, J., *Land Below the Sea: Holland in Its Age Long Fight Against the Waters*, The Hague, 1957

*FRANCE*

The basic research remains the three monumental volumes on France by Emm. de Martonne and A. Demangeon in the series *Géographie Universelle*, cited above, which were written in the late 1930s and can be updated with material from the eight volumes of the more popular series *France de Demain*, edited by F. L. Closon and P. George and covering the major regions of France.

de la Blache, Vidal, P., *Tableau de la géographie de la France*, Paris, 1902
Faucher, D. (ed.), *La France: géographie et tourisme*, 2 vols., Paris, 1956-1957
Jeanneney, J. M., *Forces et Faiblesses de l'économie française*, 2 vols., Paris, 1956-1957
de Martonne, Emm., *Geographical Regions of France*, London, 1933
Pinchemel, Ph., *Géographie de la France*, 2 vols., Paris, 2nd ed., 1967.
Siegfried, André, *France: A Study in Nationality*, London, 1930

*SWITZERLAND*

Früh, J., *Geographie der Schweiz*, 3 vols., St. Gallen, 1930-1945
Mayer, K. B., *The Population of Switzerland*, New York, 1952
Rappard, W. E., *The Government of Switzerland*, New York, 1936
Siegfried, André, *Switzerland, a Democratic Way of Life*, London, 1950
Imhof, E. (ed.), *Atlas der Schweiz*, Bern, 1965 ff.

In addition, a wealth of local details can be found in the major geographical periodicals of Western European countries and in the *Geographical Review* (New York) and *Economic Geography* (Worcester, Mass.). Extremely helpful, too, are the atlases now available for many of these countries. Finally, on the process of urban growth that becomes increasingly important the following are useful reading:

Dickinson, R. E., *The West European City*, London, 1951; *City and Region*, London, 1965
Jones, Emrys, *Cities and Towns*, London, 1966
Lavedan, P., *Histoire de l'Urbanisme*, 3 vols., Paris, 1927-1942 (a monumental work on this subject)
Rasmussen, S. E., *Towns and Buildings*, Liverpool, 1951
Self, Peter, *Cities in Flood*, London, 1957

## PART III  MEDITERRANEAN EUROPE

Here again *Géographie Universelle* is the basic reference work; in addition, the following general and specialized books may be consulted:

Houston, J. M., *The Western Mediterranean World*, London, 1964
Parain, J., *La Méditerranée; les hommes et leurs travaux*, Paris, 1936
Philippson, Alfred, *Das Mittelmeergebiet*, Leipzig, 1922
Siegfried, André, *The Mediterranean*, London, 1948

*PORTUGAL*

The best source is now the four volumes of the *Livretsguide*, Lisbon, 1949, edited by Orlando Ribeiro and prepared for the excursions of the International Geographical Congress

Birot, P. *Le Portugal*, Paris, 1949
Lautensach, H., *Portugal auf grund eigener Reise und der Literatur*, 2 vols., Gotha, 1932 and 1937
Ribeiro, Orlando, *Portugal, o Mediterraneo e o Atlantico*, Lisbon, 1963
Stanislawski, D., *The Individuality of Portugal*, Austin, Tex., 1959

Important articles on Spain, Italy, and the Balkans are assembled in Readings in *Geography of the Mediterranean Region* (American Geographical Society), New York, 1943. See also the periodical *Mediterranée: Revue Géographique des Pays Mediterranéens*, published in French by the universities of Aix en Provence and Nice, Editions Ophrys, Gap, quarterly since 1960.

*SPAIN*

Brennan, G., *The Face of Spain*, London, 1950
Houston, J. M., "Irrigation as a Solution to Agrarian Problems in Modern Spain," *Geographical Journal*, London, 1950, pp. 55–63

*ITALY*

Almagià, *L'Italia*, 2 vols., Turin, 1959
Compagna, F., *La politica della citta*, Bari, 1967
Dainelli, G., *Atlante Fisico e Economico d'Italia*, Milan, 1940
Dozier, Craig L., "Development in Sardinia," *Geographical Review*, October, 1957, pp. 400–410
Giusti, Ugo, *Lo spopolamento montano in Italia*, Rome, 1938
Jenness, Diamond, "The Recovery Program in Sicily," *Geographical Review*, April, 1950, pp. 355–363
Kish, George, "Italian Boundary Problems," *Geographical Review*, January, 1947, pp. 137–141 (bibliographical article)
———, "The 'Marine' in Calabria," *Geographical Review*, October, 1953, pp. 495–505
Longobardi, C., *Land Reclamation in Italy*, London, 1936
Lutz, V., *Italy: A Study in Economic Development*, London, 1962
Milone, F., *L'Italia: nell'economia delle sui regioni*, Turin, 1955
Sestini, Aldo, "Le regione italiane come base geografica della struttura dello Stato," *Atti del XIV Congresso Geografico Italiano*, Bologna, 1949, pp. 128–143
———, "Densità tipiche di popolazione in Italia secondo le forme di utilizzazione del suolo," *Rivista Geografica Italiana*, Florence, September, 1959, pp. 231–241

*THE BALKAN PENINSULA*

Cvijic, J., *La péninsule balkanique*, Paris, 1917
*Southeastern Europe: A Political and Economic Survey* (Royal Institute of International Affairs), London, 1939
Wolff, R. L., *The Balkans in Our Time*, Cambridge, Mass., 1956
Djordjevic, J., *La Yougoslavie, démocratie socialiste*, Paris, 1959
Hoffman, G. W., and Neal, F. W., *Yugoslavia and the New Communism*, New York, 1962

Kerner, Robert J. (ed.), *Yugoslavia* (United Nations Series), Berkeley, Calif., 1949

Lodge, Olive, *Peasant Life in Yugoslavia,* London, 1942

Markert, W. (ed.), *Jugoslawien,* Cologne, 1954

Moodie, A. E., *The Italo-Yugoslav Boundary: A Study in Political Geography,* London, 1945

Dallin, L. A. D. (ed.), *Bulgaria,* London, 1957

Rusinow, S., *Bulgaria: Land, Economy, Culture,* Sofia, 1965

Todorov, N., *et al, Bulgaria: Historical and Geographical Outline,* Sofia, 1965

Valev, E. V., *Bolgarya* (in Russian), Moscow, 1951

Wilhelmy, Herbert, *Hochbulgarien,* 2 vols., Kiel, 1935 and 1936

Allbaugh, Lelland G., *Crete: A Case Study of an Underdeveloped Area,* Princeton, N.J. 1953

Ancel, Jacques, *La Macédoine,* Paris, 1930

Kayser, B., *Géographie humaine de la Grèce,* Paris, 1964

McNeill, William H., *Greece: American Aid in Action,* New York, 1957

Noel-Baker, F., *The Land and People of Greece,* London, 1960

*Report of the F.A.O. Mission to Greece* (United Nations Food and Agriculture Organization), Washington, 1947

## PART IV  CENTRAL EUROPE

Besides the standard two-volume work by Emm. de Martonne mentioned above, which deals with the Central European countries in their boundaries of the 1930–1935 period and is still a good source for physical and historical geographic data, the following general works and books on particular countries may be consulted:

Ancel, Jacques, *Manuel géographique de politique européenne,* vol. I and vol. II, 2d part, Paris, 1938 and 1945

Caesar, A. A. L., "On the Economic Organisation of Eastern Europe," *Geographical Journal,* London, 1955, pp. 451–469

Cahnman, Werner J., "Frontiers Between East and West in Europe," *Geographical Review,* October, 1949, pp. 605–624 (suggestive maps)

George, P., and Tricart, J., *L'Europe centrale,* 2 vols. (in the "Orbis" series), Paris, 1954

Juillard, E., *L'Europe rhenane,* Paris, 1968

Kirk, Dudley, "European Migration: Prewar Trends and Future Prospects," *Milbank Memorial Fund Quarterly,* New York, April, 1947, pp. 128–152

Kulischer, Eugene M., *The Displacement of Population in Europe,* Montreal, 1943

Moore, Wilbert E., *Economic Demography of Eastern and Southern Europe* (League of Nations), Geneva, 1945

Schechtman, Joseph, *European Population Transfers,* 1939–1945, New York, 1946

Sharp, Samuel L., *Nationalization of Key Industries in Eastern Europe* (Foundation for Foreign Affairs, Pamphlet no. 1), Washington, D. C., 1946

Spulber, Nicholas and Pounds, N. J. G. (eds.), *Resources and Planning in Eastern Europe,* Bloomington, Ind., 1957

*FINLAND*

Ilvessalo, Y., *The Forests of Present-day Finland,* Helsinki, 1949

Mead, W. R., *An Economic Geography of the Scandinavian States and Finland, op. cit.;* "Finnish Farming," *Economic Geography,* January, 1957, pp. 31-40
Platt, R. R., ed., *Finland and Its Geography,* New York, 1955
Toivola, U., (ed.), *Introduction to Finland* (Ministry of Foreign Affairs), Helsinki, 1960 (with a valuable bibliography)
Westermarck, N., *Finnish Agriculture,* Helsinki, 1954

*GERMANY*

*The Effect of Strategic Bombing on the German War Economy and Final Report* (U. S. Strategic Bombing Survey), Washington, D.C., 1946 and 1947
Bathrustand, M. E. and Simpson, J. L., *Germany and the North Atlantic Community,* London, 1956
Dickinson, Robert E., *Germany, A General and Regional Geography,* New York, 1946
Erhard, L., *Germany's Comeback in the World Market,* London, 1954
Fischer, P., *Die Saar zwischen Deutschland und Frankreich,* Frankfurt, 1959
Freymond, J., *The Saar Conflict,* New York, 1960
Grosser, A., *La Démocratie de Bonn,* Paris, 1958
Harris, Chauncy D., "The Ruhr Coal Mining District," *Geographical Review,* April, 1946, pp. 194-221
Hiscocks, R., *Democracy in Western Germany,* Oxford, 1957
Hornsby, L. (ed.), *Profile of East Germany,* London, 1966
Klute, F., *Das Deutsche Reich,* 2 vols. (in the series *Handbuch der Geographischensenschaft*), Berlin, 1941
Passarge, S., *Die deutsche Landschaft,* Berlin, 1936
Pounds, Norman J. G., *The Ruhr,* Bloomington, Ind., 1953
————, *The Economic Pattern of Modern Germany,* London, 1966
Robinson, G. W. S., "West Berlin: The Geography of an Exclave," *Geographical Review,* October, 1953, pp. 540-557
Rüger, L., *Die Bodenschätze Deutschlands,* Munich, 1937
Spreng, R., *et al, Die Verfassung des Landes Baden-Würtemberg,* Stuttgart, 1954
Stolper. W. F., *The Structure of the East German Economy,* Cambridge, Mass., 1960
Wiskemann, E., *Germany's Eastern Neighbors,* London, 1956

*POLAND AND CZECHOSLOVAKIA*

Frankel, H., *Poland,* London, 1946
*Geographical Essays on Eastern Europe,* Bloomington, Ind., 1961
Karpinski, A., *Twenty Years of Poland's Economic Development,* Warsaw, 1964
Pounds, N. J. G., "The Industrial Geography of Modern Poland," *Economic Geography,* July, 1960, pp. 231-253
Schmidt, Bernadotte E. (ed.), *Poland* (United Nations Series), Berkeley, Calif., 1951, 2d ed.
Sharp, Samuel L., *Poland: White Eagle on a Red Field,* Cambridge, Mass., 1953
Staar, R. F., *Poland 1944-62,* Louisiana University Press, 1962
Stolper, W. F., *The Structure of the East German Economy,* Cambridge Mass, 1960
Taylor, J. *The Economic Development of Poland, 1919-1950,* Ithaca, N. Y., 1952

Blazek, M., *Okonomische Geographie der Tschechoslokischen Republik,* East Berlin, 1959
Braibant, Guy, *La planification en Tchécoslovaquie (Cahiers de la Fondation Nationale des Sciences Politiques no. 6),* Paris, 1948

Taskin, G. A., "The Soviet Northwest," *Geographical Review*, April, 1961, pp. 213–235

Tutaeff, D., *The Soviet Caucasus*, London, 1942

Vakar, N. P., *Belorussia*, Cambridge, Mass., 1956

Woods, E. G., *The Baltic Region: A study in Physical and Human Geography*, London, 1945

## PART VI   CONCLUSION

Beloff, Max, *The United States and the Unity of Europe*, London, 1963

Gottmann, Jean, "Le problème européen: le problème géographique," *L'Europe du XIXe et du XXe siecles* (Marzorati), vol. I, tome I, Milan, 1960, pp. 1–30

Haines, C. G. (ed.), *European Integration*, Baltimore, 1957

Lindberg, L. N., *The Political Dynamics of European Economic Integration*, Stanford, Calif., 1963

Robertson, A. H., *European Institutions*, London, 1966

Sampson, A., *The New Europeans. A Guide to the Workings, Institutions and Character of Contemporary Western Europe*, London, 1968

Servan-Schreiber, J. J., *The American Challenge*, New York, 1968

Walsh, A. E., and Paxton, J., *Trade in the Common Market Countries*, London, 1965

# *Index*

Main references are indicated by **bold face** type, illustrations by *italic* type, and maps by (M).